D0761446

# ACAPULCO
## IXTAPA & ZIHUATANEJO

BRUCE WHIPPERMAN

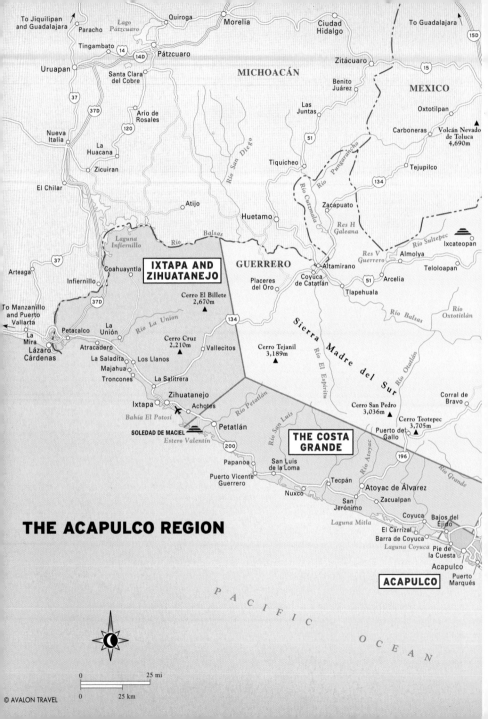

# THE ACAPULCO REGION

**IXTAPA AND ZIHUATANEJO**

**THE COSTA GRANDE**

**ACAPULCO**

MICHOACÁN

MEXICO

GUERRERO

Sierra Madre del Sur

PACIFIC OCEAN

To Jiquilpan and Guadalajara
Paracho
Quiroga
Morelia
Ciudad Hidalgo
To Guadalajara
Lago Pátzcuaro
Tingambato
Pátzcuaro
Zitácuaro
Santa Clara del Cobre
Benito Juárez
Oxtotilpan
Las Juntas
Carboneras
Volcán Nevado de Toluca 4,690m
Uruapan
Ario de Rosales
Tiquicheo
Tejupilco
Nueva Italia
La Huacana
Zicuiran
Zacapuato
El Chilar
Atijo
Huetamo
Res H Galeana
Almolya
Ixcateopan
Arteaga
Río Balsas
Altamirano
Res V Guerrero
Teloloapan
Infiernillo
Coahuayntla
Placeres del Oro
Coyuca de Catalán
Arcelia
Cerro El Billete 2,670m
Tlapehuala
Río Balsas
Río Oxtotitlán
Petacalco
La Unión
Cerro Cruz 2,210m
Vallecitos
Cerro Tejanil 3,189m
La Mira
Lázaro Cárdenas
Atracadero
Los Llanos
La Saladita
Majahua
Troncones
La Salitrera
Zihuatanejo
Achotes
Ixtapa
Bahía El Potosí
SOLEDAD DE MACIEL
Estero Valentín
Petatlán
Cerro San Pedro 3,036m
Corral de Bravo
Cerro Teotepec 3,705m
Puerto del Gallo
Papanoa
San Luis de la Loma
Puerto Vicente Guerrero
Nuxco
Tecpán
Atoyac de Álvarez
Zacualpan
San Jerónimo
Coyuca
Bajos del Éjido
Laguna Mitla
El Carrizal
Barra de Coyuca
Pie de la Cuesta
Laguna Coyuca
Acapulco
Puerto Marqués

To Manzanillo and Puerto Vallarta

Río San Diego
Río Cutzmala
Río Panzarancho
Río Balsas
Río La Unión
Río El Espíritu
Río Otatlán
Río Sultepec
Río Petatlán
Río San Luis
Río Atoyac
Río Grande

0    25 mi
0    25 km

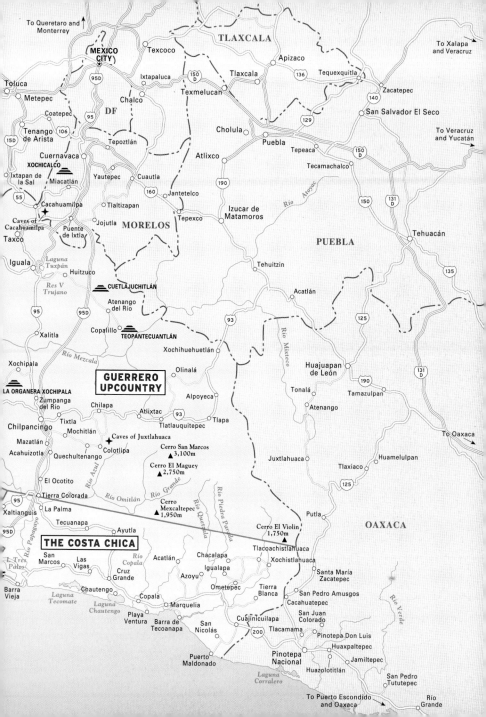

# Contents

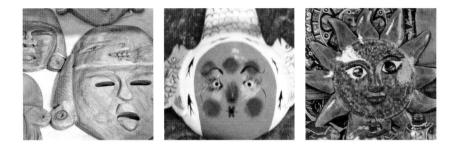

# Discover Acapulco,
## Ixtapa & Zihuatanejo

The worldwide renown of Mexico's south-seas resort trio is more deserved now than ever. The planet's original world-class tropical resort, Acapulco still shines, with an emerald-green half-moon bay by day, and a gleaming galaxy of city lights by night. Along the same shoreline lie Ixtapa and Zihuatanejo. Fashionably modern, Ixtapa is brilliant white above creamy golden sands; neighboring Zihuatanejo still resembles the old-Mexico fishing village that once slumbered on a diminutive crescent bay. Explore hidden beaches; enjoy brilliant sunsets; camp, surf, and fish on wild, open-ocean strands; and view grand flocks of seabirds, either on the beach or by boat on broad mangrove lagoons.

Although you can fully enjoy your time in the Acapulco region's beach diversions and resort comforts, you'll find there's much more to discover. Fascinating ancient sites abound, from petroglyphs within sight of downtown Acapulco to the 3,000-year-old lost Olmec city of Teopantecuantlán, to a submarine rock wall built around A.D. 1400 for Zihuatanejo's king. As for colonial history, the past blooms in old Acapulco at the banyan-shaded old-town plaza and peaks at the bastion of Fuerte San Diego, which still stands, like a sentinel of old, proudly overlooking the inner harbor shore where it once guarded the treasures of the fabled Manila galleon against a dozen generations of pirates.

The appeal expands beyond each city's limits, encompassing

virtually the entire state of Guerrero. On the northwest coast, you'll discover relaxing getaways at small resorts such as Troncones, Barra de Potosí, and Playa Escondida. On the region's southeastern side, there are the refreshingly downscale beach towns of El Carrizal, Pie de la Cuesta, and Playa Ventura. Farther southeast, you can follow paths less traveled into Guerrero's indigenous and African-Mexican heartlands, where a treasury of fetching handicrafts is for sale at native markets, Spanish is a foreign tongue, and villagers are more likely to speak Mixtec or Amusgo. Finally, all roads seem to lead to Taxco, the celebrated silver-rich colonial gem of the Sierra, set on the slope of a towering mountain. There, you can join the many folks, mostly Mexican, who stroll Taxco's narrow winding lanes, decorated with the baroque monuments of an opulent past.

The roads to the manifold delights of Acapulco, Ixtapa, and Zihuatanejo are open and easy to follow, whether you seek glamour and luxury or something offbeat and rustic — or all of the above.

# Planning Your Trip

## ▶ WHERE TO GO

### Acapulco

Acapulco has been reinventing itself for more than a decade. Many of its original hostelries, renowned for their perches on the golden beachfront, have been refurbished to welcome a new generation of travelers. The azure waters, once less than pristine, are again clean and clear. A glittering lineup of new restaurants, clubs, and shopping plazas now decorate the eastern side of the bay. And old Acapulco, the intimate, colonial-era neighborhood nestled around the west-side cove, is now being rediscovered.

### The Costa Grande

The Costa Grande extends northwest along the 150-mile (242-km) stretch of Highway 200 from Acapulco to Ixtapa and Zihuatanejo. Here you can enjoy tropical Mexico at its purest, with groves of swaying palms, wildlife-rich mangrove lagoons, endless beaches, market towns, and a sprinkling of mini-resorts.

### Ixtapa and Zihuatanejo

Zihuatanejo, with its plumy *lancha*-lined beachfront and pedestrian-friendly downtown, still resembles the original fishing village, while its high-rise cousin Ixtapa, five miles (8 km) to the northwest, appeals to those who prefer something fashionably modern. Country charms lie outside the town limits, including Troncones, about 20 miles (32 km) northwest of Ixtapa. On the opposite, southeast side, about 15 miles (24 km) from Zihuatanejo, a growing number of visitors seek heaven on earth in Barra de Potosí.

### Guerrero Upcountry

North from the tropical coast, in towns such as Chilpancingo and Iguala, a big piece of the rich tapestry of Mexican history was woven. You'll also find the pine-tufted Río Papagayo, the lush valley of the crystalline Río Azul, the craft-rich towns of Chilapa and

Zihuatanejo still resembles its fishing-village beginnings.

Brightly lacquered pottery decorates many Taxco handicrafts stalls.

Olinalá, and Taxco, Mexico's picturesque silver capital. Out-of-town must-sees include the Grutas de Cacahuamilpa limestone caverns and the legendary Xochicalco archaeological site.

## The Costa Chica

Highway 200 leaves Acapulco heading due east, traversing the Costa Chica for 200 miles (320 km) before reaching the far southern state of Oaxaca. The town of Ometepec, about 110 miles (177 km) east of Acapulco, is where you'll begin to brush shoulders with indigenous people, many speaking the Amusgo language. Southeast of Ometepec, you'll encounter many African-Mexican shoppers and sellers in the lively main market town of Cuajinicuilapa. From Cuajinicuilapa, a country road heads south to the laid-back coastal fishing hamlet of Puerto Maldonado. Another hour east into Oaxaca are the colorful market towns of Pinotepa Nacional and Jamiltepec.

## ▶ WHEN TO GO

Although temperatures and rainfall are crucial in deciding when to visit, crowds, high seasons, and low seasons are also factors. The Acapulco region has two sharply defined seasons: wet summer-fall and dry winter-spring. For folks arriving from the U.S. West Coast, the summer contrast is sharp.

Some people say this region is too hot in the summer. In fact, increased summer cloud cover and showers can actually create average daily temperatures in July, August, and September that are cooler than clear and very warm late-April, May, and early-June temperatures. And near the coast, nights never get warmer than balmy, even during the summer.

The other summer advantage is the vegetation. If you like lush green landscapes, summer–fall may be your season. This is true everywhere, but especially in the highlands, where myriad multicolored wildflowers decorate the roadsides, and the clouds seem to billow into a 1,000-mile-high blue sky.

During the sunnier and more temperate

the Costa Chica

winter, many trees are bare of leaves, grass is brown, and cactuses seem to be the only green. The landscape continues to be dry and dusty during February and March, turning hot in April and May, until the rains arrive and green breaks out again by mid-June.

If you want to avoid crowds and high prices, avoid the high Christmas to New Year's rush (Dec. 20–Jan. 3) and the Semana Santa week up through and including Easter Sunday. Sunny, temperate January, a low-occupancy mini-season, is a good bet, especially on the beach. The landscape still retains some green and hotels often offer discounts.

October through mid-December is also a good time to go. Hotel prices are cheapest, the landscape is lush, beaches are uncrowded, and it's cooler and not as rainy as July, August, and September. Although the first October weeks in Zihuatanejo may still be a bit too empty for folks who enjoy lots of company, the pace picks up by mid-October and continues through mid-December.

## ► BEFORE YOU GO

### Passports, Tourist Cards, and Visas
Your passport (or birth or naturalization certificate) is your positive proof of national identity; without it, your status in any foreign country is in doubt. Don't leave home without one. U.S. Immigration rules require that all U.S. citizens must have a valid passport in order to re-enter the United States.

For U.S. and Canadian citizens, entry by air into Mexico for a few weeks could hardly be easier. Airline attendants hand out tourist cards (*tarjetas turísticas*) en route and officers make them official by glancing at passports and stamping the cards at the immigration gate. Business travel permits for 30 days or fewer are handled by the same simple procedures.

### Immunizations and Precautions
A good physician can recommend the proper preventatives for your trip. If you are going to stay pretty much in town, your doctor will probably suggest little more than updating

your basic typhoid, diphtheria-tetanus, hepatitis, and polio shots.

For remote tropical areas—below 4,000 feet (1,200 meters)—doctors often recommend a gamma-globulin shot against hepatitis A and a schedule of chloroquine pills against malaria. Use other measures to discourage mosquitoes and other tropical pests. Common precautions include mosquito netting and rubbing on plenty of pure DEET (N,N dimethyl-meta-toluamide) "jungle juice," mixed in equal parts with rubbing (70 percent isopropyl) alcohol.

## Getting There

Most travelers fly in on regularly scheduled flights from U.S. and Canadian gateways. More options are available with a single plane change in Mexico City. Although few airlines fly directly to the Acapulco region from the northern United States and Canada, many charters do.

For cost-conscious travelers, express buses provide a safe and sure route to the Acapulco region. Hundreds of buses head south daily from central bus stations (*camioneras centrales*) in the south-of-the-border towns of Tijuana, Mexicali, Nogales, Ciudad Juárez, Nuevo Laredo, Reynosa, and Matamoros. By all means, for comfort and speed, go luxury-class (about $80–100, 20–30 hours).

Although it isn't a route for everyone, some travelers drive their cars or RVs to the Acapulco region. Driving time runs 3–5 south-of-the-border days at the wheel, and costs around $80–120 in (very worthwhile) expressway tolls for passenger cars and light trucks (about triple that for motor homes).

## What to Take

"Men wear pants, ladies be beautiful" was once the dress code of one of the Mexican Pacific Coast's classiest hotels. Today, men can get by easily without a jacket, women with simple skirts, pants, and blouses. Everyone should bring a hat for sun protection and a light jacket or sweater for the occasional cool evening. Loose-fitting, hand-washable, easy-to-dry clothes make for trouble-free coastal tropical vacationing. If you're going to the highlands (Chilpancingo, Chilapa, Olinalá, Taxco), add a medium-weight jacket. In all cases, leave showy, expensive clothes and jewelry at home. Stow valuables that you cannot lose in your hotel safe or carry them with you in a sturdy zipped purse or a waist pouch on your front side.

If you're staying the whole time at a self-contained resort, you can take the two suitcases and one carry-on allowed by airlines. If, on the other hand, you're going to be moving around a lot, you'd do better to condense everything to one easily carried bag with wheels that doubles as luggage and soft backpack.

Campers will have to be careful to accomplish one-bag packing. Fortunately, camping along the tropical coast generally requires no sleeping bag. Simply use a hammock (buy it in Mexico) or a sleeping pad and a sheet for cover. In the winter, you may, at most, have to buy a light blanket. A compact tent that you and your companion can share is a must against bugs, as is mosquito repellent. A first-aid kit is absolutely necessary.

ancient ball-ring at Petatlán

# Explore Acapulco,
## Ixtapa & Zihuatanejo

## ▶ THE BEST OF ACAPULCO

Although its golden beaches are the stuff of legend, Acapulco offers much more, both in and just outside of town.

### Days 1-2

Arrive in Acapulco, rest up for a few hours, then enjoy sunset cocktails at the Hotel Los Flamingos clifftop *mirador* and dinner in the adjacent restaurant.

The next day spend the morning around the *zócalo* (old-town plaza), the colonial-era Fuerte San Diego and museum, and the nearby Casa de la Máscara (House of Masks). Take the afternoon off, relaxing by the pool or on the beach. In the evening, join the crowd viewing the La Quebrada cliff divers.

### Days 3-4

In the morning, ride a tour boat from Playa Caleta to offshore Isla Roqueta. Walk the island trail (two hours) and snorkel, swim, and sun at hidden Playa las Palmitas. Enjoy a late lunch or dinner at Restaurant Palao on the island before returning to the mainland.

The next day you might do some browsing for handicrafts mementos at Bonita, and Linda de Taxco handicrafts stores and Mercado de Parrazal handicrafts market, all near the old-town plaza. Alternatively, taxi

Playa Caleta

up to Palma Sola Archaeological Site for a stroll and a picnic among the petrolgyphs, or head to the Jardín Botánico (botanical garden). Spend the rest of the day relaxing by your hotel pool or strolling, sunning, or swimming at the beach. Enjoy a splurge dinner at Kookaburra or Zibu (or if on a budget, at either Taco Tumbra, 100% Natural, or El Zorrito restaurants). Continue for an evening walk to sample the nightclub scene and maybe even risk a bungee jump (seniors half-price) on the Costera Miguel Alemán (also simply called the Costera) just east of the Diana Circle.

## Days 5-6

Head upcountry for either rafting at Bravo Town on the Río Papagayo, or exploring the caves of Juxtlahuaca, then the Río Azul near Colotlipa. Continue to Chilpancingo for an overnight stay. After dinner at either Nutrilite or El Portal restaurants, enjoy a stroll around the Chilpancingo plaza.

Santa Prisca church, Taxco

   If Day 6 happens to be a Sunday (or you planned it to be), spend it in Chilapa at the fabulously intense Sunday crafts market, an hour and a half by car or bus east of Chilpancingo. Otherwise, if you have kids in tow, show them a good time in Chilpancingo at the Museo La Avispa and the Zoo. If not, consider heading north an hour to the intriguing and scenic La Organera Xochipala Archaeological Zone. In any case, continue north by car or bus to Iguala for an overnight stay.

## Days 7-8

After breakfast in Iguala at La Parroquia, stroll the shady Iguala plaza, take a look around inside the gold market a block away, then spend an hour in the Museo y Santuario a la Bandera (Museum and Sanctuary of the Flag). Make the highlight of your Iguala visit a trip uphill to gaze in wonder at the colossal Hilltop Memorial Flag south of town.

   Continue north to Taxco. In the evening, after dinner at Restaurant Santa Fe, Pozolería Tía Calla, or Del Ángel Inn, stroll the Taxco zócalo (main plaza) and browse through some silver and handicrafts shops.

   The next day, after breakfast at La Parroquia on the zócalo, see the sights, such as Santa Prisca church, Museo Guillermo Spratling, the town market, and maybe ride the cableway to the top of Monte Taxco and visit more of Taxco's excellent silver and handicrafts shops.

## Days 9-10

On Day 9, be sure to at least visit Grutas de Cacahuamilpa limestone cave national park.

# BEST BEACHES

These are many of the Acapulco region's loveliest, creamiest stretches of sand. Nearly all are good for most beach delights, such as surf fishing, camping, beachcombing, swimming, snorkeling, and surfing. Beaches, however, are often good for particular reasons. Here are some of the very best.

## MOST PRISTINE

- Laguna de Mitla (Costa Grande, page 88)
- Playa Coral (Ixtapa and Zihuatanejo, page 115)

## BEST SNORKELING

- Playa Roqueta (Acapulco, page 41)
- Playa Las Gatas (Ixtapa and Zihuatanejo, page 112)

## BEST SURFING

- Playa Revolcadero (Acapulco, page 45)
- Puerto Maldonado (Costa Chica, page 252)

## BEST SURF FISHING

- Playa Pie de la Cuesta (Acapulco, page 76)
- El Carrizal (Costa Grande, page 86)
- Playa Las Pozas (Ixtapa and Zihuatanejo, page 150)

## MOST CHILD-FRIENDLY

- Playa Caleta (Acapulco, page 41)
- El Carrizal (Costa Grande, page 86)
- Playa Cuachalatate (Ixtapa and Zihuatanejo, page 115)
- Playa las Peñitas (Costa Chica, page 242)

## BEST SUNSETS

- Playa Angosta (Acapulco, page 43)
- Playa El Calvario (Costa Grande, page 98)
- Piedra Tlalcoyunque (Costa Grande, page 93)
- Playa La Ropa (Ixtapa and Zihuatanejo, page 112)

## BEST CAMPING

- Playa Luces (Acapulco, page 79)
- Playa La Barrita (Costa Grande, page 99)
- Barra de Tecoanapa (Costa Chica, page 243)

## MOST BEAUTIFUL

- Piedra Tlalcoyunque (Costa Grande, page 93)
- Playa Quieta (Ixtapa and Zihuatanejo, page 114)

## MOST INTIMATE

- Playa Las Palmitas (Acapulco, page 42)
- Playa Carey (Ixtapa and Zihuatanejo, page 115)

## BEST OVERALL

- Playa Ojo de Agua (Costa Grande, page 97)
- Playa La Ropa (Ixtapa and Zihuatanejo, page 112)
- Playa Ventura (Costa Chica, page 240)

bridge to Playa La Ropa

If you arrange a tour, start early enough with your own wheels, or hire a taxi ($40) from Cacahuamilpa. By early afternoon, you'll have time to also visit the legendary must-see Xochicalco UNESCO World Heritage site and museum 25 miles (40 km) beyond Cacahuamilpa. On the last day, return to Acapulco and head home (or continue onward to Ixtapa, Zihuatanejo, and the Costa Grande).

# ▶ THE BEST OF IXTAPA AND ZIHUATANEJO

The twin resorts of Ixtapa and Zihuatanejo crown the Guerrero Costa Grande, an alluring land of perpetual summer, where the palms always seem to be swaying in the breeze, the frigate birds soaring overhead, and the billows washing the crystalline sand.

## Days 1-2

Arrive in Ixtapa or Zihuatanejo. Rest up a few hours, then stroll around downtown Zihuatanejo and along the beachfront Paseo del Pescador. Browse some of the handicrafts shops and enjoy dinner downtown at Tamales y Atoles "Any" or Don Memo's.

The next morning, after breakfast in Zihuatanejo at Restaurant Margarita, visit the Museo Arqueología de la Costa Grande, then ride a water taxi from the pier to Playa Las Gatas for sunning on the beach, and snorkeling or maybe a scuba lesson. In the mid-afternoon, return and freshen up at your hotel, then enjoy the sunset and a splurge dinner at Il Mare or Kau Kan (or, if on a budget, Restaurant La Perla on Playa La Ropa).

## Days 3-4

On Day 3, after breakfast at restaurant Mama Norma and Deborah in Ixtapa, browse the handicrafts at the Ixtapa handicrafts market and perhaps some of the Ixtapa shops in the Los Patios shopping complex. Then, either take a taxi, drive, or ride the minibus to Playa Linda to see the crocodiles. Later, take

Zihuatanejo Bay from Hotel Irma poolside

cactus along the beachfront walkway above Zihuatanejo's Playa Madera

the ferry across to Isla Grande for sunning, strolling, swimming and/or snorkeling and a seafood lunch at a beachfront *palapa*.

On Day 4 you could kick back and simply relax, or follow your own interests. A few options include: unwinding on the beach or by the pool, renting a bike and following the Ixtapa *ciclopista* (bike path) for a few hours, going horseback riding at Playa Linda, taking a fishing trip, or shopping for local handicrafts.

## Days 5-6

On Day 5, get an early start and head northwest an hour for a getaway in Troncones. Check in at a comfortable beachfront inn, such as Casa Ki, the Inn at Manzanillo Bay, or Eden Beach Hacienda. After whiling away the afternoon strolling the beach, lazing in a hammock, or swimming beyond the breakers, enjoy dinner at either El Burro Borracho or the Cocina del Sol restaurant at the Eden Beach Hacienda.

Day 6 you might want to spend more actively, maybe trying a surfing lesson, going on a fishing trip, or simply beachcombing. Or, whether you have your own wheels or get an early start by bus, you could explore the coast northwest, checking out the mini-resort beach hamlets of La Saladita and Atracadero, and maybe even going all the way to the grand Río Balsas dam, where Highway 200 crosses the border into the state of Michoacán, and Mexico's mightiest river meanders into the Pacific.

## Days 7-8

Return southeast past Ixtapa and Zihuatanejo for a day around the village of Barra de Potosí, perhaps combined with a wildlife-viewing tour, such as with Zoe Kayak Tours, on the grand mangrove Laguna de Potosí. Stay overnight at either of the Barra de Potosí bed-and-breakfasts, Casa Frida or Casa del Encanto, or return to your hotel in Ixtapa or Zihuatanejo.

Day 8 you could simply relax, according to your own interests, in either Ixtapa, Zihuatanejo, or Barra de Potosí. If you want more activity, in Zihuatanejo you might visit the lively town market, go on a fishing trip, do either the Zihuatanejo or Ixtapa beach walk, or check out Zihuatanejo's excellent tourist handicrafts market and shops. Alternatively, from either Barra de Potosí, Ixtapa, or Zihuatanejo, you could go on an excursion south to Petatlán and visit the plaza-front gold market shops and pay your respects to Petatlán's beloved patron, Padre Jesús. Enjoy a late lunch or early dinner at Petatlán's Restaurant Mi Pueblito on the plaza.

## Days 9-10

Finally, do some genuine relaxing and let your body rest and your mind wander, whether you're spending Day 9 in Ixtapa, Zihuatanejo, or Barra de Potosí. (If, however, you crave more activity and beautiful places, you might go for an excursion-picnic south to one or both of the lovely Playa Ojo de Agua and Piedra de Tlalcoyunque.)

Day 10, head back home, or continue traveling into Acapulco and Guerrero Upcountry.

## CATCH A WAVE

The surf everywhere is highest and best during the July-November hurricane season, when big swells from storms far out at sea attract platoons of surfers to favored beaches.

Close to Acapulco Bay, **Playa Revolcadero** offers good surfing opportunities, and a few good surfing spots sprinkle the Ixtapa-Zihuatanejo area, including **Playa Las Gatas.** But surfers looking for good seasonal surfing breaks will want to head farther afield, for crystalline strands such as **Piedra Tlalcoyunque, Playa Escondida, Playa Cayaquitos, Playa El Calvario, Playa Ventura, Playa Ojo de Agua, Playa Ventura, Punta Maldonado,** and **Troncones.**

In fact, in the town of Troncones, north of Ixtapa and Zihuatanejo, surfing has become a major recreation. The most popular spot is the palm-tufted inlet known locally as **Manzanillo Bay,** location of both the Inn at Manzanillo Bay and Eden Beach Hacienda. An enterprising California couple operates **ISA (Instructional Surf Adventures) Mexico** (cell tel. 755/558-3821, U.S. tel. 514/563-6944, surf@isamexico.com, www.isamexico.com), in Troncones, offering both local on-the-spot instruction for the day and extended surfing travel packages during the fall and winter seasons (Nov.-Apr.). Classes are small and all equipment and deluxe beachfront lodging is customarily included in packages, which run about $1,000 per person, double occupancy.

Beginning surfers ride the waves at Playa El Calvario.

# ▶ TREASURES OF OLD MEXICO

The Acapulco region preserves a wealth of tradition in its museums, handicrafts galleries, cathedrals, pilgrimage shrines, native markets, and archaeological sites.

## Acapulco

In Acapulco's old town, first explore the world-class Fuerte San Diego and museum. Nearby, continue to the Casa de la Máscara, an amazing museum of masks. Back at the Acapulco old-town *zócalo,* step inside to admire the art deco–style cathedral (especially the ceiling).

Later, be sure to see the Casa de Dolores Olmedo and its monumental streetfront mosaic of Mexican mythology by celebrated artist Diego Rivera.

Finally, on a hillside overlooking the city's west-end old town, enjoy a picnic and a stroll through the leafy Palma Sola Archaeological Site, dotted with a treasury of fascinating petroglyphs.

## The Costa Grande

Moving up the coast from Acapulco, if you take the side trip to the Laguna de Mitla, be sure to stop by and see the ancient pottery remains preserved in the tiny Santa Cruz de Mitla Museo Comunitario (Community Museum) in the hamlet's municipal *kiosco* (kiosk).

Farther north, at Petatlán, step inside the pilgrimage church, Parroquia de Padre Jesús, and pay your respects to the town's fabulously beloved patron, Padre Jesús. Nearby, check out the ancient monoliths by the main plaza bandstand and the monumental stone ball-game rings (*anillos de piedra*), mounted beside the highway in town, a few blocks from the plaza.

A few miles north of town, investigate the source of Petatlán's antiquities, the Soledad de Maciel Archaeological Zone. Start by viewing the remarkable life-death motif monolith, the "King of Chole," in front of

Acapulco's art deco-style cathedral

handicrafts market, Taxco

Mochitlán church, near Chilpancingo

the village-center church. Continue to the adjacent small museum, where you can contact a guide.

## Ixtapa and Zihuatanejo
First on your list should be the regional museum, Museo Arqueología de la Costa Grande, with its treasury of ancient Costa Grande artifacts.

To see a storied on-site artifact of Zihuatanejo's past, take the water taxi over to Playa Las Gatas for a beachfront (or underwater snorkel or scuba) look at what remains of the protective "wall" that, legend says, the local pre-conquest Tarascan king built offshore.

## Guerrero Upcountry
Begin at Chilpancingo, the Guerrero state capital, to see the heroic statue of José María Morelos and the revered Templo de Santa María de la Asunción, where the Congress of Anahuac declared Mexican Independence from Spain in 1813. Then see it all colorfully illustrated by the grand historical mural in the Museo Regional de Chilpancingo.

On the way north to Iguala, the important and very ancient partly reconstructed ruined city at La Organera Xochipala Archaeological Zone is worth at least a two-hour stop.

An hour farther north, visit the Iguala plaza-front Museo y Santuario a la Bandera, and culminate your Iguala visit at the hilltop south of town, with a close-up view of the wondrous, fantastically large, quarter-ton Hilltop Memorial Flag.

Those who like ruins can have a good day exploring a pair of important archaeological sites in a side trip east of Iguala: Cuetlajuchitlán (kooay-tlah-hoo-chee-TLAHN), and another hour and a half farther east, ancient (circa 1000 B.C.) Olmec-era Teopantecuantlán (tay-oh-pahn-tay-kooan-TLAHN).

In Taxco, less than an hour north of Iguala, trace the town's colorfully rich history via a self-guided walking tour of the spectacularly baroque Santa Prisca church, the Museo Guillermo Spratling, the Casa Humboldt colonial religious art museum, and the Museo Platería (Silver Museum).

About an hour and a half outside of Taxco, you must visit the legendary Xochicalco archaeological site and museum. On another day, history enthusiasts would enjoy a half-day excursion from Taxco to Ixtcateopan village to visit the museum and shrine honoring the Aztecs' gritty last emperor, Cuauhtémoc, and his (now controversial) remains.

## The Costa Chica

The eastern Costa Chica, beginning about a hundred miles east of Acapulco and extending into Oaxaca, is a rich repository of the cultural traditions of both the indigenous (mostly Mixtec- and Amusgo-speaking) people, and a large (perhaps 50,000 strong) rural farm community of African Mexicans.

The eastern Guerrero market towns north of Highway 200, especially Ometepec (oh-may-tay-PEK) and Xochistlahuaca (soh-chees-tlah-WAH-kah), are the big indigenous centers, where thousands of folks in colorful *traje* (traditional dress) arrive for big Sunday *tianguis* (native markets, tee-AHN-geese).

By contrast, the African Mexicans, nearly all of whom live south of Highway 200, often arrive in majority numbers at the busy market town of Cuajinicuilapa (kwah-hee-nee-kwee-LAH-pah). Here, the Museo de las Culturas Afromestizos should be your priority stop.

Farther east, on the Oaxaca side of the Costa Chica, the town of Pinotepa Nacional is the big market hub for the mostly Mixtec-speaking nearby villages. The Pinotepa Nacional native market, big every day and even bigger on Wednesdays and Sundays, is where the indigenous action is.

From Pinotepa Nacional, good roads

detail of door of Santa Prisca church in Taxco

bas-relief on the Pyramid of Quetzalcoatl at Xochicalco

embroidery at San Pedro Amusgos

fan north and east to more remote indigenous villages: north to Mixtec-speaking Pinotepa Don Luis (for *pozahuancos* and masks), and Amusgo-speaking San Pedro Amusgos (for lovely hand-embroidered *huipiles*); and east along Highway 200 to Mixtec-speaking Huazolotitlán (for masks), and Jamiltepec, the coastal Mixtec capital, with a large and fascinating daily native market.

## ▶ OUTDOOR ADVENTURE

Beyond legendary beaches, the Acapulco region abounds with hills, forests, and mountains for hiking; rivers for kayaking and rafting; caves for exploring; coasts and offshore islands for boating; mangrove lagoons for birdwatching; and even an exotic natural tropical botanical garden for wandering. Moreover, the region is a veritable wildlife treasury, with everything from iguanas and crocodiles to dolphins, whales, and white herons.

### Rivers

Many of the Acapulco region's rivers, such as the Coyuca, Tecpán, and Petatlán on the Costa Grande; the Copala, Marquelia, Quetzala, and Arenas on the Costa Chica; and Balsas and Papagayo in Guerrero Upcountry, are easily navigable by experienced adventurers with their own equipment. The Río Papagayo adds the convenience of guided rafting tours from the Bravo Town ecotourism center about an hour north of Acapulco by highway.

The best of all possible inner-tubing rivers is the crystalline Río Azul, an upper tributary of the Río Papagayo system. It rises year-round

# SPORTFISHING

Acapulco and Zihuatanejo have long been world-class sportfishing grounds. Zihuatanejo in particular is known for big-game billfish (marlin, swordfish, and sailfish).

A deep-sea boat charter generally includes the boat and crew for a full or half day, plus equipment and bait for two to six people, not including food or drinks. The full-day price depends upon the season. Around Christmas and New Year's and before Easter (when reservations will be mandatory) a big boat can run $450 and up in Acapulco and Zihuatanejo. During low season, however, you might be able to bargain a captain down to as low as $250.

Renting an entire big boat is not the only choice. Winter sportfishing is sometimes so brisk in Acapulco and Zihuatanejo that travel agencies can make reservations for individuals for about $80 per person per day. In season,

boats might average one big marlin or sailfish apiece. The best month for **sailfish** (*pez vela*) is October; for **marlin,** January and February; for **dorado,** March.

But sailfish and marlin are neither the only nor necessarily the most desirable fish in the sea. Competently captained *pangas* (outboard motor launches) can typically haul in three or four large 15- or 20-pound excellent-eating **róbalo** (snook), **huachinango** (snapper), or **atún** (tuna) in two hours just outside Acapulco Bay. Seating 2–6 passengers, *pangas* are available for as little as $75, depending on the season. Once, six of my friends hired a *panga,* had a great time, and came back with a boatload of big tuna, jack, and mackerel. A restaurant cooked them as a banquet for a dozen of us in exchange for the extra fish. I discovered for the first time how heavenly fresh **sierra veracruzana** can taste.

well-equipped Acapulco sportfishing boats for rent

Stealth and patience make great white herons formidable hunters.

from springs at El Borbollón and meanders, about two feet deep, gently downhill, past a number of rustic bathing resorts, notably Balneario Santa Fe.

## Kayaking and Boating

Near the resorts, tour boats offer mangrove lagoon excursions for enjoying the breeze, the scenery, and seeing squadrons of herons, ducks, geese, cormorants, anghingas, lily walkers, gulls, sometimes even crocodiles, and much more. Find them at Laguna Coyuca at Pie de la Cuesta north of Acapulco, Laguna Tres Palos south of Acapulco, and at Laguna Barra de Potosí near Zihuatanejo.

If you want a thrilling, fast-lane version of the above, go on a jet-boat tour through Shotover Jet outfitters in Acapulco.

On the other hand, if you bring your own kayak and/or boat you can put it in the water at all of the above, in addition to at least a dozen scenic Acapulco region locations. For starters, sheltered ocean kayaking is easy right

from the beaches at Isla Grande near Ixtapa and Zihuatanejo and Isla Roqueta near Acapulco.

Other more remote but inviting mangrove lagoons, ripe for kayaking, boating, and camping, are on the Costa Grande, at El Carrizal, Laguna de Mitla, and Camalote; and on the Costa Chica at Laguna Chautengo.

## Birds and Wildlife

Although you can be on the lookout for birds and wildlife on any Acapulco-region beach or in any forest at any time, some places are consistently alive with throngs of birds and wildlife. Easiest to access are the tropical mangrove lagoons of Laguna Coyuca and Laguna Tres Palos near Acapulco. Operating out of Ixtapa, Zoe Kayak Tours offers professional wildlife-viewing tours at Laguna de Potosí, south of Zihuatanejo.

## Caves

The Acapulco region is sprinkled with

limestone caverns (called *grutas* in Spanish). The grandmother of all Mexican caves is the Grutas de Cacahuamilpa, near Taxco. Less well-known, yet equally worthy, is the smaller but exquisitely pristine Grutas de Juxtlahuaca, an hour by road east of Chilpancingo.

## Hiking and Cycling

Hiking can start right in Acapulco for visitors who follow the forested trails on Isla Roqueta, at the naturally exotic tropical Jardín Botánico (botanical garden), and the green-forested petroglyph-sprinkled Palma Sola Archaeological Site. Furthermore, adventurers who enjoy the challenge of scrambling to hidden beaches can do their thing on Isla Grande.

In Guerrero Upcountry, Bravo Town ecotourism center offers guided hiking, rapelling, climbing, and camping tours from their base on the Río Papagayo.

Furthermore, bicycling is easy and healthful on the Ixtapa and Zihuatanejo *ciclopista* (bike path). Either bring your own bike or rent one in Ixtapa.

## Tent and RV Camping

Two well-situated and equipped formal RV and tent-camping parks, the Acapulco Trailer Park and the Trailer Park and Campground Playa Luces, operate at Pie de la Cuesta, near Acapulco. The new, well-equipped Ixtapa Trailer Park is open for business on Playa Larga, north of Ixtapa. Three bare-bones sites accommodate self-contained RVs and tents on Zihuatanejo's Playa La Ropa.

Additionally, many informal but customary spots welcome self-contained RVs and tenters. These are usually on the beach, at or near *palapa* restaurants, whose owners allow you to set up beneath their *ramada* in exchange for selling you some meals. The best spots have lovely, pristine locations, the local people are welcoming, and nearby grocery stores and *palapa* restaurants are available for food and supplies.

The best spots that I've seen are El Carrizal, Laguna de Mitla, Camalote, Piedra Tlalcoyunque, La Barrita, Playa Escondida, La Saladita, and Atracadero on the Costa Grande; and Playa Ventura, Barra de Tecoanapa, and Puerto Maldonado, on the Costa Chica.

Tenting on the beach is convenient and safe beneath the *palapa* of a beachfront restaurant.

# ACAPULCO

Acapulco (pop. 1.5 million), the "Queen of Mexican Beach Resorts," is still Mexico's favorite and as sunny and breezy as ever. By day, viewed either from the shore or an airy hilltop, Acapulco's golden strand curves around its picture-perfect half-moon bay. At night, myriad twinkling city lights decorate the same space, bordered below by the bay's ebony darkness and above by the starry firmament.

In Acapulco as in its latter-day metropolitan cousins, Hollywood and Las Vegas, the new, the brash, the loud, and the bright far outshine the quiet, charming side of Acapulco that few visitors know.

But despite the hullabaloo you can easily enjoy Acapulco's hidden feast of old-Mexico diversions: intimate neighborhoods around the *zócalo,* with their upcountry traditional-food restaurants, a pair of fascinating world-class museums, and the fetching trove of handicrafts at Mercado de Parrazal.

Of course, modern Acapulco was built for people who like to party, and if you're so inclined you can sample Acapulco's best at a legion of bars, clubs, and discotheques; a shoreline nighttime bungee jump; nightclub extravaganza shows; and with the rich and famous at choice restaurants, where both the cuisine and the view—of a seeming galaxy of twinkling city lights—are equally stunning.

What's more, Acapulco offers manifold outdoor diversions, such as acquainting yourself with tropical fish either through the floor of a glass-bottomed boat or via a snorkeling or scuba diving adventure. On another day, explore the forested corners and hidden

© BRUCE WHIPPERMAN

ACAPULCO

# HIGHLIGHTS

◖ **The *Zócalo*:** Here, at the charming heart of old Acapulco, join the folks who stroll in the shade beneath the ancient *higuera* trees, people-watch from park benches, or take a look inside the art deco *zócalo*-front church (page 35).

◖ **Fuerte San Diego:** Just a few blocks from the *zócalo*, spend an interesting afternoon at the grand colonial-era fort that protected Acapulco from marauders for more than 300 years (page 35).

◖ **Casa de la Máscara:** A treasury of masks, from a tradition that still comprises an important part of ritual in indigenous Mexico, is the major attraction of this fascinating small museum (page 37).

◖ **La Quebrada:** Join the excited crowd to watch one of the intrepid cadre of divers gracefully execute a death-defying 200-foot plunge into a narrow rockbound and wave-tossed channel (page 38).

◖ **Palma Sola Archaeological Site:** Wander and wonder among the dozens of fascinating ritual petroglyphs that decorate this leafy hilltop bayview park (page 39).

◖ **Jardín Botánico de Acapulco and Capilla de la Paz:** Enjoy a picnic and a leisurely walk while getting to know the exotic natural tropical flora that adorn this pristine,

palm-shadowed botanical garden. Be sure to head uphill to view the nearby monumental cross at Capilla de la Paz, which also offers a breathtaking view of Acapulco's sparkling bay (page 39).

◖ **Isla Roqueta:** This pristine forested island that beckons across the blue channel from Playa Caleta is easily reachable by glass-bottomed boat tour. Easy trails lead uphill to the lighthouse and continue above panoramic cliff-top ocean views to hidden beach Playa Las Palmitas and relaxing Restaurant Palao, fine for lunch or an early supper (page 41).

◖ **Hotel Los Flamingos:** Its spectacular sunset-view perch would be attraction enough, but this old-Acapulco jewel offers much more. Linger to enjoy a lobby gallery of old Hollywood–Acapulco connection photos, a precious cliff-top gazebo for sunset cocktails, and an airy view *palapa* restaurant for dinner (page 42).

◖ **Laguna Coyuca Boat Tour:** Pie de la Cuesta, the beach village just northwest of Acapulco, is the jumping-off point for this relaxing day excursion. En route, as you enjoy the cooling breeze, your boat threads through mangrove-laced channels and passes islands festooned with nesting herons, cormorants, and pelicans (page 77).

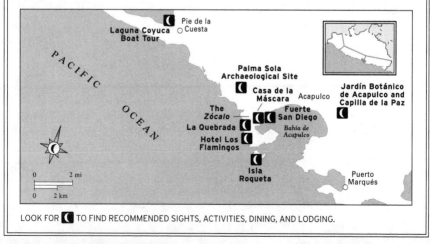

LOOK FOR ◖ TO FIND RECOMMENDED SIGHTS, ACTIVITIES, DINING, AND LODGING.

beach-nooks of offshore Isla Roqueta, and maybe hike through a sylvan mountainside park, decorated by a trove of ancient petroglyphs, and finally, at day's end, soak up the sunset vista at Hotel Los Flamingos.

With more time, you can adventure beyond the edges of the Acapulco metropolis and discover more hidden Acapulcos: such as the grand, glassy Laguna Tres Palos via either a breezy jet-boat ride or your own kayak, or by strolling the driftwood-strewn strands of Playa Larga, or by tour boat to south-seas islands such as Isla Montosa, in wildlife-rich mangrove Laguna Coyuca; and if Acapulco has persuaded you to linger, stay a night or two at the palmy, charmingly out-of-date downscale resort village of Pie de la Cuesta.

## PLANNING YOUR TIME

Of course even in a month of Sundays you won't be able to do everything that Acapulco offers, so you might as well save something for your next visit. But spend at least a day around the old-town *zócalo* neighborhood. Start out with breakfast at Café Los Amigos, and sit

© BRUCE WHIPPERMAN

the old-town *zócalo*

down and do some people-watching from a bench beneath the shady trees. Wander south a few blocks to **Fuerte San Diego** and spend a couple of hours perusing its fascinating displays, climbing to its crenellated battlements to enjoy the airy bay view. On your way back be sure to stop for a half hour at the **Casa de la Máscara.** By late afternoon, it will be time to enjoy the sunset, so taxi over to **Hotel Los Flamingos** for drinks at their sunset gazebo and perhaps supper in their adjacent restaurant. Later continue by taxi on to **La Quebrada** to ooh and aah at the divers' amazingly scary exhibition.

Having hit some of the highlights, you might concentrate on your own interests. For example, from Playa Caleta, lovers of the outdoors could take a glass-bottomed boat tour, and spend the day hiking the forested paths of **Isla Roqueta** and doing some sunning and snorkeling (bring your own gear) from the island's hidden beaches, and enjoy late lunch at super-scenic Restaurant Palao. On another day, you might taxi uphill to **Palma Sola Archaeological Site** for a picnic and a shady mountainside stroll among the petroglyphs. On a third day, head to the east side and enjoy the spectacular mountaintop vista from the **Capilla de la Paz,** followed up by a stroll around the lush, forested **Jardín Botánico** (botanical garden); or alternatively, take a scuba diving lesson from the Acapulco Scuba Center or go on a fishing trip with Fish-R-Us.

On the other hand, handicrafts shoppers could spend at least an hour at the Bonita handicrafts shop near the *zócalo,* and at least another hour at the nearby Mercado de Parrazal handicrafts market. After lunch (maybe at Sanborn's near the *zócalo*), you could taxi to Acapulco town market to see the piñatas, then continue east for a couple hours, browsing the handicrafts arcades and stores in mid-town.

If you want a party you can always find one right in Acapulco. A good place to start out would be Restaurant El Olvido for dinner (or if you're on a budget, Restaurant El Zorrito or Taco Tumbra) and continue to the lineup of clubs and the bungee jump just east of the Diana

ACAPULCO

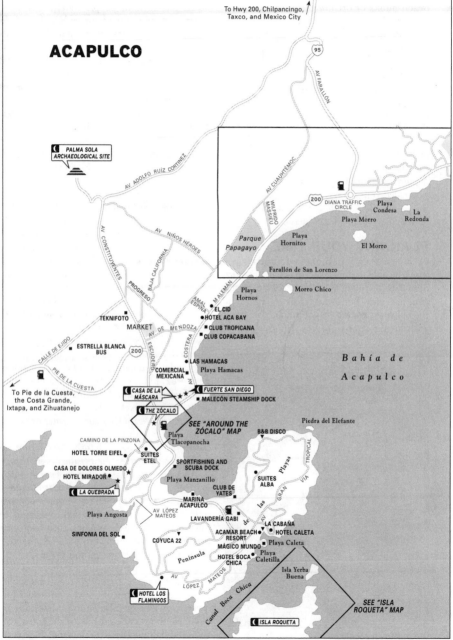

# ACAPULCO

To Hwy 200, Chilpancingo, Taxco, and Mexico City

95

AV FARALLÓN

PALMA SOLA ARCHAEOLOGICAL SITE

AV. ADOLFO RUIZ CORTINEZ

AV CUAUHTÉMOC

WILFRIDO MASSIEU

200

DIANA TRAFFIC CIRCLE

Playa Condesa

La Redonda

Playa Morro

AV. CONSTITUYENTES

AV. NIÑOS HÉROES

BAJA CALIFORNIA

PROGRESO

Parque Papagayo

Playa Hornitos

El Morro

Farallón de San Lorenzo

AV DE MENDOZA

MALEMÁN

CANAL ESPAÑA

Playa Hornos

Morro Chico

TEKNIFOTO

MARKET

EL CID

HOTEL ACA BAY

CLUB TROPICANA

CLUB COPACABANA

CALLE DE EJIDO

ESTRELLA BLANCA BUS

200

AV ESCUDERO

COSTERA

*Bahía de Acapulco*

PIE DE LA CUESTA

LAS HAMACAS

Playa Hamacas

To Pie de la Cuesta, the Costa Grande, Ixtapa, and Zihuatanejo

COMERCIAL MEXICANA

CASA DE LA MÁSCARA

FUERTE SAN DIEGO

MALECÓN STEAMSHIP DOCK

THE ZÓCALO

SEE "AROUND THE ZÓCALO" MAP

Piedra del Elefante

CAMINO DE LA PINZONA

Playa Tlacopanocha

B&B DISCO

HOTEL TORRE EIFEL

SUITES ETEL

SPORTFISHING AND SCUBA DOCK

VÍA TROPICAL

GRAN

SUITES ALBA

CASA DE DOLORES OLMEDO

HOTEL MIRADOR

Playa Manzanillo

CLUB DE YATES

las

LA QUEBRADA

MARINA ACAPULCO

de

Playa Angosta

AV LÓPEZ MATEOS

LAVANDERÍA GABI

SINFONIA DEL SOL

COYUCA 22

ACAMAR BEACH RESORT

LA CABAÑA

HOTEL CALETA

MÁGICO MUNDO

Playa Caleta

Península

HOTEL BOCA CHICA

Playa Caletilla

Isla Yerba Buena

AV LÓPEZ MATEOS

HOTEL LOS FLAMINGOS

SEE "ISLA ROQUETA" MAP

Canal Boca Chica

ISLA ROQUETA

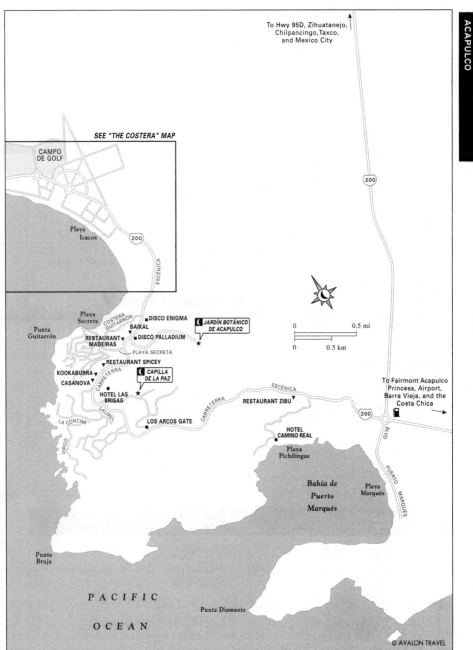

To Hwy 95D, Zihuatanejo, Chilpancingo, Taxco, and Mexico City

CAMPO DE GOLF

SEE "THE COSTERA" MAP

Playa Icacos

200

ESCÉNICA

Playa Secreta

COSTERA GUITARRÓN

DISCO ENIGMA

BAIKAL

RESTAURANT MADEIRAS

DISCO PALLADIUM

JARDÍN BOTÁNICO DE ACAPULCO

PLAYA SECRETA

Punta Guitarrón

RESTAURANT SPICEY

KOOKABURRA

CASANOVA

CAPILLA DE LA PAZ

CARRETERRA

HOTEL LAS BRISAS

LAUREL

LA CONCHA

VIRGO

LOS ARCOS GATE

ESCÉNICA

CARRETERRA

RESTAURANT ZIBU

To Fairmont Acapulco Princess, Airport, Barra Vieja, and the Costa Chica

200

BLVD

PUERTO MARQUÉS

HOTEL CAMINO REAL

Playa Pichilingue

Bahía de Puerto Marqués

Playa Marqués

Punta Bruja

0    0.5 mi

0    0.5 km

PACIFIC

OCEAN

Punta Diamante

© AVALON TRAVEL

Circle, which will probably occupy you until at least midnight. With time to spare, continue on to more clubs, such as Baby O and Nina's on the Costera, east end. And finally if the night is still young, continue to the super-disco Palladium on the far east-side Las Brisas hillside.

With another day or two you could explore some of Acapulco's country corners. For example, head northwest to Pie de la Cuesta for a boat tour of the wildlife-rich mangrove-laced **Laguna Coyuca** and its delightfully rustic mini-paradise Isla Montosa. You might linger for a day or two more in a comfortable Pie de la Cuesta beachfront hotel, such as Villa Nirvana or upscale Hotel Vayma.

Alternatively, head southeast of town for a few hours of beachcombing and a picnic on breezy Playa Larga; or continue to the palm-shaded end-of-the-road village Barra Vieja for lunch in a rustic beachfront *palapa* restaurant and a tour and some bird-watching (or a jet-boat ride) on the grand mangrove Laguna Tres Palos.

Yet another out-of-town option would be to head north for river rafting on the Río Papagayo from October through March.

## ORIENTATION

In one tremendous sweep, Acapulco curves around its dazzling half-moon bay. Face the open ocean and you are looking due south. West will be on your right hand, east on your left. (Unexpected but true, the Pacific Ocean at Acapulco lies to the south, not the west. Remember that everywhere on earth, the sun sets in the west, and then notice where the sun sets in Acapulco: not out to sea, as in San Francisco or Seattle, but in a direction approximately parallel to the shoreline.)

One continuous beachfront boulevard, appropriately named the Costera Miguel Alemán (the "Costera," for short), unites old (pre-1950) Acapulco, west of the Parque Papagayo amusement zone, with new Acapulco, the lineup of big beach hotels that stretches around the bay to the Las Brisas condo headland. There a big cross glows at night, marking the hilltop lookout, Mirador La Capilla, above the bay's east end.

On the opposite, old-town side of Parque Papagayo, the Costera curves along the palmy, uncluttered Playas Hornos and Hamacas to the steamship dock. Here the Costera, called the *malecón* as it passes the *zócalo* (town plaza), continues to the mansion-dotted hilly jumble of Peninsula de las Playas.

## GETTING AROUND

Buses run nearly continuously along the Costera. Fare averages the equivalent of about $0.40. Bus routes—indicated by such labels as Base (BAH-say, the naval base on the east end), Centro (*zócalo*), Caleta (the beach, at the far west end), Cine (movie theater near the beach before the *zócalo*), and Hornos (the beach near Parque Papagayo)—run along the Costera.

Taxis, on the other hand, cost between $2 and $6 for any in-town destination. They are not metered, so agree upon the price *before* you get in. If the driver demands too much, hailing another taxi often solves the problem.

# History

## IN THE BEGINNING

Experts believe that Acapulco Bay, with its trove of seafood ripe for the picking, was home to bands of hunter-gatherers beginning at least 4,000 years ago. They left mute testimony in the rock paintings of their gods at Puerto Marqués, Pie de la Cuesta, and the newly opened site at Palma Sola, uphill from present-day Acapulco town. Moreover, these earliest inhabitants left direct evidence of their daily life at seaside sites: stone metates and pottery utensils that experts have dated to around 2500 B.C.

Acapulco's bounty eventually led to more leisure and more sophistication. At Las Sabanas, at the northern edge of the Acapulco suburb,

# THE LEGEND OF ACAPULCO

The *Codex Mendoza* records that, in 1499, en route south from their capital of Tenochtitlán, Aztec commanders and their armies first gazed downward at the blue sweep of Acapulco Bay. Motivated by their need for tropical treasures, such as exotic bird feathers and cacao – so valuable that cacao seeds served as the Aztecs' currency – Aztec forces tried but failed to subdue the fierce Yope tribes that ruled the Acapulco coast.

Nevertheless, the Aztec-origin name, Acapulco, from *acatl*, the Náhuatl (Aztec-language) word for reed, remained. Although translations of Acapulco vary, the meaning "place where the reeds are destroyed" appears most credible. First of all, the traditional Aztec hieroglyph for Acapulco shows a pair of hands, one of which is shown breaking a reed. Moreover,

there is the Yope legend of Acapulco that tells the story of Acatl, the son of the Aztec commander. It seems that Acatl fell hopelessly in love with Quiahuitl (kwee-ahoo-WEE-tl), comely daughter of the Yope chieftain. When his father forbade him to marry Quiahuitl, Acatl screamed with sorrow. His tears flowed so profusely that they melted him, transforming Acatl into a pond bordered by a reed thicket. Meanwhile, Quiahuitl, vaporized by her all-consuming grief, rose to the heavens as a cloud, condemned to float aimlessly over land and sea. But the lovers nevertheless received fulfillment every year during the summer rains, when Quiahuitl would float over Acapulco and rain upon Acatl's pond, uniting the lovers with so much ardor that the downpour flattened and drowned the reeds lining the pond.

archaeologists unearthed a treasury of fetching female statuettes, reminiscent of early Polynesian and Asian artifacts. Such discoveries have added credence to widespread legends of early Chinese influences on the Mexican Pacific coast long before Columbus.

## Highland Influences

Evidence of other far-flung influences is equally intriguing. Among the most fascinating of finds are the ancient paintings at the caves of Juxtlahuaca, not far from Chilpancingo (see the *Guerrero Upcountry* chapter), in the mountains north of Acapulco. Here, deep in a regal limestone-draped grotto, captivating multicolored Olmec-origin paintings decorate the cavern walls. Although several similar finds all over the state of Guerrero led historians to the conclusion that Acapulco's early inhabitants were undoubtedly influenced by Mexico's high civilizations—Olmec, Mixtec, Zapotec, and Aztec—and frequented by their traders, the same experts believe that Acapulco never came under their direct control but instead remained the domain of a fiercely tenacious tribe, known as the Yopes, until the Spanish conquest.

## CONQUEST AND COLONIZATION

Enter Hernán Cortés, who in 1519 sailed in command of a small fleet west from Cuba. He didn't find the elusive passage to China, but, hearing of a grand kingdom in the mountains to the west, marched overland and boldly took the Aztec Emperor Moctezuma captive. Nearly immediately, Cortés asked Moctezuma about Mexico's southern coast and dispatched expeditions west and south, founding villages and shipbuilding ports in Oaxaca, at Huatulco and Tehuántepec, and in the Acapulco region, at Zacatula and Acapulco.

One of the earliest of those expeditions, commanded by Juan Rodríguez de Villafuerte, landed at Acapulco Bay on the feast day of Santa Lucía in 1523. Following Spanish custom, Villafuerte christened his discovery the Bahía de Santa Lucía, a name it retained for years. A safe anchorage, good fresh water, and an abundance of big trees led Villafuerte to establish an outpost and shipbuilding port by the latter 1520s. Word got back to the authorities, and by royal decree, in 1528, "Acapulco and her land...where the ships of the south will be built . . ." passed directly into the hands of the Spanish Crown.

Voyages of discovery set sail from Acapulco for Peru, the Gulf of California, and Asia. None returned from across the Pacific, however, until navigator-priest Father Andrés de Urdaneta discovered the northern Pacific trade winds, which propelled him and his ship, loaded with Chinese treasure, to Acapulco in October 1565.

## The Manila Galleon

From then on, for more than 250 years, a special yearly trading ship, renowned in Mexico as the Nao de China and in England as the Manila galleon, set sail exclusively from Acapulco for Asia. Tensely anticipating the Manila galleon's return, Acapulco authorities sent ships to scan the northwestern horizon. Runners and signal fires brought the news to Acapulco and Mexico City, setting in motion a long line of Acapulco-bound traders.

The galleon's arrival sparked an annual trade fair, swelling Acapulco's population with merchants from not only all of Mexico, but from as far as Spain and Peru. Loaded down with gold-filled purses, the traders jostled to bargain for the Manila galleon's shiny trove of silks, satins, damasks, porcelain, gold, ivory, and lacquerware. Fortunes were not only exchanged at trading; they were also gained and lost gambling at raucous cockfights and exciting horse

## THE EPIC VOYAGE OF AMBASSADOR HASEKURA TSUNENAGA

By 1600, competition with the Portuguese and Dutch for missionary and trade concessions in east Asia pushed Spanish authorities toward closer ties with Japan. In 1602, Rodrigo de Vivero, acting governor of the Philippines, initiated contact with Shogun Tokugawa Ieyasu (of *Shogun* movie and novel fame).

Vivero's efforts were successful, but literally by accident. During his return to Acapulco in 1609, Vivero's ship, the galleon *San Francisco*, was wrecked on the Japanese coast near Edo (now Tokyo). Fortunately for the Spanish this incident coincided with a serious deterioration in relations between the Tokugawa government and the Dutch trade mission. To their own detriment, the Dutch had issued impossibly stiff rules for buying Japanese silk and added insult to injury by trying to hog all Japanese foreign trade for themselves.

Vivero must have impressed the shogun, for Tokugawa ended up giving him an entire new ship (built by English samurai William Adams, also of *Shogun* movie fame), a small fortune in gold to fit out and operate the ship, a Spanish-Japanese trade treaty, and a request to the king of Spain for an exchange of ambassadors. Vivero, in his new ship, christened the *San Bue-naventura*, sailed on August 1, 1610, and landed safely in Acapulco three months later.

This set the stage for one of history's most remarkable odysseys. In reciprocation for the requested Spanish ambassador, explorer Sebastián Vizcaíno (who arrived from Acapulco on June 10, 1610), the Japanese authorities designated nobleman Hasekura Tsunenaga as ambassador-elect to the Spanish court in Madrid.

How Hasekura accomplished his task is one of history's great little-known but epic adventures. First, he needed an oceangoing ship (few if any of which were available in Japan) to carry him across the entire Pacific and return. With the enthusiastic backing of the *daimyo* (baron) of Sendai in northwest Japan, a sturdy vessel christened the *San Sebastián* was built by 7,000 workers in a mere six months, and it sailed from Sendai (where, to this day, a monument marks the event) on October 27, 1613.

Hasekura's reception in Acapulco three months later was a celebration long remembered. To the multiple booms of cannon salutes, an array of blasting harquebuses, and the rhythm of drums, fifes, and trumpets, port authorities escorted Tsunenaga's entourage of

races, in which African Mexicans soon became the star riders.

## Pirates and Forts

Acapulco's yearly treasure soon attracted marauders. In 1579, Francis Drake, during his celebrated circumnavigation of the globe, and blessed by England's Queen Elizabeth I, threatened the Spanish Pacific coast from Chile to California. One of his most notorious raids was at Huatulco, on April 13, 1579, when he even stole the church bell. Drake waited fruitlessly for the Manila galleon as far north as Cape Mendocino, in present-day Northern California, before continuing west across the Pacific.

Later, corsair Thomas Cavendish managed similar mischief, burning Huatulco in 1586. He continued northwest, where, off Cabo San Lucas, Cavendish was the first to capture the Manila galleon, the *Santa Ana*. The cash booty alone, 1.2 million gold pesos, severely depressed the London gold market.

On October 11, 1614, a five-ship Dutch fleet, consisting of the *Sun, Moon, Pechelinga, Jager,* and *Meeuve,* attacked the unfortified village of Acapulco. Already weakened by scurvy and hunger, the Dutch sailors called off the attack and, for food and water, traded two dozen hostages they had captured in Peru.

Such attacks pushed Viceroy Diego Fernández de Córdoba to build a fort overlooking Acapulco Bay. In 1615, he commissioned,

---

78 (including his entire family) to "lodgings that were ordered to be as luxurious as possible."

After a short Acapulco stay, Hasekura pushed ahead. His entire entourage, which had swollen to hundreds, continued to Mexico City, where they were likewise received with due tumult and honor and where all of the Japanese accepted baptism.

They continued to Veracruz, pushed eastward to Cuba, and finally arrived in Spain on October 5, 1614. After being feted at a number of towns, notably Seville, along the way, Hasekura continued to Madrid and presented his credentials to King Phillip III on January 30, 1615. He accepted a second baptism, this time taking the name of Felipe Francisco (in honor of both the Spanish king and the Franciscan order), on February 17. Continuing to Rome, via Barcelona and Genoa, Hasekura was declared a Roman citizen by the city fathers and received by Pope Paul V on November 3, 1615.

Despite all of the honors, pageantry, and polite talk, Hasekura's mission accomplished virtually nothing. He received no promises of trade from the Spanish authorities nor support from the pope. The reason was a feisty combination of economics and politics. Many, including rich Christian merchants in India, Macao, and the Philippines, were opposed to Spanish-Japanese

trade. The Spanish Jesuits, who already had a bishop in Japan, were opposed to Hasekura because his Christian support came from the rival Franciscans. Perhaps most devastating were the machinations of the shogun, who suspected that Spanish incursion into Japan might lead to domination. He was persecuting Japanese Christians and expelling a crowd of Spanish priests from Japan at the very moment Hasekura was conducting negotiations in Spain.

Disheartened, ill with fever, and nearly broke, Hasekura left Rome and returned quickly west. Without even stopping in Madrid, he and his entourage left Spain in July 1617, continuing via reverse route through Mexico. They departed from Acapulco in late 1617 in the *San Sebastián* and arrived in Manila in February 1618. In the Philippines, Hasekura renewed efforts on behalf of Japanese-Spanish trade and diplomatic contacts, but to no avail. He returned in August 1620, to a Japan increasingly hostile to any foreign trade or Christian missions. During the next dozen years, thousands of Japanese Christian converts were burned at the stake and all external trade, except for a trickle limited to the Dutch, was forbidden. Thus Japan remained a hermit empire, with virtually all foreign contact punishable by death, for 230 years.

ACAPULCO

© BRUCE WHIPPERMAN

view of new Acapulco (background horizon), across the blue bay from old Acapulco (foreground)

ironically, Dutch architect Adrian Bott, who completed the citadel Fuerte San Diego, with five sturdy crenellated ramparts, arranged in a formidable pentagonal array. Although the fort was mostly symbolic, it limited subsequent attacks on Acapulco throughout the 16th and 17th centuries to a few unsuccessful attempts. In reality, sun, termites, and earthquakes posed the fort's most serious hazards. Repairs seemed to be constantly necessary until a terrible earthquake in 1776 finished the old fort off.

It was resurrected in grand style by military engineers Miguel Costanzo, who drew the plans, and Ramón Panón, who supervised the construction. The entire job, completed in July 1783, cost about 600,000 gold pesos, which would amount to many tens of millions of U.S. dollars today. Now serving as a distinguished museum, the Fuerte San Diego, austere and grand, still proudly stands guard over Acapulco Bay.

## INDEPENDENCE

Scarcely a month after Miguel Hidalgo's impassioned *grito* that inspired revolt against Spain, Hidalgo's *insurgente* compatriot, José

María Morelos, was leading a rebel regiment against the royalist garrison in Acapulco. Attracted by the Manila galleon wealth he assumed was hidden there, Morelos besieged the Fuerte San Diego. Although he squeezed down on the fort, eventually surrounding it after a several-month siege, the royalist garrison broke out and scattered Morelos's soldiers. Consequently, the Manila galleon was able to land more or less annually until 1820, when rebel forces cut off all support from Mexico City, stopping the Manila galleon forever.

At the end of the war for independence, in 1821, Acapulco was almost completely in ruins. Most of its 3,000 inhabitants, the majority poor African Mexicans, were hungry and ill-clothed. Housing consisted nearly entirely of grass huts, except for the 30 or 40 stone or adobe homes of Acapulco's business and professional gentry.

By the mid-1800s, Acapulco's fine natural harbor began to turn its fortunes around. After 1850, Acapulco became a stopover for a flotilla of steamships filled with San Francisco–bound gold-rush adventurers. Subsequently Acapulco also served as a coaling station for British, American, and French navy steamers that were plying the Pacific in increasing numbers.

## MODERN ACAPULCO

On November 11, 1927, the Mexican government blasted through the first Mexico City–Acapulco automobile road, and the first cars shortly began arriving (after a six-day trip, however). The first luxury hotel, the Mirador, at La Quebrada, went up in 1933; soon airplanes began arriving.

During the late 1940s, Mexican president Miguel Alemán fell in love with Acapulco and thought everyone else should have the same opportunity. He built new boulevards, power plants, and modern Highway 95, which cut the Mexico City driving time to six hours. Investors responded with a lineup of high-rise hotels. Finally, in 1959, U.S. president Dwight Eisenhower and Mexican president Adolfo López Mateos convened their summit conference in a grand Acapulco hostelry.

Movie stars such as Elvis Presley and Lana Turner began coming, staying for weeks, and buying homes. Elizabeth Taylor married movie magnate Michael Todd in the posh Hotel Villa Vera overlooking the new Acapulco. International jet service began in 1964.

Thousands of Mexicans flocked to fill jobs in the shiny hotels and restaurants. They built shantytowns, which climbed the hills and spilled over into previously sleepy communities nearby. The government responded with streets, drainage, power, housing, and schools.

However, by the 1980s overdevelopment was beginning to tarnish Acapulco's luster. Hotels had aged; some had become rundown. Untreated sewage was beginning to pollute Acapulco's once pristine bay.

Fortunately, the government acted to reverse Acapulco's decline. New sewage works were built, clearing up the pollution. New streets and parks were constructed, and dozens of middle-aged hotels were returned to their former grandeur.

By the turn of the new millennium, Acapulco had been largely restored and was attracting new investments. Its sky was again blue, its azure waters were again clean, and it is now a magnet for millions of yearly visitors, foreign and domestic.

# Sights

## OLD ACAPULCO

In old Acapulco, traffic slows and people return to traditional ways. Couples promenade along the *malecón* dockfront, fishing boats leave and return, while in the adjacent *zócalo* families stroll past the church, musicians play, and tourists and businesspeople sip coffee in the shade of huge banyan trees.

### ◖ The *Zócalo*

Start your walk beneath those *zócalo* trees. Under their pendulous air roots, browse the bookstalls, relax in one of the cafés; at night, watch the clowns perform, listen to a band concert, or join in a pitch-penny game. Take a look inside the mod-style **cathedral** dedicated to Our Lady of Solitude. Admire its angel-filled sky-blue ceiling and visit the Virgin to the right of the altar.

Outside, cross the boulevard to the *malecón* dockside; in mid-afternoon, you may see huge marlin and swordfish being hauled up from the boats.

### ◖ Fuerte San Diego

Head out of the *zócalo* and left along the Costera and continue for about three blocks beneath the big pedestrian bridge to the uphill entrance stairway on the left. (Or, alternately, at the big signalled Costera intersection, at Sanborn's, head inland a block, and turn right at Jesús Carranza, at Woolworth's. Continue uphill about three blocks to the parking lot entrance, on the right.) Continue ahead over

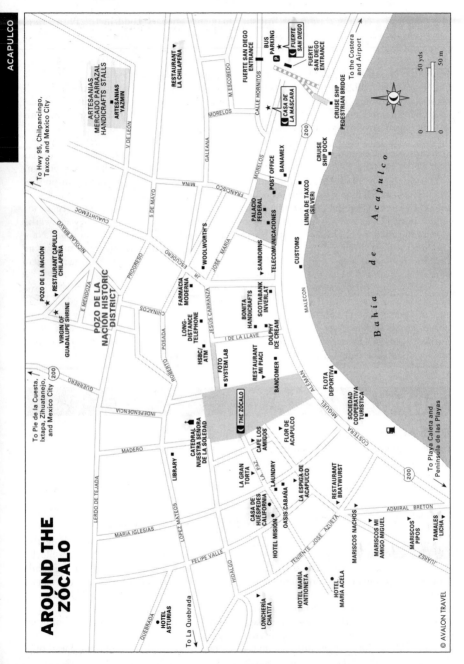

# AROUND THE ZÓCALO

To Hwy. 95, Chilpancingo, Taxco, and Mexico City

To Pie de la Cuesta, Ixtapa, Zihuatanejo, and Mexico City (200)

To La Quebrada

ARTESANÍAS MERCADO PARRAZAL HANDICRAFTS STALLS
ARTESANÍAS YAZMÍN
V. DE LEÓN

RESTAURANT LA CHILAPEÑA

M. ESCOBEDO
MORELOS
GALEANA
MINA
5 DE MAYO
CUAUHTÉMOC
NICOLÁS BRAVO
E. MENDOZA
GUERRERO

POZO DE LA NACIÓN
RESTAURANT CAPULLO CHILAPEÑA
VIRGIN OF GUADALUPE SHRINE
POZO DE LA NACIÓN HISTORIC DISTRICT

PROGRESO
ESCORRO
CHINACOS
POSADA
JR.
JESÚS CARRANZA
I DE LA LLAVE
ROBERTO
INDEPENDENCIA

FRANCISCO
JOSÉ MARÍA
WOOLWORTH'S

BANAMEX
PALACIO FEDERAL
TELECOMUNICACIONES
SANBORNS
POST OFFICE
LINDA DE TAXCO (SILVER)
CUSTOMS

FARMACIA MODERNA
BONITA HANDICRAFTS
SCOTIABANK
INVERLAT
DOLPHY ICE CREAM
LONG-DISTANCE TELEPHONE
HSBC/ATM
FOTO SYSTEM LAB
RESTAURANT MI PIACI
BANCOMER

THE ZÓCALO
CATEDRAL NUESTRA SEÑORA DE LA SOLEDAD
LIBRARY
CAFÉ LOS AMIGOS
FLOR DE ACAPULCO
LA GRAN TORTA
LA PAZ
LAUNDRY
CASA DE HUÉSPEDES CALIFORNIA
OASIS CABAÑA
HOTEL MISIÓN
LA ESPIGA DE ACAPULCO
RESTAURANT BRATWURST

MADERO
LERDO DE TEJADA
MARÍA IGLESIAS
LÓPEZ MATEOS
FELIPE VALLE
HIDALGO
QUEBRADA
TENIENTE JOSÉ AZUETA
ADMIRAL BRETON
JUÁREZ

HOTEL ASTURIAS
LONCHERÍA CHATITA
HOTEL MARÍA ANTONIETA
HOTEL MARÍA ACELA
MARISCOS NACHOS
MARISCOS MI AMIGO MIGUEL
MARISCOS PIPOS
TAMALES LICHA

MIGUEL ALEMÁN
FLOTA DEPORTIVA
SOCIEDAD COOPERATIVA TURÍSTICA
MALECÓN
COSTERA
(200)

To Playa Caleta and Península de las Playas

FUERTE SAN DIEGO ENTRANCE
BUS PARKING
FUERTE SAN DIEGO
FUERTE SAN DIEGO ENTRANCE
CALLE HORNITOS
CASA DE LA MÁSCARA
CRUISE SHIP PEDESTRIAN BRIDGE
CRUISE SHIP DOCK

To the Costera and Airport

Bahía de Acapulco

50 yds
50 m

© AVALON TRAVEL

© BRUCE WHIPPERMAN

Acapulco's cathedral is dedicated to Our Lady of Solitude.

the great moat and enter the grand Fuerte San Diego (tel. 744/482-3828, fuertedesandiego@ prodigy.net.mx, 10:30 A.M.–4:30 P.M. Tues.– Sun.), a pentagonal maze of massive walls, all topped by bristling battlements, completed by engineer Miguel Costanzo in 1783.

Inside, galleries within the original fort storerooms, barracks, chapel, and kitchen illustrate local pre-Columbian, conquest, and colonial history. The excellent, unusually graphic displays include much about pirates (such as Francis Drake, Thomas Cavendish, and John Hawkins, known as "admirals" to the English-speaking world); Spanish galleons, their history and construction; and famous visitors. One notable visitor was Japanese ambassador Hasekura Tsunenaga, who in 1613 built a ship and sailed from Sendai, Japan, to Acapulco; he continued overland to Mexico City, by sea to Spain, to the pope in Rome, and back again through Acapulco to Japan. Before you leave, be sure to visit the museum's excellent bookstore, on the right after you pass the ticket booth.

Fuerte San Diego sometimes puts on an *espectáculo* (sound and light show), using symphonic melodies and dramatic projection upon curtains of water and the old fortress walls themselves to recount Acapulco's remarkable history. Showtimes, customarily at around 7 P.M., depend on season. Confirm the schedule (*horario*) at the museum or at the tourist information office, tel. 744/484-4416 or 744/484-4583.

### ◖ Casa de la Máscara

As you exit the Fuerte San Diego, continue along the lane that begins just west of the museum parking lot. In half a block, you'll arrive at Casa de la Máscara (no phone, call *turismo* tel. 744/484-4416 to verify hours, pedriola240@ hotmail.com, 10 A.M.–4 P.M. Tues.–Sun., free). Inside, enjoy six rooms decorated with a trove of fascinating indigenous masks, all handcrafted for the myriad traditional fiestas celebrated in towns and villages all over the state of Guerrero.

Besides the well-known examples, such as the clownish Viejitos (old ones), grinning red devils, scary jaguars, and angelic cherubs, be sure to see the masks that poke fun at the

© BRUCE WHIPPERMAN

ceremonial jaguar mask

neighborhood, where the merchants that prospered from the Manila galleon trade built their homes, spreads uphill, behind the cathedral, north from the *zócalo*. The heart of the several-square-block district is the small intersection-square, at the corner of Calles Allende and Alarcón. A monument at the square's north uphill corner marks the *pozo* (well) for which the district is named. In 1850, governor Juan Álvarez ordered the well dug to furnish a clean water source and alleviate the devastating local cholera epidemic.

Acapulco people remember that wise and kindly act, especially around January 12, when droves of folks arrive to pay homage at the illuminated shrine to the Virgin of Guadalupe across the square from the *pozo*.

Behind the Guadalupe shrine, pause (especially if it's a warm day) in the cool shade beneath the great **Árbol del Fraile** (Tree of the Friar), brought from Peru as a seedling centuries ago. Locals enjoy the sweet yellow fruit that it drops from its spreading branches during the month of June.

Another good place to pause, especially if you're hungry, is at the clean *comedor*-style Restaurant El Nuevo Capullo Chilapeño, behind and to the right of the *pozo* monument.

Spanish colonials, with features such as three eyes, double noses, bald heads, and big ears.

Although in modern society masks serve merely theatrical and celebratory functions, in parts of rural Mexico certain masks retain their pre-Columbian function and significance: By donning a mask, a person soaks up the supernatural power of the god that the mask depicts. Jaguar masks, for example, are a remnant of the jaguar cult, common in Mesoamerican tradition. Many ancient Mexican and Central American stone glyphs and paper or bark codices show half human, half jaguar personages, which anthropologists commonly interpret as depictions of priests in jaguar mask and costume, thus elevated to the powerful realm of the gods.

Before leaving, be sure to visit the room of masks exotically reminiscent of West Africa, made by the *costeños,* or African Mexicans, most of whom now live along the Guerrero–Oaxaca coast east of Acapulco.

### Pozo de la Nación Historic District

Pozo de la Nación, Acapulco's oldest permanent

### ◖ La Quebrada

Head back to the *zócalo* and continue west from the front of the cathedral. After three short blocks to Avenida López Mateos, continue uphill to the La Quebrada diver's point, marked by the big parking lot at the hillcrest. There, Acapulco's energy focuses five times a day (at 1 P.M. and hourly 7–10 P.M.) as tense crowds watch the divers plummet more than 100 feet to the waves below. Admission is about $2, collected by the divers' cooperative. Performers average less than $100 per dive from the proceeds. The adjacent Hotel Mirador charges about $10 cover to view the dives from its terrace.

### Casa de Dolores Olmedo

Celebrated muralist and painter Diego Rivera (1886–1957), whose renown has received a boost from the latter-day fame of his second wife, Frida Kahlo, spent the last years of his life with his friend Dolores Olmedo, grand dame of Acapulco. Señora Olmedo, who herself died in July 2002, was perhaps the world's foremost collector of Rivera works. One of the most visible decorates the front wall of Olmedo's former home compound, on a quiet side street in the upscale Península de las Playas neighborhood, not far from La Quebrada.

The work is a rainbow-hued mosaic, dynamically depicting some of Rivera's favorite prime actors of Mexican mythology. Foremost is the feathered serpent god Quetzalcoatl, who writhes along more than half of the 100-foot length of the mosaic. Also present is the beloved Mexican hairless dog, Xoloitzciutle.

Rivera, weakened by age, toiled for a year and a half during 1956 and 1957 to complete the mosaic. Loyal to his own communist ideology, he included a red hammer and sickle; in response to a government request, Rivera removed it before he died.

Rising behind the mural is Dolores Olmedo's former house, where Rivera stayed and worked, covering the inside chamber walls with a treasury of stunning murals. Hopefully, Señora Olmedo's heirs will continue her practice of allowing public viewing tours of some of the inside rooms. For more information, contact Guerrero Turismo at tel. 744/484-4416.

Get there most easily by taxi. If you don't mind (or would welcome) a short but steep hike (best in morning or late afternoon), go from La Quebrada. Cross busy Avenida López Mateos and continue south, heading up steep, winding Camino de la Pinzona. After about a quarter mile, turn right at the first street, Camino de la Inalámbrica, and continue another quarter mile to the Olmedo house and mosaic, on the right at Inalámbrica 6.

### ◖ Palma Sola Archaeological Site

On a high hillside above Acapulco's west-side neighborhood, a trove of petroglyphs has been excavated for public viewing (approximately 9 A.M.–5 P.M. daily, $2). The site, at an elevation of about 1,200 feet, adjacent to ridgetop

© BRUCE WHIPPERMAN

**Palma Sola Archaeological Site preserves a treasury of ancient petroglyphs.**

El Veladero ecological park, displays a number of big (3–20 feet) geometric-, animal-, and human-form petroglyphs. Created by an ancient people, known generically as "Los Yopes," the stone carvings date from between 200 B.C. and A.D. 600. Get there most easily by tour or taxi, up Avenida Palma Sola to road's end before the hilltop, where a path leads you the last few hundred yards. Take a hat, water, and walking shoes. Local guides will most likely be available on-site. You may also want to arrange a tour through a travel agent, such as American Express, at the west end of the Hotel Continental Emporio (tel. 744/435-2200). For more information, contact the tourist information office (tel. 744/484-4416).

### ◖ Jardín Botánico de Acapulco and Capilla de la Paz

Tour, taxi, drive, or bus east along the Costera for a visit to one or both of these very worthwhile sights. Allow at least an hour for each, and about three hours for the entire excursion (which could easily be extended to Acapulco's east-end beach country, including breezy Playa Larga and the downscale south-seas village of Barra Vieja and Laguna Tres Palos; see listings in the *Beaches* section of this chapter).

Arrive in the morning, by 9:30, first at the botanical garden (Loyola University, Av. Heróico Militar s/n, Cumbres de Llano Largo, tel./fax 744/446-5252, esalinas@acapulcobotanico.org, www.acapulcobotanico .org, 9 A.M.–6 P.M. daily, $3). This extensive semi-wild tropical garden nestles in a pair of lush and intimate creek valleys adjacent to the small, new campus of Loyola University. Trails wind from the parking lot upward to the garden's visitors center, that includes a modest museum-gift shop and small café.

The driving force behind this all is personable director Esther Pliego de Salinas, who deserves plaudits for her expert work putting together the entire excellent project. Her efforts can be appreciated by the casual visitor at least for its lush beauty, by the serious green thumb for its exotic variety, and the professional botanist for its clearly dedicated scientific intent and achievement.

Although relatively new, the garden is fully functional and includes carefully and extensively marked self-guided trails that detail dozens of intriguingly striking tropical plants, from palms and cycads to heliconias, gingers, hardwoods, cactuses, and much more.

Get there by either bus, private car, taxi, or tour. By bus, take a "Lomas", "Barra Vieja," or "Puerto Marqués" bus heading east on the Costera. Get off the bus or pull over and stop your car at Madieras Restaurant on the right. From there, either hire a taxi, continue by car, or walk the remaining kilometer uphill to the botanical garden by following the road that cuts left beneath the overpass (watch ahead for botanical garden signs), about 100 yards (91 meters) uphill from the restaurant.

For the Capilla de la Paz, continue uphill. Turn at the first left past the Las Brisas resort and follow the Capilla de la Paz signs for about another half mile uphill.

The Ecumenical Capilla de la Paz (Non-denominational Chapel of Peace,

11 A.M.–1:30 P.M. and 4–6 P.M. daily, free) was originally built as a memorial for Milly, the wife of Las Brisas developer Carlos Trouyet. Although the Chapel eventually became the resting place of the Trouyet family (Milly and Carlos's two sons died tragically in an airplane accident in 1967), it wasn't originally intended as such. It was to be a public chapel for meditation and reflection.

The monumental (140-foot, 42-meter) bronze cross beside the chapel was added in late 1970 as a memorial to his sons by Carlos, who passed away in 1971.

The cross, chapel, and lovely hilltop garden seem to be serving their original purpose. People come quietly, stroll the garden walkways, enjoy the cooling breeze, and admire the unsurpassed view of Acapulco and its surrounding forested hills and emerald-blue bay.

Get there by bus, car, taxi, or tour, via the Los Arcos gate, which you can access by turning left off the Carretera Escénica (Hwy. 200 south toward Puerto Marqués and the airport), about a quarter mile past the Las Brisas Resort entrance. Say "Capilla de la Paz" to the guard at the Los Arcos gate, sign the entrance sheet, and continue a sharply winding half mile uphill, paying close attention to the small "Capilla de la Paz" signs.

## BEACHES
### Old Town Beaches

These start not far from the *zócalo*. At the foot of the Fuerte San Diego, the sand of **Playa Hamacas** (hammocks) begins, changing to **Playa de Los Hornos** (ovens) and curving northeasterly a mile to a rocky shoal-line called Farallón de San Lorenzo. Hornos is the Sunday favorite of Mexican families; boats buzz beyond the very tranquil waves and retirees stroll the wide, yellow sand while vendors work the sunbathing crowd.

Moving south past the *zócalo* and the fishing boats, you'll find **Playa Tlacopanocha**, a petite strip of sand beneath some spreading trees. Here, bay-tour launches wait for passengers, and kids play in the glassy water, which would be great for swimming if it weren't for the refuse from nearby fishing boats.

## Playas Caleta and Caletilla

From the inland side of the Costera, hop onto one of the parade of buses marked Caleta to gemlike Playa Caleta and its twin Playa Caletilla on the far side of the hilly peninsula (named, appropriately, Península de las Playas). The gentle blue ripples at Playa Caleta in particular are safe for the little ones. Caleta and Caletilla are for people who want company. They are often crowded, sometimes nearly packed solid on Sundays and holidays. Boats offer banana-tube rides, and snorkel gear is rentable from beach concessionaires. Dozens of stalls and restaurants serve food and refreshments. Prominent among them is the stall of Arturo "Chocolate" Castro and his oyster divers, who serve their own catch-of-the-day mussels, oysters, and octopus right on the west end of the beach.

The water park **Mágico Mundo** (tel. 744/483-1215, 9 A.M.–5 P.M. daily, $4 adult, $2 child) perches on the little peninsula between the beaches. Although old and worn, Mágico Mundo still maintains an aquarium, restaurant, water slides, and a swimming pool, plus sea lion, piranha, and turtle shows.

## ◖ Isla Roqueta

An Isla Roqueta ticket tout will often try to snare you as you get off the Caleta bus. The round-trip, which runs around $3, is usually in a boat with a glass bottom, through which you can peer at the fish as they peer back from their aqua underwater world. On the other side, you can relax on sunny little Playa Roqueta and have lunch at one of several beachside *palapas.* Sheltered **Playa Roqueta** is also a great snorkeling spot: Simply pull on your mask and snorkel and step into the water to get up close and personal with squadrons of colorful tropical fish.

Later, you might visit the small hillside **zoo,** in the forest above the beach. Animals include some of the endangered local species, such as spider monkey, jaguar, mountain lion, coatimundi, *javelín* (peccary), crocodile, and ocelot.

Other Isla Roqueta options include hiking the mid-island trail uphill from Playa Roqueta a few hundred yards through the shady tropical deciduous forest to the *faro* (lighthouse) at the island summit. The few marines who guard the place are lonely and welcome company. Say

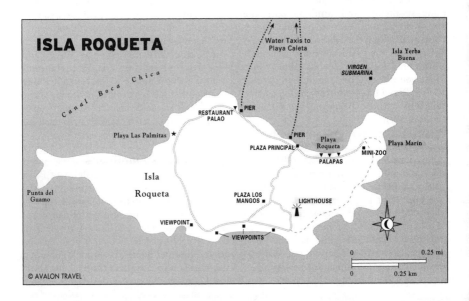

ACAPULCO

© BRUCE WHIPPERMAN

Isla Roqueta's trails lead to some of Acapulco's quiet, hidden places.

hello through the gate and they may let you in for a look around.

Afterward, you could cool off with a swimming, snorkeling, and sunning excursion at one of the island's intimate hidden beaches. For example, from the lighthouse, continue uphill a few hundred yards, then fork right at the clifftop trail and stroll downhill about a mile, where you can cool off, paddling in the tidepools at **Playa Las Palmitas,** at Roqueta's secluded western tip. (Bring your snorkel, mask, and sunscreen.)

Alternatively, on the island's east side past the zoo, a trail climbs to the hillcrest and leads steeply downhill to tiny, secluded **Playa Marin,** where you can loll to your heart's content in the waves that funnel into the narrow channel.

A **boat tour** from Playa Caleta (from the Mágico Mundo island) is another way to get to Isla Roqueta. Glass-bottomed boats leave several times an hour during mid-day, for 90-minute tours (about $5 per person, last boat back around 5 P.M.). Trips include viewing underwater life, shoreline vistas, the homes of 1940s

movie stars (Pedro Infante, John Wayne, Johnny Weismuller), the Virgen Submarina (a holy image of the Virgin of Guadalupe submerged in the Isla Roqueta channel), a stop on the island, and snorkeling. Beer and soft drinks are customarily sold onboard.

An especially nice spot to linger and kick back after your Isla Roqueta exertions is Polynesian-mode **Restaurant Palao** (noon–6 P.M. daily), perched invitingly above the island's west-side channel-front. If you've got an appetite, satisfy it with their melt-in-your mouth Hawaiian-style pork ribs.

## Hotel Los Flamingos

After a spell exploring the delights of Playa Caleta and Isla Roqueta, be sure to stop nearby (take a taxi west, uphill, along clifftop Av. López Mateos) at gorgeously out-of-date Hotel Los Flamingos for a meal, a refreshment in their airy view gazebo (*mirador*), or just a look around. Former home of Johnny Weismuller, the most famous Tarzan of them all, the Hotel Los Flamingos blooms with delights, from a

The Hotel Los Flamingos gazebo offers the best of all possible sunset views.

breathtaking clifftop ocean vista and a lusciously leafy hilltop mango garden-jungle, to a precious blue designer pool. Before you leave, be sure to take in the fascinating gallery of 1940s and '50s photos of luminaries who used to call the Hotel Los Flamingos home, such as John Wayne, Frank Sinatra, Peter Lawford, and Rory Calhoun. The place is so lovely you may be tempted to check in for a week's stay (from $65, see *Accommodations*).

## Playa Angosta

Back on the mainland, you can visit another hidden beach nearby, Playa Angosta (Narrow Beach), the only Acapulco strand with an unobstructed sunset horizon. It's a breezy dab of a beach, sandwiched between a pair of sandstone cliffs, where ocean waves roll in, swishing upon the sand. A food *palapa* occupies one side of the beach and a few fishing launches and nets are on the other. With caution, swimming, bodysurfing, and boogie boarding are sometimes possible here; otherwise, Angosta is best for scenery and picnics.

Just uphill, a few hundred yards along the southbound cliffside Avenida López Mateos, is **Sinfonia del Sol** sunset amphitheater. Here, local folks begin gathering around 5 P.M. daily during the winter (6:30 P.M. in the summer) to enjoy the sun's oft-spectacular twilight performance.

## Costera Beaches

These are the hotel-lined golden shores where affluent Mexicans and foreign visitors stay and play in the sun. They are variations on one continuous curve of sand. Beginning at the west end with **Playa Hornitos** (also known as Playa Papagayo), it continues, changing names from **Playa Morro** to **Playa Villas Acapulco** and finally **Playa Icacos,** which curves and stretches to its sheltered east end past the naval base. All of the same semi-coarse golden silica sand, the beaches begin with fairly broad 200-foot-wide Playas Papagayo and Morro. They narrow sharply to under 100 feet at Playa Villas Acapulco, then broaden again to more than 200 feet along Playa Icacos.

The surf is mostly gentle, breaking in one- or two-foot waves near the beach and receding with moderate undertow. This makes for safe swimming within float-enclosed beachside areas, but waves generally break too near the beach for bodysurfing, boogie boarding, or surfing. Beyond the swimming floats, motorboats hurry along, pulling parasailers and banana-tube riders, while personal watercraft cavort and careen over the swells.

Such motorized hubbub lessens the safety and enjoyment of quieter sports off most new-town beaches. Sailboaters and sailboarders with their own equipment might try the remote, more tranquil east end of Playa Icacos, however.

Water-skiing, officially restricted to certain parts of Acapulco Bay, has largely moved to Laguna Coyuca northwest of the city. Laguna Coyuca also has enough space for many good motorboat-free spots for sailboaters and sailboarders.

Rocky outcroppings along Playas Papagayo, Morro, and Villas Acapulco add interest and intimacy to an already beautiful shoreline. The rocks are good for tidepooling and

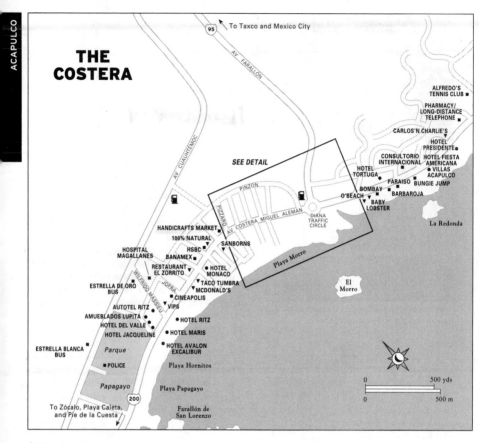

## THE COSTERA

To Taxco and Mexico City

AV FARALLON

ALFREDO'S TENNIS CLUB ■

PHARMACY/ LONG-DISTANCE TELEPHONE ■

CARLOS'N CHARLIE'S ■

HOTEL PRESIDENTE ●

CONSULTORIO INTERNACIONAL ■ HOTEL FIESTA AMERICANA ●

HOTEL TORTUGA ■ VILLAS ACAPULCO ●

PARAISO BUNGIE JUMP ●

BOMBAY ■ BARBAROJA ▼

O'BEACH ▼ BABY LOBSTER ▼

SEE DETAIL

PINZON

AV CUAUHTEMOC

PIZARRO

AV COSTERA MIGUEL ALEMAN

DIANA TRAFFIC CIRCLE

Playa Morro

La Redonda

HANDICRAFTS MARKET ■

100% NATURAL ■

SANBORNS ■

HSBC ■

HOSPITAL MAGALLANES ■

BANAMEX ■

RESTAURANT EL ZORRITO ● HOTEL MONACO

ESTRELLA DE ORO BUS ■

TACO TUMBRA ▼ MCDONALD'S ▼

CINEAPOLIS ■

AUTOTEL RITZ ●

VIPS ▼

WILFRIDO MASSIEU

JOFRA

AMUEBLADOS LUPITA ●

HOTEL DEL VALLE ● ● HOTEL RITZ

HOTEL JACQUELINE ● HOTEL MARIS

ESTRELLA BLANCA BUS ■

Parque

● HOTEL AVALON EXCALIBUR

■ POLICE

Playa Hornitos

El Morro

Papagayo

Playa Papagayo

To Zócalo, Playa Caleta, and Pie de la Cuesta 200

Farallón de San Lorenzo

0          500 yds
0          500 m

fishing by pole-casting (or by net, as locals do) above the waves.

### Beaches Southeast of Town

Drive, taxi ($10), or ride a bus marked Puerto Marqués or Lomas along the Costera eastward. Past the naval base entrance on the right, the road climbs the hill, passing a number of panoramic bay viewpoints. After the Las Brisas condo-hotel complex, the road curves around the hill shoulder and heads downward past picture-perfect vistas of **Bahía de Puerto Marqués.** At the bottom-of-the-hill intersection and overpass, a road branches right to Puerto Marqués.

This drab little bayside town is mainly a Sunday seafood and picnicking retreat for Acapulco families. Dozens of *palapa* restaurants line its motorboat-dotted sandy beach. One ramshackle hotel, at the far south end of the single main beachfront street, offers lodgings. Unless seriously limited by time, best skip this place for much better beach prospects a quarter of an hour farther southeast. If you do stay, don't linger after dark.

If you're driving, mark your odometer at the hill-bottom intersection and head east toward the airport. If traveling by bus, continue via one of the Lomas buses, which head east from Acapulco about once an hour. About a mile farther, a turn-off road goes right to the Fairmont Acapulco Princess and the Pierre Marqués hotels and golf course on Playa Revolcadero.

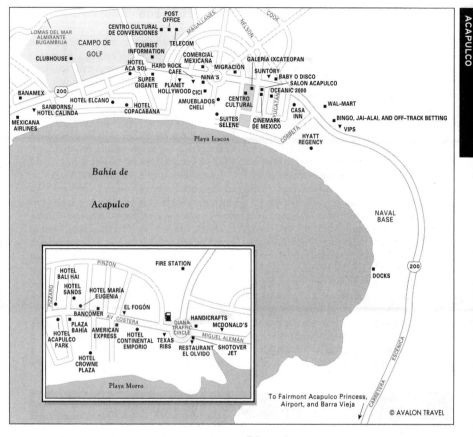

© AVALON TRAVEL

Beach access is by side roads or by walking directly through the hotel lobbies. If you come by bus, hail a taxi from the highway to the Hotel Princess door for the sake of a good entrance.

**Playa Revolcadero,** a broad, miles-long yellow-white strand, has the rolling open-ocean billows that Acapulco Bay doesn't. The sometimes-rough waves are generally good for boogie boarding, bodysurfing, and intermediate-to-advanced surfing, especially near the shoals on the northwest end. Because of the waves and sometimes hazardous currents, the hotel provides lifeguards. The Playa Revolcadero breeze is also brisk enough for sailing and sailboarding with your own boat or board. Some rentals may be available from the hotel beach concession.

## Playa Larga

About seven miles (11 km) from the Puerto Marqués traffic intersection, the Barra Vieja road forks right and heads along breezy, wild Playa Larga. The wave-tossed shoreline is rich with seabirds, nesting sea turtles (summer and fall), seasonal shells, and driftwood. If you're in the mood for some exercise, bring a bike (or rent one weekends and holidays) and take advantage of the new *ciclopista* (bike path) that begins at the Barra Vieja (Km 11) road fork and parallels the road all the way to Barra Vieja.

About two miles (3 km) from the fork, you will pass the lovely retreat Villas San Vicente, a collection of several small villas and two studio cottages, all nestled in their own palmy, private beachside park.

A rustic campground and trailer park has opened up for business on Playa Larga. Watch for their sign about four miles (6 km) from the fork. If you do camp on Playa Larga, you'll be able to share in enjoying the wide, breezy strand, whose rolling waves, with ordinary precautions, appear to be good for boogie boarding, bodysurfing, and possibly surfing. The sun sets on an unobstructed horizon, and the crab-rich beach is good for surf fishing (or by boat if you launch during morning calm). Additionally, the firm, level sand is excellent for jogging, walking, and beachcombing.

For the past several years a hardy group of eco-volunteers has patrolled Playa Larga (Long Beach). In times past, they've been camping during the summer–fall turtle season about 10 miles (16 km) from the fork at their Campamento Tortuguero Playa Larga. If you see them, stop and say a word of encouragement and perhaps donate some food or money to help them sustain their lonely vigil. Even better, set up your own tent nearby and volunteer your help recovering, incubating, and finally releasing the turtle hatchlings.

## Barra Vieja and Laguna Tres Palos

About a mile farther on, the stores (groceries and long-distance phone) and modest houses of fishing village Barra Vieja dot the roadside. Many seafood *palapas* line the beach side. The better among them include Don Beto's and Gloria del Mar, both with pools. (Prices, however, are very steep. Expect to pay $2.50 for a beer or orangeade and $12–15 for a fish plate, although buying lunch entitles you to occupy your table for the rest of the day.)

In addition to the beach, Barra Vieja visitors enjoy access to the vast Laguna Tres Palos mangrove wetland from the *estero* at the east end of town before the bridge. From there, boatmen (ask for José Organes, Beto Godoy, or Felipe Sala) take parties on fishing and wildlife-viewing excursions for about $35 for six people. Horseback rides are also available for about $20 per person.

The road continues, crossing a lagoon bridge and continues about two miles (3 km) farther east through scruffy Lomas de Chapultepec village. There it crosses the swirling Río Papagayo and connects with the Costa Chica and Oaxaca-bound Highway 200.

# Accommodations

Location largely determines the price and style of Acapulco hotels. Most of the budget hotels are in old Acapulco, near the *zócalo*. None of them are near a beach, and with only one deluxe exception, none of them have wheelchair access. Nevertheless, their doors lead directly to a nearby feast of old-Mexico sights and sounds, and their prices are certainly right.

Old Acapulco does offer beachfront hotel options, however. A number of good, moderately priced beachfront hotels are available in the Península de las Playas on Playas Caleta and Caletilla and east of the *zócalo* on Playa de Los Hornos. Here, guests enjoy semideluxe resort amenities and luscious ocean vistas.

New Acapulco hotels, by contrast, lie in new

Acapulco, along the Costera Miguel Alemán either right on the beach or within a block or two of it. Guests at the fancier beachfront hostelries enjoy a wealth of resort amenities and luxury view rooms at correspondingly luxurious prices. Most have wheelchair access.

Many Acapulco lodgings, however, defy categorization. Acapulco offers numerous choices to suit individual tastes and pocketbooks. Moreover, *Acapulco occupancy is highly seasonal.* In the new-town luxury hotels, Americans and Canadians crowd in during the winter. In old Acapulco, popular with middle- and working-class Mexican families, high season is during holidays and July and August. All hotels are full during the major Christmas–New Year's and Semana Santa (Holy Week) pre-Easter holidays, when prices approximately double. During the low seasons, you can usually save money by requesting a package (*paquete*) and four-night, weekly, or monthly discounts (*descuentos*). For high-season lodgings, always call, email, fax, or write (use global priority mail) early for reservations. More information about the hotels listed here is available at their websites.

(*Note:* Addresses along Acapulco's main boulevard, Av. Costera Miguel Alemán, do not correspond with location. Instead, numbers seem to have been mostly assigned chronologically.)

## NEAR THE *ZÓCALO*

A number of clean, budget-to-moderately priced hotels cluster in the colorful working-class neighborhood between the *zócalo* and La Quebrada divers' point.

### Under $25

Three blocks west of the *zócalo* on the quiet cul-de-sac end of Avenida La Paz stands the spartan three-story **Hotel María Acela** (Av. La Paz 19, tel. 744/482-0661, $9 s, $15 d, $30 and $40 holidays). Its family management lends a homey atmosphere more like a guesthouse than a hotel. The 21 austerely furnished fan rooms, although clean enough (but not immaculate), lack hot water. Guests enjoy a small lobby library of paperback books.

Also on quiet side street La Paz stands good budget buy **Casa de Huéspedes California** (Av. La Paz 12, tel. 744/482-2893, $15 s, $25 d low season, $25 s, $40 d holidays). Guests enjoy about 20 plainly decorated but clean rooms, in two stories surrounding a quiet, tropical inner patio.

One block farther away from the *zócalo*, the aging 1960s-vintage **Hotel María Antioneta** (Teniente Azueta 17, tel. 744/482-5024, jessyrabiitt@hotmail.com, $12 per person, $25 holidays, with fans, add $3 and $6 for a/c) fronts the busy store- and restaurant-lined Avenida Azueta. The 34 plainly furnished, somewhat worn rooms are nevertheless light, especially on the upper floor, and have fans, air-conditioning, and hot water. Bathrooms could use a good scrubbing, however. Most rooms are fortunately recessed along the leafy inner courtyard, away from street noise. Guests have the use of a handy communal kitchen and an unfurnished but potentially attractive upstairs terrace (that I suggested to the manager would be greatly improved with some tables and chairs). Credit cards are not accepted.

Uphill above and south of the La Quebrada parking lot is ◖ **Hotel Torre Eifel** (Inalámbrica 110, tel. 744/482-1683, fax 744/483-5727, $12 per person, $25 holidays, with fans, hot water, and parking). Above a hillside garden overlooking the La Quebrada divers' point tourist mecca, guests enjoy 25 simply but comfortably furnished rooms overlooking an inviting pool and patio. Guests in the uppermost rooms enjoy breezy sea views and a sunset horizon. (*Note:* The hotel's Inalámbrica address is misleading: You'll find it at the corner of Avenida Pinzona, one block uphill, on the right from the La Quebrada parking lot.)

### $25-50

The **Hotel Asturias** (Quebrada 45, tel./fax 744/483-6548, cerardoancera@aol.com, $15 per person year-round with fans, $25 per son with a/c and TV), on Avenida Quebrada a few blocks uphill from the *zócalo*, offers a relaxing atmosphere at budget rates. Its two stories hold 15 plain but tidy rooms surrounding a plant-decorated pool and patio with chairs for sunning. Get an upper room for more light and privacy. Find it four short blocks west of the cathedral, between Ramírez and Ortiz.

Arguably the most charming of *zócalo*-area hotels is the authentically colonial-era ◖ **Hotel Misión** (Felipe Valle 12, tel. 744/482-3643, fax 744/482-2076, hotelmision@hotmail.com, $20 s, $40 d with fans, $50 s, $100 d holidays), at the corner of La Paz, two blocks west of the *zócalo*. The owner, María Elena Sayago, relates the history of her hotel-home. From 1930 to 1966, it was a school, the Colegio Acapulco. When she began repairs several years ago, her workers uncovered broken antique Chinese

# OWNING PARADISE

Droves of repeat visitors have fled their northern winters and bought or permanently rented a part of their favorite Mexican Pacific paradises. They happily live all or part of the year in beachside developments that have mushroomed, especially around Acapulco, Ixtapa, Zihuatanejo, Manzanillo, and Puerto Vallarta. Deluxe vacation homes, which foreigners can own through special trusts, run upward from $100,000; condos begin at about half that. Time-shares, a type of rental, start at about $5,000.

## TRUSTS

In the past, Mexicans have feared, with some justification, that foreigners were out to buy their country. As a consequence, present laws prohibit foreigners from holding direct title to property within 30 miles (50 km) of a beachfront or within 60 miles (100 km) of a national border.

However, Mexican law does permit *fideicomisos* (trusts), which substitute for outright foreign ownership. Trusts allow you, as the beneficiary, all the usual rights to the property, such as use, sale, improvement, and transfer, in exchange for paying an annual fee to a Mexican bank, the trustee, which holds nominal title to the property. Trust ownership has been compared to owning all the shares of a corporation, which in turn owns a factory.

While not owning the factory in name, you have legal control over it.

Although some folks have been bilked into buying south-of-the-border equivalents of the Brooklyn Bridge, Mexican trust ownership is a happy reality for growing numbers of American, Canadian, and European beneficiaries who simply love Mexico. Take note, however, that *the great majority of Mexican real estate sales are cash only*. Real estate mortgage loans in Mexico, while not unheard-of, are definitely the exception.

*Bienes raíces* (bee-AY-nays rah-EE-says, real estate) in Mexico works a lot like it does in the United States and Canada. Agents handle multiple listings, show properties, assist negotiations, track paperwork, and earn commissions for sales completed. If you're interested in buying a Mexican property, work with one of the many honest and hardworking agents in Mexico, preferably a member of the Mexico National Realtors Association (AMPI) who is also recommended through a reliable firm back home or trustworthy, property-savvy friends in Mexico.

During your search, consider purchase of private property only. Communal or *ejido* property cannot legally be sold until it becomes private property. Once you have zeroed in on an

porcelain, most likely brought from Asia by the colonial-era Manila galleons. Before the 1910–1917 revolution, she says, the place housed army offices, and before that, it was a bank-like *estango* (depository) for valuables. The front-section walls and rooms were preserved in the original adobe, and the columns in the original stone. Most of the guest rooms, however, she had rebuilt, in two stories around a plant-decorated patio shaded by a spreading mango tree. When the mangoes ripen in April guests get their fill of the fragrant fruit. Rates for her 24 attractively decorated rooms include fans, hot water, and parking in an adjacent lot.

Five blocks west of the *zócalo*, up winding Avenida Pinzona, the **⬛ Hotel Etel Suites** (Av. Pinzona 92, tel. 744/482-2240 or 744/482-2241, fax 744/483-8094, etelsuites@terra.com.mx) perches on the view hillside above old Acapulco. Well-managed by friendly owner Etel Sutter Álvarez (great-granddaughter of renowned California-Swiss pioneer Johann A. Sutter) and her daughter, the three-building complex stair-steps downhill to a luxurious view garden and pool. Its airy hillside perch lends the Etel Suites a tranquil, luxurious ambience unusual in a moderately priced lodging. Chairs and sofas in a small street-level lobby invite relaxed conversation with fellow guests. The primly but thoughtfully furnished and well-maintained rooms vary from singles to multibedroom view apartments. The dozens of rooms and suites rent from about $35 s or $40 d low season, $50 holidays, with fans,

acceptable property, make sure that you and your agent are negotiating only with the owner of record or his or her attorney. With a signed sales agreement in hand, your agent should recommend a *notaria pública* (notary) who, unlike most U.S. notary publics, is an attorney skilled and licensed in property transactions.

A Mexican notary, functioning much as a title company does in the United States, is the most important person in completing your transaction. The notary traces the title, ensuring that your bank-trustee legally receives it, and makes sure the agreed-upon amounts of money get transferred between you, seller, bank, agent, and notary.

You and your agent should meet jointly with the notary early on to discuss the deal and get the notary's computation of the closing costs. For a typical trust-sale, closing costs (covering permit, filing, bank, notary, and registry fees) are considerable, typically 8-10 percent of the sale amount. After that, you will continue to owe property taxes and an approximately 1 percent annual fee to your bank-trustee.

### TIME-SHARING
Started in Europe, time-sharing has spread all over the globe. A time-share is a pre-paid rental, usually of a condominium, for a speci-fied time period per year. Agreements usually allow you to temporarily exchange your time-share rental for similar lodgings throughout the world.

Your first contact with time-sharing (*tiempo compartido*) will often be someone on a resort street corner who offers you a half-price tour for "an hour of your time." Soon you'll be attending a hard-sell session offering you tempting inducements in exchange for a check written on the spot. The basic appeal is your investment – say $10,000 cash for a two-week annual stay in a deluxe beach condo-hotel – which will earn you a handsome profit if you decide to sell your rights sometime in the future. What isn't mentioned is that time-shares have become increasingly difficult to sell and the interest or mutual fund growth that you could realize from your $10,000 cash would go far toward renting an equally luxurious vacation condo every year without entailing as much risk.

And risk there is, because you would be handing over your cash for a promise only. Read the fine print. Shop around, and don't give away anything until you inspect the condo you would be getting and talk to others who have invested in the same time-share. It may be a good deal, but don't let anyone rush you into paradise.

---

air-conditioning, and hot water. Completely furnished view apartments with kitchens go for about $80 d, $120 holidays, with discounts negotiable for monthly rentals. There is some parking, and credit cards are accepted. (*Note:* If you arrive in Acapulco on a crowded high-season weekend without a reservation, the Etel Suites will probably be the last decent place in town likely to have a room.)

## Over $100
At the cliff end of Calle Quebrada stands the *zócalo* area's only upscale hostelry, the **Hotel El Mirador Acapulco** (Plazoleta La Quebrada 74, tel. 744/483-1155, toll-free Mex. tel. 01-800/021-7557, fax 744/483-8800, mirador@hotelelmiradoracapulco.com.mx, reservaciones@hotelelmiradoracapulco.com .mx, www.hotelelmiradoracapulco.com.mx, $85 d standard, $150 deluxe, $110 and $240 holidays). Acapulco's first deluxe hotel, El Mirador was built in the early 1930s. El Mirador appropriately uses the La Quebrada diver in its logo. Directly below the hotel restaurant-bar, the divers accomplish their feat to the acclaim of hundreds of spectators five times daily. The hotel has much more to recommend than spectacle, however. Guests choose from a collection of about 50 semi-detached picturesquely perched hillside lodgings. Inside, they are attractively furnished in dark masculine tones, shiny rustic floor tiles, decorator reading lamps, and deluxe bathrooms. Two airy sunset-view restaurants, bars, and three swimming pools

complete the attractive picture. All rooms have cable TV, air-conditioning, and parking. Some rooms have wheelchair access.

## PENÍNSULA DE LAS PLAYAS HOTELS

Many of old Acapulco's mid- to high-end lodgings are spread along one continuous boulevard that winds through the plush Península de las Playas neighborhood. The boulevard starts as the Costera Miguel Alemán as it heads past the *zócalo*. A couple of miles farther southwest, the boulevard curves left as the Gran Via Tropical, rounding the Península de las Playas clockwise. Passing Playas Caleta and Caletilla, the boulevard changes to Avenida López Mateos and continues along the peninsula's sunset (southwest) side past Playa Angosta and La Quebrada divers' point before ending back in the *zócalo* neighborhood.

(*Note:* Playas Caleta and Caletilla are customarily crowded with local picnickers and vacationers all holidays and most weekends, especially Sunday. If noise is a problem for you, you had better stay at the Acamar Beach Resort or the Hotel Boca Chica weekdays only; or alternatively stay at the Hotels Los Flamingos or Caleta, both with more spacious grounds and removed from the beachfront hubbub.)

### $50-100

A quartet of recommendable semideluxe hotels decorates the peninsula's luscious southside oceanfront. Least expensive is the **Hotel Caleta** (Cerro San Martin 225, Playa Caleta, tel. 744/483-9940, toll-free Mex. tel. 01-800/700-0979, $75 d, $160 holidays), formerly Grand Meigas Acapulco, on the east headland bordering Playa Caleta. Hotel guests enjoy a big blue pool and view sundeck, an intimately private (but sometimes jetsam-strewn) rock-enfolded open-ocean beach, lush green garden, and comfortable rooms, with private panoramic view balconies. Although renovated in the mid-1990s, the hotel is now showing a bit of wear around the edges. All rooms have air-conditioning, phones, cable TV, and parking; some rooms have wheelchair access, and credit cards are accepted.

A block farther east, right on the beach, stands the **( Acamar Beach Resort** (Av. Costera M. Alemán 26, Fracc. Las Playas, tel. 744/482-0570, 744/482-0571, or 744/482-0572, toll-free Mex. tel. outside Acapulco 800/719-3684, fax 744/482-2119, rentas@acamaracapulco.com, www.acamar acapulco.com), formerly Hotel Playa Caleta. The hotel's popularity among middle-class Mexican vacationers flows from its semideluxe amenities and lovely beachfront location, all at moderate prices. Above the 1950s-style but attractively renovated lobby-restaurant-bar rise six floors of 136 rooms, invitingly decorated in white stucco, with shiny marble floors, cheery tropical-bright bedspreads, polished rattan furniture, and modern-standard shower baths. Reserve an upper room (on floors 4, 5, or 6) for more quiet, light, and a gorgeous ocean view. Rentals ordinarily run about $65 d, $75 t, street view only, or $84 d, $95 t with ocean view. Kitchenette suites sleeping up to six run about $160. Rates approximately double during pre-Easter week and Christmas–New Year's holidays. For a splurge, treat yourself to a corner suite, with panoramic 270-degree view, about $200 d. Amenities include cable TV, air-conditioning, beachfront pool-patio, some rooms with wheelchair access, parking ($3/day), and credit cards accepted.

Two blocks farther west along the beach, guests of the **( Hotel Boca Chica** (Playa Caletilla s/n, tel./fax 744/483-6601 or 744/483-6741, bocach@acabtu.com.mx, $95 d) enjoy an enviable beach vantage and semideluxe amenities. Here, views of Playa Caletilla on one hand and the green Isla Roqueta beyond an azure channel on the other are stunning. The hotel perches on a rocky point, invitingly close to the sand and clear aqua water from the pool deck and surrounding garden paths. The light, comfortably furnished rooms vary; if you have the option, look at two or three before you choose. Early reservations year-round are strongly recommended. Rates for the 45 rooms with phones and air-conditioning stay the same year-round, with breakfast, some rooms have wheelchair access;

credit cards are accepted, and parking is available. (*Note:* Hotel Boca Chica closed for extensive renovation late in 2007, and had not yet re-opened at press time. Hopefully they will be open by the time you read this.)

Half a mile farther west uphill, a different but equally attractive option is available at the **Hotel Los Flamingos** (Av. López Mateos s/n, Fracc. Las Playas, tel. 744/482-0690, 744/482-0691, or 744/482-0692, fax 744/483-9806, flamingoo@prodigy.net.mx, www.hotellosflamingos.com). Los Flamingos is the place where oldsters reminisce and youngsters find out who John Wayne, Johnny Weissmuller, and Rory Calhoun were. Personable owner-manager and musician Adolfo Santiago González enjoys playing his guitar and relating his experiences with his famous guests of yesteryear. Vintage Hollywood photos decorate the open-air lobby walls, while pathways lead through a hilltop jungle of palm, hibiscus, and spreading mangoes. The 40-odd rooms, several with private oceanview balconies, perch on a cliffside that plummets into foaming breakers hundreds of feet below. Soft evening guitar music in an open-air sunset-view restaurant and a luxurious clifftop pool and patio complete the lovely picture. The rooms, in standard, superior, and junior suite grades, ordinarily run about $60, $70, and $80 d respectively, and $65, $85, and $100 holidays. Add about $25 for an extra person. For about $300, the hotel also offers **Casa Redonda,** a secluded clifftop oceanview house sleeping six, the former Acapulco home-away-from-home of Johnny Weissmuller (the most famous Tarzan), who died in 1984. All with parking, some air-conditioning; credit cards are accepted.

On the peninsula's east side, apartment-style **Suites Alba** (Gran Via Tropical 35, tel. 744/483-0073, fax 744/483-8378, ventas@ albasuites.com.mx, www.albasuites.com.mx, toll-free U.S. tel. 866/805-4626 or Can. tel. 877/428-1327, $85 d, $105 holidays) rambles through its well-kept hilltop garden of palms and pools. The hundreds of mostly Canadian and American middle-class winter guests (Mexicans in summer, everyone holidays) enjoy

© BRUCE WHIPPERMAN

Johnny Weissmuller, the most famous actor to portray Tarzan in film, swam regularly in the Tarzan Pool when he was owner of the Hotel Los Flamingos.

a load of facilities, including a pair of pools, a whirlpool tub, a restaurant, a mini-mart, some rooms with wheelchair access, and a bayside beach club with its own saltwater pool. The 292 comfortably furnished apartments have kitchenettes, air-conditioning, and private garden-view balconies. Discounts are available for monthly rentals, credit cards are accepted, and parking is available.

## PLAYA DE LOS HORNOS

As Acapulco development moved eastward around the bay during the 1940s and '50s, a row of comfortable, multifloored hotels were built across the Costera from the long, plumy Playa de Los Hornos beachfront grove, now midway between the *zócalo* and new Acapulco. Many of these hotels, recently renovated, remain popular, especially with Mexican weekenders and savvy budget-conscious foreign vacationers, who enjoy airy, uncluttered panoramic bay views from upper-floor rooms.

### $50-100

One of the best is the very worthy **Hotel Aca Bay** (Av. Costera M. Alemán 266, Fracc. Hornos, tel. 744/485-8228, toll-free Mex. tel. 01-800/714-2762, fax 744/485-0774, acabay@prodigy.net.mx, www.hotel-acabay.com .mx). This modest 1960s-modern resort-style hotel offers 118 rooms in 20 floors. Four room grades are available: economy single for one or two people, no ocean view; double for up to four; junior suite, with room for up to six; and larger, choicer master suites, all immaculate and comfortably furnished, with attractive wood furniture, reading lamps, marble floors, shiny shower baths, and panoramic bay views. Usual non-holiday asking prices run, respectively, about $85, $110, $140, and $160. Get a 20 percent discount by reserving on the Internet. Rooms vary; look at more than one. Add about 25 percent to these rates during Easter, Christmas–New Year's and some other long-weekend holidays. Get an upper-floor room (above the 10th story) for more quiet and a better view. All with cable TV, telephones, restaurant, bar, oceanview pool-patio, kiddie

pool, some rooms with wheelchair access, and parking. Credit cards accepted.

Other Los Hornos longtime beachfront hotels that might be worth checking out include **Las Hamacas** (tel. 744/483-7006 or 744/482-2861, toll-free Mex. tel. 01-800/710-9333, fax 744/483-0575, hamas@ hamacas.com.mx, www.hamacas.com.mx, about $70 d, $100 holidays), on the Costera a couple of blocks east of the Fuerte San Diego; and **El Cid** (tel.744/485-1312 or 744/485-1410, fax 744/485-1387, about $60 d, $100 holidays), about five blocks farther east, just east of the corner of Capitán Mal Espina.

## COSTERA: WEST SIDE

With few exceptions, these hostelries line both beach and inland sides of the busy Costera Miguel Alemán, east of Papagayo amusement park. Hotels are nearly all either right on or just a short walk from the beach.

### Under $50

Among the most economical is the modest ℂ **Hotel del Valle** (G. Gomez Espinosa 8, tel. 744/485-8336 or 744/485-8388), on the side street that borders the east end of the Papagayo amusement park. Two motel-style floors of clean, comfortable rooms border a small but inviting pool-patio. On a side street just a block from the beach, away from the noisy boulevard, the del Valle is a tranquil winter headquarters for retirees and youthful budget travelers. The 20 rooms rent for about $30 s or d, with fan only; $45 s or d with a/c, about $60 and $87 holidays, all with hot-water shower baths, but with street-only parking.

If the Hotel del Valle is full, you might try its similarly budget-priced (but without pools) petite next-door neighbors, **Hotel Jacqueline** (tel./fax 744/485-9338, $50 s or d) and **Amueblados Lupita** (tel. 744/485-9412, $45 s or d); both run about $60 s or d holidays.

On the beach side of the Costera, a block or two east of McDonald's, the compact three-story **Hotel Monaco** (Av. Costera M. Alemán 137, tel./fax 744/485-6467, 744/485-6415, or 744/485-6518, monac_otel@hotmail.com,

$49 d, $57 d holidays) offers a tropical mini-retreat from the Costera noise and bustle. Past the small lobby, a big, round blue pool, decorated with shade umbrellas and edged by palms and leafy greenery, invites relaxation. (The patio's attractiveness, however, leads to its drawback: For peace and quiet, spend your time on the beach during the weekends, when families love to frolic in the pool. Weekdays by the pool are usually more tranquil.) Upstairs, the rooms are plain but clean with the basics: hot showers and two double beds. Rooms include air-conditioning, phone, TV, and parking. Hotel Monaco is close to everything, and just a block from the beach.

## $50-100

A few blocks farther east, check out the standby **Hotel Sands** (Av. Costera M. Alemán 178, tel. 744/484-2261, 744/484-2262, 744/484-2263, or 744/484-2264, toll-free Mex. tel. 01-800/710-9800, fax 744/484-1053, sands@sands.com.mx, www.sands.com.mx, $66–80 d, $140–210 holidays). In addition to a pool-patio and restaurant next to the main 1960s-modern building, the hotel's spacious grounds encompass a shady green park in the rear that leads to an attractive hidden cluster of garden *cabañas.* Of the main building rooms, the uppers are best; many have been redecorated with light, comfortable furnishings. *Cabaña guests,* on the other hand, enjoy tasteful browns, tile decor, and big windows looking out into a leafy garden. *Cabañas* 1–8 are the most secluded. The 59 rooms and 34 *cabañas* ordinarily double in price during Christmas–New Year's and Easter holidays. Low-season discounts on weekdays and for longer stays may be available for the asking. All with air-conditioning, cable TV, and phones. Parking and use of squash courts are included; credit cards are accepted.

Just east of the Hotel Sands stands the compact but nevertheless worthy and kid-friendly **Hotel Hacienda María Eugenia** (Av. Costera M. Alemán 176, tel. 744/481-0660 through 744/481-0666, fax 744/481-0669, toll-free Mex. tel. 01-800/712-6628, fax 744/481-0071, haciendamariaeugenia@prodigy.net.mx,

www.haciendamariaeugenia.com.mx, $65 d except holidays). Only a block and a half from the beach, the hotel has about 50 rooms in three stories, around a petite, leafy pool-patio, embellished with a meandering kiddie pool, small water slide, and playground equipment. A modest but well-managed boulevard-front restaurant offers a hearty, economical breakfast buffet. Upstairs, rooms are invitingly furnished, with two double beds, attractive rustic wooden furniture and floor tiles, and modern-standard shower baths. Light, however, usually must be artificial, since rooms face exterior corridors where curtains must be drawn for privacy. (However, a number of kitchenette-equipped rooms have doors opening to private side balconies, and thus more light.) Two kids stay free with parents; rooms have cable TV and air-conditioning. Parking costs $6; credit cards are accepted. The customary promotion runs about $270 for three nights, fourth night free, including daily breakfast buffet.

Just a block from Papagayo amusement park and right on the beach stands the mid-rise **Hotel Maris** (Av. Costera M. Alemán 59, tel. 744/485-8440, fax 744/485-3934, $65 d, $140 holidays). Here, guests enjoy spacious rooms with private view balconies for surprisingly reasonable rates. Lobby-level amenities include a small pool above the beach-club *palapas,* with bar and restaurant. (You may want to ask someone to turn down the TV volume.) Rates for the 85 rooms include air-conditioning, TV, and phones. Street parking only.

Also on the beachfront nearby, **Hotel Maralisa** (Alemania s/n, tel. 744/485-6677 or 744/485-7363, fax 744/485-9228, www.bestday.com/acapulco/hotels/maralisa, $65 d, about $150 holidays) nestles among its towering condo neighbors. The Maralisa is a luxuriously simple retreat, where guests, after their fill of sunning beside the palm-lined pool-patio, can step down onto the sand for a jog or stroll along the beach. Later, they might enjoy a light meal in the hotel's beachside café and go out dancing in nearby resort hotels. Several of the Maralisa's 90 comfortable rooms, tastefully decorated in whites and warm pastels, have private balconies.

Up to two kids younger than 12 stay free; be sure to ask for a discount or package. Rates include air-conditioning, cable TV, phones, and parking; credit cards are accepted.

Relax at the mid-scale **Hotel Acapulco Park** (Costera M. Alemán 127, tel. 744/485-5992, fax 744/485-5489, toll-free Mex. tel. 01-800/000-1111, hotel@parkhotel-acapulco.com, www.parkhotel-acapulco.com, $70–100 d, $150–200 holidays), with 88 comfortable rooms, some with kitchenettes, around a tranquil palm-shaded pool garden only a block from the beach. Inside, the rooms are clean, comfortable 1960s-style, with shiny, immaculate bathrooms, ceiling-to-floor drapes, and shiny tile floors, reading lamps, and two or three double beds. This place would be a special plus for tennis players, with its half-dozen night-lit tennis courts, tucked in the back. All with air-conditioning, cable TV, parking, credit cards accepted, bar but no restaurant.

Several blocks farther east on the inland side, the lovely low-rise ( **Hotel Bali-Hai** (Av. Costera M. Alemán 186, tel. 744/485-6622 or 744/485-6336, fax 744/485-7972, balihai@ balihai.com.mx, www.balihai.com.mx, $80 d) offers a bit of class at reasonable rates. The superbly maintained hotel offers 108 motel-style rooms in two floors, all enfolding a palmy interior parking-pool-patio. A pair of designer pools (one of them shallow and kid-friendly) furnished with a collection of chaise lounges set the relaxing tone. Furthermore, the hotel layout, set far back from the boulevard, produces a surprisingly tranquil ambience, shielded from the Costera traffic hubbub. Inside the rooms themselves, spotless marble and tile, handsome Polynesian-mode wood furniture, and modern standard baths complete the inviting picture. The only blot on this lovely portrait is that rooms often must be artificially lit, since they face outward onto the corridor and drapes must be drawn for privacy. Reserve an upper room in the rear for more quiet and privacy. Rooms come in two grades: standard is large and deluxe, sleeping up to four. Superior is larger and more deluxe, sleeping up to six. Standard rooms run about $80 d, decreasing to about $70 for the second, third, and fourth nights. Superior room prices

Although on the inland side of the busy Costera, the patio of the moderately priced Hotel Bali-Hai provides a tranquil haven from the Acapulco hubbub.

are about 20 percent higher; all room rates just about double during holidays. All with air-conditioning, cable TV, refrigerator, parking, bar, and quiet, cool restaurant out front.

## Over $100

A mile farther east, the super-popular long-time luxury **( Hotel Fiesta Americana Villas Acapulco** (Av. Costera M. Alemán 1220, tel. 744/484-1600, toll-free Mex. tel. 01-800/696-1313 or U.S./Can. tel. 800/343-7821, fax 744/484-1828, fiesta1@posadas.com, www .fiestamericana.com, $120–160 d, holidays $250) presides atop its rocky shoreline perch smack in the middle of the Costera action. Boulevard traffic roars nonstop past the front door and nearby nightclubs rock (on the west side; ask for an east-side room for peace and quiet). On winter days, ranks of middle-class American and Canadian vacationers sun on the hotel's spacious pool deck and downstairs at its *palapa*-shaded beach club. Resort facilities include multiple restaurants and bars, nightly live music, shops, auto rental, golf nearby, and all aquatic sports. Rooms, most with private bayview balconies, are furnished in luscious pastels, rattan, and designer lamps. Rates include air-conditioning, cable TV, phones, parking, and full wheelchair access; credit cards are accepted. Low-season promotions or discounts may be available.

## COSTERA: EAST SIDE

East of the golf course stretches the newest, shiniest part of Acapulco, where seemingly every enterprise, including Wal-Mart and McDonald's, Hooters, and Hyatt Regency, has strained to locate during the recent past. Despite the hubbub, corners of tranquillity do exist, especially among many of the high-rise hostelries and condominiums that occupy the golden beachfront.

## $50-100

A few vintage east-side remnants of Acapulco "the way it used to be" live on, seemingly oblivious to the fast-lane world around them. At the CICI water park corner, walk straight toward the beach, along Calle Cristobal Colón. Just before the beach, on the left, you'll find **( Suites Selene** (Cristobal Colón 175, tel./ fax 744/484-2977 or 744/484-3643, suitesselene@hotmail.com, $58 d, $70 with kitchenette, $70 and $89 holidays). Here, just half a block from the beach, by a shady street's-end park, stands a complex of 24 modest apartments. Exterior amenities include a leafy garden, a blue pool and patio, and parking sensitively situated in the rear, away from the garden and apartments. Most of the somewhat worn but clean units have one bedroom with two double beds, a living-dining room, bathroom, and a kitchenette, with stove, refrigerator, utensils and dishes, and purified water in a five-gallon *garafón* (demijohn) for cooking. The remaining six units have everything but the kitchenette. Rates are higher for holidays, but discounts are customarily available for weekly or monthly rentals.

Walk away from the beach two doors and find neighboring **Amueblados Cheli** (Cristobal Colón 155, tel. 744/484-3160 or 744/484-2019), also scarcely a block from the beach. The complex (*amueblados* literally means furnished) consists of about 20 apartments in two floors, set around a lovingly tended tropical garden and parking patio. On the south, beach side of the apartments is an inviting pool-patio for guest use. The whole place is set behind a sturdy security fence, probably mostly to keep beachgoers from wandering in at all hours. The only possible drawback here might be the music and noise from the CICI water park (open 10 A.M.–6 P.M. daily) across the street. Although the owner told me that she rents most apartments by the month, vacant rentals are often rented by the day, for about $55, depending on season. (The manager wasn't available to show me individual apartments, but judging from the well-tended look of the place, Amueblados Cheli is certainly worth checking out.) Contact the owner via telephone (in Spanish).

Moving several blocks farther east along the Costera, find the **Casa Inn** (Av. Costera M. Alemán 2310, tel. 744/435-2000, fax 744/435-2037, reserva@casainnacapulco.com.mx, www.casa-innacapulco.com.mx, $60–100 d, $160–220 holidays), a less refined but still good-value hostelry, especially during low season. The youngish, mostly single clientele also like the lively late-night bar and the big pool deck where they can rest and recover during the day. The 279 light and comfortable rooms come with air-conditioning, TV, views, and phones. Rooms sleep one–four people; many have kitchenettes. Be sure to ask for a discount or a package. Parking is available, and credit cards are accepted.

For a very worthy moderately priced alternative, return west a few blocks to check out the classy small **Hotel Aca Sol** (Av. Costera M. Alemán 53B, tel. 744/484-2700 or 744/484-0255, fax 744/484-0977, ventas@hotelacasol.com, www.hotelacasol.com, $75 s or d, $150 holidays and some long weekends), just a block and a half from the beach. Enter the petite but invitingly chic lobby and continue to an airy, palm-decorated rear pool-patio. To one side, an attractive small restaurant, shielded from street noise, serves guests. Upstairs, the 35 rooms in four floors enfold the patio. Inside, rooms are white, marbled, and squeaky clean. Guests in most rooms enjoy exterior balconies. Get a room overlooking Almendro, the adjacent quiet side street. Often if you stay three nights, the fourth night is free; rates include air-conditioning, parking, cable TV, in-house wireless Internet, and telephone. Credit cards are accepted.

## Over $100

Those who hanker for a party can have it, right on the beach, at **Hotel Copacabana** (Tabachines 2, Fracc. Club Deportivo, tel. 744/484-3260 or tel./fax 744/484-6268, toll-free Mex. tel. 01-800/710-9888 or U.S. tel. 800/562-0197, acapulco@hotelcopacabana.com, www.hotelcopacabana.com, $120 d, $160–200 holidays). Past the inviting, midsize lobby, guests enjoy a live music restaurant-bar, a beachview pool deck, and a squadron of private beachfront *palapas*. Everywhere inside, the marble, brass, and rattan are polished; the guests are mostly young; and the mood is upbeat.

Upstairs, the 18 floors of 400-plus rooms are deluxe, comfortable, marble-floored, and cheerily decorated in yellows and whites, with bamboo furniture and bedsteads. Third and fourth guests stay free; rates are higher holidays and July and August, but always include air-conditioning, cable TV, and parking. Boogie boards, kayaks, water polo, aerobics, and volleyball available at no extra cost. Other downstairs amenities include shops, travel agent, and business center. Credit cards accepted.

On the other hand, lovers of peace and quiet often choose the grand, dignified ( **Hotel Elcano** (Av. Costera M. Alemán 75, tel./fax 744/435-1500 or fax 744/484-2230, toll-free U.S. tel. 877/260-1765, elcano@hotel-elcano.com.mx, www.hotel-elcano.com.mx, $150 d, $210–350 holidays), two blocks removed—and with room balconies facing the ocean view, away from the Costera traffic noise. The hotel was named after Ferdinand Magellan's navigator, Sebastián Elcano (who actually was the one who first circumnavigated the globe 1519–1522; Magellan died en route but got the credit). Hotel Elcano is austerely luxurious, hued in shades of nautical blue, from the breezy, gracefully columned lobby and the spacious turquoise beachside pool to the 180 immaculate, marble-tiled view rooms. Unlike some of Acapulco's beachfront hostelries, the Elcano has plenty of space for guests to enjoy its load of extras, which includes two restaurants, three bars, poolside hot tub, beach club, kiddie pool, gym, nine-hole golf course three blocks away, and video games center. Rooms all have private oceanview balconies. Be sure to ask for possible promotional packages, or midweek or weekly rates.

Towering over the Costera's east end is the 20-story high-rise ( **Hyatt Regency Acapulco** (Av. Costera M. Alemán 1, tel. 744/469-1234, toll-free Mex. tel. 01-800/005-0000 or U.S./ Can. tel. 800/633-7313, fax 744/484-3087, acara-reservations@hyattintl.com, www .acapulco.regency.hyatt.com, about $150 lowest season, about $350 holidays). Its lavish beachfront facilities include spacious gardens, blue-lagoon swimming pool, a Tarzan-jungle waterfall, a squadron of personal beach *palapas,* restaurants, bars, frequent live music, shops, all aquatic sports, tennis, and golf nearby. The 690 rooms, all with private view balconies, are large and luxurious, with air-conditioning, cable TV, phones, parking, and full wheelchair access; credit cards are accepted.

## OUT OF TOWN
### Pie de la Cuesta

For many more budget beachfront lodgings, check out the sleepy Pie de la Cuesta downscale beach resort village on placid Laguna Coyuca (about six miles by the oceanfront Hwy. 200 northwest from the Acapulco *zócalo*). There you'll find plenty of inexpensive palm-shaded shoreline hotels and bungalows. Drive, taxi (about $10), or ride a bus marked Pie de la Cuesta, from Avenida Escudero in front of Sanborn's and Woolworth's near the *zócalo*. For details, see the *Pie de la Cuesta* section at the end of this chapter.

### East of Town

A number of luxury hostelries spread along the Playa Revolcadero oceanfront, on the beach side of the airport road.

One of the most heavenly choices is the ◖ **Villas San Vicente** (tel. 744/462-0149 or fax 744/486-6846, sanvicentevillas@aol .com, www.villassanvicente.com.mx), a mini-paradise with plenty of space, sweeping green lawns, and swaying palms, right on a long gorgeous strand. Seekers of peace and quiet can have it all: afternoons in splendid isolation, reading by the pool, long walks on the beach, savoring the tropical breeze, and watching the sun go down. Guests in the five spacious, super-deluxe mini-villas enjoy two bedrooms with king-size beds, two baths, designer living-dining room, completely equipped kitchen, hot tub, air-conditioning, and a small private pool. The two smaller units are more modest but still comfortable studios, with bath, kitchenette, and air-conditioning, set at the upper edge of the property, a bit farther from the beach. All residents share a lusciously inviting main pool and patio, with bar, tennis courts, and parking,

all on about 10 palm-shaded beachfront acres. Low season rentals run about $105, $170 holidays for the studios, upward from $340 for the mini-villas, depending on location and amenities. Holiday rates for the villas are about 40 percent more. Reservations (mandatory holidays, strongly recommended other times) are available by contacting the Villas' Acapulco office (tel. 744/486-4037, fax 744/485-6846, sanvicentevillas@aol.com). Get to Villas San Vicente by following the airport road eastbound about seven miles (11 km) past the hill-bottom Puerto Marqués traffic interchange. Instead of heading straight ahead to the airport, fork right, toward Barra Vieja. After a mile or two, you'll reach the Villas San Vicente gate, on the right.

Closer in (only about a mile east of the Puerto Marqués interchange) along the airport road, the showplace **Hotel Fairmont Acapulco Princess** (Playa Revolcadero, tel. 744/469-1000 or 744/469-1012, toll-free Mex. tel. 800/090-9900 or U.S./Can. tel. 800/441-1414, aca.reservations@fairmont.com, www.fairmont.com/acapulco, $300 d low season, $450 d holidays) provides an abundance of resort facilities (including an entire 18-hole golf course), spreading from luscious beachfront garden grounds. Although the hotel centers on a pair of grand neo-pyramids (with a total of 1,019 rooms), the impression from the rooms themselves is of super luxury; from the garden it is of Eden-like jungle tranquillity—meandering pools, gurgling cascades, strutting flamingos, swaying palms—that guests seem to soak up with no trouble at all. All rooms are deluxe with a plethora of up-to-date amenities; guests also enjoy a host of facilities, all sports, and full wheelchair access. Credit cards are accepted.

For another super-deluxe option, consider the **Mayan Palace Acapulco** (Av. de las Palmas 1121, Fracc. Playa Diamante, tel./fax 744/469-6000, toll-free Mex. tel. 01-800/366-6600, U.S. tel. 800/292-9446 or 800/996-2926, Can. tel. 800/421-4161, reservations@grupomayan.com, www.mayan resorts.com.mx, from $310 d, $600 d holidays), about a mile farther east along the beach from the Fairmont Acapulco Princess. Here, in a palace like the Mayan kings never had, you'll find an 18-hole golf course, 12 clay tennis courts, a kilometer-long swimming pool (no kidding), five bars, three restaurants, fountains, waterfalls, and an entire blue lagoon, all overlooking a gorgeous, breezy beach. Hotel rates vary for a luxurious and spacious marble and pastel room with everything; promotional packages might include discounts and/or breakfast.

## RENTALS AND REAL ESTATE

The most useful Internet site for vacation rentals is **Vacation Rentals by Owner** (www.vrbo .com), which links to a broad range of individual Acapulco rentals, from moderate to expensive. Another potentially useful source of Acapulco long-term rentals and real estate, especially high-end villas, is the (Spanish-language) website **www.acabtu.com.mx,** electronic descendant of the former community newspaper *Acapulco Heat.* (Curiously, "btu" refers to the "British thermal unit" commonly used to measure quantity of heat energy.) Go directly to the real estate (*bienes raices*) section by typing in www.acabtu .com.mx/acaweb/bienesraices.html.

For folks less familiar with the Internet, some good rental sources can also be contacted by telephone and fax. For example, in Acapulco, check out Bachur Real Estate (Av. Costera M. Alemán 20, Hotel Tropicana, Fracc. Costa Azul, tel./fax 744/484-1333, mbachur@bachur .com.mx, www.bachur.com.mx), specializing in condos and villas.

Furthermore, some U.S. and Canadian real estate networks have Acapulco branches. One of the most active is the Century 21 local branch, **Century 21 Realty Mex** (Calle Alonso Martín 43, Fracc. Magellanes, tel. 744/485-9090 or 744/486-6110, fax 744/486-4187, www .century21acapulco.com.mx) in the eastern Costera neighborhood. Although it specializes in high-end villas and condominiums, the staff also may be able to get you a moderately-priced house or villa rental (or suggest someone who can).

Finally, don't forget the three moderately priced apartment complexes recommended under *Accommodations* in this chapter: **Hotel Etel Suites,** in the *Near the Zócalo* section, and the **Amueblados Cheli** and **Suites Selene,** in the *Costera: East Side* section.

## TRAILER PARKS AND CAMPING

Although condos and hotels have crowded out virtually all of Acapulco's in-town trailer parks, good prospects exist nearby. The best are the **Acapulco Trailer Park** and the **Playa Luces RV Park and Campground,** right on the beach in Pie de la Cuesta, six miles (9 km) by the coast highway northwest of the Acapulco *zócalo.* For details, see the *Pie de la Cuesta* section at the end of this chapter.

And although development and urbanization have likewise squeezed out in-town camping, possibilities exist in the trailer parks in Pie de la Cuesta and on Playa Larga near Barra Vieja, east of town.

# Food

## SNACKS AND BREAKFAST
### Near the *Zócalo*

Eat well cheaply at 🄲 **Lonchería Chatita** (Av. Azueta, corner of Hidalgo, no phone, 8 A.M.–10 P.M. daily, $4), where a friendly female kitchen squad serves mounds of wholesome, local-style specialties. On a typical day, these may include savory *chiles rellenos,* rich

*puerco mole de Uruapan, pozole* (savory hominy soup), or potato pancakes.

Something fancier is available at **La Flor de Acapulco** (formerly Restaurant La Parroquia, cell tel. 044-744/421-7639, 8 A.M.–10 P.M. daily, $6–12) on the upstairs balcony overlooking the *zócalo,* good for a snack or a light lunch as you soak in the scene below.

For something creamy and cool (but a bit pricey—$2.50 for an ice cream cone), go to **Dolpy** (tel. 744/483-7574, noon–10 P.M. daily), one block from the *zócalo* toward the steamship dock.

Continue another block to **Sanborn's** (on the Costera corner of Escudero, tel. 744/482-4095, 7:30 A.M.–11 P.M. daily, $4–10). Here, you can enjoy the cool air-conditioning and a homestyle selection, including ham and eggs, hamburgers, roast beef, and apple pie.

Alternatively, **Woolworth's** (tel. 744/480-0072, 9:30 A.M.–8:30 P.M. daily), one block from the Costera, behind Sanborn's, also offers air-conditioned ambience and similar fare at cheaper prices.

Finally, for dessert, head back over to the opposite side of the *zócalo* to **La Espiga de Acapulco** (on Juárez, tel. 744/482-2699, 7 A.M.–10 P.M. daily, $1), a bakery a block west of the *zócalo* with tasty tarts and cakes.

## On the Costera

Snack food concentrates in Acapulco, as in many places, around **McDonald's,** with at least two branches: the original one, at the corner of Esclavo and Costera M. Alemán, a few blocks east of the landmark Hotel Ritz, and another farther east, on the Costera east of the Diana fountain and traffic circle. Here you have it all, from breakfast Egg McMuffins to Chicken McNuggets and the Big Mac, priced about a third higher than back home. Open 8 A.M.–11 P.M. daily.

For an interesting contrast, visit **Taco Tumbra** (tel. 744/485-7261, 6:30 P.M.–2 A.M. Sun.–Thurs., 6:30 P.M.–4 A.M. Fri.–Sat., $2), across the adjacent street from the original McDonald's. Here, piquant aromas of barbecued chicken, pork, and beef and strains of Latin music fill the air. For a treat, order three of the delectable tacos along with a refreshing *jugo* (fruit juice) or fruit-flavored *agua.*

A few blocks east of McDonald's and across the street, **Restaurant El Zorrito** (The Little Fox, tel. 744/485-7914 or 744/485-3744, open 24 hours daily, except 6 A.M.–1 P.M. Tues., $6–11) packs in the crowds with just about the tastiest Mexican food in town. If you're in the mood for some serious eating, fill up with a Filete Tampiqueña (beef fillet Tampico style), a *chiles rellenos* plate (enough for two), or *lomo* (roast pork loin).

A block farther east, on the beach side of the boulevard, **Sanborn's** (formerly Denny's, tel. 744/485-5360, 7 A.M.–1 A.M. daily, $4–12) provides a blessedly cool, refined, and thoroughly modern Mexican refuge from the street hustle. Here, almost around the clock daily, you can sample an international menu of either North American favorites (eggs, pancakes, bacon, and bottomless coffee), or hearty Mexican specialties. Sanborn's also offers a rack of American magazines, such as *Time, Glamour,* and *National Geographic,* and an ATM.

On the other hand, **100% Natural** (tel. 744/485-3982, 24 hours daily, $3–6), in competition directly across the Costera from Sanborn's, offers appropriately contrasting fare: many veggie and fruit drinks (try the Conga, made of papaya, guava, watermelon, pineapple, lime, and spinach), several egg breakfasts, breads, sandwiches, tacos, and enchiladas. You can also find 100% Natural branches in at least two more locations: mid-Costera (tel. 744/484-6447), next door to Carlos'n Charlie's; and on the east side (tel. 744/484-8440), next to Baby O disco.

Two miles (3 km) farther along the Costera, at Hotel Calinda, the **Sanborn's** central Costera branch (tel. 744/481-2426, 7 A.M.–1 A.M. daily) offers the same Sanborn's refined atmosphere, good food, and a big book and gift store.

## ZÓCALO AND PENÍNSULA DE LAS PLAYAS

Even though Acapulco has seemingly zillions of restaurants, only a fraction may suit your expectations. Local restaurants come and go like the Acapulco breeze, though a handful of solid longtime eateries continue, depending on a steady flow of repeat customers.

For plain good eating and homey sidewalk atmosphere morning and night, try outdoor **Café Los Amigos** (Calle La Paz, tel. 744/483-8732, 8:30 A.M.–7 P.M. daily, except 7 A.M.–10 P.M. holidays, $4–7), a few steps off the *zócalo.* Shady umbrellas beneath a spreading green tree and many familiar favorites, from tuna salad and chili to waffles, T-bone steak, and breaded shrimp, and roast pork with potatoes with gravy, attract a friendly club of Acapulco Canadian and American longtimers during the winter, and mostly local clientele in the summer, when the menu shifts to Mexican favorites, including a bountiful afternoon *comida corrida.*

Also on the *zócalo's* west side, three blocks farther west, **Restaurant Bratwurst** (Teniente Azueta 10, corner of Juárez, cell tel. 044-744/127-1523, noon–8 P.M. daily, $5–10) comprises one of the restaurant trio, including Los Amigos and Tamales Licha (described next), that comprise the budding local gourmet ghetto.

For a very popular variation on local-style cooking go a couple blocks farther west to **Tamales Licha** (Av. Costera M. Alemán 322, corner of Almirante Breton, tel. 744/482-2021, 6–11 P.M. Thurs.–Tues., $2–4). Here, appetizing south-of-the-border specialties—succulent tamales, savory *pozole,* crunchy tostadas, and tangy enchiladas—reign supreme. Portions are generous, ambience is relaxed, and hygiene standards are impeccable.

**La Gran Torta** (La Paz 6, tel. 744/483-8476, 7 A.M.–midnight daily, $3–4), one block west from the *zócalo,* is an old town headquarters for hearty local-style food at local-style prices. Specialties here are bountiful breakfasts, a four-course afternoon *comida corrida,* and *tortas*—hearty sandwiches of *pierna* (roast pork), *chorizo* (spicy sausage), or *pollo* (chicken), stuffed in a *bolillo* bun along with tomato and avocado. An additional favorite is hearty *pozole* Thursday and Friday afternoons and evenings.

Meanwhile, on the *zócalo's* opposite, east side, **Mi Piace** (tel. 744/482-5555, 9 A.M.–1 A.M. daily, $4–10) is a pizza and Italian restaurant (pronounced mee pee-AH-chay; the name means "my piece") that profits from the abundant *zócalo* foot traffic. Here, you can choose

between cool inside seating and umbrella-shaded outdoor tables. Select from several styles of pizza (veggie to seafood), four salad choices, many pastas, and more.

Although the very clean, strictly local-style **Restaurant La Chilapeña** (Cinco de Mayo 36, tel. 744/482-0498, 10 A.M.–11 P.M. daily, $2–4) requires walking a few blocks northeast from the *zócalo,* it's worth it. Friendly owner Consuela Araiz de Rosario welcomes everyone to sample her Guerrero-style *antojitos* cooked the way she learned from her mother years ago in upcountry Chilapa. It's best to organize a party so you can sample everything. Besides the tostadas, tacos, enchiladas, and *chalupas,* be sure to order the house specialty, *pozole*—which Señora Consuela claims was invented in Chilapa; see the "Origin of Pozole" wall painting—complete with its bountiful vegetable plate. Additionally, Señora Consuela is very proud of her *pata* (leg of pork vinaigrette) with *zanahorias* (carrots). Get to La Chilapeña from the *zócalo* by walking east two blocks to the Avenida Escudero corner (at Sanborn's). Turn left and walk along the east side of the street (passing Woolworth's) three blocks north to Cinco de Mayo. Turn right and walk a block and a half to Restaurant La Chilapeña on the right.

Similar and also highly recommended is the **Restaurant El Nuevo Capullo Chilapeño** (Alarcón 16, tel. 744/482-4311, 7:30 A.M.–midnight daily, $3–4), in the Pozo de la Nación district. Afternoons are good for enjoying the four-course *comida corrida* set lunch; evenings, go for the upcountry Guerrero specialties, Chilapa-style *antojitos* such as *chalupas* (or, on Thursdays only, pork or chicken *pozole verde).*

Good, reasonably priced seafood restaurants are unexpectedly hard to come by in Acapulco. An important exception is the lineup of local-style seafood eateries along Avenida Teniente Azueta, three blocks west from the *zócalo.* Situated only a block from the fishing dock, they get the freshest morsels first. Local longtimers swear by the excellence of seafood served at **El Amigo Miguel** (corner of Juárez and Azueta, tel. 744/483-2390, 10 A.M.–9 P.M.

daily, $5–25), where continuous patronage assures daily fresh shrimp; prawns; half a dozen kinds of fish, including house specialties *pescado empapelado* and *filete miguel*; and lobster. Similarly successful is rival **Mariscos Nachos** (tel. 744/482-2891, 10 A.M.–9 P.M. daily, $5–25), across the street.

If you prefer something a bit fancier, head a block farther from the *zócalo* to tourist favorite **Mariscos Pipos** (Almirante Breton 3, tel. 744/482-2696, noon–8 P.M. daily, $6–14). The freshest of everything is cooked and served to please; credit cards accepted.

Continue west to the Península de las Playas for rave-review seafood at **La Cabaña** (tel. 744/482-5007 or 744/483-7121, 9:30 A.M.–9 P.M. daily, $10–12) on Playa Caleta, next to landmark white beachfront Acamar Beach Resort. Part of the fun here is the luscious view location (arrive while it's still light), where you can choose from a number of delicious specialties. Favorites are the thick *dorado* (mahimahi) fillet, *cazuela de mariscos* (seafood casserole), and whole fish (red snapper recommended).

Many visitors' Acapulco vacations wouldn't be complete without a dinner at the luxuriously scenic clifftop *palapa* restaurant at the **◖ Hotel Los Flamingos** (Av. López Mateos s/n, tel. 744/482-0690, 8 A.M.–10:30 P.M. daily, $7–15), about a mile uphill to the west from Playa Caleta. Here all the ingredients for a memorable evening—attentive service, tasty seafood, chicken, and meat entrées, airy sunset view, and soothing instrumental melodies—come together. Credit cards are accepted. Coat not necessary (but on breezy winter evenings a windbreaker might feel cozy).

## COSTERA

Moving east, first find **VIPs** (Av. Costera M. Alemán, a block past Papagayo amusement park, tel. 744/486-8574, 8 A.M.–10:30 P.M. daily, $4–12), where you can glimpse the Mexico of the future. Here, Mexican middle-class families flock to a south-of-the-border-style Denny's that beats Denny's at its own game. Inside, the air is as fresh as a spring breeze; the windows, water glasses, and

utensils shine, the staff is both amiable and professional, and the food is tasty (but lately, a bit pricey), and credit cards are accepted. (Also, you can visit VIPs' newer Costera locations: beachside near the Hotel Calinda, and at the far east side across the boulevard from the Hyatt Regency.)

Although these days it's sometimes overlooked, in comparison with the trendy newest restaurants (that appear modeled on its successful example) enduring open-air terrace **◖ Restaurant El Olvido** (tel. 744/481-0214 or 744/481-0236, 6 P.M.–2 A.M. daily, $9–24) remains one of Acapulco's best. The Forgotten One, as its name translates, is on the mid-Costera, rear of Plaza Marbella, beach side of the Diana Circle. What's remarkable is that such a tranquil tropical mini-island could exist so close to the smoggy roar of the Costera traffic. By day, guests enjoy a palm-tufted airy bay view and by night an ebony star-studded sky bordered below by myriad twinkling city lights. The excellent cuisine, nevertheless, provides the main attraction. Choose from a very recognizable menu with lots of pasta, meat, and fish, including a number of nouveau international specialties. For example, start off with Boston lettuce with watercress and strawberries, continue with black fettuccine with smoked Norwegian salmon or quail with honey and pineapple, and finish off with tiramisu. Reservations strongly recommended, especially on weekends and holidays.

No tour of Acapulco restaurants would be complete without a stop at **Carlos 'n Charlie's** (Av. Costera M. Alemán, tel. 744/484-0039, noon–midnight daily, $7–20), across from and a block east of Hotel Fiesta Americana Villas Acapulco. Like all locations of the late Carlos Anderson's worldwide chain, it specializes in the zany. The fun begins with the screwy decor; continues via the good-natured, tongue-in-cheek antics of the staff; and climaxes with the very tasty food and drink, which is organized on the menu by categories such as "Slurp," "Munch," "Peep," "Moo," and "Zurts"; credit cards are accepted.

Another successful culinary experiment

is the Acapulco branch of the worldwide ◖ **Suntory** (tel. 744/484-8088, 2–11 P.M. daily, $8–24) Japanese restaurant chain, across from the Oceanic 2000 building, at the east end of the Costera. Although a Japanese restaurant in Mexico is as difficult to create as a Mexican restaurant in Japan, Suntory, the giant beer, whiskey, and wine producer, carries it off with aplomb. From the outside, the clean-lined wooden structure appears authentically classic Japanese, seemingly lifted right out of 18th-century Kyoto. The impression continues in the calm, cool interior, where patrons enjoy a picture-perfect tropical Zen garden, complete with lush moss, a stony brook, sago palm, and feathery festoons of bamboo. Finally comes the food, from a host of choices—vegetables, rice, fish, and meat—that chefs (who, although Mexican, soon begin to look Japanese) individually prepare for you on the grill built into your table. Credit cards are accepted.

## SPLURGE RESTAURANTS

Acapulco visitors and well-to-do residents enjoy a number of fashionable, top-of-the-line restaurants, renowned for their super-scenic locations and fine cuisine. Here's a sampling of the worthy, west to east.

Longtime favorite **Coyuca 22** (Calle Coyuca 22, tel. 744/483-5030 or 744/483-3468, 7–11:30 P.M. daily Nov. 1–Apr. 30, $20–40) is both the name and the address of the restaurant so exclusive and popular it manages to close half the year. (Coyuca is a side street that forks off from Av. López Mateos, on the Península de las Playas, near Hotel Los Flamingos—watch for the sign.) The setting is a spacious hilltop garden, where tables spread down an open-air bay- and city-view terrace. Arrive early (around 5:30 P.M. winter, 7 P.M. late spring–early summer) to enjoy the sunset sky lighting up and painting the city ever-changing colors, ending in a deep rose as finally the myriad lights shimmer and stars twinkle overhead. After that, the food (specialties such as prime rib and lobster tails) and wines seem like dessert. Credit cards are accepted and reservations are required.

The east-end bayview Las Brisas district

has acquired an exclusive sprinkling of stylish restaurants. In order, heading easterly along Highway 200 (here named Carretera Escénica), the best, in west-to-east order, are Baikal, Kookaburra, Casanova, and Zibu.

One of the finest places to be seen is **Baikal** (Carretera Escénica 22, tel. 744/446-6867, 2 P.M.–midnight Tues.–Sun., $25), near the beginning of the Las Brisas bayview strip, across from landmark Palladium disco. Join the well-heeled mostly Mexico City crowd and soak in the relaxed elegance—massive white columns, draped windows looking out on the gleaming galaxy of the Acapulco night—all to the soothing strains of live jazz. Start off with a fine overview of the entire scene, accompanied by appetizers, at the upper bar, then take a main-floor table for your entrée and dessert. After such an introduction, the food may seem like an afterthought, but for an appetizer, try fresh mussels; for salad, arugula with pear; and entrée, salmon in honey and balsamic vinaigrette. Reservations strongly recommended any time.

Next, find ◖ **Kookaburra** (tel. 744/446-6020, 6 P.M.–midnight daily, $25), where, among the beautiful people, you can gaze out on yet another view of Acapulco. In the cool of the evening, from afar, the heat, fumes, and congestion of the Costera give way to a curtain of twinkling lights, like a galaxy, sliced by the curving ebony line of the bay. The food (for example, start with crab cakes, continue with roast duck with mandarin sauce, finish with almond cake) simply embellishes the effect. Reservations are mandatory.

Nearby, at Italian gourmet **Casanova** (Carretera Escénica Las Brisas 5236, tel. 744/446-6237, 744/446-6238, or 744/446-6239, 7–11 P.M. daily, $20–40), you can join the distinguished crowd (many from the renowned Las Brisas resort across the street) evenings, at either a cool inside section or the starry, panoramic view outside, while sampling from a long list of tasty salads, pastas, meats, chicken, and seafood specialties. The house especially recommends its super-fresh shrimp fettuccine. Reservations required.

The hottest and latest of Acapulco's cadre of showplace eateries is the airy, all-outdoors seafood **❰ Restaurant Zibu** (Carretera Escénica s/n, tel. 744/433-3058 or 744/433-3068, www .zibu.com.mx, 7 P.M.–midnight daily, $24–50). The name Zibu (SEE-booh) comes from the island-city (the present-day Cebu) where Spanish explorers first landed in the Philippines, and "That gave birth to the flavor exchange between Asia and Mexico." The house menu ambitiously maps out the restaurant's flavor-fusion mission. I started with spring rolls that turned out to be the most delicious I'd ever tasted. They were accompanied by a small bowl of mild chile spice, perfect for dipping what

amounted to a pair of superb French lettuce-wrapped Asian tacos. Next came an equally delightful rigatoni pasta, dressed in piquant tomato-basil-chile-spiced sauce with goat cheese, washed down with a glass of good Domecq Baja California Cabernet, and finished off with a savory cup of café Americano. Best make up a party and share tastes of the many options, such as salmon in red curry sauce, mahi mahi baked in banana leaf, broiled lobster tail, and much more. Get there by taxi, about four miles (6 km) past the Las Brisas resort, on the east, Pichilingue side, where Highway 200 turns east and descends, above the panorama of the Bahía de Puerto Marqués.

# Entertainment and Events

The old *zócalo* is the best place for strolling and people-watching. Bookstalls, vendors, band concerts, and, on weekend nights especially, pitch-penny games, mimes, and clowns are constant sources of entertainment. When you're tired of walking, take a seat at a sidewalk café, such as La Flor de Acapulco (upstairs balcony, often with evening live music) or Cafe Los Amigos, and let the scene pass *you* by for a change.

## NIGHTLIFE

Acapulco's hottest new dance nightclub is Acapulco's "Cathedral of Salsa," the **Salon Q** (Costera M. Alemán 3117, tel. 744/484-3252 or 744/481-0114, 10 P.M.–4 A.M. daily, about $34), on the east end by the Cinemark multiplex. The fun begins quietly at around 10 P.M., the live music starts, and by midnight a platoon of folks are rocking to salsa. The climax comes with the live show at 12:45 A.M. The cover charge includes open bar.

Some of the **Costera hotels** have live music for dancing at their lobby bars. As you move east along the Costera, the best possibilities are the **Hotel Crowne Plaza** (formerly Costa Club, tel. 744/440-5555), with a medium-volume live salsa and rock band

nightly except Sunday, and the **Copacabana** (tel. 744/484-3260), from 8 P.M. nightly. Call ahead to verify programs.

On the *zócalo*, a live trio at **La Flor de Acapulco** plays everything from live oldies-but-goodies to salsa and Latin rock (call cell tel. 044-744/421-7649 to confirm) Thursday–Saturday 8 P.M.–midnight.

On the other hand, lovers of quieter music love the piano bar (evenings from 7 P.M.) at the refined but moderately priced **Café Pacífico** (tel. 744/484-8252, 5 P.M.–midnight daily, entrées $6–10) of the Hotel Tortuga (tel. 744/484-8889). Find it mid-Costera, inland side, uphill a few blocks from the Diana Circle.

**Discotheques** usually monitor their entrances carefully and are consequently safe and pleasant places for a night's entertainment (provided you are either immune to the noise or bring earplugs). They open their doors around 10 P.M. and play relatively low-volume music and videos for starters until around 11 P.M., when fogs descend, lights flash, and the thumping begins, continuing sometimes till dawn. Admission runs about $10 upwards to $30 or more for the tonier joints.

Acapulco's discos and music hangouts

concentrate in two major east-side spots. As you move east, the first is between the Diana Circle and the Hotel Fiesta Americana Villas Acapulco, a solid lineup of hangouts and discos occupies the Costera's beach side. During peak seasons, the dancing crowds spill onto the street. Stroll along and pick out the style and volume that you like.

Of the bunch, **O'Beach** disco is the loudest, brashest, and among the most popular. For the entrance fee of $5, the music and the lights go till dawn. Other neighboring discos, such as Bombay, Baby Lobster, Barba Roja, Crazy Lobster, Happy Lobster, and Mangos, while sometimes loud, are nevertheless subdued in comparison.

Of the bunch, the must-do newcomer is *Mojita,* which is hosting increasingly big crowds, right in the middle of the action.

Rising above everything is the **Bungie Jump** (tel. 744/484-7529), where dozens of spectators get goosebumps watching one soul do his or her death-defying leap (for only $55, seniors half price) daily, until about midnight.

Another mile east, Planet Hollywood and Hard Rock Cafe, both of which actually serve food, signal the beginning of a second lineup on both sides of the Costera, of about a dozen live-music or disco clubs. The energy they put out trying to outdo each other with brighter lights, louder music, and larger and flashier facades is exceeded only by the frequency at which they seem to go in and out of business. More or less permanently fixed are **Planet Hollywood** (tel. 744/484-0717, noon–1 A.M. daily, bar until 2 A.M. daily, no cover), with recorded music and videos; **Hard Rock Cafe** (tel. 744/484-0047, live music daily 10:30 P.M.–2 A.M., no cover); **Baby O** (tel. 744/484-7474, 10:30 P.M.–4 A.M., cover $20 women, $30 men)—"There's only one Acapulco and only one Baby O"—disco and concert hall; and **Nina's** (tel. 744/484-2400, 10 P.M.–4 A.M., cover about $20 for women, higher for men) "guaranteed fun" concert and *salsa* nightclub, across from the Acapulco Convention Center.

Reigning above all of these lesser centers of discomania is **Palladium** (tel. 744/446-5490), visible everywhere around the bay as the pink neon glow on the east-side Las Brisas hill. Go there, if only to look, though call for a reservation beforehand or you might not be let in. Inside, the impression is of ultramodern fantasy—a giant spaceship window facing outward on a galactic star carpet—while the music explodes, propelling you, the dancing traveler, through inner space. A mere $35 cover (women $20) gets you through the door; inside, cocktails are around $10, while French champagne runs upward of $300 a bottle. Open Tuesday, Thursday, Friday, and Saturday low season, Monday through Saturday high.

## TOURIST SHOWS

The **Salon Acapulco** (tel. 744/484-3252 or 744/484-0114), Acapulco's nightclub *espectáculo* performance, goes on two, three, or four days a week, beginning around midnight, depending on the season. Performances generally include a little bit of everything, from folkloric dance and rope twirling, to jugglers and glittering chorus lines. Tickets run about $25, including open bar. For information and reservations contact a travel agent, such as American Express (tel. 744/435-2200), or call Salon Acapulco directly. Find it on the Costera, east-end, next to the Oceanic 2000 shopping center, across from Baby O disco.

## SUNSETS

West-side hills block Acapulco Bay's sunset horizon. Sunset connoisseurs remedy the problem by gathering at oceanview points on the west-side Península de las Playas, such as the Sinfonia del Sol sunset amphitheater, La Quebrada, Playa Angosta, and especially the cliffside restaurant and gazebo/bar of the Hotel Los Flamingos before sunset.

Far east-side beach locations, especially at the Hotel Hyatt Regency beachfront restaurant-bar, and hillside east-end Las Brisas Scenic Highway (Carretera Escénica) bars at superfashionable restaurants Baikal, Kookaburra, and Casanova also provide unobstructed sunset-viewing horizons.

## BAY CRUISE PARTIES

One popular way to enjoy the sunset and a party at the same time is via a cruise aboard the steel excursion ship **Bonanza** (tel. 744/483-1803). It leaves from its bayside dock on the Costera half a mile (toward the Península de las Playas) from the zócalo. Although cruise schedules vary seasonally, offerings can include midday (11 A.M.–2 P.M.), sunset (4:30–7 P.M.), and moonlight (10:30 P.M.–1 A.M.) cruises. Tickets are available from hotels, travel agents, or at the dock. Tickets run about $30 (with open bar) per person; kids 1.4 meters (about four feet, nine inches) tall and under go for half price.

Alternatively you can go by the smaller catamaran **Aca Rey** (sunset and evening cruises 5:30 and 8 P.M. daily May–Sept., 4:30 and 7 P.M. daily Oct.–Apr., lunada moonlight cruises 10:30 P.M. and 1 A.M. daily, $35 with open bar). Get tickets at the boat dock across the Costera from the zócalo.

## MOVIES

The best cinemas are the Costera multiplexes. As you move eastward, past Papagayo amusement park, first comes **Cineapolis** (tel. 744/485-3178, $4 adults, $2 children), in the shopping plaza next to VIPs restaurant, at the corner of the Costera and Wilfrido Massieu.

Next, find **Cinema 5** (tel. 744/485-5124, $3), on the 3rd floor of the Plaza Bahía shopping center, next to the Hotel Crowne Plaza. Screenings include first-run American dramas and comedies.

Finally, at the east end, three blocks before the Hotel Hyatt Regency, is **Cinemark de Mexico** (tel. 744/481-0656, $4 adults, $2 children), in the Oceanic 2000 plaza across from Baby O disco.

## BULLFIGHTS

Bullfights are staged every Sunday at 5:30 P.M. seasonally, usually December through March, at the arena (here called a frontón) near Playa Caletilla. Avoid congestion and parking hassles by taking a taxi. Get tickets ($30–40)

through a travel agent or the ticket office (tel. 744/483-9561).

## JAI ALAI AND BINGO

About $10 gains you entrance to Acapulco's big jai alai frontón (Av. Costera M. Alemán, tel. 744/484-3195, 9 P.M.–1 A.M. Tues.–Sun.), an indoor stadium—look for the Bingo sign—on the east end of the Costera, across from the Hyatt Regency. Here, it's hard not to ooh and aah at the skill of players competing in the ancient Basque game of jai alai (Fri. and Sat. beginning at 9 P.M.). With a long, narrow curved basket tied to one arm, players fling a hard rubber ball, at lethal speeds, to the far end of the court, where it rebounds like a pistol shot and must be returned by an opposing player. You can place wagers on your favorite player, or join the hometown crowd of local folks playing bingo in the adjacent room, or head downstairs to bet on horse races and other sports events taking place far away.

## WATER PARKS

**CICI** (short for Centro Internacional de Convivencia Infantil, tel. 744/484-8210, 10 A.M.–6 P.M. daily, $10 adult, free children under 12) is the biggest and best-equipped of Acapulco's water parks. An aquatic paradise for families, CICI has acres of liquid games, where you can swish along a slippery toboggan run, plummet down a towering kamikaze slide, or loll in a gentle wave pool. Other pools contain performing whales, dolphins, and sea lions. Sea mammal performances ($1.50 for adults, free for kids) occur at 2 P.M., 4 P.M., and, in season, 5:30 P.M. Patrons also enjoy a restaurant, a beach club, and much more. CICI is on the east end of the Costera between the golf course and the Hyatt Regency.

**Mágico Mundo** (tel. 744/483-1215, 9 A.M.–6 P.M. daily, $4 adult, $3 child), Acapulco's other (older and somewhat rundown) water park, is on the opposite side of town at Playa Caleta. In addition to its very scenic rocky shoal location, it offers an aquarium, restaurant, water slides, cascades, and a pool.

# Sports and Recreation

## SWIMMING AND SURFING

Acapulco Bay's oft-tranquil and invitingly clear emerald-green waters usually allow safe swimming from hotel-front beaches. The water is often too calm for surf sports, however. Nevertheless, strong waves off open-ocean **Playa Revolcadero** southeast of the city frequently give good rides. Be aware; the waves can be dangerous. The Fairmont Acapulco Princess on the beach provides lifeguards. Check with them before venturing in. Bring your own equipment; rentals may not be available.

## SNORKELING AND SCUBA DIVING

The best local snorkeling is off **Isla Roqueta.** Closest access points are by boat from the docks at Playa Caleta and Playa Tlacopanocha. Such trips usually run about $20 per person for two hours, equipment included. Snorkel trips can also be arranged through beachfront aquatics shops at hotels such as the Ritz, Crowne Plaza, Hotel Fiesta Americana Villas Acapulco, the Hyatt Regency, and at the scuba shops listed here.

Although local water clarity is often not ideal, especially during the summer–fall rainy season, Acapulco does have a few professional dive shops. Contact instructor José Vasquez's **Acapulco Scuba Center** (tel. 744/482-9474, reserve@acapulcoscuba.com), near the Bonanza tour boat dock, about half a mile west, past the old-town *zócalo,* for PADI and NAUI. For more information, visit www.acapulcoscuba .com.

Another good option is the up-and-coming **Swiss Divers Association** (tel./fax 744/482-1357, info@swissdivers.com, www .swissdivers.com), headquartered at the Hotel Caleta above Playa Caleta. Their services range from beginner beach dives ($35) and two-tank dives for certified divers ($70) up to NAUI and PADI open-water certification courses (four days, $400).

## SPORTFISHING

Fishing boats line the *malecón* dockside across the boulevard from the *zócalo.* Activity centers on the dockside office of the 20-boat blue-and-white fleet of fishing boat cooperative **Sociedad Cooperativa Servicios Turísticos,** whose dozens of licensed captains regularly take visitors for big-game fishing trips. Although some travel agents may book you individually during high season, the Sociedad Cooperativa Servicios Turísticos office (tel. 744/482-1099, 8 A.M.–11 P.M. daily) rents only entire, captained boats, including equipment and bait. Rental prices and catches depend on the season. Drop by the dock after 2 P.M. to see what the boats are bringing in. In season, boats might average one big marlin or sailfish apiece. Best month for sailfish (*pez vela*) is October; for marlin, January and February; for dorado, March. Big 40-foot

Sailfish, while spectacular in appearance, are too tough for good eating.

© BRUCE WHIPPERMAN

boats with five or six fishing lines (and accommodating eight persons) rent for $350–400 per day. Smaller boats, with three or four lines and holding five or six passengers, rent from around $250. All of the Cooperativa boats are radio-equipped, with toilet, life preservers, tackle, bait, and ice. Customers usually supply their own food and drinks. Although the Cooperativa is generally competent, look over the boat and check its equipment before putting your money down.

Alternatively, some Internet-savvy experienced sportfishing outfitters can be contacted half a mile west along the Costera, at the dock just past the Bonzanza cruise ship landing. A very solid option is **Fish-R-Us** (tel. 744/482-8282 or 744/487-8787, toll-free Mex. tel. 01-800/347-4787 or U.S. tel. 877/347-4787, info@fish-r-us.com, www.fish-r-us.com).

Another reliable sportfishing choice is **Divers of Mexico** (tel. 744/482-1398, cristina@funfishingfactory.com, www.funfishing factory.com). Personable expatriate American owner Cristina organizes fishing trips ($400 six lines), tours, and snorkel and scuba trips, and offers tourist information at her dockside office.

Sailfish and marlin are neither the only nor necessarily the most desirable fish in the sea. Competently captained *pangas* (outboard motor launches) can typically haul in three or four large 15- or 20-pound excellent-eating *róbalo* (snook), *huachinango* (snapper), or *atún* (tuna) in two hours just outside Acapulco Bay. Such lighter boats are rentable from the Sociedad Cooperativa Servicios Turísticos cooperative for about $20 per hour or from individual fishermen on Playa Las Hamacas (east, past the steamship dock at the foot of Fuerte San Diego).

## SAILING AND BOATING

Close-in Acapulco Bay waters (except off of west-end Playa Icacos) are generally too congested with motorboats for tranquil sailing or sailboarding. Nevertheless, some beach concessionaires at the big hotels, such as the Hotel Crowne Plaza and Hyatt Regency, do rent (or

take people sailing in) simple sailboats from $20 per hour.

Outside of town, tranquil **Laguna Coyuca,** on the coast about 20 minutes' drive northwest of the *zócalo,* offers good sailboarding and sailing prospects. (See the *Pie de la Cuesta* section at the end of this chapter.)

Power sports are very popular on Costera hotel beaches. Concessionaires—recognized by their lineup of beached mini-motorboats—operate from most big hotel beaches, notably around the Ritz, the Crowne Plaza, Fiesta Americana, and the Hyatt Regency. Prices run about $60 per hour for personal watercraft, $50 per hour for water-skiing, and $20 for a 10-minute parasailing ride.

## MARINA AND BOAT DOCKING

A safe place to dock your boat is the **Club de Yates** (Av. Costera M. Alemán 215, Fracc. Las Playas, tel. 744/482-3859, fax 744/482-3846, cyates@acabtu.com.mx or gg@clubdeyatesaca .com.mx, www.clubdeyatesaca.com.mx) on the Península de las Playas's sheltered inner shoreline. The slip rate is around $2.50 per foot per day (for up to 39 feet), use of the ramp for launching runs about $75. The many services include 110/220-volt power, pump-out, toilets, showers, restaurant, repair facilities, access to the swimming pool, and more.

Get to the Club de Yates from the Gran Via Tropical on the inner, bay side of the Península de las Playas. Start out by following the Costera past the *zócalo.* About 2.5 miles (4 km) southwest of the *zócalo,* where the boulevard splits at the gas station, fork left along Gran Via Tropical. Continue straight ahead about 300 yards (275 meters), to the Club de Yates entrance gate on the left.

## ECOTOURS

**Shotover Jet** (tel. 744/484-1155, fax 744/484-2648, www.shotoverjet.com.mx), a jet-boat excursion company that originated in New Zealand, offers breezy, spray-laced jet-boat excursions on the big wildlife-rich Tres Palos mangrove lagoon at Barra Vieja, an hour drive west of Acapulco. The tariff runs about

$60, including transportation, from their office at the Plaza Marbella (beach side of the Diana Circle) in mid-Costera.

They also offer a menu of ecoadventures from their upcounty Río Papagayo canyon base, which they call "Bravo Town," 40 miles (66 km) north of Acapulco, off Highway 95 near Tierra Colorada. From Bravo Town they also offer rafting, hiking, camping, caving, rappelling, and climbing.

Like the Shotover Jet, the rafting excursions (Aug.–Jan.) take off from their Plaza Marbella headquarters. The cost is about $60 per adult, $25 kids, including transportation to and from Acapulco.

## TENNIS AND GOLF

Acapulco's tennis courts are all private and nearly all at the hotels. Try the Hotel Crowne Plaza (tel. 744/444-5555, $10/hr days only) or Acapulco Park (tel. 744/485-5437, $8/hr days, $15/hr nights), on the Costera, beach side, near the Plaza Bahía shopping center. Lessons by in-house teaching pros customarily run $20–30 an hour. The Acapulco Campo de Golf also rents tennis courts.

The Acapulco **Campo de Golf** (tel. 744/484-0781 or 744/484-0782, 6:30 A.M.–10 P.M. daily), right on the mid-Costera, is open to the public on a first-come, first-served basis. Greens fee is about $50 for nine holes and $75 for 18 holes. Caddy costs $10, club rentals are $10.

Much more exclusive are the fairways at the **Club de Golf** (tel. 744/469-1000) of hotels Fairmont Acapulco Princess and Pierre

Marqués, about five miles (8 km) past the southeast edge of town. Here, the 18-hole greens fee runs about $140 ($85 after 2 P.M.), including cart and shared caddy.

The **Vidafel Mayan Palace** (tel. 744/469-6000, golf club tel. 744/469-6042), farther east past the Fairmont Acapulco Princess, also rents tennis courts for $20/hr and has a luxury beachfront 18-hole golf course.

## WALKING AND JOGGING

The most interesting beach walking in Acapulco is along the two-mile (3-km) stretch of beach between the Hotel Fiesta Americana Villas Acapulco and the rocky point at Parque Papagayo. Avoid the midday heat by starting early for breakfast along the Costera (a good choice is Sanborn's, tel. 744/481-2426, at the Hotel Calinda) and walking west along the beach with the sun to your back. Besides the beach itself, you'll pass rocky outcroppings to climb on, tidepools to poke through, plenty of ice cream and fruit vendors, and *palapas* to rest in away from the sun. Bring a hat, shirt, and sunscreen and allow two or three hours. If you get tired, ride a taxi or bus back. You can do the reverse walk just as easily in the afternoon after about 3 P.M. from Playa Hamacas just past the steamship dock after lunch on the *zócalo* (try the Cafe Los Amigos).

Soft sand and steep slopes spoil most jogging prospects on Acapulco Bay beaches. However, the green open spaces surrounding the Centro Cultural de Convenciones, just east of the golf course, provide a good in-town substitute.

# Shopping

## MARKET

Acapulco, despite its modern glitz, has a very colorful traditional market, which is fun for strolling through even without buying anything. It is open dawn to dusk daily. Vendors arrive here with grand intentions and mounds of neon-red tomatoes, buckets of *nopales* (cactus leaves), towers of toilet paper,

and mountains of soap bars. As you wander through the sunlight-dappled aisles, past big gaping fish, bulging rounds of cheese, and festoons of huaraches, don't miss **Piñatas Uva,** one of the market's most colorful shops. You may even end up buying one of Uva's charming paper Donald Ducks, Snow Whites, or Porky Pigs. The market is at the corner of Mendoza and Constituyentes, a quarter mile inland from Playa de los Hornos. Ride a Mercado-marked bus or take a taxi.

## HANDICRAFTS

Despite much competition, asking prices for Acapulco handicrafts are relatively high. Bargaining, furthermore, doesn't always bring them down to size. **Sanborn's** (Costera M. Alemán and Escudero, tel. 744/482-4095, 8 A.M.–11 P.M. daily), two blocks from the *zócalo*, sells handicrafts. The modest all-Mexico selection includes, notably, black Oaxaca *barra* pottery, painted gourds from Uruapan, Guadalajara leather, Taxco silver jewelry, colorful plates from Puebla, and Tlaquepaque pottery and glass.

With Sanborn's prices in mind, head one block toward the *zócalo* to **Bonita** (I. de la Llave and Costera M. Alemán, local 1, tel. 744/482-0590 or 744/482-5240, 9 A.M.–7 P.M. daily) handicrafts store, where, in the basement of the big old Edificio Oviedo, glitters an eclectic fiesta of Mexican jewelry. Never mind if you find the place empty; cruise-line passengers regularly fill the aisles. Here you'll be able to see artisans adding to the acre of gleaming silver, gold, copper, brass, fine carving, and lacquerware around you. Don't forget to get your free margarita (or soft drink) before you leave.

For a treat while you're still near the *zócalo,* from Sanborn's walk directly across the Costera to class-act **Linda de Taxco** (adjacent to the cruise ship terminal, tel. 744/483-3347), a silver shop that amounts to a sight all by itself. Their amazingly huge solid-silver pieces, ranging from elephants and hippos through giant crucifixes and noble new-age gods and goddesses, are worth a visit even without buying.

Still another bountiful handicrafts source near the *zócalo* is the artisans' market **Mercado de Parrazal.** From Sanborn's, head away from the Costera a few short blocks to Vasquez de León and turn right one block. There, a big plaza of semipermanent stalls offers a galaxy of Mexican handicrafts: Tonalá and Tlaquepaque papier-mâché, brass, and pottery animals; Bustamante-replica eggs, masks, and humanoids; Oaxaca wooden animals and black pottery; Guerrero masks; and Taxco jewelry. Sharp bargaining is necessary, however, to cut the excessive asking prices down to size.

The best store in the Parrazal market is ◖ **Yazmin** (9 A.M.–6 P.M. daily), in the middle of the complex. They have an unusual collection of many one-of-a-kind jewelry, ceramics, and woodwork examples. Bargaining is necessary to lower the high asking prices.

On the new-town east side a number of handicrafts shopping centers line the Costera. Check out the pair of handicrafts arcades, **Dalia** and **Pueblito,** across the Costera from the Plaza Bahía shopping mall (just west of the Hotel Crowne Plaza). Stalls along shady interior walkways display a host of moderately priced leather, silver, hand-embroidered dresses, *huipiles,* bedspreads, napkins, and ceramics, glass, stoneware, and much more.

For a grand selection of largely inexpensive, but still attractive, native-made handicrafts, go to the large indigenous **mercado de artesanías** warren of stalls, on the mid-Costera, just east of the Diana Circle, inland side.

Moreover, not far from the Costera's eastern end, in the shady mango grove (now a park) about four blocks east of the CICI water park, visit the **Galería Ixcateopan** (9 A.M.–9 P.M. daily), which exhibits and sells paintings and sculpture of prominent local artists.

# Information and Services

## TOURIST INFORMATION AND TRAVEL AGENTS

An easily accessible local tourist information office is the **modulo** (tel. 744/484-4416, 9 A.M.–10 P.M. daily), in front of the convention center, two blocks east of the golf course. Here, workers staff a small crafts shop and money exchange office.

Acapulco is stuffed with travel agents. It's probably best to start at your hotel travel desk. Alternatively, some of the most experienced local travel agents include **Acuario Tours** (Av. Costera M. Alemán 186 #3, tel. 744/469-6100, fax 744/485-7100, 8 A.M.–9 P.M. Mon.–Sat.), in mid-Costera. Alternatively, **American Express** (tel. 744/435-2200, 9 A.M.–6 P.M. Mon.–Fri., 9 A.M.–1 P.M. Sat., check-cashing hours may be shorter), at the west end of the Hotel Continental Emporio, near the Diana Circle, cashes American Express travelers checks at near-bank rates and provides member financial services and travel agency services.

## PUBLICATIONS AND LANGUAGE INSTRUCTION

The best new-book sources in town are the three branches of **Sanborn's.** As you move west to east, you'll find the *zócalo* branch (tel. 744/482-4093, 7 A.M.–11 P.M. daily), on the Costera across from the steamship dock; the mid-Costera branch (tel. 744/482-24267, 7 A.M.–11 P.M. daily) at the Hotel Calinda; and the east-Costera branch (tel. 744/484-2035, 7:30 A.M.–1 A.M. daily) on the ground floor of the Oceanic 2000 shopping plaza, beach side of the Costera, a few blocks from the Hyatt Regency.

English-language international newspapers, such as the *News* from Mexico City, the *Los Angeles Times,* and *USA Today,* are often available in the large hotel bookshops, especially at the Hotel Fiesta Americana Villas Acapulco and the Hyatt Regency. In old town, newsstands around the *zócalo* regularly sell the *News.*

Pick up the commercial but handy and widely available American Express–sponsored tourist booklet *Acapulco Passport* free at a hotel, store, or travel agency.

Acapulco's former expatriate and tourist English-language newspaper *Acapulco Heat* has gone completely electronic as the Spanish-only website www.acabtu.com.mx. It provides a number of useful links to mostly midscale hotels, restaurants, community events and organizations, travel activities, and entertainments.

## Public Library

The small, friendly Acapulco *biblioteca* (Madero 5, corner of Quebrada, tel. 744/482-0388, 9 A.M.–9 P.M. Mon.–Fri.) is near the *zócalo* adjacent to the cathedral. Its collection, used mostly by college and high school students in the airy reading room, is nearly all in Spanish.

## Language Instruction

Get Spanish-language instruction at the reputable private **Universidad Americana** (Av. Costera M. Alemán 1756, Fracc. Magellanes, tel. 744/469-1700, 744/486-5618 ext. 1053, or 744/486-5619, info@uaa.edu.mx, www.uaa.edu.mx) on the Costera, approximately across from the Hotel Crowne Pacific.

## MONEY EXCHANGE

In the *zócalo* neighborhood, long-hours **HSBC Bank** (Jesús Carranza 8, tel. 744/483-5722, 8 A.M.–7 P.M. Mon.–Sat.) is the best bet, on the one-block side street tucked near the *zócalo*'s northeast corner. Alternatively, nearby, go to **Bancomer** (tel. 744/482-2097 or 744/480-1277, to change U.S. cash or travelers checks only, 9 A.M.–4 P.M. Mon.–Fri., 10 A.M.–3 P.M. Sat.), fronting the Costera. Although the lines at **Banamex** (tel. 744/469-4111, 9 A.M.–4 P.M. Mon.–Fri.), nearby, three blocks east of the *zócalo* a block past Sanborn's, are usually longer, it exchanges major currencies. You can avoid the lines by using the bank **ATM machines,** which are routinely connected with international networks.

On the new side of town, also change

money at **HSBC** (tel. 744/485-5309, 8 A.M.–7 P.M. Mon.–Sat.), across from the far east-end McDonald's; or at **Bancomer** (tel. 744/484-4065 or 744/484-4848), 8:30 A.M.–4 P.M. Mon.–Fri.), a few blocks west of the Diana Circle, for U.S. and Canadian currency and travelers checks.

After normal bank hours on the Costera, the **Consultorio Internacional** (tel. 744/484-3108, 9 A.M.–7 P.M. Mon.–Fri., 9 A.M.–3 P.M. Sat.), in Galería Picuda shopping center, across the street and a block west from the Hotel Fiesta Americana Villas Acapulco, exchanges currency and travelers checks.

## COMMUNICATIONS

Acapulco has at least three neighboring pairs of government post and telecommunications offices. The Acapulco main **correo** (post office, tel. 744/483-2405, 8 A.M.–8 P.M. Mon.–Sat.) is in the Palacio Federal across the Costera from the cruise ship dock, three blocks east from the *zócalo.* It provides Mexpost fast, secure mail and philatelic services. The main **Telecomunicaciones** (tel. 744/482-2622 or 744/482-0103, 8 A.M.–8 P.M. Mon.–Fri., 9 A.M.–noon Sat.–Sun.), also in the Palacio Federal, provides money order, telegram, and fax services.

There is also a joint **post and telegraph office** (Cuauhtémoc and Massieu, tel. 744/486-7952, 8 A.M.–8 P.M. Mon.–Fri., 9 A.M.–noon Sat.) at the Estrella de Oro bus terminal.

Furthermore, in mid-Costera, you can go to both the small branch **correo** (tel. 744/484-8029, 8 A.M.–4 P.M. Mon.–Fri.) and its neighboring **Telecom** (tel. 744/484-6976, 8 A.M.–3 P.M. Mon.–Fri.) at the Centro de Convenciones (Convention Center).

For the lowest **telephone** rates, use the widely available Ladatel cards in the many public street telephones. First dial 001 for long distance to the United States and Canada or 01 for Mexico. Otherwise, near the *zócalo,* you can call *larga distancia* (long distance) from the small office next to the HSBC bank (J. Carranza at Calle de la Llave, 8 A.M.–9 P.M. daily).

Connect to the **Internet** at one of the many streetfront stores scattered along the Costera and around the *zócalo.* For example, go to **Foto System Lab** (tel. 744/482-2112, 9 A.M.–10 P.M. daily), right on the *zócalo,* where, beside selling photo supplies, there is also an Internet café. Find it at the corner of J. Carranza, *zócalo* right side, as you enter the *zócalo* from the Costera.

## HEALTH AND EMERGENCIES

If you get sick, ask your hotel to call a doctor for you or contact the **Hospital Magellanes** (W. Massieu 2, corner of Colón, tel. 744/469-0270, 744/485-6544, or 744/485-6597, ext. 119 for the pharmacy), one of Acapulco's most respected private hospitals, for both office visits and round-the-clock emergencies. Get there from the mid-Costera (at the Hotel Ritz) by going one block directly inland. Facilities include a lab, 24-hour pharmacy, and an emergency room with many specialists on call.

A group of American-trained IAMAT (International Association for Medical Assistance to Travelers) physicians offers medical consultations in English. Contact them at the medical department of the Hotel Fairmont Acapulco Princess (tel. 744/469-1000, ext. 1309).

For routine medications near the *zócalo* go to one of many pharmacies, such as at **Sanborn's** (corner of Escudero and the Costera, tel. 744/482-6167) or the big **Farmacia Discuento** (at Escudero and Carranza, tel. 744/482-3552, 8 A.M.–10 P.M. daily), across Escudero from Woolworth's.

For police emergencies, contact one of the many **tourist police** (tel. 744/485-0490) on the Costera in safari pith helmets, or call the officers at the **municipal police** Papagayo station (tel. 744/485-0490), at the end of Avenida Camino Sonora, on the inland side of Parque Papagayo.

In case of fire, call the *bomberos* (tel. 744/484-4122), located on Avenida Farallón, two blocks off the Costera, uphill from the Diana Circle.

## IMMIGRATION AND CUSTOMS

If you lose your tourist card go to **Migración** (tel. 744/466-9008, 9 A.M. –1 P.M. daily) at the airport sufficiently early on your day of departure or on the Costera (tel. 744/4350102, 9 A.M.–1 P.M. Mon.–Fri.), across the traffic circle from Comercial Mexicana, same side of the Costera. Bring proof of your identity and some proof (such as your stamped passport, airline ticket, or a copy of your lost tourist card) of your arrival date in Mexico. If you try to leave Mexico without your tourist card, you may face trouble and a fine. Also report to Migración if you arrive in Acapulco by yacht.

The **Aduana** (customs, tel. 744/466-9005, 8 A.M.–3 P.M. Mon.–Fri.) is on the Costera, *zócalo* area, at the dock across from Sanborn's. If you have to temporarily leave your car in Mexico, check to see what paperwork, if any, must be completed.

## Consulates

Acapulco has several consular agents and officers. The offices of the **U.S. consular** officer, Alexander Richards (tel. 744/481-1699, 744/484-0300, or 744/481-0100, fax 744/484-0300, consular@prodigy.net.mx, 10 A.M.–2 P.M. Mon.–Fri.), are in the Hotel Continental Emporio. He's a busy man and asks that you kindly have your problem written down, together with a specific request for information or action. In genuine emergencies only, contact him at tel. 744/431-0094.

The **Canadian consul,** Diane McLean (tel. 744/484-1305, fax 744/484-1306 or 744/481-1349, acapulco@canada.org.mx, 9 A.M.–12:30 P.M. Mon.–Fri.), holds office hours at the Centro Comercial Marbella, suite 23. After hours, in an emergency, call the Canadian embassy in Mexico City, tel. 01-55/5724-7900.

For the **British consul,** check with the Canadian consul. Contact the **German consul** at Antone de Alamino 26 (tel. 744/484-1860, fax 744/484-3810). The **Netherlands consul,** Ángel Díaz, can be reached by dialing tel. 744/486-8350 or 744/486-6179.

For additional information and other consulates, see the local telephone directory yellow pages, under "Embajadas y Consulados."

## SUPERMARKETS AND DEPARTMENT STORES

In the *zócalo* area behind Sanborn's, **Woolworth's** (on Escudero, corner of Morelos, tel. 744/480-0072, 9:30 A.M.–9 P.M. daily) is a good source of a little bit of everything at reasonable prices. Its lunch counter, furthermore, provides a welcome refuge from the midday heat.

**Comercial Mexicana,** with two Acapulco branches, is a big Mexican Kmart, which, besides the expected clothes, film, cameras, auto supplies, medicines, cosmetics, and housewares, also includes groceries and a bakery. Its locations are: on the Costera at Cinco de Mayo (tel. 744/854-4924, 9 A.M.–11 P.M. daily), just east of the Fuerte San Diego; and on the Costera's east side, across from CICI water park (tel. 744/484-3373, 24 hours daily).

If you can't find what you want at Comercial Mexicana, try the huge **Walmart** (tel. 744/469-0203), open 24 hours daily at the far east end, across from the Hyatt Regency.

## PHOTOGRAPHY

Acapulco visitors enjoy the services of a number of photo stores. One of the best is the very professional **Teknifoto** (Constituyentes 245, tel. 744/483-8316 or 744/482-4741, 10 A.M.–2 P.M. and 4–7 P.M. Mon.–Fri., 10 A.M.–2 P.M. Sat.) near the fire station (*bomberos*) about half a mile northeast of the *zócalo* at the shopping plaza. Goods and services include expert camera repair, film development and printing, digital and film cameras, and a number of digital services.

For more basic photo needs (and Internet access) go to **Foto System Lab** (tel. 744/482-2112, 9 A.M.–10 P.M. daily), right on the *zócalo*, supplying photofinishing, a few cameras and accessories, and some popular film varieties. It's on the corner of J. Carranza, on the right side as you enter the *zócalo* from the Costera.

On the east end of the Costera, among the several photo stores, try **Foto Imagen** (tel. 744/484-5770, 9 A.M.–9 P.M. daily), in the basement of Gigante supermarket, across the Costera from the convention center.

## LAUNDRY

Near the *zócalo,* get your laundry done at **Lavandería Laradin** (8 A.M.–10 P.M. Mon.– Sat.), at the corner of Iglesias and La Paz, one block west of the *zócalo.* Alternatively, near Playa Caleta, try **Lavandería Gabi** (Av. Lopez Mateos 12A, 9 A.M.–7 P.M. Mon.–Sat.), two blocks inland from the beach.

# Getting There and Away

## BY AIR

Several airlines connect the **Acapulco airport** (code-designated ACA, officially the Juan N. Álvarez International Airport) with U.S. and Mexican destinations.

**Aeroméxico** (reservations tel. 744/485-1625 or 744/485-1600, flight information tel. 744/466-9296 or 744/466-9104) and associated Aerolitoral flights connect directly with Mexico City, Monterrey, and Guadalajara.

**Mexicana Airlines** (reservations tel. 744/486-7587 or toll-free Mex. tel. 01-800/502-2010, flight information tel. 744/466-9136 or 744/466-9138) flights connect five times daily with Mexico City.

**U.S. Airways** (toll-free U.S. tel. from Mexico 01-800/235-9292), formerly America West, flights connect with Phoenix.

**Continental Airlines** (reservations toll-free Mex. tel. 01-800/900-5000, flight information tel. 744/466-9063) flights connect with Houston.

**American Airlines** (reservations toll-free Mex. tel. 01-800/904-6000, flight information tel. 744/466-9227) flights connect with Dallas during the winter season.

**Aviacsa Airlines** (reservations tel. 744/484-9305 or 744/484-9306, flight information tel. 744/466-9209, 744/466-9223, or 744/466-9225) flights connect with Guadalajara, Mexico City, Tijuana, and Oaxaca.

**Delta Air Lines** (reservations toll-free Mex. tel. 01-800/902-2100) Aéromexico affiliate charter flights connect with Atlanta during the winter-spring season.

## Air Arrival and Departure

After the usually quick immigration and customs checks, Acapulco arrivees enjoy airport car rentals, efficient transportation for the 15-mile (24-km) trip to town, a post box (*buzón*), a magazine and book stand, and ATMs.

Airport car rental booths often open for arriving flights include **Hertz** (tel./fax 744/485-8947 or 744/466-9172); **Avis** (tel. 744/466-9190 or 744/485-5720); **Alamo** (tel. 744/466-9444 or 744/484-3305); and **Budget** (tel. 744/481-2433 or 744/466-9103). You can ensure availability and often save money by bargaining for a reservation with the agencies via their toll-free 800 numbers before you leave home.

Tickets for **ground transport** to town are sold by agents near the terminal exit, at the far left end as you head for the terminal door. Options include collective GMC Suburban station wagons (about $8 per person) that deposit passengers at individual hotels. Compact four-passenger *taxis especiales* run about $23–40, depending on distance. GMC Suburbans can also be hired *"especial"* as private taxis for $29–46 for up to seven passengers.

On your departure day, save money by sharing a taxi with fellow departees. Don't get into the taxi until you settle the fare. Having already arrived, you know what the airport ride should cost. If the driver insists on greed, hail another taxi.

Simplify your departure by saving $17 or its peso equivalent for your international (or $12 national) departure tax, if your ticket doesn't already cover it. If you lost your tourist permit (which an immigration clerk stamped upon your arrival) either go to Migración in town (see *Immigration and Customs* earlier in this chapter) before your departure date, or arrive early enough at the airport to iron out the problem with airport Migración officials before departure. Bring some proof of your date of arrival—either a stamped passport, airline ticket copy, or a copy of your lost tourist permit.

The Acapulco air terminal building has a number of shops upstairs for last-minute handicrafts purchases, a *buzón* (mailbox), stamp vending machine, public telephones, and a good Wings restaurant.

## BY BUS

Major competitors Estrella Blanca and Estrella de Oro operate three separate long-distance *centrales de autobús* (central bus terminals), one Estrella Blanca (the Ejido) station on the west side and two (both Estrella Blanca and Estrella de Oro) stations on the east side of town.

**Estrella Blanca** (tel. 744/469-2081, 744/469-2030) coordinates the service of its subsidiary lines Elite, Flecha Roja, Autotransportes Cuauhtémoc, Turistar, Futura, and Gacela at two separate terminals. Credit cards are accepted. Most first- or luxury-class departures use the big west-side **Ejido** terminal at Avenida Ejido 47. The airy station is so clean you could sleep on the polished onyx floor and not get dirty; bring an air mattress and blanket. Other conveniences include left-luggage lockers, food stands across the street, a deluxe and midscale hotel booking agency, and Sendatel 24-hour *larga distancia* and fax office open 6 A.M.–10 P.M. daily.

Also from the Ejido station, scores of Estrella Blanca *salidas locales* (local departures) connect with destinations in three directions: northern interior, Costa Grande (northwest), and Costa Chica (southeast) coastal destinations. Most connections are first-class Elite, Turistar, and Futura. Specific northern interior connections include Mexico City (dozens daily, some via Taxco), Toluca, Morelia via Chilpancingo and Altamirano (six daily), and Guadalajara (three daily).

Many first-class (about 10 per day) and second-class (hourly) departures connect northwest with Costa Grande destinations of Ixtapa-Zihuatanejo and Lázaro Cárdenas. Southeast Costa Chica connections with Puerto Escondido, some continuing to Huatulco and Salina Cruz, include four first-class daily (one via Ometepec) and several second-class connections per day.

Also from the Avenida Ejido Estrella Blanca terminal, one or two daily departures connect with the U.S. border (Mexicali and Tijuana) via the entire Pacific coast route, through Ixtapa-Zihuatanejo, Manzanillo, Puerto Vallarta, and Mazatlán. Other departures connect with the U.S. border at Ciudad Juárez, via San Luis Potosí, Zacatecas, Torreón, and Chihuahua.

Many additional first- and luxury-class buses depart from Estrella Blanca's separate west-side big **Papagayo** terminal, on Avenida Cuauhtémoc (tel. 744/469-2081). Facilities and services include an air-conditioned waiting room, left-luggage service, a snack bar, and hotel reservations. From the Papagayo terminal, luxury-class and first-class buses connect with northeast Mexico and the U.S. border, via Querétaro, San Luis Potosí, Monterrey, and Nuevo Laredo. Other departures connect northwest, with Guadalajara, León, Celaya, and Irapuato; and north with Puebla and Mexico City bus stations Norte and Sur; and northwest, with Zihuatanejo.

About five blocks east of the Estrella Blanca terminal, is the busy, modern **Estrella de Oro** (at Cuauhtémoc and Massieu, tel. 744/485-8758, 744/485-8705, or 744/485-9360). It provides connections only with the Mexico City corridor (Chilpancingo, Iguala, Taxco, Cuernavaca, Mexico City) and northwest Costa Grande destinations via Zihuatanejo, with Lázaro Cárdenas. Services include left-luggage lockers, but no food except sweets, chips, and drinks. A branch post office (9 A.M.–8 P.M. Mon.–Fri., 9 A.M.–noon Sat.) and *telecomunicaciones* office (8 A.M.–9 P.M. Mon.–Sat.) are on the outside upstairs walkway, west end.

Estrella de Oro departures include dozens of first- and luxury-class with destinations to Mexico City and intermediate points. Several connect directly through Taxco. Four departures connect daily with the Costa Grande, three with Zihuatanejo, one only with Lázaro Cárdenas. Estrella de Oro offers no Costa Chica (Puerto Escondido) connections southeast.

## BY CAR OR RV

Good highways connect Acapulco north with Mexico City, northwest with the Costa Grande and Michoacán, and southeast with the Costa Chica and Oaxaca.

The Mexico City Highway 95D *cuota* (toll) superhighway would make the connection via Chilpancingo easy (73 miles, 117 km, about 1.5 hrs) if it weren't for the Acapulco congestion. Avoid congestion by going via the ($6) toll tunnel (*túnel cuota*). The uncluttered extension (another 125 miles, 201 km) to Cuernavaca is a breeze in 2.5 hours. For Taxco, stay on the Mexico City–bound expressway north past Chilpancingo a total of about 100 miles (160 km) to a "Taxco *cuota*" (toll) turnoff and follow the signs about another 25 miles (40 km) uphill to Taxco. For Iguala, leave the 95D expressway by following the old Highway 95 turnoff, on the north edge of Chilpancingo. Continue another 62 miles (100 km, two hrs) to Iguala.

After reaching Cuernavaca, the over-the-mountain leg to Mexico City (53 miles, 85 km) would be simple except for possible Mexico City gridlock, which might lengthen it to two hours. Better allow a minimum of around 5.5 driving hours for the entire 251-mile (404-km) Acapulco–Mexico City trip.

The Costa Grande section of Highway 200 northwest toward Zihuatanejo is generally uncluttered and smooth (except for occasional bumps and potholes). Allow about four hours for the 150-mile (242-km) trip.

The same is true for the Costa Chica stretch of Highway 200 southeast to Ometepec (112 miles, 180 km), Pinotepa Nacional (157 miles, 253 km), and Puerto Escondido (247 miles, 398 km total). Allow about three driving hours to Ometepec, four and a half driving hours to Pinotepa, and seven hours total to Puerto Escondido.

**Avoid congestion** heading east via the coastal **Barra Vieja** bypass, across the new Río Papagayo bridge that connects directly to Highway 200, Costa Chica direction, about 20 miles (32 km) east of Acapulco. From downtown, drive east along the Costera as if you were heading to the airport. But, two miles (3 km) before the airport, fork right at the big monument-decorated Barra Vieja intersection. Continue another 15 miles (24 km) through Barra Vieja, across the Papagayo bridge to Highway 200 and the Costa Chica.

# Pie de la Cuesta

The translation of the name Pie (pee-YAY) de la Cuesta—Foot of the Hill—aptly describes this downscale resort village. Tucked around the bend a few miles northwest of Acapulco, between a broad open-ocean beach and placid Laguna Coyuca, Pie de la Cuesta appeals to those who want the excitement the big town offers and the peace and quiet that it sometimes doesn't.

Although tranquil, Pie de la Cuesta offers plenty of outdoor fun, such as mangrove-jungle boat tours, horseback riding, beach sunset-watching, hammock snoozing, water-skiing, beachcombing, boat and kayak launching, and swimming and fishing, in the adjacent palm-tufted freshwater Laguna Coyuca.

Laguna Coyuca, kept full by the sweet waters of the Río Coyuca, has long been known for its fish and birdlife, and tranquil, plumy shoreline. During the early 1400s, the Purépecha kings (who ruled from the Michoacán highlands) established a provincial capital near the town of Coyuca. After the Aztecs drove out the Purépecha a century later (and the Aztecs in turn were defeated by the Spanish), Pie de la Cuesta and its beautiful Laguna Coyuca slumbered in the shadow of Acapulco.

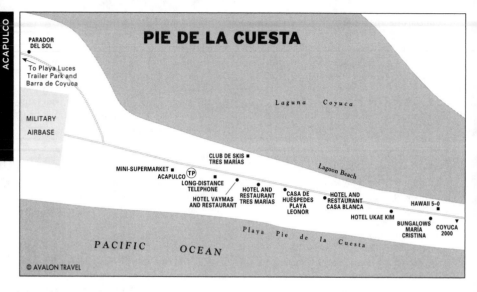

# SAFETY CONCERNS

As at all resorts, petty thievery is not unknown at Pie de la Cuesta. Keep your eyes peeled and be sure not to leave valuables such as cameras unattended, especially at the beach. It's also unwise to flash too much money in public. Some readers have also reported robberies and muggings, so take reasonable precautions.

# SIGHTS

**Laguna Coyuca** is a large sandy-bottomed lake, lined by palms and laced by mangrove channels. It stretches 10 miles (8 km) along the shoreline west from Pie de la Cuesta, which occupies the southeast (Acapulco) side. The barrier sandbar, wide Playa Pie de la Cuesta, separates the lagoon from the ocean. It extends a dozen miles west to the river outlet, which is open to the sea only during the rainy season. A road runs along the beach west the length of Laguna Coyuca to the tourist hamlet of Barra de Coyuca. There, *palapas* line the beach and serve seafood to busloads of Sunday visitors.

**Playa Pie de la Cuesta** is a seemingly endless 100-yard-wide (91-meter-wide) stretch of yellow sand. With its powerful close-in breakers, it's a fine spot for surf fishing. It's also good for beachcombing, jogging, and long sunset walks. However, its powerful (mostly March through October) open-ocean waves are unsuited for surfing and hazardous for swimming. They often break thunderously near the sand and recede with strong, turbulent undertow. Fortunately Pie de la Cuesta waves settle down to pleasantly tranquil during invitingly balmy December through February.

On the inland side, however, the tranquil Acapulco (east) end of Laguna Coyuca is an embarkation point for lagoon tours and the center for water-skiing and personal watercraft. Among the best equipped of the shoreline clubs that offer powerboat services is the **Restaurant and Club de Skis Tres Marias** (tel. 744/460-0013). Besides a pleasant lake-view shoreline *palapa* restaurant (noon–7 P.M. daily), it offers water-skiing ($40/half-hour, $60/hr) and personal watercraft riding ($80/hr).

If you want to launch your own boat, you can do so easily at Club de Skis Tres Marias and others for about $15. The boat traffic, which confines itself mostly to mid-lagoon, does not deter swimming in the lagoon's clear waters. Slip on your bathing suit and jump in anywhere along the sandy shoreline.

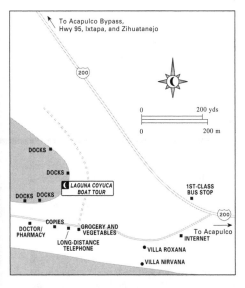

To Acapulco Bypass,
Hwy 95, Ixtapa, and Zihuatanejo

200

0          200 yds

0          200 m

DOCKS

DOCKS

LAGUNA COYUCA
BOAT TOUR

1ST-CLASS
BUS STOP

DOCKS  DOCKS

COPIES

DOCTOR/
PHARMACY

GROCERY AND
VEGETABLES

LONG-DISTANCE
TELEPHONE

200

To Acapulco
INTERNET

VILLA ROXANA

VILLA NIRVANA

## ( Laguna Coyuca Boat Tour

Lagoon tours begin from several landings dotting the Pie de la Cuesta end of the lagoon. Half-day regular excursions (maximum 10 people, about $8 per person) push off daily around 11 A.M., noon, and 1:30 P.M. Along the way, they pass islands with trees loaded with nesting cormorants, herons, and pelicans. In mid-lake, gulls dip and sway in the breeze behind your boat while a host of storks, ducks, avocets, and a dozen other varieties paddle, preen, and forage in the water nearby. Other times, your boat passes through winding channels hung with vines and lined with curtains of great mangrove roots.

At midpoint, boat tours usually stop for a bite to eat at **Isla Montosa.** (Ask ahead of time, because you shouldn't miss it.) While ashore, be sure to allow time for a stroll to restful **Restaurant Polin,** on the island's palm-shadowed south side, where you'll probably meet some descendants of the pioneer settler, known simply as Esteves. As the legend goes, he arrived during the 1930s with six women with whom he founded the present colony, which now numbers about a hundred residents, all related to their illustrious ancestor. For this reason, Isla Montosa is sometimes known as the

"La Isla del Hombre Con Seis Mujeres" (The Island of the Man with Six Women).

Judging from the happily bucolic ambience of Isla Montosa, Esteves was thoroughly successful. Here, roosters crow, pigs root, bougainvillea blooms, and a settlement of fishing families live, unencumbered by 21st-century conveniences, beneath their majestic shoreline palm grove.

## Barra de Coyuca

On another day, drive your car or ride one of the frequent *colectivo* vans that head from Pie de la Cuesta to Barra de Coyuca village at the west end of the lagoon. Along the way, you will pass several scruffy hamlets and a parade of fenced lots, some still-open meadows where horses graze while others are filled with shady gardens and big houses. Lack of potable water, local residents complain, is a continuing problem on this dry sandbar.

At road's end, 10 miles (8 km) west from Pie de la Cuesta, a few tourist stores and a colony of hammock-equipped beach *palapa* restaurants serve holiday crowds. Boats head for tours from lagoonside, where patrons at the **Restaurant Dos Vistas** enjoy a double view of both beach and lagoon.

(*Note:* Mobile travelers without a lot of

© BRUCE WHIPPERMAN

**getting ready for a Laguna Coyuca boat tour**

luggage can also continue west from here, by cross-lagoon launch to La Barra, thence to Costa Grande points west.)

## ACCOMMODATIONS

Approximately 20 bungalows, *casas de huéspedes* (guesthouses), and hotels line Pie de la Cuesta's single beachside road. Competition keeps cleanliness high, management sharp, and prices low. They all cluster along a one-mile roadfront, enjoying highly visible locations right on the beach. Telephone, fax, or email for reservations, especially for the winter season and holidays. Many, but not all of them, have tepid, room-temperature bathwater only and do not accept credit cards; exceptions are noted below. (*Note:* Although all hotels line the single road through Pie de la Cuesta, owners specify the road differently in the addresses they give, mostly either simply "Pie de la Cuesta" or "Av. Fuerza Aerea.")

Be aware that some unscrupulous Acapulco taxi drivers are trying to squeeze commissions from Pie de la Cuesta lodgings in return for bringing customers to their doorsteps. Typical tactics include outright refusal to take customers to places that don't pay commissions, or telling customers that the hotel they request *"no sirve"* ("is not running"). You can combat this, before you get into the taxi, by making sure that the driver agrees to take you to the hotel of your choice. Once in Pie de la Cuesta, make sure that he follows through—or don't pay him.

### Under $50

In approximate order of increasing price, first comes **Casa de Huéspedes Playa Leonor** (63 Pie de la Cuesta, tel. 744/460-0348), which is very popular with a loyal cadre of Canadian winter returnees. They enjoy camaraderie around the tables of the *palapa* restaurant that occupies the beachside end of a large parking-lot garden. The several breezy, more private, plain but clean units on the upper floor are most popular. All 10 rooms have two beds, showers, and fans, and rent for about $40 d year-round.

More picturesque are the **Bungalows María Cristina** (P.O. Box 607, Acapulco, Guerrero 39300, tel. 744/460-0262), with eight units

(four rooms, four kitchen-equipped bungalows) set between a street-side parking lot and a palmy beachside restaurant/garden. The clean, fixed-up, and painted rooms with toilets and hot-water showers rent for about $30 d ($40 holidays). The kitchenette units, most of which face the ocean, run about $80 for up to four people.

The enduringly lovely (( **Villa Nirvana** (302 Playa Pie de la Cuesta, tel. 744/460-1631, fax 744/460-3573, hotelvillanirvana@prodigy.net .mx, www.lavillanirvana.com) attracts a steady stream of repeat guests. A look around and the reason becomes clear: clean, comfortable semi-deluxe accommodations in an attractive garden beachfront compound, with beachfront pool and patio, restaurant, and parking intelligently screened beyond the tall garden wall, in an adjacent lot. Accommodations vary, according to season and size. Personable owners Daniel Reams and Pamela Fox offer a wide range in their 20 accommodations, from compact garden-view rooms for $30–50 d, $60 for two double beds, to airy, spacious oceanview suites accommodating up to eight, for about $80. Discounts for long-term rentals are available; holiday rates may be higher.

The adjacent **Villa Roxana** (same street address: 302 Playa Pie de la Cuesta, tel. 744/460-3252), managed by owner Roxana and her daughter Alexis, also offers attractive choices. Their dozen-odd clean, comfortable rooms, in two stories around a flowery garden with pool, run around $30 low season, $48 holidays. Although they share the same lot (Villa Nirvana in the back by the beach, Villa Roxana out front beside the road), they operate completely separately.

### Over $50

Guests at the **Hotel and Restaurant Casa Blanca** (Av. Fuerza Aerea 370, tel. 744/460-0324, fax 744/460-4027, casablanca@prodigy.net .mx) enjoy a tranquil, car-free tropical garden, small blue beachfront pool and restaurant, and French management. Rates for approximately 15 clean and comfortable rooms, all with toilets and hot-water showers and air-conditioning, run around $50 s, $80 d, add $40 per additional person, year-round. Credit cards are accepted.

Significant discounts should be available any time other than holidays. If not, read on.

Pie de la Cuesta's class-act upscale lodging is the innovative boutique ◖ **Hotel Vayma** (378 Playa Pie de la Cuesta, tel. 744/460-2882 or 744/460-5260, fax 744/460-0697, vayma@ vayma.com.mx, www.vayma.com.mx). Here, guests enjoy the best of all possible rustic chic, including a grandly intimate blue pool, romantically illuminated at night with flickering torches, and 20 individually designed super-deluxe rooms, with names such as Ravel, Berlioz, Debussy, and Pause I and Pause II. Charming Afghan-born owner-manager Parwin Kojani has decorated her rooms with soft, roomy beds, exotic dark-brown hardwood accents, designer lamps, and richly tiled bathrooms. Rentals, which are often occupied by Parwin's friends—diplomats, entertainers, politicos, and business executives—from all over Mexico and the world, rent from around $80 d upwards to about $200 d for the largest suites ($150 and $380 holidays).

### Trailer Parks and Camping

RV-equipped Pie de la Cuesta vacationers have three recommendable trailer park choices. First to consider is the homey and popular **Acapulco Trailer Park** (P.O. Box 1, Acapulco, Guerrero 39300, tel. 744/460-0010, fax 744/460-2457 or 744/485-6086, acatrailerpark@yahoo .com.mx, www.ontheroadin.com/pacificcoast/ pacificsouth/acapulcotrailerpark.htm, $30/day, $400/mo), with about 60 palm-shaded beachfront and choice lagoonside spaces, with all hookups. A congenial atmosphere, good management, and many extras, including a secure fence and gate, keep the place full most of the winter. Facilities include a boat ramp, a pool, a store, a security guard, and clean restrooms and showers. The spaces rent for about $30 per day or $400 per month; tent spaces, $10 per night. Get your winter reservation in early.

The security guard at the Acapulco Trailer Park is a reminder of former times, when muggings and theft were occurring with some frequency on Playa Pie de la Cuesta. Although bright new night lights on the beach have greatly reduced the problem, some (but not all) local folks still warn against camping or walking on the beach at night.

Next in line is the palmy but ramshackle **Quinta Dora Trailer Park** (across the road from the Acapulco Trailer Park, tel. 744/460-0600). Its pluses are an azure, palm-shaded lagoon-front location and boat ramp. Spaces rent for about $15 with low-power electricity and water only, no sewer connection.

◖ **Trailer Park Playa Luces** (playaluces@ hotmail.com, www.ontheroadin.com/pacific-coast/pacificsouth/acapulcowest.htm, $25–35) is about 2.5 miles (4 km) west out of Pie de la Cuesta village, along the Barra de Coyuca road, past the air force base. Formerly a KOA Kampground, Playa Luces is a large park, once the best equipped on the beach, but now somewhat neglected. Although most spaces (many shaded) are not right on the beach, everyone is a stone's throw from the long, silky Playa Pie de la Cuesta, fine for shells, beachcombing, and surf fishing. Facilities include a mini-store, security fence, laundry, playground, and large pool. Big motor-home spaces with all hookups run $35 by the beach, $25 in the shade away from beach, and tent spaces go for $20; all get a 20 percent discount for monthly rentals.

## FOOD

Most Pie de la Cuesta restaurants are beach-front *palapas* that line the Pie de la Cuesta road. One of the most reliable, especially for breakfast on the lagoon, is the lakeview *palapa* of the ◖ **Restaurant and Club de Skis Tres Marias** (Av. Fuerza Aerea 375, tel. 744/460-0013, weekdays noon–7 P.M., holidays and weekends open 9 A.M., $4–12). Here, you can enjoy a brunch omelette, pancakes, or eggs over easy with ham. Later, kick back and pick your favorite from their long list of super-fresh seafood entrées.

If instead you prefer an oceanfront location, you can have it, right across the street at **Hotel and Restaurant Tres Marias** (tel. 744/460-0178, 8 A.M.–8 P.M. daily, $4–12) with similar attentive service, good breakfasts, and seafood and Mexican plates.

Gourmet cuisine has arrived in Pie de la

Cuesta, at upscale ◖ **Restaurant Vayma** (tel. 744/460-5260 or 744/460-2882, 8 A.M.–11 P.M. daily, $5–17), where you can enjoy a great meal while being soothed by the murmur of the waves and the romantic flicker of tiki torches at night. A big menu lays out the finest. For example, start with Niçoise salad, continue with super-fresh oysters Rockefeller, then either a tasty broccoli-zucchini-tomato-mozzarella pizza, or a juicy rib-eye steak. Finish off with *tiramisu,* accompanied by a savory-smooth Graham's 10 year-old Portuguese port.

On the other hand, a few steps down the economic scale, but also choice, especially for enjoying the cooling afternoon offshore breeze or watching the sunset, try local favorite **Coyuca 2000** (tel. 744/460-5609, 8 A.M.–10 P.M. daily, $3–6) Here, hearty snack food is the specialty, such as savory chicken *fajitas,* rich *guacamole,* and a load of tropical margaritas (strawberry, guava, pineapple) to choose from.

## ENTERTAINMENT AND EVENTS

Pie de la Cuesta's big fiesta honors the local patron, the **Virgin of Guadalupe,** with masses, processions, fireworks, and dances on December 10, 11, and 12. The fiesta's climax, de rigueur for visitors, is the mass pilgrimage regatta around the lake by boat.

The deluxe all-inclusive resort **Parador del Sol** (tel./fax 744/444-4050 or 744/444-4049, fax 744/444-4214, parador@acabtu.com.mx, www.paradordelsol.com.mx), about a mile west of Pie de la Cuesta village—turn right at the Barra de Coyuca fork, invites visitors to buy day and/or evening guest memberships for about $47 per adult (children 4–11 half price) per eight-hour day session (10 A.M.–6 P.M.) or evening session (7 P.M.–1 A.M.). Day guests enjoy breakfast (10–11 A.M.), lunch (noon–1 P.M.), open bar, and free use of the pools, beach club, kiddie playground, exercise gym, and basketball, volleyball, mini-golf course, and tennis courts. The evening program kicks off at 7 P.M., with sports (including night-lit tennis) and swimming, continuing with supper (8:30–9:30 P.M.), open bar, and dancing at the discotheque until

after midnight. If after a day you haven't had your fill, you might want to accept the invitation to stay overnight for about $90 per person, all inclusive double occupancy, $150 holidays.

## SERVICES

Although most services are concentrated half an hour away in Acapulco, Pie de la Cuesta nevertheless provides a few essentials. For medical consultations, see either Doctora Patricia Villalobos or her husband, Doctor Luis Amados Rios (tel. 744/460-0923), at their pharmacy where the lagoon begins, right in the middle of the village. Between them, they understand both English and French.

Alternatively, telephone Doctora Paulina Casas Almanza (tel. 744/444-4076)—watch for her roadside sign, a mile west of Hotel Parador del Sol, next to Playa Luces trailer park. Furthermore, she will come to your hotel for consultation.

A scattering of minimarkets sell food and other supplies. Two public long-distance phones are available, one in front of the Acapulco Trailer Park and the other on the highway by the doctors' pharmacy. **Internet** is available at the small streetfront café on the main Pie de la Cuesta road, east end, about two blocks from the Highway 200 intersection.

For a police, fire, or medical **emergency**, simply dial 066.

## GETTING THERE AND AWAY

Pie de la Cuesta is accessible via the fork from Highway 200 near Km 10, six miles (10 km) northwest of the Acapulco old-town *zócalo* by car, taxi ($5), or local bus. The same road fork is also 144 miles (232 km), three hours by road, southeast of Zihuatanejo. First-class buses drop passengers at the roadside, where they can continue either on foot, by taxi, or one of the very frequent local *colectivos.*

Alternatively, mobile travelers can get away west toward the Costa Grande via local *colectivo,* from Pie de la Cuesta west to Barra de Coyuca, thence by launch ($1 per person) northwest across the Laguna Coyuca to La Barra landing and points west.

# THE COSTA GRANDE

The Costa Grande, the "Big Coast" of the state of Guerrero, stretches 150 miles northwest from Acapulco to Zihuatanejo. Before the highway came during the 1960s, this was a land of corn, coconuts, fish, and fruit. Although it's still that, the road added a new ingredient: a trickle of visitors seeking paradise in Zihuatanejo, a sleepy fishing village on a beautiful bay.

Now, however, that trickle of visitors is increasingly enjoying the host of country delights along the way. These include historic market towns, such as Coyuca and Tecpán de Galeana; a beloved pilgrimage shrine at Petatlán; the fascinating archaeological zone of Soledad de Maciel; breezy beaches for camping, beachcombing, and surf fishing, such as Laguna de Mitla, Playa Paraíso, Piedra Tlalcoyunque, Arroyo Seco, La Barrita, and Playa Ojo de Agua; and petite resort hideaways such as El Carrizal, Hotel Resort Villas San Luis, Playa Escondida, and Papanoa.

## PLANNING YOUR TIME

Although the temptation is to drive or bus the entire Costa Grande from Acapulco to Zihuatanejo in one quick half day, that would be a pity. Better, take the scenic route and linger at some of the Costa Grande's plumy paradises en route.

For example, spend a day or two at **El Carrizal** at its top-pick Hotel Paraíso Playa Azul, where you can enjoy both the breezy beach on one side and the hotel's lusciously

relaxing lagoonside setting on the other. Farther up the coast, you could enjoy different but equally inviting delights at the Hotel Los Arcos on invitingly petite **Playa Escondida.**

On the other hand, equipped lovers of the outdoors could be equally content with a few days camping, surf fishing, beachcombing, and maybe even surfing, on the beach at secluded **Laguna de Mitla,** or spectacular and breezy **Piedra Tlalcoyunque,** and the delightfully intimate beach hideaways Playa La Barrita and **Playa Ojo de Agua.**

Moreover, if you're into fishing, boating, canoeing, or kayaking, you might also, besides Laguna de Mitla, consider spending an overnight or more at lagoon-front informal campgrounds at Camalote and **Playa Paraíso.**

Up the coast, not far from Zihuatanejo, the area around Petatlán offers enough for a few relaxing days, starting with shopping at Petatlán's plaza-front gold jewelry market stalls, then paying your respects to Petatlán's miraculous patron Padre Jesús, enjoying some wildlife-viewing and kayaking at nearby Estero Valentín, and relaxing with a walking tour of the **Soledad de Maciel Archaeological Zone.**

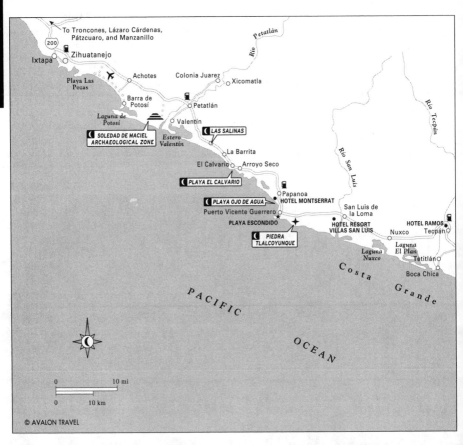

© AVALON TRAVEL

# HISTORY

Long before Zihuatanejo's latter-day popularity, people had been attracted to the Costa Grande. Their oldest remains, pottery dating from around 3000 B.C., decorates the displays at the Zihuatanejo archaeological museum. Later, around 1000 B.C., the Olmecs (famous for their monumental Gulf coast sculptures) left their unmistakable mark on regional pottery.

After them came waves of settlers, including the barbaric Chichimecs (Drinkers of Blood), the agricultural Cuitlatecs, and an early invasion of Aztecs, perhaps wandering in search of their eventual homeland in the Valley of Mexico.

None of those peoples were a match for the armies of Tarascan emperor Hiripan, who during the late 14th century A.D. invaded the Costa Grande from his Michoacán highland capital and established a coastal province, headquartered at the present town of Coyuca de Benítez, less than an hour's drive west of Acapulco.

Three generations later the star of the Aztec emperor Tízoc was rising over Mexico. His armies invaded the Costa Grande and pushed out the Tarascans. By 1500 the Aztecs ruled the coast from their provincial town capital at Cihuatlán, the "Place of Women" not far from present-day Zihuatanejo.

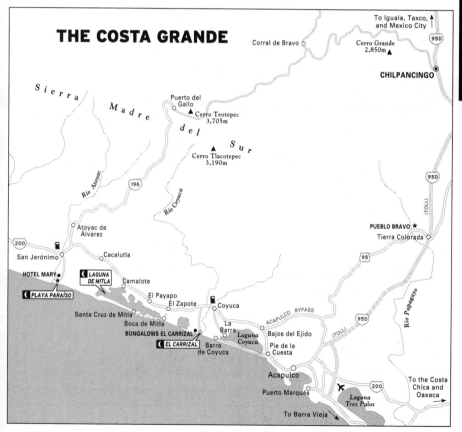

# HIGHLIGHTS

◖ **El Carrizal:** The word "charming" barely begins to describe this south-seas mini-Eden, with the advantage of a pristine open-ocean beach on one side and a rustically lovely palm-tufted lagoon on the other (page 86).

◖ **Laguna de Mitla:** This pristine wildlife-rich beach and lagoon might be heaven for adventurers who hanker for a day or a week soaking up the natural delights of sun, sea, and sand. Be sure to continue to hamlet Santa Cruz de Mitla for a look at the collection of artifacts in the village community museum (page 88).

◖ **Playa Paraíso:** This hidden, family-friendly nook offers a palmy lagoon-front setting for a breezy afternoon boat ride for lunch on the beach across the lagoon, or some restful days of camping and playing in the swimming pools at the picturesque Florentine's Garden Balneario (page 89).

◖ **Piedra Tlacoyunque:** Take a break at this spectacularly scenic, sheltering sea-rock, where in a couple of hours you can surf the waves, stroll the wild, breezy beach, visit the turtle-rescue sanctuary, poke for starfish in the wave-tossed tide pools, watch the families of cormorants, terns, and pelicans, or take it

all in at once over a refreshment at the clifftop view *palapa* restaurant (page 93).

◖ **Playa Ojo de Agua:** This intimate beach nestles beneath forested headlands and is popular for both its good restaurant and small hotel and its unique spring that provides a cooling freshwater bath for washing away the sand and saltwater after a dip in the ocean (page 97).

◖ **Playa El Calvario:** Stop for at least a drink or lunch at one of the sprinkling of clifftop restaurants and enjoy the airy panorama of waves, sun, and sand. More vigorous adventurers continue downhill to the beach for an afternoon of shells, surfing, boogie boarding, and fishing (page 98).

◖ **Las Salinas:** This village of salt harvesters combines age-old technology with ingenuity to harvest salt from nothing more than sun and seawater (page 99).

◖ **Soledad de Maciel Archaeological Zone:** The first stop in this large, ancient, but unexcavated village archaeological zone should be the village church. Later, visit the small village museum where you can contact a guide for a tour (page 102).

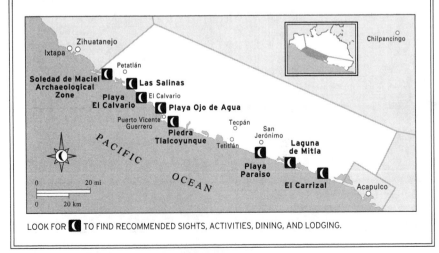

LOOK FOR ◖ TO FIND RECOMMENDED SIGHTS, ACTIVITIES, DINING, AND LODGING.

# The Road Along the Costa Grande

By bus, go by first- or second-class (whose drivers, if asked, will let you off most anywhere) from the Estrella Blanca west-side Avenida Ejido terminal in Acapulco.

Drivers, follow Avenida Ejido from Acapulco, bear right at the Avenida Pie de la Cuesta T intersection and continue northwest along the coastal Highway 200. Let the many highway signs and kilometer markers (both at roadside and painted on the highway asphalt itself, all measured from the Acapulco old-town *zócalo*) be your guide to the many palmy paradises along the way.

## COYUCA DE BENÍTEZ

Coyuca de Benítez (pop. about 20,000), 20 miles (32 km) from Acapulco, is the market and service center of the southwest Costa Grande. Besides being a trading center for the produce of upcountry *fincas cafelateras* (coffee farms) and the *copra* of coastal coconut plantations, Coyuca is famous for its Easter celebration, when folks from all over the Costa Chica crowd in for the fun. Locally known as the **Fiesta de la Palmera,** the festival climaxes the few days before Easter Sunday, with pageants of the Passion of Jesus, and a carnival of food, rides, games, fireworks, bull-roping and riding (*jaripeo*), and cockfights (*peleas de gallos*).

Traffic slows to a crawl at the stall-crowded heart of town, marked by the corner bus station.

### Accommodations and Food

The most comfortable nearby hotel accommodations are at beach resort El Carrizal. In town, the best hotel is the **Posada Coyuca** (Las Palmeras 6, tel. 781/452-0569), right on the highway, north side, a block east of the town center. The dozen-odd rooms are plainly decorated but very clean and reasonably priced, at $20 s or d in one double bed, $40 d, t, q in two double beds, all with fans, TV, and attractive open-air restaurant downstairs. Add $10 for air-conditioning. For more quiet

and privacy, get an upstairs rear room, away from the highway. In an emergency, check out the very basic but clean **Hotel Imperio** (tel. 781/452-1661, $20 d in one bed, $25 d in two beds, including TV) and **Hotel Provinciano** (tel. 781/452-0243, $25 d), both on the street bordering the south side of the town plaza.

As for **camping,** go either to the Laguna Coyuca at La Barra or the beach at El Carrizal (see the *La Barra* and *El Carrizal* sections of this chapter for details).

Coyuca is well known for its good seafood. Three restaurants are especially recommended. Try either **La Brasa,** on the highway east of the town center, or the airy **Bella Vista** view *palapa,* perched above the riverfront at the west end of town, or local favorite **Coyuca 33** across the street from Bella Vista.

Get your groceries and fruits and vegetables at the **market,** big every day, that sprawls over several town blocks north and south of the highway.

### Services

Beyond the market stalls, on the north side, find the town plaza, with the *presidencia municipal* (tel. 781/452-1164), *telégrafos* (telegraph office) and *correo.*

Back on the main street, services include a **Banamex** (tel. 781/452-0021, 9 A.M.–4 P.M. Mon.–Fri.) bank, on the Acapulco side of the highway, with 24-hour ATM; *abarrotes* (groceries), *farmacias* (pharmacies), and Ladatel card-operated street telephones. Alternatively, go to the *caseta larga distancia* (long-distance telephone office), in the center of town by the highway, south side, across from the Farmacia Padre Jesús.

Also nearby, find an *agencia de viajes* (on Guerrero, corner of Reforma, tel. 781/452-0034, 9 A.M.–8 P.M. Mon.–Sat.), and a *centro de salud* (Domínguez 36, north of the plaza uphill, tel. 781/452-0017). The **bus station** (tel. 781/452-0238) is in the center of town on the north side of the street. For police and information, visit the small but well-marked roadside office (tel. 781/452-1164) a couple blocks east of the town center.

## LA BARRA

This breezy lakefront boating, kayaking, fishing, and wildlife-viewing haven is reachable directly by car, taxi, or *colectivo*, via the paved road south from the Coyuca town-center corner of Highway 200 and Calle Guadencia Parra.

If driving, mark your odometer. At Mile 1.7 (Km 2.7) pass through Las Lomas village (stores, pharmacy); at Mile 3.8 (Km 6.1), pass palmy, riverfront *palapa* restaurant La Palma (open seasonally only). Arrive at the breezy boat jetty and local-style waterfront *palapa* restaurants at Mile 4.1 (Km 6.6).

From La Barra, the broad mangrove-fringed freshwater Laguna Coyuca spreads both a mile south across the river estuary to Barra de Coyuca ocean beach and east 10 miles to downscale Pie de la Cuesta resort village, on the edge of Acapulco.

The most popular La Barra activity is the boat ride, roaring directly across the lagoon ($1 per person in collective boat; $5 per boatload one way by private boat) a mile to the Barra de Coyuca tourist village restaurants and beach. Alternatively, and with more tranquillity, try fishing (with your own equipment) and/or viewing (bargain for about $50 per boat per day) the trove of birds and other wildlife that prowl, perch, and preen among the lake's lacy channels and palmy islets. Bring your binoculars, bird book, hat, repellent, and sunscreen. Along the way, you might visit an island or two, especially the drowsy south-sea haven Isla Montosa (for details, see the *Pie de la Cuesta* section at the end of the *Acapulco* chapter) and restaurants, in the lagoon, about four miles east of La Barra.

On the other hand, adventurers might do much the same with their own boat or kayak. It's best to hire a guide; offer $20–30 for a half day.

Camping or RV parking (bring your insect repellent) is a fertile possibility nearby. The best two or three spots appear to be on the shady Río Coyuca estuary-front, near the Restaurant Las Palmas, by the road, a quarter-mile back toward Coyuca.

## ◖ EL CARRIZAL

You know you may be in for something special when you see the Zona Ecoturística sign near the Km 37 marker three miles west of Barra de Coyuca. At the end of the road, you can have all the pleasures of easy country beach living.

If you're on foot, hire a taxi or ride a *colectivo* from the highway. If by car, mark your odometer at the highway just before turning south. At Mile 4.1 (Km 6.6) pass through Epinarillo village, with a sprinkling of stores and a pharmacy or two.

At Mile 4.6 (Km 7.4), arrive at the beach, a gorgeous miles-long medium-steep golden-yellow fine-sand shoreline with powerful, close-in breaks. Flocks of seabirds skitter along the sand, glide over the billows, and dive for fish offshore. Waves seasonally deposit shells and driftwood. The surf, although unsuitable for surfing and generally too rough for swimming, appears excellent for wading and surf fishing. Boat launching, although not impossible, appears difficult at best.

The beach at El Carrizal is a popular Sunday family destination.

© BRUCE WHIPPERMAN

THE COSTA GRANDE

The stately El Carrizal palm grove is fine for a relaxing afternoon.

At the beach, you can either go right or left. Go right for a miles-long breezy strand, ripe for tenting or RV camping. Go left for a long lineup of permanent family-friendly *palapa* restaurants and *cabaña* lodgings.

A few of the beachfront establishments stand out. Immediately on the right, find inviting **Restaurant Dunas** (no phone, 8 A.M.–9 P.M. daily, $4–8) and adjacent, away from the beach, **Bungalows El Carrizal** (tel. 781/452-1869). Owned and operated by personable Virginia Díaz, the five small, spartan but clean rooms rent for about $30 s or d, $40 weekends and holidays, with hot-water showers, TV, fans, and shaded parking. Señora Díaz also runs a snack restaurant (separate from neighbor Restaurant Dunas) whose menu features plenty of fruit, vegetables, yogurt, and granola.

Continue east along the beachfront road a few hundred yards, passing a number of *palapas,* to the inviting and popular family-friendly beach **Resort and Restaurant Nautilus** (tel. 781/452-1933). Managers rent about five plain but clean *cabañas*—two with private bath,

$30 d, three with shared bath, $20 d, $40 and $50 holidays—next to their large beachview *palapa* restaurant and blue pool. Although weekdays (except Christmas, Easter, July, and August) would generally be quiet here, seekers of peace and quiet on a weekend better stay elsewhere. Nevertheless, tent camping is customary, for a nominal fee, in the shade on the beach, right in front of the restaurant.

The Nautilus's friendly owner, Amado Fajardo Colixto, takes parties of up to eight people on lagoon tours in the adjacent Laguna Coyuca for about $25 per hour. He also sells lots for homes along the beach. (In all property transactions, work through a well-established real estate agent; see the sidebar "Owning Paradise" in the *Acapulco* chapter.)

Continue east to the palmy, picturesque road's end, at Mile 6.3 (Km 10.1), where boats line docks, ready to whisk visitors on lagoon wildlife-viewing and restaurant excursions.

Here, lagoon-front **( Hotel Paraíso Playa Azul** (tel. 781/452-2052, $60 d weekdays, $120 d weekends and holidays) offers the only deluxe local accommodations, in a cluster of about a dozen attractively decorated rooms around an invitingly grassy pool-patio. Rooms, however, are unfortunately dark (without turning on the lights) and make little use of the beautiful lagoonside setting. Nevertheless, accommodations are comfortable, each with a pair of soft double beds, hot-water shower bath, and small refrigerator. They include air-conditioning, cable TV, a lovely shaded *palapa* sitting area, and restaurant overlooking the palm-tufted lagoon; massages are available at extra cost. The gorgeous open-ocean beach is only a few steps away across the road. Additional relaxing ocean- and lagoon-view *palapa* restaurants are nearby.

## ◖ LAGUNA DE MITLA

Curiosity alone might drive adventurous lovers of tropical Mexico to explore the reaches of the grand freshwater Laguna de Mitla, a seemingly endless beachcomber's heaven of rolling breakers, delicate seasonal shells, and skittering crabs and sandpipers. Its 25-mile (40-km) high-water length makes it the longest natural lake in Guerrero, so big that it has enough room for three separate bays along its north shoreline. The rewards along the road are a lush freshwater swimming lagoon; beachfront seafood *palapa* restaurants; local fisherfolk willing to guide parties on fishing and wildlife-viewing trips; and a long, pristine, breeze-swept wild beach (but largely shadeless, except for many palm-frond beachfront *ramadas*), ready for camping or RV parking, surf-fishing, and beachcombing. At the end of the road, you'll even find a small community museum and a rancho with a freshwater well.

Get there from Highway 200, at El Zapote, 30 miles (48 km) from Acapulco. Drivers, mark your odometer. Hikers, hire a taxi, thumb a ride, or simply walk the 1.2 miles (2 km) to **Boca de Mitla.** There, cross the bridge over the channel that connects the east and west branches of the Laguna de Mitla.

You may not need to go any farther. Mangroves decorate the river; a few *lanchas* and *canoas* rest on the bank; men, waist-deep in the water, cast nets; and kids splash downstream nearby. You might either hire a *lancha* and guide, or launch your own boat or kayak

A caravan of two wagons delivers fresh water to some of Laguna de Mitla's residents.

© BRUCE WHIPPERMAN

for your private fishing or bird-watching expedition. Be equipped, however, with a hat, binoculars, insect repellent, bottled water, and fishing tackle.

Continue about a quarter mile to (closed at this writing) Restaurant Roberto at Mile 1.5 (Km 2.4). Turn right and continue past the military post on the left, at Mile 1.9 (Km 3.1). Ahead, follow along the unpaved airstrip; at Mile 2.4 (Km 3.9) fork left. At the beach, turn right (west), and arrive at attractively rustic beachfront *palapa* **( Restaurant Álvaro** (no phone, 8 A.M.–9 P.M. daily, $4–8) at Mile 3.1 (Km 5.0), with drinks, fresh seafood, and plenty of breezy space for nearly all beach delights except surfing. A fine golden-sand beach seems to stretch endlessly both west and east. Powerful waves break suddenly along long fronts and recede with strong undertow. Tiny crabs, sandpipers, and plovers scurry along the sand, sun-bleached driftwood lies for the taking, and several unused temporary palm-frond *ramadas* await new occupants. With the restaurant nearby and plenty of room to spread out, beach tenting or RV parking could hardly be better here.

Farther along, at Mile 3.4 (Km 5.5), pass the ponds of a local aquaculture cooperative where workers cultivate fish (tilapia), prawns, and shrimp, and net wild fish in the lagoon when they're not working. The gravel road continues, bumping along, paralleling the beach, through miles of short scrub and cactus. Occasional houses, remnants of a moribund Acapulco Pacífico second-home development, dot the flat, sandy landscape. Finally, at Mile 8.1 (Km 13), head inland, away from the beach, to the Santa Cruz de Mitla hamlet plaza, store, and kiosk, labeled **Santa Cruz de Mitla Museo Comunitario.** Inside, the village exhibits locally discovered ancient pottery artifacts. Nearby, beneath some trees, stands the rancho of friendly pioneer Eleuterio Diego Flores, who welcomes visitors and offers fresh sweet water from his well. If the well-cover is closed, and Eleuterio isn't around, you may have to ask someone to open it up for you.

## CAMALOTE, PLAYA PARAÍSO, AND SAN JERÓNIMO

Visit each of these little places in order to fill entirely different needs: Camalote for seafood, boating, and camping; Playa Paraíso for a picnic and a cooling swim and snooze in the shade; and San Jerónimo for supplies and essential services.

### Camalote

Reach this lagoon-shore refuge by turning left (westbound) 36 miles (58 km) northwest of Acapulco. Follow the signed dirt access road about a half mile to the pair of permanent country-style restaurants perched on the airy east shoreline of the freshwater Laguna de Mitla.

This pretty spot offers easy boating, fishing, and kayaking on the broad lagoon. Some shady sites beneath lakefront trees also invite tenting and RV parking. However, you may have to start by cleaning a bit of trash from your site.

Never mind the trash: A pair of nearby private picnic-campgrounds offer cleaner choices. At the end of the lakefront Camalote road, on the left, find **Restaurant La Bolua,** with space for picnicking, tenting, RV parking, and boat and kayak launching. Even better is the more secluded **( Cabaña Galápagos** (follow the signed dirt road that forks left from the main Camalote ingress road near the highway) with all of the above, and the additional plus of much more space to spread out, beneath shady lakefront trees. Camping charges will run about $5 per day per car during weekends and holidays, free other times when they're empty.

### ( Playa Paraíso

Formerly known as Playa Paraíso Perdido (Paradise Lost Beach), this place has now been found, and for good reason. Local folks love it for its gorgeous swimming-picnicking-camping ground and the breezy boat rides across the Río Atoyac lagoon to good seafood restaurants and a long open-ocean beach.

Get there via the Highway 200 turnoff signed Hacienda de Cabaña, near the Km 81 highway marker, 50 miles northwest of Acapulco (and two miles before San Jerónimo).

## Along the Road to Playa Paraíso

After about five miles (8 km) along a good paved road, arrive at family-friendly **Florentine's Garden Balneario** mini-resort. Cross over on its picturesque hanging bridge and enjoy a swim in the pool, a picnic, or an overnight (bring insect repellent) in the walk-in palm-shaded campground. Like virtually all places in the country, Florentine's Garden Balneario has no telephone and operates only on a drop-in basis.

Continue to the adjacent estuary-front boat landing that, on weekends and holidays, buzzes with motorboats that whisk families ($1 per person round-trip) to the restaurants and long open-ocean beach on the other side. Alternatively, rent a launch for fishing tilapia, *róbalo* (snook), and *pez gallo* (roosterfish), or launch your own boat or kayak.

If you decide to linger, tent camping space is available at the road's boat landing, on the left, beneath the palms, or better, on the open-ocean beach across the estuary.

If you want to stay overnight but lack camping gear, Playa Paraíso now has small **Hotel Mary** (tel. 742/424-2259, $20 d), oddly crowded next to the road, across the lagoon from Florentine's Garden Balneario. (This odd placement, however, allows guests to enjoy a spacious, grassy lagoon-front backyard with lovely blue pool-patio.) Hotel Mary, designed to be a "love" hotel for couples who lack a private place to sleep together, offers two stories of about 10 tiny but clean rooms with air-conditioning. Get an upper room for more light and privacy.

## San Jerónimo

The small market town of San Jerónimo (pop. 10,000), on Highway 200 52 miles (84 km) east of Acapulco, offers a modicum of services and lodging.

At the highway-center of town, find the bus station. On the town plaza nearby is **Telecomunicaciones** (public telephone, money orders, and fax), at the *presidencia municipal* (with police, tel. 781/426-0980). Nearby, also find a post office, pharmacy (Farmacia Pronto), *centro de salud,* doctor (Felipe Jesus Noguera, 17

Calle Principal, tel. 781/426-1114), Restaurant Charleston, and a pair of modest hotels, the San Francisco (at Progeso 44) and the Villa del Mar, with restaurant.

## BOCA CHICA AND TETITLÁN

For the fun and adventure of it, visit Boca Chica, a beachfront fishing village accessible sometimes by boat only. Here, camping is de rigueur, since even permanent residents are doing it. It makes no sense to pour concrete on a sandbar where palm fronds are free and the next wave may wash everything away anyway.

The jumping-off spot is near Km 98 (88 miles, 142 km southeast of Zihuatanejo and 61 miles, 98 km northwest of Acapulco), where a sign marks the road to Tetitlán (pop. 2,000). In about three miles, turn left at the T intersection at the town plaza (with long-distance phone, pharmacy, groceries) and continue a couple of miles along a wide graveled road to the Laguna Tecpán, which, during the dry season, may narrow to a river or dry completely. Here, launches will ferry you (or you can walk) the mile across to the village on the sandbar. Bargain the *viaje redondo* (return-trip) price with your boatman before you depart.

On the other side, the waves thunder upon the beach and sand crabs guard their holes, while the village's four separate societies—people, dogs, pigs, and chickens—each go about their distinct business. Shells and driftwood decorate the sand, and surf fishing with bait from the lagoon couldn't be better.

Most visitors come for the eating only: super-fresh seafood charcoal-broiled in one of the dozen *palapas* along the beach. If, however, you plan to camp overnight, bring drinking water, a valuable Boca Chica commodity.

During the summer rainy season, the Río Tecpán, which feeds the lagoon, breaks through the bar. Ocean fish enter the lagoon, and the river current sometimes washes Boca Chica, *palapas* and all, out to sea.

## TECPÁN

The major service center of the central Costa Grande, Tecpán de Galeana (pop. 25,000),

commonly shortened to Tecpán, is the birthplace of celebrated independence hero Hermenegildo (air-mah-nay-HEEL-doh) Galeana (1762–1814). Galeana, son of a prominent farming family, successfully operated his family's hacienda until he joined the *insurgente* independence cause in 1811, at the age of 49.

According to scholars, the town's name has two interpretations, both from the Náhuatl (Aztec language): either from *tetl* (stone) and *pan* (atop or on), meaning "atop the stone"; or from *tecutli* (lord) and *pan* (place of), meaning "place of the lord."

## Orientation and Sights

Tecpán spreads along the west bank of the broad south-flowing Río Tecpán. Highway 200, approaching westerly from Acapulco, bends north and continues for two miles through the town before turning west again and crossing the river.

A modern abstract stone monument on the highway's west side marks the center of town. It also marks Tecpán's main east–west street, appropriately named Hermenegildo Galeana. If from that point you head west, away from the highway, you pass the church on your right (north side) at Calle Parroquia, which continues south as Calle Reforma. After another block, you arrive at the red-and-pink-adorned

town *parque* that harmonizes cheerily with its bougainvillea floral decor.

## Accommodations and Food

Tecpán has four or five simple hotels, at least two of which are recommendable. The best is the homey, family-run ◖ **Hotel Ramos** (Ana Acostada de Ramos 3, tel. 742/425-3012 or 742/425-1515, $10 d fan only, $25 d a/c). The hotel offers 32 clean, simply but comfortably decorated rooms, built in two stories around a shady parking patio, on a quiet side street one block north of the town plaza. All with TV, private hot-water baths, and parking.

Also recommendable is the compact **Hotel Virrey** (Reforma 22, tel. 742/425-1342, $35 d fan, $45 d a/c), a block south of the HSBC bank. It offers 18 very clean, sparely but comfortably furnished rooms, all with private hot-water bathrooms, TV, and parking. (This hotel is very popular with business travelers; if you're arriving late, call ahead for a reservation.)

Tecpán's most highly recommended restaurant is the refined Mexican-style family ◖ **Restaurant Fogata** (tel. 742/425-0033, 7 A.M.–11 P.M. daily, $4–10). The restaurant, whose name means campfire, is on the through-town highway, about four blocks north of the town center, at Galeana.

## Services

Several service establishments are handily within a block or two of the plaza: the *telecom* on Galeana one block west (9 A.M.–3 P.M. Mon.–Fri., 9 A.M.–noon Sat.) and *correo* (tel. 742/425-0147, 8 A.M.–3 P.M. Mon.–Sat.) next door; **Farmacia del Centro** (tel. 742/425-2858, 9 A.M.–9 P.M. daily), across Galeana from the plaza; **HSBC bank** (on Reforma, tel. 742/425-2682, 8 A.M.–7 P.M. Mon.–Sat.), east of the plaza a block and around the corner; **Banco Santander Serfín** (9 A.M.–4 P.M. Mon.–Fri.), across the street from HSBC, both with ATMs; and photo, digital and film at **Foto Studio Albarrán** (on Calle Parroquia, tel. 742/425-2323, 8 A.M.–8 P.M. daily), across from the church.

For police or medical emergencies, dial

THE COSTA GRANDE

## HERMENEGILDO GALEANA: GENTLEMAN REBEL

Hermenegildo Galeana (1762–1814) wasted little time in rallying to Father Miguel Hidalgo's cry for Mexican independence. A well-to-do Mexican-born *hacendado*, Galeana resented having to bow to the arrogant *peninsulares* who were elevated to Mexico's ruling upper crust by the sole virtue of having been born in Spain.

Galeana was born in Tecpán on April 13, 1762, of a criollo mother and an English sea captain father who established a successful farm in the fertile Río Tecpán valley. As a youth, Hermenegildo benefited from the modicum of advantages that his landed criollo class enjoyed.

During most of his adult years, Galeana enjoyed the life of a country gentleman, successfully managing his family estate, Hacienda El Zanjón, while fathering a brood of children by a succession of six wives.

All that changed drastically when rebel priest José María Morelos, under direct orders from Hidalgo, marched into Tecpán in front of his newly recruited rebel brigade. Drawn by Morelos's charismatic determination, Galeana and his two brothers joined Morelos's force, bringing with them dozens of their workers and a swarm of their Tecpán friends and followers. Thus, at the late age of 49, Hermenegildo Galeana launched the final heroic chapter of his life.

Soon the Galeanas rose to field command rank, joining Morelos's circle of most trusted adjutants. The Spanish challenged them right away, but with little success. On January 4, 1811, the Galeanas fought bravely, achieving a rebel victory at El Veledero, which won them 800 prisoners and a load of captured arms and ammunition.

From then on, Hermenegildo Galeana fought side by side with Morelos, bravely orchestrating a series of signal victories, including the triumph at Tixtla, Vicente Guerrero's hometown.

066, or if you're only sick, see one of the several doctors—gynecologist, internist, pediatrician, and traumatologist—available at the **Centro de Especialidades** (tel. 742/425-0258) medical offices, a few blocks south on the highway downtown. After medical office hours, go to the town **Centro de Salud** (tel. 742/425-0030).

## HOTEL RESORT VILLAS SAN LUIS

Little was spared to embellish the pretty hacienda-like corner of a big mango, papaya, and coconut grove that's home to the ( Hotel Resort Villas San Luis (Carretera Zihuatanejo–Acapulco, Km 143, Buenavista de Juárez, tel. 742/427-0282, fax 742/427-0235, www.villassanluis.com.mx, $48 s, $69 d, $85 d holidays). It appears as if the owner, tiring of all work and no play, built a park to entertain his friends. Now, his project blooms with lovely swimming and kiddie pools, a big *palapa* restaurant, a smooth *palapa*-housed dance floor, a small zoo, basketball and volleyball courts, and an immaculate hotel.

Ideal for a lunch/swim break or an overnight rest, the 40 attractively furnished hotel rooms include air-conditioning and hot water. Credit cards are not accepted. If you'll be arriving on a weekend or holiday, be sure to make a reservation. Find it on the eastbound (south) side of the road near Km 142, 61 miles (98 km) southeast of Zihuatanejo, 89 miles (143 km) northwest of Acapulco.

## SAN LUIS DE LA LOMA

Nearby, two miles east of the resort, the picturesque little market town of San Luis de la Loma (pop. 5,000) perches along its hilltop main street that angles off Highway 200 near Km 140. Besides a number of groceries, fruit stalls, and pharmacies, San Luis has a clean, comfortable guesthouse, **Hotel Hermanos Ruiz** (tel. 742/427-0512, $12 s, $18 d with a/c) and recommendable **Hotel Anita** (tel. 742/427-0476, similar prices). There is also a post office, a health center, a *larga distancia,* a dentist, and doctors (gynecologist Leonarda Z. Pacheco and general practitioner Reynaldo Soria, both

Buoyed by success, Morelos led his triumphant army north, quickly capturing Cuautla, in the present state of Morelos. However, Galeana's severest challenge came when Spanish forces counterattacked and laid a 73-day siege upon the rebels. The siege climaxed when the Spanish attackers penetrated the rebels' perimeter, flanking Morelos and Galeana. A royalist colonel got near Morelos and fired his pistol but missed. Galeana returned fire with his rifle at point-blank range, saving Morelos's life.

Galeana fought on, commanding a victorious battalion in Huajuapan, Oaxaca, in July 1812. In 1813, back south on the coast, Galeana and his men surprised a Spanish force entrenched on Isla Roqueta, an action that led to the rebel capture of Acapulco.

By mid-1814, Galeana was riding a wave of victories. He had won the admiration of his men, who called him, affectionately, "Tata" (Daddy) Gildo, for his selfless, heroic devotion to them and the *insurgente* cause.

But his days were numbered. On June 27, 1814, royalist General Calleja's soldiers ambushed and killed Galeana at Salitral, near Tecpán. Aviles, the royalist commander, ordered Galeana's head cut off, placed on the point of a lance, and exhibited in the Tecpán town plaza. But, because of the riot that such barbarous action ignited, Aviles had Galeana's head taken down and buried with his body inside the Tecpán church. Later, a pair of Galeana's soldiers buried his remains in a secret location to avoid further mutilation.

The independence cause for which Galeana had fought finally prevailed. The new republican government of an independent Mexico elevated beloved Tata Gildo to the revered national rank of Benemérito de la Patria on July 19, 1823.

THE COSTA GRANDE

at tel. 742/427-0423). Both first- and second-class buses stop and pick up passengers where the main street intersects the highway.

## ◖ PIEDRA TLALCOYUNQUE

At Km 150 (94 miles, 151 km from Acapulco or 56 miles, 90 km from Zihuatanejo) a signed side road heads seaward to Piedra Tlalcoyunque and the **Carabelas Restaurant.** About a mile down the paved road, the restaurant (open weekends and holidays) appears, perching on a bluff overlooking a monumental sandstone rock, Piedra Tlalcoyunque. Below, a wave-tossed strand, ripe for beachcombing and surf fishing, stretches for miles. Powerful breakers with fine right-hand surfing angles roll in and swish up the steep beach.

For fishing, buy some bait from the net fishermen on the beach and try some casts beyond the billows crashing into the south side of the Piedra. Later, stroll through the garden of eroded-rock sea stacks on the north side. There you can poke among the snails and seaweeds in a big sheltered tide pool, under the watchful

© BRUCE WHIPPERMAN

Carabelas Restaurant's La Pinta *palapa* affords a panoramic view.

guard of the squads of pelicans roosting on the surrounding pinnacles.

The ruined house on the beach is the former headquarters of the **Campamento Playa Piedra de Tlalcoyunque,** whose mission was to rescue, incubate, and hatch as many turtle eggs as possible. Several volunteers still set up camp and patrol the beach during the summer–fall hatching (and egg-poaching) season. Although they are dedicated to their task, their vigil is a lonely one, and they welcome visitors and contributions of drinks and food.

At the Carabelas Restaurant on the bluff above, you can take in the whole breezy scene while enjoying the recommended catch of the day. The name Carabelas (caravels) comes from the owner's admiration of Christopher Columbus. He christened his restaurant's three petite oceanview gazebos after Columbus's three famous caravels: the *Niña*, the *Pinta*, and the *Santa María*.

For an overnight or a short stay, ask the restaurant owners if it's okay to set up your tent or park your (self-contained) RV in the restaurant lot or by the beach below the restaurant. For shower and dishwashing water, drop your bucket down into their well, at the bottom of the rise before the restaurant.

## SAVING TURTLES

Sea turtles were once common on the beaches of the Acapulco region. Times have changed, however. Now a determined corps of volunteers literally camps out on isolated shorelines, trying to save the turtles from extinction. This is a tricky business because their poacher opponents are invariably poor, determined, and often armed. Since turtle tracks lead right to the eggs, the trick is to get there before the poachers. The turtle-savers dig up the eggs and hatch them themselves, or bury them in secret locations where they hope the eggs will hatch unmolested. The reward – the sight of hundreds of new hatchlings returning to the sea – is worth the pain for this new generation of Mexican ecoactivists.

Once featured on dozens of Acapulco restaurant menus, turtle meat, soup, and eggs are now illegal commodities. Though not extinct, the Mexican Pacific's main sea turtle species – including the green, olive ridley, hawksbill, and leatherback – have dwindled to a small fraction of their previous numbers.

Turtle activists point out that poaching is only one of the hazards that have driven sea turtles to the edge of extinction. Beach habitat loss; ingestion of floating debris, such as plastic bags and tar balls; disease; and accidental capture by trawler nets continue to take deadly tolls.

The **green turtle** (*Chelonia mydas*), the second-largest sea turtle species, is named for the color of its fat (although in Mexico it's called the *tortuga negra* or *caguama*). Officially endangered, the prolific green turtle nevertheless remains relatively numerous. Female green turtles can return to shore up to eight times during the year, depositing 500 eggs in a single season. When not mating or migrating, the vegetarian greens can be spotted often in lagoons and bays, nipping at seaweed with their beaks. Adults, usually three or four feet long and weighing 200-300 pounds, are easily identified out of water by the four big plates on either side of their shells. Green turtle meat was once prized as the main ingredient of turtle soup.

The **olive ridley** (*Lepidochelys olivacea*,

green turtle

BOB RACE

## PLAYA ESCONDIDA

Puerto Vicente Guerrero, a small workaday fishing port and naval training center, 97 miles (156 km) from Acapulco and 52 miles (84 km) from Zihuatanejo, hides a pearl of a beach, appropriately known as Playa Escondida (Hidden Beach), beyond its southeast headland.

Two miles from the signed highway turnoff, continue through the port village, bearing uphill to the left (east) at the village-center road fork overlooking the harbor. Pass the naval training school at the road's summit, and continue ahead a few blocks downhill to the Hotel Los Arcos at Playa Escondida.

Beyond the several permanent *palapa* restaurants that populate the beachfront spreads a wide yellow-sand beach, sheltered on both sides by rocky headlands. Strong waves break and roll in along a nearly level shoreline, receding with only mild undertow.

Playa Escondida (also known locally as Playa Secreta) appears ideal for every kind of beach entertainment, from kiddie play and beachcombing, to surfing and scuba diving. The beach even has ample room for tent camping, especially on the east side.

New lodgings are receiving a growing number of visitors. Most prominent is **Hotel and**

locally *golfina*) turtle population, thanks to persistent government and local volunteer efforts, seems to be stabilizing at several hundred thousand worldwide. Olive ridleys (so-named for their dull green shells) nest in significant numbers at isolated Acapulco-region beaches, notably Playa Revolcadero, east of Acapulco, and Playa Piedra Tlalcoyunque, west on the Costa Grande. Among the smaller of sea turtles, olive ridleys (80-100 pounds, with two-foot-long shells at maturity) come ashore to nest, customarily during summer. They lay clutches of around 80-100 eggs, which they bury with their flippers, and quickly return to the sea. They hunt most of the year near shorelines for shellfish, crabs, fish, and squid.

By contrast, the severely endangered **hawksbill** (*Eretmochelys imbricata*) has vanished from many Mexican Pacific beaches. Known locally as the *tortuga carey* (kah-RAY), it was the source of both meat and the lovely translucent tortoiseshell that has been supplanted largely by plastic. Adult *careys*, among the smaller of sea turtles, run two to three feet

in length and weigh 30-100 pounds. Their usually brown shells are readily identified by shinglelike overlapping scales. During late summer and fall, females come ashore to lay clutches of eggs (around 100) in the sand. *Careys*, although preferring fish, mollusks, and shellfish, will eat almost anything, including seaweed. When attacked, *careys* can be plucky fighters, inflicting bites with their eagle-sharp hawksbills.

You'll be fortunate indeed if you glimpse the rare **leatherback** (*Dermochelys coriacea*), the world's largest turtle. Experts have learned much about the leatherback (*laut* or *tortuga de cuero*) in recent years. About 100,000 female leatherbacks are thought to nest on their favorite egg-laying ground, the Mexican Pacific coast. Tales of the leatherback – of fisherfolk catching seven- or eight-foot individuals weighing nearly a ton – are legend. If you see even a small one you'll recognize it immediately by its back of leathery skin, creased with several lengthwise ridges.

**hawksbill turtle**

BOB RACE

**Restaurant Los Arcos** (tel. 742/427-0252 or 742/424-0556, $35 s, $40 d, $50 t). Its dozen-odd modern, light rooms (somewhat neglected, take a look inside before paying) encircle an inviting pool and parking patio. On the beach side, guests also enjoy an airy beachview restaurant. Room rentals include hot-water shower baths and air-conditioning.

Folks interested in sportfishing and other water sports might want to book a stay at the **Bahía la Tortuga Fishing Lodge** (U.S. tel. 956/455-6931, www.escapeixtapa.com), which has been receiving guests (by reservation only) at Playa Escondida for several years. Owner-operators John and Angélica Lorenz advertise a number of packages, such as a three-night, four-day package that starts at $745 for two, including two days of sportfishing, all meals, and airport pickup. They also offer kayaking, snorkeling, scuba diving, surfing lessons, and whale- and turtle-watching, in season.

One or two bed-and-breakfasts and local homeowners have also rented rooms during the winter season. Follow their signs, customarily posted along the ingress street above Hotel Los Arcos.

One pristine and especially recommended local scuba diving site is El Morro, the big rock island visible off the coast northwest, offshore from Papanoa town. Although no dive shop is operating locally, experienced divers might be able to get there with John Lorenz of the Bahía la Tortuga Fishing Lodge or **Nautilus Divers** (in Zihuatanejo, tel. 755/554-9191, nautilusdivers@hotmail.com, www.nautilus-divers.com).

## PLAYA BRISAS DEL MAR

Scarcely more than a mile on the Acapulco side from Puerto Vicente Guerrero, this breezy gem of a beach spreads west from the point where Highway 200 skirts the oceanfront, at Km 154.

A dirt side road leads 100 yards past very rustic *palapa* restaurants and houses that line the near (west) end of the beach. The dirt road forks left and continues east along the beach, a pristine 200-foot-wide golden strand with rollers that break gradually about 100 yards out. All beach diversions, including surfing, boogie boarding, kiddie play, beachcombing, surf fishing, and boat launching (provided you can negotiate the soft sand) appear promising here. Although no shade is available, at least one abandoned beach *palapa* appears ready for new occupants. Tenting and RV parking also appear customary. Out of courtesy, ask locally if it's okay to camp on the beach.

## PAPANOA

The small town of Papanoa (pop. 3,000) straddles the highway 103 miles (165 km) northwest of Acapulco and 47 miles (75 km) south of Zihuatanejo. Local folks tell the tongue-in-cheek story of its Hawaiian-sounding name. It seems that there was a flood, and the son of the local headman had to talk fast to save his life by escaping in a *canoa*. Instead of saying "Papa...canoa," the swift-talking boy shortened his plea to "Papa...noa."

At least two recommendable hotels offer accommodations. At the center of town, a block north of the highway, stands the neat, family-run 🌙 **Hotel La Sirena** (on Calle Telecino Moreno, tel. 742/422-2029, $20 d, $35 with a/c, $30 and $40 holidays). Here you'll get a very spacious, clean, and comfortable room with hot-water shower bath and ceiling fan, with TV and parking in the patio. Credit cards not accepted.

Alternatively, stay at the resort-style **Hotel Club Papanoa** (Hwy. 200, tel. 742/422-0150, $60 s or d, $80 holidays.) Near the beach about a mile southeast of Papanoa town, the hotel offers about 30 spacious rooms, a restaurant, and a large, lovely pool, set in spacious oceanview garden grounds. Built to be luxurious but now aging, the hotel is often full during holidays, but nearly empty most other times. Rooms have air-conditioning.

The hotel grounds adjoin the beach, **Playa Cayaquitos.** The wide, breezy, yellow-gray strand stretches for two miles, washed by powerful open-ocean rollers with good left and right surfing breaks. Additional attractions include surf fishing beyond the breakers and driftwood along the sand. Beach access is via the off-highway driveway just north of the hotel. At the beach, a parking lot borders a sea-food restaurant. Farther on, the road narrows (but is still motorhome-accessible) through a defunct beachside home development, past several brush-bordered informal RV parking or tent camping spots.

A pair of clean restaurants, the **Annel** (8 A.M.–9 P.M. daily, $5–8) and the **Cabaña** (8 A.M.–9 P.M. daily, $5–8), in the town center on the south side of the highway, serve passable country-style food.

As for services, Papanoa offers friendly doctor Salvador Zarate (tel. 742/422-0046), with pharmacy; a photo shop, Universo (tel. 742/422-0150); a *gasolinera;* first-class bus stops; a long-distance telephone; and Ladatel card-operated public phones.

## ◖ PLAYA OJO DE AGUA

Nestled in the little nook between a pair of head-lands, about half a mile southeast of the Hotel Club Papanoa, is the petite half-moon beach named Playa Ojo de Agua for its cooling and cleansing freshwater spring. Local families flock here on weekend afternoons to play in the surf, eat fresh seafood at the beachfront *palapas,* and rinse themselves in the community spring (*ojo de agua,* literally eye of water) that trickles from a hillside spot, marked by a concrete arch, above the beach. (*Note:* If you use the spring, remember it's only a trickle, so kindly conserve water by dipping a bucket, bottle, or can in the collection basin for water to pour over yourself.)

Playa Ojo de Agua is a lovely spot, wide and level, with very surfable waves from about 200 yards out, and a number of shady possible tenting spots (but with little apparent usable space for beachfront RV parking).

### Accommodations and Food

Development has now arrived at Playa Ojo de Agua, in new beachfront **Hotel Monserrat** (cell tel. 044-742/103-0765, $85 d) with about five designer rooms built over an appealingly airy open-air beachview restaurant. The simply elegant rooms are clean and comfortable, with handsome hardwood highlights, shiny, mod bath fixtures, and king or double beds,

An arch and a stream of fresh water marks the spring behind the trees.

plus cable TV; including breakfast, excepting holidays.

The restaurant, down below, serves from a very recognizable international menu, including breakfast eggs any style, pancakes, and French toast ($4–8), soups, salads, and sandwiches ($3–6), and many entrées, mostly seafood ($6–15).

## PLAYAS ARROYO SECO, EL CALVARIO, AND CAYACAL

Between Km 178 and Km 183, Highway 200 veers spectacularly close to the ocean. Here, three long beaches, Arroyo Seco, El Calvario, and Cayacal, join in one continuously scenic sweep of sand, sea, and sky. From the Acapulco end, first comes long, wild Playa Arroyo Seco; then Playa El Calvario, stunningly viewable from any one of several clifftop *palapa* restaurants; and finally golden Playa Cayacal, seemingly extending forever west.

Along this entire stretch, conditions seem perfect for a day or season of beach diversions. Waves, fine for boogie boarding or surfing, roll in gradually with little undertow. Seasonal storms deposit a few shells and a bit of driftwood. Rock outcroppings provide resting spots for resident gulls, pelicans, boobies, and cormorants, while a sprinkling of visitors strolls the sand and plays in the surf.

### Playa Arroyo Seco
Get the best view of this breezy, palm-lined strand at headland Mirador El Calvario by clifftop **Restaurant El Mirador** (near Km 181, no phone, 7 A.M. –7 P.M. daily, $3–8), where the menu includes Mexican-style breakfasts (such as *huevos mexicanos,* omelettes, and *chilaquiles*) until noon, and fish (whole pan fried, fillet with garlic or breaded, or in tacos) the rest of the day. Below the restaurant, look along the long Playa Arroyo Seco to the petite palm grove and abandoned *palapa* restaurant at the bottom of the cliff. It currently appears ripe for RV parking or tenting. (With no one around, though, security might be questionable. Check at the restaurant to be sure.) You could also set up your tent or park your RV in the parking lot by the restaurant.

Check out Playa Arroyo Seco close-up via at least two access roads: Try the dirt road (easy by high-clearance truck or SUV, difficult by ordinary car) at the bottom of the bluff, at Km 180.5; or more easily, reach Playa Arroyo Seco via the dirt road, on the west (Zihuatanejo) side of the Río Arroyo Seco, at around Km 183. Pass through the village of the same name to the palm-lined beach after about a mile.

### ◖ Playa El Calvario
In contrast to secluded Playa Arroyo Seco, Playa El Calvario is well frequented, especially by the dozens of daily visitors who stop at one of its several clifftop restaurants perched above the beach. Playa Calvario, although especially fine for surfing and nearly everything else (except maybe surf fishing because of the flat shallows), isn't good for camping because it's only about 100 feet wide and vulnerable to flooding at high tide. Instead, camp on Playa Arroyo Seco or Playa Cayacal at either end (or stay at the hotels in Papanoa or Puerto Vicente Guerrero).

Beginning surfers ride the waves at Playa El Calvario.

Nevertheless, Playa Calvario is an irresistible spot to stop and take in the gorgeous scene. Gulls soar, pelicans dive, waves carry surfers shoreward, and cormorants preen and cackle on the Piedras Calvarios outcroppings, picturesquely visible at the Acapulco end, and Piedra Fierre, in the middle.

Furthermore, at the Playa Calvario clifftop, the sun, at dawn and sunset, graphically demonstrates why the Spanish explorers called the Pacific Ocean the Mar del Sur, the Southern Sea. Here, from the clifftop in late afternoon, you can see the sun (which everywhere in the world rises in the east and sets in the west), shining along a line parallel to the beach line. Thus, south, perpendicular to the east–west beach line, is straight out toward the ocean.

## PLAYA LA BARRITA AND LAS SALINAS
These two little roadside spots are interesting for completely different reasons. Playa La Barrita is a lovely beachside mini-paradise, while at Las Salinas, people continue to make

their living from technology whose origin is lost in time.

## Playa La Barrita

Of the several small *palapa* restaurants that decorate Playa La Barrita, around Km 188, none has such an attractive setting as █ **Restaurant Paraíso Escondido** (Hidden Paradise, no phone, 7 A.M. –8 P.M. daily, $4–10). Although the food (shrimp, octopus, fish, prawns) is good enough, the site is stunning. The fine yellow-sand beach stretches for about a mile in both directions, and waves wash in from about 100 yards out with little undertow. Surfing, boogie boarding, and surf fishing and boat launching appear very do-able. For tots, the restaurant even has a blue kiddie pool out front.

Best of all, however, are the luscious camping prospects by the restaurant's shady, forested lagoon (which also makes a fine swimming hole). What's more, the owner welcomes campers, for no more than the price of a meal or two in his restaurant. (The only drawback is the popularity of this place, especially on weekends and holidays, when, if you must have tranquillity,

you had better stay in a hotel or camp a few hundred yards away, along the beach.)

## █ Las Salinas

Families of Las Salinas (pop. 500) village of salt harvesters use the inner flats of the neighboring arm of the ocean, Estero El Cuajo, to make their living. During the dry, low-water winter–spring season, follow the off-highway side road around Km 193 or 194 to see how they do it. With long-handled wooden trowels, workers fashion diked ponds, about 10 feet (three meters) square, from the dried mud of the lagoon. They surface the ponds' bottoms with lime, which soon hardens into an impervious basin.

The salt workers channel the seawater into the ponds. The sun evaporates the water and the salt crystallizes on the edges. The workers scoop the salt crystals into small piles outside the ponds, where the salt piles dry in the sun; the salt is then wheeled in carts to the roadside warehouse to be bagged.

Along Highway 200 in the village, around Km 192, you can see the results of all this.

THE COSTA GRANDE

harvesting salt at Las Salinas

© BRUCE WHIPPERMAN

**Folks leave bowls of fruit and bags of salt for sale beside Highway 200.**

Instead of waiting by the roadside for customers, villagers let their salt bags do the waiting, perched on posts, like roadside mailboxes, for someone to stop and leave a dollar (or ten pesos) for a one-kilo sack. They don't mind doing this; the loss of an occasional dollar is small compared to long hours of waiting. And besides, every dollar they earn this way is one they didn't have in the first place.

Other Las Salinas families around Km 195 sell both salt and "colorines," yummy pastel-colored pure candied coconut cookies. They're fresh, sweet, delicious, and healthy, to boot.

# PETATLÁN

The town of Petatlán (pop. about 25,000), only 22 miles (35 km) east of Zihuatanejo, besides being Guerrero's most cherished pilgrimage shrine, has a distinguished pre-Columbian heritage that has only recently begun to be appreciated.

## Sights

All roads seem to lead to Petatlán's inviting central *parque municipal,* a few blocks south of Highway 200, around Km 207. Here, near the bright pink *kiosko* bandstand, are a pair of intriguing **monoliths,** excavated and brought from Soledad de Maciel (see later listing) to save them from looters. One is a circular stone ring, undoubtedly used in the pre-Columbian ceremonial ball game. The other, protected beneath a covered structure nearby, is a carved disk-shaped monolith, said to represent the god Tlaltecutli.

While in the *parque,* be sure to step inside the adjacent **Parroquia de Padre Jesús,** hallowed ground for the many thousands of pilgrims who arrive yearly from all over Guerrero and Mexico. Inside the innovative parabolic-arched nave, the faithful pay their respects to the venerated wooden image, known affectionately as "Papa Chuy," that arrived under miraculous circumstances as the gift of a mysterious but grateful "Christian Pirate" around 1600. The Petatlán townsfolk fete their beloved Papa Chuy at least twice a year, during the pre-Easter Semana Santa celebration and the August 6–7 Fiesta del Padre Jesús. During both occasions the *parque* is awash with merrymakers watching folkloric dances, eating traditional sweets, and thrilling to the boom and flash of fireworks overhead.

During your downtown stroll, be sure to visit the **Mercado de Oro** (Gold Market) lineup of plaza-front stalls offering a treasury of bright solid-gold necklaces, amulets, chains, bracelets, and much more.

## Accommodations, Food, and Services

A dozen-odd modest downtown hotels accommodate overnight guests. Ordinarily they're not crowded, but if you're going to stay in Petatlán during the Padre Jesús festival (around Aug. 6 and 7), the week before Easter, or Christmas–New Year's, be sure to get reservations far ahead of time.

One of the best is **Hotel Mi Pueblito** (Independencia 108, tel. 758/538-2271, $20 d fan, $30 d a/c, $40 and $50 holidays), next to Telmex. They offer about 10 comfortable,

# THE LEGEND OF PADRE JESÚS

Sometime during the late 1500s, a priest was assigned to minister to the people of Petatlán. Upon arrival, the priest sympathized with the people's sorry state. For years they had endured both the terrible ravages of smallpox and the greed and cruelty of the Spanish soldiers and colonists. The priest taught them and helped heal them, and after a few years he had gained their confidence.

During the yearly Semana Santa celebration the priest saw that the people had been carrying an old rickety image of San Antonio for the reenactment of the Stations of the Cross. In a church meeting, he convinced his congregation to take up a collection to obtain a true image of Jesus for the upcoming Semana Santa celebration.

Although the collection amounted to only a few small coins, the priest prepared to journey somewhere to get an appropriate new image of Jesus.

Meanwhile, a great storm had been blowing off the coast. Unknown to the priest and the people of Petatlán, a pirate ship, dismasted and waterlogged, was in danger of sinking. On the ship was an image of Jesus, to which the pirate sailors prayed to save their ship. The pirate captain vowed that, if they were saved, he would take the image to the nearest town and donate it to the local people.

The pirates were saved: The storm drove them aground on the Bahía de Potosí's sandy shoreline. The pirate captain, true to his vow, took the image ashore with two of his crew.

The priest, meanwhile, had been in a quandary; he did not know where he could find a suitable image of Jesus for the few coins that he had collected. Late one night, as he was praying for guidance, the priest was startled by a hard knock on his door. It was the pirate captain, who told the priest that he had the image of Jesus that the priest was looking for. Then, without further explanation, the pirate disappeared into the night.

Barely able to believe the mysterious man who became known as the "Christian Pirate," the priest nevertheless delayed his trek to find a new image.

Easter Sunday came, and the promised image had not appeared. The priest was relating the story of Jesus's death and resurrection to his congregation when a poor woodcutter pushed himself through the assembly and cried out that Jesus with a cross had appeared to him nearby.

The people followed the woodcutter to a clear stream where, under a great tree, was the sculpture of Padre Jesús. The people joyfully carried Padre Jesús back to their church, where he remains in Petatlán to this day.

*This is a synopsis of the story of Padre Jesús as researched and written by Petatlán's official historian, Señor Agapito Galeana.*

© BRUCE WHIPPERMAN

**religious goods outside the Church of Padre Jesús in Petatlán**

spacious, light and airy rooms with hot-water shower baths, TV, and parking.

Another good choice is posada-style **Hotel-Restaurant La Flor de Petatlán** (Calle N. Bravo 168, corner of Independencia, tel. 758/538-3833, about $30 d, $50 holidays). Friendly owner Aralino Chávez offers eight basic but clean, spacious, and comfortable rooms, all with two beds and fans. A plus here is the hotel's airy view veranda, overlooking the town's main plaza.

Petatlán's most highly recommended restaurant is the refined airy *palapa* ◖ **Restaurant Mi Pueblito** (tel. 758/538-3104, 9 A.M.–1 A.M. daily, $4–8), on the *parque*'s south side, serving a long menu of Mexican country-style favorites.

While downtown, you can avail yourself of a number of services. These include **Bancomer** (tel. 758/538-2977, 9 A.M.–4 P.M. Mon.–Fri.); a *correo;* Ladatel card-operated street telephones; **Agencia de Viajes Mayte** (Guerrero 4, tel. 758/538-2047); the police (at the *presidencia municipal,* tel. 758/538-4040); and a doctor, **Saul Enríquez García** (Bravo 42, tel. 758/538-2321).

## Excursions from Petatlán

Adventurers might go for an upcountry side trip to **Ximalcota** (shee-mahl-KOH-tah), about eight miles (12 km) via the country road from Petatlán's north side, to enjoy the picnicking, hiking, and other diversions possible on the bank of the cascading mountain Río Petatlán. Activity options include cooling off in a cascade or paddling in a swimming hole decorated with friendly rocks, smoothed through eons of the river's flow. Nearby, visit a tree so old and large that it requires a dozen people holding hands to encircle its base. Get there by car, taxi, or guide (contact the travel agent in town). (*Note:* This trip is best enjoyed during the drier months from October through May, when the river runs clear, in contrast to the rainy months of June, July, August, and September, when the river turns an unappealing brown.)

In the opposite, southerly direction, consider an excursion to the freshwater mangrove lake **Estero Valentín** for fresh seafood, wildlife-watching, turtle rescuing, pristine beach camping, fishing, and more. Drive or taxi the country road south from Highway 200 in mid-Petatlán. The three families in charge offer seafood dinners at their palm-shadowed lagoon-front *palapa.* Nearby, from their rustic dockfront, they take visitors on wildlife-watching tours on the mangrove-fringed expanse of Estero Valentín. During the turtle season, be sure to visit their government-sponsored **turtle sanctuary,** and, if you're equipped, camp on the pristine, boat-accessible-only barrier beach that separates the estuary from the ocean.

For a good eco-adventure tour of Estero Valentín, contact manager-owner Brian at very experienced ◖ **Zoe Kayak Tours** (tel. 755/553-0496, zoe5@aol.com, www.zoekayak tours.com), which operates out of Ixtapa.

## ◖ SOLEDAD DE MACIEL ARCHAEOLOGICAL ZONE

Find this important archaeological site five miles (8 km) south of Highway 200, via the good signed side road at Km 214, about three miles (5 km) west of Petatlán or 19 miles (31 km) east of Zihuatanejo. It was first explored by INAH (National Institute of Archaeology and History) investigators around 1925. From time to time excavations have continued, although none of the structures has yet been restored. It is only recently that local folks (who call their site El Chole) have begun to benefit from it. They now welcome visitors to their small artifact museum, introduce them to the monumental "King of Chole" monolith, and offer tours.

Investigators have identified a classic-era (circa A.D. 300) habitation and ceremonial zone that extends over at least a square mile (2 or 3 square km) around the present Soledad de Maciel village. Identified structures include three (completely unreconstructed, rubbleized) pyramids, ceremonial mounds and courtyards, a ball court, and extensive former habitation zones. Many artifacts have been uncovered; examples include pottery, on display at the Zihuatanejo archaeological

© BRUCE WHIPPERMAN

The ancient ball-ring shown by Highway 200 at Petatlán was excavated at the Soledad de Maciel archaeological site.

museum, the two monoliths at the Petatlán downtown *parque,* and two ball rings beside Highway 200 in town.

## King of Chole Monolith and Touring the Archaeological Zone

Artifacts are on display at the modest village museum, also the point of departure for the local tour (in Spanish, of course). Find the museum on the right at the first intersection inside the village. The major artifact is the "King of Chole" monolith, in front of the village church, adjacent to the museum. It represents a personage with two faces, looking in opposite right and left directions. One face, representing death, is emaciated, the other, representing life, is plump and vital.

Guides offer their services for a one- or two-hour tour of the environs. Highlight of the tour is often the 200-foot forested **Cerro de las Peñas,** or Hill of the Rocks. Ask your guide to point out the plants along the way up. These include the wild plumlike *ciruela;* the *cuachalalope* tree, with buds on the trunk that are boiled for a rejuvenating tonic; the *cacahuanache* tree, whose boiled bark makes a good shampoo; and the *paniko* tree, which makes a sedative tonic.

At the breezy summit, the broad hinterland with fields of corn and tobacco (for locally made cigars) and communal coconut groves spreads to the ocean, visible on the southern horizon. Also uphill, you will find a monumental *órgano* (organ cactus), some petroglyphs (of the Lord of the Hill), and a small cave, complete with bats and more petroglyphs. Bring a flashlight. Among the best qualified of the local guides is Adan Belez Romero, available through the museum or by local cell 044-755/551-4851. Offer $15–30 for a two-hour tour.

THE COSTA GRANDE

# IXTAPA AND ZIHUATANEJO

The resort pair of Ixtapa and Zihuatanejo present an irresistible opportunity for a season of relaxed vacationing. The choices seem nearly endless. You can sun to your heart's content on luscious beaches, choose from a feast of delicious food, and shop from a trove of fine Mexican handicrafts. Furthermore, outdoor lovers can enjoy their fill of unhurried beach walking and snorkeling, bicycling, horseback riding, kayaking, swimming, surfing, scuba diving, and caving.

Whether you stay in Ixtapa or Zihuatanejo depends on your inclinations. Zihuatanejo still resembles the small fishing village it once was, with many reminders of old Mexico, and has a mix of small to medium-size hotels. Ixtapa, on the other hand, is for modern travelers who

prefer the fashionable glitter of a luxuriously comfortable facility-rich hotel on a crystalline strand. (On the other hand, where you stay may not really matter, because Ixtapa and Zihuatanejo are only five miles/8 km apart.)

## PLANNING YOUR TIME

There's hardly a better place for a balmy winter vacation than the Ixtapa and Zihuatanejo coast, whether it be for simply a four- or five-day-long weekend or a month of Sundays.

If your stay is limited to four or five days, you'll still have time for some sunning and snoozing on the beach or by the pool, sampling some of the excellent Zihuatanejo restaurants, visiting the **Museo Arqueología de la Costa Grande,** browsing Zihuatanejo's irresistible

# HIGHLIGHTS

◀ **Museo Arqueología de la Costa Grande:** Zihuatanejo's first stop for history aficionados illustrates the prehistory of the Costa Grande with a treasury of dioramas, paintings, and precious locally discovered and donated artifacts (page 110).

◀ **Playa La Ropa:** Enjoy this best of all possible resort beaches, tucked along a golden mile of Zihuatanejo Bay's sheltered eastern flank (page 112).

◀ **Playa Las Gatas:** Only boat accessible, Playa Las Gatas seems like a remote south-seas island, a place where sun, sea, and sand and the rustle of the palms invite relaxation. When you get hungry, a lineup of *palapa* restaurants provide fresh seafood; for exercise, beach stalls rent snorkel gear, which you can use to acquaint yourself with squadrons of tropical fish a few steps offshore (page 112).

◀ *Teleférico* **and Playa del Palmar:** Late afternoon, stroll along Ixtapa's creamy resort beach, Playa del Palmar, to the south end where the *teleférico* will whisk you uphill for a panoramic sunset and cocktails and dinner at the El Faro view restaurant (page 113).

◀ **Isla Grande:** Visitors to this petite, pristine island jewel can enjoy three different beaches, Playa Cuachalatate, Playa Varadero, and Playa Coral, tucked on the island's three sheltered corners. A fourth beach – Playa Carey, for romantics only – is a petite sandy nook accessible by boat only on the island's wild open-ocean shore (page 114).

◀ **Barra de Potosí:** This rustic palm-shadowed village, with a grand, mangrove-laced,

wildlife-rich lagoon on one side and a luscious beach on the other, seems perfect for a spell of relaxed living (page 152).

◀ **Troncones:** Once an isolated fishing village on a coral-decorated shoreline, Troncones has become a winter refuge for a loyal cadre of sun-starved Americans and Canadians (page 154).

LOOK FOR ◀ TO FIND RECOMMENDED SIGHTS, ACTIVITIES, DINING, AND LODGING.

trove of handicrafts, and spending an afternoon at either secluded **Playa Las Gatas** or **Isla Grande.**

With more time, you can concentrate more on your individual interests. Handicrafts, for example, are a major Zihuatanejo specialty. Start with an hour or two at the tourist market on the west side of town, with many stalls stuffed with

tempting treasures from all over Guerrero and Mexico. Then spend the rest of the day browsing the top-pick private handicrafts shops, such as Casa Marina, Artesanías Olinalá, Cerámicas Tonalá, and Galería Maya.

On the other hand, active vacationers will want to get into Ixtapa and Zihuatanejo's great outdoors. You might start off with a day

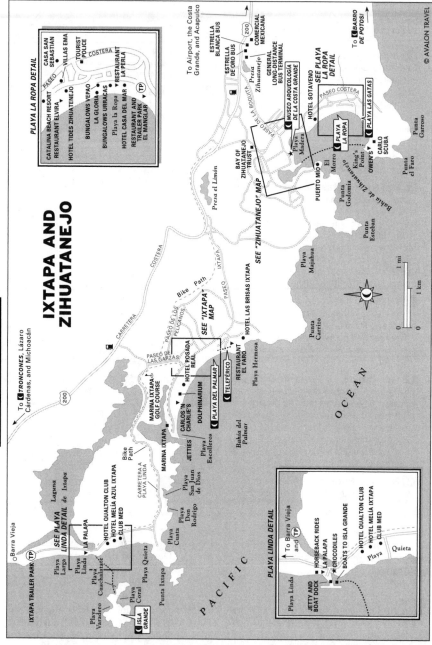

# IXTAPA AND ZIHUATANEJO

© AVALON TRAVEL

**PLAYA LA ROPA DETAIL**

- CASA SAN SEBASTIAN
- VILLAS EMA
- TOURIST POLICE
- CATALINA BEACH RESORT
- RESTAURANT ELVIRA
- HOTEL TIDES ZIHUATANEJO
- BUNGALOWS VEPAO
- LA GLORIA
- BUNGALOWS URRACAS
- Playa la Ropa
- HOTEL CASA DEL MAR
- RESTAURANT LA PERLA
- RESTAURANT AND TRAILER PARK EL MANGLAR
- TP

COSTERA
PASEO

**PLAYA LINDA DETAIL**

- Playa Linda
- JETTY AND BOAT DOCK
- LA PALAPA
- HORSEBACK RIDES
- CROCODILES
- BOATS TO ISLA GRANDE
- HOTEL QUALTON CLUB
- HOTEL MELIÁ IXTAPA
- CLUB MED
- Playa
- Quieta
- To Barra Vieja and TP

To **TRONCONES**, Lázaro
Cárdenas, and Michoacán

To Airport, the Costa
Grande, and Acapulco

To **BARRO
DE POTOSÍ**

200

ESTRELLA BLANCA BUS
ESTRELLA DE ORO BUS
COMMERCIAL MEXICANA
Presa Zihuatanejo
GENERAL LONG-DISTANCE BUS TERMINAL
MUSEO ARQUEOLOGÍA DE LA COSTA GRANDE
HOTEL SOTAVENTO

**SEE PLAYA
LA ROPA
DETAIL**

PASEO COSTERA

PLAYA
LA ROPA
PLAYA LAS GATAS
CARLO SCUBA
OWEN'S
Punta el Faro
Punta Garroso

King's Point
Punta Godonia
CARRETERA

PASEO DE LA BOQUITA

Presa el Limón

BAY OF ZIHUATANEJO TRUST

Playa Madera
PUERTO MÍO
El Morro

Bahía de Zihuatanejo

Punta Esteban

**SEE "ZIHUATANEJO" MAP**

Laguna de Ixtapa

Barra Vieja

IXTAPA TRAILER PARK  TP
Playa Larga
Playa Linda
**SEE PLAYA LINDA DETAIL**
LA PALAPA
HOTEL QUALTON CLUB
HOTEL MELIÁ AZUL IXTAPA
CLUB MED

Playa Cuachalalate
Playa Varadero
ISLA GRANDE
Playa Coral
Playa Quieta
Punta Ixtapa

CARRETERA A PLAYA LINDA

Bike Path

Playa San Juan de Dios
Playa Don Rodrigo
Playa Cuata

PASEO DE LAS GARZAS
PASEO DE LOS PELÍCANOS
Bike Path
PASEO IXTAPA

MARINA IXTAPA GOLF COURSE
MARINA IXTAPA
JETTIES
CARLOS 'N CHARLIE'S
DOLPHINARIUM
HOTEL POSADA REAL
**SEE "IXTAPA" MAP**
HOTEL LAS BRISAS IXTAPA
TELEFÉRICO
PLAYA DEL PALMAR
RESTAURANT EL FARO
Playa Escolleros
Playa Hermosa
Bahía del Palmar

Punta Carrito

Playa Majahua

OCEAN

PACIFIC

COSTERA

COSTERA

1 mi
1 km
0
0

sunning, hiking, and snorkeling off the beaches of Isla Grande. If you want more, you could try the same at Playa Las Gatas with a scuba-diving lesson thrown in. For still more outdoor adventures, do some bicycling on Ixtapa's new *ciclopista*, or head southeast to **Barra de Potosí** or northwest to **Troncones.**

With more days, head out of town south to Barra de Potosí for wildlife-viewing on the Laguna de Potosí or north to Troncones for sunning, swimming and surfing, and lingering a few nights at a comfortable bed-and-breakfast.

With a week or more, you'll have time to rent a car or take a taxi or bus northwest for an overnight or two in a comfortable **Troncones** beachfront bed-and-breakfast, or do the same by traveling southeast to **Barra de Potosí.** While in Troncones, adventurers will want to explore the limestone cave, do some deep-sea fishing, or maybe take a surfing lesson. At the village resort of Barra de Potosí, you can easily spend a couple of days sunning and beachcombing; dining on super-fresh seafood at rustic, palm-shaded *palapa* restaurants; and exploring, by boat or kayak, the grand, wildlife-rich Laguna de Potosí.

## ORIENTATION

Both Ixtapa and Zihuatanejo are small and easy to know. Zihuatanejo's little Plaza de Armas town square overlooks the main beach, Playa Municipal, that fronts the palm-lined pedestrian walkway, Paseo del Pescador. From the plaza looking out toward the bay, you are facing south. On your right is the pier (*muelle,* moo-AY-yay), and on the left the bay curves along the outer beaches Playas La Ropa, Madera, and finally Las Gatas beneath the far Punta El Faro (Lighthouse Point).

Turning around and facing inland (north), you see a narrow but busy waterfront street, Juan Álvarez, running parallel to the beach past the plaza, crossing the main business streets (actually tranquil shady lanes) Cuauhtémoc and Guerrero. A third street, bustling Benito Juárez, one block to the right of Guerrero, conducts traffic several blocks to and from the shore, passing the market and intersecting a second main street, Avenida Morelos, about 10 blocks inland from the beach. There, a right turn will soon bring you to Highway 200 and, within five miles (8 km), Ixtapa.

Most everything in Ixtapa lies along one three-mile-long (5-km-long) boulevard, Paseo Ixtapa, which parallels the main beach, hotel-lined Playa del Palmar. Heading westerly, arriving from Zihuatanejo, you first pass the Club de Golf Ixtapa, then the big Hotel Barceló on the left, followed by a succession of other high-rise hotels. Soon come the Zona Comercial shopping malls and the Paseo de las Garzas corner on the right. Turn right for both Highway 200 and the outer Playas Cuata, Quieta, Linda, and Larga. At Playa Linda, boats continue to heavenly Isla Grande.

If, instead, you continued straight ahead from the Paseo de las Garzas corner, you would soon reach the Marina Ixtapa condo development and yacht harbor.

## GETTING AROUND

In downtown Zihuatanejo, shops and restaurants are within a few blocks of the plaza. For the beaches, walk along the beachfront *andador* (walkway) to Playa Madera, take a taxi ($3) to Playa La Ropa, or take a launch from the pier ($5) to Playa Las Gatas.

For Ixtapa or the outer beaches, take a taxi (about $5) or ride one of the very frequent minibuses, labeled by destination, which leave from both Juárez, across from the market, and the northeast downtown corner of Juárez and Morelos, a few blocks farther north from the beach. In Ixtapa, walk or ride the minibuses that run along Paseo Ixtapa.

## HISTORY
### In the Beginning

The Purépecha-speaking people who lived in the area around A.D. 1400 were relative latecomers, preceded by waves of immigrants to Zihuatanejo. The local archaeological museum displays ancient pottery made by Zihuatanejo artisans as many as 5,000 years ago. Later, more sophisticated artists, influenced by the renowned Olmec mother-culture of the Gulf of Mexico coast, left their indisputable mark on local pottery styles.

## PIRATES OF ZIHUATANEJO

For 10 generations, from the late 1500s to independence in 1821, corsairs menaced the Mexican Pacific coast. They often used Zihuatanejo Bay for repair and resupply.

The earliest was the renowned and feared English privateer Sir Francis Drake (see the sidebar *Sir Francis Drake: The Pirate El Draque* in the *Background* chapter). During his circumnavigation of 1577-1580, Drake raided a number of Spanish Pacific ports.

The biggest prize, however, was the Manila galleon, for which he searched the Mexican coast for months. Finally, low on water and food, he dropped anchor and resupplied briefly at Zihuatanejo Bay before continuing northwest.

### ENTER THE DUTCH

Dutch corsairs also scoured the seas for the Manila galleon. In October 1624, a Dutch squadron commanded by Captain Hugo Schapenham grouped in a semicircle outside Acapulco Bay to intercept the departing galleon. Port authorities, however, delayed the sailing, and the Dutch began running out of food and water. They tried to trade captives for supplies, but the Spanish refused, offering only inedible gold for the captives. In desperation, Schapenham tried to attack the Acapulco fort directly, but his vessels were damaged and driven off by the fort's effective artillery fire.

The starving Dutch sailors retreated up the coast to Zihuatanejo Bay where, after a few weeks, rested and resupplied, they set sail for Asia on November 29, 1624.

Although most of them arrived in the Moluccas Islands in the East Indies, they disbanded. Most of them, including Schapenham, who was dead by the end of 1625, never returned to Europe.

### DAMPIER AND ANSON

A much more persistent and fortunate galleon hunter was English captain William Dampier (1651-1715), who, besides accumulating a fortune in booty, was renowned as a navigator and mapmaker. Lying in wait for the Manila galleon, Dampier anchored in Zihuatanejo Bay in 1704. On December 7, Dampier came upon

By the beginning of the Christian era, local people had developed more sophisticated lifestyles. Instead of wandering and hunting and gathering their food, they were living in permanent towns and villages, surrounded by fields where they grew most of what they needed. Besides their staple corn, beans, and squash, these farmers, called Cuitlatecs by the Aztecs, were also cultivating tobacco, cotton for clothes, and cacao for chocolate. Attracted by the Cuitlatecs' rich produce, the highland Aztecs, led by their emperor Tizoc, invaded the coast during the late 1400s and extracted a small mountain of tribute yearly from the Cuitlatecs.

## Conquest and Colonization

Scarcely months after Hernán Cortés conquered the Aztecs, he sent an expedition to explore the "Southern Sea" and find the long-sought route to China. In November 1522 Captain Juan Álvarez Chico set sail with boats built on the Isthmus of Tehuántepec and reconnoitered the Zihuatanejo coast all the way northeast to at least the Río Balsas, planting crosses on beaches and claiming the land for Spain.

Cortés, encouraged by the samples of pearls and gold that Chico brought back, built more ships and outfitted more expeditions. At a personal cost of 60,000 gold pesos (probably equivalent to several million dollars today) Cortés had three ships built at Zacatula, at the mouth of the Río Balsas. He commissioned Captain Álvaro Saavedra Cerón to command the first expedition to find the route to Asia. Saavedra Cerón set off from Zihuatanejo Bay on October 31, 1527. He commanded a modest force of about 110 men, with 30 cannons, in three small caravels: the flagship *Florida*, the *Espíritu Santo*, and the *Santiago*. The *Florida*, Saavedra Cerón's sole vessel to survive the fierce Pacific typhoons, reached present-day Guam on December 29, 1527, and the Philippines on February 1, 1528.

the Manila galleon *Nuestra Señora del Rosario.* However, a ferocious Spanish defense forced Dampier's squadron to retreat.

Six years later, commanding another squadron jointly with Captain Woodes Rogers, Dampier captured both the galleon *Encarnación* and the *Nuestra Señora de Begoña* between January 1 and January 5, 1710. Rogers and Dampier returned triumphantly to England in the *Encarnación,* which they had rechristened the *Batchelor.*

Luckiest of all Manila galleon treasure hunters was George Anson (1697-1762), who volunteered for the English navy at the age of 15 and rose rapidly, attaining the rank of captain at the age of 25.

In command of a small fleet of ships and hundreds of sailors, he arrived off Acapulco on March 1, 1742. After waiting three weeks for the galleon to sail, and running low on food and water, Anson sailed northwest, resupplied at Zihuatanejo, and then departed west across the Pacific. On July 1, 1743, off Guam, Anson's forces caught up with and captured

the galleon *Nuestra Señora de Covdonga,* with 1.3 million pieces of eight, 35,000 ounces of silver, and a trove of jewels. (A "piece of eight" is an old label for a famous Spanish coin, coveted by pirates the world over.)

Although suffering from the loss of 90 percent of his men, Anson finally returned to England in command of his last remaining ship, carrying booty worth 800,000 pounds sterling, a fortune worth many tens of millions of dollars today.

**William Dampier,**   **George Anson,**
**1651-1715**   **1697-1762**

As he did not know any details of the Pacific Ocean and its winds and currents, it's not surprising that Saavedra Cerón failed to return to Mexico. He died at sea in October 1529 in search of a return route to Mexico.

No fewer than seven more attempts were needed (from Acapulco in 1532, 1539, and 1540; Tehuántepec in 1535; and Barra de Navidad, two in 1542 and one in 1564) until finally, in 1565, navigator-priest Andrés de Urdaneta coaxed Pacific winds and currents to give up their secret and returned triumphantly to Acapulco from Asia.

## The Manila Galleon

Thereafter, the trading ship called the Manila galleon sailed yearly from Acapulco for Asia. For more than 250 years, it returned to Acapulco within a year, laden with a fortune in spices, silks, gold, and porcelain. Although Acapulco's prominence all but shut down

all other Mexican Pacific ports, the Manila galleon would from time to time stop off at Zihuatanejo. The same was true for the occasional pirate ship (or fleet) that lurked along the coast, hungry to capture the galleon's riches.

The most famous corsair was Francis Drake, who landed in Zihuatanejo in 1579. Later came the Dutch fleet of Hugo Schapenham in 1624. English Captain William Dampier entered Zihuatanejo Bay in 1704, recording that the shoreline village had about 40 grass huts, inhabited by about 100 unfriendly people who vigorously discouraged his disembarkation. The luckiest of all the corsairs was Captain George Anson, who, in 1715, captured the Manila galleon and returned to England with booty then worth 800,000 pounds sterling—upwards of $50 million today.

On one occasion, no one knows when exactly, a galleon evidently lost some of its precious silk cargo, which washed ashore on one of Zihuatanejo's beaches, now known as Playa La Ropa (Clothes Beach).

## Independence

In 1821, Mexico won its independence, stopping the Manila galleon forever. Deprived even of an occasional galleon or pirate ship, Zihuatanejo went to sleep and didn't wake up for more than half a century. The occasion was the arrival of ex-president Lerdo de Tejada, who, during the 1870s, embarked from Zihuatanejo for exile in the United States.

By the 20th century, some of the maritime prosperity of Acapulco, which benefited from the stream of California-bound steamers, spilled over to Zihuatanejo. During the 1920s, nearby resources were exploited, and what is now known as Playa Madera (Wood Beach) earned its label as a loading point for fine hardwood timber exports.

## Modern Ixtapa and Zihuatanejo

Recognition of Zihuatanejo's growing importance came on November 30, 1953, when the Guerrero state legislature decreed the formation of the Zihuatanejo *municipio,* whose governmental center was established at the budding town on the bay of the same name.

In the 1960s, a new airport suitable for propeller passenger airplanes, and the paved highway, which arrived from Acapulco around the same time, jolted Zihuatanejo (pop. 1,500) from its final slumber. No longer isolated, Zihuatanejo's headland-rimmed aqua bay began to attract a small colony people seeking paradise on earth.

Tourism grew steadily. Small hotels and restaurants were built to accommodate visitors. Zihuatanejo had a population of perhaps 5,000 by the late 1970s when Fonatur, the government tourism-development agency, decided to develop Zihuatanejo Bay. Local folks, however, objecting that the proposed lineup of high-rise hotels would block the view of their beautiful bay, squelched the plan.

Fonatur regrouped and alternatively proposed Ixtapa (often translated as White Place, but it more likely means White Top, for the several guano-topped offshore islets) five miles (8 km) north of Zihuatanejo as a perfect site for a world-class resort. Investors agreed, and the infrastructure—drainage, roads, and utilities—was installed. The jet airport was built, hotels rose, and by 2000, the distinct but inseparable twin resorts of Ixtapa and Zihuatanejo (combined pop. 80,000) were attracting a steady stream of Mexican and foreign vacationers.

# Sights

## ◪ MUSEO ARQUEOLOGÍA DE LA COSTA GRANDE

Zihuatanejo's smallish but fine archaeological museum (Plaza Olaf Palme, Paseo del Pescador, tel. 755/554-7552, 10 a.m.–6 p.m. Tues.–Sun., $3) at the east end of the main town beach authoritatively details the prehistory of the Costa Grande. Professionally prepared maps, paintings, dioramas, and artifacts—many donated by local resident and innkeeper Anita Rellstab—illustrate the development of local cultures, from early hunting and gathering to agriculture and, finally, urbanization by the time of the conquest.

## BEACHES AROUND ZIHUATANEJO BAY

Ringed by forested hills, edged by steep cliffs, and laced by rocky shoals, Zihuatanejo Bay would be beautiful even without its beaches. Five of them line the bay.

### Playas El Almacén, Municipal, and Madera

Zihuatanejo Bay's west side shelters narrow, tranquil Playa El Almacén (Warehouse Beach), mostly good for fishing from its nearby rocks. Moving east past the pier toward town brings you to the colorful, bustling Playa Municipal.

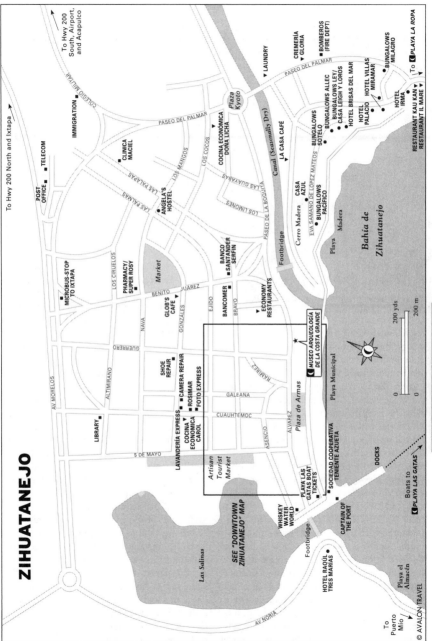

# ZIHUATANEJO

To Hwy 200 North and Ixtapa

To Hwy 200 South, Airport, and Acapulco

COLEGIO MILITAR

POST OFFICE

TELECOM

IMMIGRATION

MICROBUS-STOP TO IXTAPA

LIBRARY

CLINICA MACIEL

LAS PALMAS

LOS CIRUELOS

LOS MANGOS

ANGELA'S HOSTEL

PHARMACY/ SUPER ROSY

LOS LIMONES

LAS GUAYABAS

PASEO DE LA BOQUITA

NAVA

GUERRERO

ALTIMIRANO

AV. MORELOS

Market

BENITO    JUAREZ

GLOB'S CAFE

GONZALES

EJIDO

BRAVO

BANCO SANTANDER SERFIN

BANCOMER

ECONOMY RESTAURANTS

SHOE REPAIR

CAMERA REPAIR
ROSIMAR
FOTO EXPRESS

LAVANDERÍA EXPRESS
COCINA ECONOMICA CAROL

GALEANA

CUAUHTEMOC

RAMIREZ

Plaza de Armas

ALVAREZ

ASENCIO

5 DE MAYO

Artisan Tourist Market

SEE "DOWNTOWN ZIHUATANEJO" MAP

PLAYA LAS GATAS BOAT TICKETS

WHISKEY WATER WORLD

SOCIEDAD COOPERATIVA TENIENTE AZUETA

CAPTAIN OF THE PORT

DOCKS

★ MUSEO ARQUEOLOGÍA DE LA COSTA GRANDE

Playa Municipal

Boats to ◀ PLAYA LAS GATAS

Las Salinas

Footbridge

HOTEL RAOÚL TRES MARÍAS

Playa el Almacén

To Puerto Mío

AV. NORIA

© AVALON TRAVEL

PASEO DEL PALMAR

LAUNDRY

CREMERÍA GLORIA

BOMBEROS (FIRE DEPT)

PASEO DEL PALMAR

BUNGALOWS MILAGRO

To ◀ PLAYA LA ROPA

Plaza Kyoto

Canal (Seasonally Dry)

LA CASA CAFÉ

COCINA ECONOMICA DOÑA LICHA

LOS COCOS

BUNGALOWS ALLEC
CASA LEIGH Y LOROS

BUNGALOWS LEY

HOTEL BRISAS DEL MAR

HOTEL PALACIO

HOTEL VILLAS MIRAMAR

HOTEL IRMA

BUNGALOWS SOTELO

EVA SAMANO DE LOPEZ MATEOS

CASA AZUL

BUNGALOWS PACÍFICO

Cerro Madera

Playa Madera

Footbridge

RESTAURANT KAU KAN ▶
RESTAURANT IL MARE ▶

Bahía de Zihuatanejo

0   200 yds
0   200 m

IXTAPA AND ZIHUATANEJO

© BRUCE WHIPPERMAN

IXTAPA AND ZIHUATANEJO

**An easy beachfront walk leads from Playa Madera to Zihuatanejo's main town beach.**

Its sheltered waters are fine for wading, swimming, and boat launching (which anglers, their motors buzzing, regularly do) near the pier end. For maximum sun and serenity, continue walking east away from the pier along Playa Municipal. Cross the pedestrian bridge over the usually dry Agua de Correa creek, which marks the east end of Playa Municipal. Continue along the concrete *andador* that winds about 200 yards along the beachfront rocks that run along the west end of Playa Madera. (If you prefer, you can also hire a taxi to take you to Playa Madera, about $3.)

Playa Madera (Wood Beach), once a loading point for lumber, stretches about 300 yards, decorated with rocky nooks and outcroppings and backed by the lush hotel-dotted hill **Cerro Madera.** The beach sand is fine and gray-white. Swells enter the facing bay entrance, usually breaking suddenly in two- or three-foot waves that roll in gently and recede with little undertow. Madera's usually calm billows are good for child's play and easy swimming. Bring your mask and snorkel for glimpses of fish in the clear waters. Beachside restaurant/bars at the Hotel Brisas del Mar and the Hotel Irma, above the far east end, serve drinks and snacks.

## ◖ Playa La Ropa

Zihuatanejo Bay's favorite resort beach is Playa La Ropa (Clothes Beach), a mile-long crescent of yellow-white sand washed by oft-gentle surf. The beach got its name centuries ago from the apparel that once floated in from a galleon wrecked offshore. From the summit of the beach's clifftop approach road, **Paseo Costera,** the beach sand, relentlessly scooped and redeposited by the waves, appears as an endless line of half moons.

On the 100-foot-wide Playa la Ropa, vacationers bask in the sun, personal watercraft buzz beyond the breakers, rental sailboats ply the waves, and sailboards rest on the sand. The waves, generally too gentle and quick-breaking for surf sports, break close-in and recede with only mild undertow. With its broad horizon and *palapa* restaurants, it's a favorite spot to watch the sun go down. Joggers come out mornings and evenings.

## ◖ Playa Las Gatas

Secluded Playa Las Gatas, reachable from Playa La Ropa by taxi and a rocky one-mile shoreline hike or much more easily by launch from the town pier, lies sheltered beneath the south-end Punta El Faro headland. Legend has it that the apparent line of rock rubble visible 200 feet off the beach is what remains of a walled-in royal bathing pool that the emperor of the Purépecha people (who still inhabit the highlands of Michoacán) had built to protect his family and friends from the small cat-whiskered nurse sharks that frequent the shoreline. Although the emperor is long gone, the sharks continue to swim off Playa Las Gatas (Cats Beach), named for the sharks' whiskers. (The nurse sharks, however, are harmless; moreover, Las Gatas scuba instructors Thierry and Jean-Claude Duran told me that authoritative archaeological investigators have shown that the rocks are a natural formation.)

© BRUCE WHIPPERMAN

Playa La Ropa's sun, sand, and gentle surf seem made for child's play.

Generally calm and quiet, often with super-clear offshore waters, Playa Las Gatas is both a surfing and snorkeling haven and a jumping-off spot for dive trips to prime scuba sites. Beach booths rent gear for beach snorkelers, and a professional dive shop right on the beach, Carlo Scuba, instructs and guides both beginner and experienced scuba divers. (For more diving details, see *Sports and Recreation*.)

For a treat (high season only, however), pass the beach restaurant lineup and continue to **Owen's** (cell tel. 044-755/102-7111, 8 A.M.–7 P.M. daily, closed Sept. and Oct.) *palapa* restaurant, visible on King's Point, the palm-shaded outcropping past the far curve of the beach. There, enjoy some refreshment, watch the surfers glide around the point, and feast on the luscious beach, bay, and hill views.

## IXTAPA INNER BEACHES

Ixtapa's 10 distinct beaches lie scattered like pearls along a dozen miles of creamy, azure coastline. As you move from the Zihuatanejo end, **Playa Hermosa** comes first. The elevators of the super-luxurious clifftop Hotel Brisas Ixtapa make access to the beach very convenient. At the bottom you'll find a few hundred yards of seasonally broad white sand, with open-ocean (but often gentle) waves usually good for most water sports except surfing. Good beach-accessible snorkeling is possible off the shoals at either end of the beach. Extensive rentals are available at the beachfront aquatics shop. A poolside restaurant serves food and drinks. Hotel access is only by car or taxi.

## *Teleférico* and Playa del Palmar

For a sweeping vista of Ixtapa's beaches, bay, and blue waters, ride the *teleférico* (cableway, 7 A.M.–11 P.M. daily) to **El Faro** (tel. 755/555-2510, 8 A.M.–10 P.M. daily in high winter–spring season, shorter hours low season, breakfast $5–10, lunch $8–15, dinner entrées $14–25), a view restaurant at the south end of Ixtapa's main beach, Playa del Palmar.

Long, broad, and yellow-white, Playa del Palmar could be called the Billion-Dollar Beach for the investment money it attracted to Ixtapa. The confidence seems justified. The broad strand stretches for three gently curving miles. Even though it fronts the open ocean, protective offshore rocks, islands, and shoals keep the surf gentle most of the time. Here, most sports are of the high-powered variety—parasailing ($25), personal watercraft riding and water-skiing ($50), and banana-tubing ($10)—although boogie boards can be rented for $5 an hour on the beach.

Challenging surfing breaks roll in consistently off the jetty at **Playa Escolleros,** at Playa del Palmar's far west end. Bring your own board.

## IXTAPA OUTER BEACHES

Ixtapa's outer beaches spread among the coves and inlets a few miles northwest of the Hotel Zone. Drive, bicycle (rentals near the Hotel Emporio), taxi, or take a minibus marked Playa Linda along the Paseo de las Garzas. Drivers, heading east along the Ixtapa hotel row, at the end of the shopping complex, turn right, then fork left after a few hundred yards. After passing the Marina Golf Course (watch out for crocodiles crossing the road, no joke), the road turns toward the shoreline, winding past a trio of beach gems: Playa San Juan de Dios, Playa Don Rodrigo, and Playa Cuata. Sadly, development has now blocked access to these beaches.

Although Mexican law theoretically allows free public oceanfront access, guards might try to shoo you away from any one of these beaches on the open-ocean side, even if you arrive by boat. If somehow you manage to get there, you will discover cream-yellow strips of sand, nestled between rocky outcroppings, with oft-gentle waves and correspondingly moderate undertow for good swimming, bodysurfing, and boogie boarding. Snorkeling and fishing are equally good around nearby rocks and shoals.

On the peninsula's sheltered northern flank, **Playa Quieta** (Quiet Beach) is a place that lives up to its name: a tranquil, sheltered strand of clear water nestled beneath a forested hillside. A ribbon of fine yellow sand arcs around a smooth inlet dotted by a regatta of Club Med

kayaks and sailboats plying the water. Get there via the north-end access stairway from the parking lot, signed Playa Quieta Acceso Público. Stop by the beachfront restaurant for refreshment or a fresh seafood lunch.

## PLAYA LINDA

Playa Linda, the open-ocean yellow-sand beach at road's end, stretches for miles northwest, where it's known as Playa Larga (Long Beach). Flocks of sandpipers and plovers skitter at the surf's edge and pelicans and cormorants dive offshore while gulls, terns, and boobies skim the wavetops. Driftwood and shells decorate the sand beside a green-tufted palm grove that seems to stretch endlessly to the north.

In addition to the beach, mangrove-fringed **Laguna de Ixtapa,** an arm of which extends south to the bridge before the Playa Linda parking lot, is becoming an attraction. The lagoon's star actors are crocodiles that often sun and doze in the water and along the bank beneath the bridge.

Officially, the bicycle path ends at the bridge, but you can continue on foot or by bicycle about 1.5 miles (2.5 km) to Barrio Viejo village. Take a hat, water, insect repellent, your binoculars, and your bird-identification book. (For more bicycling information, see the *Sports and Recreation* section.)

The friendly downscale **La Palapa** beach restaurant, at pavement's end, offers beer, sodas, and seafood, plus showers, toilets, and free parking. Neighboring stable **Rancho Playa Linda** (11 A.M.–6 P.M. daily), managed by friendly "Spiderman" Margarito, provides horseback rides for about $20 per hour.

The flat, wide Playa Linda has powerful rollers often good for surfing. Boogie boarding and bodysurfing—with caution, don't try it alone—are also possible. Surf fishing yields catches, especially of *lisa* (mullet), which locals have much more success netting than hooking.

## ◖ ISLA GRANDE

Every few minutes a boat heads from the Playa Linda embarcadero to mile-long Isla Grande

Playa Linda (Beautiful Beach) always seems to live up to its name.

(formerly Isla Ixtapa, 9 A.M.–5 P.M. daily, $4 round-trip). Upon arrival, you soon discover the secret to the preservation of the island's pristine beaches, forests, and natural underwater gardens: "No trash here," the *palapa* proprietors say. "We bag it up and send it back to the mainland." And the effort shows. Great fleshy green orchids and bromeliads hang from forest branches, multicolored fish dart among offshore rocks, shady native acacias hang lazily over the shell-decorated sands of the island's little beaches.

Boats from Playa Linda arrive at **Playa Cuachalatate** (koo-ah-chah-lah-TAH-tay), the island's most popular beach, named for a local tree whose bark is said to relieve liver ailments. On the island's sheltered inner shore, it's a playground of crystal sand, clear water, and gentle ripples, perfect for families. Many visitors stay all day, splashing, swimming, and eating fresh fish, shrimp, and clams cooked at any one of a dozen beachfront *palapas*. Visitors also enjoy the many sports and equipment on offer: jet skis ($50/hr), banana-tube rides ($5),

fishing-boat rentals ($60/half day), aquatic bicycles ($6/hr), snorkel gear ($3/hr), and kayaks ($5/hr).

For a change of scene, follow the short concrete walkway over the west-side (to the right as you arrive) forested knoll to **Playa Varadero** and **Playa Coral** on opposite flanks of an intimate little isthmus. Varadero's yellow-white sand is narrow and tree-shaded, and its waters are calm and clear. Behind it lies Playa Coral, a steep coral-sand beach fronting a rocky blue bay. Playa Coral is a magnet for beach lovers, snorkelers, and the scuba divers who often arrive by boat to explore the waters around the offshore coral reef. Women offer massage to the soothing music of the waves ($25).

Isla Grande's fourth and smallest beach, secluded **Playa Carey,** is named for the sea-turtle species (see the sidebar *Saving Turtles* in the *Costa Grande* chapter). An open-ocean dab of sand nestling between petite, rocky headlands, it's easily accessible by boat from Playa Cuachalatate, but not frequently visited.

# Accommodations

The Ixtapa and Zihuatanejo area is one of the Mexican Pacific Coast's loveliest but also most highly seasonal resorts. Hotels and restaurants are most likely to be full during the sunny winter–spring high season, customarily beginning about December 20 and running through Easter week. Low season begins during the oft-hot dry months of May and June and continues until early December. Some restaurants even shut down during September and October. Nevertheless, for those who crave peace and quiet, bargain hotel prices, just-right balmy weather, and lush verdure, late fall—mid-October through mid-December—is an excellent time to visit. Hotel rates listed here as "low season" are the prices for two that you'll often encounter May through November. Prices listed as "high season" or "holidays" are the steeper tariffs that you will generally encounter during the Christmas–New Year's holidays, often extending through the Easter holiday. Hotels listed here are grouped by location—for Zihuatanejo, Downtown Zihuatanejo, Playa La Madera, and Playa La Ropa, and for Ixtapa, Ixtapa and Playa Linda—and generally listed in ascending order of low-season price.

Zihuatanejo and Ixtapa hotels divide themselves by location (and largely by price) between the budget-to-moderate downtown and more expensive Playa Madera, Playa La Ropa, and Ixtapa. For more information on Zihuatanejo and Ixtapa lodgings, visit the excellent websites www.zihuatanejo.net and www.ixtapa-zihuatanejo.net, or the individual hotel websites listed. Although Zihuatanejo hotels (with the few exceptions noted) provide little or no wheelchair access, all accommodations described in the *Ixtapa* section do.

## IXTAPA OR ZIHUATANEJO?

Your choice of local lodging sharply determines the tone of your stay. Zihuatanejo still resembles the colorful seaside village that visitors have enjoyed for years. Fishing *pangas* decorate its beach side, while *panaderías*, *taquerías*, and *papelerías* line its narrow shady lanes. Many of its hotels – budget to moderate, with spartan but clean fan-only rooms – reflect the tastes of the bargain-conscious travelers who "discovered" Zihuatanejo during the 1960s.

Ixtapa, on the other hand, mirrors the fashionwise preferences of new-generation Mexican and international vacationers. A broad boulevard fronts your Ixtapa hotel, while on the beach side thatch-shaded chairs on a wide strand, a palmy garden, blue pool, and serene outdoor restaurant are yours to enjoy. Upstairs, your air-conditioned room – typically in plush pastels, with private sea-view balcony, marble bath, room service, and your favorite TV shows by satellite – brings maximum convenience and comfort to a lush tropical setting.

Actually, you needn't be forced to choose. Split your hotel time between Ixtapa and Zihuatanejo and enjoy both worlds.

## DOWNTOWN ZIHUATANEJO
### Under $50

Right in the middle of the downtown beachfront action is **Casa de Huéspedes Elvira** (Paseo del Pescador 9, tel. 755/554-2061, casa-elvira@hotmail.com, $15 s or d, $25 holidays), operated since 1956 by its founder, Elvira R. Campos. Every day, Elvira looks after her little garden of flowering plants, feeds rice to her birds—both wild and caged—and passes the time with friends and guests. She tells of the "way it used to be" when all passengers and supplies arrived from Acapulco by boat, local *almejas* (clams) were as big as cabbages, and you could pluck fish right out of the bay with your hands. Her petite eight-room lodging divides into an upstairs section, with more light and privacy, and a lower, with private baths. The leafy, intimate lower patio leads to the airy upper level via a pair of quaint plant-decorated

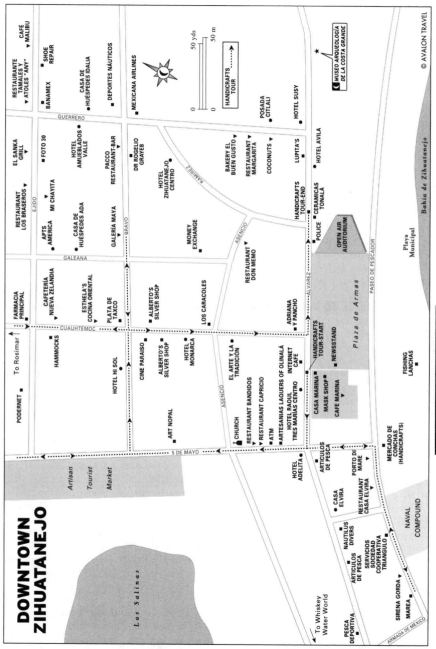

# DOWNTOWN ZIHUATANEJO

IXTAPA AND ZIHUATANEJO

© AVALON TRAVEL

*Las Salinas*

To Whiskey Water World

*Artisan Tourist Market*

To Rosimar

PODERNET

HAMMOCKS

ART NOPAL

FARMACIA PRINCIPAL

CAFETERÍA NUEVA ZELANDIA

ESTHELA'S COCINA ORIENTAL

PLATA DE TAXCO

ALBERTO'S SILVER SHOP

LOS CARACOLES

CUAUHTÉMOC

HOTEL HI SOL

CINE PARAISO

ALBERTO'S SILVER SHOP

HOTEL MONARCA

EL ARTE Y LA TRADICIÓN

ARTESANIAS LAQUERS OF OLINALÁ

INTERNET CAFE

RESTAURANT BANDIDOS

RESTAURANT CAPRICIO

CHURCH

ATM

HOTEL RAOUL TRES MARIAS CENTRO

ASENCIO

5 DE MAYO

HOTEL ADELITA

ARTICULOS DE PESCA

PORTO DI MARE

CASA ELVIRA

RESTAURANT CASA ELVIRA

MERCADO DE CONCHAS (HANDICRAFTS)

NAUTILUS DIVERS

ARTICULOS DE PESCA

SERVICIOS SOCIEDAD COOPERATIVA TRIANGULO

PESCA DEPORTIVA

SIRENA GORDA

MAREA

ARMADA DE MEXICO

NAVAL COMPOUND

RESTAURANT LOS BRASEROS

EJIDO

APTS AMERICA

MI CHAYITA

CASA DE HUÉSPEDES ADA

GALERIA MAYA

BRAVO

GALEANA

MONEY EXCHANGE

RESTAURANT DON MEMO

ADRIANA Y PANCHO

ALVAREZ

HANDICRAFTS TOUR-START

NEWSTAND

CASA MARINA

MASK SHOP

CAFE MARINA

*Plaza de Armas*

FISHING LANCHAS

PASEO DE PESCADOR

RESTAURANTE TAMALES Y ATOLES "ANY"

CAFÉ MALIBU

SHOE REPAIR

CASA DE HUÉSPEDES IDALIA

DEPORTES NÁUTICOS

BANAMEX

GUERRERO

EL SANKA GRILL

FOTO 30

HOTEL AMUEBLADOS VALLE

PACCO RESTAURANT-BAR

HOTEL ZIHUATANEJO CENTRO

RAMIREZ

DR ROGELIO GRAYEB

BAKERY EL BUEN GUSTO

RESTAURANT MARGARITA

COCONUTS

HANDICRAFTS TOUR-END

CERAMICAS TONALÁ

POLICE

OPEN AIR AUDITORIUM

MEXICANA AIRLINES

POSADA CITLALI

HOTEL SUSY

LUPITA'S

HOTEL AVILA

★ MUSEO ARQUEOLOGÍA DE LA COSTA GRANDE

*Playa Municipal*

*Bahía de Zihuatanejo*

HANDICRAFTS TOUR

0        50 yds
0        50 m

spiral staircases. The rooms themselves are small, authentically rustic, and clean. The four upper rooms share a bathroom and toilet. Rates run about $15 s or d, $25 t low season and $25 and $30 holidays. If nighttime noise bothers you, bring earplugs; TV and music from Elvira's adjoining restaurant continues until about 11 P.M. most evenings during the winter high season.

On the west side, across the lagoon mouth by footbridge from the end of Paseo del Pescador, is the **Hotel Raoúl Tres Marias** (Noria 4, Colonia Lázaro Cárdenas, tel. 755/554-2591 or 755/554-2191, $25 d). Its longtime popularity derives from its budget prices and the colorful lagoon-front boat scene, visible from porches outside some of its 25 rooms. Otherwise, facilities are strictly bare-bones, with only room-temperature water. Rooms rent for $20 s, $30 d, $35 t low season and $40 s, $50 d, $60 t holidays, with fans and most with private baths.

A few blocks north and west, find unpretentious guesthouse **( Casa de Huéspedes Idalia** (Guerrero 9, tel. 755/554-2062, $20 d). The grandmotherly owner offers two floors of about a dozen plain but clean rooms, with room-temperature-only shower baths. Idalia's guests enjoy an airy upstairs corridor-view porch, furnished with hammocks, rocking chairs, and shelves of thick paperback books. Rentals go for $15 s, $20 d, with fans only, or $30 s or d, with air-conditioning and TV, $40 for refrigerator.

Behind the town market, tucked on a quiet side street about five blocks from the beach, budget-conscious travelers will appreciate the attractive **( Angela's Hotel and Hostel** (Ascencio 10, local cell tel. 044-755/112-2191, angelashostel@hotmail.com, www.zihuatanejo .com.mx/angelas, $25 d, $35 t, $12 dorm), competently managed by friendly Angela Villalobos and Gregg Thompson. They offer a range of clean, invitingly rustic fan-only accommodations, including private rooms with beds for kids and dormitories (male, female, and mixed). Extras include a shady plant-decorated hammock-hung veranda, fine for relaxing and socializing.

Back downtown, a block from the beach, **Hotel Susy** (corner of Guerrero and Álvarez, tel./fax 755/554-2339, viajesbravo@yahoo.com) offers three floors of rooms around a shady inner patio. The seven upper-floor bayside rooms have private view balconies. Inside corridors unfortunately run past room windows, necessitating closing curtains for privacy, a drawback in these fan-only rooms. Avoid traffic noise by requesting an upper-floor room away from the street. The 20 clean but plain rooms go for $30 s, $40 d (in one bed), $50 d or t (in two beds) low season, and $40, $52, and $65 holidays, including fans and private hot-water baths.

Next door, another good moderately priced choice, if you don't mind a bit of morning noise from the adjacent school, is the popular **( Posada Citlali** (Guerrero 3, tel./fax 755/554-2043, $40 d). The hotel (Citlali means star in Náhuatl) rises in a pair of three-story tiers around a shady plant-decorated inner courtyard. The 20 plain, rather small, but clean rooms are all thankfully removed from direct street-traffic hubbub. Guests on the upper floors experience less corridor traffic and consequently enjoy more privacy. Reservations are mandatory during the high season and strongly recommended at other times. Rates run about $35 s, $40 d, $45 t low season and $40 s, $50 d, $55 t holidays, with private hot-water baths and fans.

A block west, on a leafy car-free lane, stands Ada Aburto Pineda's modest guesthouse, **( Casa de Huéspedes Ada** (Galeana 14, tel. 755/554-2186, nos@prodigy.net.mx, $25–80). Her seven rentals differ markedly. Downstairs, she offers three plain, dark, and small (barely recommendable) but clean rooms, two with fans, one with air-conditioning, for about $25 d. Her four upstairs accommodations are much larger, lighter, and more recommendable. Two are airy, multiroom kitchenette apartments with fans, accommodating up to four or five people. They open to a spacious, leafy front porch overlooking the shady street scene below. The two remaining upstairs units are in the rear and are smaller but still comfortable and clean, with fans and double beds. The larger of the two has a kitchenette. The big upstairs apartments rent for $60 d low season, $80 d high, or $700/month in low season, $1,400 high. The smaller upstairs kitchenette goes for $40 d low, $70 d high, or $400/month low, $900 high; the nonkitchenette, $35 d low, $45 d high. All units come with private baths, TV, and parking.

## $50-100

At the center of Zihuatanejo street hubbub is **Hotel Monarca** (Cuauhtémoc 13, tel./fax 755/554-2030 or 744/553-2922, $50 d). Choose from six attractive kitchenette (microwave only) studios in three floors. Units are clean, airy, and comfortable; two have private view balconies. They accommodate two to four people with combinations of double and single beds. Rentals run a reasonable $45 d low season, $65 holidays, $1,200 per month, all with TV, refrigerator, fans, and coffeemaker.

About three blocks from the beach, find **Hotel Amueblados Valle** (Guerrero 33, tel. 755/554-2084, fax 755/554-3220). Inside the front door, find eight furnished apartments, in three floors around an invitingly green inner patio. The apartments themselves, all with kitchens and either one or two bedrooms and shower baths, are clean, spacious, and comfortably appointed. Upper apartments are breezier and lighter. One-bedroom units go for about $50 low, $85 high season; two bedrooms, about $60 low, $95 high season. Discounts are possible for monthly rentals. All with TV and fans, but no parking.

Its location near the town pier draws many fishing enthusiasts to the **Hotel Raoúl Tres Marías Centro** (Juan Álvarez and Cinco de Mayo, tel./fax 755/554-6706, reservatresmarias@prodigy.net.mx, www.ixtapa-zihuatanejo .net/r3marias/, $68 s or d). Some of the 18 rooms have private balconies looking out on the street below. Newcomers might pick up some local fishing pointers after dinner at the hotel's restaurant, Los Garrobos. Rooms are $115 at holidays, and all come with hot water, cable TV, air-conditioning, and credit cards accepted.

Right in the middle of everything is Mexican family favorite **Hotel Zihuatanejo Centro** (Ramírez 2, tel. 755/554-2669, fax 755/554-6897, zihuacenter@prodigy.net.mx, www.ixtapa-zihuatanejo.net/zihuacenter, credit cards accepted, $70 s or d, $90 holidays), Although it's right smack downtown, about two blocks from the beach, guests are nevertheless sheltered from the street noise by rooms that face inward onto an inviting inner pool-courtyard. The 79 rooms, rising in four stories, are clean and simply but comfortably furnished in pastels and vinyl floor tile. Some rooms have two double beds, others have one king- or queen-sized bed. For more air and light, ask for a room with a balcony. Rates run about $85 s or d, with balcony, $70 without; $120 and $90 holidays (ask for a promotional package); with air-conditioning, fans, cable TV, hot-water shower baths, parking, restaurant, and credit cards accepted.

A block west, guests at **Apartments America** (Galeana 16, tel. 755/554-4337, zihuatanejoamerica7@hotmail.com, www .zihuatanejo.com.mx/america/, $40–80) enjoy a tranquil, shady street location. The 10 two-bedroom kitchenette apartments, of various sizes, are stacked in two floors around an inner patio-corridor. They are plainly but comfortably furnished with tile floors, bedspreads, curtains, and well-maintained shower baths. They rent, low-season, for about $40, $60, or $80 per day ($600, $800, $1,000 per month) for up to four, six, or eight persons, respectively, with fans, hot water, modest café-restaurant out front, but no parking. Add $15/day for air-conditioning and 20 percent during the Christmas–Easter winter season. Choose an upstairs apartment for more light and air.

Fishing parties are steady customers at the **Hotel Hi-Sol** (Bravo 120, tel./fax 755/554-0595), three blocks from the beach. The hotel offers two floors of around a dozen spacious, clean, semideluxe rooms. All have shiny shower baths and are invitingly decorated with tile and cheery yellow-and-blue-motif bedspreads and curtains. All rooms open to airy, private street-view balconies. Rates run about $60 s or d, and $70 t or q low season and $80 s or d, $90 t, and $100 q high; with TV, fans, and telephone.

**Hotel Ávila** (Juan Álvarez 8, tel. 755/554-2010, $60 s or d), downtown Zihuatanejo's only beachfront hostelry, is popular for its location. Rooms, although simply decorated, are comfortable. Guests in the hotel's several beachfront rooms enjoy luxurious private-patio bay and beach views. If possible avoid taking a room on the noisy streetfront side. The 27 rooms rent for about $70 s or d with view and $60 without in the low season, $85 s or d with view, $75 without high. All rooms have fans, TV, air-conditioning, phones, and hot water. Credit cards are accepted.

## PLAYA MADERA

Another sizable fraction of Zihuatanejo's lodgings spreads along and above Playa Madera on the east side of the bay, easily reachable in a few blocks on foot from the town plaza, via the scenic beachfront *andador* (walkway). Many of the lodgings are picturesquely perched along leafy Calle Eva Samano de López Mateos, which runs atop Cerro Madera, the bayfront hill just east of town, while others dot Avenida Adelita at the foot of Cerro Madera. Guests in all of the Playa Madera lodgings described here enjoy direct beach access by simply strolling a block or less downhill to luscious Playa Madera.

*Note:* Because of Zihuatanejo's one-way streets (which fortunately direct most noisy traffic away from downtown), getting to Cerro Madera by car is a bit tricky. The key is Plaza Kyoto, the traffic-circle intersection of Paseo de la Boquita and Paseo del Palmar a quarter mile east of downtown. Keep a sharp eye out and follow the small Zona Hotelera signs. At Plaza Kyoto, marked by a big Japanese *torii* gate, bear right across the canal bridge and turn right at the first street, Señora de los Remedios. Continue for another block to Avenida Adelita, address of several Playa Madera hotels, which runs along the base of Cerro Madera. At Adelita, continue straight uphill to the lane that runs atop Cerro Madera, Calle Eva Samano de López Mateos.

## $50-100

Playa Madera's only beachfront low-end lodging is the 1960s-era **Bungalows Allec** (Calle Eva Samano de López Mateos, Cerro Madera, tel./fax 755/554-2002, reservarbuallec@bungalows allec.com, www.bungalowsallec.com). Comfortable, light, and spacious although somewhat worn, the 12 clean fan-only apartments have breezy bay views from private balconies. Six of the units are very large, with two bedrooms, sleeping at least four, and kitchenettes. The others are smaller studio doubles with refrigerator. No pool, but Playa Madera is half a block downhill. The kitchenette apartments go for about $110 low season, $180 high; the smaller studios run about $50 low, $75 high, with parking and credit cards accepted. Long-term discounts may be available.

A couple of blocks inland from the beach find the family-friendly **Bungalows El Milagro** (Av. Marina Nacional s/n, Playa Madera, tel. 755/554-3045, klausbuhrer@hotmail.com, www.ixtapa-zihuatanejo.net/elmilagro/, $65 d low season, $85 d high), the life project of Dr. Niklaus Bührer and his wife, Lucina Gomes. A haciendalike walled compound of cottages and apartments, clustered around a shady pool, Bungalows El Milagro is winter headquarters for a cordial group of longtimer German returnees. The welcoming atmosphere and the inviting pool and garden account for El Milagro's success, rather than the plain but clean kitchenette lodgings, which vary in style from rustic to 1950s Bavarian motel. Look at several before you choose. The 17 units rent low season (excepting high season Christmas through Easter and July and August) for about $65 d ($900/month) for the smaller to about $140 ($1,100/month) for the larger family-sized units. Add about 25 percent high season. All with fully furnished kitchenettes with purified water, hot water, fans, pool, and parking.

On Avenida Adelita, right above the beach, stands the longtime Mexican family–run **Hotel Palacio** (Av. Adelita, Playa Madera, tel./fax 755/554-2055, hotelpalacio@prodigy .net.mx, $65 d, $80 d high) a beachfront maze of rooms connected by meandering multilevel walkways. Room windows along the two main tiers face corridor walkways, where curtains must be drawn for privacy. Upper units fronting the quiet street avoid this drawback. The rooms themselves are clean, renovated, brightly decorated, and comfortable, with fans or air-conditioning and hot water. Guests enjoy a small but pleasant bayview pool, kiddie pool, and sundeck, which perches above the waves at the hotel beachfront. Low-season rentals run about $55 s, $65 d with fan, add $10 for air-conditioning, all with TV and hot water, but street parking only. Add about 20 percent high season.

Back atop Cerro Madera, ( **Casa Azul** (tel. 755/554-3534, info@casaazul-zihuatanejo .com, www.casaazul-zihuatanejo.com, from $50 d lowest season, $115 Christmas holiday) offers a touch of luxury and restful ambience at moderate rates. Owner Marsha Gould rents three apartments, two uppers (*arriba*) and one lower (*abajo*). The larger upper (Casa Azul *arriba*) is a tropical hideaway for two, with a luxuriously rustic *palapa* roof, loft bedroom with king-sized bed, sleeping couch for one, and a private, airy bayview balcony. The other upper, El Nido (the nest), is romantic and cozy, with a rustic red-tile roof, double bed, and bayview balcony. The larger apartment *abajo* is equally comfortable, but darker, with two bedrooms sleeping up to six, living-dining room, and a town-view garden patio. All apartments have full kitchenettes and hot-water shower baths. The Casa Azul upper unit rents, double occupancy, for either $85, $95, or $115, depending on the season, the El Nido upper, similarly, for $70, $80, or $100, and the lower for $50, $60, $70, or $90; add $10 for each extra person. All accommodations are nonsmoking. Marsha leaves town June through October, although she does offer the downstairs apartment while she's gone.

Several apartment bungalow–style complexes cluster along the same scenic Cerro Madera hilltop street. Although their details differ, their basic layouts—which stair-step artfully downhill to private beachfront gardens—are similar. Typical among them is **Bungalows Sotelo** (Calle Eva Samano de López Mateos 13, tel./fax 755/554-6307, reservar@bungalows sotelo.com, www.bungalowssotelo.com, $70 d low, $90 high). Guests in a number of the clean and comfortable stucco-and-tile apartments enjoy spacious private or semiprivate terraces with deck lounges and bay views. Rents for the smaller units without kitchenette run about $70 d low season, $90 high; larger kitchenette suites rent for about $85 d low season, $130 high (for one bedroom) and $100 low season, $150 high (for two bedrooms). Rentals vary; look at more than one before deciding. No pool, street parking only, but with air-conditioning; get your winter reservations in early.

Also atop Cerro Madera, consider the spiffy ( **Bungalows Ley** (Calle Eva Samano de López Mateos s/n, Playa Madera, tel. 755/554-4087, fax 755/554-1365, bungalows ley@prodigy.net.mx). Here, several white-stucco studio apartments stair-step directly downhill to heavenly Playa Madera. Their recent decorations show nicely. Bathrooms shine with flowery Mexican tile, hammocks hang in spacious rustic-chic *palapa*-roofed view patios, and bedrooms glow with wall art, native wood details, and soothing pastel bedspreads. Except for a two-bedroom kitchenette unit at the top, all are kitchenette studios with air-conditioning and telephone. No pool, but the beach is straight down the steps from your door. The studios run about $70 d low season, $90 high. The beautiful two-bedroom unit also with air-conditioning runs $115 low season for up to four, $170 high. Long-term low-season discounts (of 15–30 percent for 6- to 21-night stays) are available.

Back downhill, the ( **Hotel Villas Miramar** (Av. Adelita, Playa Madera, tel. 755/554-2106, toll-free Mex. tel. 01-800/570-6767, fax 755/554-2149, reservaciones@hotelvillas miramar.com, www.hotelvillasmiramar.com, $75 d low season, $130 high) clusters artfully around gardens of pools, palms, and leafy potted plants. The gorgeous, manicured layout makes maximum use of space, creating both privacy and intimacy in a small setting. The designer rooms have high ceilings, split levels, built-in sofas, and large, comfortable beds. The street divides the hotel into two different but lovely sections, each with its own pool. The restaurant, especially convenient for breakfast, is in the shoreside section but still serves guests who sun and snooze around the luxurious, beachview pool-patio on the other side of the street. The garden rooms rent for about $75 d low season, $130 high; the oceanview apartments about $95 d low, $150 high; all have phones, cable TV, and air-conditioning, some have wheelchair access. Credit cards are accepted. Additional discounts may be available during May–December 15 low season. Reservations strongly recommended during the high season.

Half a block east, overlooking the beach, ◖ **Hotel Irma** (Av. Adelita, Playa Madera, tel./fax 755/554-8003 or 755/554-8472, fax 755/554-3738, toll-free U.S./Can. tel. 800/262-4500, info@mcrx.com, www.hotelirma.com.mx, $90 d low, $100 high) remains a favorite of longtime lovers of Zihuatanejo, if for no reason other than its location. Guests enjoy very comfortable renovated deluxe rooms, a

good bayview terrace restaurant and bar, and a pair of blue pools perched above the bay. A short walk downhill and you're at creamy Madera beach. Best of all, many of the front-tier rooms have private balconies with just about the loveliest view on Playa Madera. The 70 rooms rent for about $100 s or d low season, $125 high, with view ($90 low and $100 high without view), all with air-conditioning, TV, hot water, and wireless Internet connection.

## Over $100

One of the fanciest Cerro Madera options is the **Hotel Brisas del Mar** (Calle Eva Samano de López Mateos s/n, Cerro Madera, tel./fax 755/554-8332 or 755/554-2142, brisamar@prodigy.net.mx, info@hotelbrisasdelmar.com, www.hotelbrisasdelmar.com, $115 low, $134 high). Owners have completely renovated the original complex and have added a big new wing of a dozen spacious, rustic-chic view suites with native Mexico decor to the original 20 apartments. The brightest spot of this entire complex, besides its sweeping bay views, is the hotel's lovely beach club, with its shady *palapas,* lounge chairs, and big blue pool. For

© BRUCE WHIPPERMAN

**Zihuatanejo Bay, from the Hotel Irma poolside**

such amenities, Brisas del Mar asks premium prices. Its original (but upgraded) apartments rent for about $115 d low season, $134 high. Larger master suites go for $145 low, $184 high, while the spacious two-bedroom family bungalows, with kitchen, run $309 low, $370 high, all with oceanview patios, air-conditioning, and cable TV.

Also on Cerro Madera, perched atop Bungalows Ley, with the same address but completely separate, is upscale **C** **Casa Leigh y Loros** (Calle Eva Samano de López Mateos s/n, Playa Madera, tel. 755/554-3755, zihua01@ gmail.com, www.zihuatanejo-rentals.com, $155 low, $225 high), the lovely life project of friendly California resident Leigh Roth and her pet parrot, Loros. Casa Leigh y Loros, which Leigh rents when she's away, is a multilevel art-decorated white-stucco-and-tile two-bedroom, two-bath villa with roof garden, airy bayview balconies, and up-to-date kitchen appliances. High winter season (except Christmas) rent runs about $225 d, with fans, $255 with air-conditioning November 15–April 30, $155 and $180 May 1–November 14. All with cable TV and daily maid service; a cook is available at extra charge. Leigh also manages rentals for many other luxurious villas, apartments, and condominiums. See her website and/or contact Ignacio, her rental agent, in Zihuatanejo, at local cell tel. 044-755/559-8884.

A few hundred yards farther east along cliff-side Paseo Costera toward Playa La Ropa, find **C** **La Casa Que Canta** (Camino Escénico a Playa La Ropa, tel. 755/555-7030, toll-free Mex. tel. 800/710-9345 or U.S. tel. 888/523-5050, fax 755/554-7900, info@lacasaquecanta.com, www.lacasaquecanta.com), which is as much a work of art as a hotel. The pageant begins at the lobby, a luxurious soaring *palapa* that angles gracefully down the cliffside to an intimate open-air view dining room. Suite clusters of natural adobe sheltered by thick *palapa* roofs cling artfully to the craggy precipice decorated with riots of bougainvillea and gardens of cactus. From petite pool terraces perched above foamy shoals, guests enjoy a radiant aqua bay panorama in the morning and brilliant ridge-silhouetted sunsets in the evening. The 18 art-bedecked, rustic-chic suites, all with private view balconies, come in three grades: super-deluxe "terrace" rooms, more spacious "grand suites," and even more spacious and luxurious "master suites," the latter two options with their own small pools. Year-round asking rates are $590, $700, and $990, respectively. All come with air-conditioning, fans, and phone, but no TV; no kids under 16 allowed. Make winter reservations very early.

(*Note:* Casa Que Canta now offers the best of all possible upscale worlds within its present grounds: the El Murmullo super-private 10,000-square-foot four-villa inner sanctum compound, built for a maharaja. It includes complete all-exclusive staff, from gardener, chambermaids, and butler to waiters, kitchen staff, and gourmet chef, all for only about $4,500 daily.)

## PLAYA LA ROPA
## $50-100

For Playa La Ropa's most moderately priced lodging, go nearly all the way to the end of the beach, to the **Hotel Casa del Mar** (Playa La Ropa, tel./fax 755/554-3873, reserv@zihua-casadelmar.com, www.zihua-casadelmar.com or www.zihuatanejo-rentals.com/casadelmar, $85 d, $95 high), founded by master scuba diver Juan Barnard Avila and his wife, Margo. In the mid-1990s, Juan and Margo renovated a rickety old hotel, cleaned up the adjacent mangrove lagoon, and nurtured its wildlife (dozens of bird species and a number of crocodiles) back to health. They added 14 units around a rear jungle-garden and pool-patio. Now, new owners carry on Juan and Margo's ecological mission, with a restful hotel and beachfront restaurant where guests may stay and relax for a week or a season, enjoy wholesome food, friendly folks, and sample the good snorkeling, scuba diving, kayaking, turtle hatching, and fishing available right from the beach. Choose a room with an ocean view in front, or a garden view in back. All rooms are immaculate and simply but comfortably furnished with handsomely handcrafted wooden beds, lamps, and cabinets. Low-season rentals with fan only run about $95 d with ocean view, $85 d with garden view; high season, $120 and $95. Add about $15 for air-conditioning; all with hot-water baths, parking, small tank pool, and credit cards accepted. Reservations are mandatory in winter.

Back at the Zihuatanejo end of the strand, **Beach Resort Sotavento** (Playa La Ropa 01 s/n, tel. 755/554-2032, toll-free U.S. tel. 877/699-6685 or Can. tel. 877/667-3702, fax 755/554-2975, info@beachresortsotavento .com, www.beachresortsotavento.com, credit cards accepted, $65–95 d low, $70–185 d high) marks the beginning of luscious Playa La Ropa. Competent hands-on management keeps the rambling 90-room complex, which perches on a leafy bayview hillside, healthy. The Sotavento is a 1960s mod-style warren that stair-steps five stories (with no elevator) down a jungly beachfront slope. Each floor of rooms extends outward to a broad, hammock-hung communal or semi-private terrace, some with unobstructed ocean views. Inside, the Sotavento's rooms are spartan, clean, and comfortable, many with king- or queen-sized beds and all with ceiling fans. Rates vary according to season; low season: Easter–mid-July and Nov.–Dec. 15, mid-season: middle of July until middle of August, high season: Dec. 15–Easter. Accommodations, all including hot breakfast, come in four variations: large upper-level *terraza* suites, virtually all with ocean views, suitable for a couple up to a family of six ($75 low season, $95 mid-season, $145 high season); mid-sized middle-level *playa* studios, some with ocean views, with two beds, for up to four ($65, $85, and $85); smaller beach level *oceano* rooms, shaded by the beachfront forest, very few ocean views, with two beds, for up to three ($65, $70, and $70) and deluxe top-of-the-line *capitán* suites for four or more ($95, $110, and $185). (*Note:* Views, light, and shade depend on a room's vertical position in the stack. Guests in upper rooms enjoy expansive bay and sunset vistas, while guests in less pricey lower-level rooms nevertheless enjoy intimate tropical verdure-framed sunset vistas of the bay beyond. Maybe

look at both kinds of rooms before choosing.) The Sotavento's amenities include a beachside pool, room fans, parking, a restaurant, and a beach aquatics shop, but no elevator or wheelchair access.

Among the dozen-odd hotels, bungalow complexes, and restaurants that sprinkle the La Ropa beachfront is a trio of comfortable housekeeping bungalow complexes that share the same choice shoreline as the renowned Hotel Tides (described later), but offer lodging at much more modest rates.

One of these is █ **Bungalows Urracas** (Playa La Ropa, tel. 755/554-2053 in Spanish only), made up of about 15 petite brick cottages, like proper rubber planter's bungalows out of Somerset Maugham's *Malaysian Stories,* nestling in a shady jungle of leafy bushes, trees, and vines. Inside, the illusion continues: dark, masculine wood furniture, spacious bedrooms, shiny tiled kitchenettes and baths, and rustic beamed ceilings. From the bungalows, short garden paths lead to the brilliant La Ropa beachfront. About eight additional bungalows occupy beachview locations out front. Amenities include private shady front porches (use insect repellent in the evenings), hot-water baths, and fans. Rentals run a bargain $70 d low season, $80 high. Ask for a long-term discount. Telephone is their only communication option. Get your winter reservations in very early (if necessary, ask someone who speaks Spanish to call).

In contrast nearby is **Bungalows Vepao** (Playa La Ropa, tel. 755/554-3619, fax 755/554-5003, vepao@yahoo.com.mx, www .vepao.com, $75 d, $85 high). Here you can enjoy a clean, pleasantly tranquil beach lodging, simply but architecturally designed, with floor-to-ceiling drapes, modern-standard kitchenettes, tiled floors, hot-water shower baths, white stucco walls, and pastel bedspreads and shaded lamps. Guests in each of the six side-by-side apartments enjoy front patios (upper ones have some bay view) that lead right to the hotel's private row of nearby beachfront thatched *palapas.* Rates include parking and fans; long-term discounts are possible. Reserve through owner-manager Verónica Ramírez, by fax or phone (in Spanish, 7 A.M.–6 P.M. Pacific Time).

Back near the Zihuatanejo end of the beach, a block off the beach, **Villas Ema** (Calle Delfines, reserve through the Posada Citlali, Av. Guerrero 3, downtown Zihuatanejo, tel./ fax 755/554-2043, or in Spanish at the Villas tel. 755/554-4880, villasema@zihuatanejo .com.mx, $80 d, $110 high) perches at the top of a flowery hillside garden. Here, the enterprising husband-and-wife owners of downtown Posada Citlali have built about a dozen apartments, beautifully furnished with white tile floors, matching floral drapes and bedspreads, modern-standard shower baths, plenty of windows for light, and sliding doors leading to private view porches for reading and relaxing. Amenities include air-conditioning or fans, hot water, a beautiful blue pool, and the murmur of the waves on Playa La Ropa nearby. Rates for the nine smaller units, with a shared kitchen in common, run about $80 d low season, $110 high. The three top-level units, although sunnier (and consequently warmer), have the best views and most privacy. Two ground-level larger *villitas,* by the pool, each with its own kitchen and patio and sleeping four, rent for about $110 low season, $130 high. For reservations, highly recommended in winter, contact the owners through Posada Citlali. To avoid confusion, be sure to specify your reservation is for Villas Ema.

## Over $100

On the beachfront, adjacent to Bungalows Vepao, also find █ **Casa Gloria Maria** (Playa La Ropa, tel. 755/554-3510, gloriamaria@ zihuatanejo.net, www.zihuatanejo.net/casa gloriamaria, $100 d low, $120 high), a designer white-stucco beachfront house of four apartments. Each of the deluxe units (two upstairs and two down) is attractively decorated with native rustic tile floors, bright floral tile baths, and whimsical hand-painted wall designs at the head of the two queen-sized beds. Each unit has its own kitchenette in an outdoor beach-view patio. For more breeze and privacy, ask for one of the top-floor units. Rentals run about $100 low season, $120 high, with air-conditioning, hot-water baths, and parking.

Back toward Zihuatanejo, near the beginning of the beach, the **Hotel Villa Mexicana** (Playa La Ropa, tel./fax 755/554-3776, 755/554-3636, or 755/554-1331, www.villa mexicana.com.mx, from $90 d) seems to be popular for nothing more than its stunning location right in the middle of the sunny beach hubbub. Its 75 rooms, comfortable and air-conditioned, are packed in low-rise stucco clusters around an inviting beachfront pool-patio-restaurant. This seems just perfect for the mostly North American winter package-vacation clientele, who ride personal watercraft, parasail, and boogie board from the beach, snooze around the pool, and socialize beneath the *palapa* of the beachside restaurant. Low-season rates begin at about $90 d, and rise to a maximum of about $230 d around Christmas. Low-season three-night packages typically run about $250 d, including breakfast. Some rooms have wheelchair access. Parking is available; credit cards are accepted. Rooms can be reserved directly through the hotel or with the agency Mexico Hotel and Condo Reservations (toll-free U.S./Can. tel. 800/262-4500, info@ mcrx.com or reservations@mcrx.com, www .mexicocondores.com/zihuatanejo).

By contrast, the 40-odd lodgings of the hillside █ **Catalina Beach Resort** (tel. 755/554-2137 or 755/554-9321 through 755/554-9325, toll-free U.S. tel. 877/287-2411 or Can. tel. 866/485-4312, fax 755/554-9327, info@catalinabeachresort.com, www.catalina beachresort.com), next to the Beach Resort Sotavento, stair-step picturesquely all the way down to the beach. The Catalina's comfortably appointed, 1960s-era tropical-rustic accommodations maximize privacy, with individual view terraces and hammocks. The spacious lodgings, all clean and deluxe, vary from large to huge; look until you find the one that most suits you. Most have fans only (not necessarily a minus on this airy hillside); some do have air-conditioning, however. At the bottom of the hill, a beach aquatics shop offers sailing, sailboarding, snorkeling, and other rentals; those who want to simply rest enjoy chairs beneath the shady boughs of a beachside grove. The Catalina's food and drink facilities include a view restaurant, perching in the middle of the complex, a snack bar down at the beach, and an airy upper-level terrace bar. Access to all of this requires lots of stair climbing, which fitness aficionados would consider a plus. The Catalina's high-season rates for two run as follows: small casita (large room) $120 fan only; standard casita (suite) $150 fan only; deluxe bungalow (even larger suite) $187 with air-conditioning; deluxe honeymoon suite with air-conditioning $219; all with cable TV and phone. Low-season rates for the same categories run about $88, $116, $130, and $134.

German entrepreneur Helmut Leins left Munich and came to create paradise on Playa La Ropa in 1978. The result was Playa La Ropa's renowned Villa del Sol, now being operated by new owners as the **Hotel Tides Zihuatanejo** (Playa La Ropa, tel. 755/555-5500, toll-free U.S./Can. tel. 866/905-9560, fax 755/554-2758, reservations@tidueszihuatanejo .com, www.tideszihuatanejo.com). Here, in an exquisite beachside mini-Eden, a corps of well-to-do North American, European, and Mexican clients return yearly to enjoy tranquillity and the elegance of Tides Zihuatanejo's crystal-blue pools, palm-draped patios, and gourmet *palapa*-shaded restaurants. The lodgings vary, from luxuriously spacious at the high end to simply large at the low end; all have handsome rustic floor tile, handcrafted wall art, and big, luxuriously soft beds. The plethora of extras includes restaurants, bars, pools, night tennis courts, a newsstand, art gallery boutique, beauty salon, and meeting rooms. The least expensive of the approximately 70 accommodations begins at $330 s or d low season, $500 high. Super-plush room options include more bedrooms and baths, ocean views, and small private whirlpool tubs for around $800 and up. All lodgings come with cable TV, phone, air-conditioning, and parking; some have wheelchair access. Credit cards are accepted, but children are permitted in two-bedroom suites only.

## IXTAPA

Ixtapa's dozen-odd hotels line up in a luxurious strip between the beach and boulevard Paseo Ixtapa. Guests in all of them enjoy deluxe resort-style facilities and wheelchair access. All are high-end (more than $100/day) accommodations.

Near the northwest end, consider the best-buy Spanish-owned **( Hotel NH Krystal Ixtapa** (Paseo Ixtapa s/n, tel. 755/553-0333, toll-free U.S. tel. 888/726-0528 or Can. tel. 866/299-7096, fax 755/553-0216, nhix-tapa@nh-hoteles.com.mx, www.nh-hoteles .com, as little as $113 d low, $314 high). The hotel, which towers over its spacious garden compound, has an innovative wedge design that ensures an ocean view from each room. Relaxation centers on the blue pool, where guests enjoy watching each other slip from the water slide and duck beneath the waterfall all day. Upstairs, all of the 260 tastefully appointed deluxe rooms and suites have private view balconies, cable TV, air-conditioning, and phones. Check for additional discounts through extended-stay or other packages. Extras include tennis courts, racquetball, an exercise gym, and parking. Credit cards are accepted.

Another good-value choice is the Best Western **Hotel Posada Real** (Paseo Ixtapa s/n, tel. 755/553-1625 or 755/553-1745, Best Western toll-free U.S./Can. tel. 800/528-1234, fax 755/553-1805, ixtapa@posadareal.com .mx, www.bestwestern.com or www.posada real.com.mx, $135 d low, $230 high), at Paseo Ixtapa's northwest end. Get there via the street, beach side, just past the big corner restaurant on the left. With a large grassy soccer field instead of tennis courts, the hotel attracts a seasonal following of soccer enthusiasts. Other amenities include a large airy beachfront restaurant and two luscious pools. Although the 110 (rather small) rooms are clean and comfortable, many lack ocean views. Extended-stay or low-season discounts, such as a third night free, are often available. Kids under 12 stay free with parents. Amenities include air-conditioning, satellite TV, phones, and parking; credit cards are accepted.

Right in the middle of the hotel zone stands

The Hotel NH Krystal is one of Ixtapa's best-buy luxury hotels.

the **Hotel Dorado Pacífico** (Paseo Ixtapa s/n, tel. 755/553-2025, fax 755/553-0126, reserv@ doradopacifico.com.mx, www.doradopacifico .com.mx, $175 d low, $250 high). Here, three palm-shaded blue pools, water slides, a swim-up bar, and three restaurant-bars continue to satisfy a year-round crowd of vacationers. Upstairs, the rooms, all with sea-view balconies, are pleasingly decorated with sky-blue carpets and earth-tone designer bedspreads. The 285 rooms have air-conditioning, phones, and cable TV. Low-season and extended-stay discounts may be available. Other extras include tennis courts and parking; credit cards are accepted.

At the east end, **Hotel Barceló Ixtapa Beach** (Paseo Ixtapa s/n, tel. 755/555-2000, toll-free U.S. tel. 800/227-2356, fax 755/553-2438, reservas@barceloixtapa.com or ixtapa@barcelo.com, www.barceloixtapa.com), across from the golf course at the east end of the beach, rises around a soaring lobby/atrium. The Barceló, formerly the Sheraton, offers a long list of resort facilities, including pools, all sports, an exercise gym, several restaurants and bars, cooking and arts lessons, nightly dancing, and a Fiesta Mexicana show-buffet. The 330-odd rooms in standard (which include inland-view balconies only), oceanview, and junior suite grades, are spacious and tastefully furnished in designer pastels and include air-conditioning, phones, and satellite TV. The Barceló offers only all-inclusive lodging. Rates (with all drinks, food, and entertainment included) are about $195 per person, double occupancy low season, $300 d high, kids under six free, 6–12 $60.

From its east-end jungly hilltop perch, the queen of Ixtapa hotels, the ( **Hotel Las Brisas Ixtapa** (Paseo de la Roca, tel. 755/553-2121, toll-free Mex. tel. 800/227-4727 or U.S./Can. tel. 888/559-4329, fax 755/553-1038, ixtapa@ brisas.com.mx, www.brisas.com.mx) slopes downhill to the shore like a latter-day Aztec pyramid. The monumentally stark hilltop lobby, open and unadorned except for a clutch of huge stone balls, contrasts sharply with its surroundings. The hotel's severe lines immediately shift the focus to the adjacent jungle. The fecund forest aroma wafts into the lobby and the terrace restaurant where, at breakfast during the winter and early spring, guests sit watching iguanas munch hibiscus blossoms in the nearby treetops. The hotel entertains guests with a wealth of luxurious resort facilities, including pools, four tennis courts, a gym, aerobics, an intimate shoal-enfolded beach, restaurants, bars, and

IXTAPA AND ZIHUATANEJO

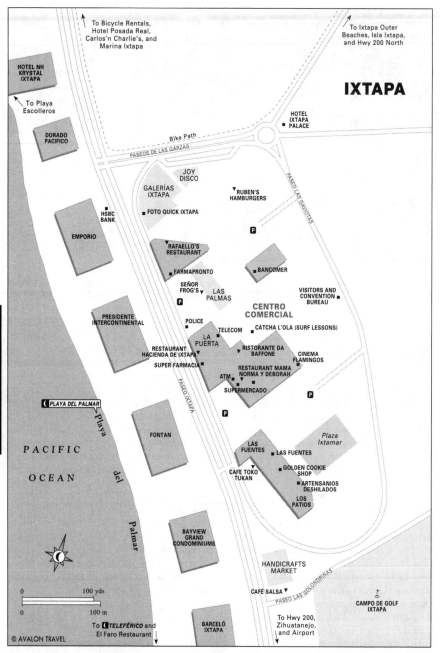

To Bicycle Rentals,
Hotel Posada Real,
Carlos'n Charlie's, and
Marina Ixtapa

To Ixtapa Outer
Beaches, Isla Ixtapa,
and Hwy 200 North

# IXTAPA

HOTEL NH
KRYSTAL
IXTAPA

To Playa
Escolleros

DORADO
PACIFICO

HOTEL
IXTAPA
PALACE

Bike Path

PASEOS DE LAS GARZAS

JOY
DISCO

GALERÍAS
IXTAPA

RUBEN'S
HAMBURGERS

PASEO LAS GAVIOTAS

HSBC
BANK

FOTO QUICK IXTAPA

EMPORIO

RAFAELLO'S
RESTAURANT

BANCOMER

FARMAPRONTO

SEÑOR
FROG'S

LAS
PALMAS

VISITORS AND
CONVENTION
BUREAU

CENTRO
COMERCIAL

PRESIDENTE
INTERCONTINENTAL

POLICE

CATCHA L'OLA (SURF LESSONS)

TELECOM

LA
PUERTA

RESTAURANT
HACIENDA DE IXTAPA

RISTORANTE DA
BAFFONE

CINEMA
FLAMINGOS

SUPER FARMACIA

ATM

RESTAURANT MAMA
NORMA Y DEBORAH

PLAYA DEL PALMAR

SUPERMERCADO

PACIFIC

OCEAN

Playa

FONTAN

Plaza
Ixtamar

LAS
FUENTES

LAS FUENTES

GOLDEN COOKIE
SHOP

del

CAFE TOKO
TUKAN

ARTENSANIOS
DESHILADOS

LOS
PATIOS

Palmar

BAYVIEW
GRAND
CONDOMINIUMS

HANDICRAFTS
MARKET

0        100 yds

0        100 m

CAFÉ SALSA

PASEO LAS GOLONDRINAS

CAMPO DE GOLF
IXTAPA

© AVALON TRAVEL

To TELEFÉRICO and
El Faro Restaurant

To Hwy 200,
Zihuatanejo,
and Airport

PASEO IXTAPA

Hotel Las Brisas Ixtapa

© BRUCE WHIPPERMAN

from sailboating and surfing to water aerobics and chess, children can also enjoy a full supervised program of child-appropriate activities. At Club Med, the usual lodging arrangement is for a minimum of one week, paid in advance. Typical winter (non-holiday) weekly rates run about $1,500 per adult, about $1,100 summer–fall low season, with discounts for kids.

Alternatively, you could consider the Club Med's worthy neighbors, the **Hotel Meliá Azul Ixtapa** (tel. 755/555-0000, toll-free U.S./Can. tel. 800/336-3542, fax 755/555-0100, www.meliaazulixtapa.solmelia.com), and the **Hotel Qualton Club** (tel. 755/552-0080, www.qualton.com/ixtapa). They both welcome children and offer deluxe amenities, food, and activities comparable to Club Med, often at reduced prices.

## TRAILER PARKS AND CAMPING

The Ixtapa and Zihuatanejo area has two equipped RV-camping parks, one small, on Playa Ropa in Zihuatanejo, and one large government-built site, on Ixtapa's far outer beach, Playa Larga. Two other small rough work-in-progress sites offer some RV hookups and camping space on Playa La Ropa. Get your winter reservations in months in advance. (The former homey Trailer Park Las Cabañas on Playa la Ropa has closed.)

Although at this writing the government-run Playa Larga RV park, officially **Ixtapa Trailer Park** (Lote 36, Real Playa Larga, tel. 755/552-0295 or 755/552-0296, trailerpark ixtapa@gmail.com, $25 low, $30 high, camping $7 per person), is still being finished, basic facilities—including high-power electricity, water, drainage, showers, toilets, and a restaurant—have been installed. The site, right by breezy, palm-shadowed Playa Larga, fine for all beach pastimes, is promising. Presently, they offer about 50 unshaded asphalt RV spaces (big enough for 35-foot rigs) inside their cyclone fence, about five miles (8 km) from Ixtapa, ten miles (16 km) to Zihuatanejo. Get there by driving to Playa Linda (see *Ixtapa Outer Beaches*, earlier in this chapter). Continue

nightly piano-bar music. The standard rooms, each with its own spacious view patio, are luxuriously spartan, floored with big designer tiles, furnished in earth tones, and equipped with big TVs, small refrigerators, phones, and air-conditioning. More luxurious options include suites with individual pools and hot tubs. The 427 rooms begin at about $250 for a standard low-season double, $540 high, and run about twice that for super-luxury suites. June–October, bargain packages can push standard-room prices as low as $150 d.

## PLAYA LINDA

A trio of all-inclusive luxury resort hotels decorate the luscious, tranquil Playa Linda beachfront about five miles (8 km) northwest of the main Ixtapa hotel zone.

The original of the three is the **Club Med Ixtapa** (toll-free U.S. tel. 800/258-2633, www .clubmed.com), which, as its long-time clients have acquired families, has become kid friendly. Besides deluxe rooms, the usual good Club Med food, and a plethora of included activities,

IXTAPA AND ZIHUATANEJO

north (follow RV park signs), past the Playa Linda bridge and parking lot, continuing about another half-mile to the RV park on the left.

A much smaller and informal spot to park your RV or put up a tent is at the far end of Playa La Ropa: **El Manglar Restaurant and RV Park** (Playa La Ropa, tel. 755/554-3752, $20 per RV, $10 for tent), on the inland side of the mangrove lagoon adjacent to the beachfront Hotel Casa del Mar. Here, the friendly restaurant owners who also run the trailer park offer parking space for about ten RVs, with all hookups, clean showers, and resident lagoon crocodiles (watch your toddlers and pets). Pluses here are a good restaurant, two-minute walk to lovely Playa la Ropa, space for about five large rigs and five small, and a locked gate at night. Minuses are lack of shade and evening no-see-ums and mosquitoes. To get to El Manglar, first follow the directions under *Playa Madera* earlier in the *Accommodations* section. Past Plaza Kyoto and the canal bridge, instead of turning right on Señora de los Remedios street, continue straight ahead two blocks. Pass the Bungalows El Milagro on the right, climb the hill for half a block and bear right for a long block, then turn left where the street forks, and you'll be on your way, with a fine bay view, along Paseo Costera. Continue about a mile, winding toward Playa La Ropa. Downhill, continue straight ahead past a traffic circle and monument on the right. Continue another mile straight ahead, passing Hotel Real de Palma on the left. After about three blocks, turn right, to the signed El Manglar gate.

If the above two RV parks are full, you might find an RV parking space and/or campsite at either of a pair of rough possibilities: **Playa La Ropa Camping and RV** (near the middle of Playa La Ropa, see Esta Campamento signpost, $15), with several spaces with all hookups, and **Costa Bella** (tel. 755/554-4967), with a few unshaded hookups and camping spaces, also for about $15; right by the beach (pass under the arch) at the far south end of the Playa La Ropa road. (For more information and photos of all of the above trailer parks and camping possibilities, visit www.ontheroadin.com/pacific coast/pacificsouth/ixtapaandzihuat.htm.)

## RENTALS

Zihuatanejo residents sometimes offer their condos and homes for rent or lease through agents. Among the most experienced and highly recommended agents is **Judith Whitehead** (tel. 755/554-6226, cell tel. 044-755/557-0078, fax 755/553-1212, jude@prodigy.net.mx, www .paradise-properties.com.mx).

Also, owner-agent **Francisco Ibarra** (tel. 755/554-4924 or 755/554-9377, donfranciscoproperties@gmail.com, www.donfrancisco properties.com) rents several moderately priced condos and houses on Playa La Ropa.

For many more vacation rentals, visit the excellent websites www.zihuatanejo.net and www.zihuatanejo-rentals.com.

For modestly priced rentals, don't forget the **Hotel Monarca, Casa de Huéspedes Ada, Apartments America,** and **Hotel Amueblados Valle** in the *Downtown Zihuatanejo* section.

# Food

## ZIHUATANEJO
### Snacks, Bakeries, and Breakfasts

For something cool in Zihuatanejo, stop by the **Paletería y Nevería Michoacana** (Álvarez, no phone, 9 A.M.–9 P.M. daily) ice shop across from the police station by the beachfront town plaza. Besides ice cream, popcorn, and safe *nieves* (ices), it offers delicious *aguas* (fruit-

flavored drinks) that make nourishing, refreshing Pepsi-free alternatives.

All roads seem to lead to the excellent downtown Zihuatanejo bakery **Buen Gusto** (Guerrero 11, 8 A.M.–10 P.M. daily, pastries about $0.30–0.80 each), on the east side of the street a few doors up from the restaurant Coconuts. Choose from a simply delicious assortment of fruit and nut tarts and cakes—pineapple, coconut, peach, strawberry, pecan—with good coffee to go with them all.

For hot sandwiches and good pizza on the downtown beach, try the **Cafe Marina** (tel. 755/554-2462, 8 A.M.–9 P.M. Mon.–Sat., closed approx. June to mid-Sept., $8), on Paseo del Pescador just west of the plaza. The friendly, hardworking owner features specials, such as spaghetti and meatballs, or ribs and potato salad, on some weeknights. The shelves of books for lending or exchange are nearly as popular as the food.

Playa Madera's prime breakfast spot is family-run **La Casa Cafe** (Av. Adelita 7, tel. 755/554-3467, 8 A.M.–1 P.M. Tues.–Sun., closed Sept. and Oct., $3–6), at the bottom of Cerro Madera, west end. Dad, mom, and the kids serve up a steady stream of bountiful omelettes, pancakes, breakfast burritos, fruit, tamales, sausage, ham, and fried potatoes to a legion of loyal customers.

A local vacation wouldn't be complete without dropping in at the **Sirena Gorda** (Fat Mermaid, tel. 755/554-2687, 9 A.M.–11 P.M. Thurs.–Tues., $4–9), near the end of Paseo del Pescador across from the naval compound. Here the fishing crowd relaxes, trading stories after a tough day hauling in the lines. The other unique attractions, besides the well-endowed sea nymphs who decorate the walls, are tempting shrimp-bacon and fish tacos, juicy hamburgers, fish *mole,* and conch and *nopal* (cactus leaves, minus the spines) plates.

On at least one Zihuatanejo day, be sure to enjoy breakfast at newcomer **( Restaurant Margarita** (on Guerrero a block from the beach, tel. 755/554-8380, 8 A.M.–11 P.M. daily, breakfast $2–3, lunch $6, dinner $7–10), across the street from the restaurant Coconuts. Besides a pleasantly refined old-world ambience including rustic beamed ceilings and soft music, they offer tasty, light entrées and attentive service. For example, for breakfast, choose an omelette or simply scrumptious *panes dulces* (pastries) along with your cappuccino and fresh-squeezed orange juice. For lunch, go for a tuna salad or *chiles*

*rellenos*; for supper try one of their excellent seafood entrées.

## Restaurants

Local chefs and restaurateurs, long accustomed to foreign tastes, operate a number of good local restaurants, mostly in Zihuatanejo (where, in contrast to Ixtapa, most of the serious eating occurs *outside* of hotel dining rooms). Note, however, that a number of the best restaurants are closed during the low-season months of September and October. If in doubt, be sure to call ahead. The recommendations here move across downtown, generally from east to west.

Local folks swear by **( Cocina Económica Doña Licha** (Calle Cocos, tel. 755/554-3933, 7 A.M.–11 P.M. daily, $3–9) in downtown Zihuatanejo's northeast neighborhood. (From Plaza Kyoto, follow Palmera west one block, turn left onto Cocos and continue half a block.) The reason is clear: tasty local-style food, served promptly in an airy, spic-and-span setting. Here customers can have it all. For breakfast try *huevos a la Mexicana* or pancakes; for *lonche,* go for the four-course *comida corrida* set lunch; for *cena* (supper), try one of their super-fresh fish fillets or a seafood brochette (shrimp, oysters, octopus, fish).

All expatriate trails seem to lead eventually to **Restaurant Glob's** (corner of Juárez and Ejido, tel. 755/554-5727, 8 A.M.–10 P.M. daily year-round, $4–8), on the east side of downtown three blocks from the beach. Here the cool coffee-shop atmosphere is refined but friendly, and the food is strictly for comfort—good American breakfasts, hamburgers, spaghetti, and salads.

Zihuatanejo has a pair of good, genuinely Mexican-style restaurants, frequented by a legion of Zihuatanejo longtimers. In the central downtown area, **( Tamales y Atoles "Any"** (corner of Guerrero and Ejido, tel. 755/554-7373, 9 A.M.–11 P.M. daily, $4–8), arguably Zihuatanejo's best, is the spot to find out if your favorite Mexican restaurant back home is serving the real thing. Tacos, tamales, quesadillas, enchiladas, *chiles rellenos,* and such goodies are called *antojitos* in Mexico. At

Tamales y Atoles "Any," they're savory enough to please even demanding Mexican palates. Incidentally, Any (AH-nee) is the co-owner, whose perch is behind the cash register, while her friendly husband cooks and tends the tables.

**Restaurant Los Braseros** (Ejido 21, tel. 755/554-8736, 4 P.M.–1 A.M. daily, $3–5), half a block farther west along Ejido, between Cuauhtémoc and Guerrero, is similarly authentic and popular. Waiters are often busy after midnight even during low season serving seven kinds of tacos and specialties such as Gringa, Porky, and Azteca, from a menu it would take three months of dinners (followed by a six-month diet) to fully investigate.

One visit and you'll wish that Zihuatanejo had more restaurants like **◖ Don Memo's** (Pedro Ascencio, local cell tel. 044-755/559-7000, 4:30–11:30 P.M. daily, $3.50–6), in the center of town a block from the beach. Here, you can enjoy a bountiful menu of no-nonsense Italian-Mexican specialties, accent on the Italian, but at Mexican prices. Tasty salads, piquant chicken chipotle, savory mushroom-tomato lasagna, tangy pulled pork smothered in tomatillo-chile *morita* sauce, and mushroom calzone: Bellisimo!

Asian-food fanciers have a choice of two good options. First, consider the very tasty offerings of Chinese restaurant **Mi Chayita** (Ejido, south side, recessed 100 feet off the street, betw. Guerrero and Galeana, tel. 755/554-5799, 11 A.M.–9 P.M. Mon.–Sat., $4–8) beneath its shady *palapa*. Here, a California-trained chef satisfies vegetable-hungry appetites, starting with bountifully delicious plates of chow mein and chop suey. On the other hand, meat eaters can choose from a list of many delicious favorites, such as sweet-and-sour pork, breaded shrimp, whole fish, broccoli beef, and much more.

For another Asian option, try **Esthela's Cocina and Express** (Cuauhtémoc betw. Ejido and Bravo, tel. 755/554-0352, 2–9 P.M. Tues.–Sun., $3–5), where local chef and Phillipine-American resident Esthela Buenaventura has relocated her popular longtime enterprise. She continues to offer her uniquely personal menu,

but now in an over-the-counter format (plastic utensils and bowls only), for either take-out or a few sit-down diners. Her tasty entrées consist of variations of stir-fried vegetables, to which she can add meat or fish for an additional price at your choice. For starters, Esthela offers such goodies as *lumpia* (Philippine-style spring rolls), cucumber salad, Buddha's Delight, and much more.

Up the street one block, families fill the tables at petite **Cocina Económica Carol** (Cuauhtémoc betw. Ejido and Gonzales, 11 A.M.–9 P.M. Mon.–Sat., $2–4). Diners enjoy country-style breakfasts such as *chilaquiles* and *huevos a la Mexicana*; *comida corrida* (set lunch of soup, rice, meat entrée, and dessert); and supper of tacos, enchiladas, tostadas, and tamales.

Down at the beach by the naval compound, longtime **Casa Elvira** (Paseo del Pescador, tel. 755/554-2061, 2–10 P.M. daily, $4–12), founded long ago by now-octogenarian Elvira Campos, is as popular as ever, still satisfying the palates of a battalion of loyal Zihuatanejo returnees. Elvira's continuing popularity is easy to explain: a palm-studded beachfront, strumming guitars, whirling ceiling fans, and a bounty of super-fresh salads and soups, hearty fish, meat and chicken entrées, and Mexican specialties, all expertly prepared and professionally served. Reservations recommended during the high season.

If Elvira's is full, an excellent seafood alternative would be **Porto de Mare** (tel. 755/554-5902, noon–11 P.M. daily, closed Sept.–Oct., $8–20) also on the beach, half a block east. It's the labor of love of its Italian architect owner, who designed and crafted its elegant open-air interior himself. As would be expected, his specialties are Italian-style pastas blended with superbly fresh local fish, shrimp, clams, scallops, and oysters.

No guide to Zihuatanejo restaurants would be complete without mention of **◖ Coconuts** (on Guerrero a block from the beach, tel. 755/554-2518, noon–3:30 P.M. daily for Mexican *comida*, regular menu 6 P.M.–midnight daily in season, closed approx. July–Oct., $12–24). Here, the food—whether it be light (pasta primavera) or hearty (rib-eye steak)—appears to be of importance equal to the airy garden setting and good cheer generated among the droves of Zihuatanejo lovers who return year after year.

The owners of up-and-coming **Restaurant Capricio** (on Cinco de Mayo by the church, tel. 755/554-3019, 11 A.M.–11 P.M. daily, $8–20), on the southwest corner of downtown, have followed the successful Coconuts example. Soft background jazz, fairy lights, and a tropical greenery-festooned patio set the scene, while the cuisine of especially good seafood pastas, hamburgers, and steaks provides the main event.

### Splurge Restaurants

**Restaurant Kau Kan** (tel. 755/554-8446, 5 P.M.–midnight daily, $16–30), on the clifftop road east and above Playa Madera, continues to be popular for both its romantic view location and its excellent food and service. While music plays softly and bay breezes gently blow, waiters scurry, bringing savory appetizers, Caesar salad, and cooked-to-perfection *dorado,* lobster, steak, and shrimp. High-season reservations mandatory.

Right next door and at least as worthy is Mediterranean boutique ◖ **Restaurant Il Mare** (tel. 755/554-9067, noon–midnight daily high season, 4 P.M.–midnight daily low season, $20). Enter and let the luscious ambience—soothing Italian arias, waves crashing against the rocks far below, the golden setting sun—transport you somewhere on the southern Amalfi coast: *O! Sole mio!* The menu extends the impression: Start with *bruschetta alla Romagna*; follow with soup *brodetta di pesce*; salad *pomodoro cipolla rossa con gorgonzola*; and *scampi al vino bianco,* accompanied by a bottle of good Chilean Sendero chardonnay. Finish off with lemon liqueur *Sogna di Sorrento.* Reservations strongly recommended on weekends and in high season.

For a nouvelle variation, head downhill to Avenida Adelita (foot of Cerro Madera) and sample the "fusion" cuisine of hot new **Restaurant La Guia** (tel. 755/554-8396, 5:30–11 P.M. Mon.–Sat., closed Aug.–Oct., $12–30) Here, chefs practice the craft of small portions and artful presentations of seafood (clams, lobster, shrimp, scallops) and pastas, steaks, and fowl. Reservations strongly recommended.

## IXTAPA
### Bakeries and Breakfasts

The perfume wafting from freshly baked European-style yummies draws dozens of the faithful to the **Golden Cookie Shop** (tel. 755/553-0310, 8 A.M.–2:30 P.M. Mon.–Fri., 8 A.M.–1 P.M. Sat., closed approx. July–Sept., $4–6), brainchild of local longtimers Helmut and his late wife, Esther Walter. On the inner patio, upper floor of Los Patios shopping complex, Helmut continues their mission of satisfying homesick palates with a continuous supply of scrumptious cinnamon rolls, pies, and hot buns, and hearty American-style breakfasts daily. In recent years, Helmut has served an authentic German buffet ($10) every Friday; call to confirm.

Alternatively, sample the good coffee and baked offerings of **Pan Nuestro** (Our Bread, in the Hotel Palacio Ixtapa, tel. 755/553-1585, 7 A.M.–midnight daily for pastries, 1 P.M.–midnight daily for pizza), at the north end of the Ixtapa shopping and restaurant complex, one block inland from the main boulevard.

### Restaurants

Restaurants in Ixtapa have to be exceptional to compete with the hotels. One such, the **Bella Vista** (tel. 755/553-2121, 7 A.M.–11 P.M. daily, breakfast buffet $12, lunch $6–12, dinner $10–20), *is* in a hotel, being the Las Brisas Ixtapa's view-terrace café. Breakfast is the favorite time to watch the antics of the iguanas in the adjacent jungle treetops. These black, green, and white miniature dinosaurs crawl up and down the trunks, munch flowers, and sunbathe on the branches. The food and service, incidentally, are exceptional. Breakfast only in low season. Call ahead to reserve a terrace-edge table; credit cards are accepted.

The latter-day Ixtapa visitor flood has resulted in more recommendable Ixtapa restaurants. Favorite Zihuatanejo eateries have added Ixtapa branches, notably **Tamales y Atoles**

**"Any"** (on the north edge of La Puerta shopping complex, behind Restaurant Mama Norma and Deborah, tel. 755/553-3370, 8 A.M.–8 P.M. daily); see the listing under *Restaurants* in the preceding *Zihuatanejo* section.

**Ruben's** (tel. 755/553-0027, 8 A.M.–midnight daily, $3–5) hamburger and taco hall, at the north end of the Ixtapa Centro Comercial shopping complex, behind the corner Galerias Ixtapa center about a block inland from boulevard Paseo Ixtapa, is by far Ixtapa's most popular eatery, especially with the new flocks of Mexican vacationers. Ruben's is a phenomenon as much as it is a restaurant, outdoing traditional *taquerías* (taco stalls) at their own game, with fresh ingredients and snappy service by a squadron of or any of a dozen variations of steaks, hamburgers, and tacos.

An Ixtapa restaurant that has customers when most others don't is **《 Restaurant Mama Norma and Deborah** (tel. 755/553-0274, 7:30 A.M.–11 P.M. daily, $12–25), in the rear of La Puerta shopping center near Ristorante Da Baffone. Canadian expatriate proprietor Deborah Thompson manages with aplomb, working from a menu of delicious specialties familiar to North American and European palates. Whatever your choice, be it Greek salad, lobster, steak, or fettuccine Alfredo, Deborah makes sure it pleases. Lately she's been open for breakfast; call to confirm morning hours.

Folks hankering for Italian-style pastas and seafood walk next door to **《 Ristorante Da Baffone** (tel. 755/553-1122, 4 P.M. until about midnight daily, $10–12). The friendly owner, a native of the Italian isle of Sardinia, claims his restaurant is the oldest in Ixtapa. He's most likely right: He served his first meal here in 1978, simultaneous with the opening of Ixtapa's first hotel. While Mediterranean-Mex decor covers the walls, marinara-style shrimp, calamari, clams with linguini, ricotta- and spinach-stuffed cannelloni, and glasses of Chianti and *pino grigio* load the tables. Call to confirm hours and for reservations.

If Da Baffone is full or closed, or for a splurge, try the highly recommended Italian gourmet restaurant **Becco Fino** (tel. 755/553-1770, 9 A.M.–11 P.M. daily) in the Marina Ixtapa. Reservations are usually necessary. Figure spending at least $30 per person for dinner.

(Other Ixtapa restaurants, popular for their party atmosphere, are described in the following *Entertainment and Events* section.)

# Entertainment and Events

In Zihuatanejo, visitors and residents content themselves mostly with quiet pleasures. Afternoons, they stroll the beachfront or the downtown shady lanes and enjoy coffee or drinks with friends at small cafés and bars. As the sun goes down, however, folks head to Ixtapa for its sunset vistas, happy hours, shows, clubs, and dancing.

## NIGHTLIFE

Nightlife lovers are blessed with a broad range of enjoyable choices, sprinkled around Ixtapa and Zihuatanejo. In Ixtapa, options vary from the zany Carlos and Charlie's to the relaxed piano bar at El Faro restaurant. Zihuatanejo choices run from raucous Restaurant Bandidos to restful Restaurant Coconuts lounge bar.

Clubs and bars in Ixtapa are spread along main boulevard Paseo del Paseo del Palmar, and have the highest-volume, latest night options. Most of the Zihuatanejo choices are downtown (and usually close before midnight) and can be best discovered on a nighttime stroll while looking and listening for what you want.

Beginning in **Ixtapa,** high on the list is the part restaurant and part wacky seasonal nightspot **Carlos 'n Charlie's** (tel. 755/553-0085). It's as wild and as much fun as all of the other Carlos Anderson restaurants from Puerto

Vallarta to Paris. Here, you can have your picture taken on a surfboard in front of a big wave for $3, or have a helmeted firefighter spray out the flames from the chili sauce on your plate. Loud recorded rock music ($10 minimum) goes on 10 P.M.–4 A.M. during the winter season. The restaurant serves daily noon–midnight. Find it on the beachfront about half a block on the driveway road west past the Hotel Posada Real.

For more of the same, but even more loud and outrageous, go to **Señor Frog's** (tel. 755/553-2282), in the Ixtapa shopping plaza across from the Hotel Presidente Intercontinental.

Other Ixtapa choices include **Liquid** (behind Rafaello's restaurant, at the north end of the Ixtapa Commercial Center, opens about midnight, cover $10), a late-night cocktail bar with a DJ spinning techno-rock-progressive music, and the blues saxophonist at **El Faro** (tel. 755/553-2525, 8–11 P.M. Tues.–Sun.) restaurant, atop the lighthouse in Marina Ixtapa.

Continuing to **Zihuatanejo** downtown, check out open-air **Restaurant Bandidos** (tel. 755/553-8072, 10 P.M.–4 A.M. nightly high season), on Cinco de Mayo near the church, colorfully decorated in faux 1910 revolution style, with plenty of old Pancho Villa and Emiliano Zapata *bandido* photos. They welcome guests to sing along to the music, both live and recorded. Call to confirm hours.

More Zihuatanejo choices (in declining order of volume) include **Black Bull** (corner of N. Bravo and V. Guerrero, tel. 755/554-2230), a younger-crowd disco; **Rick's** (on Cuauhtémoc downtown, tel. 755/554-2535), live music nightly, from around 6 P.M., sometimes shows, popular with sailboaters; the **Bay Club** (tel. 755/554-4844), on the clifftop road to Playa La Ropa, with panoramic bay view, live evening jazz; and the upscale **Coconuts Lounge-Bar** (on Guerrero, a block from the beach, tel. 755/554-2518) and restaurant, relaxing garden setting, with hammocks, sofas, and videos.

Several Ixtapa hotel lobbies bloom with dance music from around 7 P.M. during the high winter season. Year-round, however,

good medium-volume groups sometimes play for dancing evenings at the **Presidente Intercontinental** (tel. 755/553-0018); the **Barceló** (tel. 755/555-2000); and the **Las Brisas** (tel. 755/553-2121). Programs change, so call ahead to confirm.

**Christine** (in the Hotel NH Krystal, tel. 755/553-0333, open 10 P.M. Wed.–Sat., cover $10 women, $20 men) is Ixtapa's big-league discotheque. Patrons warm up by listening to relatively low-volume rock, watch videos, and talk while they can still hear each other. That stops around 11:30 P.M., when the fogs descend, the lights begin flashing, and the speakers boom forth their 200-decibel equivalent of a fast freight train roaring at trackside. Call to verify times.

## TOURIST SHOWS

Ixtapa hotels stage **Fiesta Mexicana** extravaganzas, which begin with a sumptuous buffet and go on to a whirling skirt-and-sombrero folkloric ballet. After that, the audience becomes part of the act, with piñatas, games, cockfights, and dancing, while enjoying drinks from an open bar. In the finale, fireworks often boom over the beach, painting the night sky in festoons of reds, blues, and greens.

Entrance runs about $40 per person, with kids under 12 usually half price. The most reliable and popular shows (often seasonally only, sometimes hotel guests only) are staged on Saturday at the **Presidente Intercontinental** (tel. 755/553-0018); Tuesday at the **Dorado Pacífico** (tel. 755/553-2025); and Wednesday at the **Barceló** (tel. 755/555-2000). Usually open to the public; call ahead for confirmation and reservations.

## SUNSETS

Sunsets are tranquil and often magnificent from the ◖ **Restaurant/Bar El Faro** (tel. 755/553-1027, 5:30–10 P.M. daily low season, longer hours high season), which even has a cableway (7 A.M.–7 P.M.) that you can ride uphill from the south end of the Ixtapa beach. Many visitors stay to enjoy dinner and the relaxing piano bar. Reservations are recommended during winter and on weekends. Drive or taxi via the uphill road toward the Hotel Las Brisas Ixtapa, east of the golf course; at the first fork, head right for El Faro.

For equally brilliant sunsets in a lively but refined setting, try the **( lobby bar of the Hotel Las Brisas Ixtapa** (tel. 755/553-2121). Happy hour runs 6–7 P.M.; piano bar or seasonal live music for dancing begins around 7:30 P.M. (call to confirm programs). Drive or taxi along the uphill road at the golf course, following the signs to the crest of the hill just south of the Ixtapa beach.

Zihatanejo Bay's west-side headland blocks most Zihuatanejo sunset views, except for spots at the far end of Playa La Ropa. Here, guests congregate at the longtime beachfront favorite **Restaurant La Perla** (tel. 755/554-2700, 10 A.M.–10 P.M. daily).

## CRUISES

Those who want to experience a sunset party while at sea ride the big 75-foot catamaran *Picante,* which leaves from the Zihuatanejo pier (call to confirm schedule) around 5:00 P.M. daily, returning around 8 P.M. The tariff runs about $50 per person, including open bar.

The *Picante* also heads out daily on a Sunshine Cruise around 10 A.M., returning around 2:30 P.M. Included are open bar, lunch, and snorkeling, for about $80 per person. Book tickets (high-season reservations mandatory) for both of the above cruises, which customarily include transportation to and from your hotel, through a hotel travel agent or directly through the *Picante* office (tel. 755/554-2694 or 755/554-8270, picante@picantecruises.com, www.picantecruises .com) at Puerto Mío, the small marina about half a mile across the bay from town. Get there via the road that curves around the western, right-hand shore of Zihuatanejo Bay.

## MOVIES

Head over to the petite **Cine Paraíso** (on Cuauhtémoc, tel. 755/554-2318), three blocks from the beach in downtown Zihuatanejo, to escape into American pop, romantic comedy, and adventure. About the same is available daily from 4:30 P.M. at **Cine Flamingos** (tel. 755/553-2490), in the rear of the La Puerta shopping plaza across the boulevard from the Hotel Presidente Intercontinental, behind the *supermercado.*

# Sports and Recreation

## SWIMMING AND SURFING

Oft-calm Zihuatanejo Bay is fine for swimming and sometimes good for boogie boarding and bodysurfing at Playa Madera. On Playa La Ropa, although waves generally break too near shore for either bodysurfing or boogie boarding, swimming beyond the breakers is fine. Surfing is very rewarding at Playa Las Gatas, where swells sweeping around the south-end point give good, rolling left-handed breaks.

Heading northwest to more open coast, waves improve for bodysurfing and boogie boarding along Ixtapa's main beach Playa del Palmar, while usually remaining calm and undertow-free enough for swimming beyond the breakers. As for surfing, good breaks

sometimes rise off the Playa Escolleros marina jetty at the west end of Playa del Palmar.

Along Ixtapa's outer beaches, swimming is great along oft-calm Playa Quieta; surfing, bodysurfing, and boogie boarding are correspondingly good but hazardous in the sometimes mountainous open-ocean surf of Playa Linda and Playa Larga farther north.

**Surfing lessons** have arrived in Zihuatanejo, at **Catcha L' Ola** (Catch a Wave, in Ixtapa in the Centro Comercial Kiosko, behind Mama Norma and Deborah restaurant, tel. 755/553-1384, catchalola333@prodigy .net.mx, www.ixtapasurf.com). Besides surfing lessons and luxury camping trips to the best local surfing beaches, Catcha L' Ola offers board and equipment rentals and re-pair, and for-sale accessories equipment, in-formation, and cheap beer.

## SNORKELING AND SCUBA DIVING

Clear offshore waters (sometimes up to 100-foot visibility during the dry winter–spring season) have drawn a steady flow of divers and nur-tured professionally staffed and equipped dive shops. Just offshore, good snorkel and scuba spots, where swarms of multicolored fish graze and glide among the rocks and corals, are ac-cessible from **Playa Las Gatas** in Zihuatanejo Bay and **Playa Carey** on Isla Grande.

Many boat operators take parties for off-shore snorkeling excursions. On Playa La Ropa, contact the aquatics shop at the foot of the hill beneath Beach Resort Sotavento. Playa Las Gatas, easily accessible by boat for $4 from the Zihuatanejo pier, also has snorkel and ex-cursion boat rentals. In Ixtapa, similar services are available at beachfront shops at many of the hotels, such as the Posada Real, the NH Krystal, and the Presidente Intercontinental.

Other even more spectacular offshore sites, such as Morros de Potosí, El Yunque, Bajo de Chato, Bajo de Torresillas, Piedra Soletaria, and Sacramento, are accessible with the help of professional guides and instructors.

A pair of local dive shops stands out. In Zihuatanejo, licensed long-time instructors Carlos Bustamante and L. Ricardo Gutiérrez carry on Zihuatanejo's professional scuba tradi-tion with **Nautilus Divers** (Juan Álvarez 33, tel. 755/554-9191, local cell tel. 044-755/102-3738, nautilus@nautilus-divers.com, www.nautilus-divers.com), two blocks west of the Zihuatanejo beachfront plaza. They begin with the resort course, with two hours' pool instruction and a guided dive, for $80. At the expert end, open-water NAUI certification takes three or four days and runs about $450. For certified divers (bring your certificate) they offer night, ship-wreck, deep-water, and marine biology dives at more than three dozen coastal sites.

IXTAPA AND ZIHUATANEJO

© BRUCE WHIPPERMAN

**Surfing is fine on the rollers that curl around the eastern point of Zihuatanejo Bay at Playa Las Gatas.**

**Carlo Scuba** (Playa Las Gatas, tel. 755/554-6003, carloscuba@yahoo.com, www .carloscuba.com) also provides professional scuba services. The PADI-trained instructors offer a resort course, including one beach dive ($65); a five-day open-water certification course ($450); and a two-tank dive trip for certified participants ($85, one tank $65). They also conduct student referral courses and night dives. Contact the manager-owner, friendly Jean-Claude Duran (known locally as Jack Cousteau), and his son Thierry, at their shop in the middle of Playa Las Gatas.

## FISHING

Surf or rock casting with bait or lures, depending on conditions, is generally successful in local waters. Have enough line to allow casting beyond the waves (about 50 feet out on Playa La Ropa, 100 feet on Playa del Palmar and Playa Linda).

The rocky ends of Playas La Ropa, La Madera, del Palmar, and Las Gatas on the mainland, and Playa Coral on Isla Grande, are also good for casting.

For deep-sea fishing, you can launch your own boat or rent one. *Pangas* (launches) are available for hire from individual fishermen on the beach, or the boat cooperative (see below) at Zihuatanejo pier, or aquatics shops of the Beach Resort Sotavento on Playa La Ropa or the Hotels Las Brisas Ixtapa, Barceló, NH Krystal, and others on the beach in Ixtapa. Rental for a seaworthy *panga,* including tackle and bait, should run about $100 per half day, depending upon the season and your bargaining skill. An experienced boatman can typically help you and your friends hook six or eight big fish in about four hours; local restaurants are often willing to serve them as a small banquet for you in return for your extra fish.

## BIG-GAME SPORTFISHING

Zihuatanejo has long been a center for billfish (marlin, swordfish, and sailfish) hunting. Most local captains have organized themselves into cooperatives, which visitors can contact either directly or through town or hotel travel agents. Trips begin around 7 A.M. and return 2–3 P.M. Fishing success depends on seasonal conditions. If you're not sure of your prospects, go down to the Zihuatanejo pier around 2:30 P.M. and see what the boats are bringing in. During good times they often return with one or more big marlin or swordfish per boat (although captains are increasingly asking that billfish be set free after the battle has been won). Fierce fighters, the sinewy billfish do not make the best eating and are often discarded after the pictures are taken. On average, boats bring in two or three other large fish, such as *dorado* (dolphinfish or mahimahi), yellowfin tuna, and roosterfish, all more highly prized for the dinner table.

The biggest local sportfishing outfitter is the blue-and-white fleet of the **Sociedad Cooperativa Teniente Azueta** (tel./fax 755/554-2056, 6 A.M.–6 P.M. daily), named after the naval hero Lieutenant José Azueta. You can see many of its several dozen boats bobbing at anchor adjacent to the Zihuatanejo pier. Arrangements for fishing parties can be made through hotel travel desks or at the cooperative office at the foot of the pier. The largest 36-foot boats, with four or five lines, go out for a day's fishing for about $450. Twenty-five-foot boats with three lines run about $250 per day; smaller *pangas,* about $180.

The smaller (18-boat) **Sociedad Cooperativa Triangulo** (tel./fax 755/554-3758, 9 A.M.–7 P.M. daily) is trying harder. Its 36-foot boats for six start around $350; a 25-footer for four, about $180. Contact the office across from the naval compound, near the west end of Paseo del Pescador.

A couple blocks away from the Zihuatanejo pier, find **Whiskey Water World** (Armada de Mexico 27, tel./fax 755/554-0147, local cell tel. 044-755/102-3779, U.S. tel. 661/310-3298, whiskey@prodigy.net.mx, www.zihuatanejo sportfishing.com.mx, www.ixtapasportfishing .com), that claims to employ only sober captains. Its top-of-the-line-only boats run from 25 feet ($200) upwards to 40 feet ($350), including license, bait, and soft drinks. Jack

Daniel's is extra. Proud members of the IGFA (International Game Fishing Association) and the Billfish Foundation, their captains follow marlin, swordfish, sailfish, tuna, and *dorado* tag-and-release policy.

*Note:* Prices quoted by sportfishing providers often (but not necessarily) include fishing licenses, bait, tackle, and amenities such as beer, sodas, ice, and on-board toilets. Such details should be pinned down (ideally by inspecting the boat) before putting your money down.

## SPORTFISHING TOURNAMENTS

Twice a year, usually in May and January, Zihuatanejo fisherfolk sponsor the **Torneo de Pez Vela** (Sailfish Tournament), with prizes for the biggest catches of sailfish, swordfish, marlin, and other varieties. The entrance fee runs around $800, and the prizes usually include a new pickup truck, outboard motors, and other goodies. For information, contact the local sportfishing cooperative, Sociedad Cooperativa Teniente José Azueta (Muelle Municipal, Zihuatanejo, Guerrero 40880, tel. 755/554-2056), or the fishing tournament coordinator, Crecencio Cortés (tel. 755/554-8423).

However, in recognition that mass killing of billfish and other favorite deepwater fish, such as tuna, dolphinfish (*dorado*), and roosterfish (*pez gallo*) cannot continue forever, many local fishing outfitters, in cooperation with the conservationist Billfish Foundation, have had success sponsoring an annual Ixtapa-Zihuatanejo **Fintastic Tag and Release Tournament** where fish are returned to the sea alive after being caught. For more information, contact Whiskey Water World (listed earlier), email info@fintastic.com, or visit www.fintastic.com/zih-tour.

## SAILING, SAILBOARDING, AND SEA KAYAKING

The tranquil waters of Zihuatanejo Bay, Ixtapa's Playa del Palmar, and the quiet strait off Playa

© BRUCE WHIPPERMAN

Zihuatanejo's Playa La Ropa rates as one of the loveliest best-for-everything beaches on the Mexican Pacific coast.

Quieta are good for these low-power aquatic sports. Shops on Playa La Ropa (at Beach Resort Sotavento and Catalina) in Zihuatanejo Bay and at beachfront at Ixtapa hotels, such as the NH Krystal, Presidente Intercontinental, and Dorado Pacífico, rent small sailboats, sailboards, and kayaks by the hour.

## LAGOON KAYAKING AND BIRDWATCHING

The grand Laguna de Potosí and the smaller, more remote Estero Valentin, respectively about 10 and 20 miles (16 and 32 km) southeast of Zihuatanejo, have become prime wildlife-viewing sites, due to the enterprise of Ixtapa-based **Zoe Kayak Tours** (contact Brian, tel. 755/553-0496, zoe5@aol.com, www.zoe kayaktours.com). The earnest, wildlife-sensitive operators conduct thoroughly professional excursions, designed to maximize the quality of participants wildlife-viewing experience and appreciation. Itineraries vary, from full-day (Potosi, $80; Valentin, $100) outings to extended overnights and more.

## MARINA AND BOAT LAUNCHING

**Marina Ixtapa** (tel./fax 755/553-2180, 755/553-0222, or 755/553-2365, ezuniga@ marinaixtapa.com or info@marinaixtapa.com, www.marinaixtapa.com), at the north end of Paseo Ixtapa, offers excellent boat facilities. The slip charge runs about $1 per foot per day, for 1–6 days ($0.75 for 7–29 days), subject to a minimum charge per diem. This includes use of the boat ramp, showers, pump-out, electricity, trash collection, mailbox, phone, fax, and satellite TV. For reservations and information, contact the marina 9 A.M.–2 P.M. and 4–7 P.M. daily, at the harbormaster's office in the marina-front white building on the right a block before the big white lighthouse.

The smooth, gradual Marina Ixtapa **boat ramp,** open to the public for a ramp fee (from about $40), is on the right-hand side street, leading to the water, just past the big white lighthouse. Get your ticket beforehand from the harbormaster.

## GOLF AND TENNIS

Ixtapa's 18-hole professionally designed **Campo de Golf** is open to the public. In addition to its manicured 6,898-yard course, patrons enjoy full facilities, including pool, restaurant, pro shop, lockers, and tennis courts. Golf greens fee runs about $65, cart $30, club rental $25, 18 holes with caddy $20. Play goes on 7 A.M.–5:30 P.M. daily. The clubhouse (tel. 755/553-1062) is off Paseo Ixtapa, across from the Hotel Barceló. Reservations are accepted; morning golfers, get in line early during the high winter season.

The **Marina Golf Course** (tel. 755/553-1410 or 755/553-1424) offers similar services (greens fee $55, cart $30, club rental $30, caddy $20).

Ixtapa has virtually all of the local **tennis** courts, all of them private. The Campo de Golf has some of the best. Rentals run about $7/hour days, $10 nights. Reservations (tel. 755/553-1062) may be seasonally necessary. A pro shop rents and sells equipment. A teaching professional offers lessons for about $25 per hour.

Some hotels welcome outside guests at their tennis courts. Call the **Dorado Pacífico** (tel. 755/553-2025) or the **Las Brisas** (tel. 755/553-2121) for a reservation.

## HORSEBACK RIDING

"Spiderman" Margarito, manager of the stable at **Playa Linda,** rents horses daily for beach riding for about $15 per hour low season, $20 high. Travel agencies and hotels offer the same, although for higher prices.

## BICYCLING

Ixtapa's newest popular pastime is bicycling along the new 10-mile (16-km) round-trip *ciclopista* bike path to Playa Linda. The rental station is on the main boulevard, Paseo Ixtapa, in front of the Hotel Park Royal, about two blocks north of the north end of the Ixtapa shopping and restaurant complex. Bargain for a discount on the steep $10/hour asking rate.

The *ciclopista* takes off north, at the Paseo Las Garzas intersection, at the west-end corner of the Ixtapa shopping-restaurant complex.

Officially the *ciclopista* ends five miles (8 km) west, at the wooden bridge and crocodile-viewing point at the Playa Linda parking lot, but you can go 1.5 miles (2.5 km) farther to Barrio Viejo village at the lagoon's edge. Be sure to take a hat, water, and insect repellent.

If, on your return approach to Ixtapa, you haven't enjoyed your fill of bicycling, you can rack up more mileage along the Zihuatanejo *ciclopista* leg: Heading back to Ixtapa, about 100 yards after the intersection that directs traffic left to Highway 200, bear left where Paseo de los Pelicanos forks left and follow the Zihuatanejo *ciclopista* past the back (northwest) side of the golf course, another eight miles (13 km), two hours (leisurely) to Zihuatanejo and return.

## WALKING AND JOGGING

**Zihuatanejo Bay** is strollable from Playa Madera all the way west to Puerto Mío. A relaxing half-day adventure could begin by taxiing to the Hotel Irma (Av. Adelita, Playa Madera) for breakfast. Don your hats and follow the stairs down to Playa Madera and walk west toward town. At the end of the Playa Madera sand, head left along the *andador* (walkway) that twists along the rocks, around the bend toward town. Continue along the beachfront Paseo del Pescador; at the west end, cross the lagoon bridge, head left along the bayside road to **Puerto Mío** resort and marina for a drink at the hotel's La Cala restaurant and perhaps a dip in the pool. Allow three hours, including breakfast, for this two-mile (3-km) walk; do the reverse trip during late afternoon for sunset drinks or dinner at the Irma.

**Playa del Palmar,** Ixtapa's main beach, is good for similar strolls. Start in the morning (during high winter–spring season) with breakfast (which is not served low season) at the Restaurant/Bar El Faro (tel. 755/555-2510 or 755/553-1027) atop the hill at the south end of the beach; open for breakfast high-season, 6 a.m.–noon daily. Ride the cableway or walk downhill. With the sun at your back stroll the beach, stopping for refreshments at the hotel pool patios en route. The entire beach stretches about three miles (5 km) to the marina jetty, where you can often watch surfers challenging

the waves and where taxis and buses return along Paseo Ixtapa. Allow about four hours, including breakfast.

The **reverse walk** would be equally enjoyable during the afternoon. Time yourself to arrive at the El Faro cableway about half an hour before sundown (7:30 P.M. summers, 5:30 P.M. winters) to enjoy the sunset over drinks and/ or dinner. Get to El Faro by driving or taxiing via Paseo de la Roca, which heads uphill off the Zihuatanejo road at the golf course. Follow the first right fork to El Faro.

Adventurers who enjoy ducking through underbrush and scrambling over rocks might want to explore the acacia forest and wave-tossed rocky shoreline of the uninhabited west

## ZIHUATANEJO, "PLACE OF WOMEN"

An oft-told Costa Grande story says that when Captain Juan Álvarez Chico was exploring at Zihuatanejo in 1522, he looked down on the round tranquil little bay lined with flocks of seabirds and women washing clothes in a freshwater spring. His Aztec guide told him that this place was called Cihuatlán, the "Place of Women." When Chico described the little bay, Cortés tacked "nejo" (little) on the name, giving birth to "Zihuatlanejo," which later got shortened to the present Zihuatanejo.

Investigators have offered a pair of intriguing alternative explanations for the "Place of Women" name, a handle that evokes visions of a land of Amazons. They speculate that either Isla Ixtapa (now Isla Grande) or the former royal bathing resort at Playa Las Gatas may have given rise to the name. The bathing resort, founded around 1400 by the Purépecha emperor, was most probably a carefully guarded preserve of the emperor's dozens of wives and female relatives. If not that, Isla Ixtapa may have been used as a refuge for the isolation and protection of women and children against the Aztec invaders who thus attached the label "Place of Women" to the locality.

side of **Isla Grande.** Take water, lunch, and a good pair of walking shoes.

**Joggers** often practice their art either on the smooth, firm sands of Ixtapa's main beachfront or on Paseo Ixtapa's sidewalks. Avoid crowds and midday heat by jogging early mornings or late afternoons. For even better beach jogging, try the flat, firm sands of uncrowded Playa Quieta about three miles (5 km) by car or taxi northwest of Ixtapa. Additionally, mile-long Playa La Ropa can be enjoyed by early-morning and late-afternoon joggers.

## SPORTS EQUIPMENT

**Deportes Náuticos** (corner of N. Bravo and Guerrero, downtown Zihuatanejo, tel. 755/554-4411, 10 A.M.–2 P.M. and 4–9 P.M. Mon.–Sat.) sells snorkel equipment, boogie boards, tennis racquets, balls, and a load of other general sporting goods.

A pair of shops on Álvarez, near the pier, sell fishing equipment and supplies. Check out **Pesca Deportiva** (Álvarez 66, corner of Armada de Mexico, tel. 755/554-3651, 9 A.M.–2 P.M. and 4–7 P.M. Mon.–Sat.), which specializes in sportfishing rods, reels, lines, weights, and lures.

Alternatively, another shop a block east and across the street, **Articulos de Pesca** (Álvarez 35, tel. 755/554-6451, 9 A.M.–2 P.M. and 4–8 P.M. Mon.–Sat.) offers a similar selection of heavy-duty fishing goods.

# Shopping

## ZIHUATANEJO MARKET AND SHOPS

Every day is market day at the Zihuatanejo *mercado* on Avenida Benito Juárez, four blocks from the beach. Behind the piles of leafy greens, round yellow papayas, and huge gaping sea bass, don't miss the sugar and spice stalls. There you will find big cones of raw *panela* (brown sugar); thick, homemade golden honey; mounds of fragrant *jamaica* petals; crimson dried *chiles;* and forest-gathered roots, barks, and grasses sold in the same pungent natural forms as they have been for centuries.

For a huge, handy selection of everything, go to the big Kmart-style **Comercial Mexicana** (tel. 755/554-8321 or 755/554-8384, 8 A.M.–11 P.M. daily), behind the bus terminals on Highway 200, about a mile east (Acapulco direction) of downtown. Its shelves are stacked with a plethora of quality goods, from bread and bananas to flashlights and film.

For convenience shopping downtown by the beach, go to the small grocery **Adriana y Pancho,** at the plaza-front corner of Álvarez and Cuauhtémoc.

### Handicrafts

Although stores in the Ixtapa Centro Comercial shopping center (described later) and the adjacent tourist market sell many handicrafts, Zihuatanejo shops offer the best overall selection and prices.

Sometime along your Zihuatanejo tour, be sure to visit the Zihuatanejo **Artisan Tourist Market** stalls, filled with a flood of attractive handicrafts brought by families who come from all parts of Mexico. Their goods—delicate Michoacán lacquerware, bright Tonalá papier-mâché birds, gleaming Taxco silver, whimsical Guerrero masks, rich Guadalajara leather—spread for blocks along Avenida Cinco de Mayo on the downtown west side. Compare prices; although bargaining here is customary, the glut of merchandise makes it a one-sided buyer's market, with many sellers barely managing to scrape by. If you err in your bargaining, kindly do it on the generous side.

### Along the Paseo del Pescador

Private downtown Zihuatanejo shops offer an abundance of fine handicrafts. The best place to start is on the beachfront Paseo del Pescador, at the **Casa Marina** shopping complex (tel. 755/554-2373, 10 A.M.–2 P.M. and 4–8 P.M. Mon.–Sat., credit cards generally accepted), a family project started by late community leader Helen Krebs Posse. Her adult children and their spouses own and manage stores on the bottom floor of the two-story building, just west of the beachfront town plaza.

The original store, **Embarcadero** (tel. 755/554-2373), on the lower floor, Avenida Álvarez side, has an unusually choice collection of woven and embroidered finery, mostly from Oaxaca. In addition to walls and racks of colorful, museum-quality traditional blankets, flower-embroidered dresses, and elaborate crocheted *huipiles,* they also offer wooden folk figurines and a collection of intriguing masks.

Other stores in the Casa Marina that you should visit include **La Zapoteca,** specializing in weavings from Teotitlán del Valle in Oaxaca. Also very worthwhile are **Metzli,** featuring all-Mexico crafts and resort wear selection, **El Jumil** (lacquerware and masks), and

**Costa Libre** (one-of-a-kind crafts and hammocks). Furthermore, Zapotec indigenous weavers from Oaxaca demonstrate their craft, often in the Embarcadero and La Zapoteca stores, mornings and afternoons November through April.

A block farther west on the Paseo del Pescador, find the **Mercado de Conchas** (Shell Market). Peruse the several stalls, with many fetching, priced-to-sell offerings including lovely seashells and shell jewelry, paintings, pottery, and much more.

Two blocks farther west, past the Sirena Gorda café, be sure to visit **Marea** clothing shop (8 A.M.–10 P.M. daily), across from the naval compound. It would be easy to pass, because of its mounds of ho-hum T-shirts out front, but if you look inside, you'll find racks stuffed with precious hand-crocheted *huipiles* and blouses from backcountry Guerrero and Oaxaca.

## Along Avenida Cinco de Mayo

Return east two blocks along Avenida Álvarez and turn left, inland, at the corner of Cinco

© BRUCE WHIPPERMAN

Shell necklaces make attractive gifts to take back home.

IXTAPA AND ZIHUATANEJO

de Mayo and find **Artesanías Olinalá** (Cinco de Mayo 2, tel. 755/554-9597, 9 A.M.–9 P.M. daily). Inside, you can enjoy a virtual museum of the venerable Guerrero lacquerware tradition, showcased by their seemingly endless collection of glossy boxes, trays, gourds, plates, and masks, all painstakingly crafted by age-old methods in the remote upcountry town of Olinalá. (After exiting Artesanías Olinalá you could conveniently visit the **Artisan Tourist Market** stalls on the other side of Cinco de Mayo.)

Continue up Cinco de Mayo, past the church, to **Art Nopal** (tel./fax 755/554-7530, 9 A.M.–9 P.M. daily in high season, opens 10:30 A.M. low season), the joy of the owner, who likes things from Oaxaca, especially baskets. He fills his shop with an organized clutter, including unique woven goods and ceramics.

## Along Avenida Cuauhtémoc and More

Next, head right (east) one block along Bravo, to Cuauhtémoc, for a look through several more interesting shops.

At the corner, turn left, and continue a block, passing Ejido. A few doors farther, on the right, step into **Rosimar** (tel. 755/554-2864, 9 A.M.–9 P.M. daily), the creation of Josefina and Manuel Martínez. Inside, they offer a large priced-to-sell collection of Tonalá and Tlaquepaque pottery, papier-mâché, glassware, and more.

Head back down Cuauhtémoc. Turn left at Bravo, continuing another block, past Galeana, to **Galería Maya** (tel. 755/554-4606, 10 A.M.–2 P.M. and 5–9 P.M. Mon.–Sat.) in mid-block, on the left. Here, owner Tania Scales displays a multitude of one-of-a-kind folk curios from many parts of Mexico. Her wide-ranging, carefully selected collection includes masks, necklaces, sculptures, purses, blouses, *huipiles,* ritual objects, and much more. Furthermore, be sure not to miss Tania's favorites: several regal sculptures that represent a number of indigenous female deities, such as Ixta Bay, Maya jungle goddess; Coyolxauhqui, Aztec moon goddess; and Cihuateteo, representing all the women of Zihuatanejo.

Return to Cuauhtémoc, to **Alberto's** pair of shops (tel. 755/554-2161, 9 A.M.–9 P.M. daily, credit cards accepted), a few doors below the corner of Bravo, on opposite sides of the street. They offer an extensive silver jewelry collection. As with gold and precious stones, silver prices can be reckoned approximately by weight, at between $1 and $1.25 per gram. The cases and cabinets of shiny earrings, chains, bracelets, rings, and much more are products of a family of artists, taught by master craftsman Alberto, formerly of Puerto Vallarta, now deceased. Many of the designs are original, and, with bargaining, reasonably priced.

Continue another block downhill, past the corner of Ascencio, to **El Arte y Tradición** (tel. 755/554-4625, 10 A.M.–2 P.M. and 4–8 P.M. daily, credit cards accepted), where you can admire a lovely Talavera stoneware collection. This prized ceramic style, the finest of which is made by a few families in Puebla, comes in many shapes, from plates and vases to pitchers and tea cups. Talavera's colorful floral motifs originate from a fusion of traditions, notably Moorish, Italian, Turkish, and Persian, from the Mediterranean basin.

Now that you're again near the beachfront, for a treat head east along Avenida Álvarez, half a block past the plaza to **Cerámicas Tonalá** (Av. Álvarez 12B, tel. 755/554-6733, beach side, 9 A.M.–2 P.M. and 4–8 P.M. Mon.–Sat., credit cards accepted). Here you can view one of the finest Tonalá ceramics collections outside of the renowned source itself. Kindly owner Eduardo López's graceful glazed vases and plates, decorated in traditional plant and animal designs, fill the cabinets, while a menagerie of lovable owls, ducks, fish, armadillos, and frogs, all seemingly poised to spring to life, crowd the shelves.

## IXTAPA SHOPS

Ixtapa's **Centro Comercial** complex stretches along the midsection of Paseo Ixtapa across from the hotels. Developers built about ten sub-complexes within the Centro Comercial, but several of them remain virtually empty. The good news is that the increasing stream of visitors to Ixtapa is adding new life to the Centro Comercial. At this writing, about six subcomplexes, most fronting the boulevard, are welcoming customers.

### Los Patios, Las Fuentes, El Kiosco, and Las Palmas

Moving from south to north, first come the **Los Patios** and **Las Fuentes** subcomplexes, where designer stores occupy the choice boulevard frontages. Behind them, many small handicrafts stores and ordinary crafts and jewelry shops wait for customers along back lanes and inside patios.

Some stores stand out, however. Especially worth a look is the **La Fuente** (The Source, tel. 755/553-0812, 9 A.M.–9 P.M. daily), on the ground floor at the northeast corner of the Los Patios complex. The expertly selected all-Mexico handicrafts collection includes a treasury of picture frames, ranging from polished hardwood to mother-of-pearl; droll Day of the Dead figurines; lots of tinkling glass and ceramic bells; and a trove of women's blouses,

dresses, and skirts, both traditional and stylishly up-to-date.

Also in Los Patios, you'll find at least three good Taxco silver shops and a gem of an embroidery store, **Artesanias Deshilados** (tel. 755/553-0221), with lovely tablecloths, curtains, *huipiles,* and much more.

At the **La Puerta** complex 100 yards farther on, a sprinkling of good restaurants and a cinema are open for business. There's also a **supermercado** (tel. 755/553-1514, 755/553-1508, 8 A.M.–11 P.M. daily) well stocked with veggies, fruit, groceries, and wine. An ATM, pharmacy, telecom money orders and fax are also available.

Behind the Los Patios, find the up-and-coming **El Kiosko** subcomplex, with a number of good restaurants and a surfing shop.

Next comes the boulevard-front **police station,** and, after that, the **Las Palmas** subcomplex (Señor Frog's, pharmacy, restaurant, Internet connection) and finally, the busy **Las Galerías** (mini-super, photo store, restaurant), at the corner of Paseo de las Garzas.

# Information and Services

## TOURIST INFORMATION

The local **Convention and Visitors Bureau** (Oficina de Convenciones y Visitantes, OCV, tel. 755/553-1270 or 755/553-1540, fax 755/553-0819, info@visit-ixtapa-zihuatanejo .org, www.visit-ixtapa-zihuatanejo.org, 9 A.M.–2 P.M. and 5:30–8 P.M. Mon.–Sat.) information office is in Ixtapa near the south end of Avenida Gaviotas, the street that runs behind the Ixtapa Centro Comercial shopping complex. Call ahead to confirm hours. The generally helpful and knowledgeable staff answers questions, dispenses literature and maps, and can recommend tour agencies and guides.

## PUBLICATIONS

The best local English-language book and magazine selection fills the many shelves of

the **Hotel Las Brisas** shop (Paseo de la Roca, 9 A.M.–9 P.M. daily). Besides dozens of new paperback novels and scores of popular U.S. magazines, it stocks the *News* from Mexico City and *USA Today* and a small selection of Mexico coffee table books of cultural and historical interest.

In Zihuatanejo, the **newsstand** (8 A.M.–8 P.M. daily) across Juárez from the town market (near the corner of González) sells the *News*. A second newsstand, west end of the beachfront town plaza, in high season, stocks the *News* and some popular U.S. newspapers and magazines.

The small Zihuatanejo **Biblioteca** (public library, on Cuauhtémoc, 9 A.M.–8 P.M. Mon.–Fri., 9 A.M.–5 P.M. Sat.), five blocks from the beach, also has some shelves of English-language paperbacks.

## TRAVEL AGENCIES AND TOUR GUIDES

A number of reliable local agents arrange and/or guide local excursions. One of the most experienced all-around is **Turismo International del Pacifico** (at Plaza Ixpamar in Ixtapa, tel. 755/554-2716 or 755/554-1173, tipzihua@prodigy.net.mx, www.ixtapa-zihuatanejo.net/tip, 9 A.M.–6 P.M. Mon.–Sat.). They offer air and hotel reservations, transportation, sportfishing, and many tours, from horseback riding and a one-day Acapulco tour, to a Playa Las Gatas beach party, and an all-day excursion to the cool, pine-tufted Michoacán highlands.

Eco-adventuring, including bicycling, kayaking, and snorkeling, is the specialty of **Adventours** (tel. 755/553-1069 or 755/553-1946, pablomendizabal@gmail.com, www.ixtapa-adventours.com).

Get way off the beaten track with very professional and wildlife-sensitive **Zoe Kayak Tours** (in Ixtapa, tel. 755/553-0496, zoe5@aol.com, www.zoekayaktours.com), which specializes in lagoon kayaking and birdwatching. For more information contact manager-guide Brian.

## ECOLOGICAL ASSOCIATION AND HUMANE SOCIETY

The grassroots organization **SOS BAHIA** (Paseo del Pescador 9, info@sosbahia.org, www.sosbahia.org) sponsors efforts for local beach and lagoon cleanup and tree planting, to save the turtles, to stop the cruise-liner dock, and other projects. Their headquarters shares space with the Animal Protection Society on the upper floor of Casa Marina, just west of the Zihuatanejo beachfront plaza.

The family members of the late Helen Krebs Posse are the guiding lights of the **Sociedad Protectora de Animales** (Animal Protection Society, Paseo del Pescador 9, tel. 755/554-2373, cell tel. 044-755/112-1648, spaz@zihuatanejo.net, www.zihuatanejo.net/spaz/), which is working hard to educate people about animal issues. Contact one of the family members at the family's shop complex, in Casa Marina, just west of the Zihuatanejo plaza.

## PHOTOGRAPHY

In Zihuatanejo, **Foto 30** (on Ejido, tel. 755/554-7610, 9 A.M.–8 P.M. Mon.–Sat., 10 A.M.–2 P.M. Sun.), between Galeana and Guerrero two blocks from the plaza, offers 30-minute process-and-print service and stocks lots of film and digital accessories, such as many cameras, including SLRs, and filters, tripods, and flashes.

In Ixtapa, **Foto Quick** (Paseo Ixtapa, tel. 755/553-1956, 9 A.M.–9 daily) offers approximately the same services and a modest selection of cameras and supplies, across the boulevard from Hotel Emporio.

## MONEY EXCHANGE

Several banks, all with ATMs, cluster on the east side of downtown. Find **Banamex** (tel. 755/554-7293 or 755/554-7294), at the corner of Guerrero and Ejido two blocks from the beach, open for money exchange 9 A.M.–4 P.M. Monday–Friday and 10 A.M.–2 P.M. Saturday. If the Banamex lines are too long, use the ATM or walk to **Bancomer** (corner of Bravo and Juárez, tel. 755/554-7492 or 755/554-7493, 8:30 A.M.–4 P.M. Mon.–Fri., 10 A.M.–3 P.M. Sat.); or **Banco Santander Serfín** (tel. 755/554-3941, 9 A.M.–4 P.M. Mon.–Fri., 10 A.M.–2 P.M. Sat.) across the street.

After bank hours, go to either long-hours HSBC in Ixtapa (below) or to the center of town to **Casa de Cambio Guibal** (at Galeana and Ascencio, tel. 755/554-3522, fax 755/554-2800, 8 A.M.–8 P.M. daily), with long-distance telephone and fax two blocks from the beach, to change U.S., Canadian, French, German, Swiss, and other currencies and travelers checks. For the convenience, it offers you a few percent less for your money than the banks.

In Ixtapa, for long money-changing hours, go to **HSBC** (tel. 755/553-0642 or 755/553-0646, 8 A.M.–7 P.M. Mon.–Fri., 8 A.M.–3 P.M. Sat.) in front of the Hotel Emporio right on Paseo Ixtapa. Alternatively, go to **Bancomer** (tel. 755/553-2112 or 755/553-0525, 8:30 A.M.–4 P.M. Mon.–Fri.) in the Los Portales complex behind the shops across the boulevard from the Hotel Presidente Intercontinental.

## COMMUNICATIONS

The single *correo* (post office, tel. 755/554-2192, 8 A.M.–6 P.M. Mon.–Fri., 9 A.M.–1 P.M. Sat.) that serves both Zihuatanejo and Ixtapa is in Zihuatanejo at Centro Federal, in the northeast corner of downtown, five blocks from the beach and about three blocks east of the Ixtapa minibus stop at Juárez and Morelos. Also in the post office is a sub-office of the very reliable government **Mexpost** (like U.S. Express Mail—upgraded, secure mail service).

Next door is **Telecomunicaciones,** which offers long-distance telephone, public fax (755/554-2163), telegrams, and money orders 8 A.M.–7 P.M. Monday–Friday. Another similar telecommunications office serves Ixtapa, in the La Puerta shopping center (rear side), across Paseo Ixtapa from the Hotel Presidente Intercontinental.

Money changer Casa de Cambio Guibal is also Zihuatanejo's private *larga distancia* telephone and fax office (on Galeana, corner of Bravo, tel./fax 755/554-3522, 8 A.M.–8 P.M. daily).

In both Ixtapa and Zihuatanejo, many **streetside public phone booths** provide relatively economical national and international (call the United States for about $1 per three minutes) long-distance service, using a Ladatel telephone card. Cards are readily available in grocery, drug, and liquor stores everywhere. First dial 001 for calls to the United States and Canada, and 01 for Mexico long-distance.

Beware of prominent "call home collect, dial 090" phone booths. Such calls customarily run about $30 per three minutes (whether or not you use the full three minutes.) Best ask the price before placing your call.

Get on the **Internet** in Zihuatanejo at one of several downtown spots, such as **Podernet** (on Ejido, 9 A.M.–10 P.M. daily), three blocks from the beach, between Cuauhtémoc and Cinco de Mayo.

In Ixtapa, answer your email at **Internet Connection Ixtapa** (tel. 755/553-2253,

8 A.M.–11 P.M. daily), in the Las Palmas subcomplex, behind Señor Frog's.

## HEALTH AND EMERGENCIES

For medical consultations in English, contact U.S.-trained **IAMAT associate Dr. Rogelio Grayeb** (Bravo 71A, beach side, between Guerrero and Galeana, Zihuatanejo, tel. 755/554-3334, 755/553-1711, or 755/554-2040, fax 755/554-5041).

Another Zihuatanejo medical option is the very professional **Clínica Maciel** (Palmas 12, tel. 755/554-2380), which has a dentist, pediatrician, gynecologist, and surgeon on 24-hour call, two blocks east, one block north of the market.

Neither Ixtapa nor Zihuatanejo has any state-of-the art private hospitals. However, many local people recommend the state of Guerrero *hospital general* (on Av. Morelos, corner of Mar Egeo, just off from Hwy. 200, tel. 755/554-3965, 755/554-3650) for its generally competent, dedicated, and professional staff.

For medicines and drugs in Zihuatanejo, go to one of the several downtown pharmacies, such as **Farmacia La Principal** (Cuauhtémoc, two blocks from the beach, tel. 755/554-4217, 9 A.M.–9 P.M. Mon.–Sat.). In Ixtapa, go to **Farmapronto** pharmacy (with delivery service, tel. 755/553-2423, 8 A.M.–11 P.M. daily), in the Las Palmas subcomplex across the parking lot, north, from Señor Frog's.

For police emergencies in Ixtapa and Zihuatanejo, contact the **cabercera de policía** headquarters (on Calle Limón, Zihuatanejo, near Hwy. 200, tel. 755/554-2040). Usually more accessible are the police officers at the **caseta de policía** 24-hour police booth at the Zihuatanejo plaza-front, and in Ixtapa on Paseo Ixtapa, across from the Hotel Presidente Intercontinental. On Playa La Ropa, go to the small police station on the Paseo Costera, at the north-end intersection by the Hotel Villa del Sol.

## IMMIGRATION

If you lose your tourist permit, go to **Migración** (on Colegio Militar, tel. 755/554-2795, 9 A.M.–1 P.M. Mon.–Fri.), about five blocks northeast of Plaza Kyoto, on the northeast edge of downtown. Bring your passport and some proof of the date you arrived in Mexico, such as your airline ticket, stamped passport, or a copy of your lost tourist permit. Although it's not wise to let such a matter go until the last day, you may be able to accomplish the needed paperwork at the airport Migración office (tel. 755/554-8480, 8 A.M.–9 P.M. daily). Call first.

## LAUNDRY AND DRY CLEANING

In Zihuatanejo, take your laundry to **Lavandería Express** (on Cuauhtémoc, tel. 755/554-4393, 8 A.M.–8 P.M. daily), near the corner of González, five blocks from the beach.

If you also need something dry-cleaned, take it across the street to **Lavandería Premium** (8:30 A.M.–8 P.M. daily).

# Getting There and Away

## BY AIR

Nine reliable carriers connect Ixtapa-Zihuatanejo directly with U.S. and Mexican destinations year-round. A few more operate during the winter-spring high season.

Many **Aeroméxico** (reservations tel. 755/554-2018, flight information tel. 755/554-2237 or 755/554-2634) flights (and those of affiliate airline Aeroconnect) connect daily with Mexico City, where connections with U.S. destinations may be made.

Mexicana affiliate **Click Airlines** (reservations tel. 755/554-2208 or 755/554-2209, flight information tel. 755/554-2227) flights connect directly with Mexico City.

**Alaska Airlines** (direct from Mexico tel. 001-800/426-0333) connects directly with Los Angeles and San Francisco. For flight information and reservations.

**US Airways** (direction from Mexico 001-800/235-9292) connects with Phoenix.

**Continental Airlines** (tel. 755/554-2549, toll-free Mex. tel. 1-800/900-5000) connects with Houston daily.

Furthermore, a number of newcomers now connect Zihuatanejo with U.S. and Mexican destinations: **Frontier Airlines** (tel. 755/553-7025) with Denver; **Delta Airlines** (tel. 755/553-7146) with Los Angeles; **Interjet Airlines** (tel. 755/553-7002 or 755/553-7161) with Toluca; and **Alma Airlines** (toll-free Mex. tel. 01-800/800-2562, www.alma.com.mx) with Guadalajara.

A number of **seasonal and charter** flights operated by airlines such Air Canada, Frontier, Delta, American, and Northwest connect with northern U.S. and Canadian destinations during the winter. For more information, contact a travel agent or check the airlines' respective websites.

## Air Arrival and Departure

Ixtapa and Zihuatanejo are quickly accessible, only about twenty minutes (seven miles/11 km) north of the airport via Highway 200. Arrival is generally simple—if you come with a day's worth of pesos (or an ATM card) and hotel reservations. Although the terminal does have an ATM (HSBC, in mid-terminal by the newsstand), a mailbox (*buzón,* outside the front opposite the check-in counters), restaurant, and shops for last-minute purchases, and newsstand with books, magazines, and *USA Today* (for $3.50), it has neither tourist information booth nor hotel-reservation service. Best arrive with a hotel reservation, and do not leave the choice up to your taxi driver, who will probably deposit you at a hotel that pays him a commission on your first night's lodging.

Transportation to town is usually by *taxi especial* (private taxi) or *colectivo* van. Tickets are available at booths near the terminal arrival exit. Tariff for a *colectivo* runs about $12 to both Ixtapa and Zihuatanejo, for a *taxi especial,* $28–37 for three or four people. Taxis to Troncones run about $75. Mobile budget travelers can walk the few hundred yards to the highway and flag down one of the frequent daytime Zihuatanejo-bound buses (very few, if any, continue to Ixtapa, however). At night, spend the money on a *colectivo* or taxi.

Several major **car rental** companies staff airport arrival booths. Avoid problems and save money by negotiating your car rental through the agencies' toll-free numbers before departure. Agents at the airport include **Hertz** (tel. 755/553-3338, 755/554-2255, or 755/554-2592, hertz_ixtapa@hotmail.com); **Budget** (tel. 755/554-4837 or 755/553-0397, ixtapa@budget ansa.com); **Alamo** (tel. 755/553-0206 or 755/554-8429, www.alamo-mexico.com.mx); **Thrifty** (tel. 755/553-7020 or 755/553-3019, aut zsa@prodigy.net.mx); **Dollar** (tel. 755/553-7050); and **Europcar** (tel./fax 755/553-7158 or 755/554-0869, www.europcar.com.mx).

Departure is quick and easy if you have your passport, tourist permit (which was stamped on arrival), and $19 cash (or the equivalent in pesos) international departure tax if your air ticket doesn't already cover it. Departees who've lost their tourist permits can avoid trouble and a fine by getting a duplicate from Zihuatanejo Immigration at the airport a few hours prior to departure. Simplify this procedure by being prepared with your passport and a copy of the lost permit or at least some proof of your date of arrival, such as an airline ticket.

## BY CAR OR RV

Three routes, two easy and one formerly unsafe but now marginally recommended, connect Ixtapa-Zihuatanejo with Playa Azul and Michoacán to the northwest, Acapulco to the southeast, and Ciudad Altamirano and central Guerrero to the northeast.

Traffic sails smoothly along the 76 miles (122 km) of Highway 200, either way, between Zihuatanejo and Lázaro Cárdenas/Playa Azul. Allow about an hour and a half. Several miles before Lázaro Cárdenas the new Highway 37D *cuota* (toll) expressway allows easy access to highland central Michoacán (190 miles, 312 km, 4.5 hours to Uruapan, add another half-hour to Pátzcuaro) from Zihuatanejo. The same is true of the 150-mile (242-km, allow four hours) Highway 200 southern extension to Acapulco.

The story is different, however, for the winding, sparsely populated cross-Sierra Highway 134 (intersecting with Hwy. 200 nine miles/15 km north) from Zihuatanejo to Ciudad Altamirano. Rising along spectacular ridges, the paved but sometimes potholed road leads over cool, pine-clad heights and descends to the Ciudad Altamirano high, dry valley of the grand Río Balsas after about 100 miles (160 km). The continuing leg to Iguala on the Acapulco–Mexico City highway is longer, about 112 miles (161 km), equally winding and sometimes busy. Allow about eight hours westbound and nine hours eastbound for the entire trip. Keep filled with gasoline, and be prepared for emergencies, especially along the Altamirano–Zihuatanejo leg, where no hotels and few services exist. *Warning:* This route, unfortunately, was once plagued by robberies and nasty drug-related incidents. Before attempting this trip inquire locally—at your hotel, the tourist information office, or the bus station—to see if authorities deem the road safe.

## BY BUS

Zihuatanejo has three major bus terminals. They stand side-by side on Highway 200, on the Acapulco-bound (east) side of town. The biggest and busiest is the big Estrella Blanca **Central de Autobús** station. Inside its shiny airline-style terminal, travelers have few services available: a battery of Ladatel card-operated telephones, a left-luggage service, and only a small snack bar. If you're going need supplies for a long bus trip, prepare by stocking up with water and food goodies before you depart.

**Estrella Blanca** (tel. 755/554-3477), the only carrier, computer-coordinates the service of its subsidiaries, including first-class Elite, Estrella Blanca, Futura, and luxury-class Turistar. Tickets are purchasable with either cash or credit cards for all departures from computer-assisted agents.

Many departures run along the Highway 200 corridor, connecting with Lázaro Cárdenas/ Playa Azul and northwestern destinations, such as Manzanillo, Puerto Vallarta, and the U.S. at Nogales and Tijuana, and with Acapulco and destinations southeast.

Several luxury- and first-class buses and some second-class buses connect daily with Acapulco. A number of them continue north to Mexico City, and at least one continues southeast along the Oaxaca coast all the way to Puerto Escondido and Salina Cruz. In the opposite direction, many luxury-, first-, and second-class buses (at least one an hour during the day) connect with Lázaro Cárdenas, Playa Azul junction, and northwest points.

Other departures connect north, via Michoacán. Among them, at least one daily departure connects north with points of Uruapan and Morelia, via the new 37D toll expressway. Another departure connects north by the expressway, via Uruapan, continuing northwest, via Guadalajara and Mazatlán all the way to the U.S. border at Mexicali and Tijuana.

Competing major bus carrier **Estrella de Oro** (tel. 755/554-2175) operates out of its separate station on the adjacent, west side of the Estrella Blanca station. It offers some long-distance first-class connections southeast along the coast via Acapulco, thence inland, via Chilpancingo, Iguala, and Taxco, to Mexico City.

**Transportes Autobuses del Pacifico** (TAP, tel. 755/554-2175), also operating out of the Estrella de Oro station, connects northwest, via Uruapan, Guadalajara, and Mazatlán, with Mexicali and Tijuana at the U.S. border.

**A third major terminal,** adjacent, west of the Estrella de Oro terminal, offers mostly first- and luxury-class departures, via a number of competent, well-equipped carriers, all of which can be reserved by calling 755/112-1002. They include **La Linea Plus,** with luxury-class departures connecting north with Guadalajara via Uruapan and also northwest with Puerto Vallarta, via Lázaro Cárdenas and Manzanillo; **Autovias,** with first-class departures connecting northeast with Mexico City, via Morelia and Toluca; **Parhikuni,** with first-class departures connecting northeast with Morelia, via Uruapan; **Omnibus de Mexico,** with first-class departures connecting north with Monterrey; and **Primera Plus,** with luxury-class departures connecting northeast, with Irapuato, Leon, and Aguascalientes.

# South of Ixtapa and Zihuatanejo

Playa Las Pozas, Playa Blanca, and Barra de Potosí, the trio of pocket paradises not far southeast of Zihuatanejo and long known by local people, are now being discovered by a growing cadre of off-the-beaten-track seekers of heaven on earth. Taken together, they offer a feast of quiet south-seas delights: good fishing, beachcombing, camping, wildlife-viewing, and comfortable, reasonably priced lodgings.

Playa Las Pozas, a surf-fishing and seafood haven, is reachable via the Zihuatanejo airport road. A pair of palm-shaded bungalows offers comfortable accommodation. Playa Blanca, a mile farther southeast, is a long, lovely golden-sand beach, decorated by a lovely boutique hotel and restaurant. A few miles farther, Barra de Potosí village offers the ingredients of a heavenly one-day or one-week tropical excursion: palm-shaded seafood *palapas,* room for tent or RV camping, stores for supplies, a wildlife-rich mangrove lagoon, and a long beach, ripe for swimming, surfing, fishing, and beachcombing. A trio of petite bed-and-breakfast lodgings and a downscale beachfront hotel offer accommodation.

## PLAYA LAS POZAS

Playa Las Pozas rewards visitors with a lagoon full of bait fish, space for RV or tent camping (be careful of soft sand), a wide beach, and friendly beachside *palapa* restaurants. The beach itself is 100 yards wide, of yellow-white sand, and extends for miles in both directions. It has driftwood but not many shells. Fish thrive in its thunderous, open-ocean waves. Consequently, casts from the beach can yield five-pound catches by either bait or lures. Local folks catch fish mostly by net, both in the surf

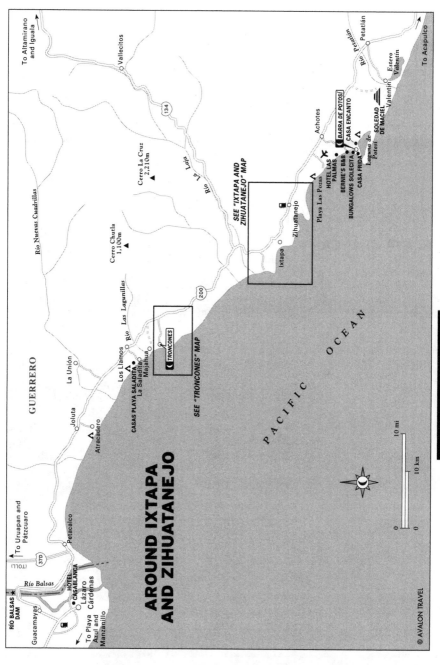

AROUND IXTAPA
AND ZIHUATANEJO

IXTAPA AND ZIHUATANEJO

SEE "IXTAPA AND ZIHUATANEJO" MAP

SEE "TRONCONES" MAP

TRONCONES

PACIFIC OCEAN

GUERRERO

To Altamirano
and Iguala

Vallecitos

Cerro La Cruz
2,210m

Cerro Churla
1,100m

134

Río Las Lagunillas

Río Nuevas Cuadrillas

La Unión

Los Llamos

CASAS PLAYA SALADITA
La Saladita
Majahua

200

Ixtapa

Zihuatanejo

Joluta

Atracadero

Petacalco

Guacamayas

Lázaro
Cárdenas

HOTEL
CASABLANCA

Río Balsas

RÍO BALSAS
DAM

370 (TOLL)

To Uruapan and
Pátzcuaro

To Playa
Azul and Manzanillo

Río Petatlán

Petatlán

Estero
Valentín

Achotes

BARRA DE POTOS

CASA ENCANTO

SOLEDAD
DE MACIEL

HOTEL LAS
PALMAS

BERNIE'S B&B

BUNGALOWS SOLECITA

CASA FRIDA

Laguna de
Potosí

Valentín

Playa Las Pozas

To Acapulco

10 mi

10 km

© AVALON TRAVEL

and the nearby lagoon. During the June–September rainy season, the lagoon breaks through the bar. Big fish, gobbling prey at the outlet, can themselves be netted or hooked at the same spot.

Camping is popular here on weekends and holidays. Other times you may have the place to yourself. As a courtesy, ask at the friendly family-run *palapa* restaurant (on the west end by the lagoon) if it's okay to camp nearby.

Get to Playa Las Pozas by following the well-marked airport turnoff road at Km 230. After one mile, turn right before the cyclone wire fence just before entering the terminal complex and follow the bumpy but easily passable straight level road 1.1 miles (1.8 km) to the beach.

## PLAYA BLANCA

In 2001, personable, savvy, and hardworking owner-builders from Phoenix, Arizona, decided to create heaven on lazy, lovely Playa Blanca. The result was ◖ **Hotel Las Palmas** (cell tel. 044-755/557-0634, from U.S. dial 011-52-1-755/557-0634, hotellaspalmas@hotmail.com, www.hotellaspalmas.net), replete with precious architecture-as-art, including polished natural tree-trunk-beamed ceilings, elegant tropical hardwood shutters, and massive overhanging thatched *palapa* roofs. A recipe for paradise? Yes, but there's even more: a big blue pool, a good restaurant and bar, all set in cool green grassy grounds overlooking a long, creamy, yellow-white strand. Their six super-comfortable handcrafted rooms, four with air-conditioning, two with ceiling fans, $225 d high season, $150 d low (June–Oct.) come with breakfast, but without TV or phones. No credit cards accepted nor kids under 18; not wheelchair accessible. Get there by continuing about 1.5 miles (2.5 km) along the beach road from Playa Las Pozas to Playa Blanca and Hotel Las Palmas. Reservations can be made through the hotel or the owners' Arizona agent, Gold Coast Travel (335 W. Virginia Ave., Phoenix, AZ 85003-1020, fax 602/253-3487, goldcoast-travel@hotmail.com).

## ◖ BARRA DE POTOSÍ

At Achotes, on Highway 200, nine miles (15 km) south of Zihuatanejo, a Laguna de Potosí sign points right to Barra de Potosí, an idyllic fishing hamlet at the sheltered south end of the Bahía de Potosí. After a few miles through green, tufted groves, the paved road parallels

Barra de Potosí offers both comfortable lodgings and tropical country ambience.

the bayside beach, a crescent of fine white sand, with a scattering of houses, a few comfortable bed-and-breakfasts, and one modest beachfront hotel.

The waves become even more tranquil at the beach's southeast end, where a sheltering headland rises beyond the village and the adjacent broad lagoon. Beneath its swaying palm grove, the hamlet of Barra de Potosí (pop. 1,000) has all the ingredients for tranquil living. Several broad, hammock-hung *palapa* restaurants (here called *enramadas*) front the bountiful lagoon.

## Sights and Recreation

Home for flocks of birds and waterfowl and shoals of fish, the **Laguna de Potosí** stretches for miles to its far mangrove reaches. Adventure out with your own boat or kayak, or go with Orlando (ask at Restaurant Teresita), who regularly takes parties out for fishing or wildlife-viewing tours. Bring water, a hat, and insect repellent.

If you want to do more but don't have your own kayak, Ixtapa-based **Zoe Kayak Tours** (tel. 755/553-0496, zoe5@aol.com, www.zoekayaktours.com) leads kayaking trips on Laguna de Potosí's pristine waters.

Bait fish, caught locally with nets, abound in the lagoon. Fishing is fine for bigger catches (jack, snapper, mullet) by boat or casts beyond the waves. Launch your boat easily in the lagoon, then head past the open sandbar like the local fishermen.

## Accommodations and Food

In the village, a pair of bed-and-breakfast-style hotels offer lodging. First consider the charming flower-bedecked **Casa del Encanto** (House of Enchantment, local cell 044-755/104-6709, from U.S. 011-52-1-755/104-6709, lauragecko2@hotmail.com, www.casadelencanto.com), on a village side street. Owner Laura Nolo rents her lovingly decorated rooms for $75–85 d low season, $90–115 d high (Oct. 31–May 1), including private hot-water bath and full breakfast; massage available at extra cost.

Beneath the plumy grove nearby, guests at **C Casa Frida** (local cell 044-755/557-0049,

from the U.S. 011-52-1-755/557-0049, casafrida@zihuatanejo.net, www.zihuatanejo.net/casafrida), life project of Mexican-French couple Anabella and François, enjoy fondly decorated rooms, built around a charmingly compact pool-patio garden. Room furnishings, based on a Frida Kahlo theme, include handcrafted art and furniture, mosquito curtains over the double beds, and bright Talavera-tiled hot-water bathrooms. François and Annabella enjoy hosting grand Christmas and Easter dinners; reserve ahead of time. Rates run about $90 d ($110 Christmas holiday), including breakfast; adults only, no pets, closed May 1–November 1.

On the beachfront, about half a mile from the village, settle into the lap of luxury at **C Bungalows Solecito** (local cell 044-755/100-5976, from U.S 011-52-1-755/100-5976, www.bungalowssolecito.com, $115 s or d, $2500 mo.). Friendly owner-builder Manuel Romo offers 10 airy, rustic-chic south-seas bungalows for two, with kitchen, all artfully arranged around a flowery, palm-shadowed beachfront garden and pool-patio. Stroll out just a few steps and you're on the lovelier-than-life Playa Barra de Potosí. Get your reservations in early.

About a mile out of the village, back toward Zihuatanejo, the downscale **Hotel Barra de Potosí** (Petatlán tel. 755/554-8290 or 755/556-8434, Zihuatanejo tel. 755/554-3445, fax 755/554-7060, reservaciones@hotelbarradepotosi.com.mx, www.hotelbarradepotosi.com.mx) perches right on the beach. The surf is generally tranquil and safe for swimming near the hotel, although the waves, which do not roll but break rather quickly along long fronts, do not appear good for surfing. The hotel, once rough and neglected, has been renovated and is maintained at a rather plain but habitable condition and the pool has been returned to a brilliant blue. The owner says that the restaurant will be open during the high winter season, but will close during the low summer and fall. The beach, however, remains inviting and kid-friendly year-round. The 14 rooms, in rising order of price, start with hot and stuffy interior rooms for about $35 d; improving to exterior rooms with view of the parking lot for $45 d, then better rooms with private oceanview balcony for $55 d, and finally kitchenette suite for four, also with oceanview balcony, $80. All come with fans, but only room-temperature water and bare-bulb lighting; bring your own lampshade or booklight.

About a mile farther from town on the same luscious beachfront, near the spot where the road from Achotes arrives at the beach, **Bernie's Bed and Breakfast** (local cell 044-755/556-6333, from U.S. 011-52-1-755/556-6333, playacalli@ hotmail.com, www.berniesbedandbreakfast .com) offers three comfortable rooms with "no TV, or piped-in-music" (says friendly owner Bernie Wittstock) that open onto a lovely palm-shadowed beachfront pool and patio. Rentals run about $90 s or d year-round except for $110 December 15–January 7 and Easter holiday, with breakfast. If you give him a day's notice, Bernie will cook a light meal for you.

**Camping** is common by RV or tent along the uncrowded edge of the lagoon. Village stores can provide basic supplies. Prepared food is available at about a dozen permanent lagoon-side *palapa* restaurants. **Restaurant Teresita** is especially recommended.

## Getting There and Away

By car, get to Barra de Potosí by following the signed turnoff road from Highway 200 at Km 225, nine miles (14 km) south of Zihuatanejo, just south of the Río Los Achotes bridge. Continue along the good, mostly paved road; pass the hotel at Mile 5 (Km 8) and continue to the village at Mile 5.5 (Km 8.9). Alternatively, get to Barra de Potosí by continuing east about three miles (5 km) along the beach road from Hotel Las Palmas at Playa Blanca.

By bus, follow the same route via a Petatlán-bound bus (Omnibus de Mexico, Estrella Blanca) either from one of the Zihuatanejo bus stations, or the local Petatlán bus from the station on Zihuatanejo Avenida Las Palmas, across from Bancrecer. In either case, ask the driver to let you off at the Barra de Potosí turn-off at Achotes and wait for the Barra de Potosí–bound covered pickup truck (about every about 30 minutes daytime).

# North of Ixtapa and Zihuatanejo

Visitors to Troncones and Majahua (mah-HAH-wah) can enjoy a long, pristine, coral-studded beach as well as the natural delights of a small kingdom of forested wildlife-rich hinterland that stretches for miles above and behind the beach. While Troncones has acquired a modicum of modern travel amenities, including a number of restful bed-and-breakfast inns and gourmet restaurants, Majahua remains charmingly rustic.

## TRONCONES

Troncones (pop. 1,000) has a little bit of everything: shady seafood *ramadas,* cozy seaside inns and houses for rent, a sprinkling of good restaurants, and room to park your RV or set up a tent by the beach. Most folks get there by bus or taxi, from Ixtapa or Zihuatanejo via the side road off of Highway 200 about 20 miles (32 km) north of Ixtapa.

But that's just the beginning. Troncones has acquired a growing colony of North Americans, some of whom operate small accommodations for lovers of peace, quiet, and the outdoors. Besides lazing in hammocks and sunning on the sand, guests at all Troncones lodgings share the same luscious shoreline. You can swim, surf, bodysurf, and boogie board the waves, jog along the sand, explore a limestone cave, and thrill to a treetop cable adventure in the adjacent jungle. Back by the shore, you can beachcomb to your heart's content while enjoying views of the wild-life trove—fish, whales (Dec.–Mar.), dolphins, turtles (Nov.–Jan.), swarms of herons, boobies, egrets, and cormorants—that abounds in the ocean and in nearby lagoons.

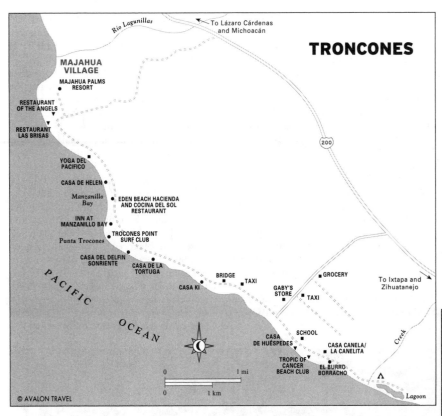

## Accommodations and Food

Many Troncones accommodations fall into the $50–100 category. As you move northwest (from the entrance road, turn right at the beach) after the bridge, first comes **◖ Casa Ki** (P.O. Box 405, Zihuatanejo, Guerrero 40880, tel. 755/553-2815, casaki@yahoo.com, www .casa-ki.com), the life project of Ed and Ellen Weston, now managed by daughter Tina Morse. Casa Ki (named after the Japanese word for energy and wholeness) offers four immaculate, charmingly rustic cottages tucked in a lovingly tended seaside garden compound. Each cottage sleeps approximately two adults and two children and comes with shower, toilet, fans, and refrigerator and daily maid service. Guests share a shady outside cooking and

dining *palapa*. High-season (Nov. 15–Apr. 30) rentals run $95–115 d ($65–85 d low season) for the cottages, including full breakfast high season only. Tina also rents a lovely two-bedroom, two-bath house that sleeps up to six, with full kitchen and daily maid service, for about $220 high, $150 low (breakfast not included). Get your winter reservations in early.

After another quarter mile find **Casa de la Tortuga** (P.O. Box 37, Zihuatanejo, Guerrero 40880, tel./fax 755/553-2812, casadelatortuga@yahoo.com or casadetortuga@troncones .net), the original Troncones lodging, built by friendly pioneer Dewey McMillin during the late 1980s. Although he used to rent individual rooms, Dewey has lately been renting the whole place (sleeping a dozen or more) for about $350/day, $2,000/week, $7,500/month during the high season, with staff; guests supply their own food. Reservations are mandatory during the winter. Rates during the low May–October season are discounted about 20 percent. If business is too slow, Casa de la Tortuga closes June, July, and August.

Continuing another half mile, you'll find one of Troncones' longstanding gems, the **( Inn at Manzanillo Bay** (tel. 755/553-2884, fax 755/553-2883, manzanillobay@aol.com, www .manzanillobay.com, $105 d low, $128 high). Here, owner-chef Michael Bensal has realized his dream of paradise: a plumy haven of eight rustic-style *palapa*-roofed *cabañas,* comfortably furnished with deluxe amenities, set around a luscious blue swimming pool and leafy patio. Here you can have it all: a gently curving, wave-washed surfable shoreline, with the murmur of the billows at night and plenty of hammock time by day. There's a good restaurant and even TV if you want it, and breakfast is included. Send deposits for the full amount to P.O. Box 5306, Concord, CA 94524.

Finally, 100 yards farther along the beach, you arrive at the **Eden Beach Hacienda and La Cocina del Sol Restaurant** (P.O Box 128, Zihuatanejo, Guerrero 40880, tel. 755/553-2802, evaandjim@aol.com, www .edenmex.com, $105–140), which shares the same luscious tropical forest oceanfront as all the other lodgings. The amenities include 14 immaculate accommodations—six comfortable rooms with fan in the original house, four spacious beachfront suites with fan, and four beamed-ceiling, air-conditioned suites—all invitingly decorated in stucco and Talavera tile, with king-size beds and private hot-water bathrooms. Rates (Oct.–May) run $105 d in the main house, $120 on the beachfront, and $140 for the air-conditioning suites, all including breakfast. Make reservations with the hotel direct by phone or email. You may also write or fax them in the United States (41 Riverview Dr., Oak Ridge, TN 37830, fax 801/340-9883). Credit cards are not accepted.

At the opposite, southeast end of the Troncones beach, **( El Burro Borracho** (The

Troncones offers a number of restful bed-and-breakfast lodgings, such as the Inn at Manzanillo Bay.

Drunken Burro, P.O. Box 37, Zihuatanejo, Guerrero 40880, tel./fax 755/553-2834, tronconesburro@yahoo.com) beachfront *palapa* restaurant and inn has become a favorite stopping place for the growing cadre of daytime visitors venturing out from Ixtapa and Zihuatanejo. Here, owner Dewey McMillin continues the standard set by former owner-chef Michael Bensal with spicy shrimp tacos, rum-glazed ribs, jumbo shrimp grilled with coconut-curry sauce, and broiled pork chops with mashed potatoes. Besides the shady ocean-view *palapa* restaurant, El Burro Borracho offers six "elegantly simple" airy rooms, each with bath, in three stone duplex beachfront cottages. Rooms include king-size bed, rustic-chic decor, hot water, and fans. Shared cooking facilities are also available. Sports and activities include swimming, surfing, and boogie boarding, plus kayaks, for use of guests. Room rentals run about $65 d high season, $45 low, with continental breakfast.

For more choices, consider some of the platoon of newer guesthouses, bed-and-breakfast inns, hotels, and vacation rental villas that have recently sprouted on the Troncones beachfront. Many choices, mostly upscale, are available. They include a cluster of jointly managed houses—**Casa Alegria, Casa Canela, La Canelita,** and **Santa Benita**—with rentals varying from individual rooms to whole houses (P.O. Box 277, Zihuatanejo, Guerrero 40880, tel. 755/553-2800, casacanela@yahoo.com, www.tronconestropic.com/alegria, from $40 to $225); bed-and-breakfast **Casa del Delfin Sonriente** (Smiling Dolphin, tel. 755/553-2803, U.S. tel. 831/688-6578, enovey@sasq.net, $70 and up); deluxe-suite **Casa Colorida** (U.S. tel. 303/400-5442, fax 303/680-9685, annmerritt@aol.com, www.casacolorida.com, $200–280); and luxurious three-bedroom house **Casa de Helen** (tel. 755/553-2800, tronconeshelen@yahoo.com, www.tronconeshelen.com, $225–300). For information on more rentals, visit websites www.troncones.com.mx and www.zihuatanejo.net.

For camping or RV parking spots, turn south (left) at the beach and follow the road half a mile past several likely spots to pull off and camp. At the far southern end, a lagoon spreads beside a pristine coral-sand beach, which curls around a low hill toward a picture-perfect little bay. Stores back by the entrance road can supplement your food and water supplies. El Burro Borracho may also let you park your RV in their lot out front for a fee.

## Sports and Recreation

Michael Bensal at the Inn at Manzanillo Bay arranges sealife-viewing tours and fully equipped launches for four hours of fishing for 2–4 people for about $150.

Surfing has become a major Troncones recreation. The most popular spot is the palm-tufted inlet, locally known as Manzanillo Bay, location of both the Inn at Manzanillo Bay and Eden Beach Hacienda. Lately, a pair of enterprising lovers of the tropics, Michael and Ann Linn of San Luis Obispo, California, operating as **ISA (Instructional Surf Adventures) Mexico** (cell tel. 044-755/558-3821, U.S. tel. 514/563-6944, surf@isamexico.com, www.isamexico.com), offer both local day instruction and extended surfing packages during the fall–winter (Nov.–Apr.) season. Classes are small and all equipment and deluxe beachfront lodging is customarily included in packages, which run about $1,000 per person, double occupancy.

## Shopping and Services

Michael Bensal maintains a shop offering fine wines, Taxco silver, Cuban cigars, and surfboards new and used at his Inn at Manzanillo Bay. Eva Robbins, at Eden Beach Hacienda, also has both a gallery offering for-sale art and a shop, **Fruity Keiko**, with a charming collection mostly of Guerrero country crafts: baskets, toys, silver jewelry, silk scarves, and more.

The **Boutique** at the Tropic of Cancer Beach Club (from the Zihuatanejo entry road, turn left and continue about two blocks, to the Beach Club on the right) offers some decorative handicrafts, beachwear, a lending library, and some drugs and medications.

Folks interested in rentals or buying

property in Troncones should contact Dewey McMillin (tel. 755/553-2812, casadela tortuga@yahoo.com).

A few local stores provide drinking water and groceries. For example, on the Zihuatanejo entrance road, on the right as you enter the village, **Gaby's** (tel. 755/553-2891 or 755/553-2892) offers some produce, basic groceries, and a long-distance telephone.

## Getting to Troncones

Follow the signed paved turnoff to Playa Troncones from Highway 200, around Km 30, about 18 miles (29 km) north of Zihuatanejo; or about 42 miles (73 km) south of the Río Balsas dam. Continue 2.2 miles (3.5 km) to the Playa Troncones beachfront *ramadas*. Turn left for the camping spots, the main part of the beach, and El Burro Borracho; turn right for the other described lodgings, beginning with Casa Ki, about a mile farther along the beachfront forest road. From there, the car-negotiable gravel road continues about 1.5 miles (2.5 km) along the beach to Playa Majahua.

## MAJAHUA

Here you can enjoy a slice of this beautiful coast as it was before tourism bloomed at Troncones nearby. Instead of cell phones and the Internet, Majahua folks still enjoy plenty of palmy shade, stick-and-wattle houses, and lots of the fresh seafood served in about half a dozen hammock-equipped *ramadas* scattered along the beach. One of the *ramadas* is competently run by a friendly family who calls it **Restaurant de Los Angeles.** Another of the best choices is *palapa* **Restaurant Las Brisas,** next door.

Camping, moreover, is welcomed by local folks (although space, especially for RVs, is limited). Water is available, but campers should bring water or purifying tablets and food.

The beach curves from a rocky southeast point, past the lagoon of Río Lagunillas, and stretches miles northwest past shoreline palm and acacia forest. The sand is soft and dusky yellow, with mounds of driftwood and a seasonal scattering of shells. Waves break far out

and roll in gradually, with little undertow. Fine left-breaking surf rises off the southern point. Boats are easily launchable (several *pangas* lie along the beach) during normal good weather.

To get to Playa Majahua either along the beach road, northeast from Troncones, or directly, by following the signed turnoff from Highway 200 at Km 33, 20 miles (32 km) northwest of Zihuatanejo (just south of the Río Lagunillas bridge), or 44 miles (70 km) southeast of the Río Balsas dam. Continue 2.9 miles (4.7 km) to the beach.

## BEYOND TRONCONES

This northwest corner of the Acapulco region hides a few small havens for those who yearn for their fill of fresh seafood, uncrowded beach camping, and plenty of swimming, surfing, fishing, and beachcombing. And finally, those who venture to Guerrero's extreme northwest edge can encounter the great Río Balsas, the Mexican Pacific's mightiest river, whose drainage basin extends over five states: Jalisco, Morelos, Michoacán, Guerrero, and Oaxaca.

### La Saladita

At La Saladita (The Little Salty Lagoon), the day used to climax when the oyster divers would bring in their afternoon catches. Now, however, the oysters are all fished out. While the oysters recover, divers go for octopus and lobster which, broiled and served with fixings, sell for about $15 for a one-pounder. You can also do your own fishing via rentable (offer $20/hour) beach *pangas,* which go out daily and routinely return with three or four 20-pound fish.

The beach itself is level far out, with rolling waves fine for surfing, swimming, boogie boarding, and bodysurfing. There are enough driftwood and shells for a season of beachcombing. The beach spreads for hundreds of yards on both sides of the road's end. Permanent *palapa* restaurants **Paco, Ilianet,** and **Sotelo** supply shade, seafood, and camping space for about $5 per person. Camping is especially popular during the Christmas and

Easter holidays. Other times, you may have the whole place to yourself. Bring your own food and water; the small stores at the highway village may help add to your supplies.

Furthermore, a colony of comfortable lodgings has been built to serve the growing crowd of visitors who now frequent this formerly undiscovered mini-paradise. Moving up the economic scale, you can choose from a number of options: the rustic beachfront *cabañas,* offered by most of the *palapa* restaurants from about $20 d; or Sotelo restaurant's modest beachfront hotel, with about four plain rooms from about $35 d.

Alternatively, check out the **House of Waves** (tel. 755/554-4532, saladita@houseofwaves.net, www.houseofwaves.net), a two-story south-seas house on stilts, with comfortable rooms with two double beds, private baths, fans or air-conditioning, and a shared kitchenette, from about $65 for up to four; or, by Ilianet beachfront restaurant, **Casas Playa Saladita** (toll-free U.S. tel. 877/927-6928, info@casasplaya saladita.com, www.casasplayasaladita.com), eight very attractive and comfortable architect-built kitchenette apartments, with two double beds, hot-water baths and air-conditioning, about $80 lower level, upper level (better ocean view and breeze), $90.

To get to La Saladita, at Km 40, 25 miles (40 km) northwest of Zihuatanejo and 39 miles (63 km) southeast of the Río Balsas, turn off at the village of Los Llanos. After 0.2 mile, turn right at the church and continue another 3.1 miles (5.1 km) to the beach, where a left fork leads you to Sotelo *palapa* and a right fork leads to the "Embarcadero" sector of the beach and Paco's and Ilianet and other *palapa* restaurants.

## Atracadero

A few miles farther northwest, Playa Atracadero is just being "discovered" and is less frequented than La Saladita. Its two or three beach *palapa* restaurants appear to operate only during weekends, holidays, and the fall–early winter surfing season. Crowds must gather sometimes, however: The main *palapa* has, over time, accumulated a five-foot pile of oyster shells.

The beach sand itself is soft and yellow-gray. The waves, with good, gradual surfing breaks, roll in from far out, arriving gently on the sand. Boat launching would be easy during calm weather. Little undertow menaces casual swimmers, bodysurfers, or boogie boarders. Lots of driftwood and shells—clams, limpets, snails—cover the sand. The beach extends for at least three miles (5 km) past palm groves on the northwest.

Furthermore, at the time of writing, workers are building a number of beachfront *cabañas* for rent, so by the time you arrive you'll probably have the company of a sprinkling of surfers and other fellow seekers of heaven on earth.

To get to Playa Atracadero, turn off at Highway 200 Km 64, near the hamlet of Joluta, 40 miles (64 km) northwest from Zihuatanejo and 24 miles (39 km) southeast from the Río Balsas. Bear left all the way, 2.1 miles (3.3 km) to the beach.

## The Río Balsas

It's hard to remain unimpressed as you follow Highway 200 over the Río Balsas Dam for the first time. The dam marks the Michoacán–Guerrero state boundary. The hulking rock-fill barrier rises in giant stair-steps to its highway summit, where a grand lake mirrors the Sierra Madre, while on the opposite, downstream side, Mexico's greatest river spurts from the turbine exit gates 500 feet below. The river's power, converted into enough electric energy for a million Mexican families, courses up great looping transmission wires, while the spent river meanders toward the sea. To experience all this, drive directly over the dam, from either the north or south, by following old Highway 200 (bear inland) instead of taking the straight-line, toll expressway direct to or from Lázaro Cárdenas.

## LÁZARO CÁRDENAS

The newish industrial port city of Lázaro Cárdenas, named for the Michoacán-born president famous for expropriating American oil companies, is an important transportation and service hub for the northwest Acapulco region. For travelers it's useful as a stopover

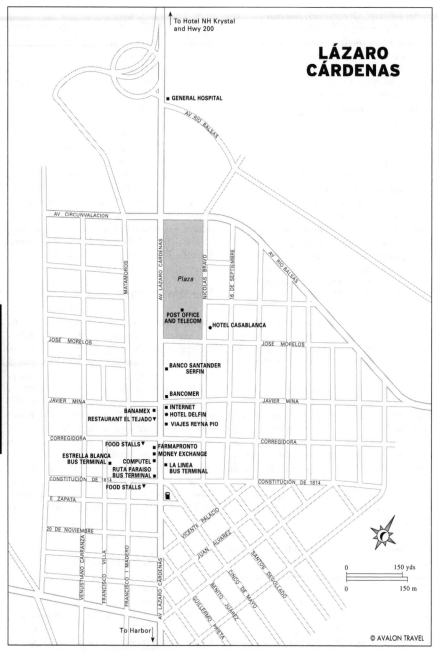

To Hotel NH Krystal and Hwy 200

GENERAL HOSPITAL

AV RÍO BALSAS

# LÁZARO CÁRDENAS

AV CIRCUNVALACIÓN

MATAMOROS

AV LÁZARO CÁRDENAS

NICOLAS BRAVO

16 DE SEPTIEMBRE

AV RÍO BALSAS

Plaza

POST OFFICE AND TELECOM

HOTEL CASABLANCA

JOSÉ MORELOS

JOSÉ MORELOS

BANCO SANTANDER SERFIN

BANCOMER

JAVIER MINA

BANAMEX

INTERNET

JAVIER MINA

RESTAURANT EL TEJADO

HOTEL DELFIN

VIAJES REYNA PIO

CORREGIDORA

FOOD STALLS

FARMAPRONTO

CORREGIDORA

ESTRELLA BLANCA BUS TERMINAL

MONEY EXCHANGE

COMPUTEL

LA LINEA BUS TERMINAL

RUTA PARAISO BUS TERMINAL

CONSTITUCIÓN DE 1814

CONSTITUCIÓN DE 1814

FOOD STALLS

E ZAPATA

20 DE NOVIEMBRE

VENUSTIANO CARRANZA

FRANCISCO VILLA

FRANCISCO I MADERO

AV LÁZARO CÁRDENAS

VICENTE PALACIO

JUAN ALVAREZ

SANTOS DEGOLLADO

CINCO DE MAYO

BENITO JUAREZ

GUILLERMO PRIETA

0          150 yds

0          150 m

To Harbor

© AVALON TRAVEL

mainly for services and bus connections, southeast with Ixtapa-Zihuatanejo, Acapulco, and Mexico City, northwest with the Michoacán coast, Manzanillo, and Puerto Vallarta, and north with the upland Michoacán destinations of Uruapan, Pátzcuaro, and Morelia. Most of its services, including banks, bus stations, post office, hospital, hotels, and restaurants, are clustered along north–south Avenida Lázaro Cárdenas, the main ingress boulevard, about three miles (5 km) from its Highway 200 intersection.

## Accommodations and Food

If you decide to stay overnight, nearby hotels offer reasonably priced lodging. The most conveniently located is the **Hotel Delfín** (Av. L. Cárdenas 1633, tel. 753/532-1418), across the street from the Ruta Paraíso bus station. The approximately 20 rooms with baths, in three stories, cluster around an inner pool and patio. Rates run about $25 d, with fans, hot water, TV, and telephone; add air-conditioning for $35.

For more class, go to the high-rise **☾ Hotel Casablanca** (on Bravo, tel. 753/537-3480, 753/537-3481, 753/537-3482, 753/537-3483, or 753/537-3484, fax 753/532-4036), a block east from Avenida Lázaro Cárdenas, visible behind and above Bancomer. It offers about six floors of light and comfortable modern-standard deluxe rooms with panoramic private-balcony views. Downstairs, past the lobby, a restaurant overlooks an inviting rear pool and patio. Rooms cost $48 s, $76 d, with air-conditioning, phones, TV, and parking.

An even fancier hotel option is the executive-class **NH Krystal Express** (Av. Circuito de las Universidades 60, tel. 753/533-2900 or 753/533-2922, toll-free U.S. tel. 888/726-0528 or Can. tel. 866/299-7096, nhlazarocardenas@nh-hotels.com, www.nh-hotels.com) on the west side of the ingress boulevard Avenida Lázaro Cárdenas, at the traffic circle, about a quarter mile before the town center. It offers 120 deluxe rooms for about $150 d, with air-conditioning, telephone, cable TV, continental breakfast, restaurant-bar, exercise gym, and whirlpool tub.

Take a break from the sun beneath the shady streetfront awning of the **Restaurant El Tejado** (8 A.M.–8 P.M. daily, $4–8), on the main street next to Banamex. (You may need to ask the staff to kindly turn the TV off or at least lower the volume.)

For more economical but wholesome country cooking, check out the *fondas* (foodstalls) on side street Constitución de 1814, adjacent to the Ruta Paraíso bus station lot, and on side street Corregidora, the next block north.

## Travel Agent

A competent and conveniently situated travel agency (and potential information source) is **Viajes Reyna Pío** (Av. L. Cárdenas, tel. 753/532-3868 or 753/532-3935, fax 753/532-0723), right across from the Ruta Paraíso bus station and Banamex.

## Money Exchange

Change your money at one of three banks, all with ATMs, clustered nearby. **Banamex** (Av. L. Cárdenas 1646, tel. 753/532-2020, 9 A.M.–4 P.M. Mon.–Fri., 10 A.M.–2 P.M. Sat.). If it's too crowded, try **Bancomer** (Av. L. Cárdenas 1555, tel. 753/532-3888, 9 A.M.–4 P.M. Mon.–Fri., 10 A.M.–2 P.M. Sat.), a block north and across the street; or **Banco Santander Serfín** (Av. L. Cárdenas 1681, tel. 753/532-0032, 9 A.M.–4 P.M. Mon.–Fri., 10 A.M.–2 P.M. Sat.), on the same side half a block farther north.

## Communications

The *correo* (tel. 753/537-2387) is in the middle of the big grassy town plaza; look for it on the left as you arrive at the town center, two long blocks after the big traffic circle.

**Telecomunicaciones,** with telegraph, money orders, telephone, and public fax (753/532-0273), is next door to the post office. For telephone, plenty of public street phones accept widely available Ladatel telephone cards. More expensive, but with long hours, is the computer-assisted long-distance telephone and fax agency **Computel** (Av. L. Cárdenas 1810, tel./fax 753/532-4806, fax 753/532-4807, 7:30 A.M.–10 P.M. daily), next to the Ruta Paraíso bus station at the corner of Constitución de 1814.

Connect to the Internet at the small store **Internet Sin Limite** (tel. 753/532-1480, 9 A.M.–10 P.M. Mon.–Sat.), corner of Javier Mina, across the street and south of Bancomer.

## Health

The **General Hospital** (tel. 753/532-0900, 753/532-0901, 753/532-0902, 753/532-0903, or 753/532-0904), known locally as "Seguro Social," is on the boulevard into town, left side, corner of H. Escuela Naval, a block before the big right-side traffic circle. Alternatively, visit highly recommended **Dr. Gustavo Cejos Pérez** (Melchor Ocampo 475, tel. 753/532-3902). For routine medicines and drugs, go to conveniently situated **Farmacia Pronto** (tel. 753/537-5002, 8 A.M.–10 P.M. daily), a few doors north of the Ruta Paraíso bus station.

## Getting There and Away

By car or RV, the options to and from Lázaro Cárdenas are virtually the same as those for Ixtapa and Zihuatanejo. Simply add or subtract the 50 miles (80 km) or 1.25-hour travel difference between Ixtapa or Zihuatanejo and Lázaro Cárdenas.

By bus, a trio of long-distance bus terminals serves Lázaro Cárdenas travelers. From the Ruta Paraíso (officially, Lineas Unidas del Sur) terminal (Av. L. Cárdenas 1810, tel. 753/532-0262 or 753/537-3868), **Ruta Paraíso** first-class and second-class local-departure buses connect north daily with Apatzingán, Uruapan, Pátzcuaro, and Morelia. Very

frequent local departures also connect northwest along the coast with nearby coastal destinations of La Mira, Playa Azul, and Caleta de Campos. Additionally, several more first- and second-class departures connect northwest with long-distance destinations of Manzanillo and intermediate points. In an adjacent booth inside the station, agents (tel. 753/532-3006) sell tickets for **Parhikuni** luxury-class buses (with a/c waiting lounge), connecting north with Michoacán destinations of Nueva Italia, Uruapan, Pátzcuaro, and Morelia.

Directly across the street, **La Linea** (tel. 753/537-1850) and associated lines maintains a small streetfront station. It offers four types of departures: executive class "Plus," connecting northeast with Guadalajara via Tecomán and Colima; first- and second-class **Sur** buses, connecting north with Uruapan and Zamora and continuing west to Guadalajara; first-class Autovia 2000 buses, connecting north, via Uruapan and Morelia, thence east with Toluca and Mexico City; and second-class Autobuses Sur de Jalisco connecting northwest with Manzanillo and also with Guadalajara, via Colima and Ciudad Guzmán.

The big **Estrella Blanca** terminal (tel. 753/532-1171) is two short blocks away, directly behind the Ruta Paraíso terminal, on Francisco Villa between Constitución de 1814 and Corregidora. From there, one or two daily first-class local departures connect north with Michoacán destinations of Uruapan, Morelia, and Mexico City. Three first-class buses stop, en route southeast to Zihuatanejo, Acapulco, and the Oaxaca coast, and northwest to Manzanillo, Puerto Vallarta, Mazatlán, and the U.S. border. In addition, three Futura luxury-class local departures connect daily with Mexico City.

# GUERRERO UPCOUNTRY

A treasury of surprises await travelers who venture out into Acapulco's pine-tufted sierra hinterland. The discoveries begin in Chilpancingo, Mexico's Home of the Brave, which basks in a banana-belt upland valley, ringed by mighty cloud-tipped mountains.

From Chilpancingo as a base, explore upcountry Acapulco's River Country, and enjoy swimming, kayaking, rafting, and camping beside clear, spring-fed rivers and investigating stalactite-draped limestone caverns.

Continue deeper into the sierra, to Acapulco's renowned Handicraft Country of Chilapa and Olinalá. Select from a treasury of soft palm baskets and sombreros, bright pottery, exotic masks, charmingly rustic furniture, and exquisite lacquerware.

Continue north to Iguala, tropical fruit and grain oasis and both a memorial to Mexican Independence and Shrine to the Flag. Wonder at Iguala's surrealistically large Mexican flag, stroll the shady downtown plazas, visit the gold market, then adventure out on a bonus side trip to a duo of fascinating ancient ruined cities.

And finally, be sure to visit Taxco, the silver-rich colonial jewel of the highlands. After exploring its winding lanes and its museums and baroque monuments, visit Taxco's trio of nearby gems—the monumental limestone Grutas de Cacahuamilpa, the legendary ruined city of Xochicalco, and Ixcateopan, believed to be the final resting place of the heroic "Descending Eagle," Cuauhtémoc, the Aztecs' last emperor.

© BRUCE WHIPPERMAN

# HIGHLIGHTS

◖ **Chilpancingo *Zócalo:*** In Chilpancingo's historic center, enjoy exploring the monuments to Mexico's independence and the Templo de Santa María de la Asunción, where much of this history was actually made (page 168).

◖ **Headwaters of the Río Azul:** It seems a miracle that every minute year-round, and especially on hot, dust-dry May afternoons, thousands of gallons of deliciously pure and cool water, enough to form a whole river, should well up from beneath the ground (page 184).

◖ **Chilapa Sunday Handicrafts Market:** Every Sunday, indigenous folks from all over central Guerrero bring their finest crafts to Chilapa for a day of bargaining and selling (page 189).

◖ **Templo de San Francisco:** Olinalá lacquerware artisans have gone all out to decorate the interior of their town church with their art. The result in the finely detailed traditional floral and animal designs that embellish the altar, the columns, the walls and the ceiling, and more is attractively unique (page 192).

◖ **Hilltop Memorial Flag:** Climax your Iguala visit atop the hillside south of town to witness Mexico's largest flag, weighing a quarter ton and requiring a platoon of men to raise it at sunrise and lower it at sunset each day (page 203).

◖ **Santa Prisca:** First stop around the Taxco *zócalo* should be the celebrated baroque-style church built with the wealth extracted from Taxco's silver mines (page 214).

◖ **Grutas de Cacahuamilpa:** Few, if any, cave systems in the world are as grand, lovely, and easily accessible as the Grutas de Cacahuamilpa (page 228).

◖ **Xochicalco:** Besides the site's world-class museum, be sure to visit the Pyramid of Quetzalcoatl, so named by modern-day archaeologists for its powerful stylized bas-relief design of Quetzalcoatl, Mexico's renowned and feared Plumed Serpent (page 228).

LOOK FOR ◖ TO FIND RECOMMENDED SIGHTS, ACTIVITIES, DINING, AND LODGING.

## PLANNING YOUR TIME

A minimum of a week would be needed to enjoy the Guerrero Upcountry highlights; visitors with more leisure could easily stretch this out to a month. If, however, you only have three or four days, you should probably enjoy them all in and around Taxco, Mexico's silver capital. Spend a day strolling the winding hillside lanes, visiting the best of the best silver jewelry shops, the Museo Guillermo Spratling, the incomparably baroque **Santa Prisca** church, and the fascinating indigenous market. The next day, ride the stunningly scary *teleférico* (cableway) for a hike, golf, or tennis and lunch or a picnic at mountaintop Hotel Monte Taxco. On a subsequent day or days, make certain to visit the spectacular limestone **Grutas de Cacahuamilpa** (Caves of Cacahuamilpa) and, if you go early enough, continue by tour or car to the storied ruined city, now world-class museum and archaeological site, of **Xochicalco.**

With three or four days more, you could add Guerrero Upcountry's River and Handicrafts Country to your itinerary. The first day, from Acapulco, go by tour, bus, or car for about 30 miles (48 km) for a rafting adventure on the Río Papagayo. Continue north for an overnight in either Chilpancingo or more conveniently, Colotlipa. The next day, head out for an adventure tour through the fascinatingly exquisite limestone Grutas de Juxtlahuaca and in the afternoon, continue to the nearby Río Azul for swimming, inner-tubing, and plenty of general frolicking in the cool, crystal-blue water. Continue back to Chilpancingo for overnight.

Head out early the next day (which must be a Sunday) and bargain for treasures at the fascinating **Chilapa Sunday Handicrafts Market.** Continue in the afternoon or the next day to the remote mountain town of Olinalá and spend at least an afternoon visiting home factory shops filled with the town's renowned glistening lacquerware.

With a day or two more, you could add Iguala, north of Chilpancingo and south of Taxco, to your itinerary. En route from Chilpancingo, you might include a three-hour side trip to an ancient lost city, now La Organera Xochipala Archaeological Zone. In the afternoon, in Iguala, a virtual shrine to the Mexican national flag, be sure to stroll around the three pleasantly shady downtown central plazas, and visit the **Museo y Santuario a la Bandera.** An hour before sunset, ride a taxi or *colectivo* to the hillside south of town to witness what must be Mexico's (if not the world's) most awesomely large national flag, powerfully rumbling and snapping, with mini–sonic booms, in the breeze.

© BRUCE WHIPPERMAN

Santa Prisca church was built with the silver fortune extracted from Taxco's mines.

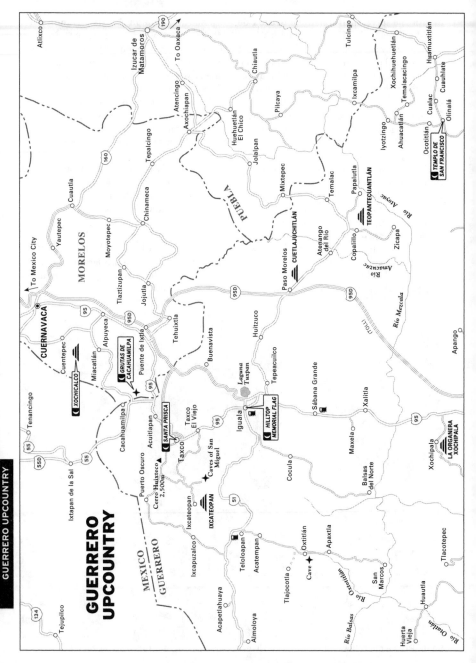

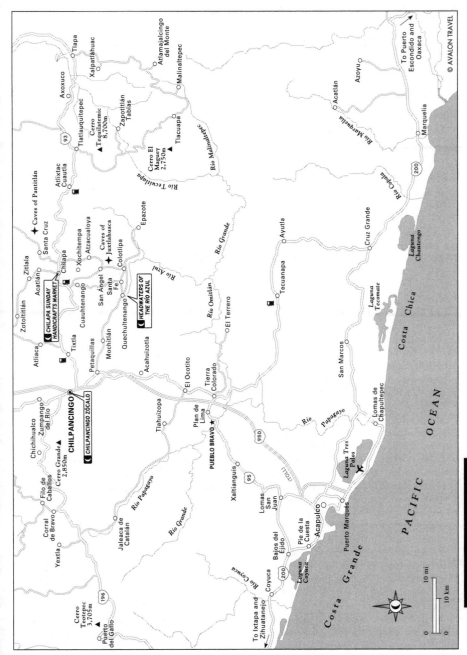

© AVALON TRAVEL

GUERRERO UPCOUNTRY

# Chilpancingo

The formal name of the Guerrero state capital, Chilpancingo de los Bravo (Chilpancingo of the Brave), reflects Mexico's kinship with the United States, "The Home of the Free and Land of the Brave." Historically, in both cases, "the Brave" was more than a mere patriotic turn of phrase. Like the Continental Congress that began meeting in Philadelphia in 1774, the members of the 1813 revolutionary Congress of Anahuac in Chilpancingo did so at the constant risk of their lives.

Chilpancingo, besides being the Guerrero state capital and the cradle of Mexican liberty, is also closely associated with Vicente Guerrero, the Mexican hero most comparable to the United States' George Washington. Probably more than any other, Guerrero, Mexico's second president, battled to win Mexico's 1821 independence and continued the struggle to ensure Mexico's 1824 constitution and resulting republican government.

Nevertheless, it's still priest-general José María Morelos who holds the hearts of Mexicans, eight generations after his death. It was Morelos who convened Mexico's first revolutionary legislature, the Congress of Anahuac, in Chilpancingo on September 14, 1813.

Morelos had earlier expressed his libertarian ideas, in the celebrated Sentimientos de la Nación, which, with as much force as the ideas of Thomas Jefferson a generation earlier, gave direction to the Congress of Anahuac's work. On November 6, 1813, the Congress declared a manifesto of principles, which notably included the idea that "sovereignty proceeds immediately from the people" and that Mexico should therefore "be free and independent."

It's interesting to note that the Mexican Act of Independence, 37 years after the American Declaration of Independence, took freedom a step farther. Among its principles, the Congress of Anahuac declared that "slavery be prohibited forever," a principle that required 52 more years and a terrible civil war to be established in the United States.

## ORIENTATION

Judging from its narrow downtown streets, Chilpancingo (pop. 200,000, elev. 4,000 feet, 1,300 meters) is a little town that grew big. Traveling the 62 miles (100 km) by *cuota* (toll) expressway from Acapulco (or 83 miles, 133 km by old Highway 95), arrivees must make an effort not to miss the downtown. Both first-class buses and the south–north thruway Avenida Vicente Guerrero bypass the town center completely.

Buses deposit passengers at the Camionera Central (a mile north of the central plaza; taxi or ride a *colectivo* from there).

Drivers, watch carefully for turnoff signs. If you're fortunate, you'll get on to main south-end ingress Avenida Lázaro Cárdenas, which begins at the Ciudad Universitaria right turnoff. About half a mile (0.8 km) from the turnoff, bear right at a big traffic circle and follow the boulevard, which becomes Bulevar Juan Álvarez and passes, via a one-block tunnel, beneath the Chilpancingo *zócalo*.

## SIGHTS
### ◖ Chilpancingo *Zócalo*

Traffic having been diverted from it and the surrounding streets, the Chilpancingo *zócalo* (central plaza) makes an enjoyable strolling ground. The best vantage point is the front steps of the tall Guerrero **Biblioteca Del Estado** (formerly the Palacio de Gobierno, statehouse). Face (or imagine you're facing) the plaza, officially the "Plaza of the First Congress of Anahuac," and you're looking east. North is on your left, south on your right. East across the plaza rises the classical facade of the Museo Regional de Chilpancingo, and to the left of that, the twin white bell towers of the Templo de Santa María de la Asunción, where the Act of Independence from Spain was declared on November 6, 1813.

Note the noble gilded statue of **José María Morelos,** at the plaza's northeast corner, below and in front of the church. It memorializes

statue of José María Morelos in front of the Templo de Santa María, where Mexican independence was declared

his Sentimientos de la Nación, with the pivotal pronouncement that "No nation has the right to prevent another from the free use of its sovereignty."

At the adjacent, southeast plaza corner, below and in front of the museum, see the grand plaque, placed on September 13, 1985, that honors the 175th anniversary of the opening of the Congress of Anahuac. Its inscription, quoting Morelos, commemorates the end of the long period of Spanish dominion from August 12, 1521, until September 14, 1813: "On that day the chains of our servitude to Mexico-Tenochtitlán were broken forever in the brave town of Chilpancingo."

Through art, antiques, artifacts, and displays, the **Museo Regional de Chilpancingo** (tel. 747/472-8088, 9 a.m.–6 p.m. Tues.–Sun., $2) illustrates Guerrero geology, flora, fauna, archaeology, history, and folkways. A major attraction is the now-faded but epic historical mural by Roberto Cueva del Río and Luis Arenal that wraps around the entire inner patio. The mural begins at the patio's northeast

(across the patio, left as you enter) corner and continues clockwise. The first panel shows the infant future emperor Cuauhtémoc (notice his birth sign, the descending eagle above the infant). Continue to the panel of the encounter of Cuauhtémoc with Cortés, then to the first corner, where another panel depicts the burial of the remains of Cuauhtémoc in Ixcateopan, near Taxco. Farther on, panels represent the independence heroes Morelos, Guerrero, and Hermenegildo Galeana (see sidebars *José María Morelos: Champion of Mexican Independence* and *Vicente Guerrero: Father of the Mexican Republic* in this chapter and *Hermenegildo Galeana: Gentleman Rebel* in the *Costa Grande* chapter), the Revolution of 1910, and, finally, the latter-day development of Guerrero state.

Step next door to the church, Templo de Santa María de la Asunción, the site revered in Mexico, not unlike Independence Hall in Philadelphia, as the place where the Congress of Anahuac formally declared Mexico's independence, on November 6, 1813. Note the polished hand-carved church doors, with reliefs

© BRUCE WHIPPERMAN

GUERRERO UPCOUNTRY

# CHILPANCINGO

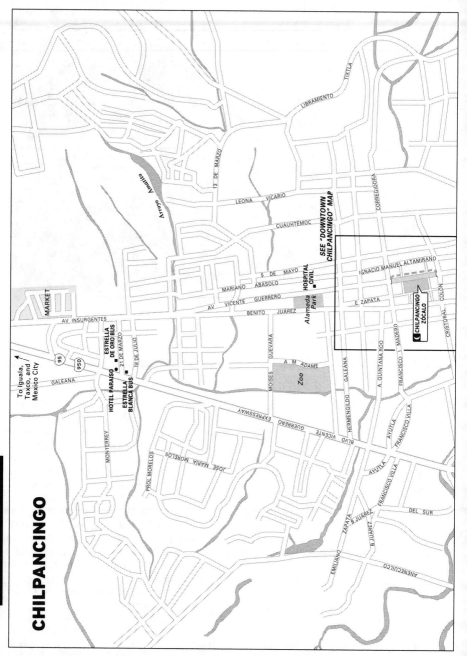

TIXTLA

LIBRAMIENTO

13 DE MARZO

Arroyo Amatillo

LEONA VICARIO

CORREGIDORA

CUAUHTÉMOC

SEE "DOWNTOWN CHILPANCINGO" MAP

5 DE MAYO

IGNACIO MANUEL ALTAMIRANO

MARIANO ABASOLO

HOSPITAL CIVIL

E. ZAPATA

AV. VICENTE GUERRERO

BENITO JUÁREZ

Alameda Park

CHILPANCINGO ZÓCALO

COLÓN

CRISTÓBAL

MARKET

AV. INSURGENTES

ESTRELLA DE ORO BUS

GUEVARA

A. QUINTANA ROO

GALEANA

HERMENGILDO

FRANCISCO I. MADERO

95

95D

21 DE MARZO

A M ADAME

Zoo

AYUTLA

HOTEL PARAÍSO

12 DE JULIO

To Iguala, Taxco, and Mexico City

GALEANA

ESTRELLA BLANCA BUS

FRANCISCO VILLA

MONTERREY

EXPRESSWAY

BLVD VICENTE GUERRERO

AYUTLA

DEL SUR

PROL MORELOS

JOSE MARIA MORELOS

FRANCISCO VILLA

ZAPATA

B. JUÁREZ

EMILIANO

B. JUÁREZ

ANENECUILCO

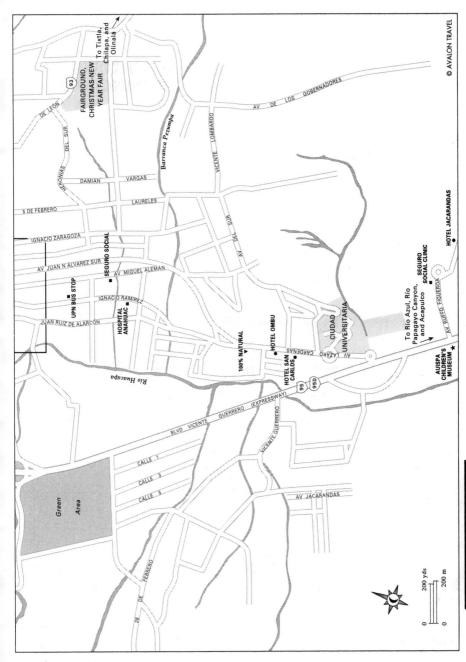

© AVALON TRAVEL

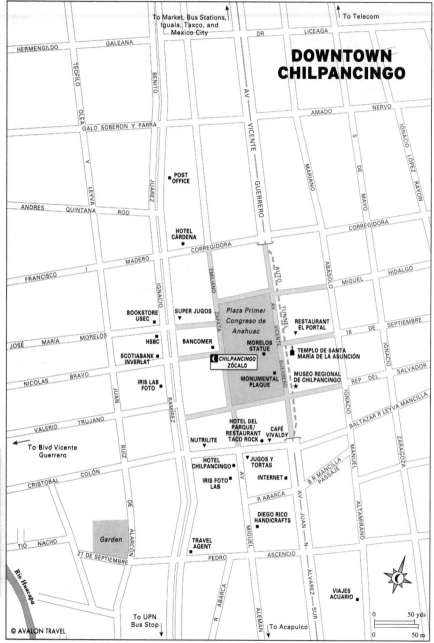

# DOWNTOWN CHILPANCINGO

To Market, Bus Stations, Iguala, Taxco, and Mexico City

To Telecom

HERMENGILDO
GALEANA
TEOFILO
OLEA
GALO SOBERON Y PARRA
Y
LEYVA
ANDRES
QUINTANA
ROO
FRANCISCO
I
MADERO
JOSÉ MARÍA MORELOS
NICOLAS BRAVO
VALERIO TRUJANO
To Blvd Vicente Guerrero
CRISTOBAL COLÓN
TIO NACHO
27 DE SEPTIEMBRE

DR LICEAGA
AV VICENTE GUERRERO
AMADO
NERVO
MARIANO
5 DE MAYO
IGNACIO LOPEZ RAYON
CORREGIDORA
CORREGIDORA
EMILIANO ZAPATA
AUTO TUNEL AV VICENTE
ABASOLO
MIGUEL
HIDALGO
16 DE SEPTIEMBRE
IGNACIO
SALVADOR
REP DEL
BALTAZAR R LEYVA MANCILLA
ZARAGOZA
B R MANCILLA PASSAJE
MANUEL
ALTAMIRANO
AV JUAN N.
ASCENCIO
ALVAREZ SUR
R ABARCA
ALEMAN

POST OFFICE

HOTEL CARDENA

BOOKSTORE USEC
SUPER JUGOS
Plaza Primer Congreso de Anahuac
RESTAURANT EL PORTAL
HSBC
BANCOMER
MORELOS STATUE
TEMPLO DE SANTA MARÍA DE LA ASUNCIÓN
SCOTIABANK INVERLAT
CHILPANCINGO ZÓCALO
IRIS LAB FOTO
MONUMENTAL PLAQUE
MUSEO REGIONAL DE CHILPANCINGO

IGNACIO
MADERO
RAMIREZ
JUAN
RUIZ
DE
ALARCÓN
PEDRO

HOTEL DEL PARQUE/ RESTAURANT TACO ROCK
CAFÉ VIVALDY
NUTRILITE
HOTEL CHILPANCINGO
JUGOS Y TORTAS
IRIS FOTO LAB
INTERNET
R ABARCA
DIEGO RICO HANDICRAFTS
Garden
TRAVEL AGENT
VIAJES ACUARIO

To UPN Bus Stop

To Acapulco

Río Huacapa

© AVALON TRAVEL

0        50 yds
0        50 m

of Mexico's independence heroes: Morelos, first president Nicolás Bravo, Guerrero, and the magnificent eagle-and-serpent national symbol.

## Beyond Downtown

Children will most certainly enjoy the small Chilpancingo **zoo** (tel. 747/472-5906, 9 A.M.–5:30 P.M. Tues.–Sun., $2) near the corner of Moises Guevara and Arturo M. Adame, about half a mile northeast of the *zócalo*. The entrance is on the north side of a large park, with plenty of room to run around and spread a picnic.

Another good place for kids is the **Museo La Avispa** (tel. 747/471-2422 or 747/471-3149, info@museolaavispa.org, www.museolaavispa .org, 9 A.M.–3 P.M. Mon.–Fri., 10 A.M.–6 P.M. Sat.–Sun., closed major holidays, $2) south of town, a block west of the corner of Bulevar Vicente Guerrero and Avenida Rulfo Figueroa. The museum's mission is to introduce technology with a host of hands-on, child-friendly (ages 4–12) activities.

## ACCOMMODATIONS

Considering its many visitors on government or commercial business, Chilpancingo has relatively few hotels. Be certain to reserve at least a day (better a week) in advance. Some, but not all, Chilpancingo hotels accept credit cards. All hotel rates fall in the under-$50 category. Most are compact, business-style hotels, with one exception: the restful, resort-style but moderately priced Hotel Jacarandas, in the southern suburb, convenient for drivers.

By location, starting downtown, the best city-center lodging choice is the busy business-style ◖ **Hotel del Parque** (Colón 5, tel. 747/472-3491 or 747/472-1364, fax 747/472-2547, alarcoma@prodigy.net.mx, $39 s, $49 d), a block south of the *zócalo*. Its 28 very clean rooms rise in four floors (but with no elevator) around a small inner lobby-patio. Inside, the rooms are comfortable, modern semideluxe, with hot-water shower baths, TV, phone, fans, and a good restaurant downstairs, but no pool. Parking nearby is extra, about $5.

In the same bustling south-of-*zócalo* neighborhood, but more economical, is the skillfully managed **Hotel Chilpancingo** (Miguel Alemán 8, tel./fax 747/472-2446). The 40 clean, invitingly decorated, compactly arranged rooms connected by a maze of blue-tiled passageways offer many options. They range from the most basic and dark, to spacious light rooms with one to three double beds. The cheapest begin at about $20 d, and range upwards to about $55 for up to six people. All include private shower baths, carpet, flowery bedspreads and comfortable mattresses, fans, some TV, some air-conditioning, and credit cards accepted.

Even more downscale but still recommendable is the homey **Hotel Cárdena** (Madero 13, tel. 747/471-6153), a block north of the *zócalo*. Rooms in this converted old family home open onto an interior patio with chairs and shade umbrellas for relaxing. The plain but clean enough (I saw only one cockroach, and it was dying) bare-bulb rooms rent for about 16 s, $22 d, and $26 t, with private hot-water shower baths and café.

Outside of the immediate downtown, visitors have a number of decent hotel choices. About a mile south of the *zócalo*, check out the newish **Hotel Ombu** (Av. L. Cárdenas 28, tel. 747/472-5382 or 747/494-7910, fax 747/474-9911, hotelombu@hotmail.com). Above the small lobby, three floors of 33 walk-up rooms rise around a spartan-chic inner atrium. Rooms themselves are simply but attractively decorated in tile, natural wood, and earth-tone bedspreads and curtains. Tariffs run about $35 s, $40 d for a smallish double-bed room and $48 d, $52 t in a larger room with two double beds. All rooms come with good cable TV, phone, portable fan available, restaurant downstairs, and parking in the basement.

Farther south, about 1.5 miles (2.5 km) south of the town center, is Chilpancingo's best: the government resort-style ◖ **Hotel Jacarandas** (Av. Jacarandas, tel. 747/472-4444, fax 747/472-4987). Guests enjoy a choice of about 50 rooms in a big, curving white jacaranda-decorated hillside block. Inside, rooms are clean, spacious, light, comfortable, and open to airy private balconies overlooking a big blue pool-patio and tropical garden. For such amenities, rates run a reasonable $40 s, $49 d, $63 t, with cable TV, fan, phone, private hot-water shower baths, good restaurant, parking, and credit cards accepted. Reserve early; this place is often booked completely by conferences.

On the other hand, car travelers interested in an immaculate, well-managed lodging might like the **Parador del Marqués** (Km 276, Carretera Mexico–Acapulco, tel. 747/472-9532 or 747/472-6773, info@parador delmarques.com, www.paradordelmarques .com) at the far southern country edge of town. The hotel's location, about two miles (3 km) south of the town center, makes it likely to have a room when no other hotel in town does. The 20-odd rooms, in an inviting leafy garden, are immaculate and impeccably maintained in traditional Mexican tile, stucco, and

## JOSÉ MARÍA MORELOS: CHAMPION OF MEXICAN INDEPENDENCE

As did his famous predecessor, George Washington, Mexican Independence general José María Morelos y Pavón convened his nation's first constitutional convention. The First Congress of Anahuac, an assemblage of leaders from all over Mexico, convened in Chilpancingo on September 14, 1813. It was virtually three years to the day after martyr-priest Miguel Hidalgo had ignited revolution from the balcony in Dolores, Guanajuato. Later, Morelos remembered: "On that day the chains of our servitude to Mexico-Tenochtitlán (Mexico City) were broken forever."

Those early days of revolution were heady times for a poor priest of such obscure origin. José María Morelos y Pavón was born in Valladolid (now Morelia, named in his honor), Michoacán, on September 30, 1765. Among experts, opinion is divided on Morelos's possible African-Mexican ancestry. Most historians go along with the major evidence: Morelos's swarthy, dark-eyed complexion and the well-known old legal document certifying that one of his grandmothers was a *"mujer libre,"* a standard legal phrase for a free, nonslave woman of African descent.

Young José no doubt was a devout Catholic. Early on, he wanted to study for the priesthood. While waiting to be admitted to seminary, he supported himself by working as a mule driver until he was admitted to the Valladolid Colegio San Nicolas in the mid-1780s.

While a student, José came under the influence of Father Miguel Hidalgo, who was the rector at San Nicolas. Hidalgo was not the usual role model for a budding acolyte. He was ambitious and much more interested in politics than in his priestly duties. Hidalgo's inner circle, which quickly included Morelos, debated the ideas of the French Enlightenment philosophers Jean-Jacques Rousseau (*The Social Contract*) and Count Montesquieu (*The Spirit of the Laws*), who had strongly influenced the founding fathers of the brand-new United States of America.

Hidalgo, always seeking advancement, got an assignment to a rich Guanajuato parish, while José went west and served in a poor isolated corner of Michoacán.

After igniting revolution on September 15, 1810, Hidalgo led his raggedy peasant army, which grew rapidly to about 100,000 at its peak. Inspired, Morelos offered his services to Hidalgo, who told him to go south, raise an army, and capture Acapulco and the riches of the Manila galleon.

Morelos returned to his Michoacán homeland, raised a scruffy platoon of volunteers, and marched toward the coast. Along the way, Morelos recruited droves of volunteers, many of them African Mexican. They passed Zacatula and followed the coast east to Acapulco, arriving as an eager but ill-equipped 3,000-man guerrilla brigade.

In Acapulco, the only point of resistance

brick decor. Choose from one king-size bed or two doubles. Rates run about $35 s or d in one bed; $49 d, t, or q in two beds, with cable TV, phone, parking, and good breakfast/lunch restaurant and pool.

On the north side of town, bus or car travelers might appreciate the convenience of the newish **Hotel Paradise Inn** (Bulevar Vicente Guerrero, Esquina 21 de Marzo, tel. 474/471-1122 or 474/472-8863, fax 474/471-4691, www.paradiseinn.com.mx) on thruway Bulevar Vicente Guerrero, across from the bus station. Find it about a mile north of the *zócalo,* at the corner of 21 de Marzo. The 100-odd rooms enclose an inner parking-patio. Inside, they're comfortable and immaculate, with all-white semi-deluxe decor and hot-water shower baths. Rooms begin at about $45 d in one bed, $55 in two beds, with cable TV, phone, exercise gym, business center, restaurant/bar, breakfast included, air-conditioning, and parking.

---

(albeit stiff resistance) was the old Fuerte San Diego, where Morelos, after weeks of besieging the fort, divided his force. He left half surrounding the fort and led the remainder north to Chilpancingo, which he captured with the help of Hermenegildo Galeana and Nicolas Bravo.

Next, Morelos marched west, capturing Chilapa. Then, with a buoyantly robust force of 4,000, he continued north to Cuautla, in the present state of Morelos. Although besieged for 73 days by a superior royalist division, Morelos broke out with most of his men and marched southeast, where he captured Oaxaca, the prize of the south.

At Oaxaca, his radical egalitarian views, source of his popularity with his troops, surfaced:

*We must eliminate the outdated classifications separating us into black, mulatto, mestizo, and criollo...and call ourselves Americans for our origin as do the English, the French, and that other European country that is oppressing us.*

The time was mid-1813, and Morelos was riding his crest of success. At 48, he was at his prime, cutting a dashing figure, topped by a colorful bandanna that wrapped his balding head. Napoleon Bonaparte is said to have paid Morelos the ultimate compliment: "With three such men as José Morelos, I could conquer the world."

Although a priest, Morelos, like his mentor Miguel Hidalgo, rejected sexual abstinence. He fathered several children by his indigenous common-law wife, Brigida Almonte, of Necupétaro, Michoacán.

One of Morelos's sons, Juan Almonte, born in 1803, gained fame, paradoxically, working for the Mexican conservative cause. He served as President Bustamante's Minister of War during the 1830s, under General Santa Anna at the Alamo in Texas, later as ambassador to the United States and Britain, and finally in Emperor Maximilian's cabinet during the 1860s.

Morelos's signal achievement was the Congress of Anahuac, Mexico's first constitutional convention, which Morelos convened in Chilpancingo on September 14, 1813. Although subsequently driven from Chilpancingo by royalist forces, the Congress reconvened in Apatzingan, Michoacán, where it promulgated Mexico's first constitution on October 22, 1814.

Continually pressed by royalist troops, Morelos fought desperately for the remainder of his days protecting the Congress, which amounted to Mexico's first republican government. Finally, royalist troops captured him and spirited him to Mexico City on November 22, 1815. After a month-long trial during which Morelos argued eloquently for the justice of the *insurgente* cause, he was defrocked and taken to the city of San Cristóbal Ecatepec, where he was executed for treason by firing squad on December 27, 1815.

## FOOD

For snacks, try one of the many very clean streetfront *jugerías* and *loncherías* around the *zócalo*. For example, try **Jugos y Tortas** on Alemán, two blocks south of the plaza, at the corner of Colón. Alternatively, a few blocks north on the *zócalo*'s northwest side, an excellent all-around choice is **Super Jugos,** with plenty of fresh *aguas,* juices, and hot *tortas* and *hamburguesas* (about $2).

As for restaurants, downtown's healthiest choice is welcoming **Nutrilite** (Colón 11, tel. 747/494-1932, 7 A.M.–8 P.M. Mon.–Fri., 8 A.M.–6 P.M. Sat., $2–3), a block south of the *zócalo,* a few doors west of the corner of Alemán. Here, you can choose from a long list of breakfasts (whole wheat pancakes, eggs any style, fruit plate), or afternoon four-course *comida corrida* (with entrées such as stuffed cactus leaves or meatballs in chipotle sauce), plus a delicious harvest of fruit drinks.

A few more sit-down restaurants provide good food in restful settings near the plaza. High marks go to refined **Restaurant El Portal** (tel. 747/472-4668, 8:30 A.M.–10 P.M. daily, $3–8) just off the *zócalo,* on the north side of the church, at the corner of Guerrero and Hidalgo. With open-air seating in view of the dramatic bust of Morelos across the street, El Portal is ideal for a relaxing snack or meal all day. In addition to a very recognizable menu of professionally prepared and served breakfasts, salads, soups, pastas, poultry, and meats, it offers a bountiful three-course *comida corrida* 1–5 P.M. daily.

The **Restaurant Taco Rock** (Colón 5, tel. 747/472-3012, 8 A.M.–midnight daily, $5–10) in the Hotel del Parque, around the block south of the *zócalo,* is a very popular breakfast and lunch stop for business and professional people. At night it becomes a TV bar and nightclub, featuring Latin "taco rock" music. Entrées from a long Mexican-style coffee-shop menu are professionally prepared and presented.

Right next to Taco Rock is the contrastingly traditional and refined class-act **Café Vivaldy** (Colón 3, tel. 747/472-2767, 8:30 A.M.–10 P.M. Mon.–Sat., $3–8), which serves up a deliciously unusual menu of breakfasts, salads, Mexican plates, meats, and baguette sandwiches, plus a dozen gourmet coffees. For dessert, sample one of their exquisite cakes (such as chocolate with pecans or strawberry cheesecake), all savored with a recording of Vivaldi's *Four Seasons* singing lightly in the background.

Although it's not strictly vegetarian or macrobiotic, the menu of **100% Natural** (Av. L. Cárdenas 12, tel. 747/472-5457, 9 A.M.–9 P.M. daily, $3–8), half a mile south of downtown, features plenty of healthy and tasty food. Choose from fruits and fruit *licuados,* granola, pancakes, eggs, yogurt, avocado, cheese, soya and meat burgers, french fries, and much more, in many styles, from scrumptious sandwiches to hearty entrée plates. Service, by a dedicated squad of twentysomethings in white, beneath an open-air *palapa,* is exemplary.

## EVENTS

Chilpancingo people unwind during the big year-end fair, **Feria de San Mateo, la Navidad, y el Año Nuevo,** December 24–January 8. The festivities kick off with the *teopancolaquio,* a ritual honoring the birth of God on Earth. Offerings include riots of flowers and regional dances, including Los Tlacoloteros, Pescados (Fish), Diablos (Devils), and Manueles. Concurrent with all this is a grand commercial and agricultural fair, bullfights, carnival, fireworks, cockfights, and plenty of hearty Guerrero country food.

In nearby Tixtla (see *Excursions from Chilpancingo*), folks whoop it up during a couple of unique local fiestas. They celebrate the birthday of their most famous native son, Vicente Guerrero, on August 9, with a feast of cultural events, including music and favorite regional dances. Three weeks later, September 1–8, the Tixtla plaza is awash with celebrants for the **Fiesta de la Natividad de María.** Indigenous folks flood into town for the parade of floats, the carnival, fireworks, *jaripeo* bull roping and riding, and favorite traditional dances Los Manueles, Moros, Diablos, Tigres, and Tlacololeros. This is probably the most

# DANCE OF
# LOS TLACOLOLEROS

The noise and excitement of the Chilpancingo regional dance Los Tlacololeros remains a favorite of campesinos, who crowd in at fiesta time. The name refers to *tlacolol*, the Aztec word meaning "preparing the fields for planting" by the age-old slash-and-burn method, still widely used in the Sierra Madre backcountry.

The compelling drama centers on the whips, which the hilariously masked cotton-and-sombrero-clothed men snap loudly on each others' padded arms, supposedly to imitate the crackle of the burning brush fire. In one version of the dance a she-dog called *la maravilla* makes a madcap chase after a *tigre* that threatens the campesinos.

All of a sudden, without warning, the fire mysteriously goes out while the dumbfounded dancers flail each other with increased desperation, trying frantically to find the culprit for the fire's failure. Soon, however, all is well that ends well as the loud rattling of chains simulates the fire's return, driving the *tigre* from the campesinos' midst.

colorful time all year to visit the Tixtla Sunday market, known for its loads of for-sale native handicrafts.

## SHOPPING

The best supermarket/department store in town is **Comercial Mexicana** (Calle Baltazar Leyva, tel. 747/472-6355, 8 A.M.–10 P.M. daily), recognizable by the tall orange-and-white pelican emblem-sign, by thruway Bulevar Vicente Guerrero (and McDonald's), about a mile north of downtown.

Although a few vendors sell handicrafts in the municipal market on Insurgentes, corner of Gardenias, about 1.5 miles north of the *zócalo*, the best source is the big Sunday *tianguis* (native market) in Tixtla.

One downtown store, however, does offer handicrafts. A couple blocks south of the plaza,

check out **Artesanías Michoacán** (Ramírez 17B, 9 A.M.–8 P.M. Mon.–Sat.) of grandfatherly Diego Rico. Although he does hail from the state of Michoacán, Diego offers curios from all over Mexico, made mostly of wood, leather, and pottery. They include a treasury of precious doodads, such as whirling *maltracas* noisemakers, sturdy huaraches, guitars both large and small, wriggling snakes, and bright lacquerware boxes.

## INFORMATION AND SERVICES
### Banks

A number of bank branches, all with ATMs, cluster around the downtown plaza. The best bet is long-hours **HSBC** (Juárez 2, tel. 747/471-2636, 8 A.M.–7 P.M. Mon.–Sat.), a block north and a block west of the plaza's northwest corner. Alternatively, go to **Bancomer** (tel. 747/472-2020, 8:30 A.M.–4 P.M. Mon.–Fri.), on the plaza's west side, corner of Bravo; or **Scotiabank Inverlat** (9 A.M.–5 P.M. Mon.–Fri.), one block west of the plaza at the corner of Bravo and Juárez.

### Communications

Buy stamps and mail letters at the downtown *correo* (Vicente Guerrero 215, tel. 747/477-2275, 8 A.M.–6 P.M. Mon.–Fri.), a block and a half north of the *zócalo*'s northeast corner.

If you need to make a phone call, buy a widely available Ladatel card and use one of the many street phones scattered around the downtown.

Internet connections are commonly available in Chilpancingo. For example, try the small Internet store **Centrinet** (tel. 747/471-6583, 9 A.M.–9 P.M. daily), on the east side of Álvarez between Colón and Abarca, a block and a half south of the *zócalo*'s southeast corner.

### Health and Emergencies

Chilpancingo has up-to-date medical facilities. If you get sick, follow your hotel's recommendation. Otherwise, hail a taxi to whisk you to the very highly recommended private **Hospital Anahuac** (on Ignacio Ramírez, tel. 747/472-9505), about seven blocks south of the downtown *zócalo*. Alternatively, go to the 24-hour public **Centro de Salud** (Vicente Guerrero 45, tel. 747/474-7077), about 4 blocks north of the downtown *zócalo*, east side of the street. For fire emergencies, call the *bomberos* (tel. 474/472-2280). For police, call the *policía municipal* at emergency number 066.

## Photography

For film and photo supplies and services, go to **Iris Lab** (tel. 747/472-6067, 9 A.M.–3 P.M. and 5–9 P.M. Mon.–Sat.), a block west of the plaza, on the west side of Ramírez between Trujano and Bravo. They stock many point-and-shoot cameras, both film and digital; camcorders; batteries; and accessories. They also develop and print color and black-and-white, and provide many digital services.

## Bookstore

The scarcity of printed matter in Chilpancingo makes the collection of the mostly Spanish-language bookstore **Librería de la U.S.E.C.** (tel. 747/472-3656, 9 A.M.–9 P.M. Mon.–Sat.), at the corner of Juárez and Morelos, one block west of the plaza, all the more precious. Even if you don't buy anything, perusing the piles of many hundreds of volumes, covering myriad subjects from Don Quixote and the history of handicrafts to Faust and French-Spanish dictionaries, can provide a relaxing diversion for book lovers.

## GETTING THERE AND AWAY
### By Bus

The main long-distance bus station, **Estrella Blanca,** is on side street 21 de Marzo, between thruway Vicente Guerrero and the municipal market, about 1.5 miles north of downtown.

Out front, a platoon of taxis, local buses, and *colectivos* ferry passengers to dozens of nearby destinations. Ladatel card-operated street telephones are available for calls.

Inside the smallish terminal, agents (tel. 474/472-0680) sell long-distance bus tickets. Both first- and second-class direct departures (including intermediate points) connect with Mexico City, Morelia, Guadalajara, Acapulco, Zihuatanejo, Puerto Vallarta, Iguala, Chilapa, Olinalá, Tlapa de Comonfort, Taxco, and the U.S. border at Nogales and Tijuana.

Outside, a few stands sell snacks, drinks, tacos, and sandwiches. For fresh items, stock up at the market, a block uphill.

Across the street, first-class **Estrella de Oro** (tel. 747/472-2130) buses connect north and south with Acapulco, Iguala, Taxco, and Mexico City.

### By Car

Good roads make connections with Chilpancingo easy. To or from Acapulco, follow the *cuota* (toll) expressway a quick 62 miles (100 km, toll a steep $20) in about an hour and a quarter. *Libre* (toll-free) Highway 95 (83 miles, 133 km) connects with Acapulco in about twice the time, with much more than twice the hazard and wear and tear.

In the opposite direction, the *cuota* expressway connects Chilpancingo with Mexico City in 148 miles (239 km, auto toll about $30 but worth it) in about 3.5 hours. Make sure you arrive in Mexico City on a permitted day. (See sidebar *Mexico City Driving Restrictions* in the *Essentials* chapter.) The old Highway 95 connection, via Iguala and Taxco, with Mexico City, adds at least two hours to this under the best of conditions.

Connect north with Iguala in 67 miles (108 km, two hours), via old Highway 95 *libre* (that forks west from the toll expressway at the north edge of Chilpancingo). From Iguala, continue to Taxco in another 24 miles (38 km, one hour), for a total of 91 miles (145 km) and three hours.

For details on the east–west connection with Chilapa, Olinalá, and Tlapa de Comonfort, see *Getting There and Away* for both Chilapa and Olinalá in the *Handicrafts Country* section of this chapter.

## EXCURSIONS FROM CHILPANCINGO

Roads fan out from Chilpancingo to a number of spots well worth visiting. These include

Tixtla de Guerrero, the historic and colorful birthplace of Vicente Guerrero; the fascinatingly exotic La Organera Xochipala Archaeological Zone; the luscious crystal springs of the Río Azul, the spectacular Grutas de Juxtlahuaca limestone caverns, and camping, rafting and kayaking adventures in the great outdoors of the Río Papagayo and canyon.

## Tixtla de Guerrero

The trip to Tixtla (pop. 20,000) is part of the fun of going there. Although it's only eight miles (12 km), Tixtla is over a mountain, whose summit has refreshing breezes and a beautiful view. The first glimpse of Tixtla is its green patchwork of orchards and fields framed by high, pine-tufted ridges.

The place to arrive is the town-center *zócalo.* Bus riders, get off at the adjacent Tixtla market, at the end of the line. Drivers, turn left on to the main north–south town street, several blocks after entering the town. Let the church's bell tower be your guide to the central *zócalo.*

The *zócalo* focuses around the **Monument to Vicente Guerrero,** a bronze likeness of the great general in a heroic cape.

Next, head across the street, south from the *zócalo,* to the house where Vicente Guerrero lived and directed Mexico's rebellion against Spain. Although it has been the Tixtla *presidencia municipal* since 1978, the house is a virtual shrine to Vicente Guerrero, not unlike Mount Vernon is for George Washington. The house's main attraction is a mural by Jaime A. Gómez de Payan that dramatically portrays major events and players in Mexican history. Moving clockwise: *insurgente* general Ignacio M. Altamirano (also born in Tixtla) with his hand on a jaguar's head; Benito Juárez surrounded by his contemporaries; José María Morelos passing the flame of liberty to Vicente Guerrero, who completes the struggle for independence; Emperor Cuauhtémoc, tortured for resisting Cortés.

From the *zócalo,* head west (away from the church) to an open ceremonial *zócalo,* fringed by market stalls and with a line of busts of eight of Tixtla's favorite sons and daughters.

All of the busts are looking west to the adjacent monument, dedicated jointly to Vicente Guerrero and Ignacio M. Altamirano. A large tablet records the words of Tixtla's most famous sons, which translate thus:

> Before friendship, stands the homeland! Before sentiment, stands the idea! Before compassion, stands justice!
>
> – Ignacio M. Altamirano
>
> Your voice, father, is sacred to me; But the voice of my homeland comes first.
>
> – Vicente Guerrero

From the Guerrero-Altamirano monument, walk south along Calle Federico Encarnación about four blocks. Turn right (west) and walk three blocks to the small park, the **Cuna (Cradle) de Vicente Guerrero.** Guerrero was born in the modest house (occupied) at the rear of the park on August 9, 1782.

If you get hungry during your Tixtla visit, a few clean plaza-front *torta* and taco *loncherías* supply wholesome snacks. For a further treat, hire a taxi to whisk you to the nearby **Centro Recreativo Tixtla** for a swim in the big spring-fed pool (and kiddie pool) and a picnic in the shade beneath a grove of big trees.

Although any day is good, Sunday is the best day to arrive in Tixtla, for the big *tianguis* (native market, tee-AHN-geese), when *campesinos* troop into town loaded with handicrafts. These include soft palm *tenates* (tumpline baskets), sombreros, leather belts and huaraches, and colorfully embroidered *huipiles,* blouses, and skirts.

From Chilpancingo, get to Tixtla by minibus from the corner of Avenida Insurgentes and 17 de Octubre (near the market) about 10 blocks (0.6 mile, 1 km) north of the *zócalo.*

Drivers, get to Tixtla from downtown Chilpancingo's Avenida Juan Álvarez, about eight blocks south of the *zócalo.* Head east, uphill, along Laureles. After two blocks, turn left on Zaragoza; continue three blocks to Heronias del Sur and turn right, uphill. Continue east, going uphill at every intersection, until you arrive at the Tixtla *libramento* highway, where you turn right and follow the traffic.

## La Organera Xochipala Archaeological Zone

The half-day (60 miles, 100 km) trip to La Organera Xochipala (named for the zone's giant organ cactuses) is typical of other sites of the Mezcala culture, which influenced the west and central inland areas of the present state of Guerrero for more than 1,000 years, until about A.D. 1400. Xochipala, which means "the flower that paints red" in the Aztec language, comprised an urban ceremonial center and defensive refuge for a community that probably lived and farmed in an adjacent river valley.

At the expertly restored site, archaeologists have partially rebuilt more than two dozen significant constructions, including colonnaded palaces, false-arched passageways, plazas,

## VICENTE GUERRERO: FATHER OF THE MEXICAN REPUBLIC

The 1849 proposal for a new Mexican state to be carved from the states of Mexico, Puebla, and Michoacán would seem improbable, except that the proposed state was to be named Guerrero in honor of Mexico's famously popular independence hero and second president, Vicente Ramón Saldana Guerrero.

Vicente Guerrero, Mexico's first African-Mexican president, was born of working-class parents in the village of Tixtla, near Chilpancingo, on August 10, 1782. In 1811, Vicente was working successfully as a gunsmith when, inspired by Father Miguel Hidalgo's *insurgente* cause, he joined with priest-general José María Morelos's ragtag southern rebel forces.

Vicente's valor in battle and natural leadership ability led to his swift promotion. By 1815, however, with most of its original leaders, including Morelos, dead, the *insurgente* cause had lost momentum. Nevertheless, Guerrero grabbed the rebel banner in the south and rallied his men. Guerrero and his *compadre* commanders, Juan Álvarez and Pedro Ascencio, kept royalist brigadier Agustín de Itúrbide's troops in frustrated disarray, chasing the ragtag rebel bands throughout the southern Sierra Madre.

Vicente Guerrero was confronted by a crucial test in 1819. When offered amnesty, the exhausted Guerrero was tempted to give up. Even his father pleaded with him to surrender. But Guerrero remained resolute. In front of his men, Guerrero answered with the now-hallowed words, "Father, to me your voice is sacred...[but] the voice of my country comes first."

In 1821, Mexican royalists, faced with a new unfriendly liberal Spanish government, swallowed hard and joined Guerrero and the rebels. Under the flag (for which Guerrero had personally chosen the colors: red, white, and green) of "Three Guarantees" – independence, Catholicism, equality – Guerrero and Itúrbide rode victoriously into Mexico City.

But quickly, Itúrbide vaulted himself to glory as Emperor Agustín I of Mexico. As could be expected, Guerrero soon revolted, defeating Itúrbide's forces in battle on January 23, 1823, forcing Itúrbide to abdicate on March 19 and later to exile in May.

Mexican republicans took over and put together a national constitution in 1824. An election elevated liberal Guadalupe Victoria to president and conservative Nícolas Bravo to vice president. Although the restless Bravo revolted in 1827, the breach was temporarily resealed with the election of Vicente Guerrero as Mexico's second president in 1828.

Guerrero, although an able general and enormously popular war hero, was ill at ease among Mexico City's blue bloods. Guerrero left most of the salon politicking to his war minister, Leonardo Zavala (who had organized a popular revolt to get Guerrero elected), and Joel Poinsett, U.S. president Andrew Jackson's savvy ambassador to Mexico.

In the last analysis, although Guerrero's

patios, temples, rooms, tombs, basements, and a ball court. Its forest of towering organ cactuses adds to La Organera Xochipala's invitingly exotic ambience.

Archaeologists have uncovered five stages in La Organera Xochipala's history. The oldest, now covered over by more recent construction, started with walls of cemented blocks, associated with pottery fragments identifiable with the Mexican classic period, A.D. 200–350. During the second stage of construction, around 200 years later, the builders added false arches, one of which formed the dome of a tomb of a young prince. Most of the visible construction was completed during the third epoch, centering around A.D. 800. Builders completed columned, circular structures that supported flat roofs. The site declined during the fourth, "decadent," stage, in which old buildings were either abandoned or merely maintained. The site was completely abandoned during the fifth stage, around A.D. 1400.

egalitarian views were bad news to Mexico's powerful conservative chosen few, his untutored working-class and mixed-race background was the clincher. He simply didn't fit into Mexico City's upper crust. As it turned out, others were more than willing to take Guerrero's place.

One of those was Antonio López de Santa Anna, who became the darling of Mexican conservatives when his regiment batted down a half-hearted Spanish invasion on the Gulf Coast in July 1829. With Santa Anna's backing, conservative general Anastasio Bustamante mounted a revolt, forcing Guerrero to step down from the presidency in December 1829.

Guerrero again retreated to his southern home territory and drummed up yet another guerrilla revolt against the Mexico City *politicos*. As usual, Guerrero was master on his own ground. His irregulars outwitted government troops for a year.

Bustamante decided that trickery was the only way to defeat Guerrero. His agents got Guerrero to board the ship *Colombo*, in Acapulco, by bribing the ship's Genoese captain, archvillain Francisco Pichaluga. He took Guerrero, under custody, to Huatulco and handed him over to Bustamante's operatives on January 20, 1831.

Guerrero was next taken to the Valley of Oaxaca; after a bogus trial, he was executed by firing squad at the old Cuilapan basilica on February 14, 1831.

Sadly, the old warrior was gone. But his cause was not lost. Others such as Juan Álvarez, Benito Juárez, Emiliano Zapata, Álvaro Obregón, Lázaro Cárdenas, and many more would carry Guerrero's banner for generations to come.

© BRUCE WHIPPERMAN

**A monument memorializes Vicente Guerrero's immortal words.**

GUERRERO UPCOUNTRY

## LA ORGANERA XOCHIPALA ARCHAEOLOGICAL ZONE

TOMB II

TEMPLE OF THE LIGHTS

NORTH PLAZA

BANQUET ROOM

PALACE OF THE THREE PILARS

WHITE PALACE

TOMB I

NORTH PLAZA

PALACE OF THE WALLS

PALACE OF THE FOUR PILLARS

PATIO OF THE ORGAN CACTUS

PLAZA OF THE CISTERN

PATIO OF THE MEZCAL

PATIO OF THE HIDDEN TOMB

TEMPLE OF SUNSET

SOUTH PATIO

BURNED PALACE

CIRCULAR EDIFICE

ALTAR

0    25 yds

0    25 m

© AVALON TRAVEL

Important clues have been discovered in the trash dumps left by the inhabitants: much pottery, similar to that still used today, stone hatchets, metates, tiles, polishing stones, arrow- and spearheads, leather, copper greenstone beads, and much more. All this, added to the evidence of trade in cotton, fruit, salt, seeds, and medicinal plants recorded at the time of the conquest, surely indicates a vibrant agricultural and commercial culture, with busy trade ties with both neighboring and distant communities.

Get there from the main Chilpancingo bus station by second-class Tlacotepec-bound bus or *colectivo*. Ask the driver to let you off at the signed Zona Arqueológica side road on the left

before Xochipala. The site is another two miles on foot.

Drivers, head north from Chilpancingo on old Highway 95 about 20 miles (33 km) to the signed Filo de Caballo paved secondary road. Turn left and continue uphill six miles (10 km) to the signed Zona Arqueológica dirt side road on the left. Continue two miles (3 km) to the signed gate on the right.

La Organera Xochipala Archaeological Zone is open approximately 9 A.M.–5 P.M. daily except holidays. Admission to the site is $5. Few facilities, except a toilet, are available. Bring drinks, food for a picnic, sturdy walking shoes, and a hat.

# River Country

Chilpancingo serves as a convenient jumping-off point to enjoy this trio of uniquely lovely natural attractions, set like gems beneath the pine-tufted Sierra Madre del Sur.

Closest to Chilpancingo is the Río Azul, a popular Sunday picnic route, decorated along the way by a winding, intimate canyon; a lush green farm valley; and colorful, petite market towns, climaxed by an azure ribbon of crystalline springs.

Although all that would be quite enough, a marvelous natural treat hides at the end of the 31-mile road: the Grutas de Juxtlahuaca, a pristine wonderland grotto of varicolored limestone formations, underground rivers, prehistoric burial remains and wall paintings, all culminating in a wondrous garden of flowery, snow-white aragonite (calcium carbonate) crystals.

South of Chilpancingo, the clear green Río Papagayo and its rocky canyon provide plenty of opportunities for swimming, kayaking, rafting, hiking, and camping.

## THE RÍO AZUL

By bus, this trip could be done from Chilpancingo in one very long day. Start out at dawn, via a Colotlipa-bound bus, from the Universidad Pedagogical Nacional (UPN, oo-pay-EN-ay) streetfront bus terminal at the corner of Ignacio Ramírez and Niños Héroes, about five blocks south of the Chilpancingo main *zócalo.*

For more leisure, hire a taxi for the day (figure about $50), or stay overnight, camping or staying in a *cabaña* at Balneario Santa Fe or in the Casa de Huéspedes Citlalí in Colotlipa.

Travelers by car could likewise do this 74-mile (119-km) round-trip in a long day. Start off around 7 A.M., drive to the Grutas de Juxtlahuaca and explore until around 1 P.M. On the return, stop for a leisurely lunch and swim at the Balneario Santa Fe. In Chilpancingo, fill up with gasoline before you leave; otherwise, gasoline is customarily available en route at the Quechultenango *gasolinera.*

## Petaquillas, Mochitlán, and Quechultenango

Drivers, follow old Highway 95 (not the expressway) south from Chilpancingo seven miles (11 km) to the signed Petaquillas–Quechultenango crossroad. Mark your odometer and turn left, east.

Immediately pass through **Petaquillas** (pop. 5,000, stores, local-style restaurants, town plaza, post office), known for its Balneario Bugambilias water slide, pool, and restaurant, a block from the town plaza. During the week before August 27, folks will also be celebrating their patronal **Fiesta de San Agustín** with bullfights, plenty of food, a carnival, and regional dances, including the Tlacololeros, Moros, Pastoras (Shepherdesses), and Diablos (Devils).

Continue east, winding through the narrow, precipitous canyon of the Río Azul. Although the riverbed will probably be dry during the winter and spring, don't worry; year-round springs keep the downstream delightfully crystal blue (except perhaps during some muddy summer rainy-season floods).

At Mile 6 (Km 10) arrive at **Mochitlán** (pop. 4,000, *centro de salud,* post office, street market, taco shops, and stores), presiding over its lush irrigated riverbottom fields. If you have an extra few minutes, take a look inside the town's venerable barrel-nave church. It's the focus of the July 26 **Fiesta de Santa Ana,** when the townsfolk stage a float parade, carnival, fireworks, and enjoy regional dances, including the Tlacololeros, Santiagueros, Diablos, and Huexquitxles.

Continue east to **Quechultenango** (pop. 4,000), the dominant town of the upper Río Azul Valley, at Mile 17 (Km 27). As if proclaiming the town's importance, the brilliantly decorated church presides over the east side of the plaza. Enter and pass the flowery *retablo* behind the Virgin of Guadalupe on the left. Overhead, paintings of the Stations of the Cross decorate the ceiling, while up front, behind the altar, Santiago, mounted on a silver horse, brandishes a sword while trampling a hapless band of defeated Moors.

Community celebration focuses yearly at that very altar during the eight-day **Fiesta of Santiago,** combined with the unique indigenous rite of **Ocozuchil,** all of which culminates on the Santiago Feast Day of July 25. People flock in from neighboring communities, among them men decked out in red leather with machetes in hand, to perform the traditional dance Los Santiagueros. Representing Christian warriors, their machetes clash menacingly and repeatedly with the swords of the Moors, whom the Santiagueros finally vanquish and force to accept baptism.

Concurrently during the Santiago fiesta, other folks journey to the sierra to collect *ocozuchil,* an aromatic wild herb. When cut, the herb oozes a strong medicinal odor, thought to be curative. They walk to Quechultenango with the *ocozuchil* branches draped over their bodies and crowd into the church atrium. Inside, a chosen group of penitents pass one by one in front of the image of Santiago, with an *ocozuchil* branch in each hand. Afterward, they dance, whirling to the mesmerizing beat of the pre-Hispanic *teponaxtli* drum.

## ◖ Headwaters of the Río Azul

The series of *manantiales* (springs) near Coxcamila, one mile farther east of Quechultenango, at Mile 18, are the marvelous main source of the Río Azul. At the Coxcamila village center, go right, south, onto the dirt side road to the springs, locally called El Borbollón. Follow the pedestrian file along the dirt entrance driveway about a quarter mile to a grove of giant old *tule* trees, from beneath whose gnarled roots cool crystal-clear water wells up, free for everyone to enjoy.

On Sunday, dozens of cars loaded with picnickers arrive and eventually fill a big parking lot, where vendors sell corn on the cob, tamales, and soft drinks from wheelbarrows, cows stand around, men fill buckets for washing their trucks, and women do laundry and bathe their children, while everyone else seems to be frolicking in the water.

The headwaters of the Río Azul flow blue and crystalline.

That this is the source is certain. Walk upstream 100 yards, and the river is a mere trickle during the dry season. But downstream, many tens of thousands of gallons a minute of clear water, delightfully cool on a warm day, flow constantly.

Camping in your own tent by the riverbank or self-contained RV in the parking lot is customary at El Borbollón. Police patrols assure nighttime security.

### Balnearios

Farther downstream, activity focuses at three *balnearios* (bathing spots) on the Río Azul. These include **Los Manantiales** (several attractive swimming pools and restaurant at Mile 19, Km 31); **Los Sauces** (at Mile 22, Km 35, but apparently abandoned); and by far the most popular, **Balneario Santa Fe,** reachable by the signed paved side road, right at Mile 19.4 (Km 31.2), about half a mile after Los Manantiales.

For Balneario Santa Fe, continue along the side road two miles (3 km), passing through

# EXPLORING THE GRUTAS DE JUXTLAHUACA

Although the Juxtlahuaca limestone cave complex, 30 miles (50 km) east of Chilpancingo, is not the world's largest, the treasures that it hides are exquisite and unique.

The cave complex, used as a burial ground and sacred site, probably by 400 B.C., was explored by latter-day investigators in 1926 and later more thoroughly by Andrés Ortega Covarrubias during the 1950s. Ortega uncovered a then-unknown entrance and eight underground branches, extending a total of about four miles (6 km).

As in all limestone caves, Juxtlahuaca's extensive stalagmites, stalactites, columns, and curtains result from the slight solubility of limestone (calcium carbonate) in water. Thus groundwater, over eons, gradually dissolved the limestone, forming hollow chambers.

The process continues with water droplets falling from the ceiling, leaving a small wet spot above and a similar wet spot below, which dry and deposit some limestone at top and bottom. The dripping continues, gradually building the deposits into long, massive formations that, after many thousands of years, often merge to form grand columns. Water dribbling down the cave walls can deposit limestone similarly, forming magnificent curtains, lovely enough for a maharaja's palace.

Moreover, variations in mineral content, especially iron, causes color variations in the deposits, from pure white to cream, dusty rose, and sienna. Explorers have named many of the formations thus created, such as the Enchanted Fountain, the Cathedral, the Salon of the Ghost, and the Tiger.

Bats and insects make up the bulk of the cave's permanent living inhabitants. Thousands of bats roost on the ceilings not far from the entrance; on the cave floor, cockroaches scurry, feasting on the bats' droppings.

Deep in the cave, humans have left their signs on the cave's walls and floors. Several burial sites, including complete petrified skeletons; much pottery; and *El Chaman, El Serpiente,* and *El Jaguar,* a trio of magnificent cave paintings, attest to the human presence that continues to the present day.

© BRUCE WHIPPERMAN

aragonite as delicate as snowflakes on the cave wall and ceiling at the Grutas de Juxtlahuaca

GUERRERO UPCOUNTRY

the small but prosperous Santa Fe town, to the river overlook, then downhill the last quarter mile to the river.

A dozen shady *palapa* restaurants line the clear two-foot-deep flowing stream, a welcome marvel, especially during the dry and oft-hot winter and spring.

Besides ready food for eating and hammocks for resting, old-fashioned water sports abound. After taking your fill of swimming, inner-tubing, and rafting, cross the river suspension bridge to the other side to the best of all possible swimming holes, complete with rope to swing out and plunge into the cool water.

If you decide to linger, the walk-in **Campamento Santa Fe,** also across the sus-pension bridge, offers some options. Choose one of the cramped (but probably fun for kids) *cabañas* ($10 for up to four people, $20 for up to eight). For a better choice, if you're equipped, set up your tent in one of the roomy camping spaces, $1.50 per person. Toilets are in shared lavatories. For a bath, jump in the river (or the swimming pool, if it's operating).

RV campers (with medium to small rigs) can park in a large riverside lot that is accessible by turning left from the downhill entrance road a couple hundred yards before the river at the driveway marked by a big tree on the left.

## GRUTAS DE JUXTLAHUACA

The lightly touristed but wondrous Grutas de Juxtlahuaca takes its name from its neighbor-ing village, Juxtlahuaca (hooks-tlah-WAH-kah). The small town of Colotlipa, four miles before the cave, is the jumping-off point for guides, food, and services.

Get to the Grutas de Juxtlahuaca (10 A.M.–4 P.M. Tues.–Sun., best during Feb.–May dry season) from Colotlipa most conve-niently by taxi (about $10). By car, drive to the eastern edge of town, where a Grutas sign directs you left onto a paved secondary road. After three miles, pass a sugar cane–pressing mill on the left, which squeezes out juice for sweet *tepache* or for fermentation into fiery *aguardiente*. After four miles, arrive at the cave parking lot. Facilities consist only of a

Curtains of stone embellish the wall of the Juxtlahuaca cave.

toilet and a *palapa* restaurant that is some-times open.

## Colotlipa

The town of Colotlipa (pop. 4,000) is not far past the Río Azul *balnearios,* 23 miles (37 km) east of old Highway 95. If you arrive during the February 18–26 **Fiesta del Señor de las Misericordias** (Lord of Mercy) festival, the plaza might be filled with celebrants who, at dawn on February 26, climax the festivities by saluting their *patrón* with jingle bells and *mañanitas.*

Besides having the usual services such as lo-cal-style restaurants, market fruits and vegeta-bles, grocery stores, *centro de salud,* post office, and street telephones, Colotlipa is the place to hire your guide.

A right-side sign, on east–west plaza-front Calle Guerrero, marks the cave guides' at-home office. Up until the late 1990s, the main guide was Profesor Andrés Ortega Casarrubias, who during the 1950s was first to explore the cave thoroughly. Andrés, known famously as

El Chivo (The Goat), passed away in 2004. Now Andrés's son Andrés, his widow, Brenda, and his second son, Enrique, continue his mission as Chivo II, Chivo III, and Chivo IV, respectively.

The Chivo guides have inherited the exclusive Grutas de Juxtlahuaca guide franchise, awarded to Andrés by the governor of Guerrero in 1958. They lead individuals and small groups for about $20 per person, $10 per person in a larger group of four to eight. Although on weekdays you can usually arrange a tour by showing up at the cave entrance, call (tel. 756/474-7006, 756/474-7034, or 756/474-7047) at least a day in advance to assure yourself a reservation.

Their standard tour (in Spanish, which lasts two to three hours and stretches about two underground miles round-trip, is fascinating, but moderately difficult, with some crawling through tight rocky passageways, and threading your way carefully down steep limestone inclines. If at all possible, try not to miss the climactic conclusion, which requires wading along a knee-to-waist-deep underground river, then crawling 100 feet along a cramped, damp passageway. You'll get wet, but at the end of the road a marvelous garden of flowery aragonite crystals will reward your effort. Be sure to take along a pair of tennis shoes for wading and a small backpack or camera holster (seal your camera in a strong watertight bag) to keep your camera dry and undamaged. For adventurers, the Chivo guides also offer extended explorations that include overnight camping in the cave. For more information (in Spanish) and some good cave photos, visit www.barragan zone.com/ultimopro.html.

For a Colotlipa overnight, you can stay at **Casa de Huéspedes Citlalí** (Calle Neri 21, no phone), run by friendly Xochi (SOH-chee) Ortega, two blocks east and half a block south of the Colotlipa zócalo. She offers clean rooms, with two double beds and shared toilet and hot-water shower, for about $15 per room for up to four people. Make reservations through the Chivo guides. Besides managing her guesthouse, Xochi also runs a brisk business selling tacos on the curb in front of her house at night.

Hearty home-cooked food is also available in Colotlipa, at home restaurant **El Latino**, half a block south of the southeast corner of the town plaza. The hard-working owner serves country-style Mexican breakfasts around 8 A.M. ($2–4), an afternoon comida (such as beef stew, or chiles rellenos, $3–5), and snacks for supper (tacos, quesadillas, or eggs, $2–4) until around 7 P.M. (Don't be put off by the trucks parked adjacent to the restaurant tables. Besides providing meals for dozens of daily satisfied customers, the friendly, hardworking owner also rents garage space.)

## RÍO PAPAGAYO

Only about 30 miles (50 km) south of Chilpancingo, both the old Highway 95 and the new cuota expressway 95D cross the free-flowing, wild Río Papagayo. Its cool waters and rocky, pine-tufted canyon provide adventurers with plenty of swimming, rafting, canoeing, kayaking, hiking, rock-climbing, and informal camping opportunities. Activity centers around the **Bravo Town** private eco-adventuring headquarters. The best time for enjoying Río Papagayo outdoor activities is during the drier (but not driest) months of October–January, when the river still has plenty of invitingly clear emerald-green water. Higher water during the rainy months of July, August, and sometimes September colors the river a muddy brown and possible flooding could put a damper on river adventure options.

Get to the Río Papagayo by second-class bus either from the Chilpancingo Estrella Blanca bus station or the Acapulco Estrella Blanca Ejido station. After an approximate hour-and-a-half trip from either city, ask the bus driver to let you off at the Bravo Town riverfront headquarters, marked by a prominent roadside arch near Km 322, a fraction of a mile north of the old Highway 95 Río Papagayo bridge.

By car, drive about 30 miles (50 km) or 45 minutes south from Chilpancingo (or the same north from Acapulco) via the Highway 95D cuota expressway to the signed Tierra

Colorada exit. For Bravo Town, exit at the Tierra Colorada interchange and head west under the expressway, along old Highway 95, about four downhill miles southwest to Bravo Town, or a fraction of a mile farther to the old Highway 95 bridge, where dirt roads lead downhill to the river.

(If you have an extra hour and enjoy handicrafts, stop by **Acahuizotla,** two miles off the Acapulco expressway, about 17 miles/28 km south of Chilpancingo. Folks make and sell fetching curios carved from the rose-colored wood of the *palo de morado* tree.)

## Bravo Town

The Río Papagayo outdoor adventure sports site, Bravo Town (Pueblo Bravo), is about 45 minutes by *cuota* expressway south of Chilpancingo (and about the same distance north of Acapulco). Bravo Town is a subsidiary branch of the popular Acapulco-based Shotover Jet boat excursion company (Shotover has nothing to with bullets; it's the name of the New Zealand inventor of their jet boats) that used to operate out of the Bravo Town river site, but now offers jet boat rides in mangrove Laguna Dos Palos east of Acapulco.

At Bravo Town (tel. 744/484-1155, fax 744/484-2648, ventas@shotoverjet.com.mx, www.shotoverjet.com.mx, open June–Dec.) you can enjoy many attractive, modestly priced features that include, for starters, a good snack restaurant, a blue pool, riverfront shade trees for picnicking, and space for tenting and RV parking ($10). Bravo Town's adventure tour offerings include river rafting, kayaking, hiking, camping, caving, rappelling, and climbing. For example, their half-day rafting excursion runs $60 per person from Bravo Town (or $70, including transportation, from their Acapulco headquarters at the Plaza Marbella on the Costera, beach side of the Diana Circle). A more extensive adventure option is a two-day (Class III and IV) rafting expedition that includes rappelling and riverside overnight camping, for $300 per adult, kids cheaper, everything included. They also offer leisurely family-oriented trips that, besides gentle rafting, include exploring a natural riverside "museum" of fantastic rock formations, hiking, animal-watching, camping, and more.

### Practicalities

Plenty of sandy riverfront is also available for independent RV parking and tent camping below the Río Papagayo bridge (at old Highway 95 Km 322). Moreover, hearty country-style meals are obtainable at nearby restaurants such as **Bello I** (cell tel. 044-744/102-3305, 8 A.M.–9 P.M. daily), on Highway 95 about half a mile uphill from Bravo Town. Groceries, drinking water, and supplies are available at stores in Tierra Colorada town, along Highway 95, a fraction of a mile east of the Highways 95–95D toll expressway interchange.

# Handicrafts Country

The renowned handicrafts of upcountry mountain towns **Chilapa** and **Olinalá** draw a steady stream of buyers and visitors. Be sure to arrive in Chilapa, only an hour's travel east of Chilpancingo, early for the Sunday *tianguis* (native market), where craftspeople from all over the Guerrero Sierra Madre bring their best for sale.

Afterward, travel a few hours farther east to Olinalá and visit the workshops of the masters of a preconquest lacquerware tradition whose intriguingly mysterious origins are lost in time.

## CHILAPA

Presiding over its rich spring-fed mountain valley, Chilapa de Álvarez (pop. 20,000, elev. 4,300 feet, 1,310 meters) was named in honor of the liberal hero general Juan Álvarez (1810–1867). The other part of the town's name comes from Chilapan, a description given by the Aztec—from *chili* (red), *atl* (water), and *pan* (on or above). It translates roughly as "on the red water," or simply, "red river."

An early historical reference to Chilapan comes from the time of Emperor Moctezuma I (Moctezuma Ilhuacamina), who, around A.D. 1450, was expanding his domain. He ordered his subordinate officer, Texcolo Tecutlique, to establish an outpost beneath the mountain Chilapantépetl, which eventually became the town of Chilapan.

In 1522, the Spanish, in the person of Hernán Cortés's lieutenant, conquistador Gonzalo Sandoval, conquered the local people. Soon, Augustinian missionaries arrived and began converting the natives and building a church and convent, which they dedicated to Saint Augustine on October 5, 1533.

The Augustinian friars encouraged the Chilapa people to expand their long-established weaving tradition. For many centuries before the conquest, their elaborately crafted blankets, *huipiles,* and skirts had been traded all over southern Mexico. Under the guidance of the Augustinians, they broadened their skills, eventually crafting the wide variety of baskets, hats, napkins, and pottery that make up the rich Chilapa handicrafts tradition that continues to the present day.

## Orientation

The prime orientation point upon Chilapa arrival is the main highway crossing by the crafts market, marked by the permanent stalls behind the fence just east of the crossing. If you arrive on a Sunday, park your car or get off the bus and head for the crafts market. Later, from the crossing, you can reach the downtown plaza either on foot (about half a mile south), *bici-taxi* (bicycle rickshaw, BEE-see), taxi, or your own wheels.

## ◖ Chilapa Sunday Handicrafts Market

Beginning Saturday afternoon, country folks loaded with handmade goods begin arriving for the renowned Sunday handicrafts market. Their wealth of offerings come in a grand array of materials—supple leather bags, handsome belts, handy coin purses, sturdy wallets, comfortable huaraches; glistening shell and horn bracelets, lovely combs, decorative ashtrays, hand-carved desk sets, attractive lampshades; iron machetes, hatchets, gleaming daggers and swords, pocket knives; many handpainted or embroidered textiles such as strong *ixtle* (agave fiber) bags, fetching *rebozos* (shawls), napkins, tablecloths, *huipiles;* basketry such as soft palm sombreros, mats, and baskets; and lacquered wooden miniature castles and bulls, scary

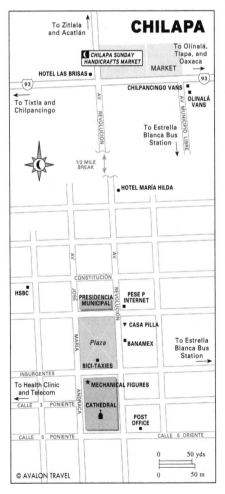

© BRUCE WHIPPERMAN

**Bright paper flowers are among the best sellers at the Chilapa Sunday Handicrafts Market.**

human tiger-masked figures, colorful paper flowers, pine furniture, select musical instruments, and enticing animal figurines.

Many crafts come from outside Chilapa—for example, shawls from Tenancingo; silver from Taxco; huaraches from Iguala and Tixtla; fireworks from Ayahualulco; lacquerware and tiger masks from Olinalá; papier-mâché from Mezcala; bright earth-red pottery from Atzcualoya; *amate* (painted bark paper) from Amayaltepec; animal figures from Temalacatzingo; and embroidered blouses and skirts from Acatlán.

You might also stroll through the colorful **main market,** adjacent (east) of the crafts market. Here, the double meaning of *tianguis,* the native name for both awning and market, becomes abundantly clear in the seeming acres of colorful awnings. The excitement begins on the market-front steps, where women sell small piles of produce (radishes, corn, small pumpkins, squash, mangoes in the March–July season, beans, and mountain herbs).

(*Note:* Although unusual most places in Guerrero, some pickpockets unfortunately seem to be operating at the Chilapa Sunday *tianguis.* Their technique, which I experienced, was distraction by jostling. Be aware, and keep your unmissable items in a secure front waist belt. Moreover, women, zip your purses, and men, keep your wallet in your front pocket with a hand on it.)

## Downtown Plaza and Cathedral

For more sights, head south to the downtown plaza and towering neo-Gothic cathedral, dedicated to St. Francis and seat of the local bishop. One of the cathedral's main attractions occurs every Sunday at noon, when the miraculous roses of the Virgin of Guadalupe are revealed to mechanical figures of Don Diego and Archbishop Zumárraga at the door on the right bell tower. Inside the cool nave, spectacularly large stained glass windows, each one donated by a Guerrero locality, add daytime cheer to the cavernous interior. Up front, contemplate the image of mother Mary above the altar being lifted to heaven by a band of angels.

Back outside the church, a fleet of *bici-taxis,* looking every bit like bicycle rickshaws from the Indian subcontinent, stop and pick up passengers at curbside.

Before leaving the Chilapa plaza, be sure to stop for a drink or snack and admire the marvelous mask collection at the plaza-front Casa Pilla restaurant.

## Accommodations and Food

Chilapa visitors enjoy a pair of recommendable hotels. About three blocks north of the plaza is ( **Hotel María Hilda** (Av. Revolución 229, tel. 756/475-1840). The hotel's 36 rooms occupy two stairway-accessible floors above street level. Rooms are cool, clean, light, and sparely but comfortably furnished with bedspreads, curtains, and tiled hot-water shower baths. They have no reading lamps, however. Most rooms have one, two, or three double beds. A few rooms have king-size beds. Rates run $16 s, $19 d (one bed); $25 s or d in king; $25 d (two beds); $28 t (two beds); and $33 t (three beds), with cable TV and parking, but no fans or air-conditioning.

Chilapa's downtown plaza

"Cleanliness Is Our Rule" at **Hotel Las Brisas** (Prolongacion Av. Revolución 2, tel. 756/475-0769), at the Chilpancingo highway intersection. Here you get to choose from 36 clean rooms, comfortably furnished with double beds, shiny wood furniture, bright bedspreads, and small but tiled hot-water shower baths. Some rooms have bedside reading lamps. Expect to pay about $15 s or d (one bed); $26 d, t, or q (two beds); $35 for 3–6 in three beds, with cable TV, parking, fans, and air-conditioning. Reserve the quietest rooms (with least highway noise): 5, 6, or 7 on the 2nd and 3rd floors.

Some of Chilapa's best budget food is available at the several permanent *jugerías* with juices, *tortas,* and *hamburguesas* ($1–3) and *fondas,* serving stews (*guisados*), soups (*sopas*), tacos, *chiles rellenos,* and enchiladas ($2–4), at the rear of the main market floor at the highway crossing north of downtown. One of the best is *fonda* **Doña Lilia** (7:30 A.M.–7 P.M. daily), which specializes in savory chicken or pork *pozole* and steaming *guisado de res* (beef stew).

Chilapa's best plaza-front eatery is restaurant-bakery ◖ **Casa Pilla** (tel. 756/475-0263, 8 A.M.–8 P.M. Mon.–Sat., 8 A.M.–7 P.M. Sun., $3–7) at the northeast downtown plaza corner. If not for the food, Casa Pilla is unforgettable for the spectacular mask collection that adorns its airy dining room. The menu is nevertheless both recognizable and appetizing for breakfast (pastries, fruit, omelettes, pancakes) and lunch and dinner (hamburgers, spaghetti, pork chops, seafood, and *pozole*).

## Events

Chilapa takes time out for a pair of colorful yearly fiestas. First comes the **Fiesta de San Juan** around June 24, when folks crowd the plaza to watch a parade of floats, listen to the oompah of country bands, watch fireworks, and enjoy their favorite regional dances, including the Pescados (Fish) and Moros y Cristianos (Moors and Christians).

Those who didn't get a chance to celebrate earlier get another opportunity when townsfolk parade their patron at the August 15 **Fiesta de la Virgen de la Asunción.**

## Services

A number of essential services are available near the Chilapa *zócalo.*

Find at least two banks with 24-hour ATMs. Best bet is long-hours **HSBC** (tel. 756/475-2398, 8 A.M.–7 P.M. Mon.–Fri., 8 A.M.–3 P.M. Sat.); walk a block north to Constitución from the plaza's northwest corner, turn left (west) and continue a block to the bank. Alternatively, go to **Banamex** (tel. 756/475-0101, 9 A.M.–4 P.M. Mon.–Fri.) on the east side of the plaza.

The *correo* (post office, Calle 5 Oriente 394, tel. 756/475-0066, 8 A.M.–3 P.M. Mon.–Fri.) is on the south side of the plaza; walk south from the plaza's southeast corner. At Calle 5 Oriente (just past the south end of the church), go left about three doors. For telephone, either buy a Ladatel phone card and use one of the plaza-front street telephones, or go to **Telecom** (9 A.M.–3 P.M. Mon.–Fri., 9 A.M.–noon Sat.–Sun.) on Calle 3 Poniente (West) for public telephone, fax, and money orders.

From the southwest (church-front) plaza corner, walk south a block to Calle 3 Poniente. Turn right and continue three blocks past the Centro de Salud. Internet access is available at **Pese P Internet** store (tel. 756/475-2400, chelisinc@hotmail.com, 9 A.M.–10 P.M. daily), at the northeast plaza corner.

For medical attention, let your hotel desk clerk call a doctor for you. Alternatively, go to the **Centro de Salud** (Calle 3 Poniente 703, tel. 756/475-0288), with a doctor on call 24 hours a block east of the Telecom.

### Getting There and Away

From Chilpancingo, connect with Chilapa via a first- or second-class bus departure from the **Estrella Blanca main bus station.** From Acapulco, Chilapa connections are available from the Estrella Blanca Ejido terminal.

For Chilapa bus departure, go by taxi or *bici-taxi* to the local **Estrella Blanca terminal** (Av. Municipio Libre 1804, tel. 756/475-0032). Either walk three blocks east of the plaza, to Avenida Municipio Libre, or from the market walk a block east along the highway-front, then right, south, about a mile.

From the terminal, a number of first- and second-class buses connect daily via Tixtla with Chilpancingo, Acapulco, and Mexico City. One bus per day connects east with Olinalá, and several with Tlapa de Comonfort, where connections are available with Puebla and Oaxaca destinations.

Frequent *colectivo* connections are also available between about 5 A.M. and 7 P.M. at a pair of terminals across Highway 93 from the Chilapa main market, at the corner of Calle Municipio Libre. **Transportes Guerrerenses** vans connect west several times per day with Chilpancingo and all intermediate points. Next door, **Ruta Chilapa-Olinalá** vans provide similar connections west with Olinalá and all intermediate points. Neither had phones at this writing.

The good, super-scenic, all-paved but winding Highway 93 connects Chilpancingo with Chilapa in 34 miles (54 km, about an hour). In the opposite direction, Highway 93 connects Chilapa with Tlapa de Comonfort over three

7,000-foot ridges, in about 75 miles (121 km) of smooth, scenic, but winding highway, in about three hours. In all cases, fill up with gasoline at the Chilapa station on the highway.

Reach Olinalá by starting out driving east toward Tlapa. After about 57 miles (92 km, 2.5 hrs), turn left (north) from Highway 93 at the signed Olinalá junction. Continue north about 25 smooth miles (40 km, 1 hr) to Olinalá, for a total of about three and a half hours from Chilapa.

## OLINALÁ

Reigning over its fertile mountain-rimmed valley on the edge of the sunny basin of the Río Balsas, Olinalá is famous not only for its lacquerware, but also for its masks and furniture. Most Olinalá families are involved in lacquerware, and a number of artisans welcome visitors into their home factory-stores.

### Orientation

Olinalá (Place of Earthquakes, pop. 5,000, elev. 4,000 feet, 1,300 meters) is basically a large, easy-to-explore village. As in most Mexican towns, Olinalá's streets run north–south and east–west.

Incoming bus travelers arrive at the Olinalá street-corner bus terminal, uphill, about five blocks south of town. Continue on foot or take a taxi ($1) to the town plaza. Drivers, turn left (west) onto Olinalá main street Ibarra, a block after the ingress highway bridge. Within about three uphill blocks, you'll arrive at the main town plaza.

Orient yourself by the *presidencia municipal* portals on the plaza's west side, and the church on the opposite (east) side. Olinalá's two main streets, Ramón Ibarra and Vicente Guerrero, run east–west along the south and north sides of the plaza, respectively.

### ◖ Templo de San Francisco

For a revealing preview of the finest of all possible Olinalá lacquerware, head first to the town showplace Templo de San Francisco, one of Mexico's most unique churches, on the plaza's east side.

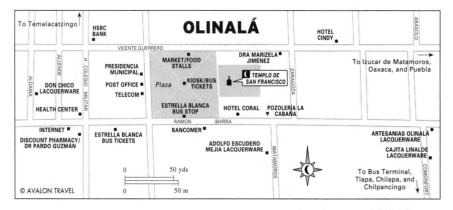

Inside, a riot of lacquerware, known locally as *linaoe* (lee-nah-OH-ay), dominates the decorations. Although many local artisans have contributed to the decorations, some features stand out. The nave columns, in contrasting cream and maroon, are the work of the acknowledged Olinalá master *artesano* Francisco Coronel.

Also, don't miss the right front side chapel, dedicated to the Virgin of Guadalupe. And before you leave, be sure to look at the mural by the front door, featuring a unique Trinity. Its deity-trio, all of whom resemble Jesus, rain avenging angels down upon devils and sinners in hell.

## Handicrafts

Next, go to the source, the workshop-store of *maestro* **Francisco "Don Chico" Coronel** (Juan Aldama 12, tel. 756/473-0084), who welcomes visitors during the day. From the plaza's southwest corner, walk west, uphill, along Ibarra, a few blocks to Aldama, turn right, and continue a few doors to Coronel's house on the right. Inside, if you're lucky, you'll get to watch him applying the finishing touches to a fine piece of work. The masterfully crafted and detailed treasury—*bateas* (trays), *cajas* (boxes), *arcas* (chests), *calabazas* (gourds)—that decorates his workshop represents the pinnacle of Olinalá craftsmanship. Collectively, the pieces represent the essence of many centuries of experience and practice. Individually, each piece is the prized product of hours of meticulous work, gathering and processing the natural raw materials, sanding, painting, burnishing, engraving, and finally the fine finish painting that *maestro* Francisco applies. The prices that he asks, typically $40–60 for small-to-medium pieces, are modest indeed.

Several other Olinalá master artisans welcome visitors. (Although they have no formal business hours, keep in mind that these aaritsans work from their homes. Out of courtesy, one shouldn't arrive too early or late; no earlier than 9 A.M. and no later than 6 P.M.) Back at the plaza's southeast corner, walk downhill (east) along Ibarra one block. Turn right at Matamoros and continue a few doors to the shop of **Adolfo Escudero Mejia** (Matomoros 5, tel. 756/473-0075). He specializes in beautiful meticulously designed and adorned boxes, chests, chairs, and trays, many of innovative decoration.

Continue east, downhill, along Ibarra a long block to the corner of Comonfort, where you'll find **Artesanías Olinalá** (tel. 756/473-0022, 8 A.M.–8 P.M. daily), the shop of personable Edilberto Jiménez Barrera. Inside, admire his collection of mostly boxes and chests, but also many unusual-motif (representing, for example, lawyers, rancheros, and cockfighters) gift clocks.

Walk a few doors south on Comonfort to find, on the left, **Cajita Linaloe** (Comonfort 3, tel. 756/473-0029), the shop of *artesana*

# THE ART OF DON CHICO CORONEL

Olinalá's native son Francisco "Don Chico" Coronel is the nationally acknowledged master of the style of lacquerware that has made Olinalá famous. Born in 1941, young Francisco was apprenticed into the traditional craft of lacquerware as it had been learned by nameless generations of Olinalá youths before him.

Originally, Olinalá craftspeople had made an art of lacquer-decorated gourds. Demand extended the original craft to trinket and jewel boxes, then trays and chests, tables and chairs, and more.

But regardless of size and variety, the method has remained constant. First, the wood is collected, cut, carved to shape, and hand-sanded. A base coat of *chia* seed oil, colored with a locally gathered and ground natural mineral pigment, is applied and left to dry. The piece is then burnished to a shine with a smooth stone, and the whole process is repeated many times over. After the last coat of oil has been applied, the piece is left to dry for a month.

Craftspeople next lay out designs that are engraved into the piece, traditionally with a natural agave thorn needle. Vivid colors are painted into the engraving to create a harmonious animal or floral design.

During the 1970s, Don Chico began adding gold to his colors, creating rich and lovely gilded flowers, birds, rabbits, and much more in his designs.

Some Olinalá craftspeople, impatient with the time-consuming traditional materials and processes, are using commercial pigments and oils and faster machine methods. In some cases quality has suffered.

But that's not true of Don Chico's art. He continues to work by the traditional methods and materials. He's become so famous that presidents have commissioned him to make gifts representative of Mexican craftsmanship. Don Chico responded by making a magnificent tray for Queen Elizabeth II of Great Britain. And when Pope John Paul came to Mexico in July 2002 to canonize the first Latin American indigenous saint, president Vicente Fox presented John Paul a regal chest made by Francisco "Don Chico" Coronel of Olinalá.

Acknowledged Olinalá lacquerware maestro Francisco "Don Chico" Coronel finishes a fine lacquerware box.

© BRUCE WHIPPERMAN

the Olinalá town square

Audelia Rendón Franco. Her factory store and workshop (visitors welcome), in the rear, is the ongoing result of more than 200 years of family tradition. It abounds with a myriad of lacquerware: mirrors, boxes large and small, *calabazas,* picture frames, jaguar masks, and much more.

For something quite different, continue two blocks east, across the bridge and uphill, to the bouganvillea-draped house and garden of portrait artist **Bernardo Rosendo** (Comonfort 13, tel. 756/473-0019 or 756/473-1108) on the left side of the street. He specializes in ink, charcoal, and Olinalá lacquer portraits of famous personages. Order a portrait of one of your Mexican heroes, or your favorite movie star, or ask him to make a portrait of you or someone you know. He has many examples of the rich and famous, but he'll need at least a photo of people he doesn't know. Call him for an appointment.

For yet more fine lacquerware, masks, and much more, visit the even more remote village of **Temalacatcingo** (pop. 2,000), 17 miles (27 km) by bus or *colectivo* via the gravel road north from Olinalá. After about 13 miles (20 km), drivers should turn right at the fork to Ahuacatlán, and continue past Ahuacatlán for about two miles.

## Accommodations and Food

Olinalá accommodates visitors with at least two acceptable hotels. If you can tolerate roosters crowing at six in the morning, the best choice is **Hotel Cindy** (Guerrero 46, tel. 756/473-0114, $20 s or d), two blocks east of the plaza. I arrived the first time at night and nearly missed the place, because its illuminated sign says "Corona Hotel" (for Corona Beer, which had installed the sign). This loosely run family establishment offers about 15 rooms (not all in operating condition as of this writing) in three exterior-corridor floors overlooking a parking lot–garden. If you make your way past the storefront-desk and the stashes of semi-trash (boxes of bottles, used lumber, rolls of wire, old tools), along hallways and in corners, you'll find the rooms decently clean and attractive, with pink bedspreads and tiled baths. With the added pluses of hot water, ceiling fan (make sure yours works), TV, parking, and airy upstairs restaurant, you'll have a deal.

Second choice goes to four-floor **Hotel Coral** (Ramón Ibarra s/n) half a block east of the plaza. A popular stopping place for truck drivers, the Coral offers about 30 plain but clean bare-bulb rooms with colorful tile, fluffy bedspreads, curtains, and hot-water showers. For privacy and a minimum of noise, take a room on the top floor, away from the street. Rates run $16 s or d (in one double bed), $20 d (two double beds), with fan and TV; street parking only.

As for food, economy meals (soups, stews, tacos, enchiladas, *pozole,* and more) are the specialties of the several **fondas** (food stalls) that set up daily (and nightly) on the north side of the plaza.

For sit-down breakfast, lunch, and supper, the best choice in town is the charming **◖ Pozolería La Cabaña** (on Ibarra, 8 A.M.–10 P.M. Mon.–Sat., 8 A.M.–3 P.M. Sun., $2–5), half a block east of the plaza. Savvy owners have turned a rustic, massive-beamed old house into a restaurant that fits its name perfectly. Part of the fun of La Cabaña is the eclectic old-time collection—masks, *cazuelas* (stewing crocks), gourds, wooden spoons, longhorn cattle skulls, and a yellowed portrait of Emiliano Zapata—that decorates the walls. Although La Cabaña's specialty is savory country-style *pozole,* your choices are more varied. For breakfast, choose among juice, Nescafé, fruits, eggs, and potatoes; for lunch, order either à la carte or a three-course set *comida corrida,* with choice of seafood, stew, or chicken; for supper, go for *pozole, chiles rellenos,* tacos, or enchiladas.

Alternatively, go to friendly **Cocina Económica La Guadalupana** (8 A.M.–6 P.M. daily, $2–4), on Ibarra across from the plaza, for breakfast, a hearty *comida* for lunch, or early supper. Friendly, hard-working owner-chef Oralia Garcia specializes in wild game, such as rabbit, opossum, wild pig, and turkey.

Evenings after 9 P.M., when everything else in town is closed, you can often get a tasty snack, such as a hamburger or *torta* and juice, at the *jugería* beneath the town plaza's elevated *kiosko* (bandstand) until 10 or 11 P.M.

## Events

If you like old-Mexico color and don't mind crowds, time your visit to coincide with either of Olinalá's big festivals, the **Fiesta de Pascua** (Passover) during the week before Easter Sunday, or the patronal **Fiesta de San Francisco de Asis,** October 2–5.

During the Easter festival, the highlight, besides plenty of food, handicrafts for sale, fireworks, cockfights, and carnival, is the procession of the Stations of the Cross that reenacts the Passion of Jesus.

Later, the San Francisco festival features much of the same, plus a big for-sale handicrafts exposition, *mojigangos* (giant dancing effigies), and favorite traditional dances, including Los Tigres, Los Tecuanes, and the French courtship Danza de los Doce Pares. (Make your hotel reservation early.)

## Services

Olinalá provides some essential services within a block of the plaza.

For ATMs and money exchange, first try **HSBC** (tel. 756/473-0602, 8 A.M.–4 P.M. Mon.–Sat.) on Guerrero, a block west of the plaza. Alternatively, go to **Bancomer** (tel. 756/473-0332, 8:30 A.M.–4 P.M. Mon.–Fri.), on Ibarra across from the southeast corner of the plaza.

Find the *correo* (8 A.M.–3 P.M. Mon.–Fri.) and **Telecom** (tel. 756/473-0259, 9 A.M.–3 P.M. Mon.–Fri., 9 A.M.–noon Sat.) beneath the *presidencia municipal* portal, west of the plaza. Longer hours for public telephone and fax are available at the Farmacia Discuento, listed below.

Internet access is available at **Café@Internet** (Ibarra 27 Poniente, tel. 756/473-1039, 10 A.M.–10 P.M. daily), a block and a half west of the plaza.

Olinalá provides a number of medical options. For simple medications and advice, try

**Farmacia Discuento** (tel. 756/473-0346, 8 A.M.–10 P.M. daily), with Dr. Pardo Guzmán in charge, on the north side of Ibarra a block west of the plaza, corner of H. Colegio Militar. If you need a doctor, drop in to the 24-hour **Centro de Salud** (tel. 756/473-0044), across the street from Farmacia Discuento. Of Olinalá's private physicians, **Dr. Cipriano López Hernandéz** (Guerrero 105) is highly recommended, about four blocks downhill, east of the plaza. Alternatively, visit **Dr. Marizela Jiménez,** also on Guerrero, half a block east of the plaza.

In an emergency, contact the *policías* (tel. 756/473-0006 or 756/473-0007), in the *presidencia municipal,* on the west side of the plaza.

## Getting There and Away
### BY BUS
To reach Olinalá, bus travelers can connect via Estrella Blanca buses from western locations of Acapulco (via Chilpancingo) and Chilapa. From eastern locations in Puebla and Oaxaca you can reach Olinalá via Tlapa de Comonfort.

In Olinalá, a ticket agent (tel. 756/473-1050) on Ibarra, across from the plaza, sells tickets for all Estrella Blanca local bus connections, including Chilapa, Chilpancingo, Cuernavaca, Mexico City, and most intermediate destinations. Catch the bus at the hilltop terminal, about five blocks south of town, most conveniently reached by taxi.

From the same uphill bus station, Sur provides two second-class departures per day, connecting with northern and eastern destinations including Mexico City and the states of Puebla (via Izucar de Matamoros), Morelos (via Cuautla), and Oaxaca (transfer at Tlapa de Comonfort).

Also from the same uphill station, vans provide connections east, with Tlapa de Comonfort, and west with Chilapa and Chilpancingo, many times per day.

### BY CAR
To or from Chilpancingo via Chilapa, drivers can connect with Olinalá, via Highway 93. Westbound, about 57 miles (92 km, 2.5 hrs) after Chilapa, head left (north) from Highway 93 at the signed Olinalá junction. Continue north about 25 smooth miles (40 km, 1 hr) to Olinalá, for a total of about three and a half hours from Chilapa (or 116 miles, 187 km, about five hours, from Chilpancingo).

To or from the north and east (Mexico City and the states of Morelos, Puebla, and Oaxaca), connect via Highway 190 via Izucar de Matamoros, Puebla; or Huajuapan de León, Oaxaca; at the Highway 190 junction with Highway 92, 37 miles (59 km) southeast of Izucar, or 57 miles (92 km) northwest of Huajuapan. Head south 78 miles (126 km) to the Olinalá junction at Huamuxtitlán. Continue via westbound secondary road another 17 miles (27 km) via Cuauhlote, Cualac, and Xhiacingo, to Olinalá. For this trip, figure a total of about four hours from Izucar, five from Huajuapan.

# Iguala

Only a tiny fraction of the vacationers hurrying south to Acapulco bothers to stop in Iguala (pop. 100,000, elev. 2,430 feet, 740 meters). Consequently, Iguala is nearly tourist-free. This is remarkable, since the town's official name, Iguala de la Independencia, is much more than a slogan. Iguala is a major patriotic-historic center of Mexico and cradle of Agustín de Itúrbide's Plan de Iguala, which spelled out Mexican independence, and his Bandera de las Trigarantías (Flag of the Three Guarantees), the red, white, and green tricolor beneath which Itúrbide finally rode triumphantly into Mexico City on September 27, 1821.

Local folks don't seem to mind the lack of tourist hullabaloo, however. They go about their business, living well from the both the local mineral riches and the agricultural

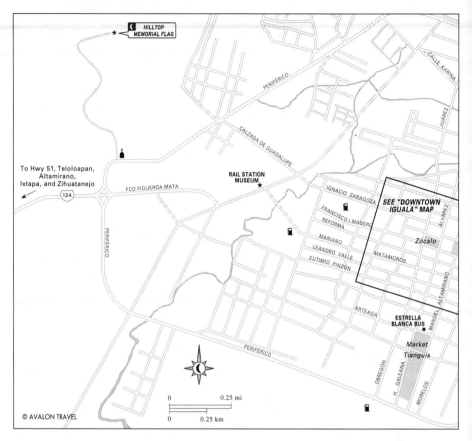

bounty—fruit, corn, cattle—of their fertile, spring-fed valley.

They also love their pedestrian-friendly downtown, with a number of good restaurants and not one but three shady plazas, sprinkled with juice- and snackstands and cafés.

All this would be easily worth an overnight, but Iguala offers much more: a whole complex of many dozens of shops selling gold jewelry, the fascinating Museo y Santuario a la Bandera, and, not to be missed atop a breezy view hillside, a spectacularly large Mexican flag billowing gracefully above a monument to the Heroes of the Independence.

Excursions nearby lead to Lake Tuxpan, for possible boating and camping, and adjacent lovely Quinta Happy bathing resort. Farther afield, ruins enthusiasts can visit Teopantecuantlán and Cuetlajuchitlán, a pair of fascinating partly restored pre-Columbian ceremonial centers.

## HISTORY

The name Iguala comes from the town's former Aztec-language label, Yohualtépetl, which means, very appropriately, "basin surrounded by mountains." After the conquest, the local Spanish missionaries shifted the name to the more pronounceable Yohuala, and finally, Iguala.

Chontal-speaking people at least as early as A.D. 800 founded the town, which was

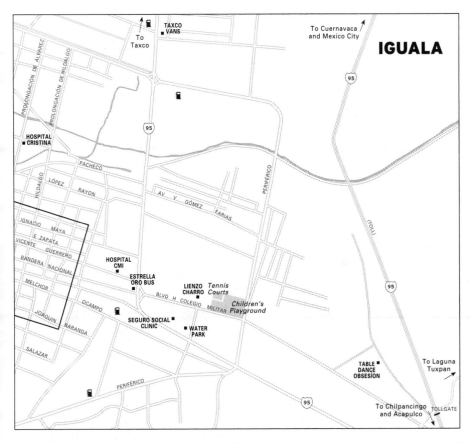

originally known as Motlacehuatl, an Iguala district still called "old town." During the Aztec expansions of the 1400s, warriors under direction of Emperor Izcoatl conquered Motlacehuatl and erected a temple. Aztec colonists arrived and prospered on the labor of their Chontal-speaking slaves and servants.

The Spanish arrived in 1522 and replaced the Aztec temple, warriors, and settlers with their own church, soldiers, and colonists. They prospered for nearly 300 years until the surrounding region, ignited by Miguel Hidalgo's 1810 cry for independence and led by generals José María Morelos and Vicente Guerrero, became a focus of anti-Spanish rebellion.

From 1811 to 1821 Spanish troops fought an aggressive but losing campaign, battling rebel guerrillas from the cool, pine-tufted high sierra to Acapulco's summery shoreline. Finally, the independence drama climaxed in Iguala on February 24, 1821, when Agustín de Itúrbide, former royalist general turned rebel, joined forces with Guerrero.

Their agreement was based on the Plan de Iguala, an independence strategy based on more than two dozen points. The Plan de Iguala was essentially a moderate compromise that both the conservative white elite that Itúrbide represented and Guerrero's indigenous and mestizo campesinos could agree upon. It called for an independent Mexico with a parliament presided over by a constitutional

Spanish monarchy, much as the 19th-century English monarchs presided over the Dominion of Canada. The Plan de Iguala even invited King Ferdinand VII of Spain to agree to all of this, which he never did.

At the core of the plan that lasted were the Trigarantías (Three Guarantees): independence, Catholicism, and equality amongst all Mexicans (men only, however).

Later, on October 27, 1849, Iguala was chosen as the first capital of the new state of Guerrero, with general Juan Álvarez as governor. Soon, in early 1850, the first state legislature met in Iguala. Later, the capital shifted to Tixtla, and finally Chilpancingo by the end of the 19th century.

## SIGHTS
### Arrival and Orientation

Most bus passengers arrive at the Estrella Blanca bus station, north side of the main market, corner of Galeana and Salazar. For the center of town, walk or taxi the seven blocks north along Galeana (to the right as you exit the terminal), or ride a *colectivo* to the zócalo. (If, however, you arrive at the east-side Estrella de Oro bus station, on Highway 95, do the same by either taxi or *colectivo* or by walking eight blocks west, away from the highway, along Bandera Nacional to the zócalo.)

Drivers arriving via Highway 95 from Taxco heading south, or from Chilpancingo heading north, follow Centro or Zócalo highway signs west after passing the *periférico* (peripheral boulevard)—heading south, turn right; heading north, turn left. Continue about eight blocks west to the zócalo.

At the Iguala town center you'll find a trio of inviting plazas: from east to west, first comes the **Plaza de Trigarantías,** bordered by Avenida Vicente Guerrero on the north and Avenida Bandera Nacional on the south. Move diagonally southwest, across the corner of Bandera Nacional and north–south Calle Altamirano, to find the broad garden **Plaza y Monumento a la Bandera,** bordered on the south by Calle Aldama.

Finally, move diagonally northwest, across the corner of Calle Juan Álvarez and Avenida Bandera Nacional, to the **zócalo,** the very heart of the town. Its bordering streets are one-block Constitución, on its north side; Juárez, on the west side; Reforma, on the south side; and Álvarez, on the east side. Note the landmarks: the Museo y Santuario a la Bandera on the Juárez (west) side and the Hotel María Isabel on its Constitución (north) side.

### The *Zócalo*

The downtown *zócalo,* one of the most excitingly pleasant in Guerrero, is a relaxing people-watching sight all in itself. Pause for a refreshment at one of the juice bars and enjoy the shade beneath the 32 leafy tamarind trees, planted in 1832 thanks to general Don Luis Gonzaga Vieyra.

### Museo y Santuario a la Bandera

From the *zócalo,* walk west across Juárez to the Museo y Santuario a la Bandera (tel. 733/333-6765, 9 A.M.–6 P.M. Tues.–Sat., 9 A.M.–3 P.M. Sun., $3). The museum has three main *salas* (exhibition halls), all worth a visit.

The **Sala de las Banderas** exhibits about two dozen historic Mexican flags, led off by the celebrated tricolor Bandera de las Trigarantías, with its diagonal white, green, and red stripes. The stripes represent the Plan de Iguala's Three Guarantees: pure white for the Catholic religion, green for independence, and red representing equality for all the races of Mexico.

Also notable is the eagle-and-serpent Aztec "flag," from the Aztec historical document the *crónica* Mexcáyotl, as preserved in the postconquest record, the Codex Duran.

The 20-odd remaining flags are remarkable partly for their evolutionary linkages to the present Mexican national flag, adopted in 1952, at the end of the hall.

Continue to the **Sala Plan de Iguala,** which exhibits, besides the words of the Mexican national anthem, a copy of the original Plan de Iguala signed by Agustín de Itúrbide on February 24, 1821, and a more readable modern copy. The Plan de Iguala is interesting, partly for its comparison with the revolutionary-period documents

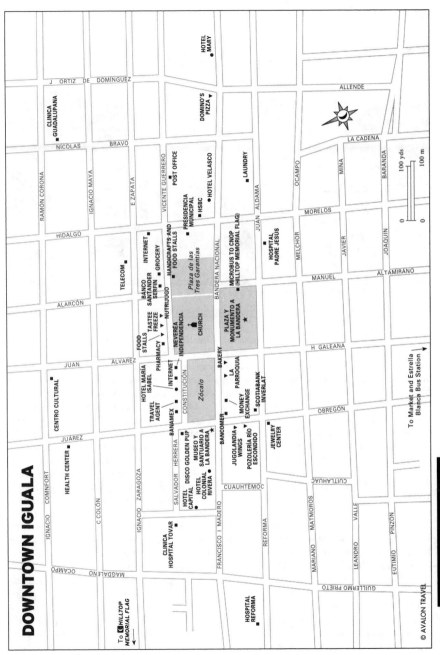

# DOWNTOWN IGUALA

GUERRERO UPCOUNTRY

© AVALON TRAVEL

To ★ HILLTOP MEMORIAL FLAG

HOTEL MARY

ALLENDE

J ORTIZ DE DOMÍNGUEZ

CLINICA GUADALUPANA

LA CADENA

NICOLÁS    BRAVO

DOMINO'S PIZZA

RAMÓN CORONA

IGNACIO MAYA

E ZAPATA

VICENTE GUERRERO

POST OFFICE

HOTEL VELASCO

LAUNDRY

BARANDA

OCAMPO

MINA

MORELOS

HIDALGO

PRESIDENCIA MUNICIPAL

HSBC

ALDAMA

JUAN

ALTAMIRANO

JOAQUIN

TELECOM

INTERNET

HANDCRAFTS AND FOOD STALLS

GROCERY

BANCO SANTANDER SERFIN

NUTRIJUGO

Plaza de las Tres Garantías

MICROBUS TO CNOP (HILLTOP MEMORIAL FLAG)

BANDERA NACIONAL

HOSPITAL PADRE JESÚS

MELCHOR

JAVIER

MANUEL

ALARCÓN

FOOD STALLS

TASTEE FREEZE

NEVERÍA INDEPENDENCIA

CHURCH

PLAZA Y MONUMENTO A LA BANDERA ★

H GALEANA

JUAN    ÁLVAREZ

PHARMACY

HOTEL MARÍA ISABEL

INTERNET

Zócalo

BAKERY

LA PARROQUIA

SCOTIABANK INVERLAT

CENTRO CULTURAL

TRAVEL AGENT

BANAMEX

CONSTITUCIÓN

MONEY EXCHANGE

OBREGÓN

To Market and Estrella Blanca Bus Station →

HEALTH CENTER

JUÁREZ

BANCOMER

JUGOLANDIA

WINGS

JEWELRY CENTER

C COLÓN

IGNACIO    ZARAGOZA

SALVADOR    HERRERA

HOTEL CAPITAL

DISCO GOLDEN PUP

MUSEO Y SANTUARIO A LA BANDERA ★

POZOLERIA RÍO ESCONDIDO

CUAUHTÉMOC

HOTEL COLONIAL RIVERA

COMNFORT

IGNACIO

CLINICA HOSPITAL TOVAR

FRANCISCO I MADERO

REFORMA

MARIANO

MATMOROS

CUITLAHUAC

VALLE

PINZON

OCAMPO

MAGDALENO

To ★ HILLTOP MEMORIAL FLAG

HOSPITAL REFORMA

GUILLERMO PRIETO

LEANDRO

EUTIMIO

100 yds    0

100 m    0

© BRUCE WHIPPERMAN

The Monumento a la Bandera decorates one of Iguala's three downtown plazas.

of the United States. While the Mexican document effectively declares Catholicism to be the religion of the land and all races to be equal, its U.S. counterparts, such as the Declaration of Independence and the Bill of Rights, say nothing about equality of the races and next to nothing about religion, except the freedom to worship (or not to worship) thereof.

The third hall is the **Santuario a la Bandera,** with a grand illuminated Mexican flag at one end of a hushed and darkened room.

## More Downtown Sights

From the museum, head due east to the *zócalo*'s southeast corner. Diagonally southeast, across the corner of Álvarez and Bandera Nacional, spreads the **Plaza y Monumento a la Bandera.** The plaza's grand central memorial, dedicated in 1942 by then president Manuel Ávila Camacho, reflects the Socialist Realism style of the day. It depicts an abnormally husky native couple, the woman with torch in hand, guarding the flag. On the monument itself, an inscription translates as: ". . . the city of Iguala, cradle of Mexican Independence, the

consummation proclaimed here, on February 24, 1821." Before moving on, you might stroll over to the plaza's northeast (church side) corner for a look at the bronze bust memorializing Francisco Gonzales Bocanegra, author of the words for the Mexican national anthem.

The **Centro Joyero de Iguala** (Jewelry Center, tel. 733/333-3778, 9 A.M.–7 P.M. daily) is both a sight and a shopping ground. Find it at the corner of Reforma and Obregón, just one block south of the *zócalo*'s southeast corner. Inside, a swarm of shops sell seemingly everything possible that can be made of gold.

The **Museo Ferrocarríl** (Rail Station Museum), in the process of being finished during the past few years, may be open for visitors by the time you read this. Check with your hotel desk. If so, find it at the west end of downtown: Taxi or walk (about a mile) beginning along Reforma, a block south of the *zócalo*. Go four blocks and turn left at the dead end (at the library), at Mariano Herrera. Continue one short block and turn right (west) at the fire station, corner of 18 de Marzo. Continue two short blocks to diagonal street Calzada del

Ferrocarril; follow it about two blocks to the old rail station, across the railroad track.

## ◖ Hilltop Memorial Flag

Although initially I didn't plan to go to the hilltop west of town for a close-up view of Iguala's big Mexican flag atop its summit, I changed my mind when one day I glanced west across town and noticed the flag for the first time. It was so fantastically huge that it dwarfed every tall building and tree (which were several times closer) in the town foreground.

The hilltop where the giant flag was first raised in 1998, known as C.N.O.P. (pronounced say-enay-oh-pay), is officially the site of the **Monumento a los Héroes de la Independencia** (Monument to the Heroes of the Independence) featuring a shrine inside a summit building (9 A.M.–5 P.M. daily), which had closed by the time I arrived around 5:30 P.M. Nevertheless, it was fortunate that I had arrived during one of Iguala's oft-breezy late afternoons. The noise alone from the flag's

graceful, slow-motion rippling was surprisingly powerful, like the repeated rumble and snap of a chorus of mini–sonic booms (which they in fact are). The flagpole, a monumental stack of welded steel about eight feet in diameter at the base, is a wonder in itself.

A small platoon of 25 men is required to carry and fold the 550-pound (250-kg) flag, which is brought down daily before sunset and raised around sunrise. To view the spectacle, arrive before approximately 5:30 A.M. or 5:30 P.M. in summer, 6:00 A.M. or 5:00 P.M. in winter.

Get to the flag by either taxi ($4 round-trip) from near the *zócalo* or *colectivo* ($0.50 one way) from the east (Av. Altimirano) side of the Plaza y Monumento a la Bandera.

By car, head west along *zócalo*-front Calle Ignacio Zaragoza from downtown. Continue for about a mile (across railroad tracks) to the Periferico four-lane thoroughfare. Turn left (south) and continue a half-mile east until you see a chapel on the right, a block before the old Highway 95 underpass. Turn right and pass in

© BRUCE WHIPPERMAN

Notice the tiny figure at the base of the pole, which is like an ant in comparison to the 200-foot length of Iguala's hilltop memorial flag.

front of the chapel, uphill. Continue up the all-paved grade, following the tricolor red, white, and green signs to the top.

## ACCOMMODATIONS

All recommendable Iguala hotels fall in the moderate under-$50 category. During Iguala's very hot and dry spring months of April, May, and June, air-conditioning, if not essential, is certainly a very desirable option if you can afford the extra expense (about $7). These recommendations start at the *zócalo* and move outward.

Start with Iguala's best all-around hotel, the **C Hotel María Isabel** (Portal Constitución 5, tel. 733/333-3233 or 733/333-3242, fax 733/333-3240). Once Iguala's pride, now a bit worn but still worthy, the hotel offers about 40 clean (but less than immaculate) conservatively but thoughtfully decorated dark-wood-paneled rooms with bath. The best and quietest are the upper rear rooms, with small balconies overlooking the tree-shaded pool-patio. Rentals cost $45 s, $54 d, $60 t with air-conditioning; $38, $43, and $48 with fan only, all with TV, fan, phone, inviting large pool and patio, parking, and convenient sidewalk restaurant downstairs. Credit cards are not accepted.

Walk west of the *zócalo* for two more recommendable hostelries. On the short north–south street a block due west of the *zócalo,* find new **Hotel Capital** (José A. Ocampo 1, tel. 733/33-1399). Here, guests have the advantage of a quiet side-street location a mere block from the downtown action. Many of the 30-odd smallish rooms in three floors are dark, but invitingly decorated in color-coordinated shades of blue, with hot-water shower baths, tile floors, and attractive wooden furniture. Rentals (with one double bed only) cost $20 s, $23 d fan only; $30 s, $35 d with air-conditioning. Two beds cost $28 d, $30 t fan only, and $38 d and $40 t with air-conditioning; all include TV, parking, and small pool and patio. Credit cards not accepted.

A block south and a block and a half farther west is the classier old-standby hostelry, **Hotel Colonial Rivera** (Madero 3, tel./fax

733/333-3464, 733/333-2587, or 733/333-2547). The hotel's builders have packed a lot of hotel into a small space. Most of the two floors of 49 rooms line an invitingly leafy but narrow interior patio-garden. Unfortunately, most rooms are dark, with only one window (which must be covered for privacy) facing the exterior corridor. A few lighter, more private rooms face the street but are consequently noisier. The good news is that the rooms are immaculate and have attractive neocolonial decor and some even have up-to-date noiseless air-conditioning. Rates, furthermore, are very moderate, at $25 s, $29 d fan only, in a one-double-bed room, $33 and $38 with air-conditioning; two double beds, $32 d and $37 t fan only, $40 d and $45 t with air-conditioning. All with TV, phone, security box, restaurant, parking, but no pool. Credit cards are accepted.

On the opposite, east side of the *zócalo* are a pair of good economy hotel choices, well managed by the same savvy owners. Two blocks east of the *zócalo,* find **Hotel Velasco** (Bandera Nacional 3, tel. 733/332-0566 or 733/332-8120, fax 733/332-5714). Clever design has placed the 30 rooms in two floors *above* (rather than beside) the noisy, smoggy parking patio. Another attractive feature is an airy front upstairs breezeway, with tables beside soft couches for relaxing. Corridors also have the same. One-double-bed rentals run a modest $18 s, $22 d, fan only; $32 s or d, with air-conditioning and ceiling fans. For two double beds, rates are $27 d, $35 t fan only; $32 d, $40 t with air-conditioning and fans. All rooms have hot-water shower baths, phones, cable TV, and parking.

Two blocks farther east, find the **Hotel Mary** (at Bandera Nacional 39A, tel. 733/332-5020 or 733/332-5320, fax 733/332-5714). The three-floor Mary has modest prices and savvy amenities similar to its brother, the Velasco: breezeways with soft chairs for relaxing; clean, well-maintained rooms, ranging from $18 s, $23 d, $28 t with fan; upwards to $32 s or d, $37 s or d, $42 t with air-conditioning, all with TV and hot-water shower baths. The Mary has the advantage of an enclosed bottom-floor garage, but the disadvantage of some noisier streetfront rooms. Reserve a quieter room in the upper rear.

Additional lodging choices are in Tuxpan (see *Excursions from Iguala*): either RV parking and/or tenting on the Laguna Tuxpan shoreline or bedding down at the inviting family resort, Quinta Happy.

## FOOD
### Snacks, Bakeries, and Food Stalls
Snacks and bakeries are plentiful downtown. For example, on one of Iguala's frequent warm afternoons, beat the heat with a *licuado* (ice, fruit, milk, and sugar, whipped to a milkshake-like froth but minus the calories) at one of the *jugerías* that dot the *zócalo* area. If you want more, they usually also serve fresh fruit, hot dogs, *hamburguesas*, and *tortas*.

For example, on the west side, pull up a stool at **Jugolandia Wings** (Juiceland Wings, 6 A.M.–11 P.M. daily), diagonally across from the *zócalo*'s southwest corner, across Madero from the Museo y Santuario a la Bandera. On the *zócalo*'s east side, enjoy about the same tasty options at **Nutrijugo** on Vicente Guerrero, across (north) from the church.

For plenty of pastries, muffins, and doughnuts, visit **Panadería San Francisco** (8 A.M.–9 P.M. Mon.–Sat., 9 A.M.–3 P.M. Sun.) at the corner of Reforma and Galeana diagonally across from the southwest corner of the Plaza y Monumento a la Bandera.

Hearty budget country-style specialties (tacos, tostadas, *tortas, sincronizadas, pinguinos, quemeyes, alambre*) and more are offered by the platoon of *fondas* (food stalls) in the **Market San Francisco Plaza** on Guerrero, a block and a half east of the *zócalo*, past the church, across from the Plaza de Trigarantías.

Finally, enjoy an ice cream at one of Iguala's quaintest and most venerable institutions, the **Nevería Independencia** (tel. 733/333-3169, 10 A.M.–9 P.M. daily) on the *zócalo*'s north side, a few doors east of the Hotel María Isabel. Here, the star of the show is an antique ice-cream freezer, complete with a 1930s-era belt-drive compressor, open for everyone to admire.

The ice cream, which is excellent (the house specialty is vanilla, in a dozen variations), seems an afterthought after witnessing in action the old machine that made it.

## Cafés and Restaurants
Of the lineup of sidewalk cafés along the *zócalo*'s north side, best (if you don't mind their TV; if so, ask them to turn down the volume) is probably **Restaurant Bambino** (tel. 733/333-6389, 8 A.M.–midnight daily, breakfast $2–5, lunch and dinner $3–9) at the front of the Hotel María Isabel. Here you can get your day started right, with a choice of fruit, good espresso coffee, *panes dulces,* eggs any style, hotcakes, and much more. For lunch and dinner, choose among plenty of sandwiches, salads, and meat, pasta, and poultry platters.

Many downtown restaurants accommodate the crowds of Iguala locals who can afford to eat out. One of the town center's best is **La Parroquia** (tel. 733/333-3400, 7 A.M.–midnight daily, breakfast $3–6, lunch and dinner $3–13), which lives up to its name, made famous by the many good like-named restaurants all over Mexico. Here, breakfasts are the main event. Choose from six, from the simple "American" (actually continental) breakfast to the hearty "Campesino" breakfast. The lunch specialty is a four-course *comida corrida.* Otherwise order from a long all-day list of fruit, eggs, poultry, soups, salads, *antojitos,* and elaborate house specialties, such as Molcajete La Parroquia (roasted meats, cactus leaves, fondue, and much more), served in a stone grinding bowl. Find La Parroquia in the small Plaza San Ángel complex, near the *zócalo*'s southeast corner.

Second restaurant choice goes to mod **Tastee Freeze-La Vaca Negra** (tel. 733/332-0177, 8 A.M.–11 P.M. daily, $4–10), on Guerrero half a block east of the *zócalo,* across from the church. Although its name sounds like that of a fast-food joint, it's actually a refined coffee shop trying to appeal to the middle- and upper-class young at heart. It does it quite well with a tasty, professionally prepared and served breakfast, lunch, and dinner menu.

A number of town-center restaurants also serve folk hungering for country fare the way *abuelita hacia* (grandma used to make). The best example is ◖ **Pozolería Río Escondido** (tel. 733/333-3362, 9 A.M.–11 P.M. daily, $2), the place for you to learn even more if you think you already know Mexican food. Start out with appetizer *pata de puerco,* continue with *tacos de longaniza,* then *tostadas de tinga,* all about $2. If, on the other hand, you hanker for something familiar, go for the house specialty *pozole con todo* (with all the fixin's). Find it on Obregón, half a block south of the southwest *zócalo* corner.

If you want a spell away from old Mexico, go to **Domino's Pizza** (tel. 733/332-4567, 9 A.M.–11 P.M. daily, $5–15), four blocks east of the *zócalo* at the corner of Ortiz de Domínguez and Bandera Nacional. Enter the cool white dining room and choose from the lineup of a dozen styles of the usual pizzas plus half a dozen local favorites you've never heard of.

## ENTERTAINMENT AND EVENTS

For child's play, Iguala has both the kid-friendly west-side park and playground **Parque Infantil del D.I.F.** (Integral Family Development) and its neighboring **CICI Parque Aquatico** water-slide park (10 A.M.–6 P.M. daily. Admission is, $3). Find them on the eastern extension of Vicente Guerrero, on opposite sides of the street a few hundred yards east of old Highway 95, by the *lienzo charro* (rodeo ring). Parque Infantil is a kiddie playground open during daylight hours. The water-slide park has two or three pools, water slides, and a restaurant (open 10 A.M.–6 P.M. daily).

Sunday afternoons (around 5 P.M., check with your hotel desk for times) at the *lienzo charro,* riders practice the art of *jaripeo* (bull riding and roping) and show off their skills of horsemanship. Sometimes young women in colorful *ropa típica* compete in a daredevil *escaramuza charra* in which they race sidesaddle, with abandon, around the ring. A frequent local treat is the noisy "oompah" wind instrument bands, known locally as the Bandas de

---

## THE FLOWER OF CHRISTMAS

Mexican people tell a story of the lovely red poinsettia flower, which they know as the Flower of Christmas:

Once upon a time, on Nochebuena (Christmas Eve) in a village of southern Mexico, a poor girl named Angelita stood outside the village church sadly watching the faithful carrying rich offerings of fruit, candy, and flowers for the infant Jesus. Angelita was weeping, because she had nothing to offer.

At that moment an angel, shining with a brilliant light, appeared and told Angelita to pick some wild plants beside the road. Angelita did this and returned with a large but humble bunch of weeds. Inside, as she approached the altar, Angelita's weeds miraculously transformed themselves into lovely scarlet flowers.

At the same time, the Virgin above the altar lowered her arm in a gesture of love, and gold stars on her blue cape showered the faithful in the nave. Simultaneously, outside in the black night sky a single star glowed a brilliant white over the little pueblo.

From that time forward, Angelita's brilliant red flowers have blossomed all over southern Mexico just before Christmas. For that reason, people have named that gorgeous bloom the *flor de Nochebuena* and always offer bunches of them to the baby Jesus on December 24.

---

Chile Frito. (Get to the *lienzo charro,* on the eastern prolongation of Bandera Nacional, past old Highway 95, about nine blocks east of the *zócalo,* by taxi.)

Iguala **Semana Santa** celebrations, in addition to the usual processions, *mañanitas,* stations of the cross, food, and carnival games, also feature a procession of dozens of *penitencias* who may be flaying themselves or crawling on hands and knees to the downtown church altar to ask for forgiveness.

The big patronal **Fiesta de San Francisco**

features an October 4 parade of *locos* throwing water and eggs and whatever else in honor of St. Francis of Assisi, who's famous for his sense of humor.

The **Day of the Dead,** celebrated November 1 and 2, is big in Iguala. Families go to cemeteries and clean up the grave sites of their loved ones. They rebuild the "houses" of the dead and bring the favorite foods of the departed, thus tempting their relatives to leave the land of the dead and be with the family once again.

If you're in Iguala around the time of Carnaval (the week before Ash Wednesday), consider visiting the important town of Teloloapan (pop. 20,000), about 17 miles (27 km) along the Altamirano highway west of Iguala. The Teloloapan Carnaval (Mardi Gras), locally called the **Paseo de los Agullis,** is unique. Beginning a week before Ash Wednesday, usually in early February, celebrants dance through the streets to the rhythm of drum and tamborine and splash themselves with paint. On Tuesday before Ash Wednesday they climax it all with a dangerous competition, climbing a high tree to claim the valuable prizes in its limbs. The merrymaking continues during the subsequent week, in the **El Segundo Viernes de Cuaresma** (Fiesta of the Second Friday of Lent), a weeklong (Mon.–Sun. after Ash Wednesday) celebration, including a daily round of traditional dances, a big handicrafts fair, and fireworks.

## SHOPPING

Iguala's prime general shopping ground is the main town market, at the corner of Salazar and Galeana six blocks south of the *zócalo.* Everything—from shoes and clothes to produce and hot food—seems to be on sale. Even if you don't buy anything, the market is an interesting place for wandering and enjoying the displays, especially the festoons of old-fashioned goods: flowers, mounds of spices, dried flower petals, cinnamon bark, *cal* (limestone), *panela* (rough brown sugar), and mountain-gathered herbs and remedies.

Iguala's handicrafts vendors cluster on the Plaza de Trigarantías, two blocks east of the *zócalo,* behind the church. Customarily about a dozen stands offer a large variety, including soft palm-leaf *tenates* (tumpline baskets) and *petates* (mats), wooden bowls and utensils, colorful pottery, masks, and much more.

Iguala is famous for its gold market, the **Centro Joyero de Iguala** (tel. 733/333-3778, 9 A.M.–7 P.M. daily), Mexico's third gold merchandising center after Taxco and Guadalajara. Find its many dozens of shops under one roof at the corner of Obregón and Reforma, a block south of the *zócalo*'s southwest corner. Inside is a budget jewelry lover's paradise, where the gold and silver is genuine, but most of the apparent rubies, diamonds, and emeralds are not. (Nevertheless, a few stores, such as Orovel's, downstairs, and Jeisha, upstairs, do carry genuine low-to-medium-quality gemstones.) If you want to check on the reasonableness of a price, ask the prospective seller to weigh it. Ordinary sterling silver pieces customarily sell reasonably for about $1 per gram, 12–22 karat (50–90 percent) gold for about $8–15 per gram.

## SERVICES
### Banks

Banks with ATMs are plentiful near the *zócalo.* Find **Banamex** (tel. 733/333-3049, 9 A.M.–4 P.M. Mon.–Fri.) at the *zócalo*'s northwest corner; **Bancomer** (tel. 733/333-3401, 8:30 A.M.–4 P.M. Mon.–Fri.) across the *zócalo* at the southwest corner; and **Banco Santander Serfín** (tel. 733/332-8770, 9 A.M.–4 P.M. Mon.–Fri., 9 A.M.–2 P.M. Sat.), one block east of the *zócalo*'s northeast corner, at the Guerrero and Alarcón corner. Find somewhat more flexible hours at the *casa de cambio* (money-exchange office) **Dimex** (tel. 733/333-6581, 8 A.M.–6 P.M. Mon.–Fri., 9 A.M.–2:30 P.M. Sat.–Sun.), on the *zócalo*'s southwest side.

## Communications

Find the *correo* (tel. 733/332-0160, 9 A.M.–5 P.M. Mon.–Fri.) on the south side of Guerrero, two and a half blocks west of the *zócalo.* For telephone, buy a Ladatel card and use one of the many street telephones. Otherwise, go to **Telecom** (local cell tel. 044/110-7439, 9 A.M.–8 P.M. Mon.–Fri.), northeast of the *zócalo* on Zapata between Alarcón and Hidalgo, for fax and money orders.

Connect to the Internet at **Cyber Vebelde** (Constitución 7, tel. 733/334-0741, 10 A.M.–9 P.M. Mon.–Sat.), two doors east of the Hotel Isabel.

## Health and Emergencies

For routine medications and remedies, try one of the many downtown pharmacies, such as **Farmacia Pronto** (on Guerrero, tel. 733/333-6855, 8 A.M.–midnight daily), half a block east of the *zócalo*'s northeast corner.

If you need a doctor, follow your hotel's recommendation. Otherwise, a handily situated internist, **Dr. Raoul Tovar** (Jose O. Ocampo 8, tel. 733/333-3624, 10 A.M.–4 P.M. and 6–8 P.M. Mon.–Fri.) is available for consultations at Clínica Tovar, his lovely garden-patio hospital-home, a block west of the *zócalo*'s northeast corner. His personable English-speaking wife, Ana, runs the reception.

Also in an emergency, a number of reliable hospitals provide round-the-clock services in the downtown area. Hire a taxi to take you to one of the following: **Hospital Reforma** (Reforma 54, tel. 733/333-5892, **Sanatorio Padre Jesús** (Aldama 24, tel. 733/332-0801), or **Hospital Cristina** (Prolongación Álvarez 153, tel. 733/333-2514 or 733/333-7386).

For police, call 733/332-8005. In case of fire, contact the *bomberos* by emergency tel. 066.

## Travel Agents

Often willing sources of information, find them in the downtown area. For example, try **Agencia de Viajes María Isabel** (tel./fax 733/333-0506, agencia_maria-isabel@hotmail .com, 9 A.M.–8 P.M. Mon.–Fri., 9 A.M.–5 P.M. Sat.–Sun.), next to the Hotel María Isabel.

## Laundry

Get your clothes washed at **Lavandería Easy** (tel. 733/332-6189, 10 A.M.–8 P.M. Mon.–Sat.). From the *zócalo*'s southeast corner, walk one block south to Aldama, turn left and walk two and a half blocks west.

## GETTING THERE AND AWAY
### By Bus

The main bus station, **Central Camionera Estrella Blanca** (tel. 733/332-3473), is at Galeana and Salazar, six blocks south of the *zócalo*'s southeast corner.

The terminal has many services, including kept luggage ($1 for 3 hours, $7/day), long-distance telephone and fax office, air-conditioned first-class waiting room, cafeteria, and money exchange. Buy fresh fruits, vegetables, groceries, and handicrafts at the market across the street.

First- and second-class buses connect with many destinations in all directions, both long-distance and semilocal.

One first-class departure connects daily northwest with the U.S. border at Mexicali and Tijuana, via Cuernavaca, Toluca, Guadalajara, Tepic, and Mazatlán, along the Pacific Coast.

One first-class **Futura** or **Turistar** departure connects daily north with the U.S. border at Nueveo Laredo, via Cuernavaca, Toluca, San Luis Potosí, Saltillo, and Monterrey.

Many first- and second-class buses connect (hourly during the day) north with Mexico City and south with Chilpancingo and Acapulco. Others connect northeast with Puebla via Izucar de Matamoros, where connections southeast with Oaxaca may be made.

Many second-class buses connect east with Altamirano and north with Toluca via Taxco.

A swarm of second-class **Flecha Roja** buses connect with dozens of small regional Guerrero and Morelos destinations, such as Huitzuco, Taxco, Zacapalco, Jojutla, Casahuatlán, and Cuautla.

First-class bus connections, north with Taxco, Cuernavaca, and Mexico City, and south with Chilpancingo and Acapulco, are also available at the alternative **Estrella de Oro** bus terminal (tel. 733/332-1029), on Highway 95 north, corner of Bandera Nacional, about eight blocks east of the *zócalo*.

### By Car

Connect north 22 miles (36 km) with Taxco via old nontoll Highway 95 in about an hour.

Alternatively connect north directly with Mexico City via Cuernavaca by *cuota* expressway Highway 95. (Find the expressway entrance along old Highway 95, on the southeast, Acapulco, end of town.) Allow about 2.5 hours for this 80-mile (129-km) trip. Make sure you arrive in Mexico City on a permitted driving day.

Connect south with Chilpancingo via old Highway 95, about 64 miles (103 km) in about two hours. Continue to Acapulco via the toll expressway 95D, an additional 62 miles (100 km), in another hour and a quarter.

Connect west with Altamirano from the *periférico*'s northwest side, via winding but scenic Highway 51, 114 miles (184 km) in about 3.5 hours.

## EXCURSIONS FROM IGUALA
### Tuxpan

Nearby Laguna Tuxpan makes an interesting excursion, if not for the lake itself, at least for the country views and the palmy Quinta Happy family resort.

Along the two-mile road to Tuxpan, a major source of Iguala's prosperity becomes immediately apparent. Irrigation has been the key, turning the Iguala valley into an oasis of lush cornfields and a grand orchard of mango trees like the ones you see overhanging the Tuxpan road.

Soon, on the right, pass the refined restaurant *campestre* (country-style) **Villa Los Ocampo** (no phone, 8 A.M.–9 P.M. daily) with plenty of shade and lots of room for kids to run around. The menu includes shrimp tacos, fish fillets, and brochettes, and also breakfast ($4–8).

Continue through the Tuxpan village (with a few small groceries, a post office, and a pharmacy or two) to the restaurants on the north Laguna Tuxpan shore. Two of the most inviting are **El Muelle** (no phone, 8 A.M.–8 P.M. daily), with a pier to walk out on; and farther on, **Restaurant El Arbolito** (no phone, 8 A.M.–8 P.M. daily), shaded by *tabachín* trees (which burst out with lovely red blossoms in season). Both restaurants offer good fish and shrimp dinners beneath airy lakeview *palapas*.

The lake itself is large, about a mile across, and spring-fed. Despite continual withdrawing of irrigation water, the lake level remains virtually constant year-round. When I was there, during the dry spring season, the lake was not very inviting. Local folks were dirtying it up washing clothes on the shoreline. Furthermore, people told me that the lake bass were small because fisherfolk are so poor that they take anything, regardless of size.

Nevertheless, the lake is cleaner and more appealing on the far west side, accessible by the lakeshore dirt road after the restaurants. Amenities include some shade trees, plenty of room for RV parking or tent camping (customary and allowed any time), and easy boat- and kayak-launching access.

Much more inviting is the family-friendly ◖ **Balneario Quinta Happy** (tel. 733/332-3562). From the Tuxpan ingress road, follow the fork to the right (signed "Quinta Alegre"). This is a gorgeous spot for at least a picnic and at most a one-week stay. Amenities include five palm-shaded blue swimming pools, three kiddie pools, restaurants, basketball, mini-market, tennis, volleyball and squash courts, and a soccer field, all surrounded by a beautiful orchard of palm, orange, *limón,* and mango trees. The Quinta Happy (*alegre* in Spanish) accommodations are no less than you would expect: about 20 clean, semi-deluxe rooms around an inviting pool-patio, separated from the oft-noisy day-use area. Room decor is invitingly rustic, embellished with interior brick and hand-hewn wood furnishings. Rates run, for adults, about $35 s or d, $45 t or q; add $5 per kid, with TV, air-conditioning, and parking. For more peace and quiet, reserve a weekday stay.

Get to Tuxpan by local bus or *colectivo* from the Estrella Blanca bus station, seven blocks south of the Iguala *zócalo*. By car from the Iguala *zócalo*, go east via Bandera Nacional; after seven blocks turn right (south) at Highway 95. Continue under the *periférico* overpass. Approximately half a mile after the overpass, at the Rotary Internacional sign on the left, fork left onto the Tuxpan road. At the signed Quinta Alegre fork either turn right to the

GUERRERO UPCOUNTRY

Quinta, or continue straight ahead for Tuxpan village and lakeshore after another mile.

## Cuetlajuchitlán Archaeological Site

Adventurous ruins enthusiasts might enjoy a day exploring at least one of a pair of important partially restored archaeological sites, the closest about an hour by car, two hours by bus, east of Iguala.

Closest is Cuetlajuchitlán (kooay-tlah-hoo-chee-TLAHN), near the small town of Paso Morelos, just off the Mexico City–Acapulco *cuota autopista*. Cuetlajuchitlán, an Aztec (Náhuatl) label, has two possible contrasting translations: either "place of red flowers" or "shriveled place."

Engineers saved the site from destruction by building the 95D expressway tunnel, Los Querendes, under the archaeological zone, which covers about 90 acres (35 hectares). Investigators believe that Cuetlajuchitlán was occupied as early as 600 B.C. and reached its cultural and economic zenith around 200 B.C. Although little is known of the ethnic identity of its founders, archaeologists believe that Cuetlajuchitlán influenced a wide region, stretching north to the valley of Morelos state, south to the Pacific Coast, and east and west along the Río Balsas basin. The reason is that the cylindrical stone monoliths found extensively at Cuetlajuchitlán are also widespread in so many far-flung regions centering on Cuetlajuchitlán. Consequently, archaeologists have begun to associate Cuetlajuchitlán with what they call the "Culture of the Cylinders."

The most fascinating part of the zone is the **Recinto Ceremonial,** a 100-by-60-foot enclosure at the heart of the ruins complex, with both a number of the stone cylinders and *tinas ceremoniales* (ceremonial baths), presumably for purification rituals.

Also very interesting, about 100 feet south of the Recinto Ceremonial, is the *taller de cantería* (stonework factory) with a number of great cylindrical monoliths lying about, apparently finished but unused.

Two **Complejos Habitacionales** (Habitational Complexes), apparently for nobles and priests, can be explored about 100 feet northeast and about 300 feet west of the Recinto respectively.

Get to Cuetlajuchitlán by bus, via Huitzuco, an hour southeast from the Iguala main bus station. From Huitzuco, continue by bus or local minivan east to Paso Morelos, just past (east of) the Mexico City–Acapulco expressway. Continue by taxi or on foot (ask local directions) to the nearby archaeological site.

By car from Iguala, drive south along Highway 95 about six miles (9 km) to the left (eastbound) turnoff road to Huitzuco. Continue another 14 miles (23 km) to Huitzuco and another 10 miles (16 km) to the expressway and Paso Morelos, just east of it. In Paso Morelos, ask directions to the site, nearby.

## Teopantecuantlán Archaeological Site

Equally fascinating, but an hour and a half more remote, is Teopantecuantlán (tay-oh-pahn-tay-kooan-TLAHN), in the valley about 30 miles east of Cuetlajuchitlán. The entire archaeological zone, including both the ceremonial center and surrounding former agricultural village, occupies nearly a square mile (about 500 acres or 200 hectares).

The site is especially interesting because of the antiquity of its two main pieces of Olmec-style monumental art, heavy with jaguar symbolism, dating from around 1400 B.C. As a result, archaeologists have inferred connections between Teopantecuantlán and the similar Olmec-style art found in the cave paintings at Juxtlahuaca, 100 miles to the south.

Archaeologists believe Teopantecuantlán reached its zenith around 900 B.C., with irrigation that in turn led to bumper crops, rising population, economic specialization, wealth, and architectural innovation. Massive stone walls were raised, culminating in a pair of grand platforms and arched passageways leading to noble tombs.

Exploration of the site reveals partly restored remains of Teopantecuantlán's grandeur:

pyramidal platforms, palaces, plazas, tombs, two ball courts, and an irrigation channel.

To get to Teopantecuantlán, follow the directions from Iguala to Cuetlajuchitlán in the previous listing. From Paso Morelos, by car or local minivan or bus, continue 22 miles (36 km) southeast to Atenango del Río, and another seven miles (12 km) to the right (south) turnoff to Copalillo village. After two more miles, at Copalillo, ask for local directions to the site, about 10 miles (16 km) farther by auto-accessible gravel road.

# Taxco

As Acapulco thrives on what's new, Taxco (pop. 150,000) luxuriates in what's old. Nestling beneath forest-crowned mountains and decorated with monuments of its silver-rich past, Taxco now enjoys an equally rich flood of visitors who stop en route to or from Acapulco. They come to enjoy its fiestas and clear pine-scented air and to stroll the cobbled hillside lanes and bargain for world-renowned silver jewelry.

And despite the acclaim, Taxco preserves its diminutive colonial charm *because* of its visitors, who come to enjoy what Taxco offers. They stay in venerable family-owned lodgings, walk to the colorful little *zócalo,* where they admire the famous baroque cathedral, and wander among the awning-festooned market lanes just downhill.

But Taxco offers even more. Travel an hour north to wander within the colossal limestone fairyland of the renowned Grutas de Cacahuamilpa. On the same day, continue another hour north to marvel at the exquisite untouristed remains of Xochicalco, legendary pre-Columbian capital and internationally acclaimed UNESCO World Heritage site.

On yet another day, travel west an hour to

Taxco, built on seven hills, affords lovely views in all directions.`

© BRUCE WHIPPERMAN

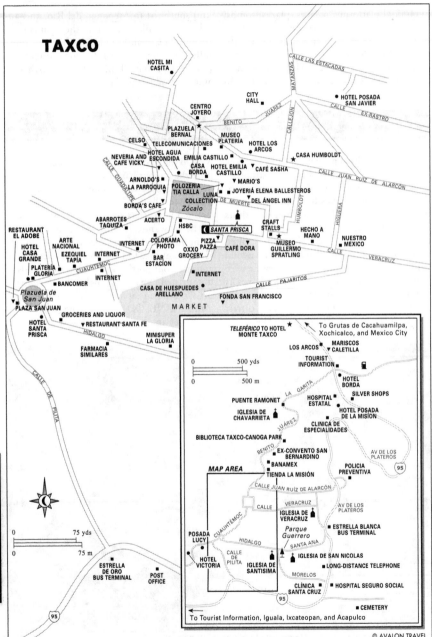

# TAXCO

HOTEL MI CASITA

CITY HALL

CENTRO JOYERO

HOTEL POSADA SAN JAVIER

CALLE LAS ESTACADAS

MATANZAS

JUAREZ

CALLEJON

CALLE EX-RASTRO

PLAZUELA BERNAL

BENITO

MUSEO PLATERÍA

TELECOMUNICACIONES

HOTEL LOS ARCOS

CASA HUMBOLDT

CELSO

NEVERIA AND CAFE VICKY

HOTEL AGUA ESCONDIDA

EMILIA CASTILLO

HOTEL EMILIA CASTILLO

CAFÉ SASHA

CALLE GUADALUPE

ARNOLDO'S LA PARROQUIA

CASA BORDA

CALLE JUAN RUIZ DE ALARCÓN

MARIO'S

POLOZERIA TIA CALLA

JOYERIA ELENA BALLESTEROS

LUNA COLLECTION

DE MUERTE

DEL ÁNGEL INN

BORDA'S CAFÉ

Zócalo

HUMBOLDT

HIGUERA

ABARROTES TAQUIZA

ACERTO

HSBC

SANTA PRISCA

CRAFT STALLS

HECHO A MANO

NUESTRO MEXICO

RESTAURANT EL ADOBE

ARTE NACIONAL

EZEQUIEL TAPÍA

INTERNET

COLORAMA PHOTO

PIZZA PAZZA

CAFÉ DORA

MUSEO GUILLERMO SPRATLING

CALLE VERACRUZ

HOTEL CASA GRANDE

OXXO GROCERY

BAR ESTACIÓN

PLATERÍA GLORIA

CUAUHTEMOC

INTERNET

INTERNET

BANCOMER

Plazuela de San Juan

CASA DE HUESPEDES ARELLANO

CALLE PAJARITOS

PLAZA SAN JUAN

FONDA SAN FRANCISCO

HOTEL SANTA PRISCA

GROCERIES AND LIQUOR

RESTAURANT SANTA FE

MARKET

HIDALGO

MINISUPER LA GLORIA

FARMACIA SIMILARES

CALLE DE PILITA

GUERRERO UPCOUNTRY

75 yds

75 m

ESTRELLA DE ORO BUS TERMINAL

POST OFFICE

95

**Inset map (MAP AREA):**

TELEFÉRICO TO HOTEL MONTE TAXCO

To Grutas de Cacahuamilpa, Xochicalco, and Mexico City

LOS ARCOS

MARISCOS CALETILLA

TOURIST INFORMATION

500 yds

500 m

HOTEL BORDA

SILVER SHOPS

LA GARITA

PUENTE RAMONET

HOSPITAL ESTATAL

IGLESIA DE CHAVARRIETA

JUAREZ

HOTEL POSADA DE LA MISIÓN

CLINICA DE ESPECIALIDADES

BIBLIOTECA TAXCO-CANOGA PARK

BENITO

AV DE LOS PLATEROS

EX-CONVENTO SAN BERNARDINO

MAP AREA

BANAMEX

TIENDA LA MISIÓN

POLICIA PREVENTIVA

95

CALLE JUAN RUÍZ DE ALARCÓN

CALLE

VERACRUZ

AV DE LOS PLATEROS

IGLESIA DE VERACRUZ

CUAUHTEMOC

Parque Guerrero

ESTRELLA BLANCA BUS TERMINAL

POSADA LUCY

HIDALGO

SANTA ANA

IGLESIA DE SAN NICOLAS

HOTEL VICTORIA

CALLE DE PILITA

IGLESIA DE SANTISIMA

LONG-DISTANCE TELEPHONE

MORELOS

CLÍNICA SANTA CRUZ

HOSPITAL SEGURO SOCIAL

95

CEMETERY

To Tourist Information, Iguala, Ixcateopan, and Acapulco

© AVALON TRAVEL

Ixcateopan village and visit the revered resting place of Cuauhtémoc, the last Aztec emperor who, at the eventual cost of his life, rallied his people against the Spanish conquest.

## ORIENTATION

Although the present city (elev. 5,850 feet, 1,780 meters) spreads much farther, the center of town encompasses the city's original seven hills, wrinkles in the slope of a towering mountain.

For most visitors, the downhill town limit is the *carretera,* the local stretch of old National Highway 95, now named Avenida de los Plateros, after the Taxco *plateros* (silversmiths) who put Taxco on Mexico's tourism map. The highway contours along the hillside from **Los Arcos** (The Arches) on the north (Mexico City) end of town about two miles, passing the Calle Pilita intersection on the south (Acapulco) edge of town. Along the *carretera,* immediately accessible to a steady stream of tour buses, lie the town's plusher hotels and many silver shops.

Be sure to pass under the picturesque Calle Los Arcos arch during your Taxco stay.

The rest of the town is fortunately insulated from tour buses by its narrow winding streets. From the *carretera,* the most important of them climb and converge, like bent spokes of a wheel, to the *zócalo* (main plaza). Beginning with the most northerly, the main streets (and directions they run) are La Garita (uphill), J. R. de Alarcón (downhill), Veracruz (downhill), Santa Ana (downhill), Salubridad (uphill), Morelos (downhill), and Pilita (downhill).

## GETTING AROUND

Although walking is by far Taxco's most common mode of transport, taxis go anywhere within the city limits for about $2 days, $3 nights. White *combi* collective vans (fare about $0.40) follow designated routes, marked on the windshields. Simply tell your specific destination to the driver. For side trips to nearby towns and villages, a fleet of **Flecha Roja** second-class local buses and *colectivo* vans leave frequently from the Estrella Blanca on the *carretera* terminal near the corner of Veracruz.

## HISTORY

The traditional hieroglyph representing Taxco shows athletes in a court competing in a game of *tlatchtli* (still locally played) with a solid natural-rubber (*hule*) ball. "Tlachco," the Náhuatl name representing the place that had become a small Aztec garrison settlement by the eve of the conquest, literally translates as "Place of the Ball Game." The Spanish, more interested in local minerals than in linguistic details, shifted the name to Taxco.

### Colonization

In 1524, Hernán Cortés, looking for tin to alloy with copper to make bronze cannon, heard that people around Taxco were using bits of metal for money. Prospectors hurried out, and within a few years they struck rich silver veins in Tetelcingo, now known as Taxco Viejo (Old Taxco), seven miles downhill from present-day Taxco. The Spanish crown appropriated the mines and worked them with generations of native forced labor.

Eighteenth-century enlightenment came to

Taxco in the person of José Borda, who, arriving from Spain in 1716, modernized the mine franchise his brother had been operating. José improved conditions and began paying the miners, thereby increasing productivity and profits. In contrast to past operators, Borda returned the proceeds to Taxco, building the monuments that still grace the town. His fortune built streets, bridges, fountains, arches, and his masterpiece, the church of Santa Prisca, which included a special chapel for the miners, who before had not been allowed to enter the church.

### Independence and Modern Times

The 1810–1821 War of Independence and the subsequent civil strife within a generation reduced the mines to but a memory. They were nearly forgotten when William Spratling, an American artist and architect, moved to Taxco in 1929 and began reviving Taxco's ancient but moribund silversmithing tradition. Working with local artisans, Spratling opened the first cooperative shop, Las Delicias.

Spurred by the trickle of tourists along the new Acapulco highway, more shops opened, increasing the demand for silver, which in turn led to the reopening of the mines. Soon silver demand outpaced the supply. Silver began streaming in from other parts of Mexico to the workbenches of thousands of artisans in hundreds of family- and cooperative-owned shops dotting the still-quaint hillsides of a new, prosperous Taxco.

## SIGHTS
### 【 Santa Prisca

All roads in Taxco begin and end on the *zócalo* at Santa Prisca church. French architect D. Diego Durán designed and built the church between 1751 and 1758 with money from the fortune of silver king Don José Borda. The facade, decorated with saints on pedestals, arches, and spiraled columns, follows the baroque churrigueresque style (after Jose Churriguera, 1665–1725, the "Spanish Michelangelo"). Interior furnishings include an elegant pipe organ, brought from Germany by muleback (via boat to Veracruz, thence overland) in 1751, and several gilded side

Santa Prisca church

© BRUCE WHIPPERMAN

altars. The riot of interior elaboration climaxes in the towering gold-leaf main altar, which seems to drip with ornamentation in tribute to Santa Prisca, the Virgin of the Immaculate Conception, the Virgin of the Rosary, and San Sebastián (on the right) who bravely and piously endures his wounds.

Dreamy Bible-story paintings by Miguel Cabrera decorate a chamber behind the main altar, while in a room to the right, portraits of Pope Benedict XIV, who sanctioned all this, José Borda, who paid for it, and his brother, Manuel Borda, Santa Prisca's first priest, hang at the head of a solemn gallery of subsequent padres.

Outside, landmarks around the plaza include the **Casa Borda** (visible, as you face away from the church facade, on the right side of the *zócalo,* open 9 A.M.–9 P.M. daily). This former Borda family town house, built concurrently with the church in typical baroque colonial style, now serves as the Taxco Casa de Cultura, featuring exhibitions by local artists and artisans in the upstairs gallery (10 A.M.–5 P.M. Tues.–Sun.).

## Downhill

Heading out and down the church steps, you can continue downhill in either of two interesting ways. If you walk left immediately downhill from the church, you reach the lane Calle Los Arcos, running alongside and below the church. From there, reach the **market** by heading right before the quaint archway over the street, down the winding staircase-lane, where you'll soon be in a warren of awning-covered stalls.

If, however, you head right from the church steps, another immediate right leads you beside the church along legendary **Calle de Muerte** (Street of Death), so named because of the former cemetery where the workers who died constructing the church were buried. (Note the skeleton on the church-front corner facing Calle de Muerte.)

## Museo Guillermo Spratling

Continuing downhill, you'll find Museo Guillermo Spratling (fronting the little plaza behind the church, tel. 762/622-1660, usually open 9 A.M.–5 P.M. Tues.–Sun., hours may vary seasonally, $3). William Spratling was instrumental in helping the community revive its silversmithing tradition in the late 1920s. On the main and upper floors of this history and archaeology museum named in his honor, the National Institute of Archaeology displays intriguing carvings and ceramics (including unusual phallic examples), such as a ball-game ring, animal masks, and a priestly statuette with knife in one hand, human heart in the other. Temporary historical, cultural, and archaeological displays are housed in the basement.

## Casa Humboldt

Nearby stands the Casa Humboldt (one block down J. R. de Alarcón, the downhill extension of Calle de Muerte, tel. 762/622-5501, 10 A.M.–6 P.M. Tues.–Sat., 10 A.M.–2 P.M. Sun., winter hours may be shorter, $3). The museum is named after the celebrated geographer (who is said to have stayed only one night, however). Now the state maintains it as the Museum of Viceregal (colonial) Art. Displays feature a

Casa Humboldt houses the Museum of Viceregal Art.

© BRUCE WHIPPERMAN

permanent collection of historical artifacts, including the Manila galleon, colonial technology, and colonial religious sculpture and painting.

## Museo Platería

Nearby, the Museo Platería (J. R. de Alarcón 4, 3rd floor, a few doors uphill from the Hotel Emilio Castillo, tel. 762/622-0658, 10 A.M.–6 P.M. daily, $3) illustrates a history of Taxco silver craft and displays a number of prizewinning pieces by renowned Taxco artists-in-silver. (Alternately, you may enter the museum through the *zócalo*-front shopping patio de Las Artesanías, next to the Casa Borda.)

## Walking Tour

A short ride, coupled with a walk circling back to the *zócalo*, provides the basis for an interesting half-day exploration. Taxi or ride a *combi* to the Hotel Posada de la Misión, where the **Cuauhtémoc Mural** glitters on a wall near the pool. Executed by renowned muralist Juan O'Gorman with a riot of pre-Columbian symbols—yellow sun, pearly rabbit-in-the-moon, snarling jaguar, writhing serpents, fluttering eagle—the mural glorifies Cuauhtémoc, the last Aztec emperor. Cuauhtémoc, unlike his uncle Moctezuma, tenaciously resisted the conquest, but was captured and later executed by Cortés in 1525. His remains were discovered in 1949 in Ixcateopan, about 24 miles away by local bus or car (see *Excursions from Taxco*).

Continue your walk a few hundred yards along the *carretera* (north, Mexico City direction) from the Hotel Posada de la Misión. There, a driveway leading right just before the gas station heads to the Hotel Borda grounds. Turn left on the road just after the gate and you'll come to an **antique brick chimney and cable-hung derrick.** These mark an inactive **mineshaft** descending to the mine-tunnel honeycomb thousands of feet beneath the town. The mines are still being worked from another entrance, but for mostly lead rather than silver. You can see the present-day works from the hilltop of the now-closed Hotel Hacienda del Solar on the south edge of town.

Now, return to the *carretera,* cross over and stroll the main town entry street, **Calle la Garita,** about a mile back to the *zócalo.* Of special interest along the way, besides a number of crafts stores and stalls, are the **Iglesia de Chavarrieta,** the **Ex-Convento San Bernardino,** and the **Biblioteca Taxco-Canoga Park** (library, 9 A.M.–1 P.M. and 3–7 P.M. Mon.–Fri., 9 A.M.–1 P.M. Sat.) with many English-language novels and reference books.

Farther on, a block before the *zócalo,* pause to decipher the stone mosaic of the **Taxco Hieroglyph,** which decorates the pavement in front of the Palacio Municipal (City Hall). Inside, climb the stairs for a balcony-front view of the hieroglyph and the wall mural for a graphic review of Mexican history. See the main actors, from left to right: stolid Benito Juárez ("Respect for the rights of all is peace"); elderly general Porfirio Díaz gives away church and communal land to foreigners; banderilla-laden Emiliano Zapata declares his Plan de Ayala; president Lázaro Cárdenas in overalls expropriates foreign oil companies; and

© BRUCE WHIPPERMAN

the Taxco Hieroglyph, in front of the Palacio Municipal

Aldolfo López Mateos declares free school textbooks; while Juárez, John F. Kennedy, Henry Kissinger, Charles de Gaulle, and Jawarlal Nehru look on.

## Cableway (*Teleférico*)

A cableway above the highway (8 A.M.–7 P.M. daily, round-trip tickets about $6, kids half price), on the north side of town where the *carretera* passes beneath Los Arcos, lifts passengers to soaring vistas of the town on one side and ponderous, pine-studded mesas on the other. The ride ends at the Hotel Monte Taxco, where you can make a day of it golfing, horseback riding, playing tennis, eating lunch, and sunning on the panoramic-view pool deck. Return by taxi if you miss the last car down.

## Cristo del Monte

Above the opposite (west) side of town, about two miles uphill from the *zócalo,* stands the colossal new stone statue of Jesus, where folks enjoy an airy panoramic town view framed by lush, green looming mountains. Get there on foot (if

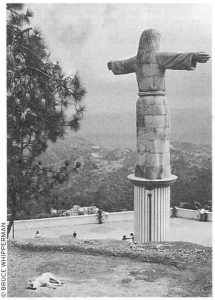
the Cristo del Monte, high above Taxco

© BRUCE WHIPPERMAN

you relish a 1,500-foot climb; wear a hat and carry water) or by taxi (about $2.50), *colectivo* ($0.40, to Casahuates village), or car or on foot, west from the *zócalo,* via Calle Cuauhtémoc, past the Hotel Victoria. After about two more uphill miles (3 km), fork right at the Huixteco sign and continue past Casahuates village about 200 yards, where a dirt driveway leads right to the Cristo del Monte park.

### In-Town Vistas

You needn't go as far afield as the Hotel Monte Taxco or the Cristo del Monte to get a good view of the city streets and houses carpeting the mountainside. Vistas depend not only on vantage point but time of day, since the best viewing sunshine (which frees you from squinting) should come generally from *behind.* Consequently, spots along the highway (more or less east of town), such as the patios of the Hotel Posada de la Misión and the *mirador* atop the Hotel Borda, provide good morning views, while afternoon views are best from points west of town, along the extension

of Cuauhtémoc past the Plazuela de San Juan uphill by (or in the hilltop garden of) the Hotel Rancho Taxco Victoria.

## ACCOMMODATIONS

Taxco's dry, temperate climate relegates air-conditioning, ceiling fans, and central heating to frills offered only in the most expensive hotels. All of the hotel recommendations listed here have hot water and private baths, however.

Taxco's low-end hotels (under $50, but nevertheless comfortable) cluster in the colorful *zócalo* neighborhood, while many of the high-end (over $100) lodgings are scattered mostly along the *carretera.*

### Under $50

Soak in your fill of Mexico delights during a stay at **Casa de Huéspedes Arrellano** (Calle de Pajaritos 23, tel. 762/622-0215), an island of graceful tranquillity, yet, surprisingly, smack in the middle of the town market. Past the hotel gate, you enter a flowery patio garden blooming with birdsong and enfolded by tropical verandas. Owner Maria Castillo Arellano offers 14 guest rooms, all opening to airy plant-decorated view portico-patios, ideal for shady relaxation. The rooms themselves, most in need of some paint and polish, are nevertheless clean and simply but comfortably furnished. Tariffs are right, at about $16 s, $28 d, $37 t with shared bath; $21, $32, and $34 with private hot-water bath; all with fans and colorful old-world Taxco just beyond the gate. Get there on foot only, by rolling your luggage a couple of long blocks along Calle Pajaritos, the lane that begins on (one-way downhill) thoroughfare Calle Veracruz (hire a taxi), across from Nuestro Mexico handicrafts shop.

Walk west of the *zócalo* half a block past Plazuela de San Juan to the **Posada Lucy** (Carlos J. Nibbi 8, tel./fax 762/622-1780, $35 d) on the left. Here, owners offer 32 budget rooms in a rambling complex, fortuitously isolated below and away from street noise. Airy patios with chairs and tables invite quiet relaxation. Inside, rooms are simply but attractively decorated with color-coordinated curtains, bedspreads, and handmade wooden furniture. Prices run a reasonable $35 s or d in one bed; $60 for 2–4 people in two double beds, all with hot-water showers, TV, parking, and credit cards accepted.

On the diagonally opposite side of the town center, five blocks northeast of the *zócalo,* find the inviting ◖ **Hotel Posada San Javier** (Estacas 32, tel. 762/622-3177, tel./fax 762/622-2351, posadasanjavier@hotmail.com, $49 d). Although it's a steep climb to the *zócalo,* this is a very popular hotel, built around a tranquil inner garden. It offers about 40 immaculate rooms, an idyllic patio with (unheated but usually swimmable) blue pool, framed in lush verdure and airy verandas for relaxing. All this for only $45 s, $49 d, $55 t; very large junior suites run $70 d. All with fans, hot water, parking, and an inviting reading room with lots of books. This hotel customarily fills up by late afternoon, especially on weekends. Best arrive very early, or reserve several days in advance.

Back by the town center, on J. R. de Alarcón just a block downhill, west of the *zócalo,* a pair of former colonial mansions, now popular hotels, face each other across the street. First choice goes to the refined ◖ **Hotel Los Arcos** (J. R. de Alarcón 4, tel. 762/622-1836, fax 762/622-7982, hotelosarcostaxco@yahoo.com, www.hotellosarcos.net, $47 d). The 21 rooms rise in three vine-draped tiers around an inner patio, replete with reminders of old Mexico. The rooms, with thoughtfully selected handmade polished wooden furniture, tile floors, rustic wall art, and immaculate hand-painted cobalt-on-white tile bathrooms, rent for about $32 s, $47 d, with hot water and fans.

Guests at the very compact **Hotel Emilia Castillo** (J. R. de Alarcón 7, tel./fax 762/622-1396, reservations2@hotelemilia castillo.com, www.hotelemiliacastillo.com, $45 d) across the street enjoy hand-carved wood embellishments, oil paintings, stone sculptures, and plants gracing virtually every wall and corner. The 14 smallish rooms, in neocolonial decor around an intimate upper balcony, are clean, comfortable, and thoughtfully furnished in old-world style, and rent for about

$40 s, $45 d, $50 t, with hot-water shower baths, TV, and fans. The owners also runs an adjacent silver boutique, whose displays decorate the downstairs lobby.

## $50–100

Picturesquely tucked on an uphill lane, just two blocks north of the *zócalo,* find ◖ **Hotel Mi Casita** (Altos de Redondo 1, tel./fax 762/627-1777, reservations@hotelmicasita .com, www.hotelmicasita.com, $55 d). A charmingly rustic retreat for a loyal cadre of longtime lovers of Mexico, the Hotel Mi Casita blooms with a treasury of delightful Mexicana. Its 12 rooms and suites, most with panoramic balcony views of the surrounding city and cloud-tipped mountains, are individually decorated with fetching designer lamps, handpainted wall art, and colorful Talavera-tiled bathrooms. Rentals, some quaintly petite, ordinarily begin at about $55 s or d and range upward to about $75 for the largest suites. Add about 25 percent during Christmas and Easter holidays.

Head uphill, past the opposite (west) side of the plaza, and follow Cuauhtémoc one block to the Plazuela de San Juan and the adjacent ◖ **Hotel Santa Prisca** (Cena Obscura 1, tel. 762/622-0080 or 762/622-0980, fax 762/622-2938, htl_staprisca@yahoo.com, credit cards accepted, $35 s, $51 d). This tranquil, dignified hostelry surrounds an oft-fragrant garden of orange trees; its off-lobby dining room shines with graceful old-world details, such as beveled glass, a fireplace, blue-white stoneware, and ivy-hung portals. Its tile-decorated rooms, in two floors around the garden just outside, are clean and comfortable. Larger junior suites go for $70 s or d; all rooms have fans, private hot-water baths, and parking.

Taxco's only *zócalo*-front hostelry, the **Hotel Agua Escondida** (Calle Guillermo Spratling 4, tel. 762/622-0726 or 762/622-1166, fax 762/622-1306, hotelaguaesc@prodigy.net .mx, $76 d), stands on the diagonally opposite corner from the church. A multilevel maze of hidden patios, rooftop sundecks, and dazzling city views, the Agua Escondida offers dozens of clean, comfortable rooms. The name, which translates as "Hidden Water," must refer to its big (but unheated) swimming pool, which is tucked away in a far rooftop corner. Rooms vary; if you have the choice, look at several. Try to avoid the oft-noisy streetfront rooms. If you don't mind climbing, some of the upper-floor rooms have airy penthouse views. The 76 rooms run about $60 s, $76 d, $103 t, with fans, TV, hot water, limited parking, and credit cards accepted.

The formerly neglected **Hotel Borda** (Cerro de Pedregal, tel. 762/622-0225, fax 762/622-0617, hotelborda@prodigy.net.mx, www.hotelborda.com, $87 d), off the *carretera* downhill, thanks to new owners has been fixed up to approximate the luxury hotel it once was. This is fortunate, for the hotel's magnificent assets—grand vistas, spacious garden, and luxurious blue pool and patio—remain as attractive as ever. The 110 clean, comfortable, and pleasingly decorated motel-modern rooms rent for about $87 s or d in one bed, $92 d in two beds, $97 and $103 weekends, two kids up to 12 go free, suites from $110, with restaurant, bar, fans, TV, parking, and credit cards accepted.

## Over $100

Resort-style ◖ **Hotel Monte Taxco** (Lomas de Taxco, tel. 762/622-1300 or 762/622-1301, fax 762/622-1428, reservaciones@montetaxco .com.mx, www.montetaxco.com.mx, credit cards accepted, $110) stands atop a towering mesa accessible by either a steep road or cableway (*teleférico*) from the highway just north of town. On weekends, the hotel is often packed with well-heeled Mexico City families, whose kids play organized games while their parents enjoy the panoramic poolside view or play golf and tennis. The 156 deluxe rooms, most with view balconies, rent from about $140 s or d weekends (Sun.–Thurs. $110), with air-conditioning, phones, and TV; facilities include restaurants, shops, a piano bar, disco, weekend live music, parking, a gym, pool, sauna, and spa. The adjacent hotel country club offers a nine-hole golf course, tennis courts, and horseback riding. To get there from Hwy. 95, look for the Hotel Monte Taxco sign about half a mile north

of town, and turn steeply uphill to the left, in the direction of Mexico City . The cableway runs 8 A.M.–7 P.M. daily; round-trip tickets cost about $6, with kids' tickets half price.

If you'd like to stay atop Monte Taxco, a good alternative to the hotel would be to rent one of the neocolonial-style apartments of the **Villas Monte Taxco** (adjacent to the golf course, 100 yards outside the Hotel Monte Taxco front door, tel. 762/622-2305, fax 762/622-5609). For about $110 per night (ask for a mid-week discount) you get a deluxe one-bedroom mountainview apartment with kitchenette, living room, dining room, use of the pool, and access to the golf course, tennis courts, horseback riding, mountain trails, and the Hotel Monte Taxco's facilities next door.

Back down on the highway in town, the **Hotel Posada de la Misión** (Cerro de la Misión 32, tel. 762/622-0063 or 762/622-0533, fax 762/622-2198, hpmreserva@posadamision .com, www.posadamision.com, credit cards accepted) spreads over a view hillside. Its guests, many on group tours, enjoy cool, quiet patios, green gardens, plant-lined corridors, a sunny pool and deck, a view restaurant, and parking. Many of the semideluxe rooms have panoramic city views; some have fireplaces. All rooms have color TV and phones. Standard rooms rent for about $200 d, $225 weekends, including breakfast. Kids under 12 are free in room with parents. Christmas and New Year's prices are higher. Some readers have complained about unkempt rooms; take a look before moving in. Find it just off the *carretera,* uphill side, 200 yards south of the Pemex gas station.

## FOOD
## Stalls and Snacks

The numerous *fondas* (foodstalls) atop the *artesanías* (ar-tay-sah-NEE-ahs) handicrafts section of the Taxco market (see *Shopping*) are Taxco's prime source of wholesome country-style food. The quality of their fare is a matter of honor for the proprietors, since among their local patrons word of a little bad food goes a long way. It's very hard to go wrong, moreover, if your selections are steaming hot and made fresh before your own eyes (in contrast, by the way, to most restaurant and hotel fare).

Choose from a potpourri that might include steaming bowls of *menudo* or *pozole,* or maybe plates of pork or chicken *mole,* or *molcajetes* (big stone grinding bowls) filled with steaming meat and broth and draped with hot nopal cactus leaves.

On the *zócalo,* stalls appear late afternoons, offering favorite evening snacks, including tacos, *pozole, menudo,* hot dogs, popcorn, potato chips (deep-fried on the spot), and sweets such as french-fried bananas and churros.

For a sit-down snack or light lunch or supper, go to the **Nevería and Cafetería Vicky** (above the *zócalo*'s northwest corner, tel. 762/622-4085, noon–10 P.M. Mon.–Sat., noon–11 P.M. Sun., $2–3), across the street from the Hotel Agua Escondida. Take a balcony seat and take in the fascinating *zócalo* view, with an espresso *café Americano,* fruit plate, hamburger, and/or ice cream. (Get there via the lane that heads steeply uphill across from the Hotel Agua Escondida. At the first street, turn a sharp left. Vicky's is one door past Arnoldo's mask shop.)

Escape from the *zócalo* hubbub to **Café Naturalito** (Plaza Borda 1, tel. 762/622-7000, 8 A.M.–10:30 P.M. Tues.–Sun., breakfast and lunch $2.50–3.50, dinner $8), a block north of the churchfront. In the shady exhaust-fume-free inner patio of the Plaza Borda shopping center, enjoy breakfast (omelettes, waffles), lunch (chicken sandwich, banana-nut crepe) or supper (salad and spaghetti Bolognese).

## Restaurants

Although its restaurants are not what draws most Taxco's visitors, Taxco nevertheless offers some very recommendable dining options.

Judging from its hundreds of daily customers, the **( Pozolería Tía Calla** (at the *zócalo*'s northeast corner, downstairs, tel. 762/622-5602, 1–10 P.M. Wed.–Mon., $2–4) seems to be Taxco's most popular restaurant. Everyone comes to feast on the delicious country-style tacos, enchiladas, *pozole* in multiple variations, and even salads (try the good tuna salad, full

of crunchy veggies, enough for two). Besides the budget prices, the final clincher here is the prompt, professional service, in an immaculate family-friendly dining room setting.

Another good bet on the *zócalo* is **Pizza Pazza** (right-hand side of the cathedral, upstairs, tel. 762/622-5500, 9 A.M.–11 P.M. daily, $5–12). Although the menu offers a little bit of everything Italian and more, the specialty is good pizza in about 15 varieties; extras include relaxed ambience, professional service, checkered tablecloths, and airy plaza-view balcony tables. If the TV bothers you, the staff won't mind turning it down to low volume (*volumen bajo*) if asked.

For both hearty and economical daytime meals, visit friendly newcomer **Café Dora** (Calle Los Arcos 13, tel. 762/622-2850, 8 A.M.–6 P.M. daily, $3–6) on the downstairs lane behind the church. The specialties here are good coffee, breakfasts, and a bountiful afternoon *comida.*

On the other hand, join in a 30-year Taxco tradition at **Mario's** (Plaza Borda 1, south side of the *zócalo,* tel. 762/622-7797, 10 A.M.–midnight daily, $3–12). Favorites here are Sicilian burritos, chili American-style, spaghettis, and pizzas in many varieties). Musician-owner Mario Esquivel (a '60s-era headliner) continues his long custom, entertaining at his piano bar along with a trio Saturdays and holidays (call to check program).

At least recommendable for its refined old-world ambience, the restaurant **( Del Ángel Inn** (Calle de Muerte—now Celso Muñoz—4, 2nd floor, tel. 762/622-5525, 8 A.M.–10:30 P.M. daily, $5–10) adds an airy view and good food to the reasons for going there. Inside, rustic old-adobe walls, regal stone columns, and baroque statuary enhance the pleasing effect. As for food, choose from a very recognizable and tasty menu of appetizers, soups, and salads, pasta, Mexican specialties, meats, and more. Find it a few steps downhill from the Santa Prisca churchfront, left side.

A block from the *zócalo,* along Calle Cuauhtémoc overlooking Plazuela de San Juan, try Mexican-style **Restaurant El Adobe**

(Plazuela de San Juan 13, tel. 762/622-1416, 8 A.M.–11 P.M. daily, $5–12) for breakfast or a lunch break. For breakfast, enjoy juice, eggs, and hotcakes; for lunch, hamburgers, tacos, and enchiladas, or, for dinner, steak Adobe-style and shrimp brochette.

Of the restaurant options, one of the best for genteel non-tourist ambience is the local favorite **❰ Restaurant Santa Fe** (on the left a few doors downhill from Plazuela de San Juan, tel. 762/622-1170, 7:30 A.M.–10 P.M. daily, $5). Tasty professionally prepared and served country fare keeps a battalion of faithful patrons happy. Although the long à la carte menu varies from *pozole* and soup to chicken and fish, the main event is the daily four-course *comida* of soup (try *crema de zanahoria*), spaghetti, main dish (try *chiles rellenos*), and dessert. Good for breakfast, too.

Customers at **Café Sasha** (on Callejon Matanzas, around the corner from Casa Humboldt, cell tel. 044-762/101-1713, 7:30 A.M.–11 P.M. daily, $4–8) enjoy both an inviting bohemian atmosphere and hearty comfort food. Pick from a unique and tasty menu of breakfasts (one cup of coffee included), with home fries; salads (such as Roquefort and spinach), pizzas, sandwiches, pastas; and specialties such as falafel, excellent chow mein, Thai chicken, and apple pie.

## ENTERTAINMENT AND EVENTS

Taxco people mostly entertain each other. Such spontaneous diversions are most likely around the *zócalo*, which often seems like an impromptu festival of typical Mexican scenes. Around the outside stand the monuments of the colonial past, while on the sidewalks sit the native people who come in from the hills to sell their onions, tamales, and pottery. Kids run between them, their parents and grandparents watching, while young men and women flirt, blush, giggle, and jostle one another until late in the evening.

### Nightlife

A number of night spots, around or near the *zócalo*, are popular with both local folks and visitors. For example, join the locals at **Bar Berta,** on the church corner, or enjoy bouncy music with a mostly tourist crowd at **Bar Estación** (on Cuauhtémoc, by Bancomer, a block west of the *zócalo*, hours vary depending on customer demand, usually noon–11 P.M. Mon.–Thurs., noon–2 A.M. Fri.–Sun.). Or, climb the economic scale, up the *zócalo*-front stairs, to fashionable **Acerto** (Plaza Borda 12, tel. 762/622-0064, noon–midnight daily, $6–16) restaurant-sports bar. Here, either thrill to the international soccer battles, enjoy a choice people-watching perch, or just relax over dinner. The food (salads, soups, pastas, meats) will, most likely, send you home satisfied.

For a contrasting but equally entertaining scene, walk downstairs to tiny **Borda's Café** (Plaza Borda 6A, tel. 762/627-2073, 8 A.M.–11 P.M. daily, $5–7), where owner Efrain fills his small space with humor and good cheer. Decor shifts seasonally—Christmas, Independence Day, Day of the Dead. His permanent exhibit is a gallery of vintage James Dean, Marlon Brando, Marilyn Monroe, and Elvis Presley portraits. Furthermore, the food, a bit of everything from enchiladas *verdes* and tuna salad to cappuccino or pork chops with guacamole, is prepared to please.

Later, or on another day, continue your Taxco party via the jazzy recorded music pouring out of the speakers at restaurant-bar **Concha** (upstairs at Hotel Casa Grande, at Plazuela de San Juan, hours vary depending on customer demand, usually noon–11 P.M. Mon.–Thurs., noon–2 A.M. Fri.–Sun.). Live music is featured on Saturdays. At **Mario's** (Plaza Borda 1, south side of the *zócalo*, tel. 762/622-7797, 10 A.M.–midnight daily) a piano accompanies a trio playing oldies but goodies Saturday from around 9 or 10 P.M. They often remain open past midnight during holidays, especially Christmas–New Year, and Easter.

For more music, in a refined, upscale setting, the **Hotel Monte Taxco** (tel. 762/622-1300 or 762/622-1301) offers a piano bar in the restaurant 8–11 P.M. Fri.–Sat. and on holidays. At the similarly upscale **Hotel Posada de la Misión** (tel. 762/622-0063 or 762/622-0533)

## *TLATCHTLI:* THE BALL GAME

Basketball fever is probably a mild affliction compared to the enthusiasm pre-Columbian crowds felt for *tlatchtli,* the ball game that was played throughout Mesoamerica and is still played in some places. Contemporary accounts and latter-day scholarship have led to a partial picture of *tlatchtli* as it was played centuries ago. Although details varied locally, the game centered around a hard natural-rubber ball called a *tlatchtli,* which players batted back and forth across a center dividing line with hip, arm, and torso blows.

Play and scoring was vaguely similar to tennis. Opponents, either individuals or small teams, tried to smash the ball past their opponents into scoring niches at the opposite ends of an I-shaped, sunken court. Players also could garner points by forcing their opponents to make wild shots that bounced beyond the court's retaining walls.

Courts were often equipped with a pair of stone rings fixed above opposite ends of the lateral center dividing line. One scoring variation awarded immediate victory to the team who could manage to bat the *tlatchtli* through the ring.

Like tennis, players became very adept at batting the ball at high speed. Unlike tennis, the ball was solid and perhaps as heavy as two or three baseballs. Although protected by helmets and leather, players were usually bloodied, often injured, and sometimes even killed from opponents' punishing *tlatchtli*-inflicted blows. Matches were sometimes decided like a boxing match, with victory going to the opponent left standing on the court.

As with everything in Mesoamerica, tradition and ritual ruled *tlatchtli.* Master teachers subjected initiates to rigorous training, prescribed ritual, and discipline not unlike the ascetic lifestyle of a medieval monastic brotherhood.

Potential rewards were enormous, however. Stakes varied in proportion to a contest's ritual significance and the rank of the players and their patrons. Champion players could win fortunes in gold, feathers, or precious stones. Exceptional games could result in riches and honor for the winner and death for the loser, whose heart, ripped from his chest on the centerline stone, became food for the gods.

---

patrons enjoy a roving trio for lunch (around 1–4 P.M.and a cozy piano bar (8–10 P.M. nightly). Programs may vary seasonally; call to confirm.

### Festivals

An abundance of local fiestas provide the excuses for folks to celebrate, starting on January 17 and 18 with the **Festival of Santa Prisca.** On the initial day, kids and adults bring their pet animals for blessing at the church. At dawn the next day, pilgrims arrive at the *zócalo* for *mañanitas* (dawn Mass) in honor of the saint, then head for folk dancing inside the church.

During the year Taxco's many neighborhood churches celebrate their saints' days (such as Chavarrieta, March 4; Veracruz, the four weeks before Easter; San Bernardino, May 20; Santísima Trinidad, June 13; Santa Ana, July 26; Asunción, Aug. 15; San Nicolas, Sept. 10;

San Miguel, Sept. 19; San Francisco, Oct. 4; and Guadalupe, Dec. 12) with food, fireworks, music, and dancing.

Religious fiestas begin with **Carnaval** the few days before Ash Wednesday (usually in February), and climax six weeks later, during Semana Santa (Easter week). On the Thursday and Good Friday before Easter, cloaked penitents proceed through the city, carrying gilded images and bearing crowns of thorns.

On the Monday after the November 2 Día de los Muertos (Day of the Dead), Taxco people head to pine-shaded **Parque Huixteco** (PAR-kay weesh-TAY-koh) atop the Cerro Huixteco behind town to celebrate their unique **Fiesta de los Jumiles.** In a ritual whose roots are lost in pre-Columbian legend, people collect and feast on *jumiles* (small crickets)—raw or roasted—along with music and plenty of beer and fixings. Since so many people go, transportation is easy. Drive or ride a *colectivo* (Huixteco on windshield) along the west-side road (westward extension of Cuauhtémoc from the *zócalo*) uphill about two miles. Fork right at the Huixteco sign. Continue for several miles to the mountaintop Parque Huixteco.

About three weeks later, the Taxco year-end holiday season kicks off in earnest, with the weeklong **National Silver Fair,** from the last Saturday in November until the first Friday in December. A month of partying continues, with the **Fiesta of the Virgin of Guadalupe** on December 12, climaxing with a week of continuous Christmas and New Year merrymaking, concluding with Day of the Kings gift-giving on January 6.

## SPORTS AND RECREATION

Stay in shape as local folks do, by walking Taxco's winding, picturesque side streets and uphill lanes. And, since all roads return to the *zócalo,* getting lost is rarely a problem.

For more formal sports, the **Monte Taxco Country Club** has horses ready for riding ($15/hr), three good tennis courts ($14/hr), and a nine-hole golf course available for use by nonguests for $50 per person. Contact the country club sports desk, in the little house about 100 yards away from the Hotel Monte Taxco's front entrance, or call the hotel (tel. 762/622-1300). Rough informal *senderos* (hiking paths) head north, uphill, into the luscious pine- and cedar-forested mesa country. Take sturdy shoes, water, and a hat.

## SHOPPING
### Market

Taxco's big market day is Sunday, when the town is loaded with people from outlying villages selling produce and live pigs, chickens, and ducks. The market is just downhill from Los Arcos, the lane that runs below the right side of the *zócalo* church (as you face the church). From the lane, head right before the arch and down the staircase. Soon you'll be descending through a warren of market stalls. Pass the small Baptist church on Sunday and hear the congregation singing like angels floating above the market. Don't miss the spice

stall, **Yerbería Castillo,** piled with the intriguing wild remedies collected by owner Elvira Castillo and her son Teodoro.

Farther on you'll pass mostly scruffy meat stalls but also some clean juice stands, such as **Licuados Memo** (7 A.M.–6 P.M. daily), where you can rest with a delicious fresh *zanahoria* (carrot), *toronja* (grapefruit), or *sandía* (watermelon) juice.

Before leaving the market, be sure to ask for *jumiles* (hoo-MEE-lays), live crickets that are sold in bags for about a penny apiece, ready for folks to pop into their mouths.

If *jumiles* don't suit your taste, you may want to drop in for lunch at one of the *fondas* upstairs, above the market's *artesanías* section.

### Handicrafts

Before visiting the individual private handicrafts shops, you might look around the submarket **Mercado de Artesanías** (watch for the sign above the main Taxco market downhill staircase) stalls that offer an abundance of priced-to-sell mini-treasures such as silver chains, necklaces, earrings, belts, huaraches, and wallets. Furthermore, if you're in town on Saturday, you might also taxi down to the Estrella Blanca bus station on the highway and browse around the **Saturday Silver Market** that spreads along the street out front of the station.

And furthermore, while in town be sure not to miss the common but colorful handicrafts such as the host of charming ceramic cats, turtles, doves, fish, and other figurines that local vendors sell very cheaply. Find them everywhere—in the market, on street corners, and especially in front of the Museo Spratling. If you buy, bargain—but not too hard, for the people are poor and have often traveled far.

Taxco abounds in private handicrafts shops, most of them specializing in silver but a number of others specializing in Guerrero and Oaxaca masks, woodcrafts, pottery, and much more. Taxco's picturesque maze of up-and-downhill lanes makes handicrafts shopping both taxing and enjoyable at the same time.

I have arranged my list of favorite handicrafts stores so that, without too much backtracking,

In Taxco, adorning yourself with your merchandise may make some quick sales.

you can get a good look at lots of lovely handicrafts in an afternoon's (mostly downhill) stroll around town. Save your energy by taxiing uphill to the first shop on the list.

Start uphill right above the *zócalo* at **Arnoldo** (Palma 1, tel. 762/622-1272, 9 A.M.–8:30 P.M. Mon.–Sat., 10 A.M.–5:30 P.M. Sun.), upstairs across the uphill lane next to Hotel Agua Escondida, where the friendly proprietors, Arnoldo Jacobo and his son Raoul, are more than willing and able to explain every detail about their fascinating array of merchandise. Masks are the prime attraction, and hundreds of masks from all over Guerrero—stone and wood, antique and new—line the walls like a museum. All of the many motifs, varying from blue-eyed sea goddesses and black men puffing cigarettes to inscrutable Aztec gods in onyx and grotesque lizard-humanoids, are priced to sell.

Next, head back downhill to the Hotel Agua Escondida curbfront, and bear right along the *zócalo*'s uphill sidewalk (across the *zócalo* from the church) to Calle Cuauhtémoc, on the *zócalo*'s west side, to the store of master silversmith **Ezequiel Tapia** (15 Cuauhtémoc, 9 A.M.–7 P.M. daily, tel. 762/622-0416), winner of a score of national prizes. His shop, as much a museum as it is store, displays a choice collection of mostly spectacular pieces, tending toward the large and the avant-garde.

A few doors farther west, check out the longtime (since 1950) silver shop **Arte Nacional** (Cuauhtémoc 9, tel. 762/622-1096, fax 762/622-2202, noon–8 P.M. daily), with a grand selection of virtually everything silver. Specialties range from a museum-quality selection of gleaming table silver (chafing dishes, large platters, tea sets, candelabras) to a treasury of necklaces, bracelets, rings, and much, much more.

Half a block farther, find **Platería Gloria** (Plazuela de San Juan 7, tel. 762/622-2047 or 762/622-0410, fax 762/622-6498, 9 A.M.–7 P.M. Mon.–Sat., 11 A.M.–4 P.M. Sun.), winner of two-dozen-odd national prizes. Besides an exquisite collection of one-of-a-kind earrings, necklaces, and cameos, his shop glows with huge, lovely sculptures in solid silver. For sheer volume and selection of everything lovely, this is the place, with literally thousands of charming silver necklaces, bracelets, rings, place settings, pendants, candlesticks: You name it, they have it, in myriad sizes, styles, and prices.

For a very carefully selected general Mexico handicrafts assortment, including of Tlaquepaque stoneware, Tonalá papier-mâché, and Guadalajara pewter, take a look inside the shop **Plaza San Juan** (tel. 762/622-1683, 10 A.M.–8 P.M. daily) beneath Restaurant Adobe, on the west side of Plazuela de San Juan.

Return east along Cuauhtémoc back to the *zócalo*'s right, downhill side. Just after the Santa Prisca churchfront, turn right at Calle de Muerte, and immediately on the left find what must be Taxco's most elegantly extravagant silver shop, the **Joyería Elena Ballesteros** (Calle de Muerte 4, tel. 762/622-3767, fax 762/622-3907, silver@ballesteros.com, 9 A.M.–7 P.M. Mon.–Sat.). More than just a labor of love, this is a virtual shrine to silver, beginning with the simply exquisite, moving to dining-room tables loaded with enough plate for a maharaja's banquet, to gleaming 10-pound $50,000 crucifixes, and a huge gold tree of life.

Return uphill to the *zócalo* corner, then turn right for a look around the grotto-like interior of **Luna Collection** (tel. 762/622-6447, 9 A.M.–8 P.M. daily) in the *zócalo*-front complex Patio de las Artesanías, on the right before the Casa Borda. Inside you'll find showrooms decorated with pendulous plaster stalacites hanging above faux stalagmites, seemingly dripping with fine silver jewelry (all of which, owners say with a smile, was the model for the Grutas de Cacahuamilpa complex).

Continue, passing the Casa Borda. At the corner, just before the Hotel Agua Escondida, head right steeply downhill a block to the petite Plazuela Bernal and the **Centro Joyero** (10 A.M.–7 P.M. Mon.–Sat., 11 A.M.–5 P.M. Sun.) on the left side of the *plazuela*. Inside, find a number of small shops with many fine priced-to-sell pieces.

Bear right, downhill, onto J. R. de Alarcón, at the fork with Avenida Juárez. Continue downhill a block to one of Taxco's most venerable institutions, the family-owned shop of **Emilia Castillo** (J. R. de Alarcón 7, tel. 762/622-3471, 10 A.M.–7 P.M. Mon.–Sat., 10 A.M.–4 P.M. Sun.), adjacent to the lobby of the Hotel Emilia Castillo on the right side of the street. Run by a branch of the industrious and prolific Castillo clan, the shop offers all in-house work, specializing in porcelain and silver, at reasonable prices. Here, unlike at many shops, you can bargain a bit.

Continue east along J. R. de Alarcón, passing Casa Humboldt; after two short blocks, turn right at Calle Higuera, arriving after one block at **Nuestro Mexico** (Veracruz 8, tel. 762/622-0976, nuestromexico@hotmail.com, 10:30 A.M.–8 P.M. Fri.–Wed.) on the left, at the corner of Veracruz. Inside, enjoy a look around at their interesting all-Guerrero clutter of wood and ceramic reproduction masks, soaring angels, ceramic coffee cups, silver, and much more.

A few doors uphill back toward the *zócalo*

along Veracruz, find elegant **Hecho a Mano** (Veracruz 4, 10 A.M.–5 P.M. Mon.–Sat.), of master silversmith Manuel Porcayo. If originality is what you prefer, he can provide you with a treasury of one-of-a-kind necklaces, bracelets, rings, collars, pendants, and much more.

Finally, continue uphill a block to Humboldt lane, on the right, in the small plaza in front of the Museo Spratling. Here, choose your favorites among a trove of priced-to-sell indigenous handicrafts: fetching painted pottery animals, cheerful Father Suns, colorful *amate* (fig-tree-bark) placemats, emerald-hued beads, cool sombreros, polished wooden bowls, and much, much more.

## INFORMATION AND SERVICES
### Tourist Information

Taxco has a pair of **tourist information offices,** both beside the highway at opposite ends of town, open approximately 9 A.M.–7 P.M. daily. The knowledgeable and English-speaking officers readily answer questions and furnish whatever maps and literature they may have. The north office (tel. 762/622-0798) is next to the north-end Pemex gas station; the south office is about a quarter mile south of the south-end Pemex station.

Personable veteran Mexico guide **Benito Flores Batalla** (tel./fax 762/622-0542), who staffs the north-side tourist information office, offers his services as a guide. For starters, he offers a 3.5-hour city tour for $35, without car; $70 with car supplied. Longer trips might include the Grutas de Cacahuamilpa, Xochicalco, and Ixcateopan (see *Excursions from Taxco*). The same is approximately true for **Enrique Viveros** (tel. 762/627-6245, cell tel. 044-762/107-9110), who staffs the south-end office. If Benito and Enrique are unavailable, they highly recommend guide **Juan Menatel** ($70 per day including car, tel. 762/622-0986).

One of the most reliable travel agents in town is **Turismo Misión** (at the Hotel Posada de la Misión reception desk, tel. 762/622-1125 or 762/622-0063, info@posadamision.com, www.posadamision.com), who provides tours ($160 for all-day tour, including car for 2–4) plus all the usual travel agency services.

## Grocery

Handicrafts have driven most groceries from the Taxco town center. However, **Oxxo** convenience store (on Cuauhtémoc, west side of the *zócalo*, 7 A.M.–midnight daily) brings in the crowd, with its decent selection of cheese, milk, yogurt, eggs, lunchmeat, bread, some fruit, wine, beer, chips, cookies, pastries, and more.

Alternatively, go to **Minisuper La Gloria** (on Hidalgo, tel. 762/622-3878, 8 A.M.–10 P.M. daily), a long block downhill from Plazuela de San Juan.

## Photography

The small **Colorama** (Cuauhtémoc 7, tel. 762/622-3394, 10 A.M.–8 P.M. Mon.–Sat.) photo shop, half a block west of the *zócalo*, offers a modest stock of merchandise, including batteries, point-and-shoot cameras, popular print film and development and digital services and accessories.

Long-time **Tienda la Misión** (Benito Juárez 216, tel. 762/622-0116, 10 A.M.–8 P.M. Mon.–Sat., 11 A.M.–3 P.M. Sun.), downhill a few blocks past City Hall, on the right, next to Banamex, offers some digital cameras and accessories, plus Kodak film and film and digital development and printing. It also does Xerox photocopying, including enlargement and reduction.

## Publications

English-language books and newspapers are hard to find in Taxco. The most convenient place to find used paperbacks will probably be your hotel.

Nevertheless, you can benefit from the collection at the small local library, **Biblioteca Taxco-Canoga Park** (9 A.M.–1 P.M. and 3–7 P.M. Mon.–Fri., 9 A.M.–1 P.M. Sat.). Browse its several shelves of English-language novels, nonfiction, magazines, and reference books. Most of the book collection has been donated by volunteers from Taxco's sister city,

Canoga Park, California. The library is a five-minute walk downhill along Juárez (east) from the *zócalo*. About a block past the city hall, turn right at an alley (watch for the Taxco–Canoga Park sign) and continue a few steps downhill to the library. (You might ask the librarian where you can get an English-language magazine or newspaper.)

## Money Exchange

Banks near the *zócalo* and their ATMs are Taxco's cheapest source of pesos. The good longest-hours option is **HSBC** (tel. 762/622-7300 or 762/622-7506, 8 A.M.–7 P.M. Mon.–Sat.), to the right of the church. Alternatively, go to **Bancomer** (tel. 762/622-2393, 8:30 A.M.–4 P.M. Mon.–Fri.), downhill on the *carretera* across from the Hotel Posada de la Misión.

## Communications

The town center *correo* (post office, tel. 762/622-8596, 9 A.M.–3 P.M. Mon.–Fri., 9 A.M.–12:30 P.M. Sat.), with after-hours mailbox out front, is in the *presidencia municipal* on Juárez, downhill (east) from the *zócalo*. The highway branch downhill (tel. 762/622-0501, 8 A.M.–3 P.M. Mon.–Fri.) is half a block north (Mexico City direction) of the Estrella de Oro bus station.

**Telecomunicaciones** (tel. 762/622-4885, fax 762/622-0001, 9 A.M.–3 P.M. Mon.–Fri.), off the *zócalo* behind the Casa Borda downhill, offers telex, money order, and public fax services.

Public street telephones all over the town center allow cheap, easy long-distance direct dialing with widely available Ladatel telephone cards. Get them everywhere, especially at pharmacies and liquor and grocery stores.

Internet access is available at **Interplaza** computer center (tel. 762/622-0789, 9:30 A.M.–9 P.M. Mon.–Sat., 10 A.M.–6 P.M. Sun.) in the town market, 200 feet down the steps below the right (west) side of the church. If Interplaza is closed, go to the hole-in-the-wall Internet store on Cuauhtémoc, upstairs, half a block west of the *zócalo;* it's open 11 A.M.–11 P.M. daily.

## Health and Emergencies

Taxco has a pair of respected private hospitals, both on the *carretera*. The **Clínica de Especialidades** (33 Av. de los Plateros, tel. 762/622-1111 or 762/622-4500) has a 24-hour emergency room, X-rays, a laboratory, a 24-hour pharmacy, and many specialists on call. The **Clínica Santa Cruz** (tel. 762/622-3012) offers similar services, also on Carretera Plateros, at the corner of Morelos, across from the government Seguro Social hospital.

For routine medicines and remedies, go to one of the good town-center pharmacies, such as **Farmacia de Ahorro** (on Cuauhtémoc, tel. 762/627-3444, 7 A.M.–11 P.M. daily) half a block west of the *zócalo*, or **Farmacia Similares** (on Hidalgo, tel. 762/627-2214, 8 A.M.–9 P.M. Mon.–Sat., 8 A.M.–8 P.M. Sun.) one block downhill from Plazuela de San Juan. Alternatively, go to the good 24-hour pharmacy at the Clínica de Especialidades, on the *carretera*.

For police emergencies, contact the *policía*, either by tel. 762/622-0007 or on duty on the *zócalo*; at the city hall, two blocks downhill (Juárez 6, tel. 762/622-0007); or at the substation on the side street Calle Fundaciones, one block below the *carretera* near the corner of J. R. de Alarcón.

## GETTING THERE AND AWAY
### By Car or RV

National Highway 95 provides a major connection south with Acapulco in a total of about 159 miles (256 km) of driving via Iguala, accessible in 22 miles (36 km) via winding old Highway 95. From there, continue south via two-lane Highway 95 to Chilpancingo (for a total of about 86 miles, 138 km). For Acapulco, continue another 73 miles (117 km) via the *cuota* (toll) *autopista*. Allow about four and a half hours' driving time for the entire Taxco–Acapulco trip, either direction.

Alternatively, you can save about an hour to Acapulco by following toll expressways the whole way, by first heading north (Cuernavaca–Mexico City direction) out of town. Follow the Mexico City *cuota* signs all the way about 25 miles (40 km) to the Mex. 95D *cuota* expressway, where you fork south, Chilpancingo–Acapulco direction. Allow about three and a half hours for this longer but quicker 192-mile (310-km) Taxco–Acapulco route.

Highway 95 also connects Taxco north via Cuernavaca with Mexico City, a total of about 106 miles (170 km). The new leg of the Taxco–Mexico City *cuota* (toll) expressway splits off from old Highway 95 about two miles north of town. For those who want to save time, the expressway cuts about half an hour off the driving time. Otherwise, follow the winding old Highway 95 about 20 miles (32 km) to its intersection with Highway 95D *cuota* (toll) superhighway. Congestion around Mexico City may lengthen the driving time to about three hours in either direction.

(*Note:* Authorities limit driving your car in Mexico City according to the last digit of your license plate; see the sidebar *Mexico City Driving Restrictions* in the *Essentials* chapter.)

Highway 55 (junction at Cacahuamilpa) gives Michoacán- and Jalisco-bound drivers the desirable option of avoiding Mexico City by connecting Taxco directly with Toluca (and thence the fast east–west toll expressway 15D, five hours to Guadalajara). The two-lane Highway 55 is paved and in good condition for its entire 74 miles (119 km). Fortunately, a faster, safer toll (*cuota*) expressway along the northern half of Highway 55 shortens the Taxco–Toluca driving time by at least an hour, compared to the old winding nontoll highway. Northbound, figure about 2.5 hours' driving time to Toluca; southbound, allow about two hours.

### By Bus

Competing lines **Estrella Blanca** (tel. 762/622-0131) and **Estrella de Oro** (tel. 762/622-0648) operate separate stations on the downhill *carretera* a few blocks apart. Both offer several luxury- and first-class connections north with Mexico City via Cuernavaca and south with Acapulco via Iguala and Chilpancingo.

Estrella Blanca also offers connections with Puebla, plus the very useful option for northwest-bound travelers of bypassing Mexico City via the superscenic Highway 55 route via Ixtapan del Sal (an interesting spa town) to Toluca. There, you can connect via Pátzcuaro, Michoacán, and Guadalajara, Jalisco, to the palmy Mexican Pacific beach destinations of Playa Azul, Manzanillo, Puerto Vallarta, San Blas, and Mazatlán.

## EXCURSIONS FROM TAXCO

The monumental duo of the Grutas de Cacahuamilpa (caves) and the ruins of ancient Xochicalco makes for a fascinating, although long, day trip, by tour or car (two days if by public transportation.) If you're going to do them both, start early; the Grutas are 15 miles (25 km) north (Mexico City direction) of town and Xochicalco is 25 miles (40 km) farther.

### ◖ Grutas de Cacahuamilpa

This trip is well worth the effort. The colossal Grutas (Grottos) de Cacahuamilpa (kah-kah-ooah-MEEL-pah) comprise one of the world's grandest cavern complexes. Forests of stalagmites and stalactites, in myriad shapes—Pluto the Pup, the Holy Family, a desert caravan, asparagus stalks, cauliflower heads—festoon a series of gigantic limestone chambers. The finale is a grand 30-story hall that meanders for half a mile, like a fairyland in stone. A few gift shops sell souvenirs; snack bars supply food.

The caves are open daily. Three-mile walking tours (each lasting two hours) in Spanish are included in the $5 admission ($3 for kids). Tours begin at 10 A.M. and continue thereafter, departing every hour until the final tour at 4 P.M. Make arrangements with guides a week ahead of time, either in person, at the cave's information and ticket booth, or by phone or by email (tel. 734/346-1716, grutascacahuamilpa@hotmail.com), or directly with chief guide Lorenzo Amates Mura (tel. 777/129-9078, 777/300-3695, amates_m@hotmail.com) or assistant guide Jo Paul (jopaul17@hotmail.com). For the adventurous, experienced guides lead more extensive entire-day Cacahuamilpa cave tours ($50 per person) for robust, determined hikers only, during the

February–May dry season. Highlights include walking (and sometimes maybe crawling) about five miles (8 km) along sinuous, sometimes steep and slippery subterranean tunnels and paths, and wading waist-deep (and perhaps even shoulder-deep) in cool underground rivers.

### GETTING THERE

*Combi* collective vans leave hourly for the caves, beginning at 8:30 A.M., just north of the Estrella Blanca bus station on the *carretera*. Watch for "Grutas" written on the windshields; expect to pay about $2 for a one-way fare. By car, get to the caves via Highway 95 north from Taxco; 10 miles (16 km) from the north-side Pemex station, fork left onto Highway 55 toward Toluca. Continue five more miles (8 km) and turn right at the signed Grutas de Cacahuamilpa junction. After a few hundred yards, turn right again into the entrance driveway.

### ◖ Xochicalco

Grand Xochicalco (soh-shee-KAHL-koh), an hour farther north from Cacahuamilpa, although lightly touristed, is a fountainhead of Mesoamerican legend. The archaeological zone, officially designated as a UNESCO World Heritage site, spreads over a half dozen terraced pyramid hilltops overlooking a natural lake-valley, which at one time sustained a large population. Xochicalco flowered during the late classic period around A.D. 800, partly filling the vacuum left by the decline of Teotihuacán, the previously dominant Mesoamerican classic city-state. Some archaeologists speculate that Xochicalco at its apex was the great center of learning, known in legend as Tamanchoan, where astronomer-priests derived and maintained calendars and where the Living Quetzalcoatl legend was born.

Your first stop should be the world-class **museum,** via the signed driveway east of the archaeological site. A grand entrance hall leads to six masterfully executed showrooms that illustrate the main currents of Xochicalco civilization: Earthly Gifts (flora, fauna, and trade); Warlords and Priests (don't miss the headless

Lord-in-Red sun god); Xochicalco, Guardian of the People (centered around a pair of calendar-glyph stelae that undoubtedly records an historic Xochicalco event); Creators and Artists (don't miss the sensitively executed jaguar and coyote pieces); World of the Gods (dramatic illustration of the ball court and ring found on the site); Daily Spaces (replica of a typical house, family altars and utensils and realistic "Lord of Xochicalco").

## EXPLORING THE SITE

Leave at least two hours (mandatory visitor exit time 5:45 P.M. daily) to cover the site highlights. After visiting the excellent bookstore (which closes at 5 P.M.), your first stop should be the unmissable **Pyramid of Quetzalcoatl** on the site's north side. From the parking lot, head south uphill for about 100 yards, where a wide path forks right, uphill. After approximately another 100 yards, when you reach level ground again, turn right and pass the beautifully reconstructed **eastern ball court** on your right. Continue another 50 yards or so, until,

on the wall about 200 feet to your left, you see some stairs that you should climb, to the next upper level where the platform-like Pyramid of Quetzalcoatl (The Plumed Serpent) rises on the hilltop.

Vermilion paint remnants hint at the pyramid's original appearance, which was perhaps as brilliant as a giant birthday cake. In bas-relief around the entire base a serpent writhes, intertwined with personages, probably representing chiefs or great priests. Above these are warriors, identified by their helmets and *atlatl,* or lance-throwers.

Most notable, however, is one of Mesoamerica's most remarkable bas-reliefs, flanking the staircase. It shows the 11th week sign, *ozomatli* (monkey), being pulled by a hand (via a rope) to join with the fifth week sign, *calli* (house). Latter-day scholars generally interpret this as describing a calendar correction that resulted from a grand conclave of chiefs and sages from all over Mesoamerica, probably at this very spot.

About 100 yards south of the Pyramid of

© BRUCE WHIPPERMAN

Xochicalco, a UNESCO World Heritage site, is both a fountainhead of Mesoamerican legend and one of Mexico's most regally restored ancient cities.

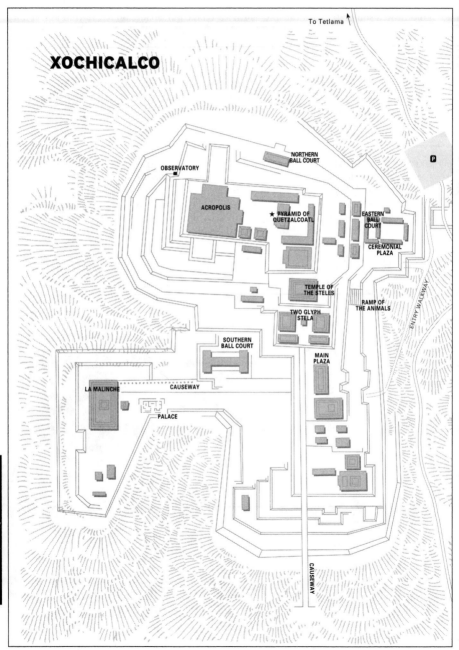

# XOCHICALCO

To Tetlama

P

NORTHERN BALL COURT

OBSERVATORY

ACROPOLIS

★ PYRAMID OF QUETZALCOATL

EASTERN BALL COURT

CEREMONIAL PLAZA

TEMPLE OF THE STELES

RAMP OF THE ANIMALS

TWO GLYPH STELA

SOUTHERN BALL COURT

MAIN PLAZA

ENTRY WALKWAY

LA MALINCHE

CAUSEWAY

PALACE

CAUSEWAY

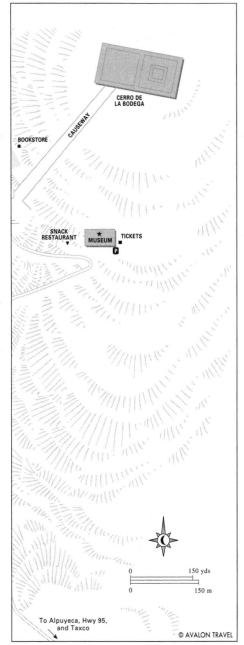

BOOKSTORE

CERRO DE
LA BODEGA

CAUSEWAY

SNACK
RESTAURANT ★ MUSEUM TICKETS
P

0       150 yds
0       150 m

To Alpuyeca, Hwy 95,
and Taxco

© AVALON TRAVEL

Quetzalcoatl rises the **Temple of the Steles,** so named for three large stone tablets found beneath the floor. They narrate the events of the Quetzalcoatl legend, wherein Quetzalcoatl (discoverer of corn and the calendar) was transformed into the morning star (the planet Venus); he continues to rule the heavens as the brightest star and the Lord of Time.

About 100 yards farther south, the **Main Plaza** was accessible to the common people via roads from below. This is in contrast to the sacrosanct **Ceremonial Plaza** by the Eastern Ball Court nearby. South of the Ceremonial Plaza, the **Ramp of the Animals** (named for the carved animal-motif stones found along its length) slopes upward from east to west.

On the south end of the zone, a faintly visible causeway once connected the La Malinche pyramid, 200 yards to the southwest, with the Ceremonial Plaza.

That causeway passed the **Southern Ball Court,** which is strikingly similar to ball courts as far away as Toltec Tula in the north and Maya Copan in Honduras, far to the south. On the opposite side of the causeway from the Ball Court lies the **Palace,** a complex marked by many rooms with luxury features such as toilet drainage, fireplaces, and steam baths.

On the far northwest side of the complex is the **Observatory,** a room hollowed into the hill and stuccoed and fitted with a viewing shaft for timing the sun and star transits essential for an accurate calendar.

### GETTING THERE

Get to Xochicalco by tour (contact an agency such as Misión Tours, at the Hotel Posada de la Misión, tel. 762/622-1125 or 762/622-0065) or taxi or car. Get there by continuing past the Caves (Grutas) of Cacahuamilpa driveway entrance (mark your odometer). The route is straightforward, continuing by a single main road generally northeast, through Coatlá del Río (12 miles, 19 km), Mazatepec (20 miles, 33 km), and finally Miacatlán (23 miles, 37 km). There you bear right (east) at a fork (watch for Xochicalco signs) and continue past Rodeo hamlet (and lake on the right) to the Xochicalco signed left side road that leads a mile or two uphill to the archaeological site, a total of 29 miles (46 km), about an hour, from Cacahuamilpa, or 48 miles (77 km), two hours, from Taxco. The ruins are open 9 A.M.–6 P.M. daily (last visitor entry at 5 P.M.). Admission (get tickets at the museum) runs about $5. Since caretakers shoo all visitors out by 5:45 P.M., arrive early enough to allow a couple of hours to explore the ruins. Although there is a restaurant by the museum, you should probably be prepared with some food and drinks, and a hat, water, and comfortable walking shoes, for sure.

## Ixcateopan

The picturesque little furniture-making town of Ixcateopan (eeks-kah-tay-OH-pan, Land of

---

# CUAUHTÉMOC: THE LAST AZTEC EMPEROR

Cuauhtémoc (koo-ah-oo-TAY-mok) is more than just a national hero; he's the celebrated Aztec leader who said no to the Spanish conquistadores and, spitting on the spineless example of his uncle Moctezuma before him, did something about it. Faced with the disastrous reality that most of imperial Tenochtitlán's population of 250,000 was either dead or sick with smallpox, Cuauhtémoc rallied his people to hold out for 75 days against Spanish cannons and their 100,000-strong army of native allies.

That the story of Cuauhtémoc was more than a legend became clear when, on September 26, 1949, official investigators announced the discovery of Cuauhtémoc's long-missing remains in the small municipality of Ixcateopan, not far from the famous Acapulco-region silver town of Taxco, Guerrero.

Cuauhtémoc was born into the comfort and privilege of the Mexican imperial family on February 23, 1501. His father, Ahuitzotl, was the son of the eighth Aztec emperor, also Ahuitzotl. His mother, princess Cuayautitalli, was the daughter of the lord of Zompancuahuitl (now Ixcateopan, Guerrero).

His given name, Cuauhtémoc, translates from the Aztec language as "descending eagle." Cuauhtémoc's traditional hieroglyph is thus marked by a stylized diving eagle.

Orphaned by his father when still an infant, Cuauhtémoc was brought up by his mother. At the age of 15 he entered Calmécac academy for sons of noble military officers and priests. His formal education initiated him into the secrets of the gods and the sciences of astronomy and the calendar.

After completing his schooling, Cuauhtémoc followed his uncle, Moctezuma II, in his infamous "War of the Flowers" conquests. During this time he proved his valor and skill, gaining the high rank of *tlacetechutli*, the command equivalent of a modern colonel.

Moctezuma II, upon returning home in glory with thousands of captives, presided over the elevation of his nephew, Cuauhtémoc, as governor of the important Tlatelolco and Teotecuhtli districts of the capital Tenochtitlán.

The good times didn't last, however, for soon Hernán Cortés and his small but determined band of armored soldiers and cavalry was entering the gates of Tenochtitlán. Cuauhtémoc's uncle, frozen by fear that Cortés might be the returned god Quetzalcoatl, quickly surrendered himself and all of his golden treasure to the wily Cortés. On July 1, 1520, angered by Spanish brutality and their emperor's fearful acquiescence, the Tenochtitlán populace rebelled, killing Moctezuma II and forcing the Spanish into their disastrous Noche Triste (Sad Night) retreat, at the end of which an exhausted Cortés sat down and cried for the loss of half of his men.

The Aztecs' triumph was short-lived, however. Although they had rid themselves of the Spanish, smallpox, the Spaniards' deadly legacy, began spreading among the people. When the Spanish, returned to Tenochtitlán in late May 1521 reinforced by a vast corps of native allies, Cuauhtémoc, by contrast, ruled a city decimated by smallpox. Nevertheless, with herculean resolve, he united his people, exhorting those who could to care for the wounded, gather rocks, or help pile bricks for a barricade.

Cotton) has become famous for the remains of the last Aztec emperor, Cuauhtémoc, which archaeologists discovered there on September 26, 1949.

## EXPLORING IXCATEOPAN

The renown has been beneficial. The town streets and plaza are smartly cobbled with the local white marble, and houses and shops are neatly painted and whitewashed. At the center of all this stands Cuauhtémoc's resting place, the venerable **Iglesia de Santa María de la Asunción** church, beside the town plaza. Inside, city workers maintain the sanctuary and its small adjoining museum (9 A.M.–3 P.M. and 4–5 P.M. Mon.–Sat., 9 A.M.–3 P.M. Sun.). Cuauhtémoc's relics themselves, which were subjected to thorough investigation when they

After a bloody siege two and a half months long, Cortés resorted to leveling the capital to capture it. On August 13, 1521, Cuauhtémoc, desperate for reinforcements, set out to find them, but he was captured and brought before Cortés and his translator-mistress, Malinche. Cuauhtémoc pointed to the dagger that Cortés held in his belt and said to Malinche, "Malintzin, since I've resisted you in the defense of my city and my people, and come by coercion and in chains before you, take that dagger and kill me with it."

Cortés, however, didn't allow Cuauhtémoc such an honorable death. Perhaps hoping that he could convince him to be his puppet emperor, Cortés kept him in captivity for another four years. He even took Cuauhtémoc and a retinue of Aztec nobles along on his ill-fated expedition to Honduras in 1523-1525. Tortured with foreboding that Cuauhtémoc and his compatriots were plotting against him, Cortés had Cuauhtémoc hanged on February 28, 1525.

Cuauhtémoc's grisly remains were still suspended in the hanging tree when Cuauhtémoc's warrior companion, Tzilactzín, rescued them. Afraid that vandals would desecrate the body, he took down Cuauhtémoc's corpse and wrapped it in aromatic leaves. He and a band of about 30 companions, all deserters of Cortés's expedition, carried the remains for 40 days and nights and buried them secretly at Ixcateopan, the home of Cuauhtémoc's mother. There, 424 years later, Cuauhtémoc's lineal descendant, Salvador Rodrigo Juárez, and historian and professor Eulalia Guzmán announced the discovery of Cuauhtémoc's remains. They are on public display before the altar of Ixcateopan town church, Santa María de la Asunción, in a glass casket above the spot where they were found.

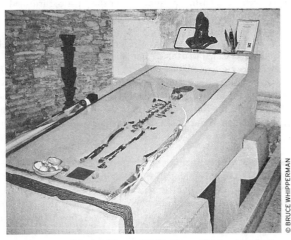

© BRUCE WHIPPERMAN

**The remains of Cuauhtémoc, the Mexicans' last emperor, lie in Santa María de la Asunción church, in Ixcateopan.**

were unearthed, were believed to authentic (although some latter-day doubters dispute this claim). The bones lie in a glass case directly over the spot where they were buried beneath the altar stones more than four centuries ago.

The museum next door details the story of Cuauhtémoc's heroic defense of the Aztec capital, Tenochtitlán, and his capture, torture, and subsequent execution by Cortés on February 28, 1525. Copies of pictograms, known as codices, such as the codex Vatican-Ríos (1528), displayed in the museum, represent Cuauhtémoc (literally, "The Descending Eagle") with an inverted, stylized eagle above his head. An excellent booklet ($3) details the fascinating story of the discovery and authentication of his ancestor's remains (in Spanish).

Outside the church, be sure to take a look about three blocks downhill past the church, on main street Calle Guerrero, at the town **archaeological site** (Wed.–Sun. 10 a.m.–5 p.m.). The main remains, called the "Temple of Cotton," echoing the name Ixcateopan, reveal a ceremonial complex, including a pair of pedestals, royal rooms, and a former spring leading through what appear to have been wash basins (presumably for the cotton the high priests may have ritually processed there).

Farther afield, you might enjoy a visit to the limestone caves called **Grutas de San Miguel,** near neighboring San Miguel village. On the highway back to Taxco, after 7 miles (11 km) fork right at the dirt road, at hamlet Plaza del Gallo (Plaza of the Rooster). Continue about three miles to San Miguel; ask a shopkeeper for someone who can lead you to the caves.

### FESTIVALS

Customarily sleepy Ixcateopan wakes up for three annual fiestas. The fun kicks off in February, when folks celebrate their indigenous roots with a weeklong party of daily flower processions, indigenous dances, and fireworks, all climaxing around the February 23 birthday of Cuauhtémoc.

The customary arrival of the governor of Guerrero, the Acapulco Symphony, and maybe even the president of Mexico, on September 26, the discovery date of Cuautémoc's remains, culminates another week of celebrating.

Finally, townsfolk bring in the New Year in grand style with a combined Christmas–carnival–New Year celebration of their patron Santo Niño de Atocha.

### ACCOMMODATIONS AND FOOD

Besides its historic interest, Ixcateopan and its environs—the rustic old church and garden, the tranquil plaza, the surrounding lush oak-forested hills—invite lingering. Moreover, the amiable, frankly curious townsfolk—who are definitely not overwhelmed by tourists—are ready for visitors. They operate some pretty fair plaza-front country eateries, such as Cocinas Económicas Amanec, at the south side of the plaza.

Accommodations are also available, on the main street, at the **Posada de los Reyes** (Calle V. Guerrero 14, tel. 736/366-2368), a block past the plaza, across the street from the church. The welcoming family owners offer eight clean rooms, around a tranquil inner patio, furnished with attractive locally crafted wood furniture and homespun bedspreads. Rooms go for about $20 s, $30 d, with private hot-water shower baths.

### GETTING THERE

Reach the town via Ixcateopan-labeled *colectivo* van ($3 one-way). Catch it in front of the Estrella Blanca bus station in Taxco, or at any point on the *carretera* before the south-side signed turnoff road to Ixcateopan.

Drivers, follow the signed fork, west (turn right if traveling south) from the *carretera,* past the Pemex *gasolinera* about a mile south of town. Mark your odometer. Continue about an hour along the very scenic (a pair of waterfalls, good for picnicking and splashing, at Mile 4.5, Km 7.2, and Mile 11, Km 17.7), sometimes potholed, paved road for 23 miles (37 km) to the town plaza.

# THE COSTA CHICA

In reality the Costa Chica, the "Little Coast," which traditionally includes the coast of Guerrero east of Acapulco and the adjoining coast of Oaxaca, isn't so little after all. Highway 200, heading out of the Acapulco hubbub, requires 150 miles to traverse the scattered groves, forests, fields, and villages to the Mixtec and Amusgo indigenous country between Ometepec, Guerrero, and Pinotepa Nacional, Oaxaca.

To many thousands of Costa Chica indigenous peoples, Spanish is a foreign language. Many of them live in remote foothill villages, subsisting as they always have on corn and beans, without telephones, sewers, schools, or roads. Those who live near towns often speak the Spanish they have learned by coming to market. In the Costa Chica town markets of Ometepec, Xochistlahuaca, and Pinotepa Nacional you will brush shoulders with them—mostly Mixtecs, Amusgos, and Chatinos—men sometimes in pure-white cottons and women in colorful embroidered *huipiles* over wrapped hand-woven skirts.

Besides the indigenous people, you will often see African Mexicans—*morenos* (brown ones)—also known as *costeños* because their settlements cluster near the coast. Descendants of African slaves imported hundreds of years ago, the *costeños* subsist on the produce from their village gardens and the fish they catch.

Costa Chica *indígenas* and *costeños* have a reputation for being unfriendly and suspicious. If true in the past (it's certainly less so in the present), they have had good reason to be wary of outsiders, who in their view have been trying

# HIGHLIGHTS

◖ **Playa Las Peñitas:** "Precious" is the best word to describe this rocky nook on a breezy strand. The main attraction, besides tasty seafood and a comfortable hotel, is a sacred tidepool-enfolded sea rock that folks visit en masse on May 3, the Día de la Cruz (page 242).

◖ **Parroquia de Santiago:** Ometepec folks are so proud of their magnificent parish church that, evenings, they illuminate its lovely baby-blue-and-white facade and the rooftop statue of the avenging Santiago for all to see (page 245).

◖ **Ometepec Sunday Market:** In Ometepec, the handicrafts action centers around the downtown plaza, while across town at the formal market a mountain of old-fashioned goods draws a big crowd of traditionally costumed Amusgo- and Mixtec-speaking country folks (page 245).

◖ **Xochistlahuaca:** Every week, thousands of Amusgo-speaking indigenous people put on their Sunday-best *traje* and converge on the awning-festooned center *tianguis* of Xochistlahuaca to bargain, gossip, and flirt (page 249).

◖ **Museo de las Culturas Afromestizos:** Besides the bustling market, make your main Cuajinicuilapa stop at this singularly important museum, which skillfully showcases the history and cultural contributions of the Acapulco region's important African-Mexican community (page 251).

◖ **Pinotepa Nacional Market:** Pinotepa Nacional, an important market town of the Oaxaca Costa Chica, is a magnet for indigenous coastal Mixtec-speaking people (page 253).

◖ **Huaxpáltepec Pre-Easter Fair:** You will not be able to avoid this best of all possible indigenous market experiences if your arrival coincides with the local festival of Jesus the Nazarene, four days preceding the fourth Friday before Easter Sunday (page 259).

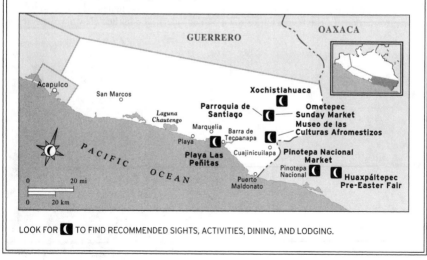

LOOK FOR ◖ TO FIND RECOMMENDED SIGHTS, ACTIVITIES, DINING, AND LODGING.

© BRUCE WHIPPERMAN

Puerto Maldonado fishing hamlet

to take away their land, gods, and lives for 400 years.

Communication is nevertheless possible. For the residents of a little mountain or shoreline end-of-road village, your arrival might be the event of the day. People are going to wonder why you came. Smile and say hello. Buy a soda at the store or *palapa*. If kids gather around, don't be shy. Draw a picture in your notebook. If a child offers to do likewise, you've succeeded.

## PLANNING YOUR TIME

Although you can traverse the Costa Chica in less than a day, try to save some time to linger a few days to soak in the local color of the market towns and enjoy the natural diversions along the way. For example, kayakers and wildlife-viewers might enjoy a whole day exploring the mangrove-laced wildlife-rich wetland Laguna Chautengo. If so, you might want to stay even longer for tenting, beachcombing, fishing, and surfing in or near the cross-lagoon breezy barrier-beach village San José de la Barra.

On the other hand, most anyone could easily enjoy an overnight or two at each of the petite south-seas beach resorts of **Playa Ventura** and **Playa Las Peñitas.** At Playa Ventura, you can choose among several beachfront hotels, especially the top-pick but modest Hotel Caracola retreat, whose owner welcomes guests with seven rustic but comfortable accommodations and a plumy beachfront pool and patio. Also at Playa Ventura, RVers and tenters could linger for a day, a week, or a season enjoying the miles-long wild Playa Ventura strand, ripe for surf fishing, camping, and beachcombing.

In contrast, **Playa Las Peñitas,** a scenically petite golden strand, offers two or three beachfront hotels (at least one with an inviting pool), a unique natural tidepool bathing spa, a luscious child-friendly lagoon, and super-fresh fish, shrimp, and oysters, from a lineup of rustic beachfront *palapa* restaurants.

Farther east, Ometepec, the capital of the indigenous Costa Chica Guerrero hinterland, deserves at least two days, one of which should be a Sunday. That will give you time to visit both the fascinating Xochistlahuaca *tianguis* and the big **Ometepec Sunday**

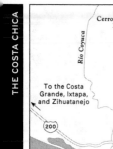

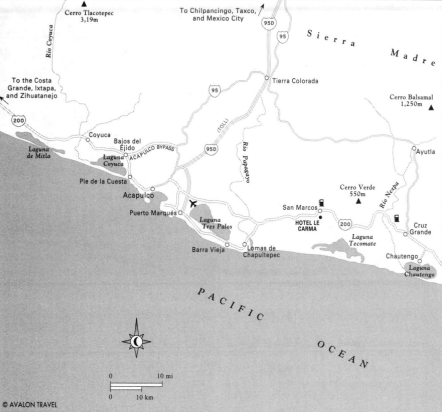

**Market** back in town on the same day. Stay overnight in the relaxing top-pick Hotel Bello Nido with pool.

Moving farther east, toward the Oaxaca border, be sure to stop in Cuajinicuilapa and visit the unique **Museo de las Culturas Afromestizos.** With another day or two you could explore the nearby African-Mexican coastal country hinterland around the breezy beach fishing hamlet of Puerto Maldonado. There, you can overnight by parking your RV or setting up your tent near the beachfront Las Brisas *palapa* restaurant or stay overnight at the modest guesthouse Casa de Huéspedes Valle Encantado nearby.

Continue east into Oaxaca and explore the coastal Amusgo- and Mixtec-speaking country around Pinotepa Nacional. Spend at least one Pinotepa Nacional overnight at the Hotel Carmona with pool; visit the big **Pinotepa Nacional Market** and maybe make a handicrafts side trip to one or two nearby upcountry towns, such as north to Pinotepa Don Luis (for *pozohuanco* wraparound skirts and masks) or San Pedro Amusgos (for *huipiles*); or east to Huazolotitlán (for masks) or maybe Huaxpáltepec, which hosts a sprawling, fascinatingly indigenous **Pre-Easter Fair** that virtually blocks Highway 200 ten miles east of Pinotepa.

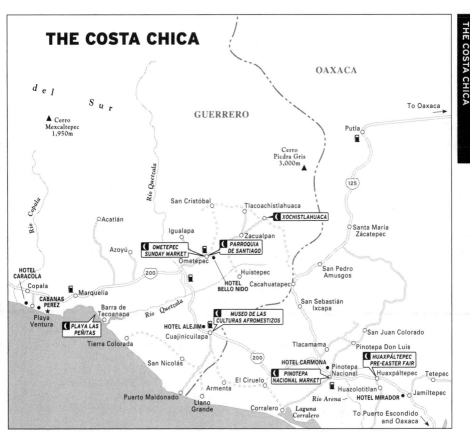

# THE COSTA CHICA

# The Road to Ometepec

If you're going by bus, ride one of the several daily first-class or second-class buses from the Estrella Blanca (Avenida Ejido) terminal in Acapulco. Let the highway kilometer markers (both at roadside and on the asphalt itself) lead you to your chosen destination. A minute ahead of time, let the driver know where to let you off.

If driving from Acapulco, mark your odometer at the traffic circle where Highways 95 and 200 intersect over the hill north from Acapulco. If, on the other hand, you bypass that congested point via the Acapulco airport road, set your odometer to zero at the east-side interchange near Puerto Marqués where the airport highway continues along the overpass, but where you either exit to the right before the overpass, and follow the Highway 200 Pinotepa Nacional sign north; or continue on the overpass, straight ahead another couple of miles, to pick up the new *cuota autopista,* on the left, which will whisk you to the Highway 200 turnoff in less than 10 minutes. Mileages and kilometer markers along the road are sometimes the only locators of side-road turnoffs to hidden villages and beaches.

Fill up the car with gas in Acapulco before starting out. After that, gas is at least available at Cruz Grande (56 miles, 91 km), Marquelia (91 miles, 146 km), Ometepec (110 miles, 177 km), Pinotepa Nacional (157 miles, 253 km), Jamiltepec (175 miles, 283 km), and Puerto Escondido (247 miles, 398 km).

## SAN MARCOS

San Marcos (pop. 10,000), 36 miles (58 km) east of Acapulco, is a frequent first stop for essential services along the Costa Chica.

### Accommodations and Food

San Marcos's best hotel, **Le Carma** (tel. 745/453-0037, $25 d with fan, $30 with a/c) on the highway, south side, is recommendable for an overnight. Although the hotel's loose management leaves something to be desired, guests enjoy a major plus: cooling off in the hotel's inviting blue pool. The approximately 20 clean rooms have fans and hot-water shower baths.

For food, try **Restaurant Ruth** (approx. 8 A.M.–9 P.M. daily, $2–4) on the highway, on the same south side and about a block east of the hotel. Although the restaurant is less than spotless, its food is plentiful and tasty and the dogs and roosters out back add a homey touch. Ruth provides country-style food, such as *huevos a la Mexicana* for breakfast, perhaps chicken in mole sauce for afternoon *comida,* and *antojitos* such as tacos and quesadillas for supper. If that's not your style, check out the immaculate, more orderly (but emptier) **Restaurant Edith** across the highway.

### Information and Services

San Marcos has a **Banamex** with 24-hour ATM (tel. 745/453-0036, 9 A.M.–3 P.M. Mon.–Fri.); Centro de Salud on the highway; a pharmacy, **Farmapronto** (tel. 745/453-1697, 8 A.M.–10 P.M. daily), near the Le Carma hotel; streetfront Ladatel card-operated telephones; a doctor (Mauricio Ibarra); a *correo* and *telecomunicaciones* (tel. 745/453-0130, 9 A.M.–3 P.M. Mon.–Fri.). Find the pharmacy, bank, doctor, *correo,* and *telecomunicaciones* on the town *jardín,* on main street Hidalgo. (Go under the highway-front entrance arch and continue about 0.3 mile/0.5 km to the *jardín.*)

## LAGUNA CHAUTENGO AND PLAYA VENTURA

These laid-back havens are attractive for different reasons: Playa Ventura is for those who enjoy civilized south-seas delights, while the broad Laguna Chautengo estuary attracts folks hankering for wild things, such as troves of wildlife for viewing and photographing, pristine beaches for camping and beachcombing, and swarms of good-eating *lisa* (mullet), *sierra* (mackerel), and *róbalo* (snook), just for the catching.

### Laguna Chautengo

Follow the good turnoff road four miles (about 6 km) east of Cruz Grande (43 miles, 69 km east of Acapulco). Continue 3.7 miles (6 km) to the boat landing. Here, the big mangrove lagoon spreads about eight miles in both directions along the coast and four miles across to the barrier sandbar. Most of the year Laguna Chautengo is a freshwater reservoir of the Ríos Nexpa, Jalapa, and Copala. But during the rainy season the lagoon breaks through the sandbar, slicing a channel at the beachfront hamlet of Pico de Monte that beckons far across the lagoon.

Boatmen customarily charge $10 one-way per person or $20 one-way per boat (of up to 10 passengers) for the cross-lagoon round-trip to the village of **San José de la Barra**, which includes waiting for the passengers to enjoy a fish dinner at one of the several beachfront *palapas*. If you're going to camp overnight on the beach, let your boatman know when to return and pick you up.

Although road's-end facilities amount to no more than a dock and a snack restaurant, alternatives exist. Rent a boat and captain (figure $10–20 per hour) and mount your own fishing trip. Or do the same with your own boat or kayak. Launching appears easily doable from the calm, gently sloping shoreline.

### Playa Ventura

Three miles east of the small town of Copala,

77 miles (123 km) from Acapulco, a roadside sign points toward Playa Ventura. Four miles down a paved road, which a truck-bus from Copala traverses regularly, you arrive at pavement's-end at Ventura village. From there, a miles-long golden-sand beach arcs gently east. Past a lighthouse, the beach leads to a point, topped by a picturesque stack of weathered granite rocks known locally as Casa de Piedra (House of Stone).

Playa Ventura can provide nearly everything for a restful day or season in the sun: a seemingly endless stretch of yellow sand, *palapa* restaurants, and friendly folks. It offers surfable rollers, turtles who nest in the summer and fall, and lots of open space for tents and RVs. Although development is gradually crowding them out, good tent or RV (maneuverable medium rigs, vans, or campers) spots still sprinkle the inviting outcropping-dotted shoreline, on the southeast side, past Casa de Piedra. There, shady *palapas* set up by former campers stand ready for rehabilitation and reuse by new arrivals.

Surf fishing (with net-caught bait fish) is fine from the beach, while *pangas* go out for deep-sea catches. Good surfing breaks angle in from the points, and, during the rainy season, the west-side behind-the-beach lagoon is good for fishing, shrimping, and wildlife-viewing. (Bring your kayak or inflatable raft.)

The palm-lined beach stretches southeast for miles. Past the Casa de Piedra outcropping, an intimate *palapa*- and *panga*-lined sandy cove curves invitingly to yet another palmy point, Pico del Monte. Past that lies still another, even more pristine, cove and beach.

## Accommodations and Food

Beside the village stores, space for tenting and RV parking and food is available at a number of family-run *loncherías* and beach *palapa* restaurants, the most visible of which is beachfront **Restaurant and Ramada Pérez.** If anyone dispels the rumor that *costeño* folks are unfriendly, it's the hospitable Pérez family team (father Bulmaro, mother Virginia, sons Luis, Reyes, and Arturo, and daughter Reina),

who have put together the modest beginnings of a little resort. The Pérezs invite visitors to park RVs in their small lot, where they offer a friendly word, showers, a homemade swimming pool, kiddie pool, and a bit of shade for a reasonable $6 per party per day. For tenters, they rent spaces beneath their shady beachfront *ramada* for the same price. Furthermore, besides the Perezs' main oceanfront restaurant, son Luis has added a breezy rooftop adjacent *palapa* hamburger restaurant, and his brother Arturo has created his life dream of a petite but elegant Discoteca Pérez.

Others have followed the Pérez example. From the Pérez compound, move east along the beach to find plumy **Las Palmeras,** which offers a shady, spacious grove for tenting and RV parking. Continue next door to beachfront restaurant and campground **Doña Maura,** with plenty of space for small-to-medium self-contained RVs and tents beneath shady palm-frond *ramadas*. Next come a trio of inviting restaurants, first **El Faro,** with a working lighthouse; next, the thatched **Jay** restaurant, and finally **Barbolumba,** with a stunning southeast shoreline view, toward Casa de Piedra.

Virtually all of Playa Ventura's lodgings are on its breezy west side. Several are recommendable. Heading west, first find beachfront **Hotel Doña Celsa** (tel. 741/411-5891), with about 20 clean, modern but smallish rooms on two floors around a parking patio. Rentals run about $25 d with fans, $40 with air-conditioning ($40 and $55 holidays), all with tiled baths and tepid-water showers, pool, restaurant, and small grocery.

Alternatively, continue west about 100 yards to restaurant and **Hotel Tomy** (local cell tel. 044-741/101-3065), also right on the beach, with about 20 rooms, some with airy ocean views, encircling a parking-pool-patio. Prices for the clean, sparely furnished but comfortable tiled rooms are certainly right, at about $30 for up to four, $40 with TV, all with fans and private baths.

For the most refined hotel choice, continue about another half mile west to [ **Hotel Caracola** (Costera Antelmo Ventura #68,

© BRUCE WHIPPERMAN

the cozy rustic-chic *cabañas* of
Playa Ventura's Hotel Caracola

Playa Ventura, local cell tel. 044-741/101-3047,
caracola_playaventura@hotmail.com, www
.playaventura.com), life project of friendly inn-
keeper Aura Elena Rodríguez. She offers her
vision of paradise, beneath a shady grove of
swaying palms, complete with café-restaurant
*palapa* and an inviting beachfront pool-patio.
Her seven designer-rustic lodgings come in
three varieties: a pair of intimate and inviting wood-covered teepee-mode rooms, $40
for two, with shared bath; and two *cabañas,*
$55 for two, with private baths; and three airy,
private rooms, nestled into a three-floor south-
seas-in-the-round wood and thatch house, $65
for up to three, with private baths. All lodgings
come with fans, mosquito nets, daily maid service, and a kitchen stove and sink for guest use.
Sorry, no kids under 15, please.

A bit farther down both the beach and the economic scale, find **Restaurant El Profe** beneath
a sleepy palm grove, with some tent spaces. Near
that is **Cabañas la Perla Coyacul** (local cell tel.
044-741/101-3080) with basic *cabañas* ($40 for
up to four) and palm-shaded space for tents and

small self-contained RVs, $6 per person, all with
shared toilets and showers and a beachfront restaurant, with pool and kiddie pool.

The increasing popularity of Playa Ventura
as a beach destination has led to a growing
colony of beachfront homes. A number of the
original Playa Ventura families are selling lots.
Luis Pérez tells me that the going price is cur-
rently about $12,000 for a 60-foot-by-60-foot
beachfront lot. Before putting your money
down, be sure to research the legal details of
owning property in Mexico in general and at
Playa Ventura in particular. Go through a reputable real estate agent, such as Century 21,
and a registered "notario," like a title company
in the United States, who researches and veri-
fies the property's title (see the sidebar *Owning
Paradise* in the *Acapulco* chapter).

## MARQUELIA

The small market town of Marquelia (pop.
10,000, 91 miles/146 km east of Acapulco) offers a number of services and is a jumping-off
point for the charming beachfront haven of Playa
Las Peñitas and the hardscrabble end-of-the-road
fishing village of Barra de Tecoanapa. You can't
miss Marquelia, since its market stalls crowd
the highway. Especially worthy is the country-
style open-air **Restaurant La Herradura** (tel.
741/416-9837, 8 A.M.–8 P.M. Tues.–Sun.), at the
eastern end of town, north side of the highway.

## ◖ PLAYA LAS PEÑITAS

Just east of Marquelia, turn south (if not driving, catch a truck ride) on the signed Playa
Las Peñitas turnoff road. After 3.5 miles (5.7
km) go right at the signed driveway 50 yards
to the beach. The main attraction, popular
with local holiday vacationers and Sunday
picnicking families, is the long, steep yellow-
sand beach, which provides plenty of opportunities for kids to scamper and splash in the
gentle waves and sheltered tidepools. It's also
lined with seafood *palapas* and Las Peñitas (the
Little Rocks), a family of sandstone rocks picturesquely perched on the shoreline.

At high tide, one of Las Peñitas becomes a
small islet, where folks have set a pilgrimage

cross around which the faithful congregate for devotions on the May 3 (Día de la Cruz) holiday. It provides a perfect playground for kids scampering and splashing in the waves that curl gently around the islet. Moreover, families frolic in a bathtublike tidepool on one side of the islet, dunking themselves in the gentle waves that fill its foamy basin.

A few small hotels embellish the lovely Las Peñitas picture. Most accessible just off the beach is the former **Hotel Puerto Palisada,** which has been taken over by new owners (who have yet to rename it). They offer four sparely but comfortably furnished detached bungalows with baths and fans in a shady beachfront palm grove, for about $40 for up to four people, $60 holidays, with a lovely blue pool and patio. For information and reservations (in Spanish) contact owner-manager Teresita Andrea Bautista, who lives in Mexico City (tel. 55/5590-9568), or her parents, David Bautista Priegro and Enerina Arizmendi, at their *ferretería* (hardware store, tel. 741/416-0012) in Marquelia, on the west-end street bordering the river, a short block off the highway, south side.

## BARRA DE TECOANAPA

Continue 1.5 miles by car (or, if without wheels, by truck; offer to pay), ford a shallow river, immediately pass a store, then bear left, passing through Guadalupe village. Continue another 4.5 miles (7.2 km) to road's end at Barra de Tecoanapa (pop. 1,000).

The village spreads for about a mile along the sandbar of the Río Quetzala, which empties into the sea from its lagoon-estuary about a quarter mile east of town. You can continue (drivers, be careful of soft sand) along the beach track to the embarcadero, decorated with a few dozen fishing *lanchas* pulled up on the lagoon-front. The river channel through the sandbar allows ocean fish (*sierra, róbalo, lisa*) to populate the lagoon.

The village appears to owe its existence to fishing and the holiday and weekend visitors who enjoy fresh seafood at its scattering of humble beachfront *palapa* restaurants. Terns and pelicans diving into onshore waves signal ideal conditions for surf fishing.

Although life on the Barra de Tecoanapa is simple and ruled by the unhurried rhythms of sun and tide, local folks, whose houses are primarily of stick and thatch, do enjoy a few 21st-century amenities, including a basketball court, two or three small stores, a kindergarten, a primary school, and a potable water system.

All this might spell heaven for experienced visitors equipped to enjoy country beachfront living. If you don't mind a few curious townsfolk, plenty of space is available for beachfront tenting and RV parking, especially west of town. Rent a boat or float your own either at the lagoon or right on the beachfront. Waves, which break gradually about 100 yards out, recede with only slight undertow, fine for wading, splashing, and boogie boarding. Although the waves I saw appeared too mild for surfing, stronger swells, a likely seasonal possibility, might produce ideal surfing conditions.

# Ometepec and Vicinity

Ometepec (pop. 20,000) is the capital of the Guerrero coastal indigenous heartland. In Ometepec's foothill backcountry, Spanish is a foreign language. About half of the Ometepec *municipio* (pop. 50,000) people are native Amusgo-speaking people. In more remote *municipios,* such as Xochistlahuaca (soh-chees-tlah-WAH-kah), more than three-quarters speak native tongues.

Vibrant markets with their piles of fruit and flowers, old-fashioned handmade goods, and crowds of folks in colorful native dress are the reward for visitors who venture uphill to spend time exploring these lively towns.

## ORIENTATION

Ometepec is readily accessible via a 10-mile paved road that branches off Highway 200 at

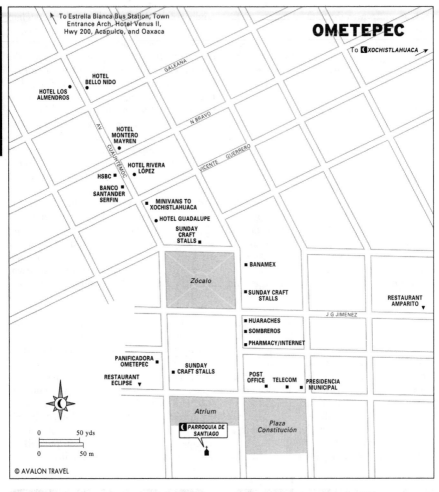

a big signed intersection 110 miles (177 km) east of Acapulco. Besides being an important market and service center that draws crowds of native peoples, notably Amusgos and Mixtecs, from outlying villages to its big Sunday market, Ometepec (elev. 1,000 feet, 304 meters) enjoys a cooler climate. Reflecting its upland location, the town's name, from the Náhuatl (Aztec) language, combines *ome* (two) and *tepec* (hill) to mean "land between two hills."

Ometepec orients itself along a single street, Avenida Cuauhtémoc. Entering town eastbound, via the ingress highway from the coast, you pass under not one, but two entrance arches. The main market is immediately on the right after the second arch.

Avenida Cuauhtémoc continues east past the main (Estrella Blanca) long-distance bus station. After about a quarter mile, the thoroughfare angles right (southeast), through the central business district, passing a parade of shops, taco restaurants, hotels, and banks. Finally, at the petite *zócalo* on the left, Cuauhtémoc bends due south and ends within a block in front of the main church, dedicated to Santiago (St. James).

## SIGHTS
### ◖ Parroquia de Santiago

Ometepec's church, although not old (it was built during the 1960s), is both popular and handsome. Evenings, spotlights keep its lovely blue-and-white facade shining long after dark. During the day, the faithful crowd through its gates and approach the facade, populated with its choir of white-shining saints and angels. Atop this all presides a sculpture of a mounted, sword-brandishing Santiago. Approach even closer and admire the church's grand polished wooden doors, climaxed in the center by yet another Santiago, this time with his horse's hooves trampling the defeated Moors. Inside, swallows swoop beneath the airy nave's ceiling

Ometepec Sunday Market

and perch and chirp in the chandeliers. Above the altar rises a grand dome whose paintings depict a vista of heaven so pleasing that it seems as pretty as the view must be through the pearly gates themselves.

### ◖ Ometepec Sunday Market

Ometepec's other famous attraction, the Sunday *tianguis,* operates in two sections: the main one on the west side, just inside the second town entrance arch, and the other around the downtown *zócalo.* At the *zócalo* are most of the handicrafts, including embroidered *huipiles,* huaraches, and sombreros. In the westside section you'll find a small mountain of everything else: forest-gathered herbs, seeds, and spices, *chiles,* homemade brooms, fruits (mangoes, grapes, and bananas), vegetables (radishes, sweet potatoes, tomatoes), tobacco (in aromatic bunches of big dried leaves), and mounds of dried fish, all in one spreading, semi-organized five-acre area. (For more market sights, see *Xochistlahuaca* in this chapter.)

Ometepec's pride and joy is its church, dedicated to Santiago (St. James).

# THE AMUSGO PEOPLE

If not the most numerous, the Amusgos are the most visible of the Acapulco region's indigenous groups. On Sunday, crowds of Amusgo-speaking people flock to easily accessible market towns in the Costa Chica foothills about 100 miles east of Acapulco.

The Amusgo homeland comprises an approximately 30-by-40-mile territory straddling the Oaxaca-Guerrero border. About a third of the 30,000 Amusgo speakers live in Oaxaca, around the small centers of Cacahuatepec and San Pedro Amusgos, while the remaining majority lives on the Guerrero side, near the centers of Ometepec, Xochistlahuaca, and Tlacoachistlahuaca.

Linguists reckon that the Amusgo language, a member of the Mixtec language subfamily, separated from Mixtec between 2000 and 1000 B.C. Around A.D. 1000 the Amusgos came under the domination of the strong coastal Oaxaca Mixtec kingdom of Tututepec. In A.D. 1457 they were conquered by the Aztecs and, not long after, by the Spanish in the 1520s. Decimation of the Amusgo population by disease during the 16th century led to the importation of African slave labor, whose descendants, known locally as *negros* or *costeños*, live along the Guerrero–Oaxaca coastline.

The Amusgo population eventually recovered; many of the old colonial-era haciendas remained intact until modern times and continued to employ Amusgo people as laborers. The Amusgos, isolated from the mainstream of modern Mexican life, retain their age-old corn-bean-squash subsistence-farming tradition. Moreover, they have received little attention from anthropologists or archaeologists, although several intriguing archaeological mounds exist near Amusgo villages.

Amusgo women are nevertheless famous for their hand-embroidered *huipiles*, whose colorful floral and animal designs fetch willing customers in the Acapulco region and Oaxaca tourist centers. Even better, Amusgo women often wear their *huipiles*, appearing as heavenly visions of spring on dusty small-town side streets.

© BRUCE WHIPPERMAN

**Amusgo-speaking men in traditional white cottons in Xochistlahuaca**

## ACCOMMODATIONS

Ometepec has a sprinkling of recommendable hotels, all of which accept cash only. They do a brisk business, accommodating the town's many market, business, and festival visitors.

The **Hotel Venus II** (Crucero de Talapa, tel. 741/412-2349, hotel_venus@hotmail.com) stands prominently, on the left, just past the statue of Vicente Guerrero and left of the second arch (about half a mile past the initial ingress highway arch) as you enter Ometepec. The hotel, at the uncongested edge of town and with a secure gated parking lot, is convenient for visitors with cars. Past the reception, the place is modern and clean, with guests in many rooms enjoying balcony vistas (of the parking lot below and hills beyond). The hotel's 20-odd rooms cost about $20 d in one bed, $25 d in two beds, with fan ($30 and $40 with a/c), all with private hot-water shower baths, good cable

TV, and a one-block walk to the main town market. The **Hotel Venus I** (tel. 741/415-8026 or 741/415-8027, hotel_venus@hotmail.com), the Venus II's sister hostelry, stands prominently at the Highway 200–Ometepec intersection, 10 miles downhill.

The remainder of Ometepec's hotels is downtown. Moving southwest along main street Avenida Cuauhtémoc, first find relaxing ◖ **Hotel Bello Nido** (Pretty Nest, Cuauhtémoc 50, tel. 741/412-0141 or 741/412-0234), about three blocks from the *zócalo.* Past the small but inviting lobby, the hotel rises in three motel-style floors around an appealing pool-patio. Rooms are clean and furnished with dark bedspreads, drapes, and tiled shower baths, but with no bedside reading lamps. Rentals run about $23 s, $27 d in one bed, with fan, $30 s and $45 d in two beds, with air-conditioning. All with TV, fans, and parking. For more tranquillity, light, and privacy, reserve a room on an upper-floor room in the back, away from the busy streetfront.

Across the street from Hotel Bello Nido is worthy newcomer business-style **Hotel Los Almendros** (Cuauhtémoc 52, tel. 741/412-2691). It offers 18 clean, attractively tiled, tan-motif rooms with shiny modern-standard hot-water bathrooms. Rentals run $30 s or d, $35 t, all with air-conditioning, cable TV, and parking.

A few cheaper hotel options cluster in the middle of the downtown action, about a block farther east. Best of the bunch is downscale **Hotel Rivera López** (Cuauhtémoc 22, tel. 741/412-0028). Choose from 33 sparely furnished rooms in three floors around an inner parking patio. Rooms cost about $19 s or $21 d in one double bed; $25 d, $30 t or q in two double beds, with TV, fans, parking, and hot-water shower bath. Add about $8 for air-conditioning.

Finally, half a block from the *zócalo,* lovers of Mexico "the way it used to be" might appreciate the **Hotel Guadalupe** (Cuauhtémoc 20, tel. 741/412-2228). The approximately 20 plain but clean rooms surround a leafy interior garden patio. They rent for about $14 s or d,

with room-temperature-water private shower baths, but no fans.

## FOOD

Most eating out in Ometepec occurs in one of two locales. The busiest of these is the west-side main market, where *fondas* offer country-style offerings of savory *guisado* (stews of chicken, pork, beef), piles of *antojitos* (*chiles rellenos, pozole,* tamales, tacos), and much more. (Permanent market *fondas* depend on repeat customers and therefore serve wholesome food. If in doubt, remember that cooked food, if it's steaming, will also be safe.)

Most of the other eateries are scattered along Cuauhtémoc near the *zócalo.* The most convenient choice is probably **Restaurant Eclipse** (7:30 A.M.–6 P.M. daily, $2–4), on the church-front street; at the end of Cuauhtémoc turn right around the corner. Restaurant Eclipse specializes in breakfasts (pancakes, omelettes, french toast) and *comida,* a set four-course lunch (noon–6 P.M.).

From late afternoon until midnight, the best food offerings are the tacos served by the platoon of stalls around the *zócalo,* in a dozen variations, from chicken and pork to barbecued beef, tongue, and brains.

Moreover, the downtown offers more than food. After the supper crowd mostly clears out around 8 or 9, the *zócalo* vicinity becomes a relaxing strolling and people-watching ground, to spend a balmy hour or two admiring the lovely illuminated churchfront view (and if you're lucky the full moon rising behind and above it).

The Ometepec downtown restaurant that everyone seems to recommend is **Amparito** (Juan Garcia Jiménez 11, tel. 741/412-2044, 7:30 A.M.–9 P.M. daily, $4–8), past Banamex, downhill two blocks east of the *zócalo.* Amparito, named after the grandmotherly owner, although specializing in seafood plates (shrimp, octopus, whole fish, fillets), does offer nonseafood specials. These might include *codorniz* (quail) or *guisado de res* (beef stew). For breakfasts, it can serve anything from eggs any style and French toast to pancakes or the good, local *pan dulce* with fresh fruit. If the TV noise bothers you, ask the staff to please lower the volume (*"favor de moderar el volumen"*—fah-VOR day moh-day-RAHR AYL vo-LOO-mayn).

For dessert, sample the fresh baked goods of **Panificadora Ometepec** (Cuauhtémoc 9, 7 A.M.–9 P.M. daily), a few doors north of the *zócalo*. On the other hand, if you're hankering for something sweet after the bakery closes, listen for someone along the street whistling, it may be the *plátano frito* (fried sweet banana) vendor with his cart.

## ENTERTAINMENT AND EVENTS

Ometepec is known for a number of festivals, notably the Easter-week **Semana Santa,** which includes, besides the usual religious Masses and processions, cattle, agricultural, and handicrafts expositions, *jaripeo* (bull riding and roping), and a carnival. Festivities climax with regional folk dance performances, including the favorite, Los Chilenos, said to have originated in Ometepec.

If you arrive in town on certain dates, join the festivities—May 3: Fiesta del Día de la Santa Cruz (Holy Cross); July 24–26: Fiesta de Santiago; September 9–11: Fiesta de San Nicolás Tolentino; September 15–16: Fiestas Patrias, including the 11 P.M. reenactment of Father Miguel Hidalgo's Grito de Dolores at the *presidencia municipal,* and the dances of El Mulo y La Tortuga (Mule and the Turtle) and El Macho.

The region's most popular festival is the **Fiesta del Señor del Perdón** at Igualapa (pop. 3,000), half an hour northwest of Ometepec. It may be worthwhile to make a special trip for this important indigenous fiesta, which local folks throw yearly on the third Friday of Lent (two weeks, two days after Ash Wednesday). The main event is a pilgrimage to pay respects to the Señor del Perdón (Lord of Pardon), visited by thousands, arriving on all fours, on their knees, by foot, or by car or bus. They arrive to ask, at least, for small favors and, at most, for miracles. And judging from the Señor del Perdón's popularity, the wishes are often granted. Miracles

notwithstanding, merrymaking abounds, especially among the swarm of campesinos—mostly speaking dialects of Amusgo, Mixtec, and Tlapanec languages—decked out in their Sunday-best *traje*. For a feast of scents, sounds, and sights, simply walk among the dozens of stalls around the Igualapa pilgrimage church, the Santuario del Señor del Perdón. Before departing, make sure to enjoy the whirl and flash of regional dances performed by a number of brightly costumed troupes. From Ometepec, get to Igualapa either via taxi or *colectivo* from the west-side market or by car. Follow the west exit road toward Highway 200. About a mile from the west edge of town, turn right at the Igualapa turnoff road; continue about 7 miles (11 km) to Igualapa.

## SHOPPING

Handicrafts are mostly sold downtown on Sunday at *zócalo*-front stores and stalls. Get huaraches and sombreros at a pair of stores on the *zócalo*'s east side. Women also sell embroidery and embroidered *huipiles* on the *zócalo,* mostly at temporary north-side stalls, on Sunday.

**Foto Alfa** (tel. 741/412-1245, 8 A.M.–7 P.M. Mon.–Fri., 9 A.M.–7 P.M. Sat.), on Cuauhtémoc a block northwest of the *zócalo,* offers developing and digital services, popular film varieties, some digital and film supplies, and point-and-shoot cameras.

The best spot for groceries and fresh fruits and vegetables in town is the main market, at the west end of Cuauhtémoc.

## SERVICES

Many establishments offer essential services near the downtown *zócalo*. (*Note:* At the *zócalo,* orient yourself by the church, which is *south* of the *zócalo*.)

Banks, all with ATMs, include **Banamex** (tel. 741/412-0880 or 741/412-1354, 9 A.M.–4 P.M. Mon.–Fri.), at the *zócalo*'s northeast corner; long-hours **HSBC** (Cuauhtémoc 52, tel. 741/412-2878 and 741/412-2879, 8 A.M.–7 P.M. Mon.–Fri., 8 A.M.–3 P.M. Sat.), a couple of blocks northwest of the *zócalo;* and neighboring **Banco Santander Serfín** (tel. 741/412-0113, 9 A.M.–4 P.M. Mon.–Fri.).

Mail letters at the *correo* (9 A.M.–1:30 P.M. Mon.–Fri.) in the *presidencia municipal,* on Plaza Constitución, two short blocks south of the *zócalo.* Money orders and public fax are available at neighboring **Telecom** (tel. 741/412-0386, 9 A.M.–2:30 P.M. Mon.–Fri., 9 A.M.–2 P.M. Sat.), also at the *presidencia municipal.* For local and long-distance calls, use Ladatel card-operated streetfront phones. Internet access and copies are available at **Super Farmacia Mexicana** (tel. 741/412-0657, 8:30 A.M.–9:30 P.M. daily) on the southeast *zócalo* corner.

If you get sick, consult with highly recommended **Dr. Alfredo Yañez Lobato** (tel. 741/412-0224). If he's not available, ask a taxi to take you to the private **Hospital de la Amistad** (tel. 741/412-0985) or **Clínica Seguro Social** (tel. 741/412-0392).

## GETTING THERE AND AWAY

**Estrella Blanca** (tel. 741/412-0035) provides a number of bus connections, most in the morning, with Acapulco and intermediate Costa Chica points. Find the terminal on Cuauhtémoc, just west of its bend toward the *zócalo.*

Although few, if any, long-distance buses from Ometepec connect directly with the very interesting easterly Costa Chica destinations of Cuajinicuilapa and Pinotepa Nacional in Oaxaca, alternatives exist. You can get an early taxi or *colectivo* downhill to the Highway 200 intersection. There, continue by *colectivo,* or wait for an Estrella Blanca (Elite, Gacela, Turistar, Flecha Roja) eastbound bus. (*Note:* The Ometepec Estrella Blanca agent may be able to tell you the bus connection times at the Highway 200 intersection.)

Driving to and from Ometepec is easy. To or from westerly Costa Chica destinations, simply follow Highway 200: one hour to/from Marquelia–Playa Las Peñitas, 33 miles (53 km); 1.5 hours to/from Copala–Playa Ventura, 48 miles (72 km); and 4.5 hours to/from Acapulco, 120 miles (194 km).

Similar good (but winding) road conditions prevail in the easterly direction: three quarters of an hour to/from Cuajinicuilapa, 25 miles (41 km); and two hours, 58 miles (93 km) to/from Pinotepa Nacional, Oaxaca.

## ◖ XOCHISTLAHUACA

Plan your Ometepec visit for a Friday or Saturday arrival (reserve your hotel room a week early) so you can visit the colorful indigenous Sunday markets at both Ometepec and Xochistlahuaca (pop. 3,000), about 17 miles (27 km) northeast. On the other hand, the things you find along the road to Xochi (SOH-chee), as Xochistlahuaca is known locally, may persuade you to linger.

The name Xochistlahuaca (soh-chees-tlah-WAH-kah), which in the Náhuatl (Aztec) language means "plain of flowers," is apt, especially during the summer rains, when wildflowers bloom all over the town's foothill *municipio* (township). Although an interesting destination all on its own, Xochi is a jumping-off point for even more remote Amusgo towns such as Chacalapa, Huistepec, and others with even less pronounceable names, such as Tlacoachistlahuaca.

Although the name Xochistlahuaca is of Aztec origin, the town is virtually all Amusgo speaking, and you can be certain that the Xochi folks have their own name for their town. At the Xochi Sunday market you may have to search around for someone who can translate Spanish into Amusgo well enough to help you bargain for one of the prized embroidered *huipiles* for which Amusgo women are renowned.

Although most Xochi young folks learn Spanish in school, and outside Spanish-speaking vendors descend to sell plastic dishes and transistor radios every Sunday, Xochistlahuaca and its surrounding *municipio* is a domain firmly rooted in Amusgo tradition. Here, *curanderos* still do much of the healing, women often recuperate from childbirth in a *temazcal* (ritual heat bath), and campesinos in their *milpas* still thank the earth spirits and the Lord of the Mountain for their harvests.

© BRUCE WHIPPERMAN

A woman rests in one of Xochistlahuaca's few quiet corners on market Sunday.

## Getting There

Get to Xochi by *colectivo* from the Ometepec downtown corner of Cuauhtémoc and Vicente Guerrero, a block north of the *zócalo*. If you have only one Sunday to visit, leave early for Xochi (buses are running by 7 A.M. and the Xochi mnarket is going strong by 9 A.M.) to allow time upon return to see the Ometepec market by 1 or 2 in the afternoon. Drivers, mark your odometer as you head northeast along Guerrero, from the same corner in Ometepec. Along the 17-mile (27-km) route are a number of interesting stops that you may want to visit on a later day.

After about three miles, pass **Balneario Camino Real** (9 A.M.–6 P.M. daily, $3 adults, $2 children under 12), with a big blue swimming pool, kiddie pool, restaurant, and shade for picnicking.

At Mile 3.5 (Km 5.6), arrive at San José village, marked by a gas station and then a road fork. (The right fork, worth exploring on its own, heads down into the lush Río Catarina valley, crosses the river, and continues uphill to indigenous Huistepec village and beyond.)

For Xochi, follow the left fork and continue about nine miles (15 km) from Ometepec, where the road splits. The left fork heads five miles (8 km) to **Tlacoachistlahuaca,** an interesting indigenous market town and *municipio,* comparable to Xochi.

For Xochi, bear right at the fork and continue straight ahead. Pass through Zacualpan village at around Mile 11 (Km 17). Continue to the Río San Pedro bridge at about Mile 15 (Km 24). Feast your eyes on the luscious procession of swimming holes decorated by giant, friendly water-sculptured rocks. (During the June–Sept. rainy season, however, the river may be a yucky muddy brown, but it will clear to an inviting jade-green as the rains abate by October.) Although swimming holes near the bridge are sometimes crowded with noisy local teens, spots upstream, via the hikeable (or 4WD-navigable) riverside trail, would probably be cleaner, more tranquil, and possible for overnight tenting.

## Exploring Xochistlahuaca

Follow the crowd to the Xochi *tianguis* that spreads over the middle of town from the intersection of Calles Morelos and Reforma. Along Reforma, a block uphill from the corner, stands the **Museo Comunitario** (10 A.M.–5 P.M. Mon.–Fri.), on the right. The museum's collection includes donated prehistoric artifacts and historical papers. Plans include adding a handicrafts store in the near future. Although the museum is not ordinarily open on Sunday, someone (try Ireneo Santana Guerrero, tel. 741/415-2149) may be available to open it up for you.

As in many backcountry areas, some men and most women wear *traje* unique to their hometowns. Xochi women distinguish themselves with a creamy-white embroidered cotton *huipil* decorated with a pair of crimson over-the-shoulder ribbons, both front and back.

Women dominate both buying and selling. Buyers bustle about, concentrating mostly on staples (fruit and vegetables and housewares),

© BRUCE WHIPPERMAN

**Amusgo-speaking folks crowd into Xochistlahuaca on market Sunday.**

perhaps pausing to pick out a bit of ribbon or jewelry as a treat. Sellers wait patiently behind their piles of offerings, which vary from flowers and pork rinds to mameys and machetes.

Sometime during your Xochi visit you might enjoy taking a look inside the attractive blue-and-white-decorated main church, atop the hill in the middle of town. Although the present (1930) structure is not old, the church it replaced, also dedicated to archangel St. Michael, dated back a good 300 years. The cool blue-and-white interior features San Miguel, sword in hand, presiding above the altar, between and above (and larger than) the Virgin Mary and Jesus.

For a rest and a good lunch, head to airy **Comedor Velé** (9 A.M.–10 P.M. daily, $2–5), Xochi's best eatery, on Morelos, half a block west of Reforma. Take a seat in the shade and choose from a very recognizable list of *tortas, hamburguesas,* enchiladas, tacos, and fresh seafood. Friendly, hardworking owner-chef Aquileo Morales López is *a su servicio* (at your service).

## CUAJINICUILAPA

Astride Highway 200, a few miles before the Oaxaca border, Cuajinicuilapa (kwah-hee-nee-kwee-LAH-pah, pop. 10,000) is the major market town and cultural center for the dozen-odd eastern Guerrero *costeño* communities. These include farming villages Los Hoyos, Montecillos, San Nicolas, and the airy, laid-back local fishing port, Puerto Maldonado.

In Cuajinicuilapa, known locally as Cuaji (koo-AH-hee), 125 miles (199 km) east of Acapulco, the market buyers and sellers crowd both the east and west ends of town. The clutter clears, however, at the town center, marked by a big covered basketball court.

### ◖ Museo de las Culturas Afromestizos

Behind the basketball court stands the Museo de las Culturas Afromestizos (10 A.M.–2 P.M. and 4–7 P.M. Tues.–Sun., free admission). The museum shouldn't be missed. If not the only, it's one of the very few Mexican museums dedicated to African-Mexican history and culture. Inside, it offers several fascinatingly graphic and insightful displays, plus a library and dance, theater, guitar, and crafts workshops.

## Accommodations and Food

A pair of town-center hotels offer comfortable accommodations. Very recommendable is the 30-room **Hotel Marin** (Calle Principal, tel. 741/414-0021), a few doors east of the basketball court. It's built along a shady corridor interspersed with lush green tropical minipatios. The comfortable, invitingly decorated rooms run $20 s, $24 d with fan, $30 s or d with air-conditioning.

First place goes to **( Hotel Alejim** (Calle Rudolfo Rodríguez, tel. 741/414-0310), on the west side of town, a block west of the gas station and half a block off the highway, north side. The hotel, kept cool by the majestic mango orchard that shades it, is an island of tranquillity. The 30 spacious, comfortable, and thoughtfully decorated rooms, in two stories, with private baths, go for $19 s, $24 d with fan; $28 s, $34 d with air-conditioning.

Cuaji's most inviting restaurant is refined **Restaurant Yvonne** (Calle Principal, tel. 741/414-0924, 8 A.M.–7 P.M. Mon.–Sat., $3–4), on the west side, about three blocks from the basketball court. Specialties are breakfasts (ham and eggs, hotcakes) and relaxing afternoon *comida* such as *guisado de puerco* (spicy pork stew), *mole de guajalote* (turkey mole).

## Services

Cuaji has a **Banamex** with ATM (9 A.M.–4 P.M. Mon.–Fri.) across from the basketball court; a **Centro de Salud** (no phone, doctor 24 hours); a pharmacy, **Farmapronto** (tel. 741/414-1074, 7 A.M.–10 P.M. daily); *correo* (8 A.M.–3 P.M. Mon.–Fri.) next to Banamex; Ladatel card-operated street telephones up and down the highway downtown, and *telecomunicaciones* (tel. 741/414-0337, 9 A.M.–3 P.M. Mon.–Fri., 9 A.M.–noon Sat.–Sun.) for money orders and public fax, by the bank.

## PUERTO MALDONADO

This country coastal fishing village (pop. 1,000), about 20 miles (32 km) south of Cuajinicuilapa, appeared on the map initially because of its lighthouse. A reassuring beacon, the lighthouse perches atop a point of land called Punta Maldonado, crowning the 100-foot-high bluff that lines this remote coast.

The lighthouse adds a picturesque aspect to the entire scene: a long, breeze-swept beach curving east, while west of the Punta (Point) a few fisherfolks' homes, a couple of stores, a small guesthouse, and a sprinkling of fishing *lanchas* decorate the strand.

Here, life goes on quietly and easily. You can stroll the beach, picking up a bit of driftwood and a shell or two, joke with the locals, play with the kids, watch the fishermen mend their nets, and rent a boat and mount your own fishing excursion.

### Getting There

Get to Puerto Maldonado by minibus from the middle of Cuaji, by the basketball court. Drivers, head east from the town. After only a mile, turn right (south) onto the signed Puerto Maldonado road near Km 201. Mark your odometer.

After about 10 miles (16 km) pass through Montecillos village (pop. about 2,000), a mixed mestizo and African-Mexican community. Farther along, at around 15 miles (24 km), at Tejastruda village, notice the apparently evangelistic church, decorated with both a Christian cross and what appears to be the Star of David. Finally, arrive at Puerto Maldonado just after 19 miles (31 km) from Highway 200.

### Sights and Recreation

Get oriented at the rustic **Las Brisas Palapa,** perched on the scenic Punta Maldonado beach-tip. From beneath the *palapa,* drink in the gorgeous panorama as the waves curl around the Punta and swish and disappear into the coral-dotted golden sand of the point's west-side beach.

THE COSTA CHICA

Use the existing posts in front of the *palapa* for a volleyball game (bring your own ball and net), explore the tidepools, or launch your own boat from the beach. **Surfing** the waves that swell inshore past the point and break diagonally along the beach line is a regular pastime here.

## Accommodations and Food

You can park your self-contained RV or set up your tent beneath the point's small but sheltering palm grove. A few village stores can supply essential groceries and water.

Travelers can also stay at the guesthouse **Casa de Huéspedes Valle Encantado,** in the beach fishing village about a quarter mile west of the point. The three plain but clean rooms rent for about $15 s or d, with private bath (but room-temperature water only). For reservations, leave a message with the *caseta* operator at long-distance satellite tel. 01-200/126-2552.

For prepared food, visit either the beachfront *palapa* or the airy oceanview *comedor* that the friendly guesthouse owner also operates, by the beach. If you need medical attention, visit the Centro de Salud on the bluff above the beach.

# Pinotepa Nacional and Vicinity

In Oaxaca, Pinotepa Nacional (pop. about 50,000; 157 miles, 253 km, east of Acapulco; 90 miles, 145 km, west of Puerto Escondido) and its neighboring communities comprise the hub of an important coastal indigenous region. Mixtec, Amusgo, Chatino, and other peoples stream into town for markets and fiestas in their *traje,* ready to combine business with pleasure. They sell their produce and crafts—pottery, masks, handmade clothes—at the market, then later get tipsy, flirt, and dance.

So many people had asked the meaning of their city's name that the town fathers wrote the explanation on a wall next to Highway 200 on the west side of town. Pinotepa comes from the Aztec words *pinolli* (crumbling) and *tepetl* (mountain)—thus "Crumbling Mountain." The second part of the name came about because during colonial times the town was called Pinotepa Real (Royal). This wouldn't do after independence, so the name became Pinotepa Nacional, reflecting the national consciousness that emerged during the 1810–1821 struggle for independence.

The Mixtecs, the dominant regional group, disagree with all this, however. To them, Pinotepa has always been Ñií Yo-oko (Little Place). Only within the town limits do the Mexicans (mestizos), who own most of the town businesses, outnumber the Mixtecs. The farther from town you get, the more likely you are to hear people conversing in the Mixtec language, a complex tongue that uses a number of subtle tones to make meanings clear.

## ORIENTATION

On Pinotepa's west side, Highway 200 splits into the town's two major arteries, which rejoin on the east side. The north, westbound branch is called Aguirre Palancares; the south, eastbound branch, the more bustling of the two branches, passes between the town-center *zócalo* and church and is called Avenida Porfirio Díaz on the west side and Avenida Benito Juárez on the east. The main north–south street, Avenida Pérez Gasga, runs past both the churchfront and the *presidencia municipal,* which faces east, toward the *zócalo.*

## ◖ PINOTEPA NACIONAL MARKET

Highway 200 passes a block north of the main town market, by the big fenced-in secondary school, on the west side, about a mile west of the *zócalo.* Despite the Pinotepa market's oft-exotic goods—snakes, iguanas, wild mountain fruits, forest herbs, and spices—its

© BRUCE WHIPPERMAN

Flowers are a popular sale item at the Pinotepa Nacional market.

## FESTIVALS

Although the Pinotepa market days are big, they don't compare to the week before Easter (Semana Santa). People get ready for the finale with processions, carrying the dead Christ through town to the church each of the seven Fridays before Easter. The climax comes on Good Friday (Viernes Santa), when a platoon of young Mixtec men paint their bodies white to portray Jews, and while intoning ancient Mixtec chants shoot arrows at Christ on the cross. On Saturday, the people mournfully take the Savior down from the cross and bury him, and on Sunday gleefully celebrate his resurrection with a riot of fireworks, food, and folk dancing.

Although not as spectacular as Semana Santa, there's plenty of merrymaking, food, dancing, and processions around the Pinotepa *zócalo* church on July 25, the day of Pinotepa's patron, Santiago (St. James).

people, nearly entirely Mixtec speaking, are its main attraction, especially on the big Monday market days. Men wear pure-white loose cottons, topped by woven palm-leaf hats. Women wrap themselves in their lovely striped purple, violet, red, and navy blue *pozahuancos.* Many women carry atop their heads a polished tan *jicara* (gourd bowl), which, although it's not supposed to, looks like a whimsical hat. Older women (and younger ones with babies at their breasts) go bare-breasted with only their white *huipiles* draped over their chests as a concession to mestizo custom. Others wear an easily removable *mandil,* a light cotton apron-halter above their *pozahuancos.* A few women can ordinarily be found offering colorful *pozahuancos* made with cheaper synthetic thread for about $20. The women told me that traditional all-handmade *pozahuancos* (hand-spun, hand-sewn, and hand-dyed with naturally gathered pigments) are more commonly available in outlying market towns, notably Pinotepa Don Luis.

## POZAHUANCOS

To a coastal Mixtec woman, her *pozahuanco* is a lifetime investment symbolizing her maturity and social status, something that she expects to pass on to her daughters. Heirloom *pozahuancos* are wraparound, horizontally striped skirts of hand-spun thread. Women dye the thread by hand, always including a pair of necessary colors: cotton dyed a light purple (*morada*) from secretions of tidepool-harvested snails, *Purpura patula pansa;* and silk dyed scarlet red with cochineal, a dye extracted from the beetle *Dactylopius coccus,* cultivated in the Valley of Oaxaca. Increasingly, women are weaving *pozahuancos* with synthetic thread, which has a slippery feel compared to the hand-spun cotton. Consider yourself lucky if you can get a traditionally made *pozahuanco* for as little as $100. If someone offers you one for $20, you know it's an imitation.

## ACCOMMODATIONS

The motel-style ◖ **Hotel Carmona** (Av. Porfirio Díaz 127, tel. 954/543-2322), about three blocks west of the *zócalo*, offers three stories of clean not fancy but comfortable rooms; arrive early to enjoy the big backyard garden with pool and sundeck. For festival dates, make advance reservations. The 50 rooms run about $25 s, $30 d, $35 t, with fan only; $35, $45, and $55, with air-conditioning. Credit cards are not accepted.

If the Carmona is full, check the two high-profile newer hotels, Pepe's and Las Gaviotas, beside the highway on the west side of town. Of the two, **Pepe's** (Carretera Pinotepa Nacional–Acapulco Km 1, tel. 954/543-4347, fax 954/543-3602) is the better choice. It offers 35 spacious semideluxe rooms for a reasonable $26 s, $34 d, with air-conditioning, cable TV, hot water, handy passable restaurant, and parking. Rooms at only-stay-in-an-emergency **Hotel Las Gaviotas** (tel. 954/543-2838, fax 954/543-2056) rent for $20 d with fan, $30 with air-conditioning.

Third choice goes to clean **Hotel Marisa** (Av. Juárez 134, tel. 954/543-2101 or 954/543-3190), downtown on the north side of the highway. Rooms are $18 s or d in one bed, $24 d in two beds, with fan; $33 s or d in one bed, $35 d in two beds with air-conditioning, all with private baths, TV, and parking.

Campers enjoy a tranquil spot (best during the dry, calm, clear-water late fall–winter–spring season) on the Río Arena about two miles east of Pinotepa. Eastbound, turn left just after the big river bridge. Continue a few hundred yards, past a pumphouse on the left, to a track that forks down to the riverbank. Notice the waterfall cascading down the rocky cliff across the river. You will sometimes find neighbors—in RVs or tents, and poor but friendly sand collectors—set up on the riverside beneath the abandoned Restaurant La Roca (now just a rock-wall ruin) a few hundred yards up the smooth stream, excellent for kayaking (if you devise some way of returning back upstream). (*Note:*

Lately the sand collectors have preempted much of the east-bank space. You might find more room to spread out on the opposite river bank. Get there just west of the bridge, by following the dirt track downhill along the southwest riverbank.)

## FOOD

For a light lunch or supper, try the very clean family-run **Burger Bonny** (11 A.M.–10 P.M. daily, $1–4), at the southeast corner of the main plaza. Besides six varieties of good hamburgers, Burger Bonny offers *tortas,* tacos, french fries, hot dogs, microwave popcorn, fruit juices, and *refrescos.*

Also worthy is traditional-style ◖ **Fonda Toñita** (7 A.M.–9 P.M. Mon.–Sat., $2–4), a block north of the churchfront, at the corner of Aguirre Palancares. Local folks flock here for the hearty afternoon *comida* (pick the entrée, and you get rice and tortillas thrown in free); it's also good for breakfast.

Third restaurant choice goes to **Tacos Orientales** (6–11 P.M. daily) with 15 styles of tacos, from fish to *carnitas,* three for $2.50. Find it on Pérez Gasga, half a block north of the churchfront.

On the other hand, consider *marisquería* **Peñitas** (8 A.M.–midnight daily, $5–8), next door, which specializes in fresh seafood however you like it: fried, baked, breaded, *al mojo,* and more.

For a quick and convenient on-the-road breakfast, lunch, or dinner, stop by the restaurant of high-profile **Pepe's Hotel** (8 A.M.–10 P.M. daily, $3–6) west of town.

## SHOPPING AND SERVICES

For the freshest fruits and vegetables, visit the town market any day, although it's biggest on Monday. For film and film-processing, step into **Arlette Foto** (tel. 954/543-2766, 8 A.M.–8 P.M. Mon.–Sat., 8 A.M.–3 P.M. Sun.) near the plaza's southwest corner.

Exchange money over the counter or use the ATM at all Pinotepa banks. Try **Bancomer** (tel. 954/543-3022 or 954/543-3190,

© BRUCE WHIPPERMAN

Old-fashioned big-top circuses remain popular in Costa Chica towns, such as Pinotepa Nacional.

8:30 A.M.–4 P.M. Mon.–Fri.), corner of Díaz and Progreso, two blocks west of the plaza; or **Banamex** (tel. 954/543-3022, 9 A.M.–4 P.M. Mon.–Fri.), across the street; or long-hours **HSBC** (tel. 954/543-3949 or 954/543-3969, 8 A.M.–7 P.M. Mon.–Fri., 8 A.M.–3 P.M. Sat.), also on Avenida Progreso, but across Porfirio Díaz and uphill a block from Bancomer.

Find the *correo* (tel. 954/543-2264, 8 A.M.–7 P.M. Mon.–Fri.) about half a mile west of downtown, a block past Pepe's Hotel and across the street. Find the *telecomunicaciones* office (tel. 954/543-2019, 8 A.M.–7:30 P.M. Mon.–Fri., 9 A.M.–noon Sat.–Sun.) one block north of the plaza church, on Avenida Pérez Gasga.

For telephone, use Ladatel card-operated street telephones, or go to the long-hours *larga distancia* Lada Central telephone and fax office (tel. 954/543-2547), on the plaza, south side. A few doors away, answer your email at **Switch Internet** store (8 A.M.–9 P.M. daily).

For a doctor, go to the **Clínica Rodriguez** (Aguirre 503 Palancares, tel. 954/543-2330), one block north, two blocks west of the central plaza churchfront. Get routine medications at one of several town pharmacies, such as the 24-hour **Super Farmacia** on Díaz, a block west of the central plaza churchfront.

## GETTING THERE AND AWAY

By car or RV, Highway 200 connects west via Cuajinicuilapa, Ometepec, and Playa Ventura, to Acapulco (160 miles, 258 km) in an easy 4.5 hours at the wheel. The easy 89-mile (143-km) eastward connection with Puerto Escondido takes about 2.5 hours. Additionally, the long 239-mile (385-km) Highway 125–Highway 190 route connects Pinotepa Nacional to Oaxaca, via Putla de Guerrero and Tlaxiaco (136 miles, 219 km), continuing by Highway 190 via Nochixtlan to Oaxaca City. Although winding most of the way and potholed at times, the road is generally uncongested. It's safely driveable in a passenger car with caution, from Pinotepa to Oaxaca City in about eight hours (under dry conditions) at the wheel, and seven hours in the reverse, downhill, direction from Oaxaca City.

By bus, from the new **Camionera Central** (Central Bus Station), about half a mile west of downtown, several long-distance bus lines connect Pinotepa Nacional with destinations north, northwest, east, and west. Dominant line **Estrella Blanca** (tel. 954/543-3194), via subsidiaries Turistar, Elite, Futura, Gacela, and Flecha Roja, offers several daily first- and second-class *salidas de paso* (departures passing through): west to Acapulco, Zihuatanejo, and Mexico City; and east to Oaxaca coastal resorts of Puerto Escondido, Pochutla (Puerto Ángel), and Bahías de Huatulco.

Other independent, mostly second-class lines also operate out of the same terminal. **Fletes y Pasajes** (tel. 954/543-6016) connects with inland points, via Putla de Guerrero, Tlaxiaco, and Teposcolula along Highway 125, continuing along Highway 190 via Nochixtlán, to Oaxaca City. **Estrella del Valle** (tel. 954/543-5476) also connects with Oaxaca City, but in the opposite direction, via Highway 200 east to Puerto Escondido and Pochutla (Puerto Ángel), thence north along Highway 175, over the high southern sierra, to Oaxaca City. On the other hand, second-class **Estrella Roja del Sureste** (tel. 954/543-6017), in addition to connecting with Oaxaca City via Highway 175 at Pochutla, also connects with Oaxaca, via Highway 200 to Puerto Escondido, thence north, along Highway 131, over the high sierra.

A welter of local buses connect with dozens of nearby towns and villages, from a streetside terminal downtown, north side of Aguirre Palancares, half a block north and half a block east of the plaza churchfront. Destinations include Jamiltepec, Huazolotitlán, Pinotepa Don Luis, San Juan Colorado, Cacahuatepec, San Pedro Amusgos, and many more.

## EXCURSIONS NORTH OF PINOTEPA

The local patronal festival year begins early, on January 20, at **Pinotepa Don Luis** (pop. 5,000), about 15 miles by back roads northeast of Pinotepa Nacional, with the uniquely Mixtec festival of San Sebastián. Village bands blare, fireworks pop and hiss, and penitents crawl until the finale, when dancers whirl the local favorite dance, Las Chilenas.

Yet another exciting time around Pinotepa Nacional is during **Carnaval**, when nearby communities put on big extravaganzas. Pinotepa Don Luis, sometimes known as Pinotepa Chica (Little Pinotepa), is famous for the wooden masks the people make for their big Carnaval. The celebration usually climaxes on the Sunday before Ash Wednesday, when everyone seems to be in costume and a corps of performers gyrates in the traditional dances: Paloma (Dove), Tigre (Jaguar), Culebra (Snake), and Tejón (Badger).

Pinotepa Don Luis bubbles over again with excitement during Semana Santa, when the faithful carry fruit- and flower-decorated trees to the church on Good Friday, explode Judas effigies on Saturday, and celebrate by dancing most of Easter Sunday.

**San Juan Colorado,** a few miles north of Pinotepa Don Luis, usually appears as just another dusty little town until Carnaval, when its festival rivals that of its neighbors. Subsequently, on November 29, droves of Mixtec people come into town to honor their patron, San Andres. After the serious part at the church, they celebrate with a cast of favorite dancing characters such as Malinche, Jaguar, Turtle, and Charros (Cowboys).

## Oaxaca Amusgo Country

**Cacahuatepec** (pop. about 5,000; on Hwy. 125 about 25 miles north of Pinotepa Nacional) and its neighboring community San Pedro Amusgos are important centers for the Amusgo-speaking people. Approximately 20,000 Amusgos live in a roughly 30-mile-square region straddling the Guerrero-Oaxaca state border. Their homeland includes, besides Cacahuatepec and San Pedro Amusgos, Ometepec, Xochistlahuaca, Zacoalpán, and Tlacoachistlahuaca on the Guerrero side.

The Amusgo language is linguistically related to Mixtec, although it's unintelligible to Mixtec speakers. Before the conquest, the Amusgos were subject to the numerically

# THE MIXTECS

Sometime during the 1980s, southern Mexico's Mixtec-speaking people regained their preconquest population of about 500,000. Of that total, around two-fifths speaks only their own language. Their villages and communal fields spread over tens of thousands of square miles of remote mountain valleys north and west of Oaxaca, east and northeast of Acapulco, and south of Puebla.

Their homeland, the Mixteca (see the map *Native Peoples of the Acapulco Region* in the *Background* chapter), speads over three distinct geocultural regions: the Mixteca Alta, Mixteca Baja, and the Mixteca Costera.

The **Mixteca Alta** centers in the high, cool plateauland of Guerrero and Oaxaca (which, on its east side, begins about 100 miles due west from Oaxaca City, and on its west side, about 100 miles due east from Chilpancingo, Guerrero), around the important market centers of Tlapa, Guerrero, and Tlaxiaco, Oaxaca.

Important **Mixteca Baja** communities, some along Highway 190, such as Huajuapan de Leó in Oaxaca, and Izucar de Matamoros in Puebla, dot the dry northwestern Oaxaca-eastern Guerrero-southern Puebla mountains and valleys.

In the **Mixteca Costera,** important Mixtec communities exist in or near Ometepec, Guerrero, and Pinotepa Nacional and Jamiltepec, Oaxaca, along Highway 200 in southwestern Oaxaca and southeastern Guerrero.

The Aztec-origin name Mixtecos (People of the Clouds) was translated directly from the Mixtecs' name for their own homeland: Aunyuma (Land of the Clouds). The Mixtecs' name for themselves, however, is Nyu-u Sabi (People of the Rain).

When the conquistadores arrived, the Mixtecs were under the thumb of the Aztecs, who, after a long, bitter struggle, had wrested control of Oaxaca from combined Mixtec-Zapotec armies in 1486. The Mixtecs naturally resented the Aztecs, whose domination was transferred to the Spanish during the colonial period, and, in turn, to the mestizos during modern times. The Mixtecs still defer to the town Mexicans, but they don't like it. Consequently, many rural Mixtecs, with little state or national consciousness, have scant interest in becoming Mexicanized.

In isolated Mixtec communities, traditions still rule. Village elders hold final authority, parents arrange marriages through go-betweens, and land is owned communally. Catholic saints are thinly disguised incarnations of old gods such as Tabayukí, ruler of nature, or the capricious and powerful *tono* spirits that lurk everywhere.

In many communities, Mixtec women exercise considerable personal freedom. At home and in villages, especially in the warm Mixteca Costa, they often still work bare-breasted. And while their men get drunk and carry on during festivals, women dance and often do a bit of their own carousing. With whom they do it is their own business.

---

superior Mixtec kingdoms until the Amusgos were conquered by the Aztecs in A.D. 1457, and later by the Spanish.

Now, most Amusgos live as subsistence farmers, supplementing their diet with occasional fowl or small game. Amusgos are best known to the outside world for their lovely animal-, plant-, and human-motif *huipiles,* which Amusgo women always seem to be hand-embroidering on their doorsteps.

Although Cacahuatepec enjoys a big market each Sunday, that doesn't diminish the importance of its big Easter-weekend festival, as well as the Día de Todos Santos (All Saints' Day, November 1), and Día de los Muertos (Day of the Dead, November 2), when, at the cemetery, people welcome their ancestors' return to rejoin the family.

**San Pedro Amusgos** celebrations are among the most popular regional fiestas. On June 29, the day of San Pedro, people participate in religious processions, and costumed participants dressed as Moors and Christians, bulls, jaguars, and mules dance before crowds of men in traditional whites and women in beautiful heirloom *huipiles*. Later, on the first

Sunday of October, folks crowd into town to enjoy the traditional processions, dances, and sweet treats of the fiesta of the Virgen del Rosario (Virgin of the Rosary).

Even if you miss the festivals, San Pedro Amusgos is worth a visit to buy *huipiles* alone. Three or four shops sell them along the main street through town. Look for the sign of **Trajes Regionales Elia** (tel. 954/582-8697), the little store run by sprightly Elia Guzmán when she's not in Oaxaca City. Besides dozens of beautiful embroidered garments, she stocks a few Amusgo books and offers friendly words of advice and local information.

## EXCURSIONS EAST OF PINOTEPA

For 30 or 40 miles east of Pinotepa Nacional, where road kilometer markers begin at zero again near the central plaza, Highway 200 stretches through the coastal Mixtec heartland. It's intriguing to explore, especially during festival times.

### ◖ Huaxpáltepec Pre-Easter Fair

For 20 miles (32 km) west of Jamiltepec, Highway 200 stretches through the coastal Mixtec heartland. The population of San Andres Huaxpáltepec (oo-wash-PAHL-tay-payk), about 10 miles east of Pinotepa, sometimes swells from about 4,000 to 20,000 or more during the three or four days before the day of Jesus the Nazarene, on the fourth Friday of Lent (or in other words, the fourth Friday after Ash Wednesday). The entire town spreads into a warren of shady stalls, offering everything from TVs to stone metates. The corn-grinding metate, which, including *mano* (stone roller), sells for about $25, is as important to a Mixtec family as a refrigerator is to an American family. A Mixtec husband and wife usually examine several of the concave stones, deliberating the pros and cons of each before deciding.

The Huaxpáltepec Nazarene fair is typical of the larger Oaxaca country expositions. Even the highway becomes a lineup of stalls; whole native clans camp under the trees, and mules, cows, and horses wait patiently around the edges of a grassy

trading lot as men discuss prices. (The fun begins when a sale is made, and the new owner tries to rope and harness his bargain steed.)

### Huazolotitlán

At nearby Santa María Huazolotitlán (ooah-shoh-loh-teet-LAN, pop. 3,000) several resident woodcarvers craft excellent **masks.** Local favorites are jaguars, lions, rabbits, bulls, and human faces. Given a photograph (or a sitting), one of them might even carve your likeness for a reasonable fee (figure perhaps $40–60). Near the town plaza, ask for Che Luna, Lázaro Gómez, or Idineo Gómez, all of whom live in the town *barrio* Ñií Yucagua.

**Textiles** are also locally important. Look for the colorfully embroidered animal- and floral-motif *huipiles, manteles,* and *servilletas* (native smocks, tablecloths, and napkins). You might also be able to bargain for a genuine heirloom *pozahuanco* for a reasonable price.

Besides all the handicrafts, Huazolotitlán people celebrate the important local **Fiesta de la Virgen de la Asunción** around August 13–16. The celebrations customarily climax

© BRUCE WHIPPERMAN

low-fired pottery at the Huaxpáltepec Pre-Easter fair

with a number of favorite traditional dances, in which you can see why masks are locally important, especially in the dance of the Tiger and the Turtle. The finale comes a day later, celebrated with the ritual dance of the Chareos, dedicated to the Virgin.

Get to Huazolotitlán in about two miles along the paved (but oft-potholed) road that forks south uphill from Highway 200 in Huaxpáltepec. Drive, hitchhike (with caution), ride the local bus, or hire a taxi for about $3.

## Santiago Jamiltepec

About 18 miles (30 km) east of Pinotepa Nacional stands the hilltop town of Jamiltepec (hah-meel-teh-PAYK). Two-thirds of its 20,000 inhabitants are Mixtec, who preserve a still-vibrant indigenous culture. A grieving Mixtec king named the town in memory of his infant son, Jamily, who was carried off by an eagle from this very hilltop.

The central plaza, about a mile (1.6 km) from the highway (follow the signed side road north), stands at the heart of the town. You can't miss it, because of the proud plaza-front clock (and sundials) and the market, always big but even bigger and more colorful on Thursday, the day of the traditional native *tianguis,* when a regiment of campesinos crowd in from the Jamiltepec hinterland.

Moreover, several big **festivals** are instrumental in preserving local folkways. They start off on New Year's Day and resume during the weeks of Cuaresma (Lent), usually during February and March. Favorite dances, such as Los Tejerones (Weavers), Los Chareos, Los Moros (Moors), and Las Chilenas, act out age-old events, stories, and fables. Los Tejerones, for example, through a cast of animal-costumed characters, pokes fun at ridiculous Spanish colonial rules and customs.

Soon after, Jamiltepec people celebrate their very popular pre-Easter **Week of Ramos** festival, featuring neighborhood candlelight processions accompanied by antique 18th-century music. Hundreds of the faithful bear elaborate wreaths and palm decorations to the foot of their church altars on Domingo de Ramos (Palm Sunday).

Later, merrymaking peaks again, between July 23 and 26 during the **Fiesta de Santiago Apóstol** (Festival of St. James the Apostle) and on September 11 with a festival honoring the Virgen de los Remedios. All this celebrating centers in the town church, the **Templo de Santiago Apóstol,** destroyed by a 1928 earthquake but brilliantly restored from 1992 to 1999. Take a look inside, where the town patron Santiago (St. James, sword in hand) and the Virgen de Los Remedios (Virgin of the Remedies) preside above the altar.

Regardless of the festivals, Jamiltepec at midday is a feast of traditional sights and sounds, accessible by simply strolling around the market and side streets. For an interesting side excursion, take a stroll to some of the local *ojos de agua* (community spring-water sources). From the plaza's northeast side, head east, downhill, along Calle 20 de Noviembre. After about a block, you'll arrive at a covered *pileta* (basin) built into the hillside rocks on the left, where folks fill bottles and jars with drinking water. Continue downhill another couple of blocks to *ojo de agua* **El Aguacate,** where another covered basin, on the left, supplies drinking water, while a cluster of folks wash clothes and bathe in a natural spring beneath an adjacent shady roof.

If you're interested in a more spectacular water diversion, follow the gravel road by local minibus or car north out of town about 15 miles (25 km) to the *cascada* (waterfall) in the foothill country near San José de las Flores village.

### PRACTICALITIES

Jamiltepec, capital of the Jamiltepec governmental district, has a number of basic hotels, restaurants, and services (but not yet a bank) near the town plaza. For an overnight, take a look at the **Hotel Díaz** (Hidalgo 4, tel. 958/582-9103, fax 958/582-8050) at the northeast plaza corner. It offers a dozen clean, basic rooms around an airy upstairs patio for about

$10 s, $14 d, with fan and private bath (but room-temperature water only). If the Hotel Díaz is full, check out the **Hotel Maris** (tel. 954/582-8042, $17 d) or Hotel Pérez (tel. 954/582-8249, $20 d), both on Calle Josefa O. Domínguez nearby.

Additionally, out on the highway, at the west edge of town, consider Jamiltepec's newish semi-deluxe **Hotel Mirador** (tel. 954/559-2448), perched on a view hillside, next to Highway 200. Fine for an overnight, the Mirador offers about 15 comfortable (if a bit dark) rooms, for about $18 s or d in one bed, $25 d with two beds with fans only; or $20 s or d in one bed, $30 d in two beds with air-conditioning. All with hot-water shower baths, parking, and an acceptable restaurant.

For medicines and drugs, go to **Farmacia del Perpetuo Socorro** (Pharmacy of Perpetual Relief, Hidalgo 2, tel. 954/582-9046, 8 A.M.–8 P.M. daily), next to Hotel Díaz, at the plaza's northeast corner, run by a team of friendly sisters. If you need a doctor, they recommend either **Dr. Manuel Mota,** on Highway 200, in *barrio* Sección 4, or the *seguro social* hospital with 24-hour emergency service, in *barrio* Las Flores.

Jamiltepec is well worth a stop if only to visit its **market handicrafts shops,** such as Santiago de la Cruz Velasco's **Yu-uku Cha-kuaa** (Hill of Darkness). Personable Santiago sells mostly locally made crafts—masks, *huipiles,* carvings, hats—at his shop on the market's northeast side (ask for Santiago by name), open until about 4 P.M. His home (where he also sells handicrafts) is located on main street Avenida Principal at Francisco Madero, by the *seguro social* (government health clinic, turn off at the highway sign). If you don't want to miss him, write Santiago at Avenida Principal, Esquina Fco. Madero, Barrio Grande, Sec. 5, Jamiltepec, Oaxaca 71700.

# BACKGROUND

## The Land

A look at a map of North America reveals that Acapulco lies very far south, at the 17th parallel of latitude, which, as seen from the north pole, places Acapulco four-fifths of the way to the equator. Furthermore, Acapulco's longitude, smack on the 100th parallel, places it both far east and far west, depending on your point of view. From Washington, D.C., Acapulco is a far 1,400 miles west; from San Francisco, Acapulco is a far 1,400 miles east. And from both, it is a far 1,400 miles south, well into the tropical land of perpetual summer: a plumy paradise, where frost never bites.

Yes, a paradise; and that dream continues to propel Acapulco to the stars among the world's renowned tropical resorts while at the same time making it Mexico's most popular beach destination.

Acapulco's popularity is well deserved. The many faces of Acapulco—its curving blue bay, framed by crystalline golden beaches and steep, green-forested ridges; the shade-dappled old-town plaza; the fine food; the continuous entertainments; and the hotels, both modest and luxurious, continue to draw millions of yearly visitors from all over the world.

# THE ACAPULCO REGION

Locally, Acapulco's influence extends far beyond its city limits into the entire Acapulco region, an ethnically and geographically diverse domain that encompasses, broadly, the entire Mexican state of Guerrero.

The deep-south state of Guerrero (pop. 3,200,000, area 25,000 square miles, 65,000 square km) is about the same size as the U.S. state of West Virginia (or the European country of Austria). It stretches about 250 miles (400 km) along Mexico's south Pacific coast and extends about 150 miles (250 km) inland. In contrast to West Virginia and Austria, however, the Acapulco region covers a vastly diverse, ruggedly corrugated landscape of coastal plain, foothills, and high sierra, interspersed with a number of large and small upland valleys, many of which drain into the basin of the grand Río Balsas, Mexico's mightiest river.

## COSTA CHICA
## AND COSTA GRANDE

Mountains notwithstanding, Acapulco's influence extends most strongly along the coast, and the Acapulco region has enough coastline for a pair of subregions that Acapulco people call the Costa Chica (Little Coast) and the Costa Grande (Big Coast). Labels aside, both coasts are big: The Costa Chica spreads 100 miles (160 km) east from Acapulco, to the state of Oaxaca border, while the Costa Grande spreads 150 miles (250 km) northwest, past Ixtapa and Zihuatanejo to the great Río Balsas, which forms the border with the state of Michoacán.

## LAGOONS, BAYS,
## COVES, AND BEACHES
### Lagoons and Barrier Beaches

The landforms that define the entire Acapulco region spread north, east, and west from Acapulco Bay's sun-drenched shoreline. For example, arrivees can enjoy from their airplane windows an aerial view of one such feature, the blue expanse of a mangrove-lined lagoon, Laguna Tres Palos, a minute before airport touchdown. This is only the beginning

of a procession of such *lagunas* that dot the Acapulco region coastline: To the east along the Costa Chica, after Laguna Tres Palos, are Laguna Tecomate and Laguna Chautengo; to the west, along the Costa Grande, first Laguna Coyuca, then Laguna Mitla, Estero Valentín, and Laguna Potosí.

Although all of the lagoons are accessible, Laguna Coyuca at Pie de la Cuesta, a few miles west of Acapulco, is most accessible and also very typically blue and placid. All the Acapulco region's *lagunas* result from the opposing forces of surging water: the ocean waves and currents pushing sand shoreward against the flow of the rivers, coursing down from the sierra, depositing many millions of gallons of fresh water at the shoreline.

It's a see-saw struggle that the rivers temporarily win, if only during the summer–early fall wet season. Freshwater floods accumulated in the lagoons break though the shoreline sandbars and open channels to the ocean. Pacific waves rush in, carrying with them a bounty of

Acapulco, on its emerald-green bay, remains the queen of Mexican beach resorts.

© BRUCE WHIPPERMAN

© BRUCE WHIPPERMAN

Flocks of birds nest, preen, splash, and flap in the Acapulco region's many coastal mangrove lagoons, such as Isla Presidio at Laguna Coyuca.

sea creatures and nutrients, and for a spell during the summer the lagoons become slightly salty (brackish).

However, when the river flood abates in the early fall, the persistent ocean waves and currents deposit their burden of sand, closing the channels through the *barras* (sandbars). Soon, the lagoons again become fresh, sweet, and clear.

On the ocean side of the lagoons lie the Acapulco region's hidden barrier beaches, with plenty of fine yellow sand, an abundance of fresh breezes, and seasonal driftwood, seashells, and sometimes even *palapa* restaurants and reusable shady palm-frond *ramadas* awaiting new occupants. All are accessible, some easily, such as Playa Revolcadero and Barra Vieja, by road about 10 miles east of Acapulco; or farther afield east, San José de la Barra, by launch from Laguna Chautengo. To the west, find Playa Pie de la Cuesta (by road) a few miles from Acapulco; the beach of Laguna de Mitla (by road); Playa Paraíso (by short launch trip); and Playa Boca Chica (by launch or road).

## Bays and Coves

Gorgeous beaches also decorate many of the Acapulco region's plumy bays and coves. Besides the famous golden resort strands of Acapulco, Zihuatanejo, and Ixtapa, many other breeze-swept sandy coasts and small bays and coves hide lovely beaches. East along the Costa Chica and especially worth exploring are the petite resort beaches of Playa Ventura, Playa Las Peñitas, and Punta Maldonado. West along the Costa Grande, likewise gorgeous are El Carrizal, Playa Tlalcoyunque, Playa Escondida, Playa Ojo de Agua, Playa Barra de Potosí, and the coral-strewn gem Playa Troncones.

## COASTAL PLAIN, FOOTHILLS, AND SIERRA

The Acapulco region's coastal plain, source of a major portion of the region's agricultural wealth, concentrates along a relatively narrow strip. It begins at the lagoons' inland edges and, crossed by many south-flowing rivers, extends inland, only about 15 miles in the west along the Costa Grande, and broadening to about twice that at the eastern, Oaxaca end of the Costa Chica.

North of the coastal strip, the cooler lush, forested foothills, about equal in width to the coastal plain, gradually rise, from an elevation of about 1,000 feet to 3,000 feet (300 to 900 meters). Several tradition-rich foothill market towns, such as Petatlán and Atoyac on the Costa Grande, and Ayutla, Acatlán, and Ometepec on the Costa Chica, are equally rich centers of lumber, produce (mangoes, papayas, tamarind, coffee, honey), and handicrafts.

## The Sierra Madre del Sur

The foothills sharply give way to the Acapulco region's great mother of ranges, the Sierra Madre del Sur, a succession of gigantic cloud-tipped mountains extending in an unbroken east–west line. Many of their jagged summits top 10,000 feet (3,000 meters). The line of rugged sentinels extends from Cerro Tejamil (10,460 feet, 3,190 meters) northeast of Zihuatanejo, all the way east to Cerro San Marcos (10,170 feet, 3,100 meters) by the Oaxaca border. In the middle, tallest of all the Acapulco region's summits, is mighty Cerro Teotepec, rising to 11,647 feet (3,550 meters), only 43 miles (70 km) as the crow flies northwest of Acapulco.

## The Río Balsas and Other Rivers

As precipitously as the sierra rises in the south, it drops in the north, into the basin of the Río Balsas, which drains a gigantic realm, including parts of five states—Jalisco, Michoacán, Morelos, Puebla, Oaxaca—and most of the Acapulco region.

The people of the Río Balsas basin are both victims and benefactors of the Sierra Madre and the Río Balsas. The mighty sierra forms a great rain shadow, blocking Pacific breeze–borne moisture and turning their homeland into the notorious Tierra Caliente: hot and desertlike most of the year. But the people, by their own ingenuity and with a little government help, benefit from the waters of the river. Aided by dams and irrigation, they have created rich oases of corn, cattle, cotton, mangoes, melons, bananas, and alfalfa by the riverbanks.

Despite the dominance of the Río Balsas, many other rivers contribute to the Acapulco region. Without exception, from the Río San Cristóbal in the west to the Río Quetzala in the east, they flow southward across the coastal plain, nurturing groves and fields and replenishing the wildlife-rich lagoons along the coast.

Most important of all these is the Río Papagayo, in the Acapulco region's center, which, joining its lovely spring-fed tributary, the Río Azul, winds southward through its precipitous scenic canyon to the sea, at Lomas de Chapultepec village, only 15 miles (25 km) east of Acapulco.

# CLIMATE

Nature has graced the Acapulco region with a microclimate tapestry. Although rainfall, offshore breezes, and vegetation introduce refreshing local variations, elevation provides the broad brush. The entire coastal strip (including the mountain slopes and plateaus up to 4,000 or 5,000 feet) luxuriates in the tropics.

The seashore is a land of perpetual summer. Winter days are typically warm and rainless, peaking at 80–85°F (27–30°C) and dropping to 60–70°F (16–21°C) by midnight.

Increasing elevation gradually decreases both temperature and humidity. In Chilpancingo (elev. 4,000 feet) you can expect warm, dry winter days at 75–80°F (24–27°C) and cooler nights around 55–65°F (14–18°C).

Similar but sometimes cooler winter weather prevails in higher 5,800-foot (1,800-meter) Taxco. Days will usually be balmy and spring-like, climbing to around 75°F (24°C) by early afternoon, with nights dropping to a temperate 45–55°F (8–15°C).

On the other hand, Iguala, in the sunny and dry Río Balsas basin, will be at least warm year-round. In the winter expect 80–85°F (27–30°C) days and 65–70°F (19–21°C) nights.

The sunny, dry spring months of April and May are customarily the Acapulco region's warmest months. By mid-June, cooling rains arrive, moderating summer temperatures.

Summer days on the beaches are warm, humid, and sometimes rainy. July, August, and September forenoons are typically bright, warming to the high 80s or low 90s (around 33°C). By afternoon, however, clouds often gather and bring short, sometimes heavy, showers. By late afternoon, the clouds part, the sun dries the pavements, and the tropical breeze is just right for enjoying a sparkling sunset.

Chilpancingo and Taxco summers are delightful. Afternoon temperatures rise to the 80s (27–32°C) and cool to the balmy 70s (21–26°C), perfect for strolling, during the evenings. In Iguala, however, late-spring and summer temperatures are often hot, typically 85–95°F (30–36°C) during the dry April and May, but cooling a few degrees during the June–September rains.

# Flora and Fauna

Abundant sun and summer rains nurture the vegetation of the Acapulco region. At some roadside spots, spiny bromeliads, pendulous passion fruits, and giant candelabra cactuses luxuriate, beckoning to admirers. Now and then visitors may stop, attracted by something remarkable, such as a riot of flowers blooming from apparently dead branches or what looks like grapefruit sprouting from the trunk of a roadside tree. More often, travelers pass by the long stretches of thickets, jungles, marshes, and dry uplands without stopping; however, a little knowledge of what to expect can blossom into recognition and discovery, transforming the humdrum into the extraordinary.

## VEGETATION ZONES

Mexico's diverse landscape and fickle rainfall have sculpted its wide range of plant forms. Botanists recognize at least 14 major Mexican vegetation zones, seven of which occur in the Acapulco region.

Directly along the coastal highway travelers often pass long sections of three of these zones: savanna, thorn forest, and tropical deciduous forest.

### Savanna

Great swaths of pasturelike savanna stretch along Highway 200 between Acapulco and Zihuatanejo. In its natural state, savanna often appears as a palm-dotted sea of grass—green and marshy during the rainy summer, dry and brown by late winter.

Although grass rules the savanna, palms give it character. Most familiar is the **coconut,** the *cocotero* (*Cocos nucifera*)—the world's most useful tree—used for everything from lumber to candy. Coconut palms line the beaches and climb the hillsides—drooping, slanting, rustling, and swaying in the breeze like troupes of hula dancers. Less familiar, but with as much personality, is the Mexican **fan palm,** or *palma real* (*Sabal mexicana*), festooned with black fruit and spread flat like a señorita's fan.

The savanna's list goes on: the grapefruitlike fruit on the trunk and branches identify the **gourd tree,** or *calabaza* (*Crescentia alata*). The mature gourds, brown and hard, are famously useful, in a dozen ways, from making music and drinking hot chocolate to carrying water and scooping corn for tortillas.

Orange-sized pumpkinlike gourds mark the **sand box tree,** or *jabillo* (*Hura polyandra*), so named because they once served as desktop boxes full of sand for drying ink. The Aztecs, however, called it the exploding tree, because the ripe gourds burst their seeds forth with a bang like a firecracker.

The waterlogged seaward edge of the savanna nurtures lagoon-front forests of the **red mangrove,** or *mangle colorado* (*Rhizophora mangle*), short trees that seem to stand in the water on stilts. Their new roots grow downward from above; a time-lapse photo would show them marching, as if on stilts, into the lagoon.

© BRUCE WHIPPERMAN

the white blossoms of the *palo del muerto* (tree of death)

## Thorn Forest

Lower rainfall leads to the hardier growth of the thorn forest—domain of the pea family—the legumes marked in late winter and spring by bursts of red, yellow, pink, and white flowers. Look closely at the blossoms and you will see they resemble the familiar wild sweet pea of North America. Even when the blossoms are gone, you can identify them by seed pods that hang from the branches. Local folks call them by many names. These include the **ta-bachín,** the scarlet Mexican bird of paradise; and its close relative the *flamboyán,* or **royal poinciana,** an import from Africa, where it's called the "flame tree."

Other spectacular members of the pea family (called "shower trees" in Hawaii) include the bright yellow **abejón,** which blooms nearly year-round; and the **coapinol,** marked by hosts of white blooms (March–July) and large dark-brown pods. Not only colorful but useful is the **fishfuddle,** with pink flowers and long pods, from which fisherfolk derive a fish-stunning poison.

More abundant (although not so noticeable) are the legumes' cousins, the **acacias** and **mimosas.** Long swaths of thorn forest sometimes grow right to the coastal highway and side-road pavements, so that the road appears tunnel-like through a tangle of brushy acacia trees. Pull completely off the road for a look and you will spot the small yellow flower balls, ferny leaves, and long, narrow pods of the **boat spine acacia,** or *quisache tempamo* (*Acacia cochliacantha*). Take care, however, around the acacias; some of the long-thorned varieties harbor nectar-feeding biting ants.

Perhaps the most dramatic member of the thorn community is the **morning glory tree,** or *palo blanco* (*Ipomoea aborescens*), which announces the winter dry season by a festoon of white trumpets atop its crown of seemingly dead branches.

If you happen upon a tree with stark grey, leafless branches, apparently lifeless except for a flock of showy white flowers, you've found the *palo del muerto,* "the tree of the dead." It is also called *palo bobo* ("fool tree") in some locales because folks believe if you take a drink from a stream near its foot, you will go crazy.

## Tropical Deciduous Forest

In rainier areas, the thorn forest grades into tropical deciduous forest. This is the "friendly" or "short-tree" forest, blanketed by a tangle of summer-green leaves that fall in the dry winter to reveal thickets of branches. Some trees show bright fall reds and yellows, later blossoming with brilliant flowers—spider lily, cardinal sage, pink trumpet, poppylike yellowsilk (*pomposhuti*), and mouse killer (*mala ratón*), which swirl in the spring wind like blossom blizzards.

The tropical deciduous forest makes up the lush jungle coat that swathes much of the Acapulco region's coastal foothills. It is especially lush during the rainy summer, in the uplands along Highway 193, above Atoyac de

Álvarez, northwest of Acapulco. Here, vine-strewn thickets overhang the road, like the edges of a lost prehistoric world, where at any moment you expect a dinosaur to rear.

The biological realities here are nearly as exotic. A four-foot-long green iguana, looking every bit as primitive as a dinosaur, slithers across the pavement. Beside the road, a spreading, solitary **strangler fig** (*Ficus padifolia*) stands, draped with hairy hanging air roots (which, in time, plant themselves in the ground and support the branches). Its Mexican name, *matapalo* (killer tree), is gruesomely accurate, for strangler figs often entwine themselves in death embraces with less aggressive tree victims.

Much more benign is the gentle giant of the Acapulco region's tropical deciduous forest, the **Mexican elm,** or *olmo* (*Chaetoptelea mexicana*). Probably Mexico's tallest tree, the *olmo*

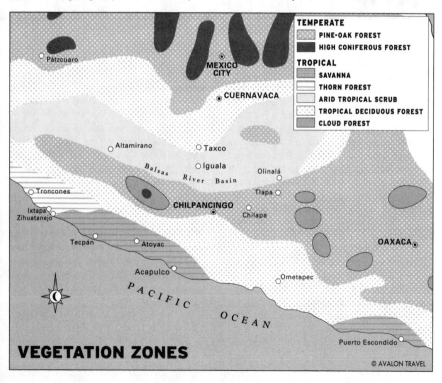

**VEGETATION ZONES**

TEMPERATE
PINE-OAK FOREST
HIGH CONIFEROUS FOREST

TROPICAL
SAVANNA
THORN FOREST
ARID TROPICAL SCRUB
TROPICAL DECIDUOUS FOREST
CLOUD FOREST

Pátzcuaro
MEXICO CITY
CUERNAVACA
Altamirano
Taxco
Iguala
Olinalá
Balsas River Basin
Troncones
Tlapa
CHILPANCINGO
Ixtapa Zihuatanejo
Chilapa
Tecpán
Atoyac
OAXACA
Acapulco
Ometepec
PACIFIC OCEAN
Puerto Escondido

© AVALON TRAVEL

# POINSETTIA

Although this lovely red flowering plant only became known and appreciated by the wider world during the 1800s, the people of Mexico have enjoyed the poinsettia for millennia. It grows in gorgeous wild profusion in semitropical mountain zones of southwestern Mexico, especially in the Acapulco region and the neighboring states of Michoacán, Morelos, Oaxaca, and Chiapas.

The Aztecs, who called the poinsettia *cuetlaxochitle*, used its sap to control fevers and its crimson red petals (actually not petals, but colored leaves, called bracts) for dye. The emperor Moctezuma II (1466-1520) especially adored the *cuetlaxochitle*. He ordered caravans of them brought to his capital at Tenochtitlán to honor an Aztec goddess who was said to have died of a broken heart. The *cuetlaxochitle*, a legend recounted, had been born from one drop of the goddess's blood.

Most present-day Mexican folks know the poinsettia as the *flor de Nochebuena* (flower of Christmas Eve). It blooms during the late autumn and early winter, just in time for people to give birthday bouquets to the baby Jesus at churches all over Mexico on December 24.

An eminent German botanist, Karl Lugwig Wilenow, was among the first outsiders to study the poinsettia, from cuttings brought to him from central America. In 1800, recognizing it as a member of the grand Euphorbia family, Wilenow christened it *Euphorbiaceae pulcherrima*, meaning "most beautiful of the Euphoribias."

Although apt, this name has been largely forgotten because of the work of Joel Robert Poinsett, amateur botanist and U.S. ambassador to Mexico during the 1820s. Poinsett, keenly interested in identifying new species wherever he traveled in Mexico, noticed the spectacularly red plant growing beside the road. He brought specimens back to the United States and nurtured them in his South Carolina greenhouse. This led to the plant's spread and ultimate immense popularity all over North and South America, Europe, and most parts of the world.

In 1836, a group of Scottish botanists proposed to honor Poinsett's work by renaming his find *Poinsettia pulcherrima*. The name stuck, and now people everywhere enjoy holiday festoons of the charmingly divine plant known simply as the poinsettia.

reaches a height of at least 285 feet (87 meters), compared to the world's tallest, the California redwood, that reaches 364 feet. It closely resembles its near relative, the American elm, notably in the shape of its serrated leaves and its hair-fringed fruit. Its tough, heavy wood, ideal for floors and door sills, makes it one of the Acapulco region's most valuable lumber trees.

Well-watered zones of the tropical deciduous forest have become home to a platoon of useful **introduced plants.** These include the common India-native **mango**, "king of fruit" (April–July), and Africa-native **plátano** (banana). Also introduced and common, but not so recognizable, is the **coffee shrub**, or locally *cafeto* (*Coffea arabica*). Coffee is widely grown in the Acapulco region, notably in the foothill forests, upcountry from Atoyac de Álvarez. Coffee shrubs grow unobtrusively, often in

an apparent wild "jungle" right next to the highway, beneath the shady canopy of taller trees. Farmers limit them to about five feet in height. They're recognizable by their camelliabush appearance, with shiny dark-green leaves, star-shaped white flowers, and red berries, in season.

Excursions by Jeep or foot along shaded offhighway tracks through the tropical deciduous forest can bestow delightful jungle scenes; however, unwary travelers must watch out for the poison oak–like **mala mujer,** the "evil woman" tree. The oil on its large five-fingered leaves can cause an itchy rash.

## Pine-Oak Forest

Along the upland highways (notably on the higher reaches of north–south Highway 95 and the Chilpancingo–Chilapa–Olinalá

Highway 93) the tropical forest gives way to temperate pine-oak forest. Here, many of Mexico's 112 oak and 39 pine species thrive. Oval two-inch cones and foot-long drooping needles (three to a cluster) make the **pino triste**, or sad pine (*Pinus lumholtzii*), appear in severe need of water. Unlike many of Mexico's pines, it produces neither good lumber nor much turpentine, although it *is* prized by guitar makers for its wood.

Much more regal in bearing and commercially important are the tall pines, including the **Mexican white pine** (*Pinus ayacahuite*), known locally as the *pinabete*. It grows to about 100 feet when mature and resembles the white pine of northern regions, with long bluish-green needles, five to a bunch, and pendulous, scaly 4- to 6-inch often reddish-brown cones that shed winged seeds. Equally notable is the **Montezuma pine** (*Pinus montezumae*), or the *ocote macho*. It likewise grows long (but gray) cones and needles, five to a bunch, but is distinguishable by its interesting drooping needles.

Pines often grow in stands, mixed at lower elevations with **oaks,** which occur in two broad classifications—*encino* (evergreen, small-leafed) and *roble* (deciduous, large-leafed)— both much like the live oaks that dot California hills and valleys. Clustered on their branches and scattered in the shade, *bellota* (acorns) distinctly mark them as oaks.

## Arid Tropical Scrub

This desertlike vegetation zone coincides with the semiarid Río Balsas basin, which sprawls for hundreds of miles east–west (reachable both along Highway 51 and north–south Highway 95) between Chilpancingo and Taxco. Although superficially appearing like the temperate deserts of the southwest United States and northern Mexico, the arid tropical scrub zone nurtures a botanic treasury of tropical, frost-sensitive plants, sculpted by extreme heat and drought.

The signature king of all these hardy plants is the spectacular **candelabra cactus** (*Lemaireocereus weberi*), or *candelabro*. Mature specimens, as wide and high as a four-story building, with a dozen or more 10-ribbed vertical columns, resemble a giant dining-table candelabra.

© BRUCE WHIPPERMAN

The fleshy cabbage agave, shown here near Chilapa, is a well-known resident of Guerrero inland mountainsides.

The candelabra's look-alike cousin is the **organ-pipe cactus** (*Marginatocereus marginatus*) or *órgano*. Distinguish it by its smaller but still formidable size (10–20 feet in height) and its five to seven ribs per vertical column.

At some spots, great forests of tall pole-straight *tetetzo* cactuses (*Pachycereus ruficeps*) inhabit the arid tropical scrubland. Up to 50 feet tall, they can collectively resemble a grand army of cactus sentinels, guarding the rocky landscape.

Although not cactuses, many of the 300-odd members of the agave family thrive in dryer areas of the Acapulco region. Although some are cultivated (for beverages, fiber, soap, and more), others grow wild. One such is the charming **cabbage agave** (*Agave perryi*), which grows in families of neat round cabbage-like plants, up to three feet in diameter, with bluish-green broad spined leaves.

## Cloud Forest and High Coniferous Forest

The Acapulco region's rarest and most exotic vegetation zones are removed from the coastal tourist centers. Adventurers who travel to certain high, dewy mountainsides, beginning around 5,000 feet, can explore the plant and wildlife community of the cloud forest. One such example lies along Highway 196, about 30 miles (50 km) uphill from Atoyac de Álvarez, past the village of El Paraíso. There, abundant cool fog nourishes a Pleistocene remnant forest of dripping tree ferns, liquid amber maples, lichen-draped pines and oaks, above a mossy carpet of orchids, bromeliads, and begonias.

About 20 miles (32 km) farther uphill along the same route, the Acapulco region's least accessible vegetation zone, the high coniferous forest, swathes the 9,000- to 11,000-foot slopes of Cerro Teotepec. This pristine alpine island, accessible only on horseback or by foot, nurtures stands of pines, spruce, and fir interspersed with grassy meadows, similar to the Rocky Mountain slopes in the United States and Canada. Here, besides the white and Montezuma pines, find hardy stands of **sacred fir** (*Abies religiosa*), or *oyamel*; **Mexican**

**cypress** (*Cupressa lusitanica*); and the high-altitude **alder** (*Alnus firmifolia*). (*Note:* Do not attempt the cloud forest and high coniferous forest explorations alone. Inquire at the Atoyac de Álvarez *presidencia municipal* for an experienced locally known guide.)

For a wealth of details, consult M. Walter Pesman's delightful *Meet Flora Mexicana* (which is out of print, but major libraries often have a copy). Also informative is the popular paperback *Handbook of Mexican Roadside Flora*, by Charles T. Mason Jr. and Patricia B. Mason.

## WILDLIFE

Despite continued habitat destruction—forests are logged, wetlands filled, and savannas plowed—great swaths of the Acapulco region still abound with wildlife. Common in the temperate pine-oak forest highlands are mammals familiar to U.S. residents such as the mountain lion (*puma*), coyote, fox (*zorro*), rabbit (*conejo*), and quail (*codorniz*).

However, the tropical coastal forests and savannas are also home to fascinating species seen only in zoos north of the border. The reality

A number of small parrots make their home in Acapulco's forests and wetlands.

of this dawns on travelers when they glimpse something exotic, such as raucous screeching swarms of small green parrots rising from the roadside, or an armadillo or coati nosing in the sand just a few feet away from them at the forested edge of an isolated beach.

Population pressures have nevertheless decreased wild habitats, endangering many previously abundant animal species. If you are lucky, you may find a tracker who can lead you to a band of now rare reddish-brown **spider monkeys** (*monos*) raiding a wild fruit tree. And deep in the mountain fastness, you may be led to a view of the endangered striped cat, the **ocelot** (*ocelotl*), or its smaller cousins, the **margay** (*tigrillo*) and the tan **jaguarundi** (*onza, leoncillo*). On such an excursion, if you are really fortunate, you may hear the "chesty" roar of, or catch a glimpse of, a jaguar, the fabled *tigre.*

## El Tigre

Each hill has its own *tigre,* a Mexican proverb says. With black spots spread over a yellow-tan coat, stretching five feet (1.5 meters) and weighing 200 pounds (90 kg), the typical jaguar resembles a muscular spotted leopard. Although hunted since prehistory, and now endangered, the jaguar lives on in the Acapulco region, where it hunts along thickly forested stream bottoms and foothills. Unlike the mountain lion, the jaguar will eat any game. Jaguars have even been known to wait patiently for fish in rivers and to stalk beaches for turtle and egg dinners. If they have a favorite food, it is probably the pig-like wild peccary, *jabalí.* Experienced hunters agree that no two jaguars will have the same prey in their stomachs.

Although humans have died of wounds inflicted by cornered jaguars, there is little or no hard evidence that they eat humans, despite legends to the contrary.

## Armadillos, Coatis, and Bats

Armadillos are cat-sized mammals that act and look like opossums but carry reptilianlike shells. If you see one, remain still, and it may walk right up and sniff your foot before it recognizes you and scuttles back into the woods.

the wild pig-like *jabalí*

A common inhabitant of the tropics is the raccoonlike coati (*tejón, pisote*). In the wild, coatis like shady stream banks, often congregating in large troops of 15–30 individuals. They are identified by their short brown or tan fur, small round ears, long nose, and straight, vertically held tail. With their endearing and inquisitive nature, coatis are often kept as pets; the first coati you see may be one on a string offered for sale at a local market.

Mexican bats (*murciélagos*) are widespread, with at least 126 species compared to 37 in the United States. In Mexico, as everywhere, bats are feared and misunderstood. As sunset approaches, many species come out of their hiding places and flit through the air in search of insects. Most people, sitting outside enjoying the early evening, will mistake their darting silhouettes for those of birds, who, except for owls, do not generally fly at night.

Bats are often locally called *vampiros,* even though only three relatively rare Mexican species actually feed on the blood of mammals—nearly always cattle—and of birds.

The many nonvampire Mexican bats carry their vampire cousins' odious reputation with forbearance. They go about their good works, pollinating flowers, clearing the air of pesky gnats and mosquitoes, ridding cornfields of mice, and dropping seeds, thereby restoring forests. Limestone caves, such as the Grutas de Juxtlahuaca, are the best places to see bats.

# BIRDS

The coastal lagoons of the Acapulco region lie astride the Pacific Flyway, one of the Americas' major north–south paths for migrating waterfowl. Many of the familiar American and Canadian species, including pintail, gadwall, baldpate, shoveler, redhead, and scaup, arrive October–January, when their numbers will have swollen into the millions. They settle near food and cover—even at the borders of cornfields, to the frustration of farmers.

Besides the migrants, swarms of resident species—**herons** and **egrets** (*garzas*), cormorantlike **anhingas, lily-walkers** (*jacanas*), and hundreds more—stalk, nest, and preen in the same lagoons.

Few spots are better for observing seabirds than the beaches of the Acapulco region. **Brown pelicans** and black-and-white **frigate birds** are among the prime actors. When a flock of pelicans spot a school of favorite fish, they go about their routine deliberately. Singly or in pairs, they circle and plummet into the waves to come up, more often than not, with fish in their gullets. Each bird then bobs and floats over the swells for a minute or two, seeming to wait for its dozen or so fellow pelicans to take their turns. This continues until they've bagged a dinner of 10–15 fish apiece. Frigate birds, the scavengers par excellence of the Mexican Pacific coast, often profit by the labor of the teams of fisherfolk who haul in nets of fish on Acapulco-region beaches. After they auction off the choice morsels of perch, tuna, red snapper, octopus, or shrimp to merchants, and the local villagers have scavenged everything else edible, the motley residue of small fish, sea snakes, skates, squid, slugs, and sharks is thrown to a screeching flock of frigate birds.

The wild blue mangrove lagoons of the Costa Chica and Costa Grande, east and west of Acapulco, nurture a trove of wildlife, especially birds, ripe for viewing on foot or by boat tours.

For more details on Mexico's mammals and birds in general, check out Les Baletsky's *Tropical Mexico: The Ecotraveler's Wildlife Guide* and other works cited in this book's *Suggested Reading.*

Mexico's native great white heron is one of the world's largest waterbirds.

brown pelicans on the rocks of the Costa Chica and Costa Grande

© BRUCE WHIPPERMAN

© BRUCE WHIPPERMAN

## REPTILES AND AMPHIBIANS
### Snakes, Gila Monsters, and Crocodiles

Mexico has 460-odd snake species, the vast majority shy and nonpoisonous; they will get out of your way if you give plenty of warning. In the Acapulco region poisonous snakes have been largely eradicated in city and tourist areas. In brush or jungle areas, carry a stick or a machete and beat the bushes ahead of you while watching where you put your feet. When hiking or rock-climbing in the country, don't put your hand in niches you can't see.

You might even see a snake underwater while swimming offshore at an isolated Acapulco region beach. The **yellow-bellied sea snake,** *Pelamis platurus* (to about two feet), although rare and shy, can inflict fatal bites. If you see a yellow-and-black snake underwater, get away, pronto.

Some eels, which resemble snakes but have gills like fish and inhabit rocky crevices, can inflict nonpoisonous bites and should also be avoided.

The Mexican land counterpart of the *Pelamis platurus* is the **coral snake** (*coralillo*), which occurs as about two dozen species, all with multicolored bright bands that always include red. Although relatively rare, small, and shy, coral snakes occasionally inflict serious, sometimes fatal, bites.

More aggressive and generally more dangerous is the Mexican **rattlesnake** (*cascabel*) and its viper relative, the **fer-de-lance** (*Bothrops atrox*). About the same in size (to six feet) and appearance as the rattlesnake, the fer-de-lance is known by various local names, such as *naughaca, cuatro narices, palanca,* and *barba amarilla.* It is potentially more hazardous than the rattlesnake because it lacks a warning rattle.

The Gila monster (confined in Mexico to northern Sonora) and its southern tropical relative, the yellow-spotted black **escorpión** (*Heloderma horridum*), are the world's only poisonous lizards. Despite its beaded skin and menacing, fleshy appearance, the *escorpión* only bites when severely provoked; and, even then, its venom is rarely, if ever, fatal.

The **crocodile** (*cocodrilo, caimán*), once prized for its meat and hide, came close to vanishing in Mexican Pacific lagoons until the government took steps to ensure its survival; it's now officially protected. A few isolated breeding populations live on in the wild (such as the very visible crocodile family at Laguna Ixtapa, north of Zihuatanejo) while government and private hatcheries are breeding more for the eventual repopulation of lagoons where crocodiles once were common.

Two crocodile species occur in the Acapulco region. The true crocodile, *Crocodilus acutus,* has a narrower snout than its local cousin, *Caiman crocodilus fuscus,* a type of alligator (*lagarto*). Although past individuals have been recorded at up to 15 feet long, wild native crocodiles and alligators are usually young and only three feet or less in length.

### Sea Turtles

The story of Mexican sea turtles is similar: They once swarmed ashore on Acapulco regional beaches to lay their eggs. Prized for their meat, eggs, hide, and shell, the turtles were severely devastated. Now officially protected, sea turtles are coming ashore in growing numbers at some isolated locations. Of the four locally occurring species, the **olive Ridley turtle** (*tortuga golfina*) and the **green turtle** (*tortuga negra* or *caguama*) are the most common. The green and olive Ridley, although officially endangered, have stabilized because of persistent government and volunteer efforts. The two other, relatively rare, locally occurring sea turtles are the **hawksbill** (*carey*) and the **leatherback** (*tortuga de cuero*). (For many more sea turtle details, see the sidebar *Saving Turtles* in the *Costa Grande* chapter.)

## FISH AND MARINE MAMMALS

Shoals of fish abound in Acapulco's waters. Four billfish species (known for their long, pointed beaks, or "bills") are found in deepsea grounds several miles offshore: **swordfish, sailfish,** and **blue** and **black marlin.** All are spirited fighters, though the sailfish and marlin are generally the toughest to bring in. The blue marlin is the biggest of the four; in the past, 10-foot specimens weighing more than 1,000 pounds were brought in at Pacific coast marinas. Lately, four feet and 200 pounds for a marlin, and 100 pounds for a sailfish, are more typical. Progressive captains (who now subscribe to the increasingly popular "tag and release") encourage victorious anglers to return these magnificent "tigers of the sea" (especially the sinewy sailfish and blue marlin, which make for poor eating) to the deep after they've won the battle.

Billfish are not the only prizes of the sea, however. Serious fish lovers also seek varieties of tunalike **jack,** such as **yellowtail, Pacific amberjack, pompano, jack crevalle,** and the tenacious **roosterfish,** named for the "comb" atop its head. These, and the **yellowfin tuna, mackerel,** and *dorado,* which Hawaiians call mahimahi, are among the delicacies sought in Acapulco waters.

Accessible from small boats offshore and by casting from shoreline rocks are varieties of **snapper** (*huachinango, pargo*) and **sea bass** (*cabrilla*). Closer to shore, **croaker, mullet,** and **groupers** can be found foraging along sandy bottoms and in rocky crevices.

**Sharks** and **rays** inhabit nearly all depths, with smaller fry venturing into beach shallows and lagoons. Huge **Pacific manta rays** appear to be frolicking, their great wings flapping like birds, not far off Acapulco shores.

Just beyond the waves, local fisherfolk bring in **hammerhead, thresher,** and **leopard sharks.**

Also common is the **stingray,** which can inflict a painful wound with its barbed tail. Experienced swimmers and waders avoid injury by both shuffling (rather than stepping) and watching their feet in shallow waters with sandy bottoms. (For more fish talk and a chart of species encountered in Acapulco waters, see *Fishing* in the *Recreation* section of the *Essentials* chapter.)

## Dolphins and Whales

The playful antics of the once numerous **Pacific bottlenosed dolphin** are nevertheless sometimes observable from Acapulco region–based tour and fishing boats, and sometimes even from beaches. (Sadly, dolphins often get caught and drown in fishing trawlers' nets.)

Although the **California gray whale** has a migration pattern extending only to the southern tip of Baja California, occasional pods stray farther south, where deep-sea fishermen and cruise- and tour-boat passengers see them in deep waters offshore.

Larger whale (*ballena*) species, such as the **humpback** and **blue** whale, appear to enjoy tropical waters even more, ranging the north Pacific tropics, from the Acapulco region coastline west to Hawaii and beyond.

# History

Once upon a time, maybe as long as 30,000 years ago, the first bands of hunters, perhaps following great game herds, crossed from Siberia to the American continent. They drifted southward, many of them eventually settling in the lush upland valleys and coastlines of present-day Mexico.

Much later, perhaps around 5000 B.C., these early people began gathering and grinding the seeds of a hardy grass that required only the summer rains to thrive. After generations of selective breeding, this grain, called *teocentli,*

the sacred seed (which we call maize or corn), led to prosperity.

## EARLY CIVILIZATIONS

With abundant food, villages grew into towns, and towns evolved into small cities. Leisure classes arose—artists, architects, warriors, and ruler-priests—who had time to think and create. With a calendar, they harnessed the constant wheel of the firmament to life on earth, defining the days to plant, harvest, feast, travel, and trade.

Of Mexico's early urban peoples, the Olmecs were foremost. Around 1500 B.C. they were establishing large ceremonial centers along the Gulf of Mexico Coast. At La Venta, in present-day Tabasco state, archaeologists have uncovered the Olmecs' most spectacular remains: giant stone heads, up to nine feet in height, with decidedly negroid features and football helmet–like caps. Other sculptures, many of lovely jade, show a strong jaguar cult influence, in the form of half-human, half-jaguar mask-like faces.

The Olmec influence arrived early in the present-day Acapulco region. Olmec-style jaguar-motif art has been uncovered at Teopantecuantlán, an upland ceremonial center dating from around 1000 B.C. Moreover, Olmec-style wall paintings decorate caves, notably the Grutas de Juxtlahuaca and Oxtotitlán, in lush highland valleys about 100 miles north of Acapulco.

## Monte Albán, Teotihuacán, and Xochicalco

After the decline of the Olmecs, around 500 B.C., other civilizations rose. Monte Albán, in Oaxaca, which was flourishing around the time of Jesus, is thought by many experts to be Mexico's first true city. Later, Teotihuacán, north of present-day Mexico City, grew into one of the world's great metropolises, with a population of about 250,000, by A.D. 500.

Teotihuacán's epic monuments still stand: the towering Pyramid of the Sun, at the terminal of a grand avenue, faces a great Pyramid of the Moon. Along the avenue sprawls a monumental temple-court, surrounded by scowling effigies of Quetzalcoatl, the feathered serpent god of gods.

Eventually both Monte Albán and Teotihuacán crumbled; they were all but abandoned by A.D. 700, leaving a host of former vassal city-states to tussle among themselves. In the Acapulco region, first among these was Xochicalco, near Taxco, 150 miles (250 km) north of present-day Acapulco.

## The Living Quetzalcoatl

Xochicalco's wise men tutored a young noble who was to become a living legend. In A.D. 947,

The Northern Ball Court at Xochicalco undoubtedly hosted many grand high-stakes ceremonial contests. Note the half-buried stone ball-ring.

© BRUCE WHIPPERMAN

Topiltzín (literally, Our Prince) was born. Records recite Topiltzín's achievements. He advanced astronomy, agriculture, and architecture and founded the city-state of Tula in A.D. 968, north of old Teotihuacán.

Contrary to the times, Topiltzín opposed human sacrifice. He ruled benignly for two decades, becoming so revered that his people knew him as the living Quetzalcoatl, the plumed serpent god incarnate.

Bloodthirsty local priests, lusting for human victims, tricked him with alcohol, however; Topiltzín awoke groggily one morning, in bed with his sister. Devastated with shame, Quetzalcoatl banished himself. He headed east from Tula with a band of retainers in A.D. 987, vowing that he would return during the anniversary of his birth year, Ce Acatl. Legends say he sailed across the eastern sea and rose to heaven as the morning star.

### The Aztecs

The civilization that Topiltzín founded, known to historians as the Toltec (People of Tula), was eventually eclipsed by others. These included the Aztecs, a collection of seven aggressive immigrant subtribes. Migrating around during the 11th century A.D., from a mysterious western land of Aztlán (Place of the Herons) into the lake-filled valley that Mexico City now occupies, the Aztecs survived by being forced to fight for every piece of ground they occupied.

Around the same time, another Aztec subtribe was migrating into the present-day Acapulco region. As did their Valley of Mexico cousins, they competed fiercely with the original inhabitants. They rose to dominance, first by war, and eventually through intermarriage with their defeated vassals. By A.D. 1100, their Náhuatl (Aztec-language) kingdom, called Coixcaltlapan, sprawled over both the central valleys of the Río Balsas basin and parts of the western coast, around Zacatula and Atoyac.

Meanwhile, to the north, the Valley of Mexico Aztecs, who called themselves the México, had also clawed their way to dominion. In A.D. 1325 they founded their capital, Tenochtitlán, on an island in the middle of the valley-lake. From there, Aztec armies, not unlike Roman legions, marched out and subdued faraway kingdoms and returned with booty of gold, brilliant feathers, precious jewels, and captives, whom they enslaved and sacrificed by the thousands as food for their gods.

Among those gods they feared was Quetzalcoatl, who, legends said, was bearded and fair-skinned. It was a remarkable coincidence, therefore, that the bearded, fair-skinned Castilian Hernán Cortés landed on Mexico's eastern coast on April 22, 1519, during the year of Ce Acatl, exactly when Topiltzín, the living Quetzalcoatl, had vowed he would return.

## THE CONQUEST

Although a generation had elapsed since Christopher Columbus founded Spain's West Indian colonies, returns had been meager. Moreover, Columbus's original goal of reaching China by sailing west had eluded the Spanish explorers. Geographers and navigators realized that, instead of China, Columbus had discovered a new continent. Perhaps, explorers hoped, China lay only a bit farther west, tantalizingly just beyond the setting sun.

Hernán Cortés, a poor Spanish nobleman, then only 34, promoted an expedition of 11 small ships and 550 men and sailed westward from Cuba in February 1519. Upon landing near present-day Veracruz, he was in trouble. His men, mostly soldiers of fortune, hearing stories of a powerful Aztec empire west beyond the mountains, had realized the impossible odds they faced and became restive.

Cortés, however, cut short any thoughts of mutiny by burning his ships. As he led his grumbling but resigned band of adventurers toward the Aztec capital of Tenochtitlán, Cortés played Quetzalcoatl to the hilt, awing local chiefs. Coaxed by Doña Marina, Cortés's native translator-mistress, local chiefs began to add their warrior-armies to Cortés's march against their Aztec overlords.

### Moctezuma, Lord of Tenochtitlán

Once inside the walls of Tenochtitlán, the Aztecs' Venicelike island-city, the Spaniards were dazzled by gardens of animals, gold and palaces, and a great pyramid-enclosed square where tens of thousands of people bartered goods gathered from all over the empire.

However, Moctezuma, the lord of that empire, was frozen by fear and foreboding, unsure if these figures truly represented the return of Quetzalcoatl. He quickly found himself hostage to Cortés and then died a few months later during a riot against Spanish greed and brutality. On July 1, 1520, on what came to be called *noche triste* (the sad night), the besieged Cortés and his men broke out, fleeing for their lives along the lake causeway from Tenochtitlán, carrying Moctezuma's treasure. Many of them drowned beneath their burdens of gold booty, while the survivors hacked a bloody retreat through thousands of screaming Aztec warriors to safety on the lakeshore.

## MALINCHE AND CORTÉS

If it hadn't been for Doña Marina (received as a gift from a local chief), Hernán Cortés may have become a mere historical footnote. Doña Marina, speaking both Spanish and native tongues, soon became Cortés's interpreter, go-between, and negotiator. She persuaded a number of important chiefs to ally themselves with Cortés against the Aztecs. Clever and opportunistic, Doña Marina was a crucial strategist in Cortés's deadly game of divide and conquer. She eventually bore Cortés a son and lived in honor and riches for many years, profiting greatly from the Spaniards' exploitation of the Mexicans.

Latter-day Mexicans do not honor her by the gentle title of Doña Marina, however. They call her Malinche, after the volcano – an ugly, treacherous scar on the Mexican landscape – and curse her as the female Judas who betrayed her country to the Spanish. *Malinchismo* has become known as the tendency to love things foreign and hate things Mexican.

## Aztec Defeat and Spanish Victory

Despite his grievous setback, Cortés regrouped and reinforced his small army with an armed sailboat fleet and 100,000 Indian warrior-allies and invaded Tenochtitlán a year later. The defenders, led by Cuauhtémoc, Moctezuma's nephew, refused to surrender, forcing Cortés to destroy the city to take it. Tenochtitlán fell on August 13, 1521.

After his triumph, Cortés took former emperor Cuauhtémoc captive. He forced Cuauhtémoc and his retainers to march with him on an ill-fated expedition to Honduras in 1523–1525. Tortured with foreboding that Cuauhtémoc and his compatriots were plotting against him, Cortés had Cuauhtémoc hanged on February 28, 1525.

But, unknown to Cortés, Cuauhtémoc's followers secretly took his remains hundreds of miles north and may have buried them at Ixcateopan, the home of Cuauhtémoc's mother, near present-day Taxco. There, 424 years later, on September 26, 1949, remains believed by many to be Cuauhtémoc's were discovered and remain enshrined there to this very day.

### New Spain

With the Valley of Mexico firmly in his grip, Cortés sent his lieutenants south, north, and west to explore and extend the limits of his domain, which eventually expanded to more than a dozenfold the size of old Spain. In a letter to his king, Charles V, Cortés christened his empire New Spain of the Ocean Sea, a label that remained Mexico's official name for 300 years.

## THE SEARCH FOR CHINA

Even during his struggle with the Aztecs, Cortés continued to dream Columbus's old dream. Somewhere west lay China, and he was determined to find it. As early as 1520 Cortés began sending his lieutenants to Mexico's southern Pacific coast to look for safe, timber-rich harbors, where he would build the ships to China.

First on the Pacific shore was Gonzalo de Uribe, who, in 1520, arrived at Zacatula, at the mouth of the Río Balsas, west of Zihuatanejo.

Besides bringing back gold samples, he told Cortés of a good harbor and plenty of timber for building ships.

## Discovery of Acapulco Bay

In 1522, conquistador Pedro de Alvarado founded the Acapulco region's first town, at Acatlán on the Costa Chica. Around the same time, Rodriguez de Villafuerte sailed into Acapulco Bay, which he named Bahía de Santa Lucia, a label that persisted on maps for generations.

After reporting to Cortés of the bay's calm anchorage and abundance of shoreline trees, Villafuerte returned, and by 1530 had built two ships, the *San Miguel* and *San Marcos,* on the shore of Acapulco Bay. For his efforts, Villafuerte was awarded *encomienda* rights (taxes and labor of an indigenous district) over Acapulco and a big slice of the present Acapulco region.

Among the dozen-odd early Pacific expeditions (several of which were personally financed by Cortés), five set out from Acapulco. In 1532, Diego Hurtado de Mendoza sailed for China via the north Pacific and never returned. Another expedition, loaded with supplies for conquistador Pizarro in Peru, sailed in 1535; in the same year, Cortés himself sailed out, searching for treasure in Baja California. Then, in 1539, Cortés sent Francisco de Ulloa northwest to search for the fabled golden Seven Cities of Cibola, but he was never heard from again. Finally, in 1540, Domingo de Castillo set out to map Mexico's Pacific coast. He returned with detailed charts and tantalizing hints of the location of Cibola.

## Cortés's Monument

Disheartened by his failure to find China (or, at least, more golden cities), and discouraged with interference by his king's Mexican representatives, Cortés returned to Spain to reassert his authority at court. But mired down by lawsuits, a small war, and his daughter's marital troubles, he fell ill and died in Spain on December 2, 1547. Cortés's remains, according to his will, were eventually laid to rest in a vault at the Hospital de Jesús, which he had founded in Mexico City.

Since latter-day Mexican politics preclude memorials to the Spanish conquest, no monument anywhere in Mexico commemorates Cortés's remarkable achievements. His single monument, historians note, is Mexico itself.

## The Manila Galleon

Although a handful of the early Spanish voyages of exploration did actually reach Asia, none had returned to Mexico until priest-navigator Andrés de Urdaneta discovered the north Pacific trade winds that pushed his ship *San Pedro* swiftly east back to America. He (together with the only other shipmate who had enough strength to do it) dropped anchor in Acapulco Bay on October 3, 1565, with a trove of Chinese treasures in his ship's hold.

Thus, more than three generations after Columbus and 40 years of failed trans-Pacific voyages from Mexico that lost dozens of ships and hundreds of lives, the western trade route to Asia was finally a reality.

Not long thereafter, authorities in Spain designated Acapulco as Mexico's sole Pacific trading port. Once a year, at least one silver-laden ship, known to the Spanish as the Nao de China, and to the English as the Manila galleon, set sail for the Spanish colony of Manila in the Philippines. It returned with an emperor's dream of rich silks, delicate porcelain, exquisite lacquerware, glittering gold, and rare spices.

For more than 250 years thereafter, merchants from all over Mexico and Peru gathered in Acapulco for a grand yearly trade fair. Bulging with bags of silver and a small mountain of trade goods, such as cochineal, cinnamon, jewels, and cacao, they camped out in Acapulco, eagerly awaiting the Manila galleon's return.

## Pirate Threats

Attracted by the Manila galleon's treasures, Dutch, French, Portuguese, and English pirates, sometimes in squadrons of several heavily armed vessels, menaced the Mexican coast.

# SIR FRANCIS DRAKE: THE PIRATE EL DRAQUE

The most renowned raider of the Spanish Main was Francis Drake, or the feared "El Draque," as the Spanish called him. The first European corsair to menace Spain's Pacific colonies, Drake left England in 1577 in command of five vessels and 166 men.

Supposedly headed on a trading mission to Africa, Drake's true purpose became clear when he ordered the attack and capture of a Portuguese merchant ship in the eastern Atlantic. By the time he had crossed westward to South America, his disillusioned crew and merchant partners on board mutinied. Executing the leader of the mutineers, Drake abandoned two of his least-seaworthy ships. Next, rallying the remainder of his men, he changed the name of his ship from the stodgy *Pelican* to the proud *Golden Hind*.

In attempting the westward passage through the stormy Strait of Magellan at the extreme southern tip of South America, he lost two of his remaining three ships. Undaunted, Drake sailed his *Golden Hind* up the west coast of South America, raiding and sacking every possible port – Valparaíso, Lima, Arica – and capturing the royal treasure ship the *Cacafuego*.

Contrary to the Spaniards' worst fears, Drake's approach to robbery was very courtly. No one, Spanish or native, was intentionally harmed. Treasure seemed to be Drake's sole objective. During his last attack on the Pacific Coast, at Huatulco on April 13, 1579, he even stole the church bell.

The ultimate prize, however, was the Manila galleon. He lurked offshore at Acapulco for a time, but seeing no treasure ship, Drake skipped northwest and dropped anchor and resupplied at undefended Zihuatanejo. He continued northwest for months, searching doggedly for the Manila galleon.

Finally, Drake stopped to rest at a safe anchorage probably somewhere on the present-day Northern California coast, at a place that he recorded had cliffs as fair as the white cliffs of Dover. He records in his log that he stayed for five weeks, traded with the native folks, repaired the *Golden Hind*, and erected his famous "plate of brass," yet to be found. On it he inscribed the claim, in the name of his queen, to the domain of "Nova Albion," now California.

The *Golden Hind* continued west across the Pacific, passing the Spice Islands and India and rounding the south Cape of Africa. Drake arrived in England on September 26, 1580, to a glorious welcome by Queen Elizabeth, having voyaged 35,000 miles and collected a booty of 50,000 pounds of silver.

---

The most famous was Francis Drake, known to the colonists as the feared El Draque. Drake raided a number of Spanish Pacific settlements during his 1578–1580 circumnavigation of the globe. After finishing with the South American colonies, Drake headed north, where he sacked Huatulco on April 13, 1579. He waited in vain for the Manila galleon outside of Acapulco, then continued northwest to California, then across the Pacific.

After a Dutch pirate fleet had attacked Acapulco in 1614, New Spain Viceroy Diego Fernández de Córdoba decided to build a fort overlooking Acapulco Bay. It successfully deterred hostile attacks, until termites, hurricanes, old age, and finally an earthquake finished the old fort off in 1776. A bigger, stronger fort, the Fuerte San Diego, replaced it in 1783 and remains to the present day.

## COLONIAL MEXICO
### The Missionaries

Even while the conquistadores subjugated the Mexicans, missionaries began arriving to teach, heal, and baptize them. A dozen Franciscan brothers impressed natives and conquistadores alike by trekking the entire 300-mile stony path from Veracruz to Mexico City in 1523. Missionary authorities generally enjoyed a sympathetic ear from Charles V and his successors, who earnestly pursued Spain's Christian mission, especially when it coincided with Spanish political and economic goals.

## The King Takes Control

Increasingly after 1525, the crown, through the Council of the Indies, began to wrest power away from Cortés and his conquistador lieutenants, many of whom had been granted rights of *encomienda:* taxes and labor of an indigenous district. From the king's point of view, tribute pesos collected by *encomenderos* from their native serfs reduced the gold that would otherwise flow to the crown. Moreover, many *encomenderos* callously enslaved and sold their native wards for quick profit. Such abuses, coupled with European-introduced diseases, began to reduce the native Mexican population at an alarming rate.

The king and his councillors, realizing that without their local labor force New Spain would vanish, acted decisively, instituting new laws and a powerful viceroy, Don Antonio de Mendoza, to enforce them.

Propelled by a near-disastrous native Mexican revolt in 1540, the Council of the Indies, through Viceroy Mendoza, promulgated its liberal New Laws of the Indies in 1542. They rested on high moral ground: The only Christian justification for New Spain was the souls and welfare of the native Mexicans. Slavery was outlawed and the colonists' *encomienda* rights over land and the Indians were to eventually revert to the crown.

Despite near-rebellion by the colonists, Mendoza and his successors kept the lid on New Spain. Although some *encomenderos* held their privileges into the 18th century, chattel slavery of native Mexicans was abolished in New Spain 300 years before Lincoln's Emancipation Proclamation.

Peace reigned in Mexico for 10 generations. Viceroys came, served, and went; settlers put down roots; friars built country churches; and the conquistadores' rich heirs played while the natives worked.

In the port of Acapulco, as the Manila galleon departed and returned safely nearly every year, a small colony of merchants took up residence, built comfortable homes, and got fat on the labor of their native servants and the profits of the Manila galleon's increasingly rich trove of silks, spices, porcelain, lacquerware, and gold.

## The Church

Apart from the missionaries, whose authority flowed directly from the pope in Rome, Mexican parish churches (*parroquias*), most of which remain to the present day, were founded and controlled by local bishops. As did the missionaries, parish churches generally moderated the native Mexicans' toil. On feast days, the natives would dress up, parade their patron saint, drink *pulque,* and ooh and aah at the fireworks.

The church nevertheless profited from the status quo. The biblical tithe—one-tenth of everything earned—filled clerical coffers. By 1800, the church owned half of Mexico.

Moreover, both the clergy and the military were doubly privileged. They enjoyed the right of *fuero* (exemption from civil law) and could be prosecuted only by ecclesiastical or military courts.

## Trade and Commerce

In trade and commerce, New Spain existed for the benefit of the mother country. For nearly the entire colonial era, exterior trade was funneled through only Veracruz on the Gulf and Acapulco on the Pacific. Trade was allowed only with Spain and certain Spanish colonies. As a result, colonists had to pay dearly for often-shoddy Spanish manufactures. The Casa de Contratación (the royal trade regulators) always ensured the colony's yearly payment deficit would be made up by bullion shipments from Mexican mines, from which the crown raked 10 percent off the top.

Despite its faults, New Spain, by most contemporary measures, was prospering in 1800. The native labor force was both docile and growing, and the galleons carried increasing tonnages of silver and gold to Spain. The authorities, however, failed to recognize that Mexico had changed in 300 years.

## Criollos—The New Mexicans

Nearly three centuries of colonial rule gave rise to a burgeoning population of more than a million criollos—Mexican-born, pure European descendants of Spanish colonists, many rich and educated—to whom power was denied.

High government, church, and military office always had been the preserve of a tiny minority of *peninsulares*—whites born in Spain. Criollos could only watch in disgust as unlettered, unskilled *peninsulares,* derisively called *gachupines* (wearers of spurs), were boosted to authority over them.

## Mestizos, *Indígenas,* and African Mexicans

Upper-class luxury existed by virtue of the sweat of Mexico's mestizo, *indígena* (indigenous), and *negro* laborers and servants. African slaves were imported in large numbers during the 17th century after typhus, smallpox, and measles epidemics had wiped out most of the *indígena* population. Although the African Mexicans, whose communities are still concentrated around Veracruz and the Costa Chica east of Acapulco, contributed significantly (crafts, healing arts, dance, cuisine, music, drums, and marimba), they had arrived last and experienced discrimination from everyone.

## POPULATION CHANGES IN NEW SPAIN

| | Early Colonial (1570) | Late Colonial (1810) |
|---|---|---|
| *peninsulares* | 6,600 | 15,000 |
| *criollos* | 11,000 | 1,100,000 |
| *mestizos* | 2,400 | 704,000 |
| *indígenas* | 3,340,000 | 3,700,000 |
| *negros* | 22,000 | 630,000 |

## INDEPENDENCE

Although the criollos stood high above the mestizo, *indígena,* and *negro* underclasses, that seemed little compensation for the false smiles, deep bows, and costly bribes that *gachupines* demanded.

The chance for change came during the aftermath of the French invasion of Spain in 1808, when Napoléon Bonaparte replaced King Ferdinand VII with his brother Joseph on the Spanish throne. Most *peninsulares* backed the king; most criollos, however, inspired by the example of the recent American and French revolutions, talked and dreamed of independence. One such group, urged by a firebrand parish priest, acted.

### El Grito de Dolores

*"¡Viva México! Death to the gachupines!"* Father Miguel Hidalgo cried passionately from the church balcony in the Guanajuato town of Dolores on September 16, 1810, igniting action. A mostly *indígena,* machete-wielding army of 20,000 coalesced around Hidalgo and his compatriots, Ignacio Allende and Juan Aldama. Their ragtag force raged out of control through central Mexico, massacring hated *gachupines* and pillaging their homes.

Hidalgo advanced on Mexico City but, unnerved by stiff royalist resistance, retreated and regrouped around Guadalajara. His rebels, whose numbers had swollen to 80,000, were no match for a disciplined 6,000-strong royalist force. On January 17, 1811, Hidalgo (now "Generalísimo") fled north toward the United States but was soon apprehended, defrocked, and executed. His head and those of his comrades hung from the walls of the Guanajuato granary for 10 years in compensation for the slaughter of 138 *gachupines* by Hidalgo's army.

### The 10-Year Struggle

Others carried on, however. Hidalgo's heroic efforts had immediately found crucial support in the Acapulco region. An African-Mexican former student of Hidalgo, José María Morelos, journeyed south from central

Mexico and recruited an entire rebel brigade in the countryside west and north of Acapulco. Attracted by the riches of the Manila galleon deposited at the port, the rebel army laid siege to Acapulco. Morelos avoided getting bogged down by the siege by splitting his force. He took half of his troops north, where he achieved signal victories, capturing Chilpancingo, Tixtla, and Chilapa in the up-country Acapulco region.

Buoyed by success, Morelos focused the independence movement in Chilpancingo, organizing the Congress of Anahuac that declared Mexican independence from Spain on November 6, 1813. Continuously threatened by Spanish counterattacks, Morelos successfully kept the Congress of Anahuac intact by moving the delegates, one step ahead of the Spanish troops, to a number of southern Mexico locations. Tragically, Morelos did not live to realize the fruits of his struggle; he was captured and executed by the Spanish in December 1815.

After Morelos's death, his compatriot, Vicente Guerrero, also of African-Mexican descent, continued their hit-and-run war of attrition for five years. In 1821, a new liberal government (which included a new constitutional monarchy) in Spain pulled the rug out from beneath Mexican royalist conservatives, who began to defect to the cause of Mexican independence. The royalist commander in the south, Brigadier Agustín de Itúrbide, asked for a meeting with Guerrero. Guerrero was amazed at Itúrbide's proposal: that Mexico should become an independent constitutional monarchy, headed by the king of Spain, and based on "Three Guarantees"—the renowned Trigarantías: independence, Catholicism, and equality—that their army would enforce.

### Mexico Wins Independence

On February 24, 1821, in the Acapulco-region town of Iguala, Guerrero and Itúrbide announced their proposal, which became known, famously, as the Plan de Iguala. The plan immediately gained wide support, and on September 21, 1821, Itúrbide rode triumphantly into Mexico City at the head of his Army of Trigarantías. Mexico was independent at last.

Independence, however, solved little except to expel the *peninsulares*. With an illiterate populace and no experience in self-government, Mexicans began a tragic 40-year love affair with a fantasy: the general on the white horse, the gold-braided hero who could save them from themselves.

### The Rise and Fall of Agustín I

After the king of Spain refused titular reign over an independent Mexico, Itúrbide was crowned Emperor Agustín I by the bishop of Guadalajara on July 21, 1822. He soon lost his charisma, however. In a pattern that became sadly predictable for generations of topsy-turvy Mexican politics, an ambitious garrison commander issued a *pronunciamiento,* or declaration of rebellion, against him; old revolutionary heroes endorsed a plan to install a republic. Itúrbide, his braid tattered and brass tarnished, abdicated in February 1823.

the Chilpancingo Regional History Museum

© BRUCE WHIPPERMAN

## The Disastrous Era of Santa Anna

The new Mexican republic, founded in 1824, teetered along, changing hands between conservative and liberal control, for nine chaotic years. But, by 1833, the government was bankrupt; mobs demanded the ouster of conservative president Anastasio Bustamante, who had executed the rebellious old revolutionary hero, Vicente Guerrero.

Antonio López de Santa Anna, the ambitious military commander whose troops had defeated an abortive Spanish counterrevolution in Veracruz, issued a *pronunciamiento* against Bustamante; Congress obliged, elevating Santa Anna to "Liberator of the Republic" and naming him president in March 1833.

Santa Anna would pop in and out of the presidency like a jack-in-the-box 10 more times before 1855. First, he foolishly lost Texas to rebellious Anglo settlers in 1836; then he lost his leg (which was buried with full military honors) fighting the emperor of France.

Santa Anna's greatest debacle, however, was to declare war on the United States with just 1,839 pesos in the treasury. With his forces poised to defend Mexico City against a relatively small 10,000-man American invasion force, Santa Anna inexplicably withdrew and the United States Marines surged into the "Halls of Montezuma," Chapultepec Castle, where Mexico's six beloved Niños Héroes cadets fell in the losing cause on September 13, 1847.

In the subsequent treaty of Guadalupe Hidalgo, Mexico lost nearly half of its territory—the present states of New Mexico, Arizona, California, Nevada, Utah, and Colorado—to the United States.

Finally, Mexican leaders decided enough was enough. General Juan Álvarez (the first governor of the new state of Guerrero, founded in 1849) and Ignacio Comonfort denounced Santa Anna; in 1854, in Ayutla, on the Costa Chica, they proposed the Plan de Ayutla to get rid of him. With virtually all of his support eroded, Santa Anna fled into permanent exile in 1855.

## REFORM, CIVIL WAR, AND INTERVENTION

While conservatives searched for a king to replace Santa Anna, liberals, led by Supreme Court Chief Justice Benito Juárez, plunged ahead with three controversial reform laws: the Ley Juárez, Ley Lerdo, and Ley Iglesias. These *reformas,* augmented by a new Constitution of 1857, directly attacked the privilege and power of Mexico's landlords, clergy, and generals. They abolished *fueros* (the separate military and church courts), reduced huge landed estates, and stripped the church of its excess property and power.

Conservative generals, priests, *hacendados* (landholders), and their mestizo and *indígena* followers revolted. The resulting War of the Reform (not unlike the U.S. Civil War) ravaged the countryside for three long years. The balance in Guerrero was tilted toward the liberal side by forces of general Juan Álvarez, whose brigades eventually won out over conservative general Miguel Miramón. Finally, the victorious army paraded triumphantly in Mexico City on New Year's Day 1861.

Later that year, at the urging of president Benito Juárez, the federal congress bestowed Mexico's highest honor, of "Benemérito de la Patria," on the old liberal soldier Juan Álvarez.

### Juárez and Maximilian

Benito Juárez, the leading *reformista,* had won the day. Like his contemporary Abraham Lincoln, Juárez, of pure Zapotec native blood, overcame his humble origins to become a lawyer, a champion of justice, and the president who held his country together during a terrible civil war. Like Lincoln, Juárez had little time to savor his triumph.

Imperial France invaded Mexico in January 1862, initiating the bloody five-year imperialist struggle known infamously as the French Intervention. After two costly years, the French pushed Juárez's liberal army into the hills and installed the king that Mexican conservatives thought the country needed. Austrian Archduke Maximilian and his wife, Carlota, the very models of modern Catholic monarchs, were crowned emperor and empress of Mexico in June 1864.

The naive Emperor Maximilian I was surprised that some of his subjects resented his presence. Meanwhile, Juárez refused to yield, stubbornly performing his constitutional duties in a somber black carriage one jump ahead of the French occupying army. The climax came in May 1867, when the liberal forces besieged and defeated Maximilian's army at Querétaro. Juárez, giving no quarter, sternly ordered Maximilian's execution by firing squad on June 19, 1867.

## RECONSTRUCTION AND THE PORFIRIATO

Juárez worked day and night at the double task of reconstruction and reform. He won reelection but died, exhausted, in 1872.

The death of Juárez, the stoic partisan of reform, signaled hope to Mexico's conservatives. They soon got their wish: General Don Porfirio Díaz, the "Coming Man," was elected president in 1876.

### Pax Porfiriana

Don Porfirio is often remembered wistfully, as old Italians remember Mussolini: "He was a bit rough, but dammit, at least he made the trains run on time."

Although Porfirio Díaz's humble Oaxaca mestizo origins were not unlike Juárez's, Díaz was not a democrat: When he was a general, his officers took no captives; when he was president, his country police, the *rurales,* shot prisoners in the act of "trying to escape."

Order and Progress, in that sequence, ruled Mexico for 34 years. Foreign investment flowed into the country; new railroads brought the products of shiny factories, mines, and farms to modernized Gulf and Pacific ports. Mexico balanced its budget, repaid foreign debt, and became a respected member of the family of nations.

The human price was high. Don Porfirio allowed more than one hundred million acres— one-fifth of Mexico's land area (including most

of the arable land)—to fall into the hands of his friends and foreigners. Poor Mexicans suffered the most. By 1910, 90 percent of the *indígenas* had lost their traditional communal land. In the spring of 1910, a smug, now-cultured and elderly Don Porfirio anticipated with relish the centennial of Hidalgo's Grito de Dolores.

## REVOLUTION AND STABILIZATION
### ¡No Reelección!

Porfirio Díaz himself had first campaigned on the slogan *No Reelección,* which expresses the idea that the president should step down after one term. Although Díaz had stepped down once in 1880, he had gotten himself reelected for 26 consecutive years. In 1910, Francisco I. Madero, a short, squeaky-voiced son of rich landowners, opposed Díaz under the same banner.

Although Díaz had jailed him before the election, Madero refused to quit campaigning. From a safe platform in the United States, he called for a revolution to begin on November 20, 1910.

### Villa and Zapata

Not much happened, but soon the millions of poor Mexicans who had been going to bed hungry began to stir. In Chihuahua, followers of Francisco (Pancho) Villa, an erstwhile ranch hand, miner, peddler, and cattle rustler, began attacking the *rurales,* dynamiting railroads, and raiding towns. Meanwhile, in the south, horse trader, farmer, and minor official Emiliano Zapata and his *indígena* guerrillas were terrorizing rich *hacendados* and forcibly recovering stolen ancestral village lands. Zapata's movement gained steam and by May had taken the Morelos state capital, Cuernavaca. Meanwhile, Madero crossed the Río Grande and joined with Villa's forces, who took Ciudad Juárez.

The *federales* (government army troops) began deserting in droves, and on May 25, 1911, Díaz submitted his resignation.

As Madero's deputy, general Victoriano Huerta, put Díaz on his ship of exile in Veracruz,

Emiliano Zapata, circa 1916

Díaz confided, "Madero has unleashed a tiger. Now let's see if he can control it."

## The Fighting Continues

Emiliano Zapata, it turned out, was the tiger Madero had unleashed. Meeting with Madero in Mexico City, Zapata fumed over Madero's go-slow approach to the "agrarian problem," as Madero termed it. By November, Zapata had denounced Madero. *"¡Tierra y Libertad!"* ("Land and Liberty!") the Zapatistas cried, as Madero's support faded. The army in Mexico City rebelled; Huerta forced Madero to resign on February 18, 1913, and then murdered him four days later.

The rum-swilling Huerta ruled like a Chicago mobster; general rebellion, led by the "Big Four"—Villa, Álvaro Obregón, and Venustiano Carranza in the north, and Zapata in the south—soon broke out. Pressed by the rebels and refused U.S. recognition, Huerta fled into exile in July 1914.

Fighting sputtered on for three years as authority see-sawed between revolutionary factions. Finally Carranza, whose forces ended

up controlling most of the country by 1917, got a convention together in Querétaro to formulate political and social goals. The resulting Constitution of 1917, while restating most ideas of the Reformistas' 1857 constitution, additionally prescribed a single four-year presidential term, labor reform, and subordinated private ownership to public interest. Every village had a right to communal *ejido* land, and subsoil wealth could never be sold away to the highest bidder.

The Constitution of 1917 was a revolutionary expression of national aspirations and, in retrospect, represented a social and political agenda for the entire 20th century. In modified form, it has lasted to the present day.

## Obregón Stabilizes Mexico

On December 1, 1920, general Álvaro Obregón legally assumed the presidency of a Mexico still bleeding from 10 years of civil war. Although a seasoned revolutionary, Obregón was also a pragmatist who recognized peace was necessary to implement the goals of the revolution. In four years, his government pacified local uprisings, disarmed a swarm of warlords, executed hundreds of *bandidos,* obtained U.S. diplomatic recognition, assuaged the worst fears of the clergy and landowners, and began land reform.

All this set the stage for the work of Plutarco Elías Calles, Obregón's minister of *gobernación* (interior) and handpicked successor, who won the 1924 election. Aided by peace, Mexico returned to a semblance of prosperity. Calles brought the army under civilian control, balanced the budget, and shifted Mexico's social revolution into high gear. New clinics vaccinated millions against smallpox, new dams irrigated thousands of previously dry acres, and campesinos received millions of acres of redistributed land.

By single-mindedly enforcing the pro-agrarian, pro-labor, and anti-clerical articles of the 1917 constitution, Calles made many influential enemies. Infuriated by the government's confiscation of church property, closing of monasteries, and deportation of hundreds of foreign priests and nuns, the clergy refused to perform marriages, baptisms, and last rites. As members of the Cristero movement, militant Catholics crying *"¡Viva Cristo Rey!"* armed themselves, torching public schools and government property and murdering hundreds of innocent bystanders.

Simultaneously, Calles threatened foreign oil companies, demanding they exchange their titles for 50-year leases. A moderate Mexican supreme court decision over the oil issue and the skillful arbitration of American ambassador Dwight Morrow smoothed over both the oil and church troubles by the end of Calles's term.

Calles, who started out brimming with revolutionary fervor and populist zeal, became increasingly conservative and dictatorial. Although he bowed out peaceably in favor of Obregón (the constitution had been amended to allow one six-year nonsuccessive term), Obregón was assassinated two weeks after his election in 1928. Calles continued to rule for six more years through three puppet presidents: Emilio Portes Gil (1928–1930), Pascual Ortíz Rubio (1930–1932), and Abelardo Rodríguez (1932–1934).

For the 14 years since 1920, the revolution had first waxed, then waned. With a cash surplus in 1930, Mexico skidded into debt as the Great Depression deepened and Calles and his cronies lined their pockets. In blessing his minister of war, general Lázaro Cárdenas, for the 1934 presidential election, Calles expected more of the same.

## Lázaro Cárdenas, President of the People

The 40-year-old Cárdenas, former governor of Michoacán, immediately set his own agenda, however. He worked tirelessly to fulfill the social prescriptions of the revolution. As morning-coated diplomats fretted, waiting in his outer office, Cárdenas ushered in delegations of campesinos and factory workers and sympathetically listened to their petitions.

In his six years of rule, Cárdenas moved public education and health forward on a broad front, supported strong labor unions, and redistributed 49 million acres of farmland, more than any president before or since.

Cárdenas's resolute enforcement of the constitution's Artículo 123 brought him the most renown. Under this pro-labor law, the government turned over a host of private companies to employee ownership and, on March 18, 1938, expropriated all foreign oil corporations.

In retrospect the oil corporations, most of which were British, were not blameless. They had sorely neglected the wages, health, and welfare of their workers while ruthlessly taking the law into their own hands with private police forces. Although Standard Oil cried foul, U.S. president Franklin Roosevelt did not intervene. Through negotiation and due process, the U.S. companies eventually were compensated with $24 million, plus interest. In the wake of the expropriation, President Cárdenas created Petróleos Mexicanos (Pemex), the national oil corporation that continues to run all Mexican oil and gas operations.

## Manuel Avila Camacho

Manuel Avila Camacho, elected in 1940, was the last general to be president of Mexico. His administration ushered in a gradual shift of Mexican politics, government, and foreign policy as Mexico allied itself with the U.S. cause during World War II. Foreign tourism, initially promoted by the Cárdenas administration, ballooned. Good feelings surged as Franklin Roosevelt became the first U.S. president to officially cross the Río Grande when he met with Camacho in Monterrey in April 1943.

In both word and deed, moderation and evolution guided President Camacho's policies. *"Soy creente"* ("I am a believer"), he declared to the Catholics of Mexico as he worked earnestly to bridge Mexico's serious church–state schism. Land-policy emphasis shifted from redistribution to utilization as new dams and canals irrigated hundreds of thousands of previously arid acres. On one hand, Camacho established IMSS (Instituto Mexicano de Seguro Social) and on the other, trimmed the power of labor unions.

As World War II moved toward its 1945 conclusion, both the United States and Mexico were enjoying the benefits of four years of governmental and military cooperation and mutual trade in the form of a mountain of strategic minerals that had moved north in exchange for a similar mountain of U.S. manufactures that moved south.

## CONTEMPORARY MEXICO
### The Mature Revolution

During the decades after World War II, beginning with moderate president Miguel Alemán (1946–1952), Mexican politicians gradually honed their skills of consensus and compromise as their middle-aged revolution bubbled along under liberal presidents and sputtered haltingly under conservatives. Doctrine required of all politicians, regardless of stripe, that they be "revolutionary" enough to be included beneath the banner of the PRI (Partido Revolucionario Institucional), Mexico's dominant political party.

Mexico's revolution hasn't been very revolutionary about women's rights, however. The PRI didn't get around to giving Mexican women,

The present-day Mexican flag was adopted in 1952.

millions of whom fought and died during the revolution, the right to vote until 1953.

Adolfo Ruíz Cortínes, Alemán's secretary of the interior, was elected overwhelmingly in 1952. He fought the corruption that had crept into government under his predecessor, continued land reform, increased agricultural production, constructed new ports, eradicated malaria, and built a number of automobile assembly plants.

Women, voting for the first time in a national election, kept the PRI in power by electing liberal Adolfo López Mateos in 1958. Resembling Lázaro Cárdenas in social policy, López Mateos redistributed 40 million acres of farmland, forced automakers to use 60 percent domestic components, built thousands of new schools, and distributed hundreds of millions of new textbooks. *"La electricidad es nuestra"* ("Electricity is ours"), Mateos declared as he nationalized foreign power companies in 1962.

Despite his left-leaning social agenda, unions were restive under López Mateos. Protesting inflation, workers struck; the government retaliated, arresting Demetrios Vallejo, the railway union head, and renowned muralist David Siqueiros, former communist party secretary.

Troubles notwithstanding, López Mateos climaxed his presidency gracefully in 1964 as he opened the celebrated National Museum of Anthropology, appropriately located in Chapultepec Park, where the Aztecs had first settled 20 generations earlier.

In 1964, as several times before, the outgoing president's interior secretary succeeded his former chief. Dour, conservative Gustavo Díaz Ordaz immediately clashed with liberals, labor, and students. The pot boiled over just before the 1968 Mexico City Olympics. Reacting to a student rebellion, the army occupied the National University; shortly afterward, on October 2, government forces opened fire with machine guns on a downtown protest, killing and wounding hundreds of demonstrators.

### Maquiladoras

Despite its serious internal troubles, Mexico's

relations with the United States were cordial. President Lyndon Johnson visited and unveiled a statue of Abraham Lincoln in Mexico City. Later, Díaz Ordaz met with president Richard Nixon in Acapulco.

Meanwhile, bilateral negotiations produced the Border Industrialization Program. Within a 12-mile strip south of the U.S.-Mexico border, foreign companies could assemble duty-free parts into finished goods and export them without any duties on either side. Within a dozen years, a swarm of such plants, called **maquiladoras,** were humming as hundreds of thousands of Mexican workers assembled and exported billions of dollars worth of shiny consumer goods—electronics, clothes, furniture, pharmaceuticals, and toys—worldwide.

Concurrently, in Mexico's interior, Díaz Ordaz pushed Mexico's industrialization ahead full steam. Foreign money financed hundreds of new plants and factories. Primary among these was the giant Las Truchas steel plant at the new industrial port and town of Lázaro Cárdenas at the Pacific mouth of the Río Balsas, at the western border of the Acapulco region.

## Oil Boom, Economic Bust

Discovery, in 1974, of gigantic new oil and gas reserves along Mexico's Gulf coast added fuel to Mexico's already rapid industrial expansion. During the late 1970s and early 1980s billions in foreign investment, lured by Mexico's oil earnings, financed other major developments—factories, hotels, power plants, roads, airports—all over the country.

The negative side to these expensive projects was the huge dollar debt required to finance them. President Luis Echeverría Alvarez (1970–1976), diverted by his interest in international affairs, passed Mexico's burgeoning financial deficit to his successor, José López Portillo. As feared by some experts, a world petroleum glut during the early 1980s burst Mexico's ballooning oil bubble and plunged the country into financial crisis. When the 1982 interest came due on its foreign debt, Mexico's largest holding company couldn't pay the $2.3 billion owed. The peso plummeted more than

fivefold, to 150 per U.S. dollar. At the same time, prices doubled every year.

But, by the mid-1980s, president Miguel de la Madrid (1982–1988) was working hard to put Mexico's economic house in order. He sliced government and raised taxes, asking rich and poor alike to tighten their belts. Despite getting foreign bankers to reschedule Mexico's debt, de la Madrid couldn't stop inflation. Prices skyrocketed as the peso deflated to 2,500 per U.S. dollar, becoming one of the world's most devalued currencies by 1988.

## Salinas de Gortari and NAFTA

Public disgust led to significant opposition during the 1988 presidential election. Billionaire PAN (National Action Party) candidate Michael Clothier and liberal National Democratic Front candidate Cuauhtémoc Cárdenas ran against the PRI's Harvard-educated technocrat Carlos Salinas de Gortari. The vote was split so evenly that all three candidates claimed victory. Although Salinas eventually won the election, his showing, barely half of the vote, was the worst ever for a PRI president.

Salinas nevertheless climaxed his presidency by negotiating the North American Free Trade Agreement (NAFTA) with U.S. president George Bush and Canadian prime minister Brian Mulroney in 1992.

## Rebellion, Assassination, and the 1994 Election

But, on the very day in early January 1994 that NAFTA took effect, rebellion broke out in the poor, remote state of Chiapas. A small but well-disciplined campesino force, calling itself Ejército Zapatista Liberación Nacional (Zapatista National Liberation Army or EZLN), or "Zapatistas," captured a number of provincial towns and held the former governor of Chiapas hostage.

To further complicate matters, while Salinas de Gortari's chief negotiator, Manuel Camacho Solís, was attempting to iron out a settlement with the Zapatista rebels, Luis Donaldo Colosio, Salinas's handpicked successor, was gunned down just months before the August balloting. However, instead of disintegrating, the nation united in grief; opposition candidates eulogized their fallen former opponent and later earnestly welcomed his replacement, stolid technocrat Ernesto Zedillo, in Mexico's first presidential election debate.

In a closely watched election relatively unmarred by irregularities, Zedillo piled up a solid plurality against his PAN and PRD opponents. By perpetuating the PRI's 65-year hold on the presidency, the electorate had again opted for the PRI's familiar although imperfect middle-aged revolution.

## New Crisis, New Recovery

Zedillo, however, had little time to savor his victory. The peso, after having been pumped up a thousand-fold by Salinas's free and easy monetary policies, crashed, losing half of its value in the few months around Christmas 1994. Mexican financial institutions were in danger of defaulting on their obligations to international investors. To stave off a worldwide financial panic, U.S. President Clinton, in February 1995, secured an unprecedented multibillion-dollar loan package for Mexico.

Although disaster was temporarily averted, the cure for the country's ills was another painful round of inflation and belt-tightening for poor Mexicans. During 1995, inflation soared, wages dropped, and malnutrition rose sixfold, while Third World diseases such as cholera and dengue fever, resurged in the countryside.

Meanwhile, as negotiations with the rebel Zapatistas sputtered on and off in Chiapas, popular discontent erupted in Guerrero, leading to the massacre of 17 unarmed campesinos at Aguas Blancas, in the hills west of Acapulco, by state police in June 1995. One year later, at a demonstration protesting the massacre, a well-armed new revolutionary group, Ejército Popular Revolucionario (People's Revolutionary Army, or EPR), appeared. A few months later, EPR guerrillas killed two dozen police and soldiers at several locations, mostly in Guerrero and Oaxaca. Although President Zedillo's immediate reaction was moderate, platoons of soldiers were soon scouring rural Guerrero, Oaxaca,

Michoacán, and other states, searching homes and arresting suspected dissidents. Public response was mostly negative, though some locals felt that they were far better off in the hands of the army than those of state or federal police.

Mexican democracy got a much-needed boost when notorious Guerrero governor Ruben Figueroa, who had tried to cover up the Aguas Blancas massacre with a bogus videotape, was removed from office in disgrace. At the same time, the Zedillo government gained momentum in addressing the Zapatistas' grievances in Chiapas, even as it decreased federal military presence, built new rural electrification networks, and refurbished health clinics.

Moreover, Mexico's economy began to improve. By mid-1996, inflation had slowed to a 20 percent annual rate, investment dollars were flowing back into Mexico, the peso had stabilized at about 7.5 to the U.S. dollar, and Mexico had paid back half the borrowed U.S. bailout money.

## Economic Recovery and Political Reforms

The best news for which the Zedillo administration could justly claim credit was the dramatically improving national economy. By mid-1998, annual inflation had dropped below 15 percent, investment dollars continued to pour into Mexico, the peso was stable at about 8 to the U.S. dollar, and Mexico had paid back every penny of the money from the 1995 U.S. bailout.

Moreover, in the political arena, although the justice system generally left much to be desired, a pair of unprecedented events signaled an increasingly open political system. In the 1997 congressional elections, voters elected a host of opposition candidates, depriving the PRI of an absolute congressional majority for the first time since 1929. A year later, in early 1998, Mexicans were participating in their country's first primary elections—in which voters, instead of politicians, chose party candidates.

Although President Zedillo had had a rough ride, he entered the twilight of his 1994–2000 term able to take credit for an improved economy, some genuine political reforms, and relative peace in the countryside. The election of 2000 revealed, however, that the Mexican people were not satisfied.

## End of an Era:
## Vicente Fox Unseats the PRI

During 1998 and 1999 the focal point of opposition to the PRI's three-generation rule had been shifting from lackluster left-of-center Cuauhtémoc Cárdenas to relative newcomer Vicente Fox, former president of Coca-Cola Mexico and clean former PAN governor of Guanajuato.

Fox, who had announced his candidacy for president two years before the election, seemed an unlikely challenger. After all, the minority PAN had always been the party of wealthy businessmen and the conservative Catholic right. But blunt-talking, six-foot-five Fox, who sometimes campaigned in cowboy boots and a ten-gallon hat, preached populist themes of coalition building and "inclusion." He backed up his talk by carrying his campaign to hard-scrabble city *barrios,* dirt-poor country villages, and traditional outsider groups, such as Jews.

Meanwhile, as the campaign heated up in early 2000, PRI candidate Francisco Labastida, former interior secretary and governor of the drug-plagued state of Sinaloa, sounded the usual PRI themes to gatherings of party loyalists. At the same time, dour PRD liberal Cuauhtémoc Cárdenas, resigning from a mediocre term as mayor of Mexico City, faded to a weak third place.

In a closely monitored election on July 2, 2000, Fox decisively defeated Labastida, 42 percent to 38 percent, while Cárdenas received only 17 percent. Fox's win also swept a PAN plurality (223/209/57) into the 500-seat Chamber of Deputies lower house (although the Senate remained PRI-dominated).

Nevertheless, in removing the PRI from the all-powerful presidency after 71 consecutive years of domination, Fox had ushered Mexico into a new, much more democratic era.

Despite stinging criticism from his own ranks, President Zedillo, who historians were already judging as the real hero behind Mexico's

new democratic era, made an unprecedented, early appeal, less than a week after the election, for all Mexicans to unite behind Fox.

On the eve of his December 1 inauguration, Mexicans awaited Fox's speech with hopeful anticipation. He did not disappoint them. Although acknowledging that he couldn't reverse 71 years of PRI entrenchment in one six-year term, he vowed to ride the crest of political reform, revamp the tax system, and reduce poverty by 30 percent, by creating a million new jobs a year through new private investment in electricity and oil production and by forming a new common market with Latin America, the United States, and Canada.

He promised, moreover, to secure Mexican democracy by a much-needed reform of police, the federal attorney general, and the army. Perhaps most difficult of all, Fox called for the formation of an unprecedented "Transparency Commission" to investigate a generation of past grievances, including the 1968 massacre of student demonstrators and assassinations of, among others, a Roman Catholic cardinal in 1993 and a presidential candidate in 1994.

## Vicente Fox, President of Mexico

After his December 1, 2000, inauguration, Fox wasted little time getting started, first heading to Chiapas to negotiate with rebellious indigenous community leaders. Along the way, he shut down Chiapas military bases and removed dozens of military roadblocks. Back in Mexico City, he sent the long-delayed peace plan, including the proposed **indigenous bill of rights,** to Congress. Zapatista rebels responded by journeying en masse from Chiapas to Mexico City, where, in their black masks, they addressed Congress, arguing for indigenous rights. Although by mid-2001 Congress had passed a modified version of the negotiated settlement, and the majority of states had ratified the required constitutional amendment, indigenous leaders condemned the legislation plan as watered down and unacceptable, while proponents claimed it was the best possible compromise between the Zapatistas' demands and the existing Mexican constitution.

Moreover, by mid-2002, Vicente Fox could claim credit for cracking down on corruption and putting drug lords in jail, negotiating a key immigration agreement with the United States, keeping the peso stable, clamping down on inflation, and attracting a record pile of foreign investment dollars.

At the same time, Fox continued to pry open the door to democracy in Mexico. In May 2002, he signed Mexico's first freedom of information act, entitling citizens to timely copies of all public documents from federal agencies. Moreover, Fox's long-promised "Transparency Commission" was taking shape. In July 2002, federal attorneys were taking unprecedented action. They were questioning a list of 74 former government officials, including ex-president Luis Echeverría, about their roles in government transgressions, notably political murders and the University of Mexico massacres during the 1960s and 1970s.

But, Mexico's economy, reflecting the U.S. economic slowdown, began to sour in 2001, losing half a million jobs and cutting annual growth to 2.5 percent, down from the 4.5 percent the government had predicted. Furthermore, a so-called "Towelgate" furor (in which aides had purchased dozens of $400 towels for the presidential mansion) weakened Fox's squeaky-clean image.

In the July 7, 2003, congressional elections, voters took their frustrations out on the PAN and gave its plurality in the Chamber of Deputies to the PRI. When the dust settled, the PRI total had risen to 225 seats, while the PAN had slipped to 153. The biggest winner, however, was the PRD, which gained more than 40 seats, to a total of about 100.

Fortunately, by 2004 the Mexican economy, reflecting that of the United States, was turning around. Exports to the United States soared to record levels in the spring of 2004.

In early 2005, reflecting Vicente Fox's victory in 2000, democracy got a big boost in Guerrero as voters broke the PRI's 76-year lock-grip on the governorship and state legislature. Furthermore, on February 6, 2005, voters swept the liberal populist PRD African-Mexican former mayor of Acapulco, Carlos Zeferino Torreblanca, into a six-year term in the governor's office. In doing so, voters expressed high hopes that the can-do Zeferino would lead Guerrero into a fresh new era of good government.

But, despite only modest gains and with his term nearly spent by late 2005, critics were increasingly claiming that Vicente Fox was a lame-duck president who had run out of time to accomplish what he promised. Fox, however, despite a hostile congress that almost continuously blocked his legislative proposals, could claim some modest accomplishments. During his first five years, he had pushed through gains in indigenous rights, national reconciliation, government transparency, drug enforcement, U.S.-Mexico immigration policy, social security reform, housing, and education. Moreover, in addition to nurturing a recovering economy, no one could deny that Fox had kept exports robust and the peso strong against the dollar, and had clamped the lid on inflation.

So, by early 2006, although many Mexican men and women in the street had mostly given up on Fox's promises to remake the economy and political system, most still believed that unseating the PRI was good for Mexico, and acknowledged that even Fox couldn't be expected to completely undo in six years what 71 years of PRI dominance had created.

## The Election of 2006

During the first half of 2006, as Vicente Fox was winding down his presidency, Mexicans were occupied by the campaign to elect his successor. Most headlines went to the PRD candidate, the mercurial leftist-populist Andres Manuel López Obrador, former mayor of Mexico City. Trying hard not to be upstaged was the steady, no-nonsense PAN candidate, Harvard-educated centrist-conservative Felipe Calderón, a leading light of President Fox's cabinet.

On Sunday, July 2, 2006, 42 million Mexicans cast their ballots. In an intensely monitored election marred by very few irregularities, unofficial returns indicated that voters had awarded Calderón a paper-thin plurality.

Four days later, after all returns were certified, the Federal Electoral Institute announced the official vote tally: only about 22 percent for the PRI candidate, Roberto Madrazo, with the remaining lion's share divided nearly evenly, with 38.7 percent going to Obrador and 39.3 percent for Calderón. This result, the Federal Electoral Institute ruled, was too close to declare a winner without a recount.

Besides the close Obrador-Calderón vote, the election results revealed much more. Not only were the 32 electoral entities (31 states and the Federal District) divided equally, with 16 going for Obrador, and 16 for Calderón, the vote reflected a nearly complete north-south political schism, with virtually all of the 16 PAN-majority states forming a solid northern bloc, while the 16 PRD-voting states did the same in the south. Furthermore, the election appeared to signal a collapse of PRI power; with no state (nor the Federal District) giving either a majority or a plurality to Roberto Madrazo.

A howl of protest came from Obrador and his PRD followers after the election results were announced. They claimed the PAN had stolen the election. They jammed the Federal Electoral Institute with lawsuits, alleging a host of irregularities and ballot stuffing incidents, and demanding a complete recount of all 42,000,000 ballots. They yelled, marched, blocked Mexico City's Paseo de la Reforma, and camped in the *zócalo* (central plaza).

## Election Aftermath

For a month, the questionable ballots, which only amounted to 9 percent of the total vote, were gathered and examined exhaustively by the Supreme Election Tribunal, an impeccable panel of federal judges. They found that the recount shifted the margin by only a few thousand votes. On September 6, the Federal Electoral Institute declared Calderón the president-elect by a margin of about 240,000 votes, or a bit more than one-half of a percent of the total vote.

Obrador and his supporters screamed foul even louder and threatened to ignore Calderón and/or block his presidency. On September 16, Mexican independence day, Obrador convened

in the Mexico City *zócalo* hundreds of thousands of his supporters that declared him the legitimate president. In the succeeding days, the PRD's obstructionist tactics reached an outrageous climax when a handful of PRD senators and deputies made such a ruckus during a joint session of the federal legislature that they prevented the president of Mexico, for the first time in history, from delivering his annual state of the union address. Mexican voters, watching the PRD's melodramatic tactics on television, began, in increasing numbers, to say enough was enough. National polls showed that more than two-thirds of Mexicans disapproved of the PRD's protest behavior. By October, many of the PRD's leaders agreed, further isolating Obrador and his rump government to a footnote in Mexican history. Mexico's new democracy, given a gentle shove forward ten years earlier by president Ernesto Zedillo and nurtured for six more years by Vicente Fox, seemed to have again surmounted a difficult crisis and emerged stronger.

An important result of the 2006 election, initially overshadowed by the intense struggle over the presidential vote, but potentially crucial, was the federal legislative vote, in which PAN emerged as the biggest winner by far. The final results showed that voters had given PAN candidates strong pluralities of 206/127/106 over the PRD and PRI, respectively, in the 500-seat federal Chamber of Deputies, and 52/29/33 in the 128-seat Senate, with the remainder of seats scattered among minor parties. This result may bode well for Mexican democracy. With some cooperation (most likely from the PRI) Felipe Calderón may be able to use his party's pluralities to further the national political and economic reform agenda Vicente Fox promised six years earlier, but could only partially deliver.

## Calderón Takes Charge

As he prepared for his December 1, 2006, inauguration, Felipe Calderón not only appeared to be both moving ahead with many of his predecessor's original proposals, but he also seemed to be reaching out to the PRI and the PRD with some new proposals. These, although containing much of PAN's pro-business pro-NAFTA ideas, also appeared to borrow considerably from the liberal-populist agenda of Obrador and the PRD and produce much-needed cooperation to push their country closer to the bright but elusive vision of a just and prosperous motherland for all Mexicans.

Calderón got started immediately, tackling Mexico's most immediate problem by declaring war on Mexico's drug lords. Right away he replaced most of the federal police chiefs, many suspected of corruption. He then put the Mexican army in charge of his war on drugs, eventually assigning 30,000 Mexican soldiers to seek and destroy criminal drug networks, especially in the most drug-infested states of Michoacán, Guerrero, and Sinaloa and the border towns of Tijuana, Ciudad Juárez, and Nuevo Laredo, where criminal drug gangs had been assassinating incorruptible judges and local police officials and officers.

Concurrently, President Calderón skillfully guided the Mexican economy and politics, at both national and international levels. Under his steady hand, during 2007, the Mexican economy continued to bubble along at a moderate annual growth rate of about 2.5 percent, inflation was kept at a low 4 percent, and the currency steadily held its value, between 10 and 11 pesos to the U.S. dollar.

## Calderón Visits the United States

On the world stage, President Calderón made his first international trip, initially to California for three days, then east to the Midwest and New York. On February 13, 2008, he addressed a joint session of the California legislature, emphasizing cooperation. "Collaboration and shared responsibility," he said, were the key to joint California-Mexico progress. In the same address, he thrust himself into the U.S. immigration debate by declaring that ". . . Mexican and Mexican-American workers are a large reason for the dynamic economy of California," and that Mexican ". . . immigration should be legal, safe, and organized."

# Government and Economy

## THE MEXICAN AND GUERRERO ECONOMIES
### Post-Revolutionary Gains

By many measures, Mexico's 20th-century revolution appears to have succeeded. Since 1910, illiteracy has plunged tenfold from 80 to 8 percent, life expectancy has risen from 30 years to more than 70, infant mortality has dropped from a whopping 40 percent to about 2 percent, and, in terms of caloric intake, Mexicans are eating about twice as much as their forebears at the turn of the 20th century.

Decades of steady economic growth account for rising Mexican living standards. The Mexican economy has repeatedly rebounded from recessions by virtue of its plentiful natural resources, notably oil and metals; diversified manufacturing, such as cars, electronics, and petrochemicals; steadily increasing tourism;

exports of fruits, vegetables, and cattle; and its large, willing low-wage workforce.

Recent Mexican governments, moreover, have skillfully exploited Mexico's economic strengths. The Border Industrialization Program has led to millions of jobs in thousands of border maquiladora factories, from Tijuana and the mouth of the Río Grande, now spreading to interior centers such as Monterrey, Guadalajara, and Mexico City. The increased manufacturing output has produced manifold economic benefits, including reduced dependency on oil exports and burgeoning job growth and foreign trade as Mexico joined in the General Agreement on Tariffs and Trade (GATT) in 1986 and NAFTA in 1994. Consequently, Mexico has become a net exporter of goods and services to the United States, its largest trading partner. Although Mexico suffered a peso collapse of about 70 percent (in relation to the

U.S. dollar) during the mid-1990s, the Zedillo administration acted quickly. Belt-tightening measures brought inflation down to 10 percent per year and restored the flow of foreign investment back into Mexico by the late 1990s.

In 2000, the new Fox administration continued its predecessor's prudent economic course, which has further reduced inflation to a healthy low of about 4 percent during 2004 through 2007 and stabilized the peso at between 10 and 11 per dollar for the entire eight-year (2000–2008) period. And despite the 2001–2003 U.S.-Mexican economic slowdown that decreased demand for Mexican products (and consequently wiped out many hundreds of thousands of Mexican jobs), the economy had recovered to a healthy 4 percent growth rate and (consequent robust job growth) during the 2004–2007 period.

## Guerrero Economic Challenges

Many of Mexico's latter 20th-century economic gains have bypassed Mexico's poor southern states of Chiapas, Oaxaca, and Guerrero. Of the three, Guerrero perennially ranks low in most indicators of quality of life, such as income, infant mortality, malnutrition, and illiteracy.

For example, although illiteracy in Guerrero is already high, running 22 percent of all adults (compared with only about 9 percent for Mexico as a whole), illiteracy is more than double that (50 percent) among Guerrero's indigenous adults, This is not surprising, since less than half of Guerrero's indigenous adults have ever completed any schooling.

As many studies show, poor education is invariably associated with poor health. Infant mortality, as high as 8 percent (one in 12 babies die) in some indigenous Guerrero communities (with one gynecologist per 17,000 women), is more than triple the (2.8 percent) Mexico average and about eleven times the 0.9 percent (one baby in 110) U.S. average. This also is not surprising, since the vast majority (95 percent in some communities) of Guerrero's indigenous people lack regular access to health care.

Although rich in sunshine, mountainous Guerrero lacks arable land and needs more

water and capital to irrigate what arable land exists. Under the right conditions, bountiful crops of sesame, corn, tomatoes, citrus, mangoes, peanuts, alfalfa, soy, and *chiles* sprout quickly from bottomland fields.

A potentially valuable crop in Guerrero is coffee, now cultivated by thousands of farmers in the vine-draped lower slopes of the coastal mountains. However, as all over the developing world, growing a crop is the easiest part of trying to make a living from it. Isolation, quality control, and lack of access to markets have kept Guerrero coffee farmers poor. To make matters even worse, the bottom has fallen out of worldwide coffee prices during recent years. It seems patently unjust that farmers can get only about $0.50 per pound for the same coffee that, after transport and roasting, sells in U.S. and European grocery stores for $6 to $8 per pound.

The bright part of the Guerrero economy is tourism, which accounts, both directly and indirectly, for most of the earnings of half of Guerrero families. If it weren't for the resorts

Coffee is an important crop in the foothill forests of the Costa Grande.

of Acapulco, Ixtapa, Zihuatanejo, and Taxco, most Guerrero people would be even poorer than they are now.

## Long-Term Economic Challenges

Despite huge gains, Mexico's Revolution of 1910 is nevertheless incomplete. Improved public health, education, income, and opportunity have barely outdistanced Mexico's population, which has increased more than sevenfold—from 15 million to 110 million—between 1910 and 2008. For example, although the illiteracy rate has decreased, the actual number of Mexican people who can't read, about 10 million, has remained about constant since 1910.

Moreover, the land reform program, once thought to be a Mexican cure-all, has long been a disappointment. The *ejidos* of which Emiliano Zapata dreamed have become mostly symbolic. The fields are typically small and unirrigated. Furthermore, *ejido* land, being communal, is not easily accepted by banks as loan collateral. Capital for irrigation networks, fertilizers, and harvesting machines is consequently lacking. Communal farms are typically inefficient; the average Mexican (and Guerrero) field produces about *one-quarter* as much corn per acre as a U.S. farm. Mexico must accordingly use its precious oil-dollar surplus to import millions of tons of corn—originally indigenous to Mexico—annually.

The triple scourge of overpopulation, lack of arable land, and low farm income has driven millions of campesino families to seek better lives in Mexico's cities and the United States. Chicago (with 300,000 Guerrero-born residents) is the world's second-largest Guerreran city, ranking only behind Acapulco.

Since 1910, Mexico has evolved from a largely rural country, where 70 percent of the population lived on farms, to an urban nation where 70 percent of the population lives in cities. Fully one-fifth of Mexico's people now live in Mexico City, and one-third of Guerrero's people live in Acapulco.

Nevertheless, the future appears bright for many privately owned and managed Mexican farms, concentrated largely in the northern border states. Exceptionally productive, they typically work hundreds or thousands of irrigated acres of crops, such as tomatoes, lettuce, *chiles,* wheat, corn, tobacco, cotton, fruits,

Earnings from their daily fish catch sustain many Costa Chica families.

alfalfa, chickens, hogs, and cattle, just like their counterparts across the border in California, New Mexico, Arizona, and Texas.

Staples—wheat for bread, corn for tortillas, milk, and cooking oil—are all imported and consequently expensive for the typical working-class Mexican family, which must spend half or more of its income (typically $400 per month) for food. Recent inflation has compounded the problem, particularly for the millions of families on the bottom half of Mexico's economic ladder.

Although average gross domestic product figures for Mexico—about $10,000 per capita (less than half that for Guerrero) compared to about $40,000 for the United States—place it above nearly all other developing countries, averages, when applied to Mexico (and especially Guerrero), mean little. A primary socioeconomic reality of Mexican history remains: the richest one-fifth of Mexican families earns about 10 times the income of the poorest one-fifth. A relative handful of people own a large hunk of Mexico, and they don't seem inclined to share much of it with the less fortunate. As for the poor, the typical Mexican and Guerrero family in the bottom one-third income bracket often owns neither car nor refrigerator, and the children typically do not finish elementary school.

## GOVERNMENT AND POLITICS
### The Constitution of 1917

Mexico's governmental system is rooted in the Constitution of 1917, which incorporated many of the features of its reformist predecessor of 1857. The 1917 document, with amendments, remains in force, both nationally and in similarly written individual state constitutions. Although drafted at the behest of conservative revolutionary Venustiano Carranza by his handpicked Querétaro "Constitucionalista" congress, it was greatly influenced by liberal Álvaro Obregón and generally ignored by Carranza during his subsequent three-year presidential term.

Although many articles resemble those of its U.S. model, the Constitution of 1917 contains provisions that stem directly from Mexican experience. Article 27 addresses the question of land. Private property rights are qualified by societal need; subsoil rights are public property, and foreigners and corporations are severely restricted in land ownership. Although the 1917 constitution declared *ejido* land inviolate, 1994 amendments allow, under certain circumstances, the sale or use of communal land as loan security.

Article 23 severely restricts church powers. In declaring that "places of worship are the property of the nation," it stripped churches of all title to real estate, without compensation. Article 5 and Article 130 banned religious missionary orders, expelled foreign clergy, and denied priests and ministers all political rights, including voting, holding office, and even criticizing the government.

Article 123 establishes the rights of labor: to organize, bargain collectively, strike, work a maximum eight-hour day, and receive a minimum wage. Women are to receive equal pay for equal work and be given a month's paid leave for childbearing. Article 123 also establishes social security plans for sickness, unemployment, pensions, and death.

On paper, Mexico's constitutional government structures appear much like their U.S. prototypes: a federal presidency, a two-house Congress (single house in Guerrero), and a Supreme Court, with their counterparts in each of the 32 states. Political parties field candidates, and citizens vote by secret ballot.

Mexico's presidents, however, have traditionally enjoyed greater powers than their U.S. counterparts. They need not seek legislative approval for many cabinet appointments, can suspend constitutional rights under a state of siege, can initiate legislation, veto all or parts of bills, refuse to execute laws, and replace state officers (as President Zedillo removed Guerrero governor Ruben Figueroa in 1995). The federal government, moreover, retains nearly all taxing authority, relegating the states to a role of merely administering federal programs.

Although ideally providing for separation of powers, the Constitution of 1917 subordinates both the legislative and judicial branches, with the courts being the weakest of all. The Supreme Court, for example, can only, with repeated deliberation, decide upon the constitutionality of legislation. Five separate individuals must file successful petitions for writs *amparo* (protection) on a single point of law to affect constitutional precedent.

## Democratizing Mexican and Guerrero Politics

Reforms in Mexico's stable but top-heavy "Institutional Revolution" came only gradually. Characteristically, street protests were brutally put down at first, with officials only later working to address grievances. Generations of dominance by the PRI, the "Institutional Revolutionary Party," led to widespread cynicism and citizen apathy. Regardless of who gets elected, the typical person on the street used to say, the officeholder was bound to retire with his or her pockets full.

Nevertheless, by 1985, movement toward more justice and pluralism seemed to be in store for Mexico. During the subsequent dozen years, minority parties increasingly elected candidates to state and federal office. Although none captured a majority of any state legislature, the strongest non-PRI parties, such as the conservative pro-Catholic Partido Acción Nacional (PAN, National Action Party) and the liberal-left Partido Revolucionario Democrático (PRD), elected governors. In 1986, minority parties were given federal legislative seats, up to a maximum of 20, for winning a minimum of 2.5 percent of the national presidential vote. In the 1994 election, minority parties received public campaign financing, depending upon their fraction of the vote.

After his 1994 inaugural address, in which he called loudly and clearly for more reforms, president Ernesto Zedillo quickly began to produce results. He immediately appointed a respected member of the PAN opposition party as attorney general—the first non-PRI cabinet appointment in Mexican history. Other Zedillo firsts were federal Senate confirmation of both Supreme Court nominees

and the attorney general, multiparty participation in the Chiapas peace negotiations, and congressional approval of the 1995 financial assistance package received from the United States. Zedillo, moreover, organized a series of precedent-setting meetings with opposition leaders that led to a written pact for political reform and the establishment of permanent working groups to discuss political and economic questions.

Perhaps most important was Zedillo's campaign and inaugural vow to separate both his government and himself from PRI decision-making. He kept his promise, becoming the first Mexican president, in as long as anyone could remember, who did not choose his successor.

## A New Mexican Revolution

Finally, in 2000, like a Mexican Gorbachev, Ernesto Zedillo, the man responsible for many of Mexico's earlier democratic reforms, watched as PAN opposition reformer Vicente Fox swept Zedillo's PRI from the presidency after a 71-year rule. Moreover, despite severe criticism from his own party, Zedillo quickly called for the country to close ranks behind Fox. Millions of Mexicans, still dazed but buoyed by Zedillo's statesmanship and Fox's epoch-making victory, eagerly awaited Fox's inauguration address on December 1, 2000.

He promised nothing less than a new revolution for Mexico and backed it up with concrete proposals: reduce poverty by 30 percent with a million new jobs a year from revitalized new electricity and oil production, a Mexican Silicon Valley, and free trade between Mexico, all of Latin America, and the United States and Canada. He promised justice for all, through a reformed police, army, and the judiciary. He promised conciliation and an agreement with the Zapatista rebel movement in the south, including a bill of rights for Mexico's native peoples.

But five years later, in early 2006, with his grand vision only fractionally fulfilled, no one can fairly say that Vicente Fox didn't try. Like few, if any, Mexican presidents before him, he remained true to his belief in a democratic presidency: negotiating, haranguing, cajoling, and compromising with a cadre of legislators who stubbornly blocked nearly all of his reform proposals.

Time and again Vicente Fox admitted the messiness and difficulty of the democratic process. But he also remained convinced and committed to the belief that there could be no turning from the democratic path for Mexico. In a 2004 interview, he pointed out that, at least, he had ended "Presidencialismo," the decades-old Mexican habit of bowing to a strong, even sometimes ruthless, president. And perhaps that is how historians will remember Vicente Fox. Maybe they will remember him as the president who with courage and honesty truly did begin a New Mexican Revolution, by earnestly leading his country along the difficult but true path to a more just and prosperous future for all Mexicans.

# People and Culture

Let a broad wooden chopping block represent Mexico; imagine hacking it with a sharp cleaver until it is grooved and pocked. That fractured surface resembles Mexico's central highlands, where most Mexicans, divided from each other by high mountains and yawning *barrancas,* have lived since before history.

The Mexicans' deep divisions, in large measure, led to their downfall at the hands of the Spanish conquistadores. The Aztec empire that Hernán Cortés conquered was a vast but fragmented collection of tribes. Speaking more than 100 mutually alien languages, those original Mexicans viewed each other suspiciously, as barely human barbarians from strange lands beyond the mountains. And even today the lines Mexicans draw between themselves—of caste, class, race, wealth—are the result, to a significant degree, of the realities of their mutual isolation.

## POPULATION

The Spanish colonial government and the Roman Catholic religion provided the glue that through 400 years has welded Mexico's fragmented people into a burgeoning nation-state. Mexico's population, about 110 million by the year 2008, increased between 2000 and 2007, but at a yearly rate diminished to about half that of the previous decade. Increased birth control and emigration largely account for the slowdown.

For similar reasons, Guerrero's population, estimated at about 3.2 million in 2008, is increasing, but at an even slower rate than Mexico in general. Compared to the 18 percent (1.8 percent yearly) increase from 1990 to 2000, Guerrero's population increase has slowed threefold, to only about a 0.6 percent average yearly increase for the 2000–2007 period. This probably represents Guerrero's large yearly emigration to other places in Mexico and the United States (where, by the beginning of 2008, about a million Guerrero-born folks were living).

Mexico's population has not always been increasing. Historians estimate that European diseases, largely measles and smallpox, wiped out as many as 25 million—perhaps 95 percent—of the *indígena* population within a few generations after Cortés stepped ashore in 1519. The Mexican population dwindled from an estimated 20 million at the eve of the conquest to a mere one million inhabitants by 1600. It wasn't until 1950, four centuries after Cortés, that Mexico's population recovered to its pre-conquest level of about 20 million.

## Mestizos, *Indígenas,* Criollos, and African Mexicans

Although by 1950 Mexico's population had recovered, it was completely transformed. The mestizo, a Spanish-speaking person of mixed blood, had replaced the pure native Mexican, the *indígena* (een-DEE-hay-nah) as the typical Mexican.

The trend continues. Perhaps three of four

Mexicans would identify themselves as mestizo, that class whose part-European blood elevates them, in the Mexican mind, to the level of *gente de razón* (people of "reason" or "right"). And there's the rub. The *indígenas* (or, mistakenly but much more commonly, Indians), by the usual measurements of income, health, or education, squat at the bottom of the Mexican social ladder.

The typical *indígena* family lives in a small adobe house in a remote valley, subsisting on corn, beans, and vegetables from its small unirrigated *milpa*. They usually have chickens, a few pigs, and sometimes a cow, but no electricity; their few hundred dollars a year in cash income isn't enough to buy even a small refrigerator, much less a truck.

The usual mestizo family, on the other hand, enjoys most of the benefits of the 21st century. They typically own a modest concrete house in town. Their furnishings, simple by developed-world standards, will often include an electric refrigerator, washing machine, propane stove, television, and car or truck. The children go to school every day, and the eldest son sometimes looks forward to college.

Sizable *negro* communities, holding around 150,000 people, descendants of 18th-century African slaves, live along the Guerrero-Oaxaca Pacific coastline. Last to arrive, the *negros* experience discrimination at the hands of everyone else and are integrating very slowly into the mestizo mainstream.

Above the mestizos, a small criollo (Mexican-born white) minority, a few percent of the total population, inherits the privileges—wealth, education, and political power—of its colonial Spanish ancestors.

## THE *INDÍGENAS*

Although anthropologists and census takers classify them according to language groups

## MEXICAN NAMES

Foreign visitors, confounded by long handles such as Doña Juana María López de Díaz, wonder how Mexican names got so complicated.

The preceding Doña Juana example is especially complicated because it's a typical woman's name, and women's names are generally more complex than typical men's names.

So, let's explain a man's name first. Take the national hero, Vicente Ramón Guerrero Saldaña. Vicente is his first given name; Ramón, his second given name, corresponding to the "middle" name in the United States. The third, Guerrero, is customarily the father's first surname, and the last, Saldaña, his mother's first surname. Only on formal occasions are men referred to with all four of their names. Simply Vicente Guerrero would do most of the time.

Now, back to Doña Juana. I threw a curve at you by introducing "Doña." It's an honorific, used as "Dame," for a distinguished woman. ("Don" is the corresponding honorific for Spanish men.)

So, skipping the honorific, women's names start out like men's: first given name, Juana; second given name, María, and father's first surname, López.

Now, things get more complicated. For unmarried women, the naming is the same as for men. But when a woman gets married, she customarily replaces her second surname with her husband's first surname, preceded by "de," meaning "of." So in the example, Juana is evidently a married woman, who has substituted "de Díaz" (her husband's first surname being Díaz) for her second surname, all adding up to "Juana María López de Díaz."

Thankfully, however, informal names for women also are simplified. Juana, above, would ordinarily shorten her name to her first given name, followed by her husband's first surname: simply Juana Díaz.

All of the above notwithstanding, many Mexican women do not go along with this male-dominated system at all and simply use their maiden names as they were known before they were married.

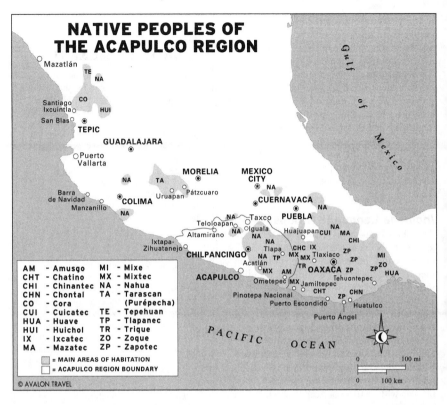

# NATIVE PEOPLES OF THE ACAPULCO REGION

| AM | – Amusgo | MI | – Mixe |
|----|----------|----|--------|
| CHT | – Chatino | MX | – Mixtec |
| CHI | – Chinantec | NA | – Nahua |
| CHN | – Chontal | TA | – Tarascan |
| CO | – Cora | | (Purépecha) |
| CUI | – Cuicatec | TE | – Tepehuan |
| HUA | – Huave | TP | – Tlapanec |
| HUI | – Huichol | TR | – Trique |
| IX | – Ixcatec | ZO | – Zoque |
| MA | – Mazatec | ZP | – Zapotec |

■ = MAIN AREAS OF HABITATION
□ = ACAPULCO REGION BOUNDARY

© AVALON TRAVEL

(such as Náhuatl, Mixtec, and Zapotec), *indígenas* generally identify themselves as residents of a particular locality rather than by language or ethnic grouping. And although as a group they are referred to as *indígenas* (native, or aboriginal), individuals are generally uncomfortable being labeled as such.

Recent census figures indicate at least 8 percent of Mexicans are *indígenas*—that is, they speak one of Mexico's 50-odd native languages. The indigenous presence in Guerrero is stronger than in Mexico in general, with four major groups, totaling about 530,000 people, or about 17 percent of the Guerrero population. The largest group, about 212,000, speak **Nahuatl** (the historical Aztec tongue); the others speak **Mixtec** (148,000), **Tlapanec** (116,000), and **Amusgo** (47,000). Of these,

a sizable fraction speak no Spanish at all. Moreover, these populations are shifting only gradually. Many *indígenas* prefer the old ways. If present trends continue, the year 2019, 500 years after the Spanish arrival, will mark the return of the Mexican indigenous population to the preconquest level of 20 million.

While the mestizos are the emergent self-conscious majority class, the *indígenas,* as during colonial times, remain the invisible people of Mexico. They are politically conservative, socially traditional, and tied to the land. On market day, the typical *indígena* family might make the trip into town. They bag tomatoes, squash, or peppers, and tie up a few chickens or a pig. The rickety country bus will often be full and the mestizo driver may wave them away, giving preference to his friends, leaving them to trudge stoically along the road. Indigenous people from all over Mexico, especially the southeast states of Michoacan, Guerrero, and Oaxaca, come to Acapulco, Taxco, and Ixtapa-Zihuatanejo to sell their crafts.

Their lot, nevertheless, has been slowly improving. *Indígena* families now sometimes have access to a local school and a clinic. Improved health has led to an increase in their population. Official census figures, however, are probably low. *Indígenas* are traditionally suspicious of government people, and census takers, however conscientious, seldom speak the local language.

### Indígena Language Groups

The Maya speakers of Yucatán and the aggregate of the Náhuatl (Aztec language) speakers of the central plateau are Mexico's most numerous *indígena* groups, totaling three million (one million Maya, two million Nahua).

Official figures of the indigenous population in the Acapulco region may be misleading. Official counts often do not measure the droves of transient folks—migrants and new arrivals—who sleep in vehicles, shantytowns, behind their crafts stalls, and with friends and relatives. Although they are officially invisible, you will see them in Acapulco, Ixtapa, and Zihuatanejo, walking along the beach, for example, laden with their for-sale fruit or handicrafts—men in sombreros and scruffy jeans, women in homemade full-skirted dresses with aprons much like your great-great-grandmother may have worn.

Immigrants in their own country, indigenous people flock to cities and tourist resorts from hardscrabble rural areas. Although of pure native blood, they will not acknowledge it or will even be insulted if you ask them if they are *indigenas*. It would be more polite to ask them where they're from. If from Michoacán, they'll usually speak Tarasco (more courteously, say Purépecha: poo-RAY-pay-chah); if from Oaxaca, they'll probably speak Zapateco, Mixteco, or Chatino; people from Guerrero will typically speak Náhuatl, Tlapaneco, Mixteco, or Amusgo.

## DUENDES: SPIRITS OF MEXICO

Once upon a time, most everyone believed that the world was full of spirits that inhabited every object in creation: trees, rocks, animals, mountains, even the wind and the stars. World mythology is replete with examples, from the leprechauns of Ireland and the fairies of Mount Tirich Mir in Pakistan to the spirits who haunt old Hawaiian *heiaus* (temples) and the *duendes* of Mexico.

Eventually many a campesino will take his children to his mountainside cornfield to introduce them to the *duendes*, the elfin beings that folks sometimes glimpse in the shadowed thickets where they hide from mortals.

At the upper end of his field, the campesino father addresses the *duendes*: "With your permission we clear your brush and use your water because it is necessary to nourish our corn and beans. Please allow us, for otherwise, we would starve."

Modernized city Mexicans, generations removed from country village life, often scoff at such antique beliefs. That is, until the family doctor fails to cure their weakened spouses or sick children. Then they often run to a *curandero* or *curandera* (folk healer).

"*Enduendado*" (affliction by an angry *duende*), the *curandero* sometimes diagnoses. Often the cure is simple and savvy: teas and poultices of forest-gathered herbs; other times it is mystical, such as "purifying" by passing an egg all over the afflicted one's body to draw out the illness, and then breaking the egg into a bowl. The shape the broken yolk takes, maybe of a snake, might determine the treatment, which could be long and intricate: massage with lotions of herbs and oils, followed by a *temazcal* (sweat bath) rubdown with rough maguey fibers, all consummated by intense prayers to the Virgin of Guadalupe to force the *duende* to cease the affliction.

Many times the folk cure fails; other times, however, it succeeds, and with enough frequency to convince millions of Mexicans of the power of the village folk healer to purge a *duende*'s poisonous spell.

As immigrants always have, they come seeking a better life. If you're interested in what they're selling, bargain with humor. And if you err, let it be on the generous side. They are proud, honorable people who prefer to walk away from a sale rather than to lose their dignity.

## Dress

Country markets are where you're most likely to see people in traditional dress. There, some elderly men still wear the white cottons that blend Spanish and native styles. Absolutely necessary for men is the Spanish-origin straw sombrero (literally, shade-maker) on their heads, loose white cotton shirt and pants, and leather huaraches on their feet.

Women's dress, by contrast, is more colorful. It can include a *huipil* (long, embroidered dress) embroidered in bright floral and animal motifs and a handwoven *enredo* (wraparound skirt that identifies the wearer with a locality, also called a *pozahuanco*). A *faja* (waist sash) and, in winter, a *quechquémitl* (shoulder cape) complete the ensemble.

## RELIGION

"God and Gold" was the two-pronged mission of the conquistadores. Most of them concentrated on gold, while missionaries tried to shift the emphasis to God. They were famously successful; more than 90 percent of Mexicans (about 77 percent of Guerrero people) profess to be Catholics.

Catholicism, spreading its doctrine of equality of all people before God and incorporating native gods into the church rituals, eventually brought the *indígenas* into the fold. Within 100 years, nearly all native Mexicans had accepted the new religion, which raised the universal God of humankind over local tribal deities.

### The Virgin of Guadalupe

Conversion of the *indígenas* was sparked by the vision of Juan Diego, a humble farmer. In 1531, on the hill of Tepayac north of Mexico City, Juan Diego saw a brown-skinned version of the Virgin Mary enclosed in a dazzling aura of light. She told him to build a shrine in her memory on that spot, where the Aztecs had long worshipped their "earth mother," Tonantzín. Juan Diego's brown virgin told him to go to the cathedral and relay her instruction to Archbishop Zumárraga.

The archbishop, as expected, turned his nose up at Juan Diego's story. The vision returned, however, and this time Juan Diego's brown virgin realized that a miracle was necessary. She ordered him to pick some roses at the spot where she had first appeared to him (a true miracle, since roses had been previously unknown in the vicinity) and take them to the archbishop. Juan Diego wrapped the roses in his rude fiber cape, returned to the cathedral, and placed the wrapped roses at the archbishop's feet. When he opened the offering, Zumárraga gasped: Imprinted on the cape was an image of the brown virgin herself—proof positive of a genuine miracle.

In the centuries since Juan Diego, the brown virgin—La Virgen Morena, or Nuestra Señora La Virgen de Guadalupe—has blended native and Catholic elements into something uniquely Mexican. In doing so, she has become the

the Virgin of Guadalupe on the banner of Miguel Hidalgo's 1810 rebel army

© BRUCE WHIPPERMAN

virtual patroness of Mexico, the beloved symbol of Mexico for *indígenas,* mestizos, *negros,* and criollos alike.

In the summer of 2002, Pope John Paul journeyed to Mexico to perform a historic gesture. Before millions of joyous faithful, on July 31, 2002, the frail aging pontiff elevated Juan Diego to sainthood, thus making him Latin America's first indigenous person to be so honored.

With few exceptions, every Acapulco regional town and village celebrates the cherished memory of its Virgin of Guadalupe on December 12. This celebration, however joyful, is but one of the many fiestas that Mexicans, especially the *indígenas,* live for. Each village holds its local fiesta in honor of its patron saint, who is often a thinly veiled sit-in for a local preconquest deity. Themes appear Spanish—Christians vs. Moors, devils vs. priests—but the native element is strong, sometimes dominant.

# Festivals and Events

Mexicans love a party. Urban families watch the calendar for midweek national holidays that create a *puente* (bridge) to the weekend and allow them to squeeze in a three- to five-day mini-vacation. Visitors should likewise watch the calendar. Such holidays (especially Christmas and Semana Santa, pre-Easter week) mean packed buses, roads, and hotels, especially around the Acapulco region's beach resorts.

Country people, on the other hand, await their local saint's or holy day. The name of the locality often provides the clue. For example, in San Marcos, on the Costa Chica, 30 miles west of Acapulco, expect a celebration in late April, around April 25, the feast day of St. Mark. People dress up in their traditional best, sell their wares and produce in a street fair, join a procession, get tipsy, and dance in the plaza.

## FIESTAS

The following calendar lists national and notable Acapulco region holidays and festivals. Dates may vary. If you want to attend a specific local fiesta, contact a local travel agent or tourism bureau for information. (But, if you happen to be where one of these is going on, get out of your car or bus and join in!)

## January

- Jan. 1: **¡Feliz Año Nuevo!** (New Year's Day); national holiday.

- Jan. 6: **Día de los Reyes** (Day of the Kings); traditional gift exchange.

- Jan. 17–18: **Fiesta de Santa Prisca** in Taxco; families bring their pet animals for blessing at the church. The next day, pilgrims arrive at the *zócalo* for *mañanitas* in honor of the saint, then head for folk dancing inside the church.

- Jan. 20–21: **Fiesta de San Sebastián;** townsfolk honor the saint martyred in Rome in A.D. 288.

- Jan. 23–Feb. 2: **Fiesta de la Virgen de la Salud;** processions, dancing, food, and fireworks.

## February

- Feb. 2: **Día de Candelaria;** plants, seeds, and candles blessed; processions and bullfights.

- February: During the four days before *Miercoles de Ceniza* (Ash Wednesday, 46 days before Easter Sunday), usually in late February, many towns and villages stage **Carnaval** (Mardi Gras) extravaganzas; especially in Teloloapan, near Iguala.

## March

- March 10–17: **Fiesta de San Patricio** (St. Patrick's Day festival).

- Fifth Friday before Easter Sunday: **Fiesta**

del Señor del Perdón; grand pilgrimage festival, in Igualapa, near Ometepec.

- Fourth Friday before Easter Sunday: **Fiesta de Jesús el Nazareno** in Huaxpáltepec; traditional Dance of the Conquest, big native country fair.

- March 19: **Día de San José** (Day of St. Joseph).

- March 21: **Birthday of Benito Juárez,** the "Hero of the Americas;" national holiday.

## April

- April 1–7: **Feria de Café** (Coffee Fair) in Atoyac de Álvarez; coffee farmers sell their best; also plenty of horse trading, handicrafts, country food, and bull riding and roping.

- April 1–19: **Fiesta de Ramos** (Palm Sunday); local area crafts fair, food, dancing, mariachis; especially in Jamiltepec.

- April: **Good Friday,** two days before Easter Sunday.

- April: **Semana Santa** (pre-Easter Holy Week culminating in Domingo Gloria, Easter Sunday, a national holiday) especially in Taxco, Pinotepa Nacional, Teloloapan, Petatlán, Ometepec, Iguala, Olinalá, and Jamiltepec.

## May

- May 1: **Fiesta del Primer de Mayo** in Atliaca, near Tixtla; age-old indigenous rite; sacrifices, praying for rain, and traditional dances at the sacred site Sótano (Sinkhole) de Oztotempa.

- May 1: **Labor Day;** national holiday.

- May 3: **Fiesta del Día de la Santa Cruz** (Holy Cross); processions to hilltops and sacred sites; many towns, but especially in Ometepec.

- May 3–15: **Fiesta of St. Isador the Farmer;** blessing of seeds, animals, and water; agricultural displays, competitions, and dancing.

- May 5: **Cinco de Mayo;** celebrates the defeat of the French at Puebla in 1862; national holiday.

- May 10: **Mother's Day;** national holiday.

## June

- June 24: **Fiesta de San Juan Bautista** (Festival of St. John the Baptist); fairs and religious festivals, playful dunking of people in water, especially in Chilapa.

- June 29: **Día de San Pablo y San Pedro** (Day of St. Peter and St. Paul).

## July

- July 20–30: **Fiesta de Santiago Apóstol** (Festival of St. James the Apostle) in many locations, but especially in Pinotepa Nacional, Quechultenango, and Ometepec.

## August

- Aug. 6–7: **Fiesta del Padre Jesús;** grand pilgrimage celebration of Petatlán's beloved *patrón,* accompanied by plenty of merrymaking, traditional dances, country food, and fireworks.

- Aug. 9: **Fiesta de Vicente Guerrero** in Tixtla; folks celebrate with cultural events, music, and traditional dances the birthday of their famous native son, Vicente Guerrero.

- Aug. 14–15: **Fiesta de la Virgen de la Asunción** (Festival of the Virgin of the Assumption); the celebration of the ascension of Mother Mary into heaven, especially in Chilapa.

## September

- Sept. 1–8: **Fiesta de la Natividad de María;** indigenous folks flood into Tixtla to sell handicrafts, get tipsy, and watch their favorite traditional dances.

- Sept. 9–11: **Fiesta de San Nicolás Tolentino** in Ometepec.

- Sept. 14: **Charro Day** (Cowboy Day) all over Mexico; rodeos.

- Sept. 15–16: **Dias Patrias** (Patriotic Days); national holiday; mayors everywhere reenact Father Hidalgo's 1810 Grito de Dolores from city hall balconies at 11 P.M. on the night of 15 September, especially in Teloloapan and Ometepec.

- Sept. 27–Oct. 2: **Fiesta de San Miguel;** often with the Danza de los Cristianos y Moros (Dance of the Christians and Moors).

## October

- Oct. 4: **Día de San Francisco** (Day of St. Francis of Assisi), especially in Iguala and Olinalá.

- Oct. 12: **Día de la Raza** (Day of the Race); national holiday that commemorates the union of the races.

## November

- Nov. 1: **Día de Todos Santos** (All Souls' Day); in honor of the souls of children; the departed descend from heaven to eat sugar skeletons, skulls, and treats on family altars.

- Nov. 2: **Día de los Muertos** (Day of the Dead); in honor of ancestors; families visit cemeteries and decorate graves with flowers and favorite food of the deceased; especially colorful in Iguala and Taxco.

- Monday after the Day of the Dead: **Fiesta de los Jumiles** in Taxco; folks collect and feast on raw or roasted *jumiles* (small crickets) and enjoy music and plenty of fixings.

- Nov. 1–15: **Feria de la Nao de China** in Acapulco; fair celebrating the galleon trade that linked colonial Acapulco with China via the Philippines.

Mexican deceased are honored in a festive Day of the Dead.

- Nov. 20: **Revolution Day;** anniversary of the Revolution of 1910–1917; national holiday.

- Nov. 28–Dec. 5: **National Silver Fair** in Taxco; Mexico's most skilled silversmiths compete for prizes amid a whirl of concerts, dances, and fireworks.

## December

- Dec. 1: **Inauguration Day;** national government changes hands every six years: 2012, 2018, 2024 . . .

- Dec. 8: **Día de la Purísima Concepción** (Day of the Immaculate Conception).

- Dec. 12: **Día de Nuestra Señora de Guadalupe** (Festival of the Virgin of Guadalupe, patroness of Mexico); processions, music, and dancing nationwide, especially around the Acapulco *zócalo* and the adjacent Pozo de la Nación neighborhood.

- Dec. 16–24: **Christmas Week;** week of *posadas* and piñatas; midnight Mass on Christmas Eve.

- Dec. 24–Jan. 8: **Feria de San Mateo, la Navidad, y el Año Nuevo** in Chilpancingo; the festivities kick off with the *teopancolaquio,* a ritual honoring the birth of God on Earth. Subsequently folks celebrate with favorite traditional dances, bullfights, carnival, fireworks, cockfights, and plenty of food.

- Dec. 25: **¡Feliz Navidad!** (Christmas Day); Christmas trees and gift exchange; national holiday.

- Dec. 31: **New Year's Eve.**

# Arts and Crafts

Mexico is so stuffed with lovely, reasonably priced handicrafts (*artesanías,* ar-tay-sah-NEE-ahs) that many crafts devotees, if given the option, might choose Mexico over heaven. A sizable fraction of Acapulco-region families still depend upon homespun items—clothing, utensils, furniture, native herbal remedies, religious offerings, adornments, toys, musical instruments—which either they or their neighbors craft at home. Many such traditions reach back thousands of years, to the beginnings of Mexican civilization. The accumulated knowledge of manifold generations of artisans has, in many instances, resulted in finery so prized that whole villages devote themselves to the manufacture of a certain class of goods.

In the Acapulco region, handicrafts shoppers who venture away from the coastal resorts to the source towns and villages will most likely benefit from lower prices, wider choices, and, most important, the privilege of encountering the artisans themselves.

The Acapulco region's three prime handicrafts source towns are **Taxco,** renowned for silver jewelry; **Olinalá,** for fine lacquerware, furniture, and jaguar masks; and **Chilapa,** for the trove of charming handicrafts that folks bring in from outlying villages and sell at the grand Sunday crafts market. Handicrafts lovers should make the extra effort to visit this Sunday market in Chilapa, 2.5 hours by car, three hours by direct bus from Acapulco. In Chilapa you often can find items made of **horn** (*cuerno*): mescal bottles, combs, pen holders, ash trays, and lampshades; **ironwork** (*hierro*): hachets, daggers, swords, and knives; **maguey fiber** (*ixtle*): hand-painted bags and purses; **embroidery** (*bordado*): napkins, tablecloths, and shawls (*rebozos*); **basketry and woven fiber** (*cestería*): palm sombreros, reed baskets, purses, mats (*petates*), and palm baskets (*tenates*); **wood** (*madera*): masks, lacquerware, miniature human and animal figurines, furniture; **leather** (*cuero*): purses, belts, wallets; and **pottery** (*alfarería*).

## BARGAINING

Bargaining will stretch your money even further. It comes with the territory in Mexico and needn't be a hassle. On the contrary, if done with humor and moderation, bargaining can be an enjoyable way to meet Mexican people and gain their respect, even friendship.

The local crafts market is where bargaining is most intense. For starters, try offering half the asking price. From there on, it's all psychology: you have to content yourself with not having to have the item. Otherwise, you're sunk; the vendor will probably sense your need and stand fast. After a few minutes of good-humored bantering, ask for *el último precio* (the final price), in which, if it's close, you may have a bargain.

## BASKETRY AND WOVEN CRAFTS

Weaving straw, leaves, palm fronds, and reeds is among the oldest of Mexican crafts traditions. Mat and basketweaving methods and designs 5,000 years old survive to the present day.

In the dry sierra and Río Balsas basin of northeastern Guerrero, people weave *petates* (straw mats) upon which vacationers stretch out on the beach and which local folks use for everything, from keeping tortillas warm to shielding babies from the sun. Palm-leaf weaving is a near-universal occupation. The craft spills over to Acapulco and the Costa Chica, where you might see a person waiting for a bus or even walking down the street while weaving creamy white palm leaf strands into a coiled basket. (Despite appearances, the product, if made of palm leaf, is not strictly a basket—*canasta* in Spanish—which is made of reeds, but instead a *tenate*, which has no handle like a basket does, but a woven tumpline that folks loop over their foreheads when carrying a load.)

Not unlike the origami paper-folders of Japan, folks who live around Lago Pátzcuaro in neighboring Michoacán have taken basketweaving to its ultimate by crafting virtually everything—from toy turtles and Christmas bells to butterfly mobiles and serving spoons—from the reeds they gather along the lakeshore.

Hatmaking has likewise attained high refinement in Mexico. Many of the same Guerrero palm-leaf weavers who craft *petates* and *tenates* also craft sombreros. Also, in Sahuayo, Michoacán (near the southeast shore of Lago Chapala), and due east across Mexico, in Becal, Campeche, workers also craft so-called Panama hats, or *jipis* (HEE-pees), of palm leaf. The measure of a fine palm leaf hat is its softness and flexibility—so pliable that you can stuff one into your purse or pants pocket without damage.

## CLOTHING AND EMBROIDERY

Although **traje** (traditional indigenous dress) has nearly vanished in urban Mexico, significant numbers of Mexican women, especially in remote districts of Michoacán, Guerrero,

## ECOTOURISM

Latter-day jet travel has brought droves of vacationing tourists to developing countries largely unprepared for the consequences. As the visitors' numbers swell, power grids black out, sewers overflow, and roads crack under the strain of accommodating more and larger hotels, restaurants, cars, buses, and airports.

Worse yet, armies of vacationers drive up local prices and begin to change native customs. While visions of tourists as sources of fast money replace traditions of hospitality, television wipes out folk entertainment, Coke and Pepsi substitute for fruit drinks and desserts, and prostitution and drugs flourish.

Some travelers have said enough is enough and are forming organizations to encourage visitors to travel with increased sensitivity to native people and customs. They have developed travelers' codes of ethics and guidelines that encourage visitors to stay at sustainable, local-style accommodations, use local transportation, and seek people- and earth-friendly vacations and tours, such as language-study and cultural programs and people-to-people work projects.

A number of especially active socially responsible travel groups sponsor tours all over the world, including the Acapulco region. These include organizations such as **Global Exchange, Green Tortoise, Green Globe,** and **Third Eye Travel.** They all have websites that can be accessed via Internet search engines, such as Google and Yahoo, or the umbrella website www.sociallyresponsible.com.

The related ecotourism movement promotes socially responsible tourism through the strategy of simultaneous enjoyment and enhancement of the natural environment. Neighboring Oaxaca and, to some extent, the Acapulco region, have become ecotourism centers partly because of the dedication of Oaxaca-based Ron Mader, moving force behind the superb website www.planeta.com. Log on and you'll find virtually everything you need to know about ecotourism, from nature tour companies and village recycling projects to indigenous handicrafts cooperatives and international conferences.

Oaxaca, Chiapas, and Yucatán, make and wear *traje*. Most common is the *huipil*, a full, square-shouldered, short- to midsleeved dress, often hand-embroidered with animal and floral designs. Notable *huipil* designs come from Xochistlahuaca, Guerrero, and San Pedro de Amusgos, Oaxaca (Amusgo tribe: white cotton, often embroidered with abstract colored animal and floral motifs); San Andrés Chicahuaxtla, Oaxaca (Trique tribe: white cotton, richly embroidered red stripes, interwoven with green, blue, and yellow, and hung with colored ribbons); Tehuántepec, Oaxaca (Zapotec tribe: white cotton, with bright multicolored flowers embroidered along two or four vertical seams). Beyond the Pacific coast, Yucatán Maya *huipiles* are among the most prized. They are of white cotton and embellished with big, brilliant machine-embroidered flowers around the neck and shoulders.

Shoppers sometimes can buy other, less common types of *traje*, such as a *quechquémitl* (shoulder cape), often made of wool and worn as an overgarment in winter. The *enredo*, a full-length skirt, wraps around the waist and legs like a Hawaiian sarong. Mixtec women on the Guerrero-Oaxaca border around Pinotepa Nacional commonly wear the *enredo*, known locally as the *pozahuanco* (poh-sah-oo-AHN-koh), below the waist and, when at home, go bare-breasted. When wearing their *pozahuancos* in public, they usually tie a *mandil*, a wide calico apron, around their front side. Women weave the best *pozahuancos* using cotton thread dyed a light purple with secretions of tidepool-harvested snails, *Purpura patula pansa*, and silk dyed deep red with cochineal, extracted from the dried bodies of a locally cultivated scale insect, *Dactylopius coccus*. On a typical day, two or three women will be selling handmade *pozahuancos* at the Pinotepa Nacional market.

Colonial-era Spanish styles have blended with native *traje*, producing a wider class of dress, known generally as **ropa típica.** Lovely embroidered *blusas* (blouses), *rebozos* (shawls), and *vestidos* (dresses) fill boutique racks and market stalls all over the Acapulco region. Among the most popular is the so-called Oaxaca wedding dress, made of cotton with a crochet-trimmed riot of diminutive flowers hand-stitched about the neck and yoke. Some of the finest examples are made in San Antonino Castillo, just north of Ocotlán in the Valley of Oaxaca.

In contrast to women, only a small fraction of Mexican men—members of remote groups, such as Amusgos in Xochistlahuaca, Guerrero; Huichol, Cora, and Tarahumara in northwest Mexico; and Maya and Lacandón in the southeast—wear *traje*. Nevertheless, shops offer some fine men's *ropa típica,* such as wool jackets and serapes for northern or highland winter wear, and *guayaberas,* hip-length pleated dress shirts.

Fine *bordado* (embroidery) embellishes much traditional Mexican clothing, as well as *manteles* (tablecloths) and *servilletas* (napkins). As everywhere, women define the art of embroidery. Although some still work by hand at home, cheaper machine-made factory lace and needlework is more commonly available in shops.

## LEATHER

Acapulco region shops offer an abundance of leather goods, which, if not manufactured locally, are shipped from the renowned leather centers. These include Guadalajara, Mazatlán, and Oaxaca (sandals and huaraches), and León (shoes, boots, and saddles). For unique and custom-designed articles you'll probably have to confine your shopping to the expensive tourist resort shops. For more usual though still attractive leather items such as purses, wallets, belts, coats, and boots, veteran shoppers go to local city markets.

## FURNITURE

Although furniture is usually too bulky to carry back home with your airline luggage, low Mexican prices allow you to ship your purchases home and enjoy beautiful, unusual pieces for a fraction of what you would pay—if you could find them—at home.

A number of classes of furniture (*muebles,* moo-AY-blays) are crafted in villages near the sources of raw materials—either wood, leather, reeds, bamboo, or wrought iron.

Sometimes it seems as if every house in Mexico is furnished with wood **colonial-style furniture.** The basic design of much of it dates at least back to the Middle Ages. Although variations exist, most colonial-style furniture is heavily built. Table and chair legs are massive, often lathe-turned; chair backs are usually straight and vertical. Although usually varnished, colonial-style tables, chairs, and chests sometimes shine with inlaid wood or tile, or animal and flower designs. Family shops turn out good furniture, usually in the highlands, where suitable wood is available. Among the Acapulco region's best-known places to find these products are Zihuatanejo, Taxco, Ixcateopan (near Taxco), Chilapa (near Chilpancingo), and Olinalá (via Chilapa).

A second, very distinctive class of Mexican furniture is **equipal,** usually roundish tables, chairs, and sofas, made of brown pigskin or cowhide stretched over wooden frames. Factories are mostly in Jalisco towns of Guadalajara, Zacoalco, Tlaquepaque, and Tonalá.

It is intriguing that **lacquered furniture,** in both process and design, has much in common with lacquerware produced half a world away in China. Moreover, Mexican lacquerware tradition both predated the conquest and was originally practiced only on the Pacific, where legends persist of preconquest contact with Chinese traders. Consequently, a number of experts believe that the Mexicans learned the craft of lacquerware from Chinese artists, centuries before Columbus.

Today, artisan families in and around Pátzcuaro, Michoacán, and Olinalá carry on the tradition. The process, which at its finest resembles cloisonné manufacture, involves carving and painting intricate floral and animal designs, followed by repeated layerings of lacquer, clay, and sometimes gold and silver to produce satiny jewel-like surfaces.

A few villages produce furniture made of plant fiber, such as reeds, raffia, and bamboo. In some cases, entire communities, such as Ihuatzio (near Pátzcuaro), and Villa Victoria (in Mexico state, west of Toluca), have long harvested the bounty of local lakes and marshes as the basis for their products.

© BRUCE WHIPPERMAN

Taxco offers more than fine silver, such as these unusual wooden deer.

**Wrought iron,** produced and worked according to Spanish tradition, is used to produce tables, chairs, and benches. Ruggedly fashioned in a riot of baroque scrollwork, pieces often decorate garden, patio, and park settings. Many colonial cities, notably San Miguel de Allende, Toluca, Guanajuato, Guadalajara, and Oaxaca are wrought-iron manufacturing centers.

## GLASS AND STONEWORK

Glass manufacture, unknown in pre-Columbian times, was introduced by the Spanish. Today, factories scattered all over the country turn out mountains of *burbuja* (boor-BOO-hah) bubbled glass tumblers, goblets, plates, and pitchers, usually in blue, green, or red. Finer glass is manufactured around Guadalajara; especially in suburban Tlaquepaque and Tonalá villages, you can watch artisans blow glass into a number of shapes, notably, paper-thin balls in red, green, or blue.

Artisans usually work stone near sources of supply. Puebla, Mexico's main source of onyx (*onix,* OH-neeks), is the manufacturing center for the galaxy of mostly rough-hewn cream-colored items, from animal charms and chess pieces to beads and desk sets, that crowd curio-shop shelves throughout the country. *Cantera,* a volcanic tufa stone occurring in pastel shades from pink to green, is used similarly.

For a keepsake from a truly ancient Mexican tradition, don't forget the hollowed-out stone metate (may-TAH-tay), a corn-grinding basin, and the three-legged *molcajete* (mohl-kah-HAY-tay), a mortar for grinding *chiles.*

## HUICHOL ART

Growing demand, especially around Guadalajara and Puerto Vallarta, has greatly stimulated the supply of Huichol art. Originally produced by shamans for ritual purposes, pieces such as beaded masks, *cuadras* (rectangular yarn paintings), gourd rattles, arrows, and yarn *cicuri* (God's eyes) have a ritual symbolism. Eerie beaded masks of wood often represent the Huichols' earth mother, Tatei Urianaka. The larger *cuadras,* of colored acrylic yarn painstakingly glued in intermeshing patterns to a plywood base, customarily depict the drama of life being played out between the main actors of the Huichol pantheon. For example, as Tayau (Father Sun) radiates over the land, alive with stylized cactus, flowers, peyote buds, snakes, and birds, antlered "Brother Deer" Kauyumari heroically battles the evil sorcerer Kieri, while nearby Tatei Urianaka gives birth.

## JEWELRY

Gold and silver were once the basis for Mexico's wealth. Her Spanish conquerors plundered a mountain of gold—religious offerings, necklaces, pendants, rings, bracelets—masterfully crafted by a legion of native metalsmiths and jewelers. Unfortunately, much of that indigenous tradition was lost because, for generations, the Spanish denied the Mexicans access to precious metals while they introduced Spanish methods. Nevertheless, a small goldworking tradition survived the dislocations of the 1810–1821 War of Independence and the 1910–1917 revolution. Silvercrafting, moribund during the 1800s, was revived in the Acapulco region in Taxco, principally through the joint efforts of architect-artist William Spratling and the local community.

Today, spurred by the tourist boom, jewelry-making is thriving in Mexico. Taxco, where a swarm of local families, guilds, and cooperatives produce sparkling silver and gold adornments, is the acknowledged center. Scores of Taxco shops display the results—shimmering ornamental butterflies, birds, jaguars, serpents, turtles, and fish from ancient native tradition. Pieces, mostly in silver, vary from humble but attractive trinkets to glittering necklaces, candelabras, and place settings for a dozen, sometimes embellished with precious stones.

Additionally, Iguala, not far south of Taxco, and Petatlán, a short drive southeast of Zihuatanejo, are thriving market centers of affordable 14-carat-gold rings, necklaces, chains, bracelets, and pendants.

### Buying Silver and Gold

One hundred percent pure silver is rarely sold because it's too soft. Silver (sent from processing mills in the north of Mexico to be worked in Taxco shops) is nearly always alloyed with 7.5 percent copper to increase its durability. Such pieces, identical in composition to sterling silver, should have ".925," together with the initials of the manufacturer, stamped on their back sides. Other, less common grades, such as "800 fine" (80 percent silver), should also be stamped.

If silver is not stamped with the degree of purity, it probably contains no silver at all and is an alloy of copper, zinc, and nickel, known by the generic label "alpaca," or "German" silver. Once, after haggling over the purity and prices of his offerings, a street vendor handed me a shiny handful and said, "Go to a jeweler and have them tested. If they're not real, keep them." Calling his bluff, I took them to a jeweler, who applied a dab of hydrochloric acid to each piece. Tiny telltale bubbles of hydrogen revealed the cheapness of the merchandise, which I returned the next day to the vendor.

Some shops price sterling silver jewelry simply by weighing, which typically translates to about $1 per gram. If you want to find out if a price is fair, ask the shopkeeper to weigh the item for you.

People prize pure gold, partly because, unlike silver, it does not tarnish. Gold, nevertheless, is rarely sold pure (24 karat); for durability, it is alloyed with copper. Typical purities, such as 18 karat (75 percent) or 14 karat (58 percent), should be stamped on the pieces. If not, chances are they contain no gold at all.

## METALWORK

Bright copper, brass, and tinware, sturdy ironwork, and razor-sharp knives and machetes are made in a number of regional centers. Copperware, from jugs, cups, and plates to candlesticks—and even the town lampposts and bandstand—all comes from Santa Clara del Cobre, a few miles south of Pátzcuaro, Michoacán.

Although not the source of brass itself, Tonalá, in the Guadalajara eastern suburb, is the place where brass is most abundant and beautiful, appearing as menageries of brilliant fetching birds and animals, sometimes embellished with shiny nickel highlights.

A number of Oaxaca family factories turn out fine cutlery—swords, knives, machetes—scrolled cast-iron grillwork, and a swarm of bright tinware or *hojalata* mirror frames, masks, and glittering Christmas decorations.

Be sure not to miss the miniature *milagros,* one of Mexico's most charming forms of metalwork. Usually of brass, they are of homely shapes—a horse, dog, or baby, or an arm, head, or foot—and, accompanied by a prayer, are pinned by the faithful to the garment of their favorite saint who they hope will intercede to cure an ailment or fulfill a wish.

## POTTERY AND CERAMICS

Although Mexican pottery tradition is as diverse as the country itself, some varieties stand out. Among the most prized is the so-called Talavera (or Majolica), the best of which is made by a few family-run shops in Puebla. The labels Talavera and Majolica derive from Talavera, the Spanish town from which the

brightly painted pottery in Taxco

© BRUCE WHIPPERMAN

tradition migrated to Mexico; before that it originated on the Spanish Mediterranean island of Mayorca (thus Majolica), from a combination of still older Arabic, Chinese, and African ceramic styles. Shapes include plates, bowls, jugs, and pitchers, hand-painted and hard-fired in intricate bright yellow, orange, blue, and green floral designs. Shops in Taxco and Zihuatanejo (especially El Arte y Tradición) sell authentic Talavera.

So few shops make true Talavera these days that other cheaper look-alike grades, made around Guanajuato, are more common, selling for as little as one-tenth of the price of the genuine article.

More practical and nearly as prized is the hand-painted, high-fired stoneware from Tonalá in Guadalajara's eastern suburbs. Although made in many shapes and sizes, such stoneware is often sold as complete dinner place settings. Decorations are usually in abstract floral and animal designs, hand-painted over a reddish clay base.

From the same tradition come the famous

*bruñido* pottery animals of Tonalá. Round, smooth, and cuddly as ceramic can be, the Tonalá animals—very commonly doves and ducks, but also cats and dogs and sometimes even armadillos, frogs, and snakes—seem to embody the essence of their species. One Zihuatanejo shop, Cerámicas Tonalá, carries a large, lovely selection.

Some of the most charming Mexican pottery, made from a ruddy low-fired clay and crafted following pre-Columbian traditions, comes from western Mexico, especially Colima. Charming figurines in timeless human poses—flute-playing musicians, dozing grandmothers, fidgeting babies, loving couples—and animals, especially Colima's famous playful dogs, decorate the shelves of a sprinkling of shops.

The Acapulco region also sustains a vibrant pottery tradition. In crafts shops and street displays in Acapulco, Taxco, and Zihuatanejo, you'll find the humble but very attractive unglazed but brightly painted animals—cats, ducks, fish, and many others—that folks bring to resort centers from their village family workshops.

Even more acclaimed are various types of pottery from the valley surrounding the city of Oaxaca. The village of Atzompa is famous for its green-glazed clay pots, dishes, and bowls. Nearby San Bártolo Coyotepec village has acquired equal renown for its black pottery, sold all over the world. Doña Rosa, now deceased, pioneered the crafting of big round pots without using a potter's wheel. Now made in many more shapes by Doña Rosa's descendants, the pottery's exquisite silvery black sheen is produced by the reduction (reduced air) method of firing, which removes oxygen from the clay's red (ferric) iron oxide, converting it to black ferrous oxide.

Although most latter-day Mexican potters have become aware of the health dangers of lead pigments, some for-sale pottery may still contain lead. The hazard comes from low-fired pottery in which the lead has not been firmly melted into the glaze. Acids in foods such as lemons, vinegar, and tomatoes dissolve the lead pigments, which, when ingested, eventually result in lead poisoning. In general, the hardest, shiniest pottery, which has been twice fired—such as the high-quality Tonalá stoneware used for dishes—is the safest.

## WOOLEN WOVEN GOODS

Mexico's finest wool weavings come from Teotitlán del Valle, in the Valley of Oaxaca, less than an hour's drive east of Oaxaca city. The weaving tradition, carried on by Teotitlán's Zapotec-speaking families, dates back at least 2,000 years. Many families still carry on the arduous process, making everything from scratch. They gather the dyes from wild plants and the bodies of insects and sea snails. They hand-wash, card, spin, and dye the wool and even travel to remote mountain springs to gather water. The result, they say, *vale la pena* (is worth the pain): intensely colored tightly woven carpets, rugs, and wall hangings that retain their brilliance for generations. Casa Marina textiles shop in Zihuatanejo carries such fine Oaxaca textiles.

Rougher, more loosely woven blankets, jackets, and serapes come from other parts, notably mountain regions, especially around San Cristóbal Las Casas, in Chiapas, and Lago Pátzcuaro in Michoacán.

## MASKS

Spanish and native Mexican traditions have blended to produce a multitude of masks—some strange, some lovely, some scary, some endearing, all interesting. The tradition flourishes in the strongly indigenous southern Pacific states of Michoacán, Guerrero (especially in Chilapa and Olinalá), and Oaxaca (especially in Pinotepa Don Luis and Huazolotitlán), where campesinos gear up all year for the village festivals. These include Semana Santa (Easter week), Carnaval (Mardi Gras, usually in February), early December (Virgin of Guadalupe), and the festival of the local patron, whether it be San José, San Pedro, San Pablo, Santa María, Santa Barbara, or one of a host of others. Every local fair has its favored dances, such as the Dance of the Conquest, the Christians and Moors, the Old Men, or

onyx masks in the ancient Olmec style

the Jaguar, in which masked villagers act out age-old allegories of fidelity, sacrifice, faith, struggle, sin, and redemption. For a singularly fascinating display of Acapulco region masks, be sure to visit the Casa de la Máscara (House of Masks) in Acapulco.

Although masks are made of many materials—from stone and ebony to coconut husks and paper—wood, where available, is the medium of choice. For the entire year, village master-carvers cut, shave, sand, and paint to ensure that each participant will be properly disguised for the festival.

The popularity of masks has led to an entire made-for-tourist mask industry of mass-produced duplicates, many cleverly antiqued. Many shops in Taxco and Zihuatanejo sell attractive reproductions. Examine the goods carefully; if the price is high, don't buy unless you're convinced it's a real antique.

## ALEBRIJES

Tourist demand has made *alebrijes* (zany wooden animals) a Oaxaca growth industry.

Virtually every family in certain Valley of Oaxaca villages—notably Arrazola and San Martín Tilcajete—runs a factory studio. There, piles of *copal* wood, which men carve and women finish and intricately paint, become whimsical giraffes, dogs, cats, iguanas, gargoyles, dragons, and most of the possible permutations in between. The farther from the source you get, the higher the *alebrije* price becomes; what costs $5 in Arrazola will probably run about $10 in the Acapulco region and $30 in the United States or Canada.

Others commonly available are the charming colorfully painted wooden fish carved mainly in Guerrero, and the burnished, dark hardwood animal and fish sculptures of desert ironwood from the state of Sonora.

## MUSICAL INSTRUMENTS

The great majority of Mexico's guitars and other stringed instruments are made in Paracho in Michoacán. There, scores of cottage factories turn out guitars, violins, mandolins, *viruelas,* ukuleles, and a dozen more variations every day. They vary widely in quality, so look carefully before you buy. Make sure that the wood is well cured and dry; damp, unripe wood instruments are more susceptible to warping and cracking.

## PAPER AND PAPIER-MÂCHÉ

Papier-mâché has become a high art in Tonalá, Jalisco, where a swarm of birds, cats, frogs, giraffes, and other animal figurines are meticulously crafted by building up repeated layers of glued paper. The result—sanded, brilliantly varnished, and polished—resembles fine sculpture rather than the humble newspaper from which it was fashioned.

Other paper goods you shouldn't overlook include piñatas (durable, inexpensive, and as Mexican as you can get), available in every town market; colorful decorative cutout-banners (string overhead at your home fiesta) from San Salvador Huixcolotla, Puebla; and **amate,** wild fig tree bark paintings in animal and flower motifs, from Xalitla and Ameyaltepec, Guerrero.

# ESSENTIALS

## BY AIR
### From the United States and Canada

The vast majority of travelers reach the Acapulco region by air. Flights are frequent and reasonably priced. Competition sometimes shaves prices down as low as $500 for an Acapulco or Ixtapa-Zihuatanejo round-trip; air-hotel packages sometimes do even better.

Air travelers can save lots of money by shopping around. Don't be bashful about asking for the cheapest price. Make it clear to the airline or travel agent you're interested in a bargain. Ask the right questions: Are there special-incentive, advance-payment, night, midweek, tour package, or charter fares? Peruse the ads in the Sunday newspaper travel section for bargain-oriented travel agencies. Check airline and bargain-oriented travel websites, such as **www.priceline.com, www.orbitz.com, www .expedia.com,** and **www.travelocity.com.**

Although some agents charge booking fees and don't like discounted tickets because their fee depends on a percentage of ticket price,

© BRUCE WHIPPERMAN

# AIRLINES TO THE ACAPULCO REGION

A number of airlines offer direct flights to Acapulco (AC) or Ixtapa-Zihuatanejo (IX), or Mexico City (MX), where quick air or bus connections with Acapulco and Ixtapa-Zihuatanejo may be made. The airlines with the most flights, in approximate descending order of activity, are **Mexicana, Aeroméxico, American, Delta, Aviacsa, Continental, U.S. Airways (formerly America West), Alaska,** and **Air Canada.** Others offering flights are Azteca, Aerocalifornia, Allegro, and Canadian World of Vacations charter. Some flights may be seasonal (usually winter–spring) only.

| AIRLINE | ORIGIN | DESTINATIONS |
| --- | --- | --- |
| **Mexicana** | Los Angeles | MX |
| tel. 800/531-7921 | San Francisco | MX |
| www.mexicana.com | San Jose | MX |
| | Oakland | MX |
| | Las Vegas | MX |
| | Portland | MX |
| | Tijuana | MX |
| | Denver | MX |
| | San Antonio | MX |
| | Chicago | MX |
| | New York | MX |
| | Miami | MX |
| | Toronto | MX |
| | Montreal | MX |
| **Aeroméxico** | Los Angeles | MX |
| tel. 800/237-6639 | San Diego | MX |
| www.aeromexico.com | Ontario | MX |
| | Seattle | MX |
| | Tucson | MX |
| | Tijuana | MX |
| | Phoenix | MX |
| | San Antonio | MX |
| | Houston | MX |
| | Dallas | MX |
| | Chicago | MX |
| | New York | MX |
| | Atlanta | MX |
| | Orlando | MX |
| | Miami | MX |

| AIRLINE | ORIGIN | DESTINATIONS |
|---|---|---|
| **Delta**<br>tel. 800/221-1212<br>www.delta.com | Los Angeles<br>Dallas<br>Atlanta<br>New York | MX<br>MX<br>MX<br>MX |
| **Aviacsa**<br>tel. 800/967-5263<br>tel. 800/258-0755<br>www.aviacsa.com<br>www.aviacsa-usa.com | Las Vegas<br>Houston<br>Tijuana | MX<br>MX<br>AC |
| **Continental**<br>tel. 800/231-0856<br>www.continental.com | Houston<br>Newark | AC, IX, MX<br>MX |
| **American**<br>tel. 800/433-7300<br>www.aa.com | Dallas<br>Miami<br>Miami | AC, MX<br>MX<br>MX |
| **USAirways**<br>tel. 800/363-2597<br>www.usairways.com | Phoenix | AC, IX, MX |
| **Alaska Airlines**<br>tel. 800/426-0333<br>www.alaskaair.com | Los Angeles<br>San Francisco | IX<br>IX |
| **Air Canada**<br>tel. 888/247-2262<br>www.aircanada.com | Toronto | MX |
| **Aerocalifornia**<br>tel. 800/237-6225<br>www.aerocalifornia.com | Tijuana | MX |

many will nevertheless work hard to get you a bargain, especially if you book an entire air/hotel package with them.

Although few airlines fly directly to the Acapulco region from the northern United States and Canada, many charters do. In locales near Vancouver, Calgary, Ottawa, Toronto, Montreal, Minneapolis, Chicago, Detroit, Cleveland, and New York, consult a travel agent or website for charter flight options. Be aware that charter reservations, which often require fixed departure and return dates and provide minimal cancellation refunds, decrease your flexibility. If available charter choices are unsatisfactory, then you might choose to begin your vacation with a connecting flight to one of the Acapulco-region gateways, such as Seattle, San Francisco, Los Angeles, Phoenix, Dallas, Houston, or Chicago.

You may be able to save money by booking an air/hotel package through one of the airlines that routinely offer them from their Acapulco region gateway cities:

- **Aeroméxico:** tel. 800/245-8585
- **Alaska:** tel. 800/468-2248
- **American:** tel. 800/321-2121
- **America West:** tel. 800/356-6611
- **Continental:** tel. 800/634-5555
- **Delta:** tel. 800/872-7786
- **Mexicana:** tel. 866/380-8741

It's wise to reconfirm both departure and return flight reservations, especially during the busy Christmas and Easter seasons. This is a useful strategy, as is prompt arrival at check-in, against getting "bumped" (losing your seat) by the tendency of airlines to overbook the rush of high-season vacationers. For further protection, always try to get your seat assignment and boarding pass included with your ticket.

Airlines generally try hard to accommodate travelers with dietary or other special needs. When booking your flight, inform your travel agent or carrier of the necessity of a low-sodium, low-cholesterol, vegetarian, or lactose-reduced meal, or other requirements.

## From Europe, Latin America, and Australasia

A few airlines fly across the Atlantic directly to Mexico City. These include **Lufthansa,** which connects directly from Frankfurt, and **Aeroméxico,** which connects directly from Paris and Madrid. In Mexico City, several connections with the Acapulco region are available, mostly via Mexicana and Aeroméxico airlines.

From Latin America, **Aeroméxico** connects directly with Mexico City from São Paulo, Brazil; Santiago, Chile; and Lima, Peru. A number of other Latin American flag carriers also fly directly to Mexico City.

Very few flights cross the Pacific directly to Mexico, except for **Japan Airlines,** which connects Tokyo-Osaka to Mexico City with a fueling stop in Vancouver. More commonly, travelers from Australasia routinely transfer at San Francisco, Los Angeles, or Phoenix for the Acapulco region.

## Baggage

The tropical Acapulco region makes it easy to pack light. Use my packing checklist at the end of this chapter at the last minute to make certain that you're not leaving something important behind. Veteran tropical travelers condense their luggage to carry-ons only. Airlines routinely allow one carry-on (not exceeding 45 inches in combined length, width, and girth), a small book bag, and a purse. Thus relieved of heavy burdens, your trip will become much simpler.

Even if you can't avoid checking luggage, loss of it needn't ruin your vacation. *Always carry your irreplaceable items in the cabin with you.* These should include all money, credit cards, travelers checks, keys, tickets, cameras, passport, prescription drugs, and eyeglasses.

At the X-ray security check, insist that your film and cameras be hand-inspected. Regardless of what attendants claim, repeated X-ray scanning will fog any undeveloped film, especially the sensitive ASA 400, 800, and 1600 high-speed varieties.

## Travel Insurance

Travelers packing lots of expensive baggage, or who (because of illness, for example) may have to cancel a nonrefundable flight or tour, might consider buying travel insurance. Travel agents routinely sell packages that include baggage, trip cancellation, and default insurance. Baggage insurance covers you beyond the airlines' liability limits (typically $1,000 domestic, $500 international, check with your carrier).

Trip cancellation insurance pays if you must cancel your prepaid trip, while default insurance protects you if your carrier or tour agent does not perform as agreed. Travel insurance, however, can be expensive. Traveler's Insurance Company, for example, offers $1,000 of baggage insurance per person for two weeks for about $50. (For more information, see the *Internet Resources* in this book or call a travel agent.) Carefully weigh your options and the cost against benefits before putting your money down.

## BY BUS

As air travel rules in the United States, bus travel rules in Mexico. Hundreds of gleaming luxury- and first-class buses with names such as Elite, Turistar, Futura, Omnibus de Mexico, Primera Plus, Transportes Pacífico, and Estrella Blanca (White Star) depart the border daily, headed for the Acapulco region.

Since North American bus lines ordinarily terminate just north of the Mexican border, you must usually disembark and walk to the Mexican *migración* (immigration) office just across the border. After having completed the necessary but very simple paperwork, proceed to the nearby *sitio taxi* (taxi stand) and hire a taxi (agree upon the price before getting in) to take you the few miles to the *camionera central* (central bus station).

First- and luxury-class bus service in Mexico is much cheaper and more frequent than in the United States. Tickets for comparable trips in Mexico cost a fraction of what you'd pay in the

United States (as little as $75 for a 1,000-mile trip, compared to $150 in the United States).

Nevertheless, in Mexico, as on U.S. buses, you often have to take it as you find it. *Asientos reservados* (seat reservations), *boletos* (tickets), and information must generally be obtained in person at the bus station, and credit cards and travelers checks are not often accepted. Neither are reserved bus tickets typically refundable, so don't miss the bus. On the other hand, plenty of buses roll south almost continually.

## From California and the West

Cross the border to Tijuana, Mexicali, or Nogales, where you can ride one of several bus lines south along the Mexican Pacific coast route (National Highway 15): Estrella Blanca subsidiaries first-class Elite (which connects the whole way to Ixtapa, Zihuatanejo, and Acapulco), deluxe-class Turistar, second-class Transportes Norte de Sonora; or first-class independent Transportes del Pacífico.

At Mazatlán or Tepic, depending on the line, you transfer or continue on the same bus, west via Guadalajara, or south via Puerto Vallarta (the longer but more scenic option). If you choose Guadalajara, you have a pair of options: If your first destination is Zihuatanejo, transfer there to the Estrella Blanca affiliate bus south via Uruapan (in Michocáan) to the coast at Zihuatanejo. If, however, your first destination is Acapulco, take the Estrella Blanca affiliate bus that bypasses Mexico City, via Toluca, thence south via expressway 95D to Acapulco.

If however, you choose to go via Puerto Vallarta, from Tepic, continue south through Manzanillo, along the gorgeously scenic Michoacán coast, to Ixtapa, Zihuatanejo, or Acapulco. Allow a minimum of two full 24-hour days for either option. Carry liquids and food (which might only be minimally available en route) with you.

Instead of doing the trip in one big bite, you might stop overnight or more for a rest in Guadalajara (go to semideluxe Hotel La Serena adjacent to the bus station, tel. 33/3600-0910, fax 33/3600-1974, $45 d) or better, in Puerto

Vallarta (Hotel Rosita on the beach, tel. 322/223-2177, tel./fax 322/223-2000, $45) en route.

## From the U.S. Midwest, South, and East

From the U.S. Midwest, cross the border from El Paso to Ciudad Juárez and ride one of the Estrella Blanca subsidiaries (luxury-class Turistar or Transportes Chihuahuenses) via Chihuahua and Torreón to either Mexico City Norte (North), or preferably, the Mexico City Sur (South) bus terminal.

From the Sur (sometimes known as Taxqueña) terminal, many buses connect directly with Taxco (Futura, Estrella de Oro), Acapulco via Chilpancingo (independent Estrella de Oro, or Estrella Blanca deluxe-class affiliates Turistar or Futura and second-class Transportes Cuauhtémoc), and Zihuatanejo. If you go from the Norte terminal, ride Estrella Blanca affiliates Turistar or Futura, or independent Estrella de Oro to Acapulco, Ixtapa, or Zihuatanejo. For the entire trip, allow at least two full days to Acapulco, a few hours longer for Ixtapa or Zihuatanejo.

From southern and eastern parts of the United States (and alternatively from the Midwest), cross the border at Laredo, Texas, to Nuevo Laredo and ride one of the Estrella Blanca deluxe-class subsidiaries Turistar, Elite, or Futura to the Mexico City Norte (or possibly Sur) terminal. Continue south, exactly as described above. Allow a minimum of a day and a half (36 hours) for the trip to Acapulco.

## BY CAR OR RV

If you're adventurous and like going to out-of-the-way places, but still want to have all the comforts of home, you may enjoy driving your car or RV to the Acapulco region. On the other hand, consideration of cost, risk, wear on both you and your vehicle, and the congestion hassles in towns may change your mind.

### Mexican Car Insurance

Mexico does not recognize foreign insurance. When you drive into Mexico, Mexican auto insurance is at least as important as your passport. At the busier crossings, you can get it at insurance "drive-ins" just north of the border. The many Mexican auto insurance companies are government-regulated; their numbers keep prices and services competitive.

**Sanborn's Mexico Insurance** (Sanborn's Mexico, P.O. Box 310, McAllen, TX 78502, tel. 956/686-3601, toll-free tel. 800/222-0158, www.sanbornsinsurance.com), one of the best-known agencies, certainly seems to be trying hardest. It offers a number of books and services, including the *Recreational Guide to Mexico,* a good road map, "smile-by-mile" *Travelog* guide to "every highway in Mexico," hotel discounts, and more. Much of the above is available to members of Sanborn's Sombrero Club.

Alternatively, look into **Vagabundos del Mar** (tel. 800/474-2252, www.vagabundos .com), an RV-oriented Mexico travel club offering memberships that include a newsletter, caravaning opportunites, discounts, insurance, and much more.

Mexican car insurance runs from a bare-bones rate of about $6 a day for minimal $10,000/$50,000 (property damage/medical payments) coverage to a more typical $12 a day for more complete $20,000/$100,000 coverage. On the same scale, insurance for a $50,000 RV and equipment runs about $30 a day. These daily rates decrease sharply for six-month or one-year policies, which run from about $200 for the minimum to $400–1,600 for complete high-end coverage.

If you get broken glass, personal effects, and legal expenses coverage with these rates, you're lucky. Mexican policies don't usually cover them.

You should get something for your money, however. The deductibles should be no more than $300–500, the public liability per occurrence/medical payments per person/per occurrence should be about double the ($25,000/$25,000/$50,000) legal minimum, and you should be able to get your car fixed in the United States and receive payment in U.S. dollars for losses. If not, shop around.

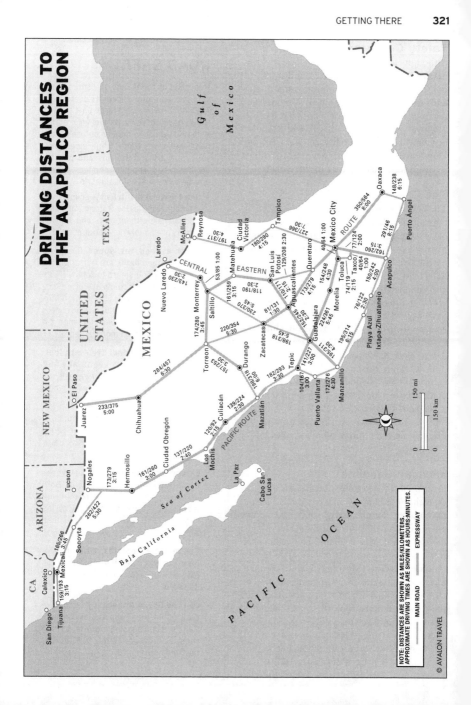

DRIVING DISTANCES TO
THE ACAPULCO REGION

NOTE: DISTANCES ARE SHOWN AS MILES/KILOMETERS.
APPROXIMATE DRIVING TIMES ARE SHOWN AS HOURS:MINUTES.
━━━ MAIN ROAD    ━━━ EXPRESSWAY

© AVALON TRAVEL

## Safety Concerns in Sinaloa

Although *bandidos* no longer menace Mexican roads (but loose burros, horses, and cattle still do), be cautious in the infamous marijuana- and opium-growing region of Sinaloa state north of Mazatlán. It's best not to stray from Highway 15 between Culiacán and Mazatlán or from Highway 40 between Mazatlán and Durango. Curious tourists have been assaulted in the hinterlands adjacent to these roads.

## The Green Angels

The Green Angels have answered many motoring tourists' prayers in Mexico. Bilingual teams of two, trained in auto repair and first aid, help distressed tourists along main highways. They patrol fixed stretches of road at least twice daily by truck. To make sure they stop to help, pull completely off the highway and raise your hood. You may want to hail a passing motorist or trucker with a Mexican cell phone to call the Mexico Tourism–Green Angels hotline, tel. 01-800/903-9200, or all-purpose emergency direct tel. 078, for you.

If, for some reason, you have to leave your vehicle on the roadside, don't leave it unattended. Hire a local teenager or adult to watch it for you. Unattended vehicles on Mexican highways are quickly stricken by a mysterious disease, the symptom of which is rapid loss of vital parts.

## Mexican Gasoline

Pemex, short for Petróleos Mexicanos, the government oil monopoly, markets diesel fuel and two grades of unleaded gasoline: 92-octane *premio* (PRAY-mee-oh) and 87-octane Magna (MAHG-nah). Magna is good gas, yielding performance similar to that of U.S.-style regular unleaded gasoline. (My original car, whose manufacturer recommended 91-octane, ran well on Magna.) On main highways, Pemex makes sure that major stations (typically spaced about 30 miles apart in the countryside) stock Magna.

At this writing, Mexican gas runs about $0.65 per liter, or about $2.50 per gallon. Although this price will most certainly rise, for the foreseeable future, petroleum-rich

## ROAD SAFETY

Hundreds of thousands of visitors enjoy safe Mexican auto vacations every year. Their success is due in large part to their frame of mind: Drive defensively, anticipate and adjust to danger before it happens, and watch everything – side roads, shoulders, the car in front, and cars far down the road. The following tips will help ensure a safe and enjoyable trip.

- **Don't drive at night.** Range animals, unmarked sand piles, pedestrians, one-lane bridges, cars without lights, and drunken drivers are doubly hazardous at night.

- **Don't exceed the speed limit.** Although speed limits are not often enforced, it's still smart to follow them. Mexican country roads are often narrow and shoulderless. Poor markings and macho drivers who pass on curves are best faced at a speed of 40 mph (64 kph) rather than 75 mph (120 kph).

- **Don't drive on sand.** Even with four-wheel-drive, you'll eventually get stuck if you drive often or casually on beaches. When the tide comes in, who'll pull your car out?

- **Slow down** at the *topes* (speed bumps) at the edges of towns and for *vados* (dips), which can be dangerously bumpy and full of water.

- **Extend courtesy of the road.** This goes hand-in-hand with safe driving. Both courtesy and machismo are more infectious in Mexico; on the highway, it's much safer to spread the former than the latter.

- **Use *cuota autopistas*.** When convenient for your destination, these toll expressways allow for maximum speed and safety.

- **Call the Green Angels.** If you do have car trouble, the Green Angels can help. Call (or ask a passing motorist to call) them at emergency tel. 078, during daytime hours.

Mexico will probably enjoy gasoline costing a dollar less per gallon than gas back in the United States.

## Gas Station Thievery

Although the problem has abated considerably in recent years (by the hiring of young female attendants), boys who hang around gas stations to wash windows are notoriously light-fingered. When stopping at the *gasolinera,* make sure that your cameras, purses, and other moveable items are out of reach. Also, make sure that your car has a lockable gas cap. If not, insist on pumping the gas yourself, or be super-watchful as you pull up to the gas pump to make certain that the pump reads zero before the attendant pumps the gas.

## A Healthy Car

Preventive measures spell good health for both you and your car. Get that tune-up (or that long-delayed overhaul) *before,* rather than after, you leave.

Carry a stock of spare parts, which will be more difficult to get and more expensive in Mexico than at home. Carry an extra tire or two, a few quart bottles of motor oil, oil and gas filters, fan belts, spark plugs, tune-up kit, ignition points, and fuses. Be prepared with basic tools and supplies, such as screwdrivers, pliers including Vise-Grip, lug wrench, jack, adjustable wrenches, tire pump, tire pressure gauge, steel wire, and electrical tape. For breakdowns and emergencies, carry a folding shovel, a husky rope or chain, a gasoline can, and flares or red highway markers.

## Car Repairs in Mexico

The American big three—General Motors, Ford, and Chrysler—as well as Nissan and Volkswagen are represented by extensive dealer networks in Mexico. Latecomers Toyota and Honda are also represented, although to a lesser extent. Getting your car or truck serviced at such agencies is straightforward. While parts will probably be higher in price, shop rates run about one-third to one-half U.S. prices, so repairs will generally come out cheaper than back home.

© BRUCE WHIPPERMAN

Competent tire repair shops (*llantera* or *vulcanizadora*) are common everywhere in Mexico.

The same may not be true for repairing other makes, however. Mexico has few, if any, other car or truck dealers; consequently, officially certified mechanics for other Japanese, British, and European makes are hard to find.

Nevertheless, many ingenious Mexican independent mechanics can fix any car that comes their way. Their humble *talleres mecánicos* (tah-YER-ays may-KAH-nee-kohs) dot town and village roadsides everywhere.

Although the great majority of Mexican mechanics are honest, beware of unscrupulous operators who try to collect double or triple their original estimate. If you don't speak Spanish, find someone who can assist you in negotiations. *Always* get a cost estimate, including needed parts and labor, in writing, even if you have to write it yourself. Make sure the mechanic understands, then ask him to sign it before he starts work. Although this may be a hassle, it might save you a much nastier hassle later. Shop labor at small, independent repair shops should run $10–20 per hour. For much more information, and for entertaining anecdotes of car and RV travel in Mexico, consult Carl Franz's *The People's Guide to Mexico*.

### Bribes (*Mordidas*)

The usual meeting ground of the visitor and Mexican police is in the visitor's car on a highway or downtown street. To the tourists, such an encounter may seem mild harassment by the police, accompanied by vague threats of going to the police station or impounding the car for such-and-such a violation. The tourist often goes on to say, "It was all right, though . . . we paid him $20 and he went away. . . . Mexican cops sure are crooked, aren't they?"

And, I suppose, if people want to go bribing their way through Mexico, that's their business. But calling Mexican cops crooked isn't exactly fair. Police, like most everyone else in Mexico, have to scratch for a living, and they have found that many tourists are willing to slip them a $20 bill for nothing. Rather than crooked, I would call them hungry and opportunistic.

Instead of paying a bribe, do what I've done a dozen times: Remain cool, and if you're really

## MEXICO CITY DRIVING RESTRICTIONS

To reduce smog and traffic gridlock, authorities have limited which cars can drive on which days in Mexico City, depending upon the last digit of their license plates. If you violate these rules, you risk getting an expensive ticket. On Monday, no vehicle may be driven with final digits 5 or 6; Tuesday, 7 or 8; Wednesday, 3 or 4; Thursday, 1 or 2; Friday, 9 or 0. Weekends, all vehicles may be driven.

guilty of an infraction, calmly say, "Ticket, please." (*"Boleto, por favor"*). After a minute or two of stalling, and no cash appearing, the officer most likely will not bother with a ticket, but will wave you on with only a warning. If, on the other hand, the officer does write you a ticket, he will probably keep your driver's license, which you will be able to retrieve at the *presidencia municipal* (city hall) the next day in exchange for paying your fine.

### Crossing the Border

Squeezing through the border-traffic bottlenecks during peak holidays and rush hours can easily take two or three hours. Avoid crossing 7–9 A.M. and 4:30–6:30 P.M. Moreover, with latter-day increased U.S. homeland security precautions, the northbound return border crossing, under the best of conditions, generally takes at least an hour waiting in your car, along with a hundred or more other frustrated drivers. (Note: Do not cross the border into Mexico without a **valid passport** for everyone in your party. U.S. border authorities will probably not let you return without them.)

### Highway Routes from the United States

If you decide to drive to the Acapulco region, you have your choice of three general routes. Maximize comfort and safety by following the broad *cuota* expressways that often parallel the old narrow *libre* routes. Despite the increased cost (about $150 total to Acapulco for a car, double or triple that for a motorhome) the *cuota* expressways will save you at least two days (including the extra food and hotel tariffs) and wear and tear on both your vehicle and your nerves. Most folks in passenger cars should allow at least three (more likely four or five, depending on the route) full south-of-the-border driving days to Acapulco, Ixtapa, or Zihuatanejo. Larger RVs and motorhomes should allow at least a day or two more.

## PACIFIC ROUTE

From the U.S. Pacific Coast and West, follow National Highway 15 (called 15D as the toll expressway) from the border at Nogales, Sonora, an easy hour's drive south via Interstate 19 from Tucson, Arizona. **California drivers,** unless you have some special reason for doing so, do not cross the border farther west at Tijuana or Mexicali; access by U.S. Interstate Highways 8 and/or 10 to Nogales via Tucson is half a day quicker than the corresponding two-lane south-of-the-border route.

From Nogales, Highway 15D continues southward smoothly, leading you through cactus-studded mountains and valleys that turn into lush farmland and tropical coastal plain and forest by the time you arrive at Mazatlán. Watch for the peripheral bypasses (*periféricos*) and truck routes that guide you past the congested downtowns of Hermosillo, Guaymas, Ciudad Obregón, Los Mochis, and Culiacán. Between these centers, you speed along, via the *cuota* expressway, all the way to Mazatlán. If you prefer not to pay the high tolls (about $60 Nogales–Mazatlán for a car, much more for motorhome), stick to the old *libre* highway. Hazards, bumps, and slow going might force you to reconsider, however.

From Mazatlán, continue along the narrow two-lane route (soon to be replaced by a toll expressway) to Tepic. There, you can either fork left (east) along Highway 15D east to Guadalajara, or fork right (south) along Highway 200 to Puerto Vallarta.

If you opt for the Guadalajara route, continue east past Tepic along the easy *cuota autopista* 15D to Guadalajara. There, you link eastward, via crosstown expressway (watch for signs) Avenida Lázaro Cárdenas to Mexico City–bound expressway 15D on the east side of town. Continue east on 15D past Morelia to Toluca, where you *do not continue ahead for Mexico City.* Instead connect, winding through the southeast side of town, with Highway 55 (Boulevard José M. Pino Suárez to Metepec) that, after continuing several miles southeast, connects directly with southbound *cuota autopista* 55D to spa resort Ixtapan del Sal. Continue south on Highway 55 and connect directly with either old Highway 95 to Taxco and Iguala, or expressway 95D south, via Chilpancingo, to Acapulco (total about 1,700 miles, 2,730 km, minimum 36 hours at the wheel to Acapulco, 40 hours to Ixtapa or Zihuatanejo).

Although slower, the Puerto Vallarta route to the Acapulco region is more scenic and easier to follow. From Tepic, simply continue south, via two-lane Highway 200, through the palmy coastal resorts of Puerto Vallarta, Manzanillo, and the spectacularly scenic Michoacán coast, to Ixtapa, Zihuatanejo, and Acapulco (total about 1,600 miles, 2,580 km, minimum 40 hours at the wheel to Acapulco, 36 hours to Zihuatanejo).

Although choosing between the Puerto Vallarta and Guadalajara options appears to be a toss-up, the Guadalajara route, via expressway nearly all the way, allows for safer driving more hours per day. In effect, this might amount to as little as four days of south-of-the border traveling, in comparison to about five or six days via Puerto Vallarta. However, the extra day or two required by the Puerto Vallarta option might be well worth the scenery and the opportunity to stop in beautiful oceanfront spots along the way. But never mind, you can have it both ways: go one way coming and the other way going.

## CENTRAL-EASTERN ROUTE

From the U.S. Midwest, South, and East, a number of routes are possible. Probably fastest and most direct is the route via the southern Texas Laredo–Nuevo Laredo border crossing. Continue south via *cuota autopistas* 85D, 40D, and 57D to Mexico City, thence to Acapulco via *cuota autopista* 95D. Along the way, keep an eye out for the Mexico (meaning Mexico City) signs that mark suburban bypasses (commonly labeled *libramiento* or *periférico*): before Monterrey (*periférico* Highway 40 or 40D); before Saltillo (*libramiento* Highway 57 or 57D); before San Luis Potosí (Highway 57 or 57D); and before Querétaro (Highway 57D).

At the Mexico City northern outskirt, bypass the congested Mexico City downtown the same way by following the right fork Cuernavaca- or Acapulco-direction *periférico*; after several miles also fork right along Boulevard Avila Camacho *periférico,* until finally you see the sign for *cuota* Cuernavaca/Acapulco Highway 95D. From there, you can breeze all the way to Acapulco either direct or via the smooth, wide, and scenic two-lane Taxco–Iguala Highway 95 toll cutoff.

Also, make sure that you're not in Mexico City on your forbidden day, determined by the last digit of your car's license plate (see sidebar "Mexico City Driving Restrictions").

# BY TOUR, CRUISE, AND SAILBOAT

For travelers on a tight time budget, prearranged tour packages can provide a hassle-free route for sampling the attractions of Acapulco-region coastal resorts and upcountry towns and cities. If, however, you prefer a self-paced vacation, or desire thrift over convenience, you should probably defer tour arrangements until after arrival. Many Acapulco-region travel and tour agencies are as close as your hotel telephone or front-lobby tour desk and can customize a tour for you. Options vary from city highlight tours and bay snorkeling adventures to shopping in inland colonial cities and sightseeing overnights to boat adventures through wildlife-rich mangrove jungle hinterlands.

## By Cruise or Sailboat

Travel agents and websites advertise many cruises that include Acapulco and/or Ixtapa and Zihuatanejo on their itineraries. Vacationers who enjoy being pampered with lots of food and ready-made entertainment (and who don't mind paying for it) can have great fun on cruises. Accommodations on a typical 10-day winter tour or cruise (which would include several days in Ixtapa and Zihuatanejo and/or Acapulco) can run as little as $100 per day per person, double occupancy, to as much as $1,000 or more.

If, however, you want to get to know Mexico and the local people, a cruise is not for you. Included lodging, food, and entertainment are the main events of a cruise; guided shore sightseeing excursions, which generally cost plenty extra, are a sideshow.

Sailboats, on the other hand, offer an entirely different kind of sea route to the Acapulco region. **Ocean Voyages** (1709 Bridgeway, Sausalito, CA 94965, tel. 415/332-4681 or 800/299-4444, fax 415/332-7460, sail@ocean voyages.com, www.oceanvoyages.com), a California-based agency, arranges passage on a number of sail and motor vessels that regularly depart to Ixtapa, Zihuatanejo, and Acapulco from ports such as San Diego, Los Angeles, San Francisco, Seattle, and Vancouver, British Columbia. It offers customized itineraries and flexible arrangements that can vary from complete round-trip voyages to weeklong coastal idylls between Acapulco-region ports of call. Some captains allow passengers to save money by signing on as crew.

# Getting Around

## BY BUS

The bus is the king of the Mexican road. Dozens of lines connect virtually every town in the Acapulco region. Three distinct levels of service—deluxe, first-class, and second-class—are generally available. **Deluxe-class** (called Turistar, Futura, Diamante, and Primera Plus, depending upon the line) express coaches speed between major towns, seldom stopping en route. In exchange for relatively high fares (about $40 Acapulco–Zihuatanejo or $50 Acapulco–Taxco, for example), passengers often enjoy rapid passage and airline-style amenities: plush reclining seats, air-conditioning, an on-board toilet, video, and aisle attendant.

Although less luxurious, for about two-thirds the price **first-class** service is frequent and always includes reserved seating. Additionally, passengers enjoy soft reclining seats and air-conditioning (if it is working).

Besides their regular stops at or near most towns and villages en route, first-class bus drivers, if requested, will usually stop and let you off anywhere along the road.

**Second-class** bus seating is unreserved. In outlying parts of the Acapulco region, there is even a class of bus beneath second-class, but given the condition of many second-class buses, it seems as if third-class buses wouldn't run at all. Such buses are the stuff of travelers' legends: the recycled old GMC, Ford, and Dodge schoolbuses that stop everywhere and carry everyone and everything to even the smallest villages tucked away in the far mountains. As long as there is any kind of a road, the bus will most likely go there.

Now and then you'll read a newspaper story of a country bus that went over a cliff somewhere in Mexico, killing the driver and a dozen unfortunate souls. The same newspapers, however, never bother to mention the

© BRUCE WHIPPERMAN

If there's a road to it, there's usually a second-class bus that goes there.

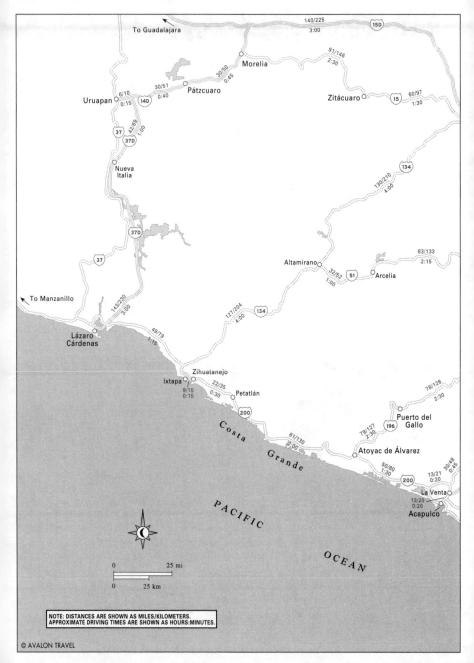

To Guadalajara

140/225
3:00

15D

Morelia

91/146
2:30

30/50
0:45

Pátzcuaro

Zitácuaro

15

60/97
1:30

Uruapan

6/10
0:15

30/51
0:40

14D

37
37D

42/69
1:00

134

Nueva
Italia

37D

37

130/210
4:00

Altamirano

32/52
1:00

51

Arcelia

83/133
2:15

To Manzanillo

143/230
3:00

127/204
4:00

134

Lázaro
Cárdenas

49/79
1:15

Ixtapa

Zihuatanejo

22/35
0:30

9/15
0:15

Petatlán

200

78/126
2:30

Puerto del
Gallo

196

79/127
2:30

Atoyac de Álvarez

81/130
2:00

Costa

Grande

50/80
1:30

200

30/48
0:45

13/21
0:20

La Venta

13/20
0:20

Acapulco

PACIFIC

OCEAN

0        25 mi
0        25 km

NOTE: DISTANCES ARE SHOWN AS MILES/KILOMETERS.
APPROXIMATE DRIVING TIMES ARE SHOWN AS HOURS:MINUTES.

© AVALON TRAVEL

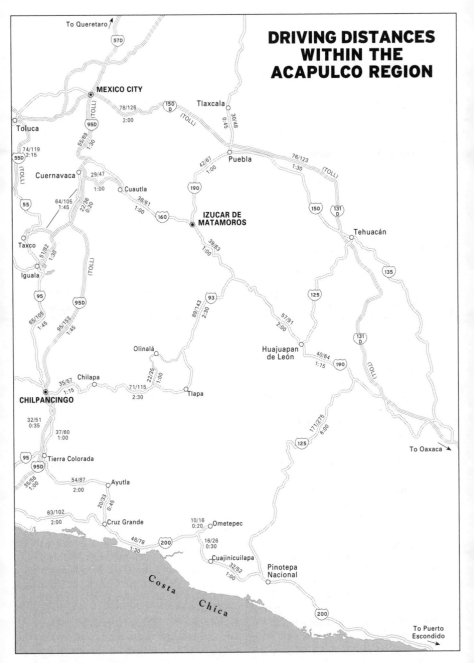

# DRIVING DISTANCES WITHIN THE ACAPULCO REGION

half-million safe passengers for whom the same bus provided trips during its 15 years of service before the accident.

Second-class buses are not for travelers with weak knees or stomachs. Often, you will initially have to stand, cramped in the aisle, in a crowd of campesinos. They are warm-hearted but poor people, so don't tempt them with open, dangling purses or wallets bulging in back pockets. Stow your money safely away. After a while, you will be able to sit down. Such privilege, however, comes with obligation, such as holding an old woman's bulging bag of carrots or a toddler on your lap. But if you accept your burden with humor and equanimity, who knows what favors and blessings may flow to you in return.

## Tickets, Seating, and Baggage

Mexican bus lines do not usually publish schedules or fares. You have to ask someone who knows (such as your hotel desk clerk), or call the bus station. Only a sprinkling of travel agents bother handling bus tickets. If you don't want to spend the time to get a reserved ticket yourself, hire someone trustworthy to do it for you. Another option is to get to the bus station early enough on your traveling day to ensure that you'll get a bus to your destination.

Although most luxury and first-class lines accept credit cards and issue computer-printed tickets at their major stations, a sizable fraction of reserved bus tickets are sold for cash and are handwritten, including an assigned *número de asiento* (specific seat number). If you miss the bus, you lose your money. Furthermore, airlines-style automated reservations systems have not yet arrived at minor Mexican bus stations. Consequently, you can generally buy reserved tickets only at the *salida local* (local departure) station. (An agent in Iguala, for example, may not be able to reserve you a ticket on a bus that originates in Acapulco, 100 miles to the south.)

Request a reserved seat, if possible, with numbers 1–25 in the *delante* (front) to *medio* (middle) of the bus. The rear seats are often occupied by smokers, drunks, and rowdies. At night, you will sleep better on the *lado derecho* (right side), away from the glare of oncoming traffic lights.

Baggage is generally secure on Mexican buses. Label it, however. Overhead racks are generally too cramped to accommodate airline-sized carry-ons. Carry a small bag with your money and irreplaceables on your person; pack clothes and less-essentials in your checked luggage. For peace of mind, watch the handler put your checked baggage on the bus and watch to make sure it is not mistakenly taken off the bus at intermediate stops.

If your baggage gets misplaced, remain calm. Bus employees are generally competent and conscientious. If you are patient, recovering your luggage will become a matter of honor for many of them. Baggage handlers are at the bottom of the pay scale; a tip for their mostly thankless job is very much appreciated.

On long trips, carry food, beverages, and toilet paper. Station food may be dubious, and the sanitary facilities may be ill-maintained.

If you are waiting for a first-class bus at an intermediate *salida de paso* (passing departure), you have to trust to luck that there will be an empty seat. If not, your best option may be to ride a more frequent second-class bus.

## BY CAR OR RV
### Rental Car

Car and Jeep rentals are an increasingly popular transportation option for Acapulco-region travelers. They offer mobility and independence for local sightseeing and beach excursions. In the resorts, most of the gang's there: Hertz, Avis, Alamo, and Budget, plus several local outfits. They generally require drivers to have a valid driver's license, passport, a major credit card, and may require a minimum age of 25. Some local companies do not accept credit cards, but offer lower rates in return.

Base prices of international agencies such as Hertz and Avis are not cheap. With a 17 percent value-added tax and mandatory insurance, rentals run more than in the United States. The cheapest possible rental car, usually a used, stick-shift VW Beetle, or better, Nissan Tsuru, runs $35–60 per day or $220–400 per week, depending on location and season. Prices are highest and availability lowest during

© BRUCE WHIPPERMAN

The Acapulco-Mexico City expressway crosses over the Río Papagayo via an unusual solid, triangular, concrete truss bridge.

Christmas and pre-Easter weeks. Before departure, use the international agencies' toll-free numbers and websites for availability, prices, and reservations. During nonpeak seasons, you may save lots of pesos by waiting until arrival and renting a car through a local agency. Shop around, starting with the agent in your hotel lobby or with the local Yellow Pages (under *"Automoviles, renta de"*).

Car insurance that covers property damage, public liability, and medical payments is a legal requirement with your rental car. If you get into an accident without insurance, you will be in deep trouble, and probably sent to jail. Narrow, rough roads and animals grazing at roadside make driving in Mexico more hazardous than back home. (For important car safety and insurance information, see *By Car or RV* under *Getting There* earlier in this chapter.)

## BY TAXI, LOCAL TOUR, AND HITCHHIKING
### Taxis

The high prices of rental cars make taxis a viable option for local excursions. Cars are luxuries, not necessities, for most Mexican families. Travelers might profit from the Mexican money-saving practice of piling everyone in a taxi for a Sunday outing. You may find that an all-day taxi and driver, who, besides relieving you of driving, will become your impromptu guide, will cost no more than a rental car.

The magic word for saving money by taxi is *colectivo:* a taxi you share with other travelers. The first place you'll practice getting a taxi will be at either the Acapulco or Ixtapa-Zihuatanejo airport, where *colectivo* tickets are routinely sold from booths at the terminal door.

If, however, you want your own private taxi, ask for a *taxi especial,* which will run about three or four times the per-person tariff for a *colectivo.*

Your airport experience will prepare you for in-town taxis, which I've never seen with a meter anywhere in the Acapulco region. You must establish the price before getting in. Bargaining comes with the territory in Mexico, so don't shrink from it, even though it seems a hassle. If you get into a taxi without an agreed-upon price, you are letting yourself in for a more serious and potentially nasty hassle later. If your driver's price is too high, he'll probably come to his senses as soon as you hail another taxi.

After a few days, getting taxis around town will be a cinch. You'll find that you don't have to take the more expensive taxis lined up in your hotel driveway. If the price isn't right, walk toward the street and hail a regular taxi.

In town, if you can't find a taxi, it may be because taxis are waiting for riders at the local stand, called a taxi *sitio*. Ask someone to direct you to it: *"Disculpe. ¿Dónde está el sitio taxi, por favor?"* ("Excuse me. Where is the taxi stand, please?").

## Local Tours and Guides

For many Acapulco-region travelers, locally arranged tours offer a hassle-free alternative to sightseeing by rental car or taxi. Hotels and travel agencies, many of whom maintain front-lobby travel and tour desks, offer a bounty of sightseeing, water sports, bay cruise, fishing, and wildlife-viewing tour opportunities. See the destination chapters for recommendations.

## Hitchhiking

Most everyone agrees hitchhiking is not the safest mode of transport. If you're unsure, don't do it. Hitchhiking doesn't make for a healthy steady travel diet, nor should you hitchhike at night.

The recipe for trouble-free hitchhiking requires equal measures of luck, savvy, and technique. The best places to catch rides are where people are arriving and leaving anyway, such as bus stops, highway intersections, gas stations, and on the highway out of town.

Male/female hitchhiking partnerships seem to net the most rides (although it is technically illegal for women to ride in commercial trucks). The more gear you and your partner have, the fewer rides you will get. Pickup and flatbed truck owners often pick up passengers for pay. Before hopping onto the truck bed, ask how much the ride will cost.

# Visas and Officialdom

The Mexican government welcomes visitors into their country. Certain rules do apply, however. If you require more information than the guidelines presented here, you can contact the Mexico Tourism Board hotline at toll-free U.S./Can. tel. 800/44-MEXICO (800/446-3942) or visit www.visitmexico.com. For more detailed help, you can contact either your closest office of the Mexico Tourism Board (see the sidebar "Mexico Tourism Board Offices") or contact one of the many North American Mexico consulates or embassies (for a list of them, visit www.mexonline.com/consulate.htm).

## PASSPORTS, TOURIST CARDS, AND VISAS
### Your Passport

Your passport (or birth or naturalization certificate) is your positive proof of national identity; without it, your status in any foreign country is in doubt. Don't leave home without one. In fact, U.S. Immigration rules require that all **U.S. citizens must have a valid passport in order to reenter the United States.** U.S. citizens may apply for passports (allow four to six weeks) at local post offices. For-fee private passport agencies can speed this process and get you a passport within a week, maybe less.

## Entry into Mexico

For U.S. and Canadian citizens, entry by air into Mexico for a few weeks could hardly be easier. Airline attendants hand out tourist cards (*tarjetas turísticas*) en route and officers make them official by glancing at passports and stamping the cards at the immigration gate. Business travel permits for 30 days or fewer are handled by the same simple procedures.

Mexican immigration rules require that all entering U.S. citizens 15 years old or over must present proper identification—either a valid U.S. passport, original (or notarized copy) of your birth certificate, military ID, or state driver's license, while naturalized U.S. citizens must show naturalization papers (or a laminated naturalization card) or valid U.S. passport.

Canadian citizens must show a valid passport or original birth certificate. Nationals of other countries (especially those such as Hong Kong, which issues more than one type of passport) may be subject to different or additional regulations. For advice, consult your regional Mexico Tourism Board Office (see sidebar "Mexico Tourism Board Offices") or local Mexican consulate. Very complete and up-to-date Mexico visa and entry information for nationals of virtually all of the world's countries is available at the Toronto, Canada, Consulate website, www.consulmex.com.

For more complicated cases, get your tourist card early enough to allow you to consider the options. Tourist cards can be issued for multiple entries and a maximum validity of 180 days; photos are often required. If you don't request multiple entry or the maximum time, your card will probably be stamped single entry, valid for some shorter period, such as 90 days. If you are not sure how long you'll stay in Mexico, request the maximum (180 days is the absolute maximum for a tourist card; long-term foreign residents routinely make semiannual "border runs" for new tourist cards).

**Don't lose your tourist card.** If you do, be prepared with a copy of the original, which you should present to the nearest federal Migración (Immigration) office (on duty in Acapulco and Zihuatanejo, both in town and at the airports) and ask for a duplicate tourist permit. Be prepared with some dated evidence of arrival, such as a stamped passport or airline ticket. Savvy travelers carry copies of their tourist cards, while leaving the original safe in their hotel rooms.

## Student and Business Visas
A visa is a notation stamped and signed on your passport showing the number of days

and entries allowable for your trip. Apply for a student visa at the consulate nearest your home well in advance of your departure; the same is true if you require a business visa of longer than 30 days. One-year renewable student visas are available (sometimes with considerable red tape). An ordinary 180-day tourist card may be the easiest option, if you can manage it.

## Entry for Children
Children under 15 can be included on their parents' tourist cards, but complications occur if the children (by reason of illness, for example) cannot leave Mexico with both parents. Parents can avoid such red tape by getting a passport and a Mexican tourist card for each of their children.

Acapulco travelers should hurdle all such possible delays far ahead of time in the cool calm of their local Mexican consulate rather than the hot, hurried atmosphere of a border or airport immigration station.

## Entry for Pets
A pile of red tape may delay the entry of dogs, cats, and other pets into Mexico. Be prepared with veterinary-stamped health and rabies certificates for each animal. For more information, contact your regional Mexico Tourism Board, or your local Mexican Consulate.

## Car Permits
If you drive to Mexico, you will need a permit for your car. Upon entry into Mexico, be ready with originals and copies of your proof-of-ownership or registration papers (state title certificate, registration, or notarized bill of sale), current license plates, and current driver's license. The auto permit fee runs about $30, payable only by non-Mexican-bank MasterCard, Visa, or American Express credit cards. (The credit-card-only requirement discourages those who sell or abandon U.S.-registered cars in Mexico without paying customs duties.) Credit cards must bear the same name as the vehicle proof-of-ownership papers.

The resulting car permit becomes part of the owner's tourist card and receives the same length of validity. Vehicles registered in the name of an organization or person other than the driver must be accompanied by a notarized affidavit authorizing the driver to use the car in Mexico for a specific time.

Border officials generally allow you to carry or tow additional motorized vehicles (motorcycle, another car, large boat) into Mexico but will probably require separate documentation and fee for each vehicle. If a Mexican official desires to inspect your trailer or RV, go through it with him.

Accessories, such as a small trailer, boat shorter than six feet, CB radio, or outboard motor, may be noted on the car permit and must leave Mexico with the car.

For more details on motor vehicle entry and what you may bring in your baggage to Mexico, you might also consult the AAA (American Automobile Association) *Mexico TravelBook;* see the "Unique Guide and Tip Books" section in *Suggested Reading* at the end of this book.

Since Mexico does not recognize foreign automobile insurance, you must buy Mexican

## MEXICO TOURISM BOARD OFFICES

More than a dozen Mexico Tourism Board (Consejo de Promoción Turístico de Mexico, CPTM) offices and scores of Mexican government consulates operate in the United States, Canada, Europe, South America, and Asia. Consulates generally handle questions of Mexican nationals abroad, while Mexico Tourism Boards serve travelers heading for Mexico.

For straightforward questions and Mexico regional information brochures, contact the Tourism Board (U.S./Can. tel. 800/446-3942, Europe tel. 00-800/111-2266, www.visit mexico.com). If you need more details and read a bit of Spanish, you might also find www .cptm.com.mx helpful. Otherwise, contact one of the North American, European, South American, or Asian Mexico Tourism Boards directly for guidance.

### IN NORTH AMERICA
From Alaska, Arizona, California, Colorado, Hawaii, Idaho, Montana, Nevada, Utah, Washington, and Wyoming, contact the **Los Angeles** office (1880 Century Park East, Suite 511, Los Angeles, CA 90067, tel. 310/282-9112, fax 310/282-9116, losangeles@visitmexico.com).

From Alberta, British Columbia, Alberta, Saskatchewan and the Yukon and Northwest Territories, contact the **Vancouver** office (999 W. Hastings St., Suite 1110, Vancouver, B.C. V6C 2W2, tel. 604/669-2845, fax 604/669-3498, mgto@telus.net).

From Arkansas, Colorado, Louisiana, New Mexico, Oklahoma, and Texas, contact the **Houston** office (4507 San Jacinto, Suite 308, Houston TX 77004, tel. 713/772-2581, fax 713/772-6058, houston@visitmexico.com).

From Alabama, Florida, Georgia, Mississippi, Tennessee, North Carolina, Puerto Rico, and South Carolina, contact the **Miami** office (5975 Sunset Dr. #305, Miami, FL 33143, tel. 786/621-2909, fax 786/621-2907, miami@visitmexico.com).

From Illinois, Indiana, Iowa, Kansas, Kentucky, Michigan, Minnesota, Missouri, Nebraska, North Dakota, Ohio, South Dakota, and Wisconsin, contact the **Chicago** office (225 North Michigan Ave., 18th Floor, Suite 1850, Chicago, IL 60601, tel. 312/228-0517, fax 312/228-0515, chicago@visitmexico.com).

From Connecticut, Delaware, Kentucky, Maine, Maryland, Massachusetts, New Hampshire, New Jersey, New York, Pennsylvania, Rhode Island, Vermont, Virginia, Washington D.C., and West Virginia, contact the **New York** office (400 Madison Ave., Suite 11C, New York, NY 10017, tel. 212/308-2110, fax 212/308-9060, newyork@visitmexico.com).

From Ontario, Manitoba, and the Nunavut Territory, contact the **Toronto** office (2 Bloor St. West, Suite 1502, Toronto, Ontario M4W 3E2, tel. 416/925-0704, fax 416/925-6061, toronto@visitmexico.com).

automobile insurance. (For more information on this and other details of driving in Mexico, see the *Getting There* section earlier in this chapter.)

## Crossing the Border and Returning Home

Squeezing through border bottlenecks during peak holidays and rush hours can be time-consuming. Avoid crossing 7–9 A.M. and 4:30–6:30 P.M.

Just before returning across the border with your car, park and have a customs (*aduana*) official *remove and cancel the holographic identity sticker that you received on entry*. If possible, get a receipt (*recibo*) or some kind of verification that it's been canceled (*cancelado*). Tourists have been fined hundreds of dollars for inadvertently carrying uncanceled car entry stickers on their windshields.

At the same time, return all other Mexican permits, such as tourist cards and hunting and fishing licenses. Also, be prepared for Mexico exit inspection, especially for cultural

---

From New Brunswick, Newfoundland, Nova Scotia, Prince Edward Island, and Quebec, contact the **Montreal** office (1 Place Ville Marie, Suite 1931, Montreal, Quebec H3B2C3, tel. 514/871-1052 or 514/871-1103, fax 514/871-3825, montreal@visitmexico.com).

### IN EUROPE

In Europe, travelers may either contact the all-Europe Mexico tourism information (tel. 00-800/111-2266, www.visitmexico.com) or contact the local offices directly:

**London:** Wakefield House, 41 Trinity Square, London EC3N 4DJ, England, UK, tel. 207/488-9392, fax 207/265-0704, uk@visitmexico.com.

**Frankfurt:** Taunusanlage 21, D-60325 Frankfurt-am-Main, Deutschland, tel. 697/103-3383, fax 697/103-3755, germany@visitmexico.com.

**Paris:** 4 Rue Notre-Dame des Victoires, 75002 Paris, France, tel. 1/428-69612 or 1/428-69613, fax 1/428-60580, france@visitmexico.com.

**Madrid:** Calle Velázquez 126, 28006 Madrid, España, tel. 91/561-3520 or 91/561-1827, fax 91/411-0759, spain@visitmexico.com.

**Rome:** Via Barbarini 3-piso 7, 00187 Roma, Italia, tel. 06/487-4698, fax 06/487-3630 or 06/420-4293, italy@visitmexico.com.

### IN SOUTH AMERICA

Contact the Mexico Tourism Board in either Brazil, Argentina, or Chile:

**Sao Paulo:** Alameda Administrativo, Rocha Azevedo 882, Conjunto 31, Tercer Andador, São Paulo, Brazil, 01410-002, tel. 3088-2129, fax 3083-5005, brasil@visitmexico.com.

**Buenos Aires:** Avenida Santa Fe 920, 1054 Capital Federal, Argentina, tel. 1/4393-7070, 1/4393-8235, fax 1/4393-6607, argentina@visitmexico.com.

**Santiago:** Felix de Amesti #128, primer piso, Los Condes, Santiago de Chile, tel. 562/583-8426, fax 562/583-8425, chile@visitmexico.com.

### IN ASIA

Contact the Mexico Tourism Board in either Japan or China:

**Tokyo:** 2-15-1-3F, Nagata-Cho, 2-chome, Chiyoda-ku, Tokyo, Japan 100-0014, tel. 335/030-290, fax 335/030-643, japan@visitmexico.com.

**Beijing:** San Li Dongwajie 5, Chaoyang 100600, Beijing, People's Republic of China, tel./fax 106/532-1717 or 106/532-1744, jamezcua@visitmexico.com.

artifacts and works of art, which may require exit permits. Certain religious and pre-Columbian artifacts, legally the property of the Mexican government, cannot be taken from the country.

If you entered Mexico with your car, you cannot legally leave without it, except by permission from local customs authorities, usually the Aduana (Customs House) or the Oficina Federal de Hacienda (Federal Treasury Office).

All returnees are subject to U.S. immigration and customs inspection. These inspections have become generally more time-consuming since September 11, 2001. The worst bottlenecks are at busy border crossings, especially Tijuana and to a lesser extent Mexicali, Nogales, Juárez, Nuevo Laredo, and Matamoros, all of which should be avoided during peak hours.

U.s. law allows a fixed value ($400 at present) of duty-free goods per returnee. This may include no more than one liter of alcoholic spirits, 200 cigarettes, and 100 cigars. A flat 10 percent duty will be applied to the first $1,000 (fair retail value, save your receipts) in excess of your $400 exemption. You may, however, mail packages (up to $100 value each) of gifts duty-free to friends and relatives in the United States. Make sure to clearly write "unsolicited gift" and a list of the value and contents on the outside of the package. Perfumes (over $5), alcoholic beverages, and tobacco may not be included in such packages.

Improve the security of such mailed packages by sending them by Mexpost class, similar to U.S. Express Mail service. Even better (but much more expensive), send them by Federal Express or DHL international couriers, which maintain offices in Acapulco, Ixtapa-Zihuatanejo, Chilpancingo, Iguala, Taxco, and other larger Acapulco region towns.

## U.S. Government Customs and Wildlife Information

For more information on U.S. customs regulations important to travelers abroad, read or download the useful pamphlet *Know Before You Go,* by visiting the U.S. Customs and Border Patrol website, www.cpb.gov. Click on "travel" at the top of the home page, then scroll down to *Know Before You Go.*

For more information on the importation of endangered wildlife products, contact the Fish and Wildlife Service (1849 C St. NW, Washington, DC 20240, toll-free tel. 800/344-9453, www.fws.gov).

# Recreation

## BEACHES

Their soft sand, gentle waves, and south-seas ambience have made the golden shores of Acapulco, Ixtapa, and Zihuatanejo a magnet for a generation of seekers of paradise. And while those brilliant strands are justly renowned, travelers are increasingly discovering the many small beach hideaways, such as Pie de la Cuesta, Troncones, Barra de Potosí, Playa Escondida, El Carrizal, Playa Ventura, and Playa Las Peñitas, that beckon beyond the famous resorts.

Other travelers take adventure a step further and set up camp to enjoy the solitude and the rich wildlife of even more pristine shorelines. They explore beaches that vary from pristine driftwood-strewn barrier dunes and wildlife-rich jungle lagoons to foamy tidepools and sand of seemingly innumerable colors and consistencies.

Sand makes the beach—and the Acapulco region has plenty—from warm golden quartz to cool, velvety white coral. Some beaches drop steeply to turbulent, close-in surf, fine for fishing. Others are level, with gentle, rolling breakers, made for surfing and swimming.

Beaches are fascinating for the surprises they yield. The Acapulco region's beaches, especially the hidden strands near resorts and the dozens of miles of wilderness beaches and tidepools, yield troves of shells and treasures of flotsam and jetsam for those who enjoy looking for them. Beachcombing is more rewarding during the summer–fall storm season, when big waves deposit acres of fresh shells—among them conch, scallop, clams, combs of Venus, whelks, limpets, olives, cowries, starfish, and sand dollars.

During the summer rainy season, beaches near river mouths are often fantastic outdoor galleries of wind- and water-sculpted snags and giant logs deposited by the downstream flood.

### Viewing Wildlife

Wildlife-watchers should keep quiet and always be on the alert. Animal survival depends on their seeing you first. Occasional spectacular offshore sights, such as whales, porpoises, and manta rays, or an onshore giant constrictor, beached giant squid or Pacific octopus, crocodile, or even a jaguar looking for turtle eggs are the reward of those prepared to recognize them. Don't forget your binoculars and Steve Howell's *Bird-Finding Guide to Mexico*.

## WATER SPORTS

Swimming, surfing, sailboarding, snorkeling, scuba diving, kayaking, sailing, and personal watercraft riding are the Acapulco region's water sports of choice.

### Safety First

Viewed from Acapulco region beaches, the Pacific Ocean usually lives up to its name. Many protected inlets, safe for child's play, dot the coastline. Unsheltered shorelines, on the other hand, can be deceiving. Smooth water in the calm forenoon often changes to choppy in the afternoon; calm ripples that lap the shore in March can grow to hurricane-driven walls of water in November. Such storms can wash away sand, temporarily changing a wide, gently sloping beach into a steep one plagued by turbulent waves and treacherous currents.

Undertow, whirlpools, cross-currents, and occasional oversized waves can make ocean swimming a fast-lane adventure. Getting unexpectedly swept out to sea or hammered onto the beach bottom by a surprise breaker are potential hazards.

Never attempt serious swimming when tipsy or full of food; never swim alone where someone can't see you. Always swim beyond big breakers (which come in sets of several, climaxed by a huge one, which breaks highest and farthest from the beach). If you happen to get caught in the path of such a wave, avoid it by *diving directly toward and under it,* letting it roll harmlessly over you. If you are unavoidably swept up in a whirling, crashing breaker, try to roll and tumble with it, as football players tumble, to avoid injury.

Look out for other irritations and hazards. Now and then swimmers get a nettlelike (but usually harmless) jellyfish sting. Be careful around coral reefs and beds of sea urchins; corals can sting (like jellyfish) and you can additionally get infections from coral cuts and sea-urchin spines. *Shuffle* your feet along sandy bottoms to scare away stingrays rather than stepping on one. If you're unlucky, its venomous tail spines may inflict a painful wound.

### Snorkeling and Scuba Diving

A number of exciting clear-water sites, especially around Ixtapa and Zihuatanejo, and offshore Isla Roqueta in Acapulco, await both beginner and expert scuba divers. Veteran divers usually arrive during the dry winter and early spring when river outflows are mere trickles, leaving offshore waters clear. In Acapulco, Ixtapa, and Zihuatanejo, professional dive shops rent equipment, provide lessons and guides, and transport divers to choice sites.

While convenient, rented equipment is often less than satisfactory. To be sure, serious divers bring their own gear. This should probably include wetsuits in the winter, when many swimmers begin to feel cold after an unprotected half-hour in the water.

### Surfing, Sailing, Sailboarding, and Kayaking

Although Acapulco Bay itself seldom if ever offers any good surfing opportunities, nearby Playa Revolcadero does. Moreover, a few good surfing spots sprinkle the Ixtapa-Zihuatanejo area. Farther afield, a number of crystalline strands, such as Troncones, Piedra Tlalcoyunque, Playa Escondida, Playa Cayaquitos, Playa El Calvario, Playa Ventura, and Punta Maldonado, offer good seasonal surfing breaks.

The surf everywhere is highest and best during the July–November hurricane season, when big swells from storms far out at sea attract platoons of surfers to favored beaches.

Sailboarders, sailboaters, and kayakers—who, by contrast, require more tranquil waters—do best in the Acapulco region's winter or spring. Aquatics shops rent sailboarding outfits, sailboats, and kayaks at a number of resort hotel beaches on both Acapulco and Zihuatanejo Bays and Ixtapa's main beach.

The Acapulco region's many coastal lagoons offer fine sailboating and kayaking opportunities. Very accessible examples are Laguna Coyuca at Pie de la Cuesta, just northwest of Acapulco, and Laguna Barra de Potosí, just southeast of Zihuatanejo. (Bring your own equipment, however; few if any rentals are available.)

## FISH

A bounty of fish darts, swarms, jumps, and wriggles in the Acapulco region's surf, reefs, lagoons, and offshore depths. While many make delicious dinners (albacore, dorado, pompano, red snapper, roosterfish), others are tough (sailfish), bony (bonefish), and even poisonous (puffers). Some grow to half-ton giants (marlin, grouper), while others are diminutive reef-grazers (parrot fish, damselfish, angelfish) whose bright colors delight snorkelers and divers. Here's a sampling of what you might find underwater or on your dinner plate:

- **albacore** (*albacora, atún*): 2-4 feet in size; blue; deep waters; excellent taste
- **angelfish** (*ángel*): one foot; yellow, orange, blue; reef fish*
- **barracuda** (*barracuda, picuda*): two feet; brown; deep waters; good taste
- **black marlin** (*marlin negro*): six feet; blue-black; deep waters; good taste
- **blue marlin** (*marlin azul*): eight feet; blue; deep waters; poor taste
- **bobo** (*barbudo*): one foot; blue, yellow; surf; fair taste
- **bonefish** (*macabi*): one foot; blue or silver; inshore; poor taste
- **bonito** (*bonito*): two feet; black; deep waters; good taste
- **butterfly fish** (*muñeca*): six inches; black, yellow; reef fish*
- **chub** (*chopa*): one foot; gray; reef fish; good taste
- **croaker** (*corvina*): two feet; brownish; inshore bottoms; rare and protected

- **damselfish** (*castañeta*): four inches; brown, blue, orange; reef fish*
- **dolphinfish, mahimahi** (*dorado*): three feet; green, gold; deep waters; good taste
- **grouper** (*garropa*): three feet; brown, rust; offshore and in reefs; good taste
- **grunt** (*burro*): eight inches; black, gray; rocks, reefs*
- **jack** (*toro*): 1-2 feet; bluish-gray; offshore; good taste
- **mackerel** (*sierra*): two feet; gray with gold spots; offshore; good taste
- **mullet** (*lisa*): two feet; gray; sandy bays; good taste
- **needlefish** (*agujón*): three feet; blue-black; deep waters; good taste
- **Pacific porgy** (*pez de pluma*): 1-2 feet; tan; sandy shores; good taste
- **parrot fish** (*perico, pez loro*): one foot; green, pink, blue, orange; reef fish*
- **pompano** (*pómpano*): one foot; gray; inshore bottoms; excellent taste

While beginners can have fun with the equipment available from rental shops, serious surfers, sailboarders, sailboaters, and kayakers should pack their own gear.

## FISHING

Experts agree: The Acapulco region (and increasingly Zihuatanejo) is a world-class deep-sea and surf fishing ground. Sportspeople routinely bring in dozens of species from among the hundreds that have been hooked in Acapulco region waters.

## Surf Fishing

Most good fishing beaches away from the immediate resort areas will typically have only a few locals (mostly with nets) and fewer visitors. Mexicans typically do little sportfishing. Most either make their living from fishing, or they do none at all. Consequently, few shops (only in Acapulco and Zihuatanejo) sell fishing equipment in the Acapulco region; plan to bring your own surf-fishing tackle, including net, poles, hooks, lures, line, and weights.

Your best general information source before you leave home is a good local bait-and-tackle

- **puffer** (*botete*): eight inches; brown; inshore; poisonous
- **red snapper** (*huachinango, pargo*): 1-2 feet; reddish pink; deep waters; excellent taste
- **roosterfish** (*pez gallo*): three feet; black, blue; deep waters; excellent taste
- **sailfish** (*pez vela*): five feet; blue-black; deep waters; poor taste
- **sardine** (*sardina*): eight inches; blue-black; offshore; good taste
- **sea bass** (*cabrilla*): 1-2 feet; brown, ruddy; reef and rock crevices; good taste
- **shark** (*tiburón*): 2-10 feet; black to blue; in- and offshore; good taste

- **snook** (*róbalo*): 2-3 feet; black-brown; brackish lagoons; excellent taste
- **spadefish** (*chambo*): one foot; black-silver; sandy bottoms; reef fish*
- **swordfish** (*pez espada*): five feet; black to blue; deep waters; good taste
- **triggerfish** (*pez puerco*): 1-2 feet; blue, rust, brown, black; reef fish; excellent taste
- **wahoo** (*peto, guahu*): 2-5 feet; green to blue; deep waters; excellent taste
- **yellowfin tuna** (*atún amarilla*): 2-5 feet; blue, yellow; deep waters; excellent taste
- **yellowtail** (*jurel*): 2-4 feet; blue, yellow; offshore; excellent taste

*generally too small to be considered edible*

© BRUCE WHIPPERMAN

Pink ocean carp, on the left, grey carp and tuna, center, and red snapper (*huachinango*) are plentiful along the Guerrero coast.

Well-equipped Acapulco sportfishing boats rent for about $400 a day, in season.

shop. Tell the folks there where you're going, and they'll often know the best lures and bait to use and what fish you can expect to catch with them.

In any case, the cleaner the water, the more interesting your catch. On a good day, your reward might be *sierras, cabrillas,* porgies, or pompanos pulled from the Acapulco region surf.

You can't have everything, however. Foreigners cannot legally take Mexican abalone, coral, lobster, clams, rock bass, sea fans, shrimp, turtles, or seashells. Neither are they supposed to buy them directly from fishermen.

## Deep-Sea Fishing

Zihuatanejo and Acapulco have long been world-class sportfishing grounds. A deep-sea boat charter generally includes the boat and crew for a full or half day, plus equipment and bait for two to six people, not including food or drinks. The full-day price depends upon the season. Around Christmas and New Year's

and before Easter (when reservations will be mandatory) a big boat can run $450 and up at Acapulco and Zihuatanejo. During low season, however, you might be able to bargain a captain down to as low as $250.

Renting an entire big boat is not the only choice. Winter sportfishing is sometimes so brisk at Acapulco and Zihuatanejo that travel agencies can make reservations for individuals for about $80 per person per day.

*Pangas* (outboard launches), seating 2–6 passengers, are available for as little as $75, depending on the season.

## Bringing Your Own Boat

If you're going to do lots of fishing, your own boat may be your most flexible and economical option. One big advantage is that you can go to the many excellent fishing grounds the charter boats do not frequent. Keep your equipment simple, scout around the dock, and keep your eyes peeled and ears open for local regulations and customs, plus tide, wind, and fish-edibility information.

## Fishing Licenses and Boat Permits

Anyone, regardless of age, who is either fishing or riding in a fishing boat in Mexico is required to have a fishing license. Although Mexican fishing licenses are obtainable from certain bait-and-tackle stores and car insurance agents or at government fishing offices everywhere along the coast, save yourself time and trouble by getting both your fishing licenses and boat permits by mail ahead of time from the Mexican Department of Fisheries. Call at least a month before departure (U.S. tel. 619/233-4324, fax 619/233-0344) and ask for (preferably faxed) applications and the fees (which are reasonably priced, but depend upon the period of validity and the fluctuating exchange rate). On the application, fill in the names (exactly as they appear on passports) of the people requesting licenses. Include a cashier's check or a money order for the exact amount, along with a stamped, self-addressed envelope. Address the application to the Mexican Department of Fisheries (Oficina de Pesca), 2550 5th Ave., Suite 15, San Diego, CA 92103-6622.

## POWER SPORTS

Acapulco, and to a lesser extent Ixtapa, has long been a center for motorboating, water-skiing, parasailing, and personal watercraft riding. Crowded conditions on Acapulco Bay have fortunately pushed most water-skiing to spacious Laguna Coyuca (at Playa Pie de la Cuesta) east of town. There, a few well-equipped providers offer equipment and lessons for about $100 per hour.

In parasailing, a motorboat pulls while a parachute lifts you, like a soaring gull, high over the ocean. After 5 or 10 minutes the driver deposits you—usually gently—back on the sand.

Personal watercraft (such as WaveRunners) are like snowmobiles except that they operate on water, where, with a little practice, beginners can quickly learn to whiz over the waves.

Although Acapulco and Ixtapa resort hotels' aquatic shops generally provide experienced power-sports crews and equipment, crowded conditions increase the hazard to both participants and swimmers. You, as the patron, are paying plenty for the privilege; you have a right to expect that your providers and crew are well-equipped, sober, and cautious.

## Beach Buggies and ATVs

Some visitors enjoy racing along the beach and rolling over dunes in beach buggies and ATVs (all-terrain vehicles—*motos* in Mexico), balloon-tired, three-wheeled motor scooters. While certain resort rental agencies cater to the growing use of such vehicles, limits are in order. Of all the proliferating high-horsepower beach pastimes, these are the most intrusive. Noise, exhaust, and gasoline pollution, injuries to operators and bystanders, scattering of wildlife and destruction of their habitats have led (and I hope will continue to lead) to the restriction of dune buggies and ATVs on beaches.

## TENNIS AND GOLF

Most Mexicans are working too hard to be playing much tennis and golf. Consequently, nearly all courses and courts are private. Acapulco golfers enjoy one public *campo de golf* (golf course) and at least two plush private ones. In Ixtapa, one public and one private course serve golfers.

As for tennis, plenty of private courts are available in both Acapulco and Ixtapa. If you are planning on a lot of golf and tennis, check into (or inquire about court rental at) one of the many hotels with these facilities. Use of hotel tennis courts is often, but not always, included in your hotel tariff. If not, fees will run about $10 per hour. Golf greens fees, which begin at about $50 for 18 holes, are always extra.

## BULLFIGHTING

It is said there are two occasions for which Mexicans arrive on time: funerals and bullfights.

Bullfighting is a recreation, not a sport. The bull is outnumbered seven to one and the outcome is never in doubt. Even if the matador (literally, killer) fails in his duty, his assistants will entice the bull away and slaughter it in private beneath the stands.

### La Corrida de Toros

Moreover, Mexicans don't call it a "bullfight"; it's the *corrida de toros,* during which six bulls are customarily slaughtered, beginning at around 5 P.M. After the beginning parade, featuring the matador and his helpers, the picadores and the banderilleros, the first bull rushes into the ring in a cloud of dust. Clockwork *tercios* (thirds) define the ritual: the first, the *puyazos* (stabs), requires that two picadores on horseback thrust lances into the bull's shoulders, weakening it. During the second *tercio,* the banderilleros dodge the bull's horns to stick three long, streamered darts into its shoulders.

Trumpets announce the third *tercio* and the appearance of the matador. The bull—weak, confused, and angry—is ready for the finish. The matador struts, holding the red cape, daring the bull to charge. Form now becomes everything. The expert matador takes complete control of the bull, which rushes at the cape, past its ramrod-erect opponent. For charge after charge, the matador works the bull to exactly the right spot in the ring—in front of the judges, a lovely señorita, or perhaps the governor—where the matador mercifully delivers the precision *estocada* (killing sword thrust) deep into the drooping neck of the defeated bull.

Most sizable Acapulco region towns, including Zihuatanejo, Taxco, Chilpancingo, Iguala, and Ometepec, stage *corridos de toros.*

In Acapulco, *corridas de toros* are staged late Sunday afternoons seasonally, usually January–March, at the arena (here called a *frontón*) near west-side Playa Caletilla.

# Accommodations

The Acapulco region has many hundreds of lodgings to suit every style and pocketbook: world-class resorts, small beachside hotels, homey *casas de huéspedes* (guesthouses), palm-shaded trailer parks, and many dozens of miles of pristine beaches, ripe for camping.

## HIGH AND LOW SEASONS

Acapulco-region high seasons depend on whether the visitors are international or domestic: international visitors, mostly from the United States, Canada, and Europe, begin arriving in droves around December 20 and remain in significant numbers through Easter. Mexican vacationers, on the other hand, concentrate in the resorts during holidays, especially Christmas–New Year's and Semana Santa (pre-Easter week), and weekends, especially during *puentes* (long weekends) around national holidays, and July and August.

As for resort preferences, the new-town district of Acapulco is most popular with most international visitors; both the old town and the new town with Mexicans. Ixtapa and Zihuatanejo are mostly popular with international visitors, less so with Mexicans. Taxco, on the other hand, is mostly popular with Mexico City Mexicans, especially during holidays and weekends.

So, make sure you arrive with reservations in Acapulco, Ixtapa, and Zihuatanejo during the winter–spring season and Taxco during Christmas–New Year's, pre-Easter week, weekends, and July and August.

## PICKING A HOTEL

The hundreds of accommodations described in this book are positive recommendations—checked out in detail—good choices, from which you can pick according to your taste and purse.

### Hotel Rates

The rates listed in the destination chapters are U.S. dollar equivalents of peso prices, 15 percent IVA (value-added taxes) included, as quoted by the hotel management at the time of writing. Where many hotels are available—Acapulco,

Ixtapa, Zihuatanejo, and Taxco—hotels are listed in ascending order of high-season double-occupancy rates. Both low- and high-season rates are quoted whenever possible and are intended as a general guide only. Since rates fluctuate sharply according to local demand, quoted figures will probably only approximate the asking rate when you arrive. (Some readers, unfortunately, try to bargain by telling desk clerks that, for example, the rate should be $30 because they read it in this book. This is unwise, because it makes hotel managers and clerks reluctant to quote rates for fear readers might hold their hotels responsible for such quotes years later.)

In the Acapulco region, hotel rates depend strongly upon inflation and season. To cancel the effect of relatively steep Mexican inflation, rates are reported in U.S. dollars. However, when settling your hotel bill, *you should always pay in pesos.*

## Saving Money

The hotel prices quoted in this book are rack rates: the maximum tariff, exclusive of packages and promotions, that you would pay if you walked in and rented an unreserved room for a night. Savvy travelers seldom pay the maximum. Always inquire if there are any discounts or packages (*descuentos o paquetes,* des-koo-AYN-tohs OH pah-KAY-tays). At most times other than the super-high Christmas–New Year's and Easter weeks, you can usually get at least one or two free days for a one-week stay. Promotional packages available during slack seasons may include free extras such as breakfast, a car rental, a boat tour, or a sports rental. A travel agent or travel website can be of great help in shopping around for such bargains.

You nearly always save additional money if you deal in pesos only. Insist on both booking your lodging for an agreed price in pesos and paying the resulting hotel bill in the same pesos, rather than dollars. The reason is that dollar rates quoted by hotels are often based on the hotel desk exchange rate, which is customarily about 5 percent, or even as much as 15 percent, less than bank rates. For example, if the clerk tells you your hotel bill is $1,000,

instead of handing over the dollars, or having him mark $1,000 on your credit card slip, ask him how much it is in pesos. Using the desk conversion rate, he might say something like 10,000 pesos (considerably less than the 11,000 pesos that the bank might give for your $1,000). Pay the 10,000 pesos in cash or make sure the clerk marks 10,000 pesos on your credit card slip, and save yourself $100.

For stays of more than two weeks, you'll most likely save money and add comfort with an apartment or condominium rental. Monthly rates range $500–1,500 (less than half the comparable hotel per diem rate) for comfortable one-bedroom furnished kitchenette units, often including resort amenities such as pool and sundeck, beach club, and private view balcony.

Airlines regularly offer air/hotel packages, which, by combining your hotel and air fees, may save you lots of pesos. Accommodations are usually, but not exclusively, in luxury resorts.

For accommodations details, see the destination chapters of this book, travel websites, travel agents, and *Internet Resources* at the end of this book.

## GUESTHOUSES AND LOCAL HOTELS

As did most of the celebrated Mexican Pacific coast resorts, both Acapulco and Zihuatanejo began with an old town, which expanded to a new *zona hotelera* (hotel strip) where big hostelries rise along a golden strand. In the old town, near the piquant smells, sights, and sounds of traditional Mexico, are the *casas de huéspedes* and smaller local hotels where rooms are often arranged around a plant-decorated patio.

Such lodgings vary from scruffy to spic-and-span, and humble to semideluxe. At minimum, you can expect a plain room, a shared toilet and hot-water shower, and plenty of atmosphere for your money. High-season rates, depending on the resort and amenities, are typically between $30 and $50 for two. Discounts are often available for long-term stays. *Casas de huéspedes* will rarely be near the beach, unlike many of the medium-to-high-end local hotels.

## Medium-to-High-End Local Hotels

Locally owned and operated hotels make up most of the recommendations of this book. Many veteran travelers find it hard to understand why people come to Mexico and spend $200–400 a day for a hotel room when good alternatives run between $60 and $120, high season, depending upon the resort.

Many locally run hostelries are right on the beach, sharing the same velvety sand and golden sunsets as their much more expensive international-class neighbors. Local hotels, which depend as much on Mexican tourists as foreigners, generally have clean, spacious rooms, often with private view balconies, ceiling fans, and toilet and hot-water bath or shower. What they often lack are the plush extras—air-conditioning, cable TV, phones, tennis courts, exercise gyms, and golf courses—of the luxury resort hotels.

Booking these hotels is straightforward. All can be dialed direct (from the United States, dial 011-52, then the local area code and number) for information and reservations; like the big resorts, many have websites and email addresses, and some even have U.S. and Canada toll-free phone numbers. Always ask about money-saving packages (*paquetes*) and promotions (*promociones*) when reserving.

## INTERNATIONAL-CLASS RESORTS

The Acapulco region has many beautiful, well-managed international-class resort hotels. They spread along the pearly strands of Acapulco Bay, Zihuatanejo, and Ixtapa. Their super-deluxe amenities, moreover, need not be overly expensive. During the right time of year you can vacation at many of the big-name spots, such as Barceló (formerly Sheraton), Fairmont, Meliá, Las Brisas, Hyatt, Fiesta Americana, NH Krystal, Best Western—for surprisingly little. While high-season room tariffs ordinarily run $150–350, low-season (May–Nov., and to a lesser degree, Jan.–Feb.) packages and promotions can cut these prices to as low as $100. Shop around for savings via your Sunday newspaper travel section, travel agents, and by contacting the hotels directly through their toll-free phone numbers or website that you'll find in the destination chapters of this book.

## APARTMENTS, BUNGALOWS, CONDOMINIUMS, AND VILLAS

For longer stays, many visitors prefer the convenience and economy of an apartment or condominium or the luxurious comfort of a villa vacation rental. Choices vary, from spartan studios to deluxe beachfront suites and rambling view homes big enough for entire extended families. Prices depend strongly upon season and amenities, from $500 per month for the cheapest to at least 10 times that for the most luxurious.

A Mexican variation on the apartment style of accommodation is called a bungalow, although, in contrast to English-language usage, it does not usually imply a detached dwelling. Common in Zihuatanejo, a bungalow accommodation generally means a kitchenette-suite with less service, but with more space and beds. For families or for long stays by the beach, where you want to save money by cooking your own meals, such an accommodation might be ideal.

At the low end, you can expect a clean, furnished apartment within a block or two of the beach, with kitchen and regular maid service. More luxurious condos, very common in Acapulco and Ixtapa and which usually rent for $500 per week and up, are typically high-rise oceanview suites with hotel-style desk services and resort amenities, such as a pool, whirlpool tub, sundeck, and beach-level restaurant.

Higher up the scale, villas and houses vary from moderately luxurious homes to sky's-the-limit beachview mansions, blooming with built-in designer luxuries, private pools and beaches, tennis courts, and gardeners, cooks, and maids.

### Shopping Around

You'll generally find the most economical apartment, condo, and house rental deals through on-the-spot local contacts, such as local newspaper want-ad sections, neighborhood For Rent ("Renta") signs, or local listing agents.

Be smart and let your fingers do the walking with the very useful website for finding affordable long-term vacation rentals, **Vacation Rentals by Owner, www.vrbo.com,** with dozens of leads in Acapulco, Zihuatanejo, Ixtapa, and Troncones.

If you prefer, you can often write, fax, email, or telephone rental managers—many of whom speak English—directly, using the numbers given in the destination chapters of this book.

Rentals are also available through agents who will make long-distance rental agreements. Local real estate agents such as Century 21, which specializes in nationwide and foreign contacts, sometimes list (or know someone who does list) Acapulco region vacation rentals. Such rentals are becoming increasingly available through the Internet; see *Internet Resources* at the end of this book.

## Home Exchange and Renting Out Your Own House

You may also want to consider using the services of a home exchange agency/website whereby you swap homes with someone in the Acapulco region for an agreed-upon time. For a list of agencies, see the Internet Resources at the back of this book, or simply enter "home exchange" into an Internet search engine.

On the other hand, it may be easier to rent or lease your own house and use the income to rent a house or apartment in the Acapulco region. (Although some people—including myself—have found this strategy successful, talk to someone who's done it to find out if it's your cup of tea.)

## CAMPING AND TRAILER PARKS
### Beach Camping

Informal beach camping is popular among middle-class Mexican families, especially during the Christmas–New Year's week and during Semana Santa. The crowds even overflow onto the resort beaches of Acapulco, Zihuatanejo Bay, and Ixtapa, where folks set up tents or simply sleep under the stars.

On nearly all other Acapulco-region beaches plenty of camping space is always available. The choice spots, such as Playa Ventura, Playa Las Peñitas, and Playa Puerto Maldonado on the Costa Chica; and Playa El Carrizal, Playa Paraíso, the Laguna de Mitla beach, Playa Escondida, Playa La Barrita, and Playa Ojo de Agua on the Costa Grande, typically have a shady palm grove for camping and at least one *palapa* restaurant that serves drinks and fresh seafood. (Heads up for falling coconuts, especially when it's windy.) Cost for parking and tenting is often minimal, typically only the price of food at the restaurant.

© BRUCE WHIPPERMAN

Tenting on the beach is safe beneath the *palapa* of a beachfront restaurant.

Days are often perfect for swimming, strolling, and fishing, and nights are balmy—too warm for a sleeping bag, but fine for a hammock (which allows the air circulation that a tent does not). However, good tents keep out mosquitoes and other pesties, which may be further discouraged by a good bug repellent. Tents can get hot, requiring only a sheet or very light blanket for sleeping cover.

As for the safety of camping on isolated beaches, opinions vary from dire warnings of *bandidos* to bland assurances that all is peaceful along the coast. The truth is somewhere in between. Trouble is most likely to occur in the vicinity of resort towns, where a few local thugs sometimes harass isolated campers.

When scouting out an isolated beach for camping, a good rule is to arrive early enough in the day to get a feel for the place. Buy a soda at the *palapa* or store and take a stroll along the beach. Say *"Buenos días"* to the people along the way; ask if the fishing is good (*"¿Pesca buena?"*). Above all, use your common sense and intuition. If the people seem friendly, ask if it's *seguro* (safe). If so, ask permission: *"¿Es bueno acampar acá?"* ("Is it okay to camp around here?"). You'll rarely be refused.

## Camping Upcountry

Scenic river canyons provide some of the most inviting camping opportunities in the Acapulco region's vast upcountry hinterland. Two of the best are at Campamento Santa Fe and El Borbollón on the spring-fed Río Azul (Blue River) about 20 miles east of Chilpancingo. Another promising spot is on the Río Papagayo at Pueblo Bravo (on old Highway 95, about 30 miles south of Chilpancingo).

You can enjoy one of the most informative and entertaining discussions of camping in Mexico in *The People's Guide to Mexico* by Carl Franz.

## Trailer Parks

Campers who prefer company to isolation usually stay in trailer parks. Unfortunately, development has squeezed out many Acapulco-region trailer parks. Nevertheless, two good trailer parks remain nearby, on breezy Playa Pie de la Cuesta a few miles northwest of Acapulco.

A decent well-equipped beachfront trailer park, the Ixtapa Trailer Park, is newly open, a few miles north of Ixtapa. The bare-bones but popular Trailer Park and Restaurant El Manglar, with all hookups, is operating on Playa La Ropa in Zihuatanejo.

# Food and Drink

Some travel to the Acapulco region for the food. True Mexican food is old-fashioned, home-style fare requiring many hours of loving preparation. Such food is short on meat and long on corn, beans, rice, tomatoes, onions, eggs, and cheese.

Mexican food is the unique product of thousands of years of native tradition. It is based on corn—*teocentli,* the Aztec "holy food"—called *maíz* (mah-EES) by present-day Mexicans. In the past, a Mexican woman spent much of her time grinding and preparing corn: soaking the grain in lime water, which swells the kernels and removes the tough seed-coat, and grinding the bloated seeds into meal on a stone metate. Finally, she patted the meal into tortillas and cooked them on a hot baked-mud griddle.

Sages (men, no doubt) wistfully imagined that gentle pat-pat-pat of women all over Mexico to be the heartbeat of Mexico, which they feared would cease when women stopped making tortillas.

Fewer women these days make tortillas by hand. The gentle pat-pat-pat has been replaced by the whir and rattle of the automatic tortilla-making machine in myriad *tortillerías,* where women and girls line up for their family's daily kilo-stack of tortillas.

Tortillas are to the Mexicans as rice is to the Chinese and bread to the French. Mexican food is invariably some mixture of sauce, meat, beans, cheese, and vegetables wrapped in a tortilla, which becomes the culinary be-all: the food, the dish, and the utensil wrapped into one.

If a Mexican man has nothing to wrap in his lunchtime tortilla, he will content himself by rolling a thin filling of salsa (*chile* sauce) in it.

## HOT OR NOT?

Much food served in Mexico is not "Mexican." Eating habits, as most other customs, depend upon social class. Upwardly mobile Mexicans typically shun the corn-based *indígena* fare in favor of the European-style food of the Spanish colonial elite: chops, steaks, cutlets, fish, clams, omelettes, soups, pasta, rice, and potatoes.

Such fare is often as bland as Des Moines on a summer Sunday afternoon. *No picante*—not spicy—is how the Mexicans describe bland food. *Caliente*, the Spanish adjective for "hot" (as in hot water), does not, in contrast to English usage, imply spicy, or *picante*.

## VEGETARIAN FOOD

Although the availability of healthy food is increasing, strictly vegetarian and vegan cooking is the exception in Mexico, as are macrobiotic restaurants, health-food stores, and organic produce. Meat is such a delicacy for most Mexicans that they can't understand why people would give it up voluntarily. If, as a vegetable-lover, you can manage with corn, beans, cheese, eggs, *legumbres* (vegetables), and fruit, Mexican cooking will suit you fine.

Furthermore, wholesome **Chinese food** is a good source of veggies at several Acapulco, Ixtapa, and Zihuatanejo locations, plus at least one each in Chilpancingo, Iguala, and Taxco.

## SEAFOOD

Early chroniclers wrote that Aztec Emperor Moctezuma employed a platoon of runners to bring fresh fish 300 miles every day from the sea to his court. In the Acapulco region, fresh seafood is fortunately much more available from many dozens of shoreline establishments, varying from thatched beach *palapas* to five-star hotel restaurants.

Despite the plenty, Acapulco region seafood prices reflect high worldwide demand, even at the humblest seaside *palapa*. The freshness and

---

## CATCH OF THE DAY

**Ceviche** (say-VEE-chay): A chopped raw-fish appetizer as popular on Acapulco region beaches as sushi is on Tokyo side streets. Although it can contain anything from conch to octopus, the best ceviche consists of diced *tiburón* (young shark) or *sierra* (mackerel) fillet and plenty of fresh tomatoes, onions, garlic, and *chiles*, all doused with lime juice (the acid of which "cooks" the fish).

*Filete de pescado:* A fish fillet, sautéed *al mojo* (ahl MOH-hoh) – with butter and garlic.

*Pescado frito*: Fish, pan-fried whole; if you don't specify that it be cooked *a medio* (lightly), the fish may arrive well done, like a big, crunchy french fry.

*Pescado veracruzana:* A favorite everywhere. Best with *huachinango* (red snapper), smothered in a savory tomato, onion, *chile*, and garlic sauce. *Pargo* (snapper), *mero* (grouper), and *cabrilla* (sea bass) are also popularly used in this and other specialties.

**Shellfish:** These are abundant and include *ostiones* (oysters) and *almejas* (clams) by the dozen; *langosta* (lobster) and *langostina* (crayfish) *asado* (broiled), *al vapor* (steamed), or fried. Pots of fresh-boiled *camarones* (shrimp) are sold on the street by the kilo; cafés will make them into *cóctel*, or prepare them *en gabardinas* (breaded) at your request.

---

variety, however, make even the typical dishes seem bargains at any price.

## FRUITS AND JUICES

Squeezed vegetable and fruit juices (*jugos,* HOO-gohs) are among the widely available delights of the Acapulco region. Among the many establishments—restaurants, cafés, and *loncherías*—willing to supply you with your favorite *jugo*, the *jugerías* (juice bars) are often the most fun. Colorful fruit piles usually mark *jugerías*. If you don't immediately spot your

## MEXICAN FOOD

On most Mexican-style menus, diners will find variations on a number of basic themes:

**Carnes** (meats): **Carne asada** is grilled beef, usually chewy and well-done. Something similar you might see on a menu is *cecina* (say-SEE-nah), dried salted beef grilled to a shoeleather-like consistency. Much more appetizing is **birria,** a Guadalajara specialty. Traditional *birrias* are of lamb or goat, often wrapped and pit-roasted in maguey leaves, with which it is served, for authenticity. In addition to *asada,* meat cooking styles are manifold, including *guisado* (stewed), *al pastor* (spit barbecue), and *barbacoa* (grill barbecued). Cuts include *lomo* (loin), *chuleta* (chop), *milanesa* (cutlet), and *albóndigas* (meatballs).

**Chiles rellenos:** Fresh roasted green chiles, usually stuffed with cheese but sometimes with fish or meat, coated with batter, and fried. They provide a piquant, tantalizing contrast to tortillas.

**Enchiladas** and **tostadas:** variations on the filled-tortilla theme. Enchiladas are stuffed with meat, cheese, olives, or beans and covered with sauce and baked, while tostadas consist of toppings served on crisp, open-faced tortillas.

**Guacamole:** This luscious avocado, onion, tomato, lime, and salsa mixture remains the delight it must have seemed to its indigenous inventors centuries ago. In nontourist Mexico it's served sparingly as a garnish, rather than in appetizer bowls as is common in the U.S. Southwest (and Mexican resorts catering to North Americans). (Similarly, in nontourist Mexico, burritos and fajitas, both stateside inventions, seldom if ever appear on menus.)

**Moles** (MOH-lays): uniquely Mexican specialties. *Mole poblano,* a spicy-sweet mixture of chocolate, *chiles,* and a dozen other ingredients, is cooked to a smooth sauce, then baked with chicken (or turkey, a combination called *mole de pavo*). So *típica* it's widely regarded as the national dish.

**Quesadillas:** made from soft flour tortillas, rather than corn, quesadillas resemble tostadas and always contain melted cheese.

**Sopas:** Soups consist of vegetables in a savory chicken broth, and are an important part of both *comida* (afternoon) and *cena* (evening) Mexican meals. *Pozole,* a rich steaming stew of hominy, vegetables, and pork or chicken, often constitutes the prime evening offering

---

favorite fruit, ask anyway; it might be hidden in the refrigerator.

Besides your choice of pure juices, a *jugería* will often serve *licuados.* Into the juice, they whip powdered milk, your favorite fruit, and sugar to taste for a creamy afternoon pick-me-up or evening dessert. One big favorite is a cool banana-chocolate *licuado,* which comes out tasting like a milkshake minus the calories.

## ALCOHOLIC DRINKS

The Aztecs sacrificed anyone caught drinking fermented beverages without permission. The later, more lenient, Spanish attitude toward getting *borracho* (soused) has led to a thriving Mexican renaissance of native alcoholic beverages: tequila, mescal, Kahlúa, pulque, and *aguardiente.* Tequila and mescal, distilled from the fermented juice of the maguey, originated in

Oaxaca, where the best are still made. Quality tequila (named after the Guadalajara-area distillery town) and mescal come 76 proof (38 percent alcohol) and up. A small white worm, endemic to the maguey, is customarily added to each bottle of factory mescal for authenticity.

Pulque, although also made from the sap of the maguey, is locally brewed to a modest alcohol content between that of beer and wine. The brewing houses are sacrosanct preserves, circumscribed by traditions that exclude women and outsiders. The brew, said to be rich in nutrients, is sold to local *pulquerías* and drunk immediately. If you are ever invited into a *pulquería,* it is an honor you cannot refuse.

*Aguardiente,* by contrast, is the notorious fiery Mexican "white lightning," a locally distilled, dirt-cheap ticket to oblivion for poor Mexican men.

of small side-street shops. *Sopa de taco,* an ever-popular country favorite, is a medium-spicy cheese-topped thick *chile* broth served with crisp corn tortillas.

**Tacos** or **taquitos:** tortillas served open or wrapped around any ingredient.

**Tamales:** as Mexican as apple pie is American. This savory mixture of meat and sauce imbedded in a shell of corn dough and baked in a wrapping of corn husks is rarely known by the singular, however. They're so yummy that one *tamal* invariably leads to more *tamales.*

**Tortas:** the Mexican sandwich, usually broiled beef, pork, or chicken, topped with fresh tomato and avocado, and stuffed between two halves of a crisp *bolillo* (boh-LEE-yoh) or Mexican bun.

**Tortillas y frijoles refritos:** cooked brown or black beans, mashed and fried in pork fat, and rolled into tortillas with a dash of vitamin C-rich salsa to form a near-complete combination of carbohydrate, fat, and balanced protein.

### BEYOND THE BASICS
Mexican food combinations seem endless. Mexican corn itself has more than 500 recognized culinary variations, all from indigenous tradition. This has led to a myriad of permutations on the taco, such as *sopes* (with small and thick tortillas), *garnacho* (flat taco), *chilaquile* (breakfast specialty: shredded tortilla, smothered in sauce and baked with grated cheese and onion), *chalupa* (like a tostada), and *gorditas* (thick corn tortillas).

Taking a lesson from California nouveau cuisine, avante-garde Mexican chefs are returning to traditional ingredients. They're beginning to use more and more *chiles* – habanero, poblano, jalapeño, serrano – prepared in many variations, such as chipotle, ancho, *piquín,* and *mulato. Flor de calabaza* (squash flowers) and *nopal* (cactus) leaves are increasingly finding their way into soups and salads.

More often chefs are serving the wild game – *venado* (venison), *conejo* (rabbit), *guajalote* (turkey), *codorniz* (quail), *armadillo,* and *iguana* – that country Mexicans have always depended upon. As part of the same trend, *cuitlacoche* (corn mushroom fungus), *chapulines* (small french-fried grasshoppers), and *gusanos de maguey* (maguey worms) are being increasingly added as ingredients in fancy restaurants.

While pulque comes from age-old indigenous tradition, beer (introduced by 19th-century German brewers) is the beverage of modern mestizo Mexico. More full-bodied than "light" U.S. counterparts, Mexican beer enjoys an enviable reputation.

Those visitors who indulge usually know their favorite among the many brands, from light to dark: Superior, Corona, Pacífico, Tecate, Carta Blanca, Modelo, Dos Equis, Bohemia, Tres Equis, and Negro Modelo. Nochebuena, a hearty dark brew, becomes available only around Christmas.

Mexicans have yet to develop much of a taste for *vino tinto* or *vino blanco* (red or white table wine), although some domestic wines (such as the Baja California labels Cetto and Domecq and the boutique Monte Xanic) and newcomer Chilean (Concha y Toro and more) are at least very drinkable and at best excellent.

## BREAD AND PASTRIES
Wonderful locally baked bread is a delightful surprise to many first-time visitors to the Acapulco region. Small bakeries everywhere put out trays of hot, crispy-crusted *bolillos* (rolls) and *panes dulces* (sweet bread). The pastries vary from simple cakes, muffins, cookies, and doughnuts to fancy fruit-filled turnovers and puffs. Half the fun occurs before the eating: grab a tray and tongs, peruse the goodies, and pick out the most scrumptious. With your favorite dozen or so finally selected, you take your tray to the cashier, who deftly bags everything up and collects a few pesos (two or three dollars) for your entire mouthwatering selection.

# A TROVE OF FRUITS AND NUTS

Besides carrying the usual temperate fruits, *jugerías* and especially markets are seasonal sources of a number of exotic (followed by an *) varieties.

- **avocado** (*aguacate* – ah-wah-KAH-tay): Aztec aphrodisiac

- **banana** (*plátano*): many kinds – big and small, red and yellow

- **chirimoya\*** (*chirimoya*): green scales, white pulp, sometimes called an *anona*

- **ciruela\***: looks like (but tastes better than) a small yellow-to-red plum

- **coconut** (*coco*): coconut "milk," called *agua coco*, is a wonderful and healthy thirst quencher

- **grapes** (*uvas*): August–November season

- **guanabana\***: looks, but doesn't taste, like a green mango

- **guava** (*guava*): delicious juice, widely available as all-natural Jumex yummy canned juice

- **lemon** (*lima real* – LEE-mah ray-AHL): uncommon and expensive; use lime instead

- **lime** (*limón* – lee-MOHN): abundant and cheap; douse salads with it

- **mamey\*** (*mamey* – mah-MAY): yellow, juicy fruit; excellent for jellies and preserves

- **mango** (*mango*): king of fruit, in a 100 varieties April–September

- **orange** (*naranja* – nah-RAHN-ha): greenish skin but sweet and juicy

- **papaya** (*papaya*): said to aid digestion and healing

- **peach** (*durazno* – doo-RAHS-noh): delicious and widely available as Jumex all-natural canned juice

- **peanut** (*cacahuate* – kah-kah-WAH-tay): home roasted and cheap

- **pear** (*pera*): fall season

- **pecan** (*nuez*): for a treat, try freshly ground pecan butter

- **piña anona\***: looks like a thin ear of corn without the husk; tastes like pineapple

- **pineapple** (*piña*): huge, luscious, and cheap

- **strawberry** (*fresa* – FRAY-sah): local favorite

- **tangerine** (*mandarina*): common around Christmas

- **watermelon** (*sandía* – sahn-DEE-ah): perfect on a hot day

- **yaca\*** (YAH-kah): a relative of the Asian jackfruit, with pebbly green skin, round and as large as a football; yummy mild taste

- **zapote\*** (sah-POH-tay): yellow, fleshy fruit, said to induce sleep

- **zapote colorado\***: brown skin, red, puckery fruit, like persimmon; commonly, but incorrectly, called *mamey*

© BRUCE WHIPPERMAN

# Tips for Travelers

## BRINGING THE KIDS

Children are treasured like gifts from heaven in Mexico. Traveling with kids will ensure your welcome most everywhere. On the beach, take extra precautions to make sure they are protected from the sun.

A sick child is no fun for anyone. Fortunately, clinics and good doctors are available even in most small towns. When in need, ask a storekeeper or a pharmacist, *"¿Dónde hay un doctor, por favor?"* (*"¿DOHN-day eye oon doc-TOHR por fah-VOHR?"*). In most cases, within five minutes you will be in the waiting room of the local physician or hospital.

Children who do not favor typical Mexican fare can easily be fed with always-available eggs, cheese, *hamburguesas,* milk, oatmeal (*avena*), corn flakes, bananas, cakes, and cookies.

Your children will generally have more fun if they have a little previous knowledge of Mexico and a stake in the trip. For example, help them select some library picture books and magazines so they'll know where they're going and what to expect, or give them responsibility for packing and carrying their own small travel bag.

Be sure to mention your children's ages when making air reservations; child discounts of 50 percent or more are often available. Also, if you can arrange to go on an uncrowded flight, you can stretch out and rest on the empty seats.

For more details on traveling with children, check out the classic *Adventuring with Children* by Nan Jeffrey (see *Suggested Reading* at the end of this book).

## TRAVEL FOR PEOPLE WITH DISABILITIES

Mexican airlines and hotels (especially the large ones) have become sensitive to the needs of travelers with disabilities. Open street-level lobbies and large wheelchair-accessible elevators and rooms are available in nearly all Pacific Mexico resorts (and some smaller, especially boutique, hotels). Furthermore, most street-corner curbs accommodate wheelchairs.

Both Mexican and U.S. law forbids travel discrimination against otherwise qualified people with disabilities. As long as your disability is stable and not liable to deteriorate during passage, you can expect to be treated like any passenger with special needs.

Make reservations far ahead of departure and ask your agent to inform your airline of your needs, such as boarding wheelchair or in-flight oxygen. Be early at the gate to take advantage of the preboarding call.

For many helpful details to smooth your trip, get a copy of *Survival Strategies for Going Abroad* by Laura Hershey, published in 2005 by **Mobility International USA** (132 E. Broadway, Suite 343, Eugene, OR 97401, tel. 541/343-1284 voice/TDD, fax 541/343-6812, www.miusa .org). Furthermore, Mobility International is a valuable resource for many disabled lovers of Mexico, for it encourages disabled travelers with a goldmine of information and literature and can provide them with valuable Mexico connections. They publish a regular newsletter and provide information and referrals for international exchanges and homestays.

Similarly, **Partners of the Americas** (1424 K St. NW, Suite 700, Washington, DC 20005, tel. 202/628-3300 or 800/322-7844, fax 202/628-3306, info@partners.net, www .partners.net), with chapters in 45 U.S. states, works to improve understanding of disabilities and facilities in Mexico and Latin America. It maintains communications with local organizations and individuals whom disabled travelers may contact at their destinations.

## GAY AND LESBIAN TRAVEL

The great majority of visitors find Acapulco region people both gracious and tolerant. This extends from racial color-blindness to being broad-minded about sexual preference. As long as gay and lesbian visitors don't flaunt their own preference, they will find acceptance most anywhere in the Acapulco region.

As a result, both Acapulco and Ixtapa-Zihuatanejo

coastal resorts have acquired a growing company of gay- and lesbian-friendly hotels, bars, and entertainments. For example, for Acapulco region hotel, restaurant, and nightlife details, visit the gay-oriented travel website www .casacondesa.com/gay.acapulco.directory.htm.

Some gay- and lesbian-oriented Internet and print publishers also offer excellent travel guidebooks. One of the most experienced is **Damron Company** (tel. 415/255-0404 or 800/462-6654, www.damron.com), which publishes, both in print and by Internet subscription, the *Damron Women's Travel* and *Damron Men's Travel* guidebooks, containing a wealth of gay and lesbian travel information, including listings in Acapulco and Zihuatanejo.

If you're interested in more gay and lesbian travel information, advice, and services, check out the very complete San Francisco **Purple Roofs** Internet travel agency (wheretostay@ purpleroofs.com, www.purpleroofs.com). They offer Acapulco and Zihuatanejo hotel, nightlife, and travel agent listings, plus a multitude of services, from tours and air tickets to travel insurance and hotel reservations.

## TRAVEL FOR SENIOR CITIZENS

Age, according to Mark Twain, is a question of mind over matter: If you don't mind, it doesn't matter. Mexico is a country where whole extended families, from babies to great-grandparents, live together. Senior travelers will often benefit from the respect and understanding Mexicans accord to older people. Besides these encouragements, consider the number of foreign retirees already in havens in Puerto Vallarta, Guadalajara, Manzanillo, Acapulco, Zihuatanejo, Taxco, Oaxaca, and other regional centers.

Certain organizations support and sponsor senior travel. Leading the field is **Elderhostel** (11 Ave. de Lafayette, Boston, MA 02111-1746, toll-free tel. 800/454-5768, www.elderhostel .org); contact them for information and/or one of their catalogs of special tours, study, homestays, and people-to-people travel programs.

Some books also feature senior travel opportunities. One of the pithiest is *Unbelievably Good Deals and Great Adventures You Can't Have Unless You're Over 50,* by Joan Rattner Heilman, published by McGraw Hill (2003). Its 200 pages are packed with details of how to get bargains on cruises, tours, car rentals, lodgings, and much, much more.

For seniors with online access (as close as your neighborhood library these days) the **Internet** is a gold mine of senior-oriented travel information. For example, on the Google search engine (www.google.com) home page, I typed in "Senior Travel" and netted more than 90 million responses. Near the top of the list was the **Transitions Abroad** site, www.transitions abroad.com, which offers a gold mine of a subsite (www.transitionsabroad.com/listings/travel/ senior) with a load of useful resources centering around senior traveling and living abroad.

# Health and Safety

## STAYING HEALTHY

In the Acapulco region as everywhere, prevention is the best remedy for illness. For those visitors who confine their travel to the beaten path, a few basic common-sense precautions will ensure vacation enjoyment.

Resist the temptation to dive headlong into Mexico. It's no wonder that people get sick— broiling in the sun, gobbling peppery food, guzzling beer and margaritas, then discoing half the night—all in their first 24 hours. An alternative is to give your body time to adjust. Travelers often arrive tired and dehydrated from travel and heat. During the first few days, drink plenty of bottled water and juice, and take siestas.

### Immunizations and Precautions

A good physician can recommend the proper preventatives for your Acapulco region trip. If

---

## MEDICAL TAGS AND AIR EVACUATION

Travelers with special medical problems should consider wearing a medical identification tag. For a reasonable fee, **Medic Alert** (2323 Colorado Ave., Turlock, CA 95382, tel. 209/668-3333 or 888/633-4398, www.medicalert.org) provides such tags, as well as an information hotline that will inform doctors of your vital medical background.

In life-threatening emergencies, highly recommended **Aeromedevac** (Gillespie Field Airport, 681 Kenney St., El Cajon, CA 92020, 800/462-0911, from Mexico 24-hr. toll-free tel. 001-800/832-5087, www.aeromedevac.com) provides high-tech jet ambulance service from any Mexican locale to a U.S. hospital for roughly $20,000.

Alternatively, you might consider the similar services of **Med-Jet Assistance** (Birmingham, Alabama, Intl. Airport, 4900 69th St., Birmingham AL, 35206, 800/963-3538, www.medjet.com; in emergencies, worldwide, call U.S. tel. 205/595-6626 collect).

---

super-effective, 100 percent DEET dries and irritates the skin.

### Sunburn

For sunburn protection, use a good sunscreen with a sun protection factor (SPF) rated 15 or more, which will reduce burning rays to one-fifteenth or less of direct sunlight. Better still, take a shady siesta-break from the sun during the most hazardous midday hours. If you do get burned, applying your sunburn lotion (or one of the "caine" creams) after the fact usually decreases the pain and speeds healing.

### Safe Water and Food

Although municipalities have made great strides in sanitation, food and water are still potential sources of germs in some parts of the Acapulco region. Although it's probably safe most everywhere, except in a few upcountry localities, it's still probably best to drink bottled water only. Hotels, whose success depends vitally on their customers' health, generally provide *agua purificada* (purified bottled water). If, for any reason, the available water is of doubtful quality, add a water purifier, such as "Potable Aqua" brand (get it at a camping goods store before departure) or a few drops per quart of water of *blanqueador* (household chlorine bleach) or *yodo* (tincture of iodine) from the pharmacy.

Pure bottled water, soft drinks, beer, and fresh fruit juices are so widely available it is easy to avoid tap water, especially in restaurants. Ice and *paletas* (iced juice-on-a-stick) may be risky, especially in small towns.

Washing hands before eating in a restaurant is a time-honored Mexican ritual that visitors should religiously follow. The humblest Mexican eatery will generally provide a basin to *lavar las manos* (wash the hands). If it doesn't, don't eat there.

Hot, cooked food is generally safe, as are peeled fruits and vegetables. These days milk and cheese in Mexico are generally processed under sanitary conditions and sold pasteurized (ask, "*¿Pasteurizado?*") and are virtually always safe. Mexican ice cream used to be both

you are going to stay pretty much in town, your doctor will probably suggest little more than updating your basic typhoid, diphtheria-tetanus, hepatitis, and polio shots.

For camping or trekking in remote tropical areas—below 4,000 feet or 1,200 meters—doctors often recommend a gamma-globulin shot against hepatitis A and a schedule of chloroquine pills against malaria. While in backcountry areas, use other measures to discourage mosquitoes—and fleas, flies, ticks, no-see-ums, "kissing bugs" (see *Chagas' Disease and Dengue Fever* later in this section), and other tropical pesties—from biting you. Common precautions include sleeping under mosquito netting, burning *espirales mosquito* (mosquito coils), and rubbing on plenty of pure DEET (n,n dimethyl-meta-toluamide) "jungle juice," mixed in equal parts with rubbing (70 percent isopropyl) alcohol. Although bad-tasting and of dubious safety, but national brands available in supermarkets are so much improved that it's no longer necessary to resist ice cream while in town.

In recent years, much cleaner public water and increased hygiene awareness have made salads—once shunned by Mexico travelers—generally safe to eat in tourist-frequented Acapulco region cafés and restaurants. Nevertheless, lettuce and cabbage, particularly in country villages, are more likely to be contaminated than tomatoes, carrots, cucumbers, onions, and green peppers. In any case, you can douse your salad in *vinagre* (vinegar) or plenty of sliced *limón* (lime) juice, the acidity of which kills most (but not all) bacteria.

### First-Aid Kit

In the bug-friendly tropical outdoors, ordinary cuts and insect bites are more prone to infection and should receive immediate first aid. A first-aid kit with aspirin, rubbing alcohol, hydrogen peroxide, water-purifying tablets, household chlorine bleach or iodine for water purifying, swabs, bandages, gauze, adhesive tape, Ace bandage, chamomile (*manzanilla*) tea bags for upset stomachs, Pepto-Bismol, acidophilus tablets, antibiotic ointment, hydrocortisone cream, mosquito repellent, knife, and good tweezers is a good precaution for any traveler and mandatory for campers.

## HEALTH PROBLEMS
### Traveler's Diarrhea

Traveler's diarrhea (known in Southeast Asia as "Bali Belly" and in Mexico as *turista* or "Montezuma's Revenge") sometimes persists, even among prudent vacationers. You can suffer *turista* for a week after simply traveling from California to Philadelphia or New York. Doctors say the familiar symptoms of runny bowels, nausea, and sour stomach result from normal local bacterial strains to which newcomers' systems need time to adjust. Unfortunately, the dehydration and fatigue from heat and travel reduce your body's natural defenses and sometimes lead to a persistent cycle of sickness at a time when you least want it.

Time-tested protective measures can help your body either prevent or break this cycle. Many doctors and veteran travelers swear by Pepto-Bismol for soothing sore stomachs and stopping diarrhea. Acidophilus, the bacteria found in yogurt, is widely available in the United States in tablets and aids digestion. Warm *manzanilla* (chamomile) tea, used widely in Mexico (and by Peter Rabbit's mother), provides liquid and calms upset stomachs. Temporarily avoid coffee and alcohol, drink plenty of *manzanilla* tea, and eat bananas and rice for a few meals until your tummy can take regular food.

Although powerful antibiotics and antidiarrhea medications such as Lomotil and Imodium are readily available over *farmacia* counters, they may involve serious side effects and should not be taken in the absence of medical advice. If in doubt, consult a doctor.

### Chagas' Disease and Dengue Fever

Chagas' disease, spread by the "kissing" (or, more appropriately, "assassin") bug, is a potential hazard in the Mexican tropics. Known locally as a *vinchuca,* the triangular-headed three-quarter-inch (two-centimeter) brown insect, identifiable by its yellow-striped abdomen, often drops upon its sleeping victims from the thatched ceiling of a rural house at night. Its bite is followed by swelling, fever, and weakness and can lead to heart failure if left untreated. Application of drugs at an early stage can, however, clear the patient of the trypanosome parasites that infect victims' bloodstreams and vital organs. See a doctor immediately if you believe you're infected.

Most of the precautions against malaria-bearing mosquitoes also apply to dengue fever, which does occur (although uncommonly) in outlying tropical areas of Mexico. The culprit here is a virus carried by the mosquito species *Aedes aegypti.* Symptoms are acute fever, with chills, sweating, and muscle aches. A red, diffuse rash frequently results, which may later peel. Symptoms abate after about five days, but fatigue may persist. A particularly serious, but fortunately rare, form, called dengue hemorrhagic fever, afflicts children and can be fatal. See a doctor immediately. Although no vaccines or preventatives, other than deterring mosquitoes, exist, you should nevertheless see a doctor immediately.

For more good tropical preventative information, get a copy of the excellent pamphlet distributed by the International Association of Medical Advice to Travelers (IAMAT, see *Medical Care* later in this section).

### Scorpions and Snakes

While camping or staying in a *palapa* or other rustic accommodation, watch for scorpions, especially in your shoes, which you should shake out every morning. Scorpion stings and snakebites are rarely fatal to an adult but are potentially very serious for a child. Get the victim to a doctor calmly but quickly. (For more snakebite details, see *Reptiles and Amphibians* in the *Flora and Fauna* section of the *Background* chapter.)

### Sea Creatures

While snorkeling or surfing, you may suffer a coral scratch or jellyfish sting. Experts advise you to wash the afflicted area with ocean water and pour alcohol (rubbing alcohol or tequila) over the wound, then apply hydrocortisone cream available from the *farmacia.*

Injuries from sea-urchin spines and sting-ray barbs are painful and can be serious. Physicians recommend similar first aid for both: remove the spines or barbs by hand or with tweezers, then soak the injury in as-hot-as-possible fresh water to weaken the toxins and provide relief. Another method is to rinse the area with an antibacterial solution—rubbing alcohol, vinegar, wine, or ammonia diluted with water. If none are available, the same effect may be achieved with urine, either your own or someone else's in your party. Get medical help immediately.

### Tattoos

All health hazards don't come from the wild. A number of Mexico travelers have complained of complications from black henna tattoos. When enhanced by the chemical dye PPD, an itchy rash results that can lead to scarring. It's best to play it safe: If you must have a vacation tattoo, get it at an established, professional shop.

## MEDICAL CARE

For medical advice and treatment, let your hotel (or if you're camping, the closest *farmacia*) refer you to a good doctor, clinic, or hospital. Mexican doctors, especially in medium-sized and small towns, practice like private doctors in the United States and Canada once did before health insurance, liability, and group practice. They will come to you if you request it; they often keep their doors open even after regular hours and charge reasonable fees.

You will receive generally good treatment at the many local hospitals in the Acapulco region's tourist centers and larger towns. If you must have an English-speaking, American-trained doctor, contact the International Association for Medical Assistance to Travelers (IAMAT, 1623 Military Road, #279, Niagra Falls, NY 14304, tel. 716/754-4883, in Canada 40 Regal Rd., Guelph, Ontario N1K 1B5, tel. 519/836-0102, or 1287 St. Clair Ave. W., Toronto, Ontario M6E 1B8, tel. 416/652-0137, info@iamat.org, www.iamat.org). IAMAT publishes an updated booklet of qualified member physicians, one of whom practices in Acapulco, and another in Zihuatanejo. IAMAT also distributes a very detailed *How to Protect Yourself Against Malaria* guide, together with worldwide malaria risk and communicable disease charts.

For more useful information on health and safety in Mexico, consult Drs. Robert H. Paige and Curtis P. Page's *Mexico: Health and Safety Travel Guide* (Tempe, AZ: Med to Go Books, 2007) and Dirk Schroeder's *Staying Healthy in Asia, Africa, and Latin America* (Berkeley, CA: Avalon Travel, 2000.)

## SAFETY
### Safe Conduct

Mexico is an old-fashioned country where people value traditional ideals of honesty, fidelity, and piety. Crime rates are low; visitors are often safer in Mexico than in their home cities.

This applies even more strongly in the Acapulco region. Don't be scared away by headlines about kidnappings and drug-related murders in border cities such as Tijuana and Ciudad Juárez, or car hijackings in bad Mexico City neighborhoods. Violent crime, while not unknown in Acapulco, is nearly always associated with drug turf wars. In the major centers of Ixtapa-Zihuatanejo, Taxco, Chilpancingo, and Iguala, violent crime is rare.

In Acapulco, around the *zócalo,* women are often seen walking home alone at night. Nevertheless, some Acapulco neighborhoods are friendlier than others. If you find yourself walking in a locality at night that doesn't feel too welcoming, do not hesitate to hail a taxi.

Although the Acapulco region is very safe with respect to violent crime, you should still take normal precautions against petty theft. Stow your valuables in your hotel safe, don't wear showy jewelry and display wads of money, and especially at a crowded market, keep your camera and valuables protected in a waist belt, secure purse, or zipped pockets. If you're parking your car for the night, do it in a secure garage or a guarded hotel parking lot.

Even though four generations have elapsed since Pancho Villa raided the U.S. border, the image of a Mexico bristling with *bandidos* persists. And similarly for Mexicans: Despite the century and a half since the *yanquis* invaded Mexico City and took half their country, the communal Mexican psyche still views gringos (and, by association, all white foreigners) with revulsion, jealousy, and wonder.

Fortunately, the Mexican love-hate affair with foreigners does not usually apply to individual visitors. Your friendly *"buenos días"* ("good morning") or *"por favor"* ("please"), when appropriate, is always appreciated, whether in the market, the gas station, or the hotel. The shy smile you will most likely receive in return will be your small, but not insignificant, reward.

## Women

Your own behavior, despite low crime statistics, largely determines your safety in Mexico. For women traveling solo, it is important to realize that the double standard is alive and well in Mexico. Dress and behave modestly and you will most likely avoid embarrassment. Whenever possible, stay in the company of friends or acquaintances; find companions for beach, sightseeing, and shopping excursions. Ignore strange men's solicitations and overtures. A Mexican man on the prowl will invent the sappiest romantic overtures to snare a gringa. He will often interpret anything but a firm "no" as a "maybe," and a "maybe" as a "yes."

## Men

For male visitors, alcohol often leads to trouble. Avoid bars and cantinas; and if, given Mexico's excellent beers, you can't abstain completely, at least maintain soft-spoken self-control in the face of challenges from macho drunks.

## The Law and Police

While Mexican authorities are tolerant of alcohol, they are decidedly intolerant of other substances such as marijuana, psychedelics, cocaine, and heroin. Getting caught with such drugs in Mexico usually leads to swift and severe results.

Equally swift is the punishment for nude sunbathing, which is both illegal in public and offensive to Mexicans. Confine your nudist colony to very private locations.

Although with decreasing frequency lately, traffic police in Acapulco and Zihuatanejo sometimes seem to watch foreign cars with eagle eyes. Officers seem to inhabit busy intersections and one-way streets, waiting for confused tourists to make a wrong move. If they whistle you over, stop immediately or you will really get into hot water. If guilty, say *"Lo siento"* ("I'm sorry") and be cooperative. Although the officer probably won't mention it, he or she is usually hoping that you'll cough up a $20 *mordida* (bribe) for the privilege of driving away. Don't do it. Although he may hint at confiscating your car, calmly ask for an official *boleto* (written traffic ticket, if you're guilty) in exchange for your driver's license (have a copy), which the officer will probably

# MACHISMO

I once met an Acapulco man who wore five gold wristwatches and became angry when I quietly refused his repeated invitations to get drunk with him. Another time, on the beach near San Blas, two drunk campesinos nearly attacked me because I was helping my girlfriend cook a picnic dinner. Outside Taxco I once spent an endless hour in the seat behind a bus driver who insisted on speeding down the middle of the two-lane highway, honking aside oncoming automobiles.

Despite their ethnic and socioeconomic differences, all four men shared the common affliction of machismo, an affliction that seems to possess many Mexican men. Machismo is a sometimes-reckless obsession to prove one's masculinity, to show how macho you are. Men of many nationalities share the instinct to prove themselves. Japan's *bushido* samurai code is one example.

When confronted by a Mexican braggart, male visitors should remain careful and controlled. If your opponent is yelling, stay cool, speak softly, and withdraw as soon as possible. On the highway, be courteous and unprovoking – don't use your car to spar with a macho driver. Drinking often leads to problems. It's best to stay out of bars or cantinas unless you're prepared to deal with the macho consequences. Polite refusal of a drink may be taken as a challenge. If you visit a bar with Mexican friends or acquaintances, you may be heading for a no-win choice between a drunken all-night *borrachera* (binge) or an insult to the honor of your friends by refusing.

For women, machismo requires even more cautious behavior. In Mexico, women's liberation is long in coming. Although a handful of Mexican women have risen to positions of political or corporate power, they constitute a small minority.

Female visitors should keep a low profile and wear bathing suits and brief shorts only at the beach. They can follow the example of their Mexican sisters by making a habit of going out in the company of friends or acquaintances, especially at night. Many Mexican men believe an unaccompanied woman wants to be picked up. Ignore their offers; any response, even refusal, might be taken as an encouraging sign. If, on the other hand, there is a Mexican man whom you'd genuinely like to meet, the traditional way is an arranged introduction through family or friends.

Mexican families, as a source of protection and friendship, should not be overlooked – especially on the beach or in the park, where, among the gaggle of kids, grandparents, aunts, and cousins, there's room for one more.

keep if he writes a ticket. If after a few minutes no money appears, the officer will most likely give you back your driver's license rather than go to the trouble of writing the ticket. If not, the worst that will usually happen is you will have to go to the *presidencia municipal* (city hall) the next morning and pay the $20 to a clerk in exchange for your driver's license.

## Political Protest

The Acapulco region's customary tranquillity has occasionally undergone episodes of public unrest. Recent protests have been the result of the longstanding backlog of unsettled grievances that run from local land disputes and strikes by underpaid teachers and government workers, to rough anti-drug military searches, all the way up to unsolved kidnappings and political assassinations.

In recent years, the aggrieved, usually local community delegations, have both petitioned state and city authorities for redress and set up camp in plain view for visitors to see, in the Acapulco and Chilpancingo central plazas. There is no reason for visitors to be concerned by such peaceful demonstrations. During recent years, political protests have been generally tolerated by local authorities and could be considered a positive sign of a maturing Mexican democracy.

## Pedestrian and Driving Hazards

Although the Acapulco region's potholed pavements and "holey" sidewalks won't land you in jail, one of them might send you to the hospital if you don't watch your step, especially at night. "Pedestrian beware" is especially good advice on Mexican streets, where it is rumored that some drivers speed up rather than slow down when they spot a tourist stepping off the curb. Falling coconuts, especially frequent on windy days, constitute an additional hazard to unwary campers and beachgoers.

Driving Mexican country roads, where slow trucks and carts block lanes, campesinos stroll the shoulders, and horses, burros, and cattle wander at will, is hazardous—doubly so at night.

# Information and Services

## MONEY
### The Peso: Down and Up

Overnight in early 1993, the Mexican government shifted its monetary decimal point three places and created the "new" peso (now known simply as the "peso"), which, at this writing, trades between 10 and 11 per U.S. dollar. Since the peso value sometimes changes rapidly, U.S. dollars have become a much more stable indicator of Mexican prices; for this reason they are used in this book to report prices. You should, nevertheless, always use pesos to pay for everything in Mexico.

Since the introduction of the new peso, the centavo (one-hundredth of a new peso) has reappeared, in coins of 10, 20, and 50 centavos. Incidentally, the dollar sign, "$," also marks Mexican pesos. Peso coins (*monedas*) in denominations of 1, 2, 5, 10 and 20 pesos, and bills, in denominations of 20, 50, 100, 200 and 500 pesos, are common. Since banks like to exchange your travelers checks for a few crisp large bills rather than the often-tattered smaller denominations, ask for some of your change in 50- and 100-peso notes. A 500-peso note, while common at the bank, may look awfully big to a small shopkeeper, who might be hard-pressed to change it.

### Banks, ATMs, and Money-Exchange Offices

Mexican banks, like their North American counterparts, have lengthened their business hours. Hong Kong Shanghai Banking Corporation (HSBC) maintains the longest hours: as long as Monday–Saturday 8 A.M.–7 P.M. Banamex (Banco Nacional de Mexico), generally the most popular with local people, usually posts the best in-town dollar exchange rate in its lobbies; for example: *Tipo de cambio: venta 10.799, compra 10.933,* which means it will sell pesos to you at the rate of 10.799 per dollar and buy them back for 10.933 per dollar.

ATMs (automated teller machines), or *cajeros automáticos* (kah-HAY-rohs ahoo-toh-MAH-tee-kohs), have become the money sources of choice in Mexico. Virtually every bank has a 24-hour ATM, accessible (with proper PIN) by a swarm of U.S. and Canadian credit and ATM cards. *Note:* Some Mexican bank ATMs will "eat" your ATM card if you don't retrieve it within about 15 seconds of completing your transaction. Retrieve your card *immediately* after getting your cash.

Although one-time bank charges, typically about $2 per transaction, for ATM cash remain small, the money you can usually get from a single card is limited to about $300 or less per day.

Even without an ATM card, you don't have to go to the trouble of waiting in long bank service lines. Opt for a less-crowded bank, such as Bancomer, Banco Serfín, HSBC, or a private money-exchange office (*casa de cambio*). Often most convenient, such offices often offer long hours and faster service than the banks for a fee (as little as $0.50 or as much as $3 per $100).

### Keeping Your Money Safe

Travelers checks, the traditional prescription

for safe money abroad, are accepted, but not as widely as before in the Acapulco region. Nevertheless, even if you plan to use your ATM card, you could buy some U.S. dollar travelers checks (a well-known brand such as American Express or Visa) for an emergency reserve. Canadian travelers checks and currency are not as widely accepted as U.S. travelers checks, and European and Asian travelers checks even less so. Unless you like signing your name or

paying lots of per-check commissions, buy denominations of $50 or more.

In the Acapulco region as everywhere, thieves circulate among the tourists. Keep valuables in your hotel *caja de seguridad* (security box). If you don't particularly trust the desk clerk, carry what you cannot afford to lose in a money belt. Pickpockets and purse-snatchers love crowded markets, buses, and airport terminals where they can slip a wallet out of a back pocket or

---

# PACKING CHECKLIST

Use this list as a last-minute check to make sure that you've packed all of the items essential to your Mexico trip:

## NECESSARY ITEMS

___ camera, film, extra memory card (expensive in Mexico)
___ comb, brush
___ guidebook, reading books
___ inexpensive watch, clock
___ keys, tickets
___ lightweight clothes, hat for sun
___ money, ATM card, and/or travelers checks
___ mosquito repellent
___ prescription eyeglasses, contact lenses
___ prescription medicines and drugs
___ purse, waist-belt carrying pouch
___ sunglasses, sunscreen
___ swimsuit
___ toothbrush, toothpaste
___ passport
___ windbreaker

## USEFUL ITEMS

___ address book
___ birth control
___ checkbook, credit cards
___ dental floss
___ earplugs
___ first-aid kit
___ flashlight, batteries
___ immersion heater
___ lightweight binoculars
___ portable radio/cassette player
___ razor

___ travel booklight
___ vaccination certificate

## NECESSARY ITEMS FOR CAMPERS

___ collapsible gallon plastic bottle
___ dish soap
___ first-aid kit
___ hammock (buy in Mexico)
___ insect repellent
___ lightweight hiking shoes
___ lightweight tent
___ matches in waterproof case
___ nylon cord
___ plastic bottle, quart
___ pot scrubber/sponge
___ sheet or light blanket
___ Sierra Club cup, fork, and spoon
___ single-burner stove with fuel
___ Swiss army knife
___ tarp
___ toilet paper
___ towel, soap
___ two nesting cooking pots
___ water-purifying tablets or iodine

## USEFUL ITEMS FOR CAMPERS

___ compass
___ dishcloths
___ hot pad
___ instant coffee, tea, sugar, powdered milk
___ moleskin (Dr. Scholl's)
___ plastic plate
___ poncho
___ short (votive) candles
___ whistle

dangling purse or a camera from its case in a blink. Guard against this by carrying your wallet in your front pocket, your camera in your purse or backpack, and your purse, waist pouch, and daypack (which clever crooks can sometimes slit open) on your front side.

Don't attract thieves by displaying wads of money or flashy jewelry. Don't get sloppy drunk; if so, you may become a pushover for a determined thief.

Don't leave valuables unattended on the beach; share security duties with trustworthy-looking neighbors, or leave a bag with a shop-keeper nearby.

## Tipping

Without their droves of visitors, Mexican people would be even poorer. Deflation of the peso, while it makes prices low for outsiders, makes it rough for Mexican families to get by. The help at your hotel typically get paid only a few dollars a day. They depend on tips to make the difference between dire and bearable poverty. Give the *camarista* (chambermaid) and floor attendant 20 pesos every day or two. And whenever uncertain of what to tip, it will probably mean a lot to someone—maybe a whole family—if you err on the generous side.

In restaurants and bars, Mexican tipping customs are similar to those in the United States: Tip waiters, waitresses, and bartenders about 15 percent for satisfactory service.

## Credit Cards

Credit cards, such as Visa, MasterCard, and, to a lesser extent, American Express and Discover, are widely honored in the hotels, restaurants, craft shops, and boutiques that cater to foreign tourists. You will generally get better bargains, however, in shops that depend on local trade and do not so readily accept credit cards. Such shops sometimes offer discounts for cash sales.

Whatever the circumstance, your travel money will usually go much further in the Acapulco region than back home. Despite the national 17 percent sales tax (IVA), local lodging, food, and transportation prices will often seem like bargains compared to the developed

world. Outside of the pricey high-rise beach-front strips, pleasant, palmy hotel room rates often run $50 or less.

## COMMUNICATIONS
### Using Mexican Telephones

Although Mexican phone service has improved in the last decade, it's still sometimes hit-or-miss. If a number doesn't get through, you may have to redial it more than once. When someone answers (usually *"Bueno"*), be especially courteous. If your Spanish is rusty, say, *"¿Por favor, habla inglés?"* (¿POR fah-VOR, AH-blah een-GLAYS?, "Please, do you speak English?" If you want to speak to a particular person (such as María), ask, *"¿María se encuentra?"* (¿mah-REE-ah SAY ayn-koo-AYN-trah?).

Since November 2001, when telephone numbers were standardized, Mexican phones operate pretty much the same as in the United States and Canada. In Acapulco, for example, a complete telephone number is generally written like this: 744/485-4709. As in the United States, the "744" denotes the telephone area code, or *(lada)* (LAH-dah), and the 485-4709 is the number (except in the case of calling a cell phone, see below) that you dial locally. If you want to dial this number long distance (*larga distancia*) in Mexico, **first dial "01" (like "1" in the United States),** then 744/485-4709. All Mexican telephone numbers, with only three exceptions, begin with a three-digit *lada,* followed by a seven-digit local number. (The exceptions are Monterrey, Guadalajara, and Mexico City, which have two-digit *ladas* and eight-digit local numbers. The Mexico City *lada* is 55; Guadalajara's is 33; Monterrey's is 81. (For example, a complete Guadalajara phone number would read 33/6897-2253.)

Although **Mexican cellular telephones** are as universally used as those in the United States and Canada, at this writing, they operate a bit differently. Generally, in order to call a cellular number locally (from within its local Mexican dialing area) you must prefix it with "044". For example, in Acapulco, call Acapulco cell phone number 744/485-4709, by dialing 044-744/485-4709. The same is true for other locales; for example, in Zihuatanejo, with area code 755, call the cellular number 755/554-3822 locally by dialing 044-755/554-3822.

However, if you're calling a cell phone long distance (from outside the cell phone's local area), you must first dial "045" instead of "044." For example, in Taxco, with area code 762, you must call the above cited Zihuatanejo cell phone by dialing 045-755/554-3822. The same is true of the above cited Acapulco cell phone by dialing 045-744/485-4709. This procedure is necessary for calling all cell phones throughout Mexico.

In Acapulco region towns and cities, direct long-distance dialing is the rule—from hotels, public phone booths, and efficient private computerized telephone offices. The cheapest, often most convenient, way to call is by buying and using a public telephone **Ladatel telephone card** (*tarjeta telefónica*). Buy them in 30-, 50-, and 100-peso denominations at the many outlets—minimarkets, pharmacies, liquor stores—that display the blue-and-yellow Ladatel sign.

## Calling Mexico and Calling Home

To call a Mexico (non-cellular) phone direct from the United States, first dial 011 (for international access), then 52 (Mexico country code), followed by the Mexican area code and local number. For example, to call an Acapulco local number, such as 744/485-4709, from the U.S., dial 011-52-744/485-4709. Again, you must **dial cellular phone numbers a bit differently,** by entering a "1" before the area code. Thus, if the Acapulco number 744/485-4709 were a cellular number, from the U.S. you must dial 011-52-1-744/485-4709.

For station-to-station **calls to the United States and Canada from Mexico,** dial 001 plus the U.S. or Canadian area code and the local number. For example to call San Diego (area code 619) local number 388-5390, from Mexico, simply dial 001-619/388-5390. For calls to other countries, ask your hotel desk

Much more economical options exist than the common "Call Home Collect" telephones.

© BRUCE WHIPPERMAN

clerk or see the easy-to-follow directions in the local Mexican telephone directory (*directorio telefónico*).

By far the cheapest way to call home (about $0.50 per minute) is via one of the many public telephones with your Ladatel phone card.

**Beware** of certain private "To Call Long Distance to the U.S.A. Collect" (or "by Credit Card") telephones installed prominently in airports, tourist hotels, and shops. Tariffs on these phones often run as high as $10 per minute (with a three-minute minimum), for a total of $30, whether you talk three minutes or not. Always ask the operator for the rate (*tipo*), and if it's too high, buy a 30-peso ($3) Ladatel phone card for a (six-minute) call home.

In smaller towns, with no public street telephones, you must often do your long-distance phoning in the *larga distancia* (local phone office). Typically staffed by a young woman and often connected to a café, the *larga distancia* becomes an informal community social center as people pass the time waiting for their phone connections.

## Post, Telegraph, and Internet Access

Mexican *correos* (post offices) operate similarly, but more slowly and less securely, than most of their counterparts all over the world. Mail services usually include *lista de correo* (general delivery, address letters *"a/c lista de correo,"*), *servicios filatelicas* (philatelic services), *por avión* (airmail), *giros* (postal money orders), and Mexpost secure and fast delivery service, sometimes from separate Mexpost offices.

Mexican ordinary (non-Mexpost) mail is sadly unreliable and pathetically slow. If, for mailings within Mexico, you must have security, use the efficient, reformed government Mexpost (like U.S. Express Mail) service. For international mailings, check the local Yellow Pages for widely available DHL, Federal Express, and UPS courier service.

*Telégrafos* (telegraph offices), usually near the post office, send and receive *telegramas* (telegrams) and *giros* (money orders). *Telecomunicaciones* (Telecom), the new high-tech telegraph offices, add computerized telephone, public fax, and sometimes Internet connection to the available services.

**Internet service,** including personal email access, has arrived in Acapulco region cities and larger (and even smaller) towns. Internet "cafés" are becoming increasingly common, especially in Acapulco, Ixtapa-Zihuatanejo, Taxco, Iguala, and Chilpancingo towns. Access rates run $1–2 per hour.

## ELECTRICITY AND TIME

Mexican electric power is supplied at U.S.-standard 110 volts, 60 cycles. Plugs and sockets are generally two-pronged, nonpolar (like the pre-1970s U.S. ones). Bring adapters if you're going to use appliances with polar two-pronged or three-pronged plugs. A two-pronged polar plug has different-sized prongs, one of which is too large to plug into an old-fashioned non-polar socket.

The entire Acapulco region, all surrounding states, and Mexico City operate on U.S. Central Time, the same as central U.S. states such as Nebraska, Illinois, Tennessee, and Louisiana.

# RESOURCES

## Glossary

Many of the following words have a social-historical meaning; others you will not find in the usual English–Spanish dictionary.

**abarrotesía** grocery store

**aguardiente** Mexican "white lightning": cheap distilled liquor made from sugarcane

**alcalde** mayor or municipal judge

**alebrije** fanciful wooden animal, mostly made in Arrazola and Tilcajete villages

**alfarería** pottery

**andador** walkway, or strolling path

**antojitos** native Mexican snacks, such as tamales, chiles rellenos, tacos, and enchiladas

**artesanías** handicrafts

**artesano, artesana** craftsman, craftswoman

**asunción** the assumption of the Virgin Mary into heaven (as distinguished from the *ascención* of Jesus into heaven)

**atole** a popular nonalcoholic drink made from corn juice

**audiencia** one of the royal executive-judicial panels sent to rule Mexico during the 16th century

**autopista** expressway

**ayuntamiento** either the town council or the building where it meets

**barrio** a town or village district or neighborhood, usually centered around its own local plaza and church

**bienes raíces** literally "good roots," but popularly, real estate

**boleto** ticket, boarding pass

**brujo, bruja** male or female witch doctor or shaman

**caballero** literally "horseman," but popularly, gentleman

**cabaña ecoturísticas** bungalow lodging for tourists

**cabercera** head town of a municipal district, or headquarters in general

**cabrón** literally, a cuckold, but more commonly, bastard, rat, or S.O.B.; sometimes used affectionately

**cacique** local chief or boss

**calenda** procession, usually religious, as during a festival

**camionera** bus station

**campesino** country person; farm worker

**canasta** basket, usually of woven reeds, with handle

**cantera** local volcanic stone, widely used for colonial-era Oaxaca monuments

**Carnaval** celebration preceding Ash Wednesday, the beginning of the fasting period called Lent. Carnaval is called Mardi Gras in the United States

**casa de huéspedes** guesthouse, often operated in a family home

**cascada** waterfall

**caudillo** dictator or political chief

**centro de salud** health center/clinic

**charro** gentleman cowboy

**chingar** literally, to "rape," but also the universal Spanish "f" word, the equivalent of "screw" in English

**churrigueresque** Spanish Baroque architectural style incorporated into many Mexican colonial churches, named after José Churriguera (1665-1725)

*científicos* literally, scientists, but applied to President Porfirio Díaz's technocratic advisers

*coa (estaca)* digging stick, used for planting corn

**Cocijo** Zapotec god of rain, lightning, and thunder

*cofradía* Catholic fraternal service association, either male or female, mainly in charge of financing and organizing religious festivals

*colectivo* a shared public taxi or minibus that picks up and deposits passengers along a designated route

*colegio* preparatory school or junior college

*colonia* suburban subdivision/satellite of a larger city

*comal* a flat pottery griddle, for cooking/heating tortillas

*comida casera* home-cooked food

*comida corrida* economical afternoon set meal, usually with four courses – soup, rice, entrée, and dessert

*compadrazgo* the semi-formal web of village and barrio *compadre* and *padrino* relationships that determine a person's lifetime obligations and loyalties

*compadre* a semi-formalized "best friend" relationship that usually lasts for life

*comunal* refers to the traditional indigenous system of joint decision-making and land ownership and use

**Conasupo** government store that sells basic foods at subsidized prices

*copra* sun-dried coconut meat; processed for its oil

*correo* mail, post, or post office

*criollo* person of all-European, usually Spanish, descent born in the New World

**Cuaresma** Lent (the 46 days of pre-Easter fasting, beginning on Ash Wednesday)

*cuota* toll, as in *cuota autopista,* toll expressway

*curandero, curandera* indigenous medicine man or woman

*damas* ladies, as in "ladies room"

**Domingo de Ramos** Palm Sunday

*ejido* a constitutional, government-sponsored form of community, with shared land ownership and cooperative decision-making

*encomienda* colonial award of tribute from a designated indigenous district

*farmacia* pharmacy, or drugstore

*finca* farm

*finca cafetelera* coffee farm

*fonda* foodstall or small restaurant, often in a traditional market complex

*fraccionamiento* city sector or subdivision, abbreviated "Fracc."

*fuero* the former right of Mexican clergy and military to be tried in separate ecclesiastical and military courts

*gachupín* "one who wears spurs"; a derogatory term for a Spanish-born colonial

*gasolinera* gasoline station

*gente de razón* "people of reason"; whites and mestizos in colonial Mexico

*gringo* once-derogatory but now commonly used term for North American whites

*grito* impassioned cry, as in Hidalgo's Grito de Dolores

*hacienda* large landed estate; also the government treasury

*hamaca* hammock

*hechicero* a "wizard" who often leads native propitiatory ceremonies

*hidalgo* nobleman or noblewoman; called honorifically by "Don" or "Doña"

*hojalata* tinware

*indígena* indigenous or aboriginal inhabitant of all-native descent who speaks his or her native tongue; commonly, but incorrectly, an *indio* (Indian)

*jacal* native label for thatched, straw, and/or stick country house

*jaripeo* bull roping and riding

*jejenes* "no-see-um" biting gnats, most common around coastal wetlands

*judiciales* the federal "judicial," or investigative police, best known to motorists for their highway checkpoint inspections

*jugería* stall or small restaurant providing a large array of squeezed vegetable and fruit *jugos* (juices)

*juzgado* the "hoosegow," or jail

*lancha* launch (small boat)

*larga distancia* long-distance telephone service, or the *caseta* (booth or office) where it's provided

**licencado** academic degree (abbrev. Lic.) approximately equivalent to a bachelor's degree in the United States

**lonchería** small lunch counter, usually serving juices, sandwiches, and *antojitos*

**machismo; macho** exaggerated sense of maleness; person who holds such a sense of himself

**manañita** early-morning mass

**mano** a hand, or the stone roller used to grind corn on the flat stone *metate*

**mayordomo** community leader responsible for staging a local Catholic religious festival

**mescal** alcoholic beverage distilled from the fermented hearts of maguey (century plant)

**mestizo** person of mixed native and European descent

**metate** a slightly concave, horizontal stone basin for grinding corn for tortillas

**milagro** literally a miracle, but also a small religious wish medal, often pinned to an altar saint by someone requesting divine intervention

**milpa** a small, family-owned field, traditionally planted in corn, beans, and squash

**mirador** viewpoint, overlook

**molcajete** a stone mortar and pestle, used for hand-grinding, especially chilies and seeds

**mordida** slang for bribe; "little bite"

**olla** a pottery jug or pot, used for stewing – vegetables, meats, beans, coffee

**padrino, padrina** godfather or godmother, often the respective *compadres* of the given child's parents

**palapa** an open, thatched-roof structure, usually shading a restaurant

**panela** rough brown cane sugar, sold in lumps in the market

**panga** outboard motor-launch *(lancha)*

**papier-mâché** the craft of glued, multilayered paper sculpture, centered in Tonalá, Jalisco, where creations can resemble fine pottery or lacquerware

**Pemex** acronym for Petróleos Mexicanos, the national oil corporation

**peninsulares** the Spanish-born ruling colonial elite

**peón** a poor wage-earner, usually a country native

**periférico** peripheral boulevard

**petate** all-purpose woven mat, from palm fronds

**piciete** wild tobacco

**piñata** papier-mâché decoration, usually in animal or human form, filled with treats and broken open during a fiesta

**plan** political manifesto, usually by a leader or group consolidating or seeking power

**Porfiriato** the 34-year (1876–1910) ruling period of president-dictator Porfirio Díaz

**posada** Christmas Eve procession in which participants, led by costumed Holy Mary and Joseph, knock on neighborhood doors and implore, unsuccessfully, for a room for the night

**pozahuanco** horizontally striped hand-woven wraparound skirt, commonly worn in the Oaxaca's coastal Mixtec district

**pozole** stew of hominy in broth, usually topped by shredded meat, cabbage, and diced onion

**presidencia municipal** the headquarters, like a U.S. city or county hall, of a Mexican *municipio*, county-like local governmental unit

**preventiva** state-funded local police

**principal, anciano** a respected elder, often a member of a council of elders, whom the community consults for advice and support

**pronunciamiento** declaration of rebellion by an insurgent leader

**pueblo** town or people

**puente** literally a "bridge," but commonly a holiday weekend, when hotel reservations are highly recommended

**pulque** the fermented juice of the maguey plant, approximately equivalent in alcoholic content to wine or strong beer

**puta** whore, bitch, or slut

**quinta** a villa or upscale country house

**quinto** the colonial royal "fifth" tax on treasure and precious metals

**ramada** a temporary shade roof, usually of palm fronds

**regidor** a community official, often a town council member, responsible for specific government functions, such as public works

**retablo** altarpiece, often of ornately carved and gilded wood

**retorno** cul-de-sac

***ropa típica*** traditional dress, derived from the Spanish colonial tradition (in contrast to *traje*, traditional indigenous dress)

***rurales*** former federal country police force created to fight *bandidos* (bandits) and suppress political dissent

**Sabi** Mixtec god of rain

***sabino*** Mexican cypress tree

**Semana Santa** Holy Week, the week preceding Easter Sunday

***servicios*** the ladder of increasingly responsible public tasks that, if successfully performed, leads to community approval, prestige, and leadership for a given individual by middle age

***tapete*** wool rug, made in certain east-side Valley of Oaxaca villages

***taxi especial*** private taxi, as distinguished from *taxi colectivo*, or collective taxi

***telégrafo*** telegraph office, lately converting to high-tech *telecomunicaciones (telecom)*, that also offers computerized telephone and public fax services

***temazcal*** traditional indigenous sweat room, rock-enclosed and heated by a wood fire, usually used for healing, especially by women after childbirth

***tenate*** basket of woven palm leaf, with tumpline instead of a rigid handle

***tepache*** a wine, fermented from *panela* (sugarcane juice)

***tequio*** an obligatory communal task, such as local road work, street sweeping, or child care, expected of all adult villagers from time to time

***tianguis*** literally "awning," but now has come to mean the awning-decorated native town market

***tono*** a usually benign animal guardian spirit

***topil*** lowest municipal job, of messenger, filled by youngest teenage boys

***vaquero*** cowboy

***vecinidad*** neighborhood

***yanqui*** Yankee

***zócalo*** the popular label originally for the Mexico City central plaza; now the name for central plazas all over Mexico, including Oaxaca.

## ABBREVIATIONS

**Av.** *avenida* (avenue)

**Blv.** *bulevar* (boulevard)

**Calz.** *calzada* (thoroughfare, main road)

**Fco.** Francisco (proper name, as in "Fco. Villa")

**Fracc.** *Fraccionamiento* (subdivision)

**Nte.** *norte* (north)

**Ote.** *oriente* (east)

**Pte.** *poniente* (west)

**s/n** *sin número* (no street number)

# Spanish Phrasebook

Your Mexico adventure will be more fun if you use a little Spanish. Mexican folks, although they may smile at your funny accent, will appreciate your halting efforts to break the ice and transform yourself from a foreigner to a potential friend.

Spanish commonly uses 30 letters – the familiar English 26, plus four straightforward additions: ch, ll, ñ, and rr, which are explained in "Consonants," below.

## PRONUNCIATION

Once you learn them, Spanish pronunciation rules – in contrast to English – don't change.

Spanish vowels generally sound softer than in English. (*Note:* The capitalized syllables below receive stronger accents.)

## Vowels

**a** like ah, as in "hah": *agua* AH-gooah (water), *pan* PAHN (bread), and *casa* CAH-sah (house)

**e** like ay, as in "may:" *mesa* MAY-sah (table), *tela* TAY-lah (cloth), and *de* DAY (of, from)

**i** like ee, as in "need": *diez* dee-AYZ (ten), *comida* ko-MEE-dah (meal), and *fin* FEEN (end)

**o** like oh, as in "go": *peso* PAY-soh (weight), *ocho* OH-choh (eight), and *poco* POH-koh (a bit)

**u** like oo, as in "cool": *uno* OO-noh (one), *cuarto* KOOAHR-toh (room), and *usted* oos-TAYD (you); when it follows a "q" the **u** is silent; when it follows an "h" or has an umlaut, it's pronounced like "w"

## Consonants

**b, d, f, k, l, m, n, p, q, s, t, v, w, x, y, z, and ch**
pronounced almost as in English; **h** occurs, but is silent – not pronounced at all.

**c** like k as in "keep": *cuarto* KOOAR-toh (room), Tepic tay-PEEK (capital of Nayarit state); when it precedes "e" or "i," pronounce **c** like s, as in "sit": *cerveza* sayr-VAY-sah (beer), *encima* ayn-SEE-mah (atop).

**g** like g as in "gift" when it precedes "a," "o," "u," or a consonant: *gato* GAH-toh (cat), *hago* AH-goh (I do, make); otherwise, pronounce **g** like h as in "hat": *giro* HEE-roh (money order), *gente* HAYN-tay (people)

**j** like h, as in "has": *Jueves* HOOAY-vays (Thursday), *mejor* may-HOR (better)

**ll** like y, as in "yes": *toalla* toh-AH-yah (towel), *ellos* AY-yohs (they, them)

**ñ** like ny, as in "canyon": *año* AH-nyo (year), *señor* SAY-nyor (Mr., sir)

**r** is lightly trilled, with tongue at the roof of your mouth like a very light English d, as in "ready": *pero* PAY-doh (but), *tres* TDAYS (three), *cuatro* KOOAH-tdoh (four).

**rr** like a Spanish r, but with much more emphasis and trill. Let your tongue flap. Practice with *burro* (donkey), *carretera* (highway), and Carrillo (proper name), then really let go with *ferrocarril* (railroad).

*Note:* The single small but common exception to all of the above is the pronunciation of Spanish **y** when it's being used as the Spanish word for "and," as in "Ron y Kathy." In such case, pronounce it like the English ee, as in "keep": Ron "ee" Kathy (Ron and Kathy).

## Accent

The rule for accent, the relative stress given to syllables within a given word, is straightforward. If a word ends in a vowel, an n, or an s, accent the next-to-last syllable; if not, accent the last syllable.

Pronounce *gracias* GRAH-seeahs (thank you), *orden* OHR-dayn (order), and *carretera* kah-ray-TAY-rah (highway) with stress on the next-to-last syllable.

Otherwise, accent the last syllable: *venir* vay-NEER (to come), *ferrocarril* fay-roh-cah-REEL (railroad), and *edad* ay-DAHD (age).

Exceptions to the accent rule are always marked with an accent sign: (á, é, í, ó, or ú), such as *teléfono* tay-LAY-foh-noh (telephone), *jabón* hah-BON (soap), and *rápido* RAH-pee-doh (rapid).

## BASIC AND COURTEOUS EXPRESSIONS

Most Spanish-speaking people consider formalities important. Whenever approaching anyone for information or some other reason, do not forget the appropriate salutation – good morning, good evening, etc. Standing alone, the greeting *hola* (hello) can sound brusque.

**Hello.** *Hola.*
**Good morning.** *Buenos días.*
**Good afternoon.** *Buenas tardes.*
**Good evening.** *Buenas noches.*
**How are you?** *¿Cómo está usted?*
**Very well, thank you.** *Muy bien, gracias.*
**Okay; good.** *Bien.*
**Not okay; bad.** *Mal o feo.*
**So-so.** *Más o menos.*
**And you?** *¿Y usted?*
**Thank you.** *Gracias.*
**Thank you very much.** *Muchas gracias.*
**You're very kind.** *Muy amable.*
**You're welcome.** *De nada.*
**Goodbye.** *Adios.*
**See you later.** *Hasta luego.*
**please** *por favor*
**yes** *sí*
**no** *no*
**I don't know.** *No sé.*
**Just a moment, please.** *Momentito, por favor.*
**Excuse me, please (when you're trying to get attention).** *Disculpe* or *Con permiso.*

**Excuse me (when you've made a boo-boo).** *Lo siento.*

**Pleased to meet you.** *Mucho gusto.*

**How do you say...in Spanish?** *¿Cómo se dice...en español?*

**What is your name?** *¿Cómo se llama usted?*

**Do you speak English?** *¿Habla usted inglés?*

**Is English spoken here? (Does anyone here speak English?)** *¿Se habla inglés?*

**I don't speak Spanish well.** *No hablo bien el español.*

**I don't understand.** *No entiendo.*

**How do you say...in Spanish?** *¿Cómo se dice...en español?*

**My name is . . .** *Me llamo . . .*

**Would you like . . .** *¿Quisiera usted . . .*

**Let's go to . . .** *Vamos a . . .*

## TERMS OF ADDRESS

When in doubt, use the formal *usted* (you) as a form of address.

**I** *yo*

**you (formal)** *usted*

**you (familiar)** *tu*

**he/him** *él*

**she/her** *ella*

**we/us** *nosotros*

**you (plural)** *ustedes*

**they/them** *ellos* (all males or mixed gender); *ellas* (all females)

**Mr., sir** *señor*

**Mrs., madam** *señora*

**miss, young lady** *señorita*

**wife** *esposa*

**husband** *esposo*

**friend** *amigo* (male); *amiga* (female)

**sweetheart** *novio* (male); *novia* (female)

**son; daughter** *hijo; hija*

**brother; sister** *hermano; hermana*

**father; mother** *padre; madre*

**grandfather; grandmother** *abuelo; abuela*

## TRANSPORTATION

**Where is . . . ?** *¿Dónde está . . . ?*

**How far is it to . . . ?** *¿A cuánto está . . . ?*

**from...to . . .** *de...a . . .*

**How many blocks?** *¿Cuántas cuadras?*

**Where (Which) is the way to . . . ?** *¿Dónde está el camino a . . . ?*

**the bus station** *la terminal de autobuses*

**the bus stop** *la parada de autobuses*

**Where is this bus going?** *¿Adónde va este autobús?*

**the taxi stand** *la parada de taxis*

**the train station** *la estación de ferrocarril*

**the boat** *el barco*

**the launch** *lancha; tiburonera*

**the dock** *el muelle*

**the airport** *el aeropuerto*

**I'd like a ticket to . . .** *Quisiera un boleto a . . .*

**first (second) class** *primera (segunda) clase*

**roundtrip** *ida y vuelta*

**reservation** *reservación*

**baggage** *equipaje*

**Stop here, please.** *Pare aquí, por favor.*

**the entrance** *la entrada*

**the exit** *la salida*

**the ticket office** *la oficina de boletos*

**(very) near; far** *(muy) cerca; lejos*

**to; toward** *a*

**by; through** *por*

**from** *de*

**the right** *la derecha*

**the left** *la izquierda*

**straight ahead** *derecho; directo*

**in front** *en frente*

**beside** *al lado*

**behind** *atrás*

**the corner** *la esquina*

**the stoplight** *la semáforo*

**a turn** *una vuelta*

**right here** *aquí*

**somewhere around here** *por acá*

**right there** *allí*

**somewhere around there** *por allá*

**road** *el camino*

**street; boulevard** *calle; bulevar*

**block** *la cuadra*

**highway** *carretera*

**kilometer** *kilómetro*

**bridge; toll** *puente; cuota*

**address** *dirección*

**north; south** *norte; sur*

**east; west** *oriente (este); poniente (oeste)*

## ACCOMMODATIONS

**hotel** *hotel*
**Is there a room?** *¿Hay cuarto?*
**May I (may we) see it?** *¿Puedo (podemos) verlo?*
**What is the rate?** *¿Cuál es el precio?*
**Is that your best rate?** *¿Es su mejor precio?*
**Is there something cheaper?** *¿Hay algo más económico?*
**a single room** *un cuarto sencillo*
**a double room** *un cuarto doble*
**double bed** *cama matrimonial*
**twin beds** *camas gemelas*
**with private bath** *con baño*
**hot water** *agua caliente*
**shower** *ducha*
**towels** *toallas*
**soap** *jabón*
**toilet paper** *papel higiénico*
**blanket** *frazada; manta*
**sheets** *sábanas*
**air-conditioned** *aire acondicionado*
**fan** *abanico; ventilador*
**key** *llave*
**manager** *gerente*

## FOOD

**I'm hungry** *Tengo hambre.*
**I'm thirsty.** *Tengo sed.*
**menu** *carta; menú*
**order** *orden*
**glass** *vaso*
**fork** *tenedor*
**knife** *cuchillo*
**spoon** *cuchara*
**napkin** *servilleta*
**soft drink** *refresco*
**coffee** *café*
**tea** *té*
**drinking water** *agua pura; agua potable*
**bottled carbonated water** *agua mineral*
**bottled uncarbonated water** *agua sin gas*
**beer** *cerveza*
**wine** *vino*
**milk** *leche*
**juice** *jugo*
**cream** *crema*
**sugar** *azúcar*

**cheese** *queso*
**snack** *antojo; botana*
**breakfast** *desayuno*
**lunch** *almuerzo*
**daily lunch special** *comida corrida* (or *el menú del día* depending on region)
**dinner** *comida* (often eaten in late afternoon); *cena* (a late-night snack)
**the check** *la cuenta*
**eggs** *huevos*
**bread** *pan*
**salad** *ensalada*
**fruit** *fruta*
**mango** *mango*
**watermelon** *sandía*
**papaya** *papaya*
**banana** *plátano*
**apple** *manzana*
**orange** *naranja*
**lime** *limón*
**fish** *pescado*
**shellfish** *mariscos*
**shrimp** *camarones*
**meat (without)** *(sin) carne*
**chicken** *pollo*
**pork** *puerco*
**beef; steak** *res; bistec*
**bacon; ham** *tocino; jamón*
**fried** *frito*
**roasted** *asada*
**barbecue; barbecued** *barbacoa; al carbón*

## SHOPPING

**money** *dinero*
**money-exchange bureau** *casa de cambio*
**I would like to exchange traveler's checks.** *Quisiera cambiar cheques de viajero.*
**What is the exchange rate?** *¿Cuál es el tipo de cambio?*
**How much is the commission?** *¿Cuánto cuesta la comisión?*
**Do you accept credit cards?** *¿Aceptan tarjetas de crédito?*
**money order** *giro*
**How much does it cost?** *¿Cuánto cuesta?*
**What is your final price?** *¿Cuál es su último precio?*

**expensive** *caro*
**cheap** *barato; económico*
**more** *más*
**less** *menos*
**a little** *un poco*
**too much** *demasiado*

# HEALTH

**Help me please.** *Ayúdeme por favor.*
**I am ill.** *Estoy enfermo.*
**Call a doctor.** *Llame un doctor.*
**Take me to . . .** *Lléveme a . . .*
**hospital** *hospital; sanatorio*
**drugstore** *farmacia*
**pain** *dolor*
**fever** *fiebre*
**headache** *dolor de cabeza*
**stomach ache** *dolor de estómago*
**burn** *quemadura*
**cramp** *calambre*
**nausea** *náusea*
**vomiting** *vomitar*
**medicine** *medicina*
**antibiotic** *antibiótico*
**pill; tablet** *pastilla*
**aspirin** *aspirina*
**ointment; cream** *pomada; crema*
**bandage** *venda*
**cotton** *algodón*
**sanitary napkins** use brand name, e.g., Kotex
**birth control pills** *pastillas anticonceptivas*
**contraceptive foam** *espuma anticonceptiva*
**condoms** *preservativos; condones*
**toothbrush** *cepilla dental*
**dental floss** *hilo dental*
**toothpaste** *crema dental*
**dentist** *dentista*
**toothache** *dolor de muelas*

# POST OFFICE AND COMMUNICATIONS

**long-distance telephone** *teléfono larga distancia*
**I would like to call . . .** *Quisiera llamar a . . .*
**collect** *por cobrar*
**station to station** *a quien contesta*
**person to person** *persona a persona*
**credit card** *tarjeta de crédito*

**post office** *correo*
**general delivery** *lista de correo*
**letter** *carta*
**stamp** *estampilla, timbre*
**postcard** *tarjeta*
**aerogram** *aerograma*
**air mail** *correo aereo*
**registered** *registrado*
**money order** *giro*
**package; box** *paquete; caja*
**string; tape** *cuerda; cinta*

# AT THE BORDER

**border** *frontera*
**customs** *aduana*
**immigration** *migración*
**tourist card** *tarjeta de turista*
**inspection** *inspección; revisión*
**passport** *pasaporte*
**profession** *profesión*
**marital status** *estado civil*
**single** *soltero*
**married; divorced** *casado; divorciado*
**widowed** *viudado*
**insurance** *seguros*
**title** *título*
**driver's license** *licencia de manejar*

# AT THE GAS STATION

**gas station** *gasolinera*
**gasoline** *gasolina*
**unleaded** *sin plomo*
**full, please** *lleno, por favor*
**tire** *llanta*
**tire repair shop** *vulcanizadora*
**air** *aire*
**water** *agua*
**oil (change)** *aceite (cambio)*
**grease** *grasa*
**My...doesn't work.** *Mi...no sirve.*
**battery** *batería*
**radiator** *radiador*
**alternator** *alternador*
**generator** *generador*
**tow truck** *grúa*
**repair shop** *taller mecánico*
**tune-up** *afinación*
**auto parts store** *refaccionería*

# VERBS

Verbs are the key to getting along in Spanish. They employ mostly predictable forms and come in three classes, which end in *ar*, *er*, and *ir*, respectively:

**to buy** *comprar*
**I buy, you (he, she, it) buys** *compro, compra*
**we buy, you (they) buy** *compramos, compran*
**to eat** *comer*
**I eat, you (he, she, it) eats** *como, come*
**we eat, you (they) eat** *comemos, comen*
**to climb** *subir*
**I climb, you (he, she, it) climbs** *subo, sube*
**we climb, you (they) climb** *subimos, suben*
Here are more (with irregularities indicated):
 **to do or make** *hacer* (regular except for *hago*, I do or make)
**to go** *ir* (very irregular: *voy, va, vamos, van*)
**to go (walk)** *andar*
**to love** *amar*
**to work** *trabajar*
**to want** *desear, querer*
**to need** *necesitar*
**to read** *leer*
**to write** *escribir*
**to repair** *reparar*
**to stop** *parar*
**to get off (the bus)** *bajar*
**to arrive** *llegar*
**to stay (remain)** *quedar*
**to stay (lodge)** *hospedar*
**to leave** *salir* (regular except for *salgo*, I leave)
**to look at** *mirar*
**to look for** *buscar*
**to give** *dar* (regular except for *doy*, I give)
**to carry** *llevar*
**to have** *tener* (irregular but important: *tengo, tiene, tenemos, tienen*)
**to come** *venir* (similarly irregular: *vengo, viene, venimos, vienen*)
Spanish has two forms of "to be":
**to be** *estar* (regular except for *estoy*, I am)
**to be** *ser* (very irregular: *soy, es, somos, son*)
Use *estar* when speaking of location or a temporary state of being: "I am at home." *"Estoy en casa."* "I'm sick." *"Estoy enfermo."* Use *ser* for a permanent state of being: "I am a doctor." *"Soy doctora."*

# NUMBERS

**zero** *cero*
**one** *uno*
**two** *dos*
**three** *tres*
**four** *cuatro*
**five** *cinco*
**six** *seis*
**seven** *siete*
**eight** *ocho*
**nine** *nueve*
**10** *diez*
**11** *once*
**12** *doce*
**13** *trece*
**14** *catorce*
**15** *quince*
**16** *dieciseis*
**17** *diecisiete*
**18** *dieciocho*
**19** *diecinueve*
**20** *veinte*
**21** *veinte y uno* or *veintiuno*
**30** *treinta*
**40** *cuarenta*
**50** *cincuenta*
**60** *sesenta*
**70** *setenta*
**80** *ochenta*
**90** *noventa*
**100** *ciento*
**101** *ciento y uno* or *cientiuno*
**200** *doscientos*
**500** *quinientos*
**1,000** *mil*
**10,000** *diez mil*
**100,000** *cien mil*
**1,000,000** *millón*
**one half** *medio*
**one third** *un tercio*
**one fourth** *un cuarto*

# TIME

**What time is it?** *¿Qué hora es?*
**It's one o'clock.** *Es la una.*

**It's three in the afternoon.** *Son las tres de la tarde.*
**It's 4 A.M.** *Son las cuatro de la mañana.*
**six-thirty** *seis y media*
**a quarter till eleven** *un cuarto para las once*
**a quarter past five** *las cinco y cuarto*
**an hour** *una hora*

## DAYS AND MONTHS
**Monday** *lunes*
**Tuesday** *martes*
**Wednesday** *miércoles*
**Thursday** *jueves*
**Friday** *viernes*
**Saturday** *sábado*
**Sunday** *domingo*
**today** *hoy*
**tomorrow** *mañana*

**yesterday** *ayer*
**January** *enero*
**February** *febrero*
**March** *marzo*
**April** *abril*
**May** *mayo*
**June** *junio*
**July** *julio*
**August** *agosto*
**September** *septiembre*
**October** *octubre*
**November** *noviembre*
**December** *diciembre*
**a week** *una semana*
**a month** *un mes*
**after** *después*
**before** *antes*

# Suggested Reading

Some of these books are informative, others are entertaining, and all of them will increase your understanding of both Mexico and the Acapulco region. Some are easier to find in Mexico than at home, and vice versa. Many of them are out of print, but www.amazon.com, www.barnesandnoble.com, or libraries may have used copies. Take some along on your trip. If you find others that are especially noteworthy, let us know.

## HISTORY

Brunk, Samuel. *Emiliano Zapata: Revolution and Betrayal in Mexico.* Albuquerque: University of New Mexico Press, 1995. A detailed narrative of the renowned revolutionary's turbulent life, from his humble birth in Anenecuilco village in Morelos, through his de facto control of Mexico City in 1914–1915, to his final betrayal and assassination in 1919. The author authoritatively demonstrates that Zapata, neither complete hero nor complete villain, was simply an incredibly determined native leader who paid the ultimate price in his selfless struggle for land and liberty for the campesinos of southern Mexico.

Calderón de la Barca, Fanny. *Life in Mexico, with New Material from the Author's Journals.* New York: Doubleday, 1966. Edited by H. T. and M. H. Fisher. An update of the brilliant, humorous, and celebrated original 1913 book by the Scottish wife of the Spanish ambassador to Mexico.

Casasola, Gustavo. *Seis Siglos de Historia Gráfica de Mexico (Six Centuries of Mexican Graphic History).* Mexico City: Editorial Gustavo Casasola, 1978. Six fascinating encyclopedic volumes, in Spanish, of Mexican history in pictures, from 1325 to the present.

Coe, Michael D., and Rex Koontz. *Mexico: From the Olmecs to the Aztecs.* London: Thames and Hudson, 2002. An authoritative history of the foundations of Mexican civilization. Clearly traces the evolution of Mexico's successive worlds—Olmec, Teotihuacán, Toltec, and Aztec, that set the stage for present-day Mexico.

Collis, Maurice. *Cortés and Montezuma.* New York: New Directions Publishing Corp., 1999. A reprint of a 1954 classic piece of well-researched storytelling, Collis traces Cortés's conquest of Mexico through the defeat of his chief opponent, Aztec Emperor Montezuma. He uses contemporary eyewitnesses—notably Bernal Díaz del Castillo—to revivify one of history's greatest dramas.

Cortés, Hernán. *Letters from Mexico.* Translated by Anthony Pagden. New Haven, CT: Yale University Press, 1986. Cortés's five long letters to his king, in which he describes contemporary Mexico in fascinating detail, including, notably, the remarkably sophisticated life of the Aztecs at the time of the conquest.

De las Casas, Bartolome. *A Short Account of the Destruction of the Indies.* New York: Penguin Books, 1992. The gritty but beloved Dominican bishop, renowned as Mexico's "Apostle of the Indians," writes passionately of his own failed attempt to moderate and humanize the Spanish conquest of Mexico. Undoubtedly, de las Casas' sad tale made a great impression on Spain's King Charles V, who, in 1542, the same year the book was written, promulgated the liberal New Laws of the Indies, that outlawed slavery 320 years before Abraham Lincoln's Emancipation Proclamation.

Díaz del Castillo, Bernal. *The Discovery and Conquest of Mexico.* Translated by Albert Idell. London: Routledge (of Taylor and Francis Group), 2005. A soldier's still-fresh tale of the conquest from the Spanish viewpoint.

Fernández, Miguel Ángel. *The China Galleon.* Translated by Debra Nagao. Photographs by Michel Zabé. Monterrey, Mexico: Vitro Corporativo, S.A. de C.V., 2000. This authoritatively researched, masterfully translated, and gorgeously illustrated coffee-table volume traces the colorful history of the Manila galleon, and consequently Acapulco, from the fall of Constantinople in A.D. 1453 to the present day. The author shows how the allure of Asia's aromatic spices, glistening lacquerware, smooth silks, glittering gold and gems, and radiant porcelains propelled the Spanish to realize Columbus's old dream and transform the Pacific into the Spanish lake that it remained for 300 years.

Garfias, Luis. *The Mexican Revolution.* Mexico City: Panorama Editorial, 1985. A concise Mexican version of the 1910–1917 Mexican revolution, the crucible of present-day Mexico.

Gugliotta, Bobette. *Women of Mexico.* Encino, CA: Floricanto Press, 1989. Lively legends, tales, and biographies of remarkable Mexican women.

León-Portilla, Miguel. *The Broken Spears: The Aztec Account of the Conquest of Mexico.* New York: Beacon Press, 1962. Provides an intriguing contrast to Díaz del Castillo's account.

Meyer, Michael, and William Sherman. *The Course of Mexican History.* New York: Oxford University Press, 2003. An insightful 700-plus-page college textbook in paperback. A bargain, especially if you can get it used.

Novas, Himilce. *Everything You Need to Know About Latino History.* New York: Plume Books (Penguin Group), 1994. Chicanos, Latin rhythm, La Raza, the Treaty of Guadalupe Hidalgo, and much more, interpreted from an authoritative Latino point of view.

Reed, John. *Insurgent Mexico.* New York: International Publisher's Co., 1994. Re-publication of 1914 original. Fast-moving, but not unbiased, description of the 1910 Mexican revolution by the journalist famed for his reporting of the subsequent 1917 Russian revolution. Reed, memorialized by the Soviets, was resurrected in the 1981 film biography *Reds.*

Ridley, Jasper. *Maximilian and Juárez.* New York: Ticknor and Fields, 1999. This authoritative historical biography breathes new life into one of Mexico's great ironic tragedies, a drama that pitted the native Zapotec "Lincoln of Mexico" against the dreamy, idealistic

Archduke Maximilian of Austria-Hungary. Despite their common liberal ideas, they were drawn into a bloody no-quarter struggle that set the Old World against the New, ended in Maximilian's execution, the insanity of his wife, and the emergence of the United States as a power to be reckoned with in world affairs. The defeat of France and Maximilian in Mexico was aided by U.S. support of the Juárez government. The Monroe Doctrine became a reality; and never again would a European power invade Mexico or any other country in the Americas.

Ruíz, Ramon Eduardo. *Triumphs and Tragedy: A History of the Mexican People.* New York: W. W. Norton, Inc., 1992. A pithy, anecdote-filled history of Mexico from an authoritative Mexican-American perspective.

Simpson, Lesley Bird. *Many Mexicos.* Berkeley: University of California Press, 1962. A much-reprinted, fascinating broad-brush version of Mexican history.

## GOVERNMENT, POLITICS, AND ECONOMY

Dillon, Samuel, and Julia Preston. *Opening Mexico: The Making of a Democracy.* New York: Farrar, Straus and Giroux, 2005. Former Mexico City *New York Times* bureau chiefs use their rich personal insights and investigative journalistic skill to tell the story of the latter-day evolution of Mexico's uniquely imperfect democracy. Their story begins during the 1980s, tracing the decay of the 71-year-rule of the PRI, to its collapse, with the election of opposition candidate Vicente Fox in 2000. The actors are vivid and manifold, from rebellious anti-government campesinos to high federal officials conspiring with drug lords, to teachers striking for fair pay and an end to political assassination of their colleagues.

## UNIQUE GUIDE AND TIP BOOKS

American Automobile Association. *Mexico TravelBook.* Heathrow, FL: 2003. Published by the American Automobile Association (1000 AAA Dr., Heathrow, FL 32746-5063). Short but sweet summaries of major Mexican tourist destinations and sights. Also includes information on fiestas, accommodations, restaurants, and a wealth of information relevant to car travel in Mexico. Available in bookstores, or free to AAA members at affiliate offices.

Church, Mike, and Terry Church. *Traveler's Guide to Mexican Camping.* Kirkland, WA: Rolling Homes Press (P.O. Box 2099, Kirkland, WA 98083-2099, tel. 425/825-7846, www.rollinghomes.com). An unusually thorough guide to trailer parks all over Mexico, with much coverage of the Pacific Coast. Detailed maps guide you accurately to each trailer park cited and clear descriptions tell you what to expect. The book also provides very helpful information on car travel in Mexico, including details of insurance, border crossing, highway safety, car repairs, and much more.

Franz, Carl. *The People's Guide to Mexico.* Berkeley, CA: Avalon Travel, 13th edition, 2006. An entertaining and insightful A-to-Z general guide to the joys and pitfalls of independent economy travel in Mexico.

Guilford, Judith. *The Packing Book.* Berkeley, CA: Ten Speed Press, 4th edition, 2006. The secrets of the carry-on traveler, or how to make everything you carry do double and triple duty. All for the sake of convenience, mobility, economy, and comfort.

Graham, Scott. *Handle With Care: Guide to Socially Responsible Travel in Developing Countries.* Chicago: The Noble Press, 1991. Should you accept a meal from a family who lives in a grass house? This insightful guide answers this and hundreds of other tough questions for people who want to travel responsibly in the third world.

Jeffrey, Nan. *Adventuring With Children*. Ashland, MA: Avalon House Publishing, 1995. This unusually detailed book starts where most travel-with-children books end. It contains, besides a wealth of information and practical strategies for general travel with children, specific chapters on how you can adventure—trek, kayak, river-raft, camp, bicycle, and much more—successfully with the kids in tow.

Mader, Ron. *Adventures in Nature: Mexico*. Berkeley, CA: Avalon Travel, 1998. An internationally acknowledged expert on ecotravel in Mexico details dozens of environmentally sensitive adventure tours in Mexico. Destinations range widely, from scuba diving off Cozumel and exploring lost Mayan cities to jeeping through the Copper Canyon to rescuing turtle eggs on Guerrero beaches. (Although used copies are available from www.amazon.com and at libraries, this book, a classic, is out of print. Nevertheless, author Ron Mader has updated much of the book in his superb website www.planeta.com.)

Werner, David. *Where There Is No Doctor*. Berkeley, CA: Hesperian Foundation, 1992 (1919 Addison St., Berkeley, CA 94704, tel. 888/729-1796, www.hesperian.org). How to keep well in the tropical backcountry.

Whipperman, Bruce. *Moon Oaxaca*. Berkeley, CA: Avalon Travel, 5th edition, 2008. The most comprehensive guidebook of Oaxaca, the Acapulco region's neighboring state. It's chock full of useful details of not only Oaxaca's both renowned and relaxing capital city and valley, but also its little-known untouristed treasures, from the mountains to the sea.

Whipperman, Bruce. *Moon Pacific Mexico*. Berkeley, CA: Avalon Travel, 8th edition, 2007. A wealth of information for traveling the Pacific Coast route, through Mazatlán, Guadalajara, Puerto Vallarta, Manzanillo, Colima, Michoacán, Ixtapa-Zihuatanejo, Acapulco, and Oaxaca.

# FICTION

Bowen, David, ed. *Pyramids of Glass*. San Antonio, TX: Corona Publishing Co., 1994. Two dozen-odd stories that lead the reader on a month-long journey through the bedrooms, barracks, cafés, and streets of present-day Mexico.

Boyle, T. C. *The Tortilla Curtain*. New York: Penguin-Putnam 1996; paperback edition, Raincoast Books, 1996. A chance intersection of the lives of two couples, one affluent and liberal Southern Californians, the other poor homeless illegal immigrants, forces all to come to grips with the real price of the American Dream.

Cisneros, Sandra. *Caramelo*. New York: Alfred A. Knopf, 2002. A celebrated author weaves a passionate yet funny multigenerational tale of a Mexican-American family and of their migrations, which, beginning in Mexico City, propelled them north, all the way to Chicago and back.

De la Cruz, Sor Juana Inez. *Poems, Protest, and a Dream*. New York: Penguin, 1997. Masterful translation of a collection of love and religious poems by the celebrated pioneer Mexican feminist-nun (1651–1695).

De Zapata, Celia C., ed. *Short Stories by Latin American Women: The Magic and the Real*. New York: Random House Modern Library, 2003. An eclectic mix of more than 30 stories by noted Latin American women. The stories, which a number of critics classify as "magical realism," were researched by editor Celia de Zapata, who got them freshly translated into English by a cadre of renowned translators; includes a foreword by celebrated author Isabel Allende.

Doerr, Harriet. *Consider This, Señor*. New York: Harcourt Brace, 1993. Four expatriates tough it out in a Mexican small town, adapting to the excesses—blazing sun, driving rain, vast untrammeled landscapes—while interacting with the local folks and while the local folks observe them, with a mixture of fascination and tolerance.

Finn, María, ed. *Mexico in Mind.* New York: Vintage Books, 2006. The wisdom and impressions of two centuries of renowned writers, from D. H. Lawrence and John Steinbeck to John Reed and Richard Rodríguez, who were drawn to the timelessness and romance of Mexico.

Fuentes, Carlos. *Where the Air Is Clear.* New York: Farrar, Straus and Giroux, 1971. The seminal work of Mexico's celebrated novelist.

Fuentes, Carlos. *The Years with Laura Díaz.* Translated by Alfred MacAdam. New York: Farrar, Straus and Giroux, 2000. A panorama of Mexico from independence to the 21st century through the eyes of one woman, Laura Díaz, and her great-grandson, the author. One reviewer said that she, "as a Mexican woman, would like to celebrate Carlos Fuentes; it is worthy of applause that a man who has seen, observed, analyzed and criticized the great occurrences of the century now has a woman, Laura Díaz, speak for him."

Jennings, Gary. *Aztec.* New York: Atheneum, 1980. Beautifully researched and written monumental tale of lust, compassion, love, and death in preconquest Mexico.

Nickles, Sara, ed. *Escape to Mexico.* San Francisco: Chronicle Books, 2002. A carefully selected anthology of 20-odd stories of Mexico by renowned authors, from Steven Crane and W. Somerset Maugham to Anaïs Nin and David Lida, who all found inspiration, refuge, adventure, and much more in Mexico.

Peters, Daniel. *The Luck of Huemac.* New York: Random House, 1981. An Aztec noble family's tale of war, famine, sorcery, heroism, treachery, love, and, finally, disaster and death in the Valley of Mexico.

Rulfo, Juan. *The Burning Plain.* Austin: University of Texas Press, 1967. Stories of people torn between the old and new in Mexico.

Rulfo, Juan. *Pedro Paramo.* Evanston, IL: Northwestern University Press, 1994. Rulfo's acknowledged masterpiece, first published in 1955, established his renown. The author, thinly disguised as the protagonist, Juan Preciado, fulfills his mother's dying request by returning to his shadowy Jalisco hometown, Comala, in search of this father. Although Preciado discovers that his father, Pedro Páramo (whose surname implies "wasteland"), is long dead, Preciado's search resurrects his father's restless spirit, which recounts its horrific life tale of massacre, rape, and incest.

Traven, B. *The Treasure of the Sierra Madre.* New York: Hill and Wang, 1967. Campesinos, *federales,* gringos, and *indígenas* all figure in this modern morality tale set in Mexico's rugged outback. The most famous of the mysterious author's many novels of oppression and justice in Mexico's jungles.

Villaseñor, Victor. *Rain of Gold.* New York: Delta Books (Bantam, Doubleday, and Dell), 1991. The moving, best-selling epic of the gritty travails of the author's family. From humble rural beginnings in the Copper Canyon, they flee revolution and certain death, struggling through parched northern deserts to sprawling border refugee camps. From there they migrate to relative safety and an eventual modicum of happiness in Southern California.

## PEOPLE AND CULTURE

Castillo, Ana, ed. *Goddess of the Americas.* New York: Riverhead Books, 1996. Here a noted author has selected from the works of seven interpreters of Mesoamerican female deities to provide readers with visions of goddesses that range as far and wide as Sex Goddess, the Broken-Hearted, the Subversive, and the Warrior Queen.

Cordrey, Donald, and Dorothy Cordrey. *Mexican Indian Costumes*. Austin: University of Texas Press, 1968. A lovingly photographed, written, and illustrated classic on Mexican native peoples.

Lewis, Oscar. *Children of Sanchez*. New York: Random House, 1961. Poverty and strength in the Mexican underclass, sympathetically described and interpreted by renowned sociologist Lewis.

Medina, Sylvia López. *Cantora*. New York: Ballantine Books, 1992. Fascinated by the stories of her grandmother, aunt, and mother, the author seeks her own center by discovering a past that she thought she wanted to forget.

Meyerhoff, Barbara. *Peyote Hunt: The Sacred Journey of the Huichol Indians*. Ithaca, NY: Cornell University Press, 1974. A description and interpretation of the Huichol's religious use of mind-bending natural hallucinogens.

Palmer, Colin A. *Slaves of the White God: Blacks in Mexico*. Cambridge, MA: Harvard University Press, 1976. A scholarly study of why and how Spanish authorities imported African slaves into the Americas and how they were used afterward. Replete with poignant details taken from Spanish and Mexican archives describing how the Africans struggled from bondage to eventual freedom.

Toor, Frances. *A Treasury of Mexican Folkways*. New York: Bonanza Books, 1947, reprinted 1985. An illustrated encyclopedia of vanishing Mexicana—costumes, religion, fiestas, burial practices, customs, legends—compiled during the celebrated author's 35 years of residence in Mexico in the early 20th century.

Wauchope, Robert, ed. *Handbook of Middle American Indians*. Vols. 7 and 8. Austin: University of Texas Press, 1969. Authoritative but aging surveys of important native-speaking groups in northern, central (vol. 8), and southern (vol. 7) Mexico.

## ARTS, ARCHITECTURE, AND CRAFTS

Berrin, Kathleen. *The Art of the Huichol Indians*. New York: Harry N. Abrams Publishing, 1978. Lovely, large photographs and text by a symposium of experts provide a good interpretive introduction to Huichol art and culture.

Covarrubias, Miguel. *Indian Art of Mexico and Central America*. New York: Knopf, 1957. A classic work by the renowned interpreter of *indígena* art and design.

Martínez Penaloza, Porfirio. *Popular Arts of Mexico*. Mexico City: Editorial Panorama, 1981. An excellent pocket-sized exposition of Mexican art and handicrafts.

Morrill, Penny C., and Carol A. Berk. *Mexican Silver*. Atglen, PA: Shiffer Publishing Co., 2001 (4880 Lower Valley Road, Atglen, PA 19310). Lovingly written and photographed exposition of the Mexican silvercraft of Taxco, Guerrero, that was revitalized through the initiative of Frederick Davis and William Spratling in the 1920s and 1930s. Color photos of many beautiful museum-quality pieces supplement the text, which describes the history and work of a score of silversmithing families who developed the Taxco craft under Spratling's leadership. Greatly adds to the traveler's appreciation of the beautiful Taxco silvercrafts.

Mullen, Robert James. *Architecture and Its Sculpture in Viceregal Mexico*. Austin: University of Texas Press, 1997. The essential work of Mexican colonial-era cathedrals and churches. In this lovingly written and illustrated life work, Mullen breathes new vitality into New Spain's preciously glorious colonial architectural legacy.

Sayer, Chloë. *Arts and Crafts of Mexico*. San Francisco: Chronicle Books, 1990. All you ever wanted to know about your favorite Mexican crafts, from papier-mâché and pottery to toys and Taxco silver. Beautifully illustrated by traditional etchings and David Lavender's crisp black-and-white and color photographs.

## FLORA AND FAUNA

Goodson, Gar. *Fishes of the Pacific Coast.* Stanford, CA: Stanford University Press, 1988. More than 500 beautifully detailed color drawings highlight this pocket version of all you ever wanted to know about the ocean's fishes (including common Spanish names) from Alaska to Peru.

Howell, Steve N. G. *Bird-Finding Guide to Mexico.* Ithaca, NY: Cornell University Press, 1999. A unique portable guide for folks who really want to see birds in Mexico. Unlike other bird books, the author presents a unique and authoritative site guide, with dozens of clear maps and lists of birds seen at sites all over Mexico. Use this book along with Howell and Webb's *A Guide to the Birds of Mexico and Northern Central America.*

Howell, Steve N. G., and Sophie Webb. *A Guide to the Birds of Mexico and Northern Central America.* Oxford: Oxford University Press, 1995. All the serious bird-watcher needs to know about Mexico's rich species treasury. Includes authoritative habitat maps and 70 excellent color plates that detail the male and females of about 1,500 species.

Mason Jr., Charles T., and Patricia B. Mason. *Handbook of Mexican Roadside Flora.* Tucson: University of Arizona Press, 1987. Authoritative identification guide, with line illustrations, of all the plants you're likely to see in your travels in Mexico.

Morris, Percy A. *A Field Guide to Pacific Coast Shells.* Boston: Houghton Mifflin, 1974. The complete beachcomber's Pacific shell guide.

Pesman, M. Walter. *Meet Flora Mexicana.* Globe, AZ: D. S. King, 1962. Delightful anecdotes and illustrations of hundreds of common Mexican plants. Out of print.

Wright, N. Pelham. *A Guide to Mexican Mammals and Reptiles.* Mexico City: Minutiae Mexicana, 1989. Pocket-edition lore, history, descriptions, and pictures of commonly seen Mexican animals.

## Internet Resources

A number of websites may be helpful in preparing for your Acapulco-Ixtapa-Zihuatanejo adventure.

## GENERAL TRAVEL

### U.S. Department of State
**www.state.gov/travel**
The U.S. State Department's very complete information website. Lots of subheadings and links to a swarm of topics, including Mexican consular offices in the United States, U.S. consular offices in Mexico, travel advisories, and links to other government information, such as importation of food, plants, and animals; U.S. customs; health abroad; airlines; and exchange rates.

### Travelocity
**www.travelocity.com**

### Expedia
**www.expedia.com**

### Tripadvisor
**www.tripadvisor.com**
Major sites for airline and hotel bookings

# TRAVEL INSURANCE

## Travel Insurance Services
www.travelinsure.com

## World Travel Center
www.worldtravelcenter.com
Both good for general travel insurance and other services

# MEXICO CAR INSURANCE

## Sanborns Insurance
www.sanbornsinsurance.com
Site of Sanborn's Insurance, the longtime, very reliable Mexico auto insurance agency, with one of the few north-of-the-border adjustment procedures. Get your quote online, order their many useful publications, and find out about other insurance you many have forgotten.

# SPECIALTY TRAVEL

## Elderhostel
www.elderhostel.org
Site of Boston-based Elderhostel, Inc., with a huge catalog of ongoing study tours.

## Mobility International
www.miusa.org
Wonderfully organized and complete site with a flock of services for travelers with disabilities, including many people-to-people connections in Mexico.

## Purple Roofs
www.purpleroofs.com
One of the best general gay-and-lesbian travel websites is maintained by San Francisco travel agency Purple Roofs. It offers, for example, details of several lesbian- and gay-friendly Acapulco and Ixtapa-Zihuatanejo hotels, restaurants, and bars, in addition to a wealth of lesbian- and gay-friendly travel-oriented links worldwide.

# MEXICO IN GENERAL

## Mexico Tourism Board
www.visitmexico.com
The official website of the public-private Mexico Tourism Board; a good general site for official information, such as entry requirements. It has lots of summarily informative subheadings, not unlike an abbreviated guidebook. If you can't find what you want here, call the toll-free information number 800/44-MEXICO (800/446-3942) or email contact@visitmexico.com. Or, if you can read a bit of Spanish, visit www.cptm.com.mx, the more detailed Mexican version of the same website.

## Mexico Online
www.mexonline.com
Very extensive, well-organized commercial site with many subheadings and links. For the Acapulco region, they cover Acapulco, Ixtapa-Zihuatanejo, Troncones, and Taxco, including dozens of accommodations, from luxury hotels to modest bed-and-breakfasts. Excellent.

## MexConnect
www.mexconnect.com
An extensive Mexico site, with dozens upon dozens of subheadings, links, and forums, most helpful for folks thinking of traveling, working, living, or retiring in Mexico. For example, I typed "Zihuatanejo" into their very useful search box and got 71 hits, on topics ranging from building construction to cooking schools.

## Mexico Desconocido
www.mexicodesconocido.com.mx
The site of the excellent magazine *Mexico Desconocido* (Undiscovered Mexico) that often features unusual, untouristed destinations. It links to a large library of past articles, in a style not unlike a Mexican version of *National Geographic Traveler*. Solid, hard-to-find information, in good English translation, if you can get it. (The site is so voluminous that the Google automatic translator tends to bog down at the effort.)

On the initial home page, find the small magnifying glass and dialog box labeled "buscar" ("find") at the upper right. I typed in Acapulco and got dozens of hits about places and things in and around Acapulco, each linked to an article in the magazine.

### On the Road in Mexico
### www.ontheroadin.com

Very helpful information and photos of hundreds of Mexico RV and camping parks. Includes accurate and very usable maps to out-of-the-way, hard-to-find locations, six around Acapulco and another three around Ixtapa-Zihuatanejo. Information, however, tends to be two or three years old.

### Planeta.com
### www.planeta.com

Life project of Latin America's dean of ecotourism, Ron Mader, who furnishes a comprehensive clearinghouse of everything ecologically correct, from rescuing turtle eggs in Jalisco to preserving cloud forests in Peru. Contains dozens of subheadings competently linked for maximum speed. For example, check out the Mexico travel directory for ecojourneys, maps, information networks, parks, regional guides, and a mountain more.

### Vacation Rentals By Owner
### www.vrbo.com

A very useful site, fine for picking a vacation rental house, condo, or villa, with photos, information, and reservations links to many individual owners. Prices vary from moderate to luxurious. Coverage extends over much of the Mexican Pacific coast, with dozens of rentals in Troncones, Ixtapa-Zihuatanejo, and Acapulco.

# DESTINATIONS

## Acapulco

### Acapulco Convention and Visitors Bureau
### www.visitacapulco.com.mx

This Spanish-only site, of the Acapulco Convention and Visitor's Bureau, broadly covers the ground from sightseeing and shopping to hotels and transportation. The information is usually available via links to individual providers' websites, with quick email contact for services and hotel bookings. It's especially useful for locating budget-to-moderate one-, two-, and three-star lodgings.

### Acapulco Heat
### www.acabtu.com.mx

Website of the former tourist newspaper *Acapulco Heat,* now electronic. It provides useful links (some in English, most in Spanish) to many mid-scale hotels, rental condos, houses, apartments, real estate agencies, restaurants, community events and organizations, travel activities, and entertainments.

## Ixtapa-Zihuatanejo

### Zihuatanejo.net
### www.zihuatanejo.net

A top-notch, very complete, and well-maintained commercial site listing nearly everywhere to stay (with reservation and email links) and dine, everything to do, and much more in Zihuatanejo, Ixtapa, Troncones, and Barra de Potosí. In English or Spanish.

### Zihua.net
### www.zihua.net

Similar to, but smaller than, www.zihuatanejo.net, this site (along with its twin, www.ixtapa.net) nevertheless has lots of useful, mostly commercial, travel-oriented information and links.

### Zihuatanejo Rentals
### www.zihuatanejo-rentals.com

The site of savvy local resident Leigh Roth, who lists (with gorgeous photos) several high-end (and a few moderately priced) condo, apartment, and villa rental options, most near Playas La Madera and La Ropa. She also includes informative sections on restaurants, shopping, activities, personal anecdotes, and stories.

## Ixtapa and Zihuatanejo Convention and Visitor's Bureau
### www.visit-ixtapa-zihuatanejo.org

The official site of Ixtapa and Zihuatanejo Convention and Visitor's Bureau, with listings of many hotels, restaurants, tours, sports, and more. At this writing, it's still a work in progress; a number of links lead to dead ends. Although it was not possible to book all hotel reservations directly, hotel email and web links to many hotel websites, especially the upscale ones, were available.

## Troncones and Barra de Potosí

### Troncones
### www.troncones.com.mx

Good site, especially for hotels, with many links to Troncones's small beachfront hotels and bed-and-breakfasts. Also links to a number of restaurants, services, real estate, and much more.

### Troncones.net
### www.troncones.net

A good alternative to www.troncones.com.mx, also with several hotel, bed-and-breakfast, restaurant, and activities links.

### Barra de Potosí
### www.barra-potosi.com

A good site, with several links to Barra de Potosí bed-and-breakfasts, hotels, activities, and services.

# Index

# Map Index

# www.moon.com

## DESTINATIONS | ACTIVITIES | BLOGS | MAPS | BOOKS

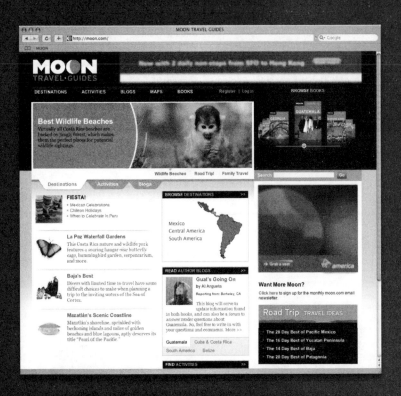

**MOON.COM** is all new, and ready to help plan your next trip! Filled with fresh trip ideas and strategies, author interviews, informative blogs, a detailed map library, and descriptions of all the Moon guidebooks, Moon.com is all you need to get out and explore the world—or even places in your own backyard. As always, when you travel with Moon, expect an experience that is uncommon and truly unique.

# MAP SYMBOLS

| | | | | | | | |
|---|---|---|---|---|---|---|---|
| ▨▨▨ | Expressway | **【** | Highlight | ✗ | Airfield | ⅃ | Golf Course |
| ▨▨▨ | Primary Road | ○ | City/Town | ✈ | Airport | **P** | Parking Area |
| ▨▨▨ | Secondary Road | ◉ | State Capital | ▲ | Mountain | ▰ | Archaeological Site |
| ------ | Unpaved Road | ⊛ | National Capital | ✛ | Unique Natural Feature | ♠ | Church |
| - - - - - | Trail | ★ | Point of Interest | | | ₩ | Gas Station |
| ············ | Ferry | • | Accommodation | 🦃 | Waterfall | | Glacier |
| ⬝⬝⬝⬝ | Railroad | ▼ | Restaurant/Bar | ▲ | Park | | Mangrove |
| ▨▨▨ | Pedestrian Walkway | ■ | Other Location | 🛈 | Trailhead | | Reef |
| ⅏⅏⅏ | Stairs | Λ | Campground | ⛷ | Skiing Area | | Swamp |

# CONVERSION TABLES

°C = (°F - 32) / 1.8
°F = (°C x 1.8) + 32
1 inch = 2.54 centimeters (cm)
1 foot = 0.304 meters (m)
1 yard = 0.914 meters
1 mile = 1.6093 kilometers (km)
1 km = 0.6214 miles
1 fathom = 1.8288 m
1 chain = 20.1168 m
1 furlong = 201.168 m
1 acre = 0.4047 hectares
1 sq km = 100 hectares
1 sq mile = 2.59 square km
1 ounce = 28.35 grams
1 pound = 0.4536 kilograms
1 short ton = 0.90718 metric ton
1 short ton = 2,000 pounds
1 long ton = 1.016 metric tons
1 long ton = 2,240 pounds
1 metric ton = 1,000 kilograms
1 quart = 0.94635 liters
1 US gallon = 3.7854 liters
1 Imperial gallon = 4.5459 liters
1 nautical mile = 1.852 km

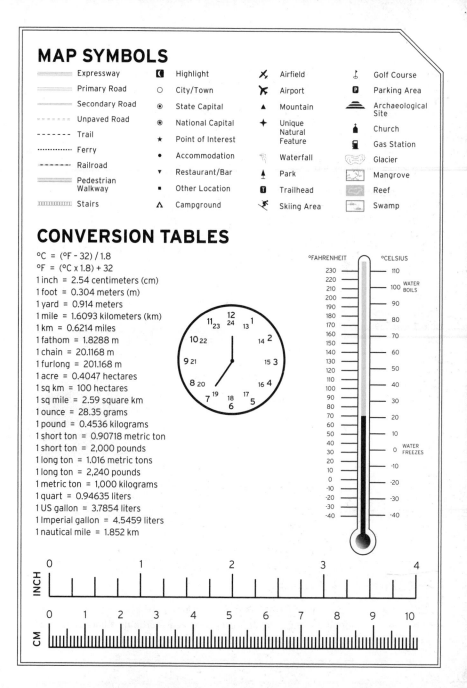

**MOON ACAPULCO,**
**IXTAPA & ZIHUATANEJO**
Avalon Travel
a member of the Perseus Books Group
1700 Fourth Street
Berkeley, CA 94710, USA
www.moon.com

Editors: Kevin McLain, Annie M. Blakley
Series Manager: Kathryn Ettinger
Copy Editor: Amy Scott
Graphics Coordinator: Elizabeth Jang
Production Coordinator: Elizabeth Jang
Cover Designer: Elizabeth Jang
Map Editor: Kevin Anglin
Director of Cartography: Mike Morgenfeld
Cartographers: Chris Markiewicz, Jon Niemczyk,
   Kat Bennett
Indexer: Greg Jewett

ISBN-10: 1-59880-087-6
ISBN-13: 978-1-59880-087-6
ISSN: 1548-8012

Printing History
1st Edition – 2004
3rd Edition – March 2009
5 4 3 2 1

## KEEPING CURRENT

If you have a favorite gem you'd like to see included in the next edition, or see anything
that needs updating, clarification, or correction, please drop us a line. Send your
comments via email to feedback@moon.com, or use the address above.